Human–Computer Interaction Series

Editors-in-Chief

Desney Tan
Microsoft Research, Redmond, USA

Jean Vanderdonckt
Université catholique de Louvain, Louvain-La-Neuve, Belgium

More information about this series at http://www.springer.com/series/6033

Jianlong Zhou · Fang Chen
Editors

Human and Machine Learning

Visible, Explainable, Trustworthy
and Transparent

 Springer

Editors
Jianlong Zhou
DATA61
CSIRO
Eveleigh, NSW, Australia

Fang Chen
DATA61
CSIRO
Eveleigh, NSW, Australia

ISSN 1571-5035   ISSN 2524-4477   (electronic)
Human–Computer Interaction Series
ISBN 978-3-030-08007-5   ISBN 978-3-319-90403-0   (eBook)
https://doi.org/10.1007/978-3-319-90403-0

Printed on acid-free paper

This Springer imprint is published by the registered company Springer International Publishing AG
part of Springer Nature
The registered company address is: Gewerbestrasse 11, 6330 Cham, Switzerland

Foreword

Machine learning has transitioned from an arcane and obscure research area to one of the hottest technologies around. Like other new and general purpose technologies, this rise to prominence brings social issues to the forefront. When electricity was the plaything of eccentric hobbyists, it was of little concern to most people. When it became infrastructure, many more took an interest because it directly started affecting their lives. Machine learning is now affecting everyone's lives, and reasonably, higher demands are being made about the technology as a consequence.

Thus, the book you hold in your hand is timely and important. Machine learning is arcane. It makes use of sophisticated mathematics and unimaginably complex data to seemingly magically ascertain patterns that were previously hidden from the view. As it becomes widely deployed, this arcaneness becomes a problem.

Machine learning offers the opportunity for great good, but also for great harm. A first step in taming the new technology is to better understand it, and in particular understand each of its manifestations when embedded in a social context. That is the focus of this book. This is not a *simple* problem. Neither is it a *single* problem, and that plurality and messiness is reflected in the diverse approaches in the book. There is not (and cannot be) a single solution to this problem. Indeed, at present, I do not believe we have an adequate handle on what 'the problem' is. We can wave our arms about the need for transparency and understandability and accountability, but what do those big words really mean? We can only find out by hard analysis and thinking, and by attempting to build real systems, and importantly, doing rigorous scientific experiments with such systems.

This is a new chapter for machine learning researchers, necessitating the mastery of a much richer set of ways of knowing. The editors of the book have been at the forefront of this richer view, and they have assembled an eclectic set of contributions that start to make sense of the exciting problem situation we now find ourselves in. This is not the last word on the subject. But it is a very important first step.

Canberra, Australia   Robert C. Williamson
March 2018   Professor, Australian National University

Preface

With the rapid boom of data from various fields such as infrastructure, transport, energy, health, education, telecommunications and finance, data analytics-driven solutions are increasingly demanded for different purposes. From management service delivery to customer support and all the way to specialised decision support systems, domain users are looking to integrate 'Big Data' and advanced analytics into their business operations in order to become more analytics-driven in their decision-making (which is also known as predictive decision-making). Rapid advances in Machine Learning (ML) research have been inspired by such expectations. While we continuously find ourselves coming across ML-based appealing systems that seem to work (or have worked) surprisingly well in practical scenarios (e.g. AlphaGO's beating with professional GO players, and the self-driving cars for deciding to choose among different road conditions), ML technologies are currently still facing prolonged challenges with user acceptance of delivered solutions as well as seeing system misuse, disuse or even failure.

These fundamental challenges can be attributed to the nature of the 'black-box' of ML methods for domain experts and a lack of consideration of the human user aspects when offering ML-based solutions. For example, for many non-ML users, they simply provide source data to an ML-based predictive decision-making system, and after selecting some menu options on screen, the system displays colourful viewgraphs and/or recommendations as output. It is neither clear nor well understood how ML algorithms processed input data to get predictive probabilities, how trustworthy was this output, or how uncertainties were handled by underlying algorithmic procedures. That is, explanation and transparency of ML are significant for domain users to trust and use ML confidently in their practices. To this end, visual representation plays a significant role in fostering the understanding of ML mechanisms. As a result, demands for visible, explainable, trustworthy and transparent ML are increasing as the use of predictive decision-making systems grows and as people realise the potential impact of these systems in society. For example, Google launched a new initiative of 'People + AI Research' (PAIR) in 2017 to study and redesign the ways human interact with AI systems. The PAIR focuses on the 'human side' of AI: the relationship between humans and technology, the new applications it enables and how to make it broadly inclusive.

The above observations and discussions motivate the editing of this book: *Human and Machine Learning: Visible, Explainable, Trustworthy and Transparent*. This edited book makes a systematic investigation into the relations between human and machine learning, and reports the state-of-the-art advances in theories, techniques and applications of transparent machine learning. The book specifically focuses on four aspects of ML from a human user's perspective: visible, explainable, trustworthy and transparent. The book consists of six parts, which are based on the systematic understanding of the current active research activities and the outcomes related to the topic of human and machine learning. The six parts cover the areas of transparency in machine learning, visual explanation of ML processes/results, algorithmic explanation of ML models, human cognitive responses in ML-based decision-making, human evaluation of machine learning and domain knowledge in transparent ML applications.

Part I investigates the *Transparency* in machine learning when applying ML to real-world applications. This part presents a 2D transparency space which integrates domain users and ML experts to translate ML into impacts. It demonstrates that transparency not only includes ML method transparency but also means input influence transparency and user response transparency. The transparency in ML is investigated from various perspectives in this part. From the perspective of fairness, the involvement of the human in ML stages such as collecting data, building a model and reporting the results introduces various bias, for example, data can be collected and labelled in a biased way which is discriminative against a certain race, gender, ethnicity or age, resulting in unfair models. The transparency in ML is the first step towards ethical and fair ML models. From the end-user's perspective, the End-User Development (EUD) models are used to create an end-user data analytics paradigm for transparent machine learning. From the cognitive perspective, the knowledge transfer in human deep cognitive learning benefits the transparency in ML by considering human cognitive processes in the ML design and implementation. From the communication perspective, the impediment to a human's situation awareness of ML-based systems often results in the disuse or over-reliance of ML-based autonomous systems. The Situation Awareness-based Agent Transparency (SAT) aims to communicate ML in autonomous systems.

Part II features *visualisation* for the explanation and understanding of ML models. The visualisation is not simply to make ML models visible but to foster understanding by the viewer. This part specifically focuses on the visual explanation of the neural network which is one of the most complex ML models to understand. For example, with the use of saliency map visualisation, it is possible to localise the regions that affect image classifications to understand and interpret the Convolutional Neural Network (CNN) classification mechanisms. Six case studies are also discussed to investigate visual representation and explanation of neural networks crossing disciplinary boundaries, focusing on extracting semantic encodings, developing interactive interfaces, discovering critical cases and negotiating cultural images of neural networks.

Part III reports the *algorithmic explanation* and interpretation of ML models from different perspectives. From the popular feature importance/contribution's perspective, with the use of quasi-nomograms, prediction models can be explained based on the feature importance visually. From the methodology's perspective, different from the gradient-based approaches limited to neural networks, the perturbation-based approaches, by perturbing the inputs in the neighbourhood of given instance to observe effects of perturbations on model's output, allow the explanation of an arbitrary prediction model decision process for each individual predicted instance as well as the model as a whole. From the perspective of a linguistic explanation, fuzzy models serve as a basic model architecture to offer linguistically understandable explanations both on a local level and a global level.

Part IV focuses on the transparency in ML by communicating *human cognitive responses* such as trust with multimodal interfaces for *trustworthy* ML solutions. The communication of human cognitive responses could help understand to what degree humans accept ML-based solutions. On the other hand, through understanding human cognitive responses during ML-based decision-making, ML-based decision attributes/factors and even ML models can be adaptively refined in order to make ML transparent. To this end, this part investigates trust dynamics under uncertainty in predictive decision-making to reveal relations between system performance and user trust. Since inappropriate trust in ML may result in system disuse, misuse or failure (e.g. the medical error in clinical decision support), this part discusses significant factors such as code structure, algorithm performance and transparency of learning affordance to foster appropriate trust in ML. Furthermore, the level of transparency of ML impacts trust in ML-based systems. It is demonstrated that different levels of transparency are needed depending on the risk levels in domains and the ability of a domain expert to evaluate the decision. Group cognition is also introduced in pursuit of natural collaboration of ML-based systems with humans.

Part V discovers the relations between human and machine learning from the perspective of *evaluation of machine learning*. Since humans are the key stakeholders as the ultimate frontline users of ML-based systems, this part presents user-centred evaluation of machine learning for model optimisation, selection and validation in order to best address the user experience as a whole. Furthermore, this part couples two types of validation for interactive machine learning to benefit the transparency in ML: algorithm-centred analysis, to study the computational behaviour of the system; and user-centred evaluation, to observe the utility and effectiveness of the application for end-users.

Part VI introduces the attempts and efforts of the use of *domain knowledge* in machine learning for ML explanation and ML performance improvement with case studies covering domains and areas including infrastructure, transport, food science and others. The domain knowledge is utilised to help extract meaningful features, interpret ML models, and explain ML results. This part shows that human domain experts play an active role in ML-based solutions from phrasing a practical problem as an ML program, feature definition, ML model building to the ML results' interpretation and deployment, resulting in visible, explainable, trustworthy and transparent ML for the impact of ML in real-world applications.

This edited book sets up links between human and machine learning from the perspectives of visualisation, explanation, trustworthiness, and transparency. Such links not only help human users proactively use ML outputs for informative and trustworthy decision-making but also inspire ML experts to passionately develop new ML algorithms which incorporate humans for human-centred ML algorithms resulting in the overall advancement of ML. The book creates a systematic view of relations between human and machine learning in this timely field for further active discussions to translate ML into impacts in real-world applications.

The book aims to serve as the first dedicated source for the theories, methodologies and applications of visible, explainable, trustworthy and transparent machine learning, establishing state-of-the-art research, and providing a groundbreaking textbook to graduate students, research professionals and machine learning practitioners.

Sydney, Australia   Jianlong Zhou
March 2018   Fang Chen

Acknowledgements

Our timely research on 'human and machine learning' for transparent machine learning was originally motivated for investigation at National ICT Australia (NICTA) (now DATA61) in early 2012. Our research outcomes together with the increasing significance of transparent machine learning in the community as well as the yearly consistent support from DATA61 inspire the editing of this volume *Human and Machine Learning: Visible, Explainable, Trustworthy and Transparent*. We would like to express our sincere appreciation to NICTA/DATA61 for its continuous strong support to this research.

This edited book represents the state-of-the-art advances in the area of 'human and machine learning', to which all authors contributed their excellent wisdom to make it an integrated volume from both research and application's perspectives. We express our deepest gratitude to all authors for their outstanding contributions and effective collaborations.

Our appreciation is also given to our reviewers, who voluntarily spent many of hours to give insightful comments and suggestions. We would also like to thank Springer Editorial Director Beverley Ford and her colleagues for their highest level of professional support to this book's publication.

We would also like to thank Air Force Office of Scientific Research (AFOSR) through Asian Office of Aerospace R&D (AOARD) for research grants to supporting editors in their different projects on human–machine interactions exploring human behaviours and responses to automation systems and predictive decision-making.

Sydney, Australia
March 2018

Jianlong Zhou
Fang Chen

Contents

Contributors

Behnoush Abdollahi Knowledge Discovery and Web Mining Lab, Computer Engineering and Computer Science Department, University of Louisville, KY, USA

Gene Alarcon Air Force Research Laboratory, Airman Systems Directorate, Wright-Patterson AFB, OH, USA

Ali Anaissi School of IT, The University of Sydney, Sydney, NSW, Australia

Marko Arsenovic Faculty of Technical Sciences, University of Novi Sad, Novi Sad, Serbia

Marc Barnabé INRA, Université Paris-Saclay, Thiverval-Grignon, France

Michael J. Barnes Human Research and Engineering Directorate, US Army Research Laboratory, Orlando, FL, USA

Shlomo Berkovsky DATA61, CSIRO, Eveleigh, NSW, Australia

Anastasia Bezerianos Univ Paris-Sud, CNRS, INRIA, Université Paris-Saclay, Orsay, France

Marko Bohanec Salvirt Ltd., Ljubljana, Slovenia

Kamel Boukhalfa Department of Computer Science, USTHB University, Algiers, Algeria

Nadia Boukhelifa INRA, Université Paris-Saclay, Thiverval-Grignon, France

Mohammed Brahimi Department of Computer Science, USTHB University, Algiers, Algeria; Department of Computer Science, Mohamed El Bachir El Ibrahimi University, Bordj Bou Arreridj, Algeria

Kieran Browne Australian National University, Canberra, ACT, Australia

Scott Allen Cambo Northwestern University, Evanston, IL, USA

Thomas Chabin INRA, Université Paris-Saclay, Thiverval-Grignon, France

Fang Chen DATA61, CSIRO, Eveleigh, NSW, Australia

Jessie Y. C. Chen Human Research and Engineering Directorate, US Army Research Laboratory, Orlando, FL, USA

Dan Conway DATA61, CSIRO, Eveleigh, NSW, Australia

Jeremy Friedman California State University, Northridge, CA, USA

Henry Gardner Australian National University, Canberra, ACT, Australia

Benoît Génot INRA, Université Paris-Saclay, Thiverval-Grignon, France

Darren Gergle Northwestern University, Evanston, IL, USA

Kevin Greenberg University of Utah, Salt Lake City, UT, USA

Cosima Gretton University College London, School of Management, London, UK

Ting Guo DATA61, CSIRO, Eveleigh, NSW, Australia

Svyatoslav Guznov Air Force Research Laboratory, Airman Systems Directorate, Wright-Patterson AFB, OH, USA

Nhut Ho California State University, Northridge, CA, USA

Nguyen Lu Dang Khoa DATA61, CSIRO, Eveleigh, NSW, Australia

Le Minh Kieu DATA61, CSIRO, Eveleigh, NSW, Australia

Janin Koch Department of Communications and Networking, School of Electrical Engineering, Aalto University, Espoo, Finland

Igor Kononenko Faculty of Computer and Information Science, University of Ljubljana, Ljubljana, Slovenia

Sohaib Laraba TCTS Lab, Numediart Institute, University of Mons, Mons, Belgium

Zhidong Li DATA61, CSIRO, Eveleigh, NSW, Australia

Peng Lin DATA61, CSIRO, Eveleigh, NSW, Australia

Edwin Lughofer Department of Knowledge-Based Mathematical Systems, Johannes Kepler University Linz, Linz, Austria

Evelyne Lutton INRA, Université Paris-Saclay, Thiverval-Grignon, France

Joseph Lyons Air Force Research Laboratory, Airman Systems Directorate, Wright-Patterson AFB, OH, USA

Mehrisadat Makki Alamdari School of Civil and Environmental Engineering, University of New South Wales, Kensington, NSW, Australia

Abdelouhab Moussaoui Department of Computer Science, Setif 1 University, Setif, Algeria

Olfa Nasraoui Knowledge Discovery and Web Mining Lab, Computer Engineering and Computer Science Department, University of Louisville, KY, USA

Antti Oulasvirta Department of Communications and Networking, School of Electrical Engineering, Aalto University, Espoo, Finland

Nathalie Perrot INRA, Université Paris-Saclay, Thiverval-Grignon, France

David V. Pynadath Institute for Creative Technologies, University of Southern California, Los Angeles, CA, USA

Thierry Rakotoarivelo DATA61, CSIRO, Eveleigh, NSW, Australia

Marko Robnik-Šikonja Faculty of Computer and Information Science, University of Ljubljana, Ljubljana, Slovenia

Patrick C. Shih Department of Informatics, School of Informatics Computing and Engineering, Indiana University Bloomington, Bloomington, IN, USA

Srdjan Sladojevic Faculty of Technical Sciences, University of Novi Sad, Novi Sad, Serbia

Erik Štrumbelj Faculty of Computer and Information Science, University of Ljubljana, Ljubljana, Slovenia

Ben Swift Australian National University, Canberra, ACT, Australia

Ronnie Taib DATA61, CSIRO, Eveleigh, NSW, Australia

Alberto Tonda INRA, Université Paris-Saclay, Thiverval-Grignon, France

Ning Wang Institute for Creative Technologies, University of Southern California, Los Angeles, CA, USA

Yang Wang DATA61, CSIRO, Eveleigh, NSW, Australia

Kun Yu DATA61, CSIRO, Eveleigh, NSW, Australia

Bang Zhang DATA61, CSIRO, Eveleigh, NSW, Australia

Lelin Zhang DATA61, CSIRO, Eveleigh, NSW, Australia

Robert Zheng University of Utah, Salt Lake City, UT, USA

Jianlong Zhou DATA61, CSIRO, Eveleigh, NSW, Australia

Acronyms

ADES	Appropriate Distance to the Enclosing Surface
AI	Artificial Intelligence
ANN	Artificial Neural Nets
AP	All Pairs
ARPI	Autonomy Research Pilot Initiative
ASM	Autonomous Squad Member
B2B	Business-to-Business
BN	Bayesian Network
BVP	Blood Volume Pulse
CAD	Computer-Aided Diagnosis
CART	Classification and Regression Trees
CDSS	Clinical Decision Support Systems
CF	Collaborative Filtering
CPPN	Compositional Pattern Producing Network
CV	Cross-Validation
CWM	Critical Water Main
DBN	Dynamic Bayesian Network
DNA	Deoxyribonucleic Acid
DQN	Deep Q-Network
EA	Evolutionary Algorithm
EAs	Evolutionary Algorithms
EC	Evolutionary Computation
ECG	Electrocardiograph
EEG	Electroencephalography
EFS	Evolving Fuzzy Systems
EIL	Expert-in-The-Loop
EMF	Explainable Matrix Factorisation
EUD	End-User Development
EUDA	End-User Data Analytic
EVE	Evolutionary Visual Exploration

FDD	Frequency Domain Decomposition
FLEXFIS	Flexible Fuzzy Inference Systems
FRF	Frequency Response Function
FS	Fuzzy Systems
FWNB	Feature-Weighted Nearest Bi-cluster
GSR	Galvanic Skin Response
GUI	Graphical User Interface
HBP	Hierarchical Beta Process
HCI	Human–Computer Interaction
HIEM	Human-Inspired Evolving Machines
HITL	Human-in-the-Loop
HMM	Hidden Markov Models
IEA	Interactive Evolutionary Algorithm
IEC	Interactive Evolutionary Computation
IME	Interactions-based Method for Explanation
iML	Interactive Machine Learning
IMPACT	Intelligent Multi-UxV Planner with Adaptive Collaborative/Control Technologies
IR	Information Retrieval
ISE	Influence Style Explanation
KA	Knowledge Acquisition
KB	Knowledge Base
KSE	Keyword Style Explanation
LIDeOGraM	Life science Interactive Development of Graph-based Models
LIME	Local Interpretable Model-agnostic Explanations
LSTM	Long Short-Term Memory
LVQ	Learning Vector Quantisation
LWL	Locally Weighted Learning
MARS	Multivariate Adaptive Regression Splines
MEMS	Microelectromechanical Systems
MF	Matrix Factorisation
MII	Mixed-Initiative Interaction
ML	Machine Learning
ML-CDSS	Machine Learning based Decision Support Systems
MLS	Machine Learning Systems
NID	Neural Interpretation Diagram
NSE	Neighbour Style Explanation
OLSR	Ordinary Least Squares Regression
PCA	Principle Component Analysis
POMDP	Partially Observable Markov Decision Process
PSD	Power Spectral Density
RBM	Restricted Boltzmann Machines
RGD	Recursive Gradient Descent
RL	Reinforcement Learning
RLM	Recursive Levenberg–Marquardt

RWM	Reticulation Water Main
SA	Situation Awareness
SAT	SA-based Agent Transparency
SHB	Sydney Harbour Bridge
SHM	Structural Health Monitoring
SMDP	Semi-Markov Decision Process
SM	Spectral Moments
SparseFIS	Sparse Fuzzy Inference Systems
STEM	Science, Technology, Engineering, and Mathematics
SVD	Singular Value Decomposition
SVM	Support Vector Machine
TML	Transparent Machine Learning
TS	Takagi-Sugeno
t-SNE	t-Distributed Stochastic Neighbour Embedding
UxV	Unmanned Vehicles
XAI	eXplainable Artificial Intelligence

Part I
Transparency in Machine Learning

Chapter 1
2D Transparency Space—Bring Domain Users and Machine Learning Experts Together

Jianlong Zhou and Fang Chen

Abstract Machine Learning (ML) is currently facing prolonged challenges with the user acceptance of delivered solutions as well as seeing system misuse, disuse, or even failure. These fundamental challenges can be attributed to the nature of the "black-box" of ML methods for domain users when offering ML-based solutions. That is, transparency of ML is essential for domain users to trust and use ML confidently in their practices. This chapter argues for a change in how we view the relationship between human and machine learning to translate ML results into impact. We present a two-dimensional transparency space which integrates domain users and ML experts together to make ML transparent. We identify typical Transparent ML (TML) challenges and discuss key obstacles to TML, which aim to inspire active discussions of making ML transparent with a systematic view in this timely field.

1.1 Introduction

With the rapid boom of data from various fields such as biology, finance, medicine, and society, data analytics-driven solutions are increasingly demanded for different purposes. From government service delivery to commercial transactions and all the way to specialised decision support systems, domain users are looking to integrate "Big Data" and advanced analytics into their business operations in order to become more analytics-driven in their decision making (which is also known as predictive decision making) [29]. Rapid advances in Machine Learning (ML) research have been inspired by such expectations. While we continuously find ourselves coming across ML-based appealing systems that seem to work (or have worked) surprisingly

J. Zhou (✉) · F. Chen
DATA61, CSIRO, 13 Garden Street, Eveleigh, NSW 2015, Australia
e-mail: jianlong.zhou@data61.csiro.au

F. Chen
e-mail: fang.chen@data61.csiro.au

© Crown 2018

J. Zhou and F. Chen (eds.), *Human and Machine Learning*, Human–Computer Interaction Series, https://doi.org/10.1007/978-3-319-90403-0_1

well in practical scenarios (e.g. AlphaGO's beating with professional GO players, and the self-driving cars for choosing between different road conditions), ML technologies are currently still facing prolonged challenges with user acceptance of delivered solutions as well as seeing system misuse, disuse, or even failure. These fundamental challenges can be attributed to the nature of the "black-box" of ML methods for domain experts and a lack of consideration of the human aspects when offering ML-based solutions [39]. For example, for many of non-ML users, they simply provide source data to an ML-based predictive decision making system, and after selecting some menu options on screen, the system displays colourful viewgraphs and/or recommendations as output [48]. It is neither clear nor well understood that how ML algorithms processed input data to get predictive probabilities, how trustworthy was this output, or how uncertainties were handled by underlying algorithmic procedures. That is, *transparency* of ML is significant for domain users to trust and use ML confidently in their practices. As a result, demands for ML transparency are increasing as the use of predictive decision making systems grows and as humans realise the potential impact of these systems in society.

Therefore, besides the development of ML algorithms, the research of introducing humans into the ML loop and making ML transparent has emerged recently as one of the active research fields recently [18, 20, 45]. Other terms are also used to refer to such researches, e.g. human-in-the-loop machine learning [19], human interpretability in machine learning [18], or eXplainable Artificial Intelligence (XAI) [14] and others. We use *Transparent Machine Learning* (TML) in this chapter. TML aims to translate ML into impacts by allowing domain users understand ML-based data-driven inferences to make trustworthy decisions confidently based on ML results, and allowing ML to be accessible by domain users without requiring training in complex ML algorithms and mathematical concepts. TML results in evolutionary improvements of the existing state of practice, for example,

- TML not only helps domain users proactively use ML outputs for informative and trustworthy decision making, but also allows users to see if an artificial intelligence system is working as desired;
- TML can help detect causes for an adverse decision and therefore can provide guidance on how to reverse it;
- TML allows effective interactions with ML algorithms, thus providing opportunities to the improve impact of ML algorithms in real-world applications.

Various approaches ranging from visualisation of the ML process to algorithmic explanations of ML methods have been investigated to make ML understandable and transparent [2, 9]. Yet these efforts are highly biased towards explaining ML algorithms, and are largely based on abstract visualisation or statistical algorithms, which introduce further complexities to domain users.

According to Wagstaff's [39] three-stage model of presenting an ML research program (the stage 1 is the preparation stage for an ML research program, the stage 2 is the development of ML algorithms, and the stage 3 is the impact stage of ML methods on real-world applications), the ML algorithm development is only one of three stages in the overall pipeline. Therefore the current highly biased ML algorithm explanation ignores the other two critical stages to translate ML results into impact. The success of the other two stages of preparation of an ML program and deployment of ML results is highly dependent on human users and therefore human factors. This is because that the judgement of ML results as "right" or "wrong" is an activity that comes after apprehension, which needs a very human intervention [36, 40]. Furthermore, the current visualisation or algorithmic explanations of ML are isolated from the two other stages and are rarely accompanied by an assessment of whether or how human factors from the preparation stage and deployment stage affect ML algorithm explanations or how the three stages interact with each other.

This also occurs because there is no a systematic understanding of the problem of making ML transparent. A systematic view of TML can be used as the guidance for future investigations in this timely field in order to translate ML results into impact in real-world applications. Furthermore, many TML or ML explanation approaches are phrased in terms of answering why a prediction/classification is made. It is time for us to ask questions of a larger scope: What is TML's ideal objective? What are the roles of domain users in TML? Can we maximize the transparency of ML by approaches besides explaining ML algorithms? Or can we characterise ML-based solutions in a more meaningful way that measures the user's cognitive responses because of ML transparency?

In this chapter, we argue for a change in how we view the relationship between human and machine learning to translate ML results into impact. The contributions of this work include: (1) identifying a fundamental problem in making ML transparent: a lack of connection between domain users and ML experts; (2) suggesting a two-dimensional (2D) transparency space which integrates the domain users and ML experts together to make ML transparent; (3) introducing transparent questions and transparent uses as well as feedback into the 2D transparency space from domain user's perspective to make ML transparent; (4) identifying example TML challenges to the community; and (5) finding several key obstacles to TML. This chapter does not propose ML algorithms or present experimental results but inspires a systematic view of making ML transparent in this timely field for further active discussions to improve the impact of ML in real-world applications.

1.2 Can Only Explanation Make ML Transparent?

This section highlights related work conducted recently and demonstrates their limitations in making ML transparent.

1.2.1 Hyper-focus on Visualisation of ML Process

In the early years, visualisation is primarily used to explain the ML process of simple ML algorithms in order to make ML transparent. For example, different visualisation methods are used to examine specific values and show probabilities of picked objects visually for Naïve–Bayes [5, 26], decision trees [3], Support Vector Machines (SVMs) [7], or Hidden Markov Models (HMMs) [10]. Advanced visualisation techniques are then proposed to present more complex ML processes. Erra et al. [12] introduced a visual clustering which utilises a collective behavioral model. Each data item is represented by an agent visualised with a metaphor in 3D domain. Visualisation helps users to understand and guide the clustering process. Huang et al. [17] used a visual clustering for assisting the analysis of email attacks. Paiva et al. [30] presented an approach that employs the similarity tree visualisation to distinguish groups of interest within the data set.

Visualisation is also used as an interaction interface for users in data analysis. For example, Guo et al. [15] introduced a visual interface named Nugget Browser allowing users to interactively submit subgroup mining queries for discovering interesting patterns dynamically. Talbot et al. [38] proposed EnsembleMatrix allowing users to visually ensemble multiple classifiers together and provides a summary visualisation of results of these multiple classifiers. Zhou et al. [48] revealed states of key internal variables of ML models with interactive visualisation to let users perceive what is going on inside a model.

More recent work tries to use visualisation as an interactive tool to facilitate ML diagnosis. ModelTracker [2] provides an intuitive visualisation interface for ML performance analysis and debugging. Chen et al. [8] proposed an interactive visualisation tool by combining ten state-of-the-art visualisation methods in ML (shaded confusion matrix, ManiMatrix, learning curve, learning curve of multiple models, McNemar Test matrix, EnsembleMatrix, Customized SmartStripes, Customized ModelTracker, confusion matrix with sub-categories, force-directed graph) to help users interactively carry out a multi-step diagnosis for ML models. Krause et al. [23, 24] presented an interactive visual diagnostic tool for ML models based on the concept of partial dependence to communicate how features affect the prediction, as well as support for tweaking feature values and seeing how the prediction responds.

Visualisations comprise the major body of ML process explanations. However, the abstract visualisations may introduce more complexities to users. Furthermore, without the consideration of how a domain problem is phrased as an ML task and what user cognitive responses on ML-based decisions are, users still have difficulty understanding the overall ML process with abstract visualisations.

1.2.2   Hyper-focus on Algorithmic Explanation of ML

Besides visualisation, various algorithmic approaches are proposed to explain ML models. At least two types of algorithmic explanation approaches can be categorised:

- **Feature/instance contributions to ML models**: The approach of feature contributions reveals each feature contributions to ML models to explain ML models. For example, Robnik-Sikonja et al. [34] explained classification models by evaluating contributions of features to classifications based on the idea that the importance of a feature or a group of features in a specific model can be estimated by simulating lack of knowledge about the values of the feature(s). Besides feature contributions, an explanation of individual instance contributions to ML models was investigated to allow users to understand why a classification/prediction is made. For example, Landecker et al. [27] developed an approach of contribution propagation to give per-instance explanations of a network's classifications. Baehrens et al. [4] used local gradients to characterise how an instance has to be moved to change its predicted label in order to explain individual classification decisions.

- **Mathematical models for ML model explanation**: This kind of explanation uses mathematical models to explain why certain ML results are obtained. For example, Chen et al. [9] developed statistical models to give online users of social network sites (e.g. Facebook) transparency into why certain inferences are made about them and control to inhibit those inferences by hiding certain personal information from inference. Zahavy et al. [43] explained the success of Deep Q-Network (DQN) based on its learned representation, by showing that DQN is mapping states to sub-manifolds with mutual spatial and temporal structure and learning specific policies at each cluster using a t-Distributed Stochastic Neighbor Embedding (t-SNE) map. Zrihem et al. [49] further developed approaches to automatically learn an internal Semi-Markov Decision Process (SMDP) model in the DQN's learned representation and visualized SMDP for the explanation of DQN's policy. Koh and Liang [22] used influence functions to trace a model's prediction back to its training data, and identify the training points which most contribute to a given prediction.

These approaches explain ML models mostly from an ML expert's perspective, which introduce further complexities to domain users and make it more difficult for users to understand complex algorithms. Furthermore, these explanations only focus on one stage of ML method development and ignore the other two stages of an ML program.

1.2.3 Limited User Cognitive Response Communication

As the ultimate frontline users of ML-based systems, humans are the key stakeholders and human factors such as user trust are essential in extracting and delivering more sensible and effective insights from data science technologies [13]. From this perspective, Zhou et al. [44, 47] argued that communicating human cognitive responses such as user trust (on ML results) and confidence (in decision making based on ML results) benefit the evaluation of effectiveness of ML approaches. On the one hand, human cognition status could help understand to what degree humans accept innovative technologies. On the other hand, through understanding human cognition status in predictive decision making, ML-based decision attributes and even

ML models can be adaptively refined in order to make ML transparent. Therefore, different approaches are investigated to reveal human cognition states such as user trust and confidence in a predictive decision making scenario [44, 48].

Moreover, various researches have been investigated to learn user trust variations in ML-based decision making. Kizilcec [21] proposed that the transparency of algorithm interfaces can promote awareness and foster user trust. It was found that appropriate transparency of algorithms through explanation benefited user trust whereas too much explanatory information on algorithms eroded user trust. Ribeiro et al. [33] explained predictions of classifiers by learning an interpretable model locally around the prediction visualising importance of the most relevant instances/features to improve user trust in classifications. Kulesza et al. [25] investigated the soundness and completeness of explanations to end users to build mental models and demonstrated that end users trusted intelligent assistants more in explanations with high soundness and completeness.

However, these investigations focus more on the user cognitive responses during the stage of deployment of ML-based solutions, i.e. during the predictive decision making. It is highly necessary to feed user cognitive responses back into the loop to improve the understanding of ML program preparation and ML method development, and thus improve the overall transparency of ML.

1.2.4 Lack of Domain Knowledge Use in Transparency

Usually, it is more acceptable for domain users to get an understanding of data and their analysis with the use of domain knowledge. Therefore, domain knowledge is used in ML for different purposes. For example, Sun and DeJong [37] proposed explanation-augmented SVMs by incorporating domain knowledge into SVMs to identify the "important" features in the explained instance that are allowed to contribute to the kernel inner product evaluation. In the Bayesian network, domain knowledge is used to judge the form of linear inequality and approximate equality constraints on Bayesian network parameters to improve learning accuracy [46]. Domain knowledge is also used as a form of restrictions (e.g. existence or absence of arcs or edges between nodes) to improve Bayesian network structure (e.g. in less time) [11]. Altendorf et al. [1] used domain knowledge on qualitative monotonicity to guide the process of finding the maximum likelihood parameters. Williams and Mostafa [42] used domain knowledge of anticipated changes between the source and target tasks to reduce prediction uncertainty in active transfer learning. Interestingly, Harrison et al. [16] used sociocultural knowledge presented in stories to train virtual agents and robots to exhibit desired behaviours using reinforcement learning. Peng et al. [32] investigated the strategy of non-expert humans in curriculum learning and showed its potentials in the reinforcement learning process to improve the learning performance.

The previous work primarily focuses on the improvement of ML performance with the incorporation of domain knowledge into the learning process. Little work has been done on the use of domain knowledge to explain input data or to phrase practical problems into an ML program in order to make ML transparent.

1.3   Workflow of Applying ML to a Practical Problem

Before giving more details on TML, this section presents the current workflow of applying ML technologies to a practical problem with the use of water pipe failure prediction as a case study, in order to motivate TML approaches. Water supply networks constitute one of the most crucial and valuable urban assets. The combination of growing populations and ageing pipe networks requires water utilities to develop advanced risk management strategies in order to maintain their distribution systems in a financially viable way [28]. Especially for critical water mains (generally >300 mm in diameter), failure of defining based on the network location (e.g. a single trunk line connecting distribution areas or under a major road) or size which infers impact potential, failure of them typically bring severe consequences due to service interruptions and negative economic and social impacts, such as flooding and traffic disruption, which can cost millions of dollars [28]. From an asset management perspective there are two goals for critical mains management [41]: (1) minimise unexpected critical mains failure by prioritising timely renewals; (2) avoid replacing a pipe too early before the end of its economic life. Thus, utility companies use outcomes from failure prediction models, to make renewal plans based on risk levels of pipes and reasonable budget plans for pipe maintenance.

Figure 1.1 illustrates the workflow of phrasing water pipe failures as an ML program in the current practice. In this workflow, original domain data (in the format of various spread sheets and images) are firstly collected from customers. Interviews with domain experts are then arranged to learn details of the water pipes, such as what factors affect pipe failures from the domain experts' view, how domain experts predict pipe failures in their routine work. After this stage, the original domain data are cleaned in order to be processed easily by future stages, such as removing records with missing information or inputting default values in records with missing information. After cleaning the data, ML method developers try to get an overview of domain data and learn some patterns in the data. Based on the overview of the cleaned data, various data features are derived and ML models are developed. In order to allow users to easily perceive ML results, visualisation of ML results is then presented. The results need to be explained to users using domain knowledge. According to the explanation of ML results, decisions are made to practice domain actions such as digging out and replacing high risk pipes. From the practice actions, significant information can be gathered such as whether pipes predicted as high risk ones are confirmed or violated from actual digging. The information can be used as feedback to the pipeline to improve effectiveness of the ML analysis, such as feature definition and ML modeling.

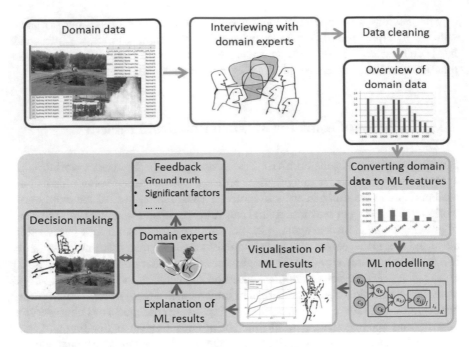

Fig. 1.1 Workflow of applying ML to water pipe failure predictions

From this workflow, we have the following observations:

- Domain users and ML experts collaborate closely in applying ML to practical problems.
- All stages of preparation of an ML program, deployment of ML, as well as feedback loop affect the effectiveness of ML-based solutions.
- Interviews with domain experts, which are based on questions/answers and domain knowledge, play a significant roles in applying ML to practical problems.

Based on these observations, this chapter proposes a two-dimensional transparency space to make ML transparent as presented in the following sections.

1.4 Making Machine Learning Transparent

Instead of just explaining why a certain prediction is being made with abstract visualisation or more complex mathematical algorithms which add additional complexities to domain users, can domain users play a greater role as they are the key stakeholders of ML-based solutions? This is also not simply a matter of user studies on different ML algorithms. A fundamental change is highly necessary in the overall workflow of making ML transparent in applying ML to domain applications.

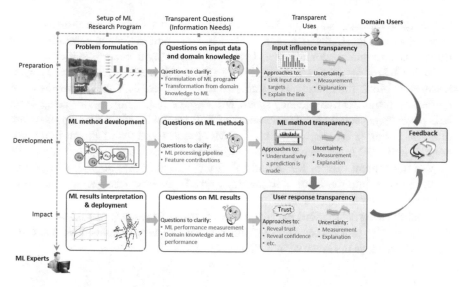

Fig. 1.2   The uncertainty-aware 2D transparency space of ML-based solutions

This chapter argues that making ML transparent can be framed into a two-dimensional (2D) transparency space by integrating both ML experts and domain users as active participants into the overall workflow (see Fig. 1.2). In this transparency space, the horizontal axis from left to right represents how ML-based solutions are used from a domain user's perspective, while the vertical axis from top to bottom shows the view of phrasing an ML-based solution from an ML expert's perspective. This 2D transparency space implies that domain users and ML experts need to collaborate closely to make ML transparent.

From a domain user's perspective, the process of using an ML-based solution can be divided into three steps (see the horizontal axis in Fig. 1.2): (1) setup of an ML research program, (2) understanding transparent questions (information needs) for the effective use of ML-based solutions, and (3) transparent uses of ML-based solutions. Transparent questions are those questions and information needs domain users may have for the effective use of ML-based solutions. Transparent uses focus on providing answers for transparent questions for the effective use of ML-based solutions. From an ML expert's perspective, the process of phrasing an ML program can be divided into three stages (see the vertical axis in Fig. 1.2): (1) preparation of an ML research program, (2) development of ML methods, and (3) deployment and impact of ML methods. For the purpose of clearances, the terms of "step" and "stage" are used for the horizontal and vertical axis respectively to show different points on each axis.

Furthermore, uncertainty is inherent to the whole process of ML-based data analytics from data collection, data preprocessing, ML modelling to the deployment. It has been shown that uncertainty awareness positively influences human trust building in ML-based decision making [6, 35]. In the 2D transparency space, uncertainty is integrated into each stage of ML-based solutions so that domain users are aware of uncertainty and its effects in order to make ML transparent. Such uncertainty-aware transparent ML allows domain users to make trustworthy decisions confidently.

In this 2D transparency space, domain users and ML experts collaborate to implement each block for making ML transparent. However, they may have different emphases in this 2D transparency space: ML experts focus more on the setup of an ML program especially the development of ML methods, while domain users are more interested in the transparent uses of ML-based solutions as shown in the last column in the 2D transparency space. Furthermore, a feedback loop is set up in the step of transparent uses of ML-based solutions, allowing user cognitive responses to be fed back into the input transparency and ML method transparency stages to improve the overall transparency.

The following subsections introduce more details of each step of ML-based solutions in the 2D transparency space from the domain user's perspective since the domain user plays the key role in TML.

1.4.1 Setup of ML Research Program

The setup of an ML research program is the starting step of applying ML approaches to practical problems (see the first column in Fig. 1.2). During the preparation stage of setting up the ML research program, business requirements are presented and related data are provided. The data are preprocessed (e.g. cleaning, transformation, feature extraction) and then an ML task is phrased based on the data. This stage requires close collaboration between ML experts and domain users. Based on the data acquired at the preparation stage, ML experts develop ML methods at the second stage and choose metrics to evaluate ML algorithms. The third stage of ML impact focuses on the interpretation and deployment of ML results to create impact.

1.4.2 Transparent Questions

Instead of utilising the ML research program directly which hinders the effective use of ML-based solutions, this chapter argues that questions on (and information needs to understand) the ML research program from the domain user's perspective at each stage both help transparent uses of ML-based solutions effectively and motivate ML experts to develop approaches meaningfully. Therefore, in the 2D transparency space, the introduction of "transparent questions" connects the "ML research program" and "transparent uses" of ML-based solutions (see the second column in Fig. 1.2). Transparent questions demonstrate the problems domain users may have in order to use ML-based solutions transparently. From this perspective, the step of "transparent questions" helps to transfer the use of ML-based solutions from the ML's perspective to the domain's perspective.

Domain users may have different questions corresponding to different stages of the ML research program. Taking the water pipe failure prediction as an example (see the previous section), domain users may have questions [41]:

- At the preparation stage, domain users may have questions such as how the pipe failure problem is formulated and explained as an ML program, and how domain knowledge on pipe failures is transformed into the ML program.
- At the development stage, domain users are concerned with how the pipe failure records are processed to get the future failure predictions, what are the influences of different pipe attributes (e.g. pipe environment, length, size) on pipe failures, or how the prediction process is interpreted with domain knowledge.
- At the impact stage, domain users have concerns such as how, when, and where pipes will fail within the entire network (i.e. how to interpret the ML performance measurement based on the domain knowledge), how to interpret the prediction and its uncertainty with domain knowledge, or how to transfer the new knowledge from the ML-based data analysis to the industry for optimal pipe management.

These transparent questions are proposed based on domain knowledge and delivered along the horizontal axis of domain users in the 2D transparency space to the next step of "transparent uses" in order to develop approaches to answer these questions. Part VI in this book features the efforts of the use of domain knowledge in machine learning. The questions from domain experts help to define meaningful features in ML, explain ML results, and improve ML performance in real-world applications.

1.4.3 Transparent Uses

Depending on different transparent questions, various approaches are then developed to provide answers for those corresponding questions. The approaches for transparent uses of ML-based solutions (see the third column in Fig. 1.2) are detailed as follows:

- **Input influence transparency**: This stage focuses on the presentation of input influences on the system output to make ML transparent. It needs to present understanding of the business requirements, feature space definition, and the process of phrasing real-world problems as ML tasks to domain users. The input influence transparency uses this understanding and domain knowledge, and sets up a domain specific input influence transparency report. For example, in the water pipe failure prediction, this stage helps domain users understand how the water pipe failure is phrased as an ML task and what influence each attribute of input data has on failures based on domain knowledge. Part II and Part III in this book discuss different approaches on input influence transparency from visualisation and algorithmic perspectives.
- **ML method transparency**: This stage reveals how ML methods work for problems to be solved, and why a prediction is made based on the domain knowledge. The ML method transparency also defines meaningful evaluation metrics based

on domain knowledge. For example, in the water pipe failure prediction, this stage communicates why certain pipes are predicted as high risk pipes based on domain knowledge. Part II and Part III in this book cover approaches on ML method transparency.

- **User cognitive response transparency**: In this stage, user cognitive responses such as trust and confidence in ML-based solutions are communicated to show the acceptance of ML-based solutions by domain users. These are based on the meaningful definition of the measurement of ML performance. For example, in the water pipe failure prediction, domain users are more interested in whether the ML-based solutions help them make trustworthy decisions in pipe risk management thus saving management costs in practice. Part IV in this book presents studies on user cognitive response transparency in predictive decision making.
- **Feedback loop**: In the step of transparent uses, a feedback loop is introduced into the pipeline, which links the three stages of input influence transparency, ML method transparency, and user cognitive response transparency together. Such link allows the adaptation of transparency at each stage to make ML transparent. For example, in the water pipe failure prediction, when domain users have low trust in ML-based pipe failure management (e.g. in the case where predictions of risk pipes are not consistent with the actual pipe failures), user cognitive responses are used as the feedback to the input and ML method development stages to modulate corresponding parameters until domain users are satisfied with ML-based solutions with appropriate cognitive response levels. Part V in this book tries to introduce users into the feedback loop from the perspectives of evaluation of ML.

1.4.4 Uncertain But Verified for Transparency

This subsection shows the importance of uncertainty and its effects on transparency at each stage of ML-based solutions.

At the preparation stage of ML-based solutions, uncertainty is mainly from the input data and its preprocessing actions. The uncertainty from these sources needs to be quantified and explained based on the domain knowledge. The clarification of uncertainty at this stage helps users better understand the input influence transparency. At the ML method development stage, uncertainty is mainly from ML models. Uncertainty from the preparation stage is propagated to this stage. The revealing and explanation of these uncertainties allow domain users to perceive the transparency of ML methods in ML-based solutions. At the impact stage, ML results and their visualisations cause uncertainties. These uncertainties as well as uncertainty propagated from the ML method development stage together affect user responses to ML-based solutions. The revealing of the effects of uncertainty on user responses such as user trust helps both domain users and ML experts understand the effectiveness and transparency of ML-based solutions. The uncertainties at each stage may be modulated in the feedback loop in order to allow domain users make trustworthy decisions confidently based on ML solutions.

Finally, the flow of uncertainty generation, propagation, transformation, and aggregation during the overall process of ML-based solutions can be revealed to users. By communicating uncertainty at each stage, the 2D transparency space allows users to verify results at each stage to make ML transparent.

1.5   TML Challenges

TML is an ambitious framework for improving ML impact in real-world applications. By considering both dimensions of domain users and ML experts in the 2D transparency space as shown in Fig. 1.2, we propose following research challenges as examples to make ML transparent:

- **Problem formulation**: General protocols are set up to link input data and targets, and phrase practical problems into ML tasks based on domain knowledge.
- **ML process explanation**: The domain knowledge is incorporated into the ML process. The explanation of the ML process becomes a part of routine domain work without the use of ML knowledge.
- **User cognitive response communication**: User cognitive responses such as trust and confidence in ML-based solutions are automatically communicated to show the acceptance of ML by domain users.
- **User cognitive response feedback**: User cognitive responses in ML-based solutions are used as feedback to the input stage and ML development stage to modulate corresponding parameters from the domain user's perspective in order to make ML acceptable to domain users with appropriate levels of cognitive responses.
- **User cognitive responses in ML**: User cognitive responses from the feedback loop are integrated into the ML method development and result in the user cognition-driven ML method.
- **Uncertainty communication**: ML transparency strongly depends on the extent of a domain user's awareness of the inherent underlying uncertainties. Users understand uncertainty in the ML process, and its relationships to use domains and expertise. However, there are still challenges in uncertainty analysis during ML-based solutions: first, uncertainty may originate from different states of the ML-based data analytics (e.g. preprocessing, training, visualisation), and thus it is difficult to effectively quantify the uncertainty. Second, it is difficult to model different types (e.g. input data uncertainty, model uncertainty, human uncertainty during interaction) of uncertainty with a unified framework.
- **ML-based decision making**: Users understand how ML results are effectively used in decision making, and how knowledge of uncertainty influences ML-based decision making. The outcomes of decision making are used to evaluate effectiveness of ML-based solutions.

These transparent challenges differ from existing challenges such as [31, 38] which focus more on parameter selections and performance evaluations, or [39] which ignore user cognitive responses and therefore do not put those responses into a feedback loop. The challenges phrased in this chapter try to capture the entire pipeline of a successful ML-based solution, from preparation of ML tasks, ML method development and deployment, to the feedback loop from both the ML expert and domain user's perspectives. The purpose is to make domain users aware that uncertainty is coupled in the pipeline and thus make ML an integral part of the overall domain problem exploration.

These TML challenges act as inspiring examples and additional transparent challenges are to be formulated to benefit both the ML field and domain applications.

1.6   Obstacles to TML

The obstacles to the success of TML we can foresee lie in different aspects ranging from fundamental research to the generalisation of approaches.

- **Fundamentals**: User cognitive responses such as trust and confidence play significant roles in TML. Despite the conspicuous progress in neuroscience for understanding human's neural activities, there are still many unsolved questions on quantitative evaluation of human cognition. This is one of the major obstacles in understanding human cognition in predictive decision making. Current research in neuroscience uses various techniques such as imaging techniques (e.g. fMRI) or other physiological signals to understand differences in user cognitions when conducting tasks. However, these are not as precise as expected. There are still no concrete theories or evidence for the quantitative evaluation of human cognition states, and for the linking of human cognition with predictive decision making. These obstacles may not always be there, but are more likely to be understood precisely with the advancement of neurobiological and genome research with modern tools such as imaging or microscopic techniques.
- **Uncertainty and risk**: Uncertainty is coupled with the entire ML process. Despite the improvement of ML technologies, humans can still feel at risk when making decisions relying on machines because of uncertainties. For instance, how can this uncertainty be solved in and delivered to different stages? When an error from the system occurs, to where can we track back the error sources? What is the cost when making a false decision? How risky is it to take actions based on decisions from the system? These concerns are especially significant in modern complex high-risk domains such as aviation, medicine, and finance. These concerns could be addressed by communicating uncertainty and risk from the domain user's perspective.
- **Generalisation**: Human cognition may be different in conducting the same task because of differences of users' social background such as culture, education, gender and other factors. People from different domains may also show differences in their attitude while conducting the same task. Therefore, the generalization becomes one obvious obstacle if predictive decision making with user cognition state communication is conducted by different users from different domains.

1.7   Conclusion

Machine learning offers a large number of powerful ways to approach problems that otherwise require manual solutions. However, significant barriers to widespread adoption of ML approaches still exist because of the "black-box" of ML to domain users. Different investigations have been conducted to make "black-box" ML transparent ranging from visualisation and algorithmic explanations to user cognitive response communication in ML-based solutions. However, many current approaches of making ML transparent suffer from the abstract visualisation-based and more complex algorithmic explanations for domain users, which continuously isolate domain users from ML in ML-based solutions for widespread impact in real-world applications. This chapter integrated domain users and ML experts into a 2D transparency space, where the introduction of transparent questions and transparent uses from the domain user's perspective makes ML transparent meaningfully based on domain knowledge. This chapter also identified examples of TML challenges and several key obstacles for TML in the hope of inspiring active discussions of how ML can be made transparent to best benefit domain applications.

Acknowledgements This work was supported in part by AOARD under grant No. FA2386-14-1-0022 AOARD 134131.

References

1. Altendorf, E.E., Restificar, A.C., Dietterich, T.G.: Learning from sparse data by exploiting monotonicity constraints. In: Proceedings of the Twenty-First Conference on Uncertainty in Artificial Intelligence (UAI'05), pp. 18–26. Arlington, US (2005)
2. Amershi, S., Chickering, M., Drucker, S.M., Lee, B., Simard, P., Suh, J.: ModelTracker: redesigning performance analysis tools for machine learning. In: Proceedings of the 33rd Annual ACM Conference on Human Factors in Computing Systems, pp. 337–346 (2015)
3. Ankerst, M., Elsen, C., Ester, M., Kriegel, H.P.: Visual classification: an interactive approach to decision tree construction. In: Proceedings of KDD '99, pp. 392–396 (1999)
4. Baehrens, D., Schroeter, T., Harmeling, S., Kawanabe, M., Hansen, K., Möller, K.R.: How to explain individual classification decisions. J. Mach. Learn. Res. **11**, 1803–1831 (2010)
5. Becker, B., Kohavi, R., Sommerfield, D.: Visualizing the simple bayesian classifier. In: Fayyad, U., Grinstein, G.G., Wierse, A. (eds.) Information visualization in data mining and knowledge discovery, pp. 237–249 (2002)
6. Boukhelifa, N., Perrin, M.E., Huron, S., Eagan, J.: How data workers cope with uncertainty: a task characterisation study. In: Proceedings of the 2017 CHI Conference on Human Factors in Computing Systems, CHI '17, pp. 3645–3656 (2017)
7. Caragea, D., Cook, D., Honavar, V.G.: Gaining insights into support vector machine pattern classifiers using projection-based tour methods. In: Proceedings of KDD '01, pp. 251–256 (2001)
8. Chen, D., Bellamy, R.K.E., Malkin, P.K., Erickson, T.: Diagnostic visualization for non-expert machine learning practitioners: A design study. In: 2016 IEEE Symposium on Visual Languages and Human-Centric Computing (VL/HCC), pp. 87–95 (2016)

9. Chen, D., Fraiberger, S.P., Moakler, R., Provost, F.: Enhancing transparency and control when drawing data-driven inferences about individuals. In: ICML 2016 Workshop on Human Interpretability in Machine Learning, pp. 21–25 (2016)
10. Dai, J., Cheng, J.: HMMEditor: a visual editing tool for profile hidden Markov model. BMC Genomics **9**(Suppl 1), S8 (2008)
11. de Campos, L.M., Castellano, J.G.: Bayesian network learning algorithms using structural restrictions. Int. J. Approx. Reason. **45**(2), 233–254 (2007)
12. Erra, U., Frola, B., Scarano, V.: An interactive bio-inspired approach to clustering and visualizing datasets. In: Proceedings of the 15th International Conference on Information Visualisation 2011, pp. 440–447 (2011)
13. Fisher, D., DeLine, R., Czerwinski, M., Drucker, S.: Interactions with big data analytics. Interactions **19**(3), 50–59 (2012)
14. Gunning, D.: Explainable artificial intelligence (xai). https://www.darpa.mil/program/explainable-artificial-intelligence (2017). Accessed 1 Aug 2017
15. Guo, Z., Ward, M.O., Rundensteiner, E.A.: Nugget browser: visual subgroup mining and statistical significance discovery in multivariate datasets. In: Proceedings of the 15th International Conference on Information Visualisation, pp. 267–275 (2011)
16. Harrison, B., Banerjee, S., Riedl, M.O.: Learning from stories: using natural communication to train believable agents. In: IJCAI 2016 Workshop on Interactive Machine Learning. New York (2016)
17. Huang, M.L., Zhang, J., Nguyen, Q.V., Wang, J.: Visual clustering of spam emails for DDoS analysis. In: Proceedings of the 15th International Conference on Information Visualisation, pp. 65–72 (2011)
18. ICML: ICML 2016 Workshop on Human Interpretability in Machine Learning. https://sites.google.com/site/2016whi/ (2016). Accessed 30 Jan 2017
19. ICML: ICML 2017 Workshop on Human in the Loop Machine Learning. http://machlearn.gitlab.io/hitl2017/ (2017). Accessed 1 Aug 2017
20. IJCAI: IJCAI 2016 Interactive Machine Learning Workshop. https://sites.google.com/site/ijcai2016iml/home (2016). Accessed 30 Jan 2017
21. Kizilcec, R.F.: How much information?: effects of transparency on trust in an algorithmic interface. In: Proceedings of the 2016 CHI Conference on Human Factors in Computing Systems, pp. 2390–2395 (2016)
22. Koh, P.W., Liang, P.: Understanding black-box predictions via influence functions. In: Proceedings of ICML2017, pp. 1885–1894. Sydney, Australia (2017)
23. Krause, J., Perer, A., Bertini, E.: Using visual analytics to interpret predictive machine learning models. In: 2016 ICML Workshop on Human Interpretability in Machine Learning, pp. 106–110 (2016)
24. Krause, J., Perer, A., Ng, K.: Interacting with predictions: visual inspection of black-box machine learning models. In: Proceedings of the 2016 CHI Conference on Human Factors in Computing Systems, pp. 5686–5697 (2016)
25. Kulesza, T., Stumpf, S., Burnett, M., Yang, S., Kwan, I., Wong, W.K.: Too much, too little, or just right? Ways explanations impact end users' mental models. In: 2013 IEEE Symposium on Visual Languages and Human-Centric Computing (VL/HCC), pp. 3–10 (2013)
26. Kulesza, T., Stumpf, S., Wong, W.K., Burnett, M.M., Perona, S., Ko, A., Oberst, I.: Why-oriented end-user debugging of naive bayes text classification. ACM Trans. Interact. Intell. Syst. **1**(1), 2:1–2:31 (2011)
27. Landecker, W., Thomure, M.D., Bettencourt, L.M.A., Mitchell, M., Kenyon, G.T., Brumby, S.P.: Interpreting individual classifications of hierarchical networks. In: 2013 IEEE Symposium on Computational Intelligence and Data Mining (CIDM), pp. 32–38 (2013)
28. Li, Z., Zhang, B., Wang, Y., Chen, F., Taib, R., Whiffin, V., Wang, Y.: Water pipe condition assessment: a hierarchical beta process approach for sparse incident data. Mach. Learn. **95**(1), 11–26 (2014)
29. McElheran, K., Brynjolfsson, E.: The rise of data-driven decision making is real but uneven. Harvard Business Review (2016)

30. Paiva, J.G., Florian, L., Pedrini, H., Telles, G., Minghim, R.: Improved similarity trees and their application to visual data classification. IEEE Trans. Vis. Comput. Graph. **17**(12), 2459–2468 (2011)
31. Patel, K., Fogarty, J., Landay, J.A., Harrison, B.: Examining difficulties software developers encounter in the adoption of statistical machine learning. In: Proceedings of the 23rd national conference on Artificial intelligence, pp. 1563–1566. Chicago, USA (2008)
32. Peng, B., MacGlashan, J., Loftin, R., Littman, M.L., Roberts, D.L., Taylor, M.E.: An empirical study of non-expert curriculum design for machine learners. In: IJCAI 2016 Workshop on Interactive Machine Learning. New York, USA (2016)
33. Ribeiro, M.T., Singh, S., Guestrin, C.: Why Should I Trust You?: Explaining the Predictions of Any Classifier [cs, stat] (2016). arXiv: 1602.04938
34. Robnik-Sikonja, M., Kononenko, I., Strumbelj, E.: Quality of classification explanations with PRBF. Neurocomputing **96**, 37–46 (2012)
35. Sacha, D., Senaratne, H., Kwon, B.C., Ellis, G.P., Keim, D.A.: The role of uncertainty, awareness, and trust in visual analytics. IEEE Trans. Vis. Comput. Graph. **22**(1), 240–249 (2016)
36. Scantamburlo, T.: Machine learning in decisional process: a philosophical perspective. ACM SIGCAS Comput. Soc. **45**(3), 218–224 (2015)
37. Sun, Q., DeJong, G.: Explanation-augmented SVM: an approach to incorporating domain knowledge into SVM learning. In: Proceedings of ICML2005, pp. 864–871 (2005)
38. Talbot, J., Lee, B., Kapoor, A., Tan, D.S.: EnsembleMatrix: interactive visualization to support machine learning with multiple classifiers. In: Proceedings of the SIGCHI Conference on Human Factors in Computing Systems, pp. 1283–1292 (2009)
39. Wagstaff, K.: Machine learning that matters. In: Proceedings of ICML2012, pp. 529–536 (2012)
40. Watanabe, S.: Pattern Recognition: Human and Mechanical. Wiley, USA (1985)
41. Whiffin, V.S., Crawley, C., Wang, Y., Li, Z., Chen, F.: Evaluation of machine learning for predicting critical main failure. Water Asset Manag. Int. **9**(4), 17–20 (2013)
42. Williams, M.O., Mostafa, H.: Active transfer learning using knowledge of anticipated changes. In: IJCAI 2016 Workshop on Interactive Machine Learning (2016)
43. Zahavy, T., Zrihem, N.B., Mannor, S.: Graying the black box: Understanding DQNs [cs] (2016). arXiv: 1602.02658
44. Zhou, J., Bridon, C., Chen, F., Khawaji, A., Wang, Y.: Be informed and be involved: effects of uncertainty and correlation on user confidence in decision making. In: Proceedings of ACM SIGCHI Conference on Human Factors in Computing Systems (CHI2015) Works-in-Progress. Korea (2015)
45. Zhou, J., Chen, F.: Making machine learning useable. Int. J. Intell. Syst. Technol. Appl. **14**(2), 91 (2015)
46. Zhou, Y., Fenton, N., Neil, M.: Bayesian network approach to multinomial parameter learning using data and expert judgments. Int. J. Approx. Reason. **55**(5), 1252–1268 (2014)
47. Zhou, J., Sun, J., Chen, F., Wang, Y., Taib, R., Khawaji, A., Li, Z.: Measurable decision making with GSR and pupillary analysis for intelligent user interface. ACM Trans. Comput. Human Interact. **21**(6), 33 (2015)
48. Zhou, J., Khawaja, M.A., Li, Z., Sun, J., Wang, Y., Chen, F.: Making machine learning useable by revealing internal states update a transparent approach. Int. J. Comput. Sci. Eng. **13**(4), 378–389 (2016)
49. Zrihem, N.B., Zahavy, T., Mannor, S.: Visualizing dynamics: from t-SNE to SEMI-MDPs. In: ICML 2016 Workshop on Human Interpretability in Machine Learning (2016)

Chapter 2
Transparency in Fair Machine Learning: the Case of Explainable Recommender Systems

Behnoush Abdollahi and Olfa Nasraoui

Abstract Machine Learning (ML) models are increasingly being used in many sectors, ranging from health and education to justice and criminal investigation. Therefore, building a fair and transparent model which conveys the reasoning behind its predictions is of great importance. This chapter discusses the role of explanation mechanisms in building fair machine learning models and explainable ML technique. We focus on the special case of recommender systems because they are a prominent example of a ML model that interacts directly with humans. This is in contrast to many other traditional decision making systems that interact with experts (e.g. in the health-care domain). In addition, we discuss the main sources of bias that can lead to biased and unfair models. We then review the taxonomy of explanation styles for recommender systems and review models that can provide explanations for their recommendations. We conclude by reviewing evaluation metrics for assessing the power of explainability in recommender systems.

2.1 Fair Machine Learning and Transparency

2.1.1 Fairness and Explainability

ML models make predictions that affect decision making. These decisions can have an impact on humans, either individually (for a single person) or collectively for a group of people. Such an impact can be unfair if it is based on an inference that is

B. Abdollahi · O. Nasraoui (✉)
Knowledge Discovery and Web Mining Lab, Computer Engineering and Computer Science Department, University of Louisville, KY, USA
e-mail: olfa.nasraoui@louisville.edu

B. Abdollahi
e-mail: b.abdollahi@louisville.edu

© Springer International Publishing AG, part of Springer Nature 2018   21
J. Zhou and F. Chen (eds.), *Human and Machine Learning*, Human–Computer Interaction Series, https://doi.org/10.1007/978-3-319-90403-0_2

biased against a certain group of people. Hence fairness is an important criterion in ML. Fairness in ML is a nascent topic that has only recently attracted attention [19, 34]. How to achieve this fairness is therefore still a matter of debate and there have recently been only a few attempts to define fairness and design fair algorithms within the ML context [18, 19, 26]. In our view, fairness can be achieved in multiple ways and either completely or partially. In particular, fairness can be addressed by changing the data that models ingest, the ways (i.e. algorithms) that models are learned, or the predictions that are made by these models. Another way that fairness can be achieved is by completely transparent models and thus scrutable predictions; in other words, predictions that can be justified as to the reasons why a particular prediction has been made and scrutinized for potential biases or mistakes. This is because such a scrutiny provides a certain level of accountability. For this reason, we believe that explainability can play an important role in achieving fairness in ML. Figure 2.1 presents a diagram that shows the relation between explainability, transparency and fairness. Figures 2.2 and 2.3 show two forms of designing explainable ML systems. In Fig. 2.2, the predictions are explained to the user using a model that is different from the ML model, while in Fig. 2.3, explainability is incorporated at the design level within the ML model.

2.1.2 Fair Machine Learning

ML models are increasingly being used in many sectors ranging from health and education to justice and criminal investigation. Hence, they are starting to affect the lives of more and more human beings. Examples include risk modeling and decision making in insurance, education (admission and success prediction), credit scoring, health-care, criminal investigation and predicting recidivism, etc [19, 54]. These models are susceptible to bias that stems from the data itself (attribute or labels

Fig. 2.1 Explainability leads to transparency and both lead to improving fairness of ML models

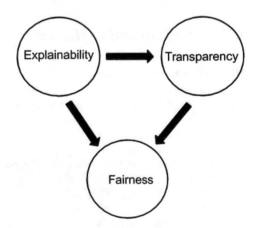

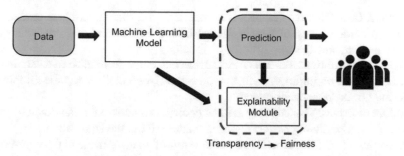

Fig. 2.2 In this form of fair ML, explainability occurs at the prediction step which results in more transparency and increasing fairness by presenting justified results to the user

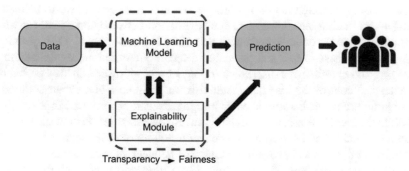

Fig. 2.3 In this form of fair ML, explainability occurs in the modeling phase which results in designing transparent ML models and consequently having more transparent and fair models

are biased) or from systemic social biases that generated the data (e.g. recidivism, arrests). As such, models that are learned from real world data can become unethical. Data can be collected and labeled in a biased way such that it is discriminative against a certain race, gender, ethnicity or age. As bias in the data can result in unfair models, ML algorithms are also susceptible to strategic manipulation [6, 24]. Therefore, they can be built such that the model creates bias against a certain group of people. The involvement of the human in all the stages of collecting data, building a model, and reporting the results, creates the setting for various types of bias to affect the process. Some of the sources of human bias in the stages of collecting and processing the data and reporting the results are [39]:

- Confirmation bias: It is a tendency to intentionally search for and include certain data and perform analysis in such a way as to make a predefined conclusion and prove a predetermined assumption.
- Selection bias: This happens when the sample is not collected randomly and because of a subjective selection technique, the data does not represent the whole population under study. Based on the elimination of samples or inclusion of certain samples, the resulting bias can be of the omission or inclusion type, respectively.

- Implicit bias: This type of bias is associated with the unconscious tendency to favor a certain group of people against others based on characteristics such as race, gender, and age.
- Over-generalization bias: This form of bias can come from making a certain conclusion based on information that is too general, especially when the sample size is small or is not specific enough.
- Automation bias: The tendency to favor decisions made from an automated system over the contradictory correct decision made without the automation.
- Reporting bias: This form of bias is the result of an error made in the reporting of the result when a certain positive finding is favored over the negative results.

Recent studies proposed techniques for building fair models by alleviating the effect of bias. Avoiding the use of sensitive features has been shown to be insufficient for eliminating bias, because of the correlation between some features which can indirectly lead to oriented and unfair data [32]. Kamishima et al. [33] formulated causes of unfairness in ML and presented a technique based on regularization by penalizing the classifier for discrimination and building discriminative probabilistic models to control the bias that resulted from prejudice. Since their solution as the prejudice remover is formulated as a regularizer, it can be used in a variety of probabilistic models such as the logistic regression classifier. Fish et al. [20] proposed a method based on shifting the decision boundary in the learning algorithm for achieving fairness and providing a trade-off between bias and accuracy.

In addition to designing fair algorithms, [32] proposed an approach for removing bias and generating fair predictions by changing the data before training the model. This method is based on modifying the dataset in order to transform the biased data into an unbiased one. The authors used a ranking function learned on the biased data to predict the class label without considering the sensitive attribute. Using this technique, they estimate the probability of the objects belonging to the target class. Their results showed that they could reduce the discrimination by changing the labels between the positive and negative class.

2.2 Explainable Machine Learning

Conventional evaluation metrics such as accuracy or precision do not account for the fairness of the model. Thus, to satisfy fairness, explainable models are required [36]. While building ethical and fair models is the ultimate goal, transparency is the minimum criterion that ML experts can directly contribute to and this could be the first step in this direction. Therefore, designing explainable intelligent systems that facilitate conveying the reasoning behind the results is of great importance in designing fair models. Note that we do not make a distinction between "explainability" and "interpretability" and use both terms interchangeably.

In the context of machine learning, interpretability means "explaining or presenting in understandable terms" [4]. In addition, interpretability and explanations can help to determine if qualities such as fairness, privacy, causality, usability and trust are met [18]. Doshi-Velez and Kim [18] presented a taxonomy of approaches for the evaluation of interpretability in ML models in general: application-grounded, human-grounded, and functionality-grounded. Application-grounded and human-grounded evaluation approaches are both user-based, while the functionality-grounded approach does not require human evaluation and uses some definition of the explainability for the evaluation. Experiments can be designed based on different factors, such as global versus local, which considers the general patterns existing in the model as global, while considering local reasoning behind the specific prediction of the model as local [18]. The global pattern is usually helpful for the designer and developer of the model when understanding or detecting bias or causality in the model. The local pattern, on the other hand, can be aimed at the end user of the systems to understand the justifications of the system decisions.

Explainability-aware ML techniques can generally be categorized into two main groups:

1. Models that explain their predictions in a way that is interpretable by the user. These types of methods usually only justify their output without providing an in depth understanding of the ML algorithm. This form of explanation is usually helpful when the user of the system is not an expert such as in the case of recommender systems. The explanation generation module can be located in a separate module relative to the predictor.
2. Models that incorporate interpretable models in the building of the automated systems. White-box models, such as decision trees where the ML model is intuitive for the user, can be categorized in this group, although, in these models the model is usually kept simple and in many cases they might not be as accurate as the more powerful black-box techniques.

Ribeiro et al. [42] proposed an explanation technique that explains the prediction of the classifiers locally, using a secondary learned white box model. Their proposed explanation conveys the relationship between the features (such as words in texts or parts in images) and the predictions; and helps in feature engineering to improve the generalization of the classifier. This can help in evaluating the model to be trusted in real world situations, in addition to using the offline accuracy evaluation metrics. Freitas [21] reviewed comprehensibility or interpretability of five classification models (decision trees, decision tables, classification rules, nearest neighbors, and Bayesian network classifiers). It is important to distinguish understanding or interpreting an entire model (which the paper does) from explaining a single prediction (which is the focus of this chapter). In addition, we note that Freitas overviews the problem from several perspectives and discusses the motivations for comprehensible classier models, which are:

1. Trusting the model: Regardless of accuracy, users are more prone to trusting a model if they can comprehend why it made the predictions that it did.
2. Legal requirements, in some cases like risk modeling, where a justification is required in case of denying credit to an applicant.
3. In certain scientific domains such as bioinformatics, new insights can be obtained from understanding the model, and can lead to new hypothesis formation and discoveries.
4. In some cases, a better understanding can help detect learned patterns in the classification model that are not really stable and inherent in the domain, but rather result from overfitting to the training data, thus they help detect the data shift problem: i.e., when the new instances deviate in their distribution from past training data; we note that concept drift (when a previously learned and accurate model no longer fits the new data because of changes in patterns of the data) can be considered as a special case of the data shift.

Understanding the logic behind the model and predictions (in other words, comprehension) can reveal to the user the fact that the (new) data has outpaced the model. The user can then realize that the model has become old and needs to be updated with a new round of learning on new data. Various interpretation methods exist depending on the family of classier models: decision trees, rule sets, decision tables, and nearest neighbors. Different studies have shown that the interpretability of entire classier models depends on the application domain and the data, with findings that sometimes contradict each other. Regardless of all the findings in interpreting models, we note that the task of interpreting an "entire classifier model" (e.g. a complete decision tree or a set of 500 rules) is different from that of one user trying to understand the rationale behind a "single prediction/recommendation" instance. That said, we find Freitas' review to be very important for transparency, fairness and explainability: first, he argues that model size alone is not sufficient to measure model interpretability, as some models' complexity is beyond mere size and small models can actually hurt the user's trust in the system (a notorious example is decision stump models [1-level trees]). Also, extremely small models would likely suffer in accuracy. Second, the work on interpreting rule-based models and nearest neighbor models can be useful to us because it is closest to the Collaborative Filtering (CF) recommendation mechanisms we study. For nearest neighbor models, Freitas [21] mentions that attribute values of nearest neighbors can help provide explanations for predictions, and that showing these values in decreasing order of relevance (based on an attribute weighting mechanism) is a sensible strategy. Another strategy is to show the nearest prototypes of training instances, for example after clustering the training instances. However, in both of these strategies, Freitas [21] was motivating interpretations of entire models rather than individual prediction explanations in the context of recommending items.

2.3 Explainability in Recommender Systems

2.3.1 Transparency and Fairness in Recommender Systems

Dascalu et al. [15] presented a survey of educational recommender systems and Thai-Nghe et al. [54] presented a recommender system for predicting student performance. Because the data in the education setting can be biased due to the underrepresentation of women in Science, Technology, Engineering, and Mathematics (STEM) topics [7, 23, 49], the predictive models resulted in an unfair system when evaluated using fairness metrics [58]. This form of bias can be dominant when the demographic profile of the user, consisting of features such as gender, race and age, is used in the model. To avoid unfairness or bias in the recommendations, the influence of specific information should be excluded from the prediction process of recommendation and for this reason CF techniques can be preferable to content-based recommender systems. While using CF models with only rating data can eliminate this bias, rating data can include another form of bias. For example in the MovieLens data [27], the ratings are obtained from the users who have rated a sufficient number of movies and the data is inherently biased towards the "successful users" [27]. This shows the serious problem of unfairness that can happen in a recommender model due to the bias in the data. This setting provides a motivation for designing transparent models and generating explainable recommendations. Sapiezynski et al. [43] studied the fairness of recommender systems used for predicting the academic performance of students. They showed that because of the gender imbalance in many data sets, the accuracy for female students was lower than male students and a different selection of features can result in a fair model.

2.3.2 Taxonomy of Explanations Styles

Recommender systems are a prominent example of a ML model that interacts directly with humans (users). This is in contrast to for instance, traditional medical decision making systems that interact with health-care providers/experts. Explanations have been shown to increase the user's trust in a recommender system in addition to providing other benefits such as scrutability, meaning the ability to verify the validity of recommendations [29]. This gap between accuracy and transparency or explainability has generated an interest in automated explanation generation methods. Explanations can be given using words related to item features or user demographic data, but these cannot be done easily in CF approaches. They vary from simple explanation formats such as: "people also viewed" in e-commerce websites [55] to the more recent social relationships and social tag based explanations [44, 57]. Bilgic and Mooney [8] showed how explaining recommendations can improve the user's estimation of the item's quality and help users make more accurate decisions (i.e. user satisfaction). Based on [8], three different approaches to explanations can be delineated:

1. Neighbor Style Explanation (NSE): this explanation format compiles a chart in CF that shows the active user's nearest CF neighbors' ratings on the recommended item. A histogram of these ratings among the nearest neighbors can be presented to the user. Figure 2.4 (1) and (3) show two different formats of the neighbor style explanation.
2. Influence Style Explanation (ISE): this explanation format presents a table of those items that had the most impact on computing the current recommendation. They can be used in both CBF and CF. An example is shown in Fig. 2.4 (2).
3. Keyword Style Explanation (KSE): this explanation format analyzes the content of recommended items and the user's profile (interests) to find matching words in CBF. An example of the KSE format which is obtained from the MovieLens benchmark dataset is shown in Fig. 2.4 (4). Figure 2.4 (3), shows an example of a neighbor style explanation (NSE) for a recommended movie based on the user's neighbors. This user-based example presents the ratings distribution of the user's neighbors on three rating levels.

Giving the user information about what type of data is used in the system encourages the user to provide more helpful data of that kind, such as preference ratings. Information about the neighbors selected as the predictors could give the user a chance to examine their ratings and to disregard the recommendations if the right neighborhood is not selected. A good explanation could also help discover weak predictions. The distribution of the ratings of the neighbors on a target item is helpful in identifying whether the prediction is based on enough data or not. Herlocker et al. [29] compared 20 other explanation systems and found histograms to perform best based on promotion only. Abdollahi and Nasraoui [3] presented an Explain-

Ratings of Your Neighbors for This Movie

Rating	Number of Neighbors
☆	0
☆☆	0
☆☆☆	3
☆☆☆☆	4
☆☆☆☆☆	2

(1)

Our recommendation is "Pulp Fiction", because you rated similar movies:

Movie	Your Rating
From Dusk Till Dawn (1996)	2
Seven (Se7en) (1995)	4
Usual Suspects The (1995)	4

(2)

Ratings of the People Who Share Your Interests and Have Watched This Movie

(3)

Our Justified Recommendations:

Movie	The reason is	Because you rated
Scream 2	horror	25 movies with this feature
Kiss the Girls	Freeman, Morgan	19 movies with this feature
The Peacemaker	Clooney, George	10 movies with this feature

(4)

Fig. 2.4 Four different explanation style formats: (1) NSE, (2) ISE, (3) NSE, (4) KSE

able Matrix Factorization (EMF) technique that proposed a metric for evaluating the explainability of the NSE and ISE style explanations and proposed to precompute explanations in a graph format and then incorporate them in a matrix factorization-based recommender system. NSE can be formulated based on the empirical density distribution of the similar users' ratings on a recommended item. Therefore, for user u, given the set of similar users as N_u, the conditional probability of item i having rating k can be written as:

$$\mathbf{P}(r_{u,i} = k | N_u) = \frac{|N_u \cap U_{i,k}|}{|N_u|} \tag{2.1}$$

where $U_{i,k}$ is the set of users who have given rating k to item i [3]. For each explanation, the expected value of the ratings given by N_u to the recommended item i can be calculated as follows:

$$\mathbf{E}(r_{u,i} | N_u) = \sum_{k \in \kappa} k \times \mathbf{P}(r_{u,i} = k | N_u) \tag{2.2}$$

where κ is the set of rating values [3]. Higher expected values indicate higher NSE explainability of item i for user u. Similarly, ISE can be formulated based on the empirical density distribution of the ratings given by user u to the items that are similar to the recommended item i. Given the set of similar items to item i, N_i, the conditional probability of item i having rating k can be written as:

$$\mathbf{P}(r_{u,i} = k | N_i) = \frac{|N_i \cap I_{u,k}|}{|N_i|} \tag{2.3}$$

where $I_{u,k}$ is the set of items that were given rating k by user u [3]. The expected value of the ratings of user u to the items in the set N_i can be calculated as follows:

$$\mathbf{E}(r_{u,i} | N_i) = \sum_{k \in \kappa} k \times \mathbf{P}(r_{u,i} = k | N_i) \tag{2.4}$$

The expected rating of similar users or similar items, obtained using Eqs. 2.2 or 2.4 gives a reasonable and intuitive measure of goodness or strength of a neighbor-based explanation.

Abdollahi and Nasraoui [2] expanded the EMF technique to Restricted Boltzmann Machines (RBM) and presented an explainability-aware RBM for CF. Bilgic and Mooney [8] proposed a book recommendation system (LIBRA). They argued that the quality of explanation can be measured using two different approaches: the promotion approach or the satisfaction approach. The promotion approach favors the explanation that would convince the user to adopt an item, while the satisfaction approach favors an explanation that would allow the user to assess the quality of (or how much they like) an item best. The conclusion from Bilgic and Mooney is that while the NSE style explanations were top performers in Herlocker et al.'s [29] experiments from the point of view of "promotion", KSE and next ISE explanations were found to be the top performers from a "satisfaction" perspective. Other than [8], Vig et al. [57] proposed a KSE explanation by introducing tagsplanation, which is generating explanations based on community tags. In their method, they consider a form of content-based explanation. The average of a given user's ratings of the movies with a specific tag defines how relevant a tag is for that user.

Another KSE approach was presented by McCarthy [37]. Their explanation is knowledge and utility based; that is, based on the users' needs and interests. The explanation is presented by describing the matched item for the specified requirements from the user. Zhang et al. [59] proposed an Explicit Factor Model (LFM) to generate explainable recommendations. They extracted explicit product features and user opinions using sentiment analysis. Ardissono et al. [5] built a recommendation system that suggests places to visit based on the travelers' type (e.g. children, impaired). In this case, the explanation comes in the form of the presentation of the recommendation to the user. The demographic information of the user is utilized to group users, and the explanation is focused on the most meaningful types of information for each group.

Billsus and Pazzani [9] presented a keyword style and influence style explanation approach for their news recommendation system which synthesizes speech to read stories to the users. The system generates explanations and adapts its recommendation to the user's interests based on the user's preferences and interests. They ask for a feedback from the user on how interesting the story had been to the user or if the user needs more information. The explanation is then constructed from the retrieved headlines that are closest to the user's interests. An example of their explanation is: "This story received a [high | low] relevance score, because you told me earlier that you were [not] interested in [closest headline]."

Symeonidis et al. [53] proposed a recommendation system that was based on the Feature-Weighted Nearest Bi-cluster (FWNB) algorithm, and they measured the accuracy of the recommendation using precision and recall. Their recommendation is based on finding bi-clusters containing item content features that have strong partial similarity with the test user. The item content features can later be used for justifying the recommendations. Their survey-based user study measured the user satisfaction against KSE, ISE and their own style, called KISE. They designed a user study with 42 pre- and post-graduate students of Aristotle University, who filled out an online survey. Each target user was asked to provide ratings for at least five movies that exist in the MovieLens data set. They then recommended a movie to each target user, justifying their recommendation by using the three justification styles (a different style each time). Finally, target users were asked to rate (in 1–5 rating scale) each explanation style separately to explicitly express their actual preference among the three styles. Subsequent analysis of the mean and standard deviation of the users' ratings for each explanation style, found KISE to outperform all other styles.

Paired t-tests also concluded that the difference between KISE and KSE and ISE was statistically significant at p-value $= 0.01$ level. Although the findings in [8, 53] did not compare with NSE, their study and experiments were similar to those of Bilgic and Mooney [8] who previously found KSE to be the top performer, followed closely by ISE (then by a margin, NSE). However it is worth mentioning that the data sets in the two studies were different: MovieLens for [53] versus books for [8]. Thus, their item content features are different (genre, keywords, directors, actors collected from the Internet and Movie Database (IMDb) for movies versus keywords in the author, title, description, subject, related authors, related titles, that are crawled from Amazon for books). It is easy to see that the content features for the books in LIBRA draw significantly more on Human Expert knowledge (subject, related authors and book titles) compared to the IMDB-sourced content features of movies in Symeonidis (no related movie titles or related producers).

Regardless of the type of explanation used for CF approaches, most explanation generation techniques reported in the literature are designed for transparent, or white-box methods, such as classical neighborhood-based CF. The prediction is performed as the process of aggregation of the ratings of the neighbor. This process could end up giving weak recommendations which might be discovered with good explanations. Other explanation methods, designed for opaque models such as latent factor models, assume some form of content data or an additional data source for explanations. Therefore, their explanation module is a separate approach from the recommender module which does not reflect the algorithm behind the suggestion made. Therefore, the explanation may, or may not reflect the underlying algorithm used by the system.

Thus it is of great interest to propose explainable CF techniques that computes the top-n recommendation list from items that are explainable in the latent space. To generate latent factors, some well-known latent factor models can be used such as: Matrix Factorization (MF) and Restricted Boltzmann Machines (RBM) methods [1–3].

2.4 Evaluation Metrics for Explainability in Recommender Systems

Evaluation of explanations in recommender systems require user-based metrics to evaluate the perceived quality of the explanation and the efficiency of the justification of the recommendation provided to the user by the explanation. Pu et al. [41] proposed a method that consists of 60 questions to assess the perceived quality of the recommendations such as usefulness, user satisfaction, influence on the users' intention to purchase the recommended product, and so on. However, this questionnaire was designed for user-based evaluation of the recommender system and not the explanation. Herlocker et al. [29] provided some initial explorations into measuring how explanations can improve the filtering performance of users, but their study was more focused on different aspects of the explanation generation than their evaluation. The user-based experiments in the two studies are different in two perspectives: Symeonidis et al. [53] used both (i) a quantitative (objective) metric for justification (coverage ratio) which is based on the amount of influence from content features in the justified recommendation list, and (ii) direct user's 1–5 scale ratings about how satisfied they are with each explanation style (KSE, ISE or KISE), while Bilgic and Mooney [8] collected the user's satisfaction via analysis of their ratings of the explanations before and after examining the recommended item in question. Furthermore [8] collected the user satisfaction without showing them which explanation method was used and most importantly, they collected the user satisfaction by providing an explanation of why the item was recommended before being shown and examining the item, thus allowing measurement of the user's satisfaction with the explanation itself and not merely the recommendation. Bilgic and Mooney's measure of the quality of an explanation is based on how similar the user's ratings of the recommendation are before and after examining the recommended item, thus measuring the power of the explanation to convey the true nature of the recommended item, even in cases where the recommended item was rated low by the user, and not merely a promotion-based explanation (which accounts only for highly rated recommended items). Despite the apparent limitation of [53], it remains easier to implement because it does not require the user to examine the item being recommended, and because it also computes an objective quantitative measure (based on total contribution of the influence of recommended items' dominant content features relative to the dominant user profile features). These can be computed directly from the ratings data, recommended lists, and explanations, none of which require actual user-based tests.

2.5   Conclusion

Machine learning models are increasingly reliant on data that is being generated at a fast pace. In particular, more and more of this data is related to humans or generated by human activity, and this in turn makes the data susceptible to various forms of human bias. Bias that can originate from the data or the design of the algorithm itself can result in building unfair machine learning models. Therefore, it is important to study and recognize the source of the bias before designing ML models. One way to determine if a model is fair is by incorporating explainability which results in transparency. Prominent examples of ML models are recommender system models that interact directly with humans and whose outputs are consumed directly by humans. Designing explainable recommender system models and explaining recommendations can help enhance the scrutability of the learned models and help detect potential biases, in addition to offering, as additional output, the reasoning behind the predictions. In this chapter, we presented our definition of fairness and transparency in ML models in addition to the main sources of bias that can lead to unfair models. We further reviewed the taxonomy of explanation styles for recommender systems, and reviewed existing models that can provide explanations for their recommendations. We concluded by reviewing several evaluation metrics for assessing the power of explainability in recommender systems.

Acknowledgements This research was partially supported by KSEF Award KSEF-3113-RDE-017 and NSF Grant NSF IIS-1549981.

References

1. Abdollahi, B., Nasraoui, O.: Explainable Matrix Factorization for Collaborative Filtering. In: Proceedings of the 25th International Conference Companion on World Wide Web. International World Wide Web Conferences Steering Committee (2016)
2. Abdollahi, B., Nasraoui, O.: Explainable Restricted Boltzmann Machines for Collaborative Filtering (2016). arXiv preprint arXiv:1606.07129
3. Abdollahi, B., Nasraoui, O.: Using Explainability for Constrained Matrix Factorization. In: Proceedings of the Eleventh ACM Conference on Recommender Systems, pp. 79–83. ACM (2017)
4. Antunes, P., Herskovic, V., Ochoa, S.F., Pino, J.A.: Structuring dimensions for collaborative systems evaluation. ACM Comput. Surv. (CSUR) **44**(2), 8 (2012)
5. Ardissono, L., Goy, A., Petrone, G., Segnan, M., Torasso, P.: Intrigue: personalized recommendation of tourist attractions for desktop and hand held devices. Appl. Artif. Intell. **17**(8–9), 687–714 (2003)
6. Baeza-Yates, R.: Data and algorithmic bias in the web. In: Proceedings of the 8th ACM Conference on Web Science, pp. 1–1. ACM (2016)
7. Beede, D.N., Julian, T.A., Langdon, D., McKittrick, G., Khan, B., Doms, M.E.: Women in STEM: A Gender Gap to Innovation (2011)
8. Bilgic, M., Mooney, R.J.: Explaining recommendations: satisfaction versus promotion. In: Beyond Personalization Workshop, IUI, vol. 5, 153 p. (2005)
9. Billsus, D., Pazzani, M. J.: A personal news agent that talks, learns and explains. In: Proceedings of the Third Annual Conference on Autonomous Agents, pp. 268–275. ACM (1999)
10. Brown, B., Aaron, M.: The politics of nature. In: Smith, J. (ed.) The Rise of Modern Genomics, 3rd edn. Wiley, New York (2001)
11. Broy, M.: Software engineering – from auxiliary to key technologies. In: Broy, M., Dener, E. (eds.). Software Pioneers, pp. 10–13. Springer, Berlin (2002)
12. Calfee, R.C., Valencia, R.R.: APA guide to preparing manuscripts for journal publication. American Psychological Association, Washington, DC (1991)
13. Cameron, D.: Feminism and Linguistic Theory. St. Martin's Press, New York (1985)
14. Cameron, D.: Theoretical debates in feminist linguistics: questions of sex and gender. In: Wodak, R. (ed.) Gender and Discourse, pp. 99–119. Sage Publications, London (1997)
15. Dascalu, M.I., Bodea, C.N., Mihailescu, M.N., Tanase, E.A., Ordoez de Pablos, P.: Educational recommender systems and their application in lifelong learning. Behav. Inf. Technol. **35**(4), 290–297 (2016)
16. Dod, J.: Effective substances. In: The Dictionary of Substances and Their Effects. Royal Society of Chemistry (1999) Available via DIALOG. http://www.rsc.org/dose/ titleofsubordinatedocument. Cited 15 Jan 1999
17. Dod, J.: Effective substances. In: The dictionary of substances and their effects. Royal Society of Chemistry (1999). Available via DIALOG. http://www.rsc.org/dose/Effectivesubstances. Cited 15 Jan 1999
18. Doshi-Velez, F., Kim, B.: Towards a rigorous science of interpretable machine learning (2017)
19. Dwork, C.: What's Fair?. In: Proceedings of the 23rd ACM SIGKDD International Conference on Knowledge Discovery and Data Mining, pp. 1–1. ACM (2017)
20. Fish, B., Kun, J., Lelkes, D.: A confidence-based approach for balancing fairness and accuracy. In: Proceedings of the 2016 SIAM International Conference on Data Mining, pp. 144–152. Society for Industrial and Applied Mathematics (2016)

21. Freitas, A.A.: Comprehensible classification models: a position paper. ACM SIGKDD Explor. Newsl. **15**(1), 1–10 (2014)
22. Geddes, K.O., Czapor, S.R., Labahn, G.: Algorithms for Computer Algebra. Kluwer, Boston (1992)
23. Griffith, A.L.: Persistence of women and minorities in STEM field majors: is it the school that matters? Econ. Educ. Rev. **29**(6), 911–922 (2010)
24. Hajian, S., Bonchi, F., Castillo, C.: Algorithmic bias: from discrimination discovery to fairness-aware data mining. In: Proceedings of the 22nd ACM SIGKDD International Conference on Knowledge Discovery and Data Mining, pp. 2125–2126. ACM (2016)
25. Hamburger, C.: Quasimonotonicity, regularity and duality for nonlinear systems of partial differential equations. Ann. Mat. Pura. Appl. **169**, 321–354 (1995)
26. Hardt, M., Price, E., Srebro, N.: Equality of opportunity in supervised learning. In: Advances in Neural Information Processing Systems, pp. 3315–3323 (2016)
27. Harper, F.M., Konstan, J.A.: The movielens datasets: history and context. ACM Trans. Interact. Intell. Syst. (TiiS) **5**(4), 19 (2016)
28. Harris, M., Karper, E., Stacks, G., Hoffman, D., DeNiro, R., Cruz, P., et al.: Writing labs and the Hollywood connection. J Film Writing **44**(3), 213–245 (2001)
29. Herlocker, J.L., Konstan, J.A., Riedl, J.: Explaining collaborative filtering recommendations. In: Proceedings of the 2000 ACM Conference on Computer Supported Cooperative Work, pp. 241–250. ACM (2000)
30. Ibach, H., Lüth, H.: Solid-State Physics, 2nd edn, pp. 45–56. Springer, New York (1996)
31. John, Alber, O'Connell, Daniel C., Kowal, Sabine: Personal perspective in TV interviews. Pragmatics **12**, 257–271 (2002)
32. Kamiran, F., Calders, T.: Classifying without discriminating. In: 2nd International Conference on Computer, Control and Communication, 2009. IC4 2009, pp. 1-6). IEEE, New York (2009)
33. Kamishima T., Akaho, S., Sakuma, J.: Fairness-aware learning through regularization approach. In: 2011 IEEE 11th International Conference on Data Mining Workshops (ICDMW), pp. 643–650. IEEE, New York (2011)
34. Kleinberg, J., Mullainathan, S., Raghavan, M.: Inherent trade-offs in the fair determination of risk scores (2016). arXiv preprint arXiv:1609.05807
35. Kreger, M., Brindis, C.D., Manuel, D.M., Sassoubre, L. (2007). Lessons learned in systems change initiatives: benchmarks and indicators. Am. J. Commun. Psychol. https://doi.org/10.1007/s10464-007-9108-14
36. Lipton, Z.C.: The Mythos of Model Interpretability (2016). arXiv preprint arXiv:1606.03490
37. McCarthy, K., Reilly, J., McGinty, L., Smyth, B.: Thinking positively-explanatory feedback for conversational recommender systems. In: Proceedings of the European Conference on Case-Based Reasoning (ECCBR-04) Explanation Workshop, pp. 115–124 (2004)
38. O'Neil, J.M., Egan, J.: Men's and women's gender role journeys: metaphor for healing, transition, and transformation. In: Wainrig, B.R. (ed.) Gender Issues Across the Life Cycle, pp. 107–123. Springer, New York (1992)
39. Pohl, R. (ed.).: Cognitive Illusions: A Handbook on Fallacies and Biases in Thinking, Judgement and Memory. Psychology Press (2004)
40. S. Preuss, A. Demchuk Jr., M. Stuke, Appl. Phys. A **61** (1995)
41. Pu, P., Chen, L., Hu, R.: A user-centric evaluation framework for recommender systems. In: Proceedings of the Fifth ACM Conference on Recommender Systems, pp. 157–164. ACM, Chicago (2011)
42. Ribeiro, M.T., Singh, S., Guestrin, C.: Why should i trust you?: explaining the predictions of any classifier. In: Proceedings of the 22nd ACM SIGKDD International Conference on Knowledge Discovery and Data Mining, pp. 1135-1144. ACM (2016)
43. Sapiezynski, P., Kassarnig, V., Wilson, C.: Academic performance prediction in a gender-imbalanced environment (2017)
44. Sharma, A., Cosley, D.: Do social explanations work?: studying and modeling the effects of social explanations in recommender systems. In: Proceedings of the 22nd International Conference on World Wide Web, pp. 1133–1144. ACM (2013)

45. Slifka, M.K., Whitton, J.L.: Clinical implications of dysregulated cytokine production. J. Mol. Med. (2000). https://doi.org/10.1007/s001090000086
46. Slifka, M.K., Whitton, J.L.: Clinical implications of dysregulated cytokine production. J. Mol. Med. (2000). https://doi.org/10.1007/s001090000086
47. M.K. Slifka, J.L. Whitton, J. Mol. Med. https://doi.org/10.1007/s001090000086
48. S.E. Smith, in *Neuromuscular Junction*, ed. by E. Zaimis. Handbook of Experimental Pharmacology, vol 42 (Springer, Heidelberg, 1976), p. 593
49. Smith, E.: Women into science and engineering? gendered participation in higher education STEM subjects. Br. Educ. Res. J. **37**(6), 993–1014 (2011)
50. Smith, J., Jones Jr., M., Houghton, L., et al.: Future of health insurance. N. Eng. J. Med. **965**, 325–329 (1999)
51. South, J., Blass, B.: The Future of Modern Genomics. Blackwell, London (2001)
52. Suleiman, C., O'Connell, D.C., Kowal, S.: If you and I, if we, in this later day, lose that sacred fire…': Perspective in political interviews. J. Psycholinguist. Res. (2002). https://doi.org/10.1023/A:1015592129296
53. Symeonidis, P., Nanopoulos, A., Manolopoulos, Y.: Justified recommendations based on content and rating data. In: WebKDD Workshop on Web Mining and Web Usage Analysis (2008)
54. Thai-Nghe, N., Drumond, L., Krohn-Grimberghe, A., Schmidt-Thieme, L.: Recommender system for predicting student performance. Procedia Comput. Sci. **1**(2), 2811–2819 (2010)
55. Tintarev, N., Masthoff, J.: Designing and evaluating explanations for recommender systems. In: Recommender Systems Handbook, pp. 479–510 (2011)
56. Tintarev, N., Masthoff, J.: Evaluating the effectiveness of explanations for recommender systems. User Model. User-Adap. Inter. **22**(4), 399–439 (2012)
57. Vig, J., Sen, S., Riedl, J.: Tagsplanations: explaining recommendations using tags. In: Proceedings of the 14th International Conference on Intelligent User Interfaces, pp. 47–56. ACM (2009)
58. Yao, S., Huang, B.: New Fairness Metrics for Recommendation that Embrace Differences (2017). arXiv preprint arXiv:1706.09838
59. Zhang, Y., Lai, G., Zhang, M., Zhang, Y., Liu, Y., Ma, S.: Explicit factor models for explainable recommendation based on phrase-level sentiment analysis. In: Proceedings of the 37th International ACM SIGIR Conference on Research and Development in Information Retrieval, pp. 83–92. ACM (2014)

Chapter 3
Beyond Human-in-the-Loop: Empowering End-Users with Transparent Machine Learning

Patrick C. Shih

Abstract Advances in data analytics and human computation are transforming how researchers conduct science in domains like bioinformatics, computational social science, and digital humanities. However, data analytics requires significant programming knowledge or access to technical experts, while human computation requires in-depth knowledge of crowd management and is error-prone due to lack of scientific domain expertise. The goal of this research is to empower a broader range of scientists and end-users to conduct data analytics by adopting the End-User Development (EUD) models commonly found in today's commercial software platforms like Microsoft Excel, Wikipedia and WordPress. These EUD platforms enable people to focus on producing content rather than struggling with a development environment and new programming syntax or relying on disciplinary non-experts for essential technical help. This research explores a similar paradigm for scientists and end-users that can be thought of as End-User Data Analytics (EUDA), or Transparent Machine Learning (TML).

3.1 Introduction

The scientific method is based on empirical measures that provide evidence for hypothesis formation and reasoning. The process typically involves "systematic observation, measurement, and experiment, and the formulation, testing, and modification of hypotheses" [74]. Critical thinking—"the intellectually disciplined process of actively and skillfully conceptualizing, applying, analyzing, synthesizing, and/or evaluating information gathered from, or generated by, observation, experience, reflection, reasoning, or communication, as a guide to belief and action" [84]—is key to the process.

In empirical research, the scientific method typically involves a scientist collecting data based on interviews, observations, surveys, or sampling of specimens. Once the

P. C. Shih (✉)
Department of Informatics, School of Informatics Computing and Engineering,
Indiana University Bloomington, Bloomington, IN 47408, USA
e-mail: patshih@indiana.edu

© Springer International Publishing AG, part of Springer Nature 2018
J. Zhou and F. Chen (eds.), *Human and Machine Learning*, Human–Computer
Interaction Series, https://doi.org/10.1007/978-3-319-90403-0_3

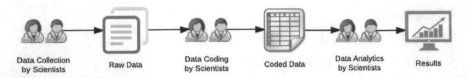

Fig. 3.1 Traditional process of scientific inquiry

raw data sample is collected, a data cleaning and coding process identifies outliers and erroneous data resulting from sampling error, and the researcher synthesises raw data points into aggregated clusters or themes that suit the research focus. A data analytics and validation process typically follows, involving statistical or inter-coder reliability checks to ensure the quality of the findings. Finally, the results are formatted in a fashion appropriate for the intended audience, be it a research or public community. Figure 3.1 provides a simplified view of the traditional scientific inquiry process.

With the improvement of data collection instruments (e.g., space imaging for astrophysicists, environmental sampling for climate scientists, etc.) and the emergence and wide adoption of consumer Information and Communication Technologies (ICTs), researchers are turning to a broad variety of data sources to infer sample population characteristics and patterns [46]. Although improvements in data collection have enabled scientists to make more accurate generalisations and ask novel questions, the sheer amount of available data can exceed scientists' ability to utilise or process it. Some have described this as the "Big Data" phenomena, defined by the three V's: volume, variety, and velocity [67]. To cope, the scientific community has enlisted the help of citizen science and crowdsourcing platforms to engage the public in both data collection and data analysis [109]. However, this naturally results in a crowd management problem in which factors like task modulation, task coordination, and data verification have added to the issues that scientists must actively manage [57]. Advances in computational infrastructure and the availability of big datasets have also led to a new set of computational techniques and data analytical tools capable of processing and visualising large scale datasets [15]. This imposes a further burden on scientists, however, in the form of having to constantly learn new computational techniques and manage new visualisation tools.

Thus, crowd management and computational data analytics have become vital skillsets that the scientific workforce is starting to develop as basic building blocks of the modern day scientific method. Scientists using Big Data are increasingly dependent on knowledge of computational skillsets or on having access to technical experts in all aspects of the scientific method (e.g., data gathering, data generation, data collection, data storage, data processing, data analysis, data verification, data representation, data sharing, data preservation, etc.). They also find themselves leveraging crowd workers who may not possess relevant scientific knowledge to provide a ground truth label of large datasets, known as "Human-in-the-Loop" (HITL) machine learning [18, 82], and scientists to correct data errors and fine-tune algorithms, known as "Interactive Machine Learning" (IML) [25, 107]. In fact, the incumbent skillsets

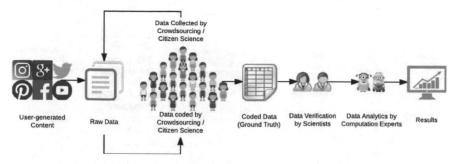

Fig. 3.2 Emerging process of scientific inquiry

have become so necessary and in such high demand that the White House has issued a call for a Science, Technology, Engineering, and Mathematics (STEM) initiative to make these areas of inquiry and practice more accessible to the general public [44]. Figure 3.2 provides an overview of this newer, emerging process of scientific inquiry.

Although the demand for STEM skillsets is increasing, enrolment in computer science has remained stagnant [17], which may be attributable to perceived race and gender stereotypes, or unequal access to computer science education [43, 108]. Computer education researchers have investigated how to effectively integrate computational thinking into education in order to craft, "the thought processes involved in formulating a problem and expressing its solution(s) in such a way that a computer-human or machine-can effectively carry out" [111, 112]. One approach involves motivating student interests with gamification [22, 32]. Another approach focuses on removing the technical barrier to content creation with user-friendly End-User Development (EUD) platforms [27, 62]. The latter view includes the belief that end-users with little or no technical expertise will be more willing to participate in tinkering, hacking, or other STEM activities if the barrier to entry is lowered. This research follows this second approach by proposing an end-user data analytics paradigm to broaden the population of researchers involved in this work, extending prior efforts to make computationally complex data analytics algorithms more accessible to end-users. This exploratory study focuses on examining the impact of interface design for eliciting data input from end-users as a segue into future work that will generate insights for designing end-user data analytics mechanisms.

The initial goal of this research is to create a transparent machine learning platform prototype to assist the scientists and end-users in processing and analysing real-time data streams and to understand opportunities and challenges of developing an end-user data analytics paradigm for future scientific workforces. Ultimately, the goal is to empower scientists and end-users to train supervised machine learning models to pre-process other sensor and device data streams along with those from cameras, and interactively provide feedback to improve model prediction accuracy. In this sense, the proposed end-user data analytics paradigm replaces human observers taking and coding data by hand with computational labour, where scientists or trained observers

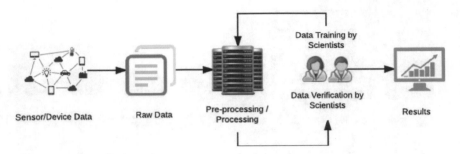

Fig. 3.3 Proposed process of scientific inquiry (End-User Data Analytics)

become end-users training the system by providing the system with ground truth labels for the data. In the process, the system frees the scientists from having to depend on highly technical programming expertise. In the context of a scientific workforce, this could potentially replace the onerous, labour-intensive system commonly used in observation research around the world. The same applies to domain applications with similar care and monitoring mandates, such as nursing homes, hospital intensive care units, certain security and military-related environments, and space and deep sea exploration vessels. Figure 3.3 provides an overview of the proposed end-user data analytics paradigm.

3.2 Background

The emergence, adoption, and advances of ICTs in the past several decades have revolutionised the scientific method and the process of scientific inquiry. This section provides a general overview of the roles of ICTs in scientific inquiry along two dimensions: the scientific domain expertise of the users and the technical functions of the ICT platforms. ICT use in the scientific workforce evolved from collaboratories in the late 1980s that created communication infrastructures for scientists to share resources and early results, to citizen science platforms in the 1990s that allowed the public to contribute to scientific data collection, analysis, and interpretation. The citizen science platforms have led more recently to crowdsourcing platforms that allow online crowd workers to analyse modularised datasets (e.g., human computation and HITL machine learning). The proposed end-user data analytics platform—a transparent machine learning platform prototype that assists animal behavioural scientists to analyse multi-channel high-definition video camera data-is an effort to now provide scientists with computational capabilities to process and analyse large datasets. Figure 3.4 shows the overview of ICT use in scientific inquiry.

		Functions of ICTs	
		Infrastructure & Information Sharing	Coordination & Computation
Scientific Domain Expertise	Low Expertise	Citizen Science (1990's)	Crowdsourcing, Human Computation, & HITL Machine learning (2000's)
	High Expertise	Collaboratory (1980's)	End-user Data Analytics (2010's)

Fig. 3.4 Overview of ICT use in scientific inquiry

3.2.1 Collaboratory and Large-Scale Scientific Workforce

The term "collaboratory" was coined by William Wulf while he worked for the National Science Foundation by merging the notion of traditional laboratory and collaboration that is afforded by ICT platforms that emerged in the late 1980s [59]. The shift in scientific inquiry occurred naturally out of the need to overcome physical limitations of instrument, infrastructure, and information sharing, such as results collected by scarce research instruments [1], or annotated electronic editions of 16th-century manuscripts [49]. Bos et al. (2007) describes a taxonomy of seven types of collaboratories that are differentiated by the nature of activities (loose coupling & asynchronous vs. tight coupling, synchronous) and resource needs (infrastructure and research instruments, open data, and virtual learning and knowledge communities) [8]. The early collaboratory platforms typically included functionalities such as electronic whiteboards, electronic notebooks, chatrooms, and video conferencing to facilitate effective coordination and interactions between dispersed scientists in astrophysics, physics, biology, medicine, chemistry, and the humanities [26].

3.2.2 Citizen Science

Citizen science is a two-part concept that focuses on (1) opening science and science policy processes to the public and (2) public participation in scientific projects under the direction of professional scientists [80]. Unfortunately, discussions of the public understanding of science tend to dismiss citizen expertise as uninformed or irrational, and some have advocated for involving the public in citizen projects to facilitate more sustainable development of the relationship between science, society, and the environment [51, 52]. Although research has attempted to involve the public in citizen science projects, without proper research framing and training prior to the project, most people will not recognise scientifically relevant findings [16, 96]. Citizen science projects are also limited to those that could be broken down into modular efforts in which laypeople could reasonably participate [96]. This limits the complexity of the projects that citizens could participate in. There have been reports of mild success in terms of scientific discoveries, but the actual impact of involving citizens in scientific projects remains fairly minimal [9]. The intent in many citizen science projects is to involve volunteers in data collection or interpretation, such as the large volume of video data of animals at the zoo, that are difficult for scientists to process. These citizen science efforts are viewed as "complementary to more localized, hypothesis-driven research" [20]. Nonetheless, citizen science is generally seen as a positive factor in raising awareness of science and is frequently used as a mechanism for engaging people in civic-related projects [7, 24]. Earlier citizen science platforms typically employed traditional technologies that are commonly found in asynchronous collaboratories mentioned in the previous section [8, 26]. Modern citizen scientist platforms are starting to incorporate features found in common crowdsourcing platforms [99], and those will be described in the section below.

3.2.3   Crowdsourcing, Human Computation, and Human-in-the-Loop

Although citizen science taps into people's intrinsic motivation to learn and contribute to science by providing labour for scientific inquiry, other crowdsourcing platforms have emerged as a way for people to outsource other kinds of labour at an affordable cost [45]. Research has linked gamification to crowdsourcing projects—if people can be incentivised to spend countless hours on playing highly interactive and engaging video games, this motivation can be harnessed as free work using progress achievement and social recognition [29, 30, 32, 85, 98]. Proponents also argue that if a task can be broken down finely enough, anyone can spend just a short moment to complete a simple task while also making a little bit of extra income. As such, crowdsourcing and human computation platforms primarily focus on task structure and worker coordination relating to workflow, task assignment, hierarchy, and quality control [57], whereas communication features between clients and workers and among workers themselves are practically nonexistent [50].

In terms of getting citizens to contribute to science projects, research has leveraged crowd workers on crowdsourcing platforms to provide ground truth label of large datasets to improve HITL prediction models [18, 25, 82, 107]. In contrast with the citizen science platforms that typically fulfil workers' desires for educational or civic engagement activities, workers on crowdsourcing platforms are typically underpaid and have no opportunity to learn or become more engaged with the project after task completion [57]. The ethics of crowdsourcing platforms are heavily debated for these reasons [41, 50, 81]. These platforms have also sparked a growth of peer-to-peer economy platforms that undercut existing worker wages[66].

3.2.4 *From Human-in-the-Loop to Transparent Machine Learning*

With the increase in available user-generated content and sensor data along with significant improvement in computing infrastructure, machine learning algorithms are being used to create prediction models that both recognise and analyse data. HITL machine learning attempts to leverage the benefits of human observation and categorisation skills as well as machine computation abilities to create better prediction models [18, 25, 82, 107]. In this approach, humans provide affordable ground truth labels while the machine creates models based on the humans' labels that accurately categorise the observations. However, HITL machine learning suffers similar issues of crowdsourcing and citizen science platforms. For example, similar to the workers on crowdsourcing platforms, the human agents in these cases are typically used to simply complete mundane work without deriving any benefits from participation in the project. In addition, human labels suffer from errors and biases [60, 61]. Similar to the participants of the citizen science program, crowd workers are prone to making incorrect labels without domain knowledge and proper research training and framing. Accuracy in the correct identification of data and the training of the system remain two major issues in the field of HITL machine learning and machine learning as a field in general [4, 60, 61, 78]. To empower scientists with mitigating the aforementioned issues, a research agenda on an end-user data analytics paradigm is necessary for investigating issues relating to the design, implementation, and use of a transparent machine learning platform prototype to make computationally complex data analytics algorithms more accessible to end-users with little or no technical expertise.

3.3 Impact of Interface Design for Eliciting Data Input from End-Users

The goal of this research is to learn about the barriers that scientists and end-users face in conducting data analytics and to discover what kinds of interaction techniques and end-user technological platforms will help them overcome these barriers. As an initial step to understand current problems and practices that scientists and end-users encounter throughout the data analytics process, the following experiment was conducted to demonstrate the impact of interface design for eliciting data input from end-users.

The experiment uses NeuralTalk2 [56, 102], a deep learning image caption generator, to generate 5 most likely captions for each of 9 images. In a between-subject experiment, a total of 88 college students were randomly assigned to one of the three interface groups—Yes/No (31 students), multiple-selection (34), and open-ended questions (23).

- In the Yes/No group, participants answered whether the generated caption accurately describes an image. This was repeated for all 5 captions for each of the 9 images, totalling 45 questions.
- In the multiple-selection group, all five captions were presented to the participants at the same time. The participants were asked to select all the captions that accurately described an image. This was repeated for all 9 images, totalling 9 questions.
- In the open-ended group, participants were asked to describe what they saw in an image. This was repeated for all 9 images, totalling 9 questions.

Participants were asked to rate their confidence level after answering each question. Participants' feedback accuracy was assessed manually after the experiment was conducted. Selection consensus across participants and time spent were also compared and analysed. Figure 3.5 illustrates the design of the experimental conditions. Below are results that detail how different feedback interfaces influence feedback accuracy, feedback consensus, confidence level, and time spent in how participants provide feedback to machine learning models.

Figure 3.6 illustrates the feedback accuracy of the captions selected by the participation. An ANOVA test followed by post-hoc comparisons revealed that the open-ended group produced higher feedback accuracy than both the Yes/No group and the multiple-selection group, and the Yes/No group outperformed the multiple-selection group ($F(2,85) = 20.44$, $p < .0001$).

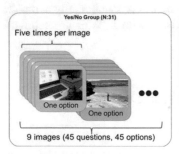 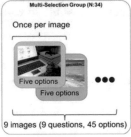 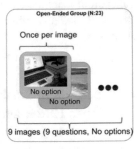

Fig. 3.5 Experimental design

Fig. 3.6 Feedback accuracy: open-ended > Yes/No > multiple-selection

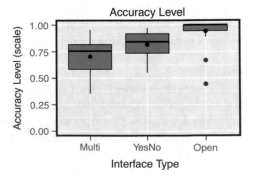

Fig. 3.7 Feedback consensus

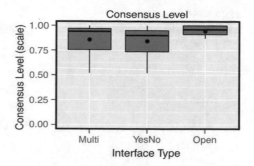

Fig. 3.8 Feedback confidence: Yes/No > open-ended and multiple-selection

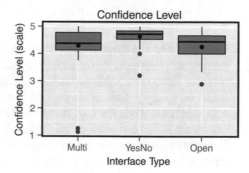

Although the feedback accuracy varied significantly across groups, participants achieved similarly high within-group consensus across all 3 conditions (non-sig., see Fig. 3.7). This indicates that the differences in the feedback provided by the participants were indeed caused by the interface design conditions.

In terms of feedback confidence, although the open-ended group provided the highest level of feedback accuracy, their self-perceived confidence level (U = 372.5, p < 0.05) is as low as the multiple-selection group (U = 197.5, p < 0.01) when compared to the Yes/No group. Figure 3.8 shows that the Yes/No group reported the highest self-perceived confidence level. This is likely due to the fact that there leaves less room for self-doubt when the participants are presented with only Yes/No options.

Figure 3.9 illustrates the difference in time spent for providing feedback across the 3 groups. It took the Yes/No group significantly more time to rate 45 captions (5 per 9 images) than the multiple-selection group (F(2,85) = 6.15, p < 0.05), whereas there is no significant difference between the open-ended and the multiple-selection groups. This is likely due to the fact that the captions in the Yes/No group were presented across a series of 45 questions instead of 9 questions presented to the multiple-selection and the open-ended groups.

Based on the results presented above, future transparent machine learning research should account for the following trade-offs when eliciting user feedback.

Fig. 3.9 Time spent on
providing feedback: Yes/No
> multiple-selection

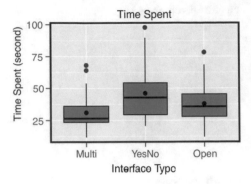

- The open-ended group achieved the highest level of feedback accuracy, and the participants also reported the highest level of confidence in their feedback. The fact that this can be accomplished within a similarly short time frame as the multiple-selection group points to the potential of utilising an open-ended form to elicit user feedback when the task demands such high level of accuracy. The biggest drawback is that the open-ended feedback requires active human involvement to interpret the data. A future transparent machine learning model could utilise current state-of-the-art natural language processing efforts to pre-process the open-ended responses to generate a list of possible labels before a second round of human coding. This essentially reduces the effort of analysing open-ended responses into two rounds of Yes/No or multiple-selection coding efforts for the users. The cumulative time spent in the proposed multi-round effort will not greatly exceed that of the Yes/No group based on the results demonstrated in this experiment, and the superb accuracy may justify the usage of the multi-round effort in some cases.
- While the multiple-selection group may appear to be promising due to the ease of data processing of user feedback relative to the open-ended group, the results show that it produced the lowest feedback accuracy and the participants are less confident of their feedback. One advantage of this user feedback elicitation method is that it gives the users the ability to view and provide feedback on multiple machine-generated labels at the same time, which results in the lowest cumulative time spent for the participants in our experiment. This method may be desirable in situations where feedback accuracy is less critical and the goal is to process through a large amount of data in a short period of time.
- The Yes/No group produced the medium level of feedback accuracy. Although the participants in the Yes/No group spent the highest cumulative time to provide feedback, it took the participants much less time to rate the individual options with the highest self-reported confidence level compared to the multiple-selection and the open-ended groups. The flexibility of adjusting the number of options that the users rate at any given time (e.g., users can stop after rating through 2 options instead of having to view all of the options at once in the multiple-selection group) can be especially desirable when user commitment is unknown and the intention is to minimise user burden to provide feedback. The human-labelled results are

also easy for machine learning models to process, making the Yes/No group the most flexible and adaptable method.

These experimental findings show that interface design significantly affects how end-users transform information from raw data into codified data that can be processed using data analytics tools, and the insights can inform the design, implementation, and evaluation of a usable transparent machine learning platform in the future. Future transparent machine learning could expand the study to different user feedback scenarios and contexts that require human feedback.

3.4   Design for End-User Data Analytics

Currently, there are many popular, general-purpose open-source scientific numerical computation software libraries such as NumPy [103], Matplotlib [47], and Pandas [69] that users can import into their software development environment to conduct numerical analysis programmatically. However, the use of these software libraries requires significant programming knowledge. To make data analytics more user-friendly, popular machine learning and data mining software suites such as Weka [31, 113], Orange [19], KNIME [6], and Caffe [55] provide users with command-line and/or graphical user interfaces to access a collection of visualisation tools and algorithms for data analysis and predictive modelling. Yet these software suites do not provide label suggestions based on the currently trained model, typically operating under the assumption that ground truth labels are error-free. Functionalities of these software suites are typically limited to training static rather than real-time live-stream datasets and lack the ability to allow users to interactively train machine learning models in order to more effectively explore data trends and correct label errors. In other words, these platforms neglect data collection and data (pre-)processing phases, both of which are essential steps throughout data analytics. A new paradigm is needed to more effectively disseminate the data science mindset more holistically and make data analytics more accessible to learners and end-users.

To realise intuitive, easy-to-learn, and user-friendly interfaces for data collection, processing, and analytics, it is necessary to create a series of software front-end prototypes, increasing in complexity but all sharing the same basic framework for interaction. The goal of the prototypes will be to learn about how different interaction techniques can replace or enhance the current paradigm of data processing by scientists and end-users. In the spirit of end-user development paradigms such as Scratch [79], combining interaction techniques used in interactive machine learning [25, 107] and direct manipulation interfaces [48] to create a novel interface to ease the training process of supervised learning models could potentially yield a more usable transparent machine learning platform. The goal is to create a system that allows the user to smoothly move between data and a list of inferred behaviours, allowing scientists and end-users to visually preview and make corrections to the prediction model. Although the prototypes will vary, the interactions will share the same basic features. Users will use the platform to select the input data streams to be worked and then overlay these with behavioural data previously coded by trained scientists and end-users.

3.5 Conclusion

Successful investigations of transparent machine learning require multidisciplinary expertise in (1) human-computer interaction and end-user oriented design processes such as participatory design, interaction design, and scenario-based design [2, 3, 10, 11, 23, 28, 58, 63–65, 73, 83, 91, 94, 97, 104], (2) human computation and crowdsourcing[5, 12, 14, 21, 34, 36, 37, 39, 40, 75, 86, 90, 100, 105, 106, 114], (3) end-user visualisation interfaces and computational data analytics [33, 35, 38, 42, 53, 54, 70–72, 87–89, 92, 93, 95, 101, 110, 116], and (4) computer science education [13, 68, 76, 77, 115, 117, 118]. This research reveals the initial insights on how to make data analytics more accessible to end-users, to empower researchers in scientific inquiry, and to involve the public in citizen science. This research also will provide trained end-users opportunities to participate in citizen science efforts, allowing them to contribute directly to citizen science as well as become more familiar with the scientific method and data literacy, heightening awareness of how STEM impacts the world.

There are numerous potential applications of this work. Sensor and surveillance technologies have made great strides in behaviour profiling and behavioural anomaly detection. Such technologies may allow scientists and end-users to closely observe real-time data streams around the clock. Although the proposed end-user data analytic and transparent machine learning platform is currently targeted toward scientists and end-users, the platform and the resulting knowledge could be used most immediately to make data analytics more accessible for other domain applications with similar care and monitoring mandates, such as nursing homes, hospital intensive care units, certain security and military-related environments, and space and deep sea exploration vessels.

References

1. Abramovici, A., Althouse, W.E., Drever, R.W., Gürsel, Y., Kawamura, S., Raab, F.J., Shoemaker, D., Sievers, L., Spero, R.E., Thorne, K.S., et al.: Ligo: the laser interferometer gravitational-wave observatory. Science **256**(5055), 325–333 (1992)
2. Baglione, A.N., Girard, M.M., Price, M., Clawson, J., Shih, P.C.: Mobile technologies for grief support: prototyping an application to support the bereaved. In: Workshop on Interactive Systems in Health Care (2017)
3. Baglione, A.N., Girard, M.M., Price, M., Clawson, J., Shih, P.C.: Modern bereavement: a model for complicated grief in the digital age. In: ACM Conference on Human Factors in Computing Systems (2018)

4. Batista, G.E., Prati, R.C., Monard, M.C.: A study of the behavior of several methods for balancing machine learning training data. ACM SIGKDD Explor. Newsl. **6**(1), 20–29 (2004)
5. Bellotti, V.M., Cambridge, S., Hoy, K., Shih, P.C., Handalian, L.R., Han, K., Carroll, J.M.: Towards community-centered support for peer-to-peer service exchange: rethinking the time-banking metaphor. In: Proceedings of the SIGCHI Conference on Human Factors in Computing Systems, pp. 2975–2984. ACM (2014)
6. Berthold, M.R., Cebron, N., Dill, F., Gabriel, T.R., Kötter, T., Meinl, T., Ohl, P., Thiel, K., Wiswedel, B.: Knime-the konstanz information miner: version 2.0 and beyond. ACM SIGKDD Explor. Newsl. **11**(1), 26–31 (2009)
7. Bonney, R., Cooper, C.B., Dickinson, J., Kelling, S., Phillips, T., Rosenberg, K.V., Shirk, J.: Citizen science: a developing tool for expanding science knowledge and scientific literacy. BioScience **59**(11), 977–984 (2009)
8. Bos, N., Zimmerman, A., Olson, J., Yew, J., Yerkie, J., Dahl, E., Olson, G.: From shared databases to communities of practice: a taxonomy of collaboratories. J. Comput.-Mediat. Commun. **12**(2), 652–672 (2007)
9. Brossard, D., Lewenstein, B., Bonney, R.: Scientific knowledge and attitude change: the impact of a citizen science project. Int. J. Sci. Educ. **27**(9), 1099–1121 (2005)
10. Carroll, J.M., Shih, P.C., Hoffman, B., Wang, J., Han, K.: Presence and hyperpresence: implications for community awareness. Interacting with Presence: HCI and the Sense of Presence in Computer-mediated Environments, pp. 70–82 (2014)
11. Carroll, J.M., Shih, P.C., Kropczynski, J., Cai, G., Rosson, M.B., Han, K.: The internet of places at community-scale: design scenarios for hyperlocal. Enriching Urban Spaces with Ambient Computing, the Internet of Things, and Smart City Design **1** (2016)
12. Carroll, J.M., Shih, P.C., Kropczynski, J.: Community informatics as innovation in sociotechnical infrastructures. J. Commun. Inf. **11**(2) (2015)
13. Carroll, J.M., Wu, Y., Shih, P.C., Zheng, S.: Re-appropriating a question/answer system to support dialectical constructivist learning activity. Educ. Technol. Res. Dev. **64**(1), 137–156 (2016)
14. Carroll, J.M., Shih, P.C., Han, K., Kropczynski, J.: Coordinating community cooperation: integrating timebanks and nonprofit volunteering by design. Int. J. Des. **11**(1), 51–63 (2017)
15. Chen, H., Chiang, R.H., Storey, V.C.: Business intelligence and analytics: from big data to big impact. MIS Q. pp. 1165–1188 (2012)
16. Cohn, J.P.: Citizen science: can volunteers do real research? AIBS Bull. **58**(3), 192–197 (2008)
17. Computer Research Association: Taulbee survey. Comput. Res. News **28**(5), 19 (2015)
18. Dautenhahn, K.: The art of designing socially intelligent agents: Science, fiction, and the human in the loop. Appl. Artif. Intell. **12**(7–8), 573–617 (1998)
19. Demšar, J., Curk, T., Erjavec, A., Gorup, Č., Hočevar, T., Milutinovič, M., Možina, M., Polajnar, M., Toplak, M., Starič, A., et al.: Orange: data mining toolbox in python. J. Mach. Learn. Res. **14**(1), 2349–2353 (2013)
20. Dickinson, J.L., Zuckerberg, B., Bonter, D.N.: Citizen science as an ecological research tool: challenges and benefits. Annu. Rev. Ecol. Evol. Syst. **41**, 149–172 (2010)
21. Ding, X., Shih, P.C., Gu, N.: Socially embedded work: A study of wheelchair users performing online crowd work in china. In: Proceedings of the ACM Conference on Computer Supported Cooperative Work and Social Computing, pp. 642–654. ACM (2017)
22. DomíNguez, A., Saenz-De-Navarrete, J., De-Marcos, L., FernáNdez-Sanz, L., PagéS, C., MartíNez-Herráiz, J.J.: Gamifying learning experiences: practical implications and outcomes. Comput. Educ. **63**, 380–392 (2013)
23. Dunbar, J.C., Connelly, C.L., Maestre, J.F., MacLeod, H., Siek, K., Shih, P.C.: Considerations for using the asynchronous remote communities (arc) method in health informatics research. In: Workshop on Interactive Systems in Health Care (2017)
24. Evans, C., Abrams, E., Reitsma, R., Roux, K., Salmonsen, L., Marra, P.P.: The neighborhood nestwatch program: participant outcomes of a citizen-science ecological research project. Conserv. Biol. **19**(3), 589–594 (2005)

25. Fails, J.A., Olsen Jr, D.R.: Interactive machine learning. In: Proceedings of the 8th international conference on Intelligent user interfaces, pp. 39–45. ACM (2003)
26. Finholt, T.A., Olson, G.M.: From laboratories to collaboratories: a new organizational form for scientific collaboration. Psychol. Sci. **8**(1), 28–36 (1997)
27. Fischer, G., Giaccardi, E., Ye, Y., Sutcliffe, A.G., Mehandjiev, N.: Meta-design: a manifesto for end-user development. Commun. ACM **47**(9), 33–37 (2004)
28. Gao, G., Min, A., Shih, P.C.: Gendered design bias: Gender differences of in-game character choice and playing style in league of legends. In: Australian Conference on Computer-Human Interaction. ACM Press (2017)
29. Ghose, A., Ipeirotis, P.G., Li, B.: Designing ranking systems for hotels on travel search engines by mining user-generated and crowdsourced content. Mark. Sci. **31**(3), 493–520 (2012)
30. Goncalves, J., Hosio, S., Ferreira, D,, Kostakos, V.: Game of words: tagging places through crowdsourcing on public displays. In: Proceedings of the 2014 Conference on Designing Interactive Systems, pp. 705–714. ACM (2014)
31. Hall, M., Frank, E., Holmes, G., Pfahringer, B., Reutemann, P., Witten, I.H.: The weka data mining software: an update. ACM SIGKDD Explor. Newsl. **11**(1), 10–18 (2009)
32. Hamari, J., Koivisto, J., Sarsa, H.: Does gamification work?–a literature review of empirical studies on gamification. In: 2014 47th Hawaii International Conference on System Sciences (HICSS), pp. 3025–3034. IEEE (2014)
33. Han, K., Cook, K., Shih, P.C.: Exploring effective decision making through human-centered and computational intelligence methods. In: ACM Conference on Human Factors in Computing Systems: Workshop on Human-Centred Machine Learning (2016)
34. Han, K., Shih, P.C., Bellotti, V., Carroll, J.M.: Timebanking with a smartphone application. In: Collective Intelligence Conference (2014)
35. Han, K., Shih, P., Carroll, J.M.: Aggregating community information to explore social connections. In: When the City Meets the Citizen Workshop, ICWSM 2013: 7th International AAAI Conference On Weblogs And Social Media, pp. 8–11 (2013)
36. Han, K., Shih, P.C., Rosson, M.B., Carroll, J.M.: Enhancing community awareness of and participation in local heritage with a mobile application. In: Proceedings of the 17th ACM conference on Computer supported cooperative work and social computing, pp. 1144–1155. ACM (2014)
37. Han, K., Shih, P.C., Beth Rosson, M., Carroll, J.M.: Understanding local community attachment, engagement and social support networks mediated by mobile technology. Interact. Comput. **28**(3), 220–237 (2014)
38. Han, K., Shih, P.C., Carroll, J.M.: Local news chatter: augmenting community news by aggregating hyperlocal microblog content in a tag cloud. Int. J. Hum.-Comput. Interact. **30**(12), 1003–1014 (2014)
39. Han, K., Shih, P.C., Bellotti, V., Carroll, J.M.: It's time there was an app for that too: a usability study of mobile timebanking. Int. J. Mob. Hum. Comput. Interact. (IJMHCI) **7**(2), 1–22 (2015)
40. Hanna, S.A., Kropczynski, J., Shih, P.C., Carroll, J.M.: Using a mobile application to encourage community interactions at a local event. In: ACM Richard Tapia Celebration of Diversity in Computing Conference (2015)
41. Hansson, K., Muller, M., Aitamurto, T., Irani, L., Mazarakis, A., Gupta, N., Ludwig, T.: Crowd dynamics: Exploring conflicts and contradictions in crowdsourcing. In: Proceedings of the 2016 CHI Conference Extended Abstracts on Human Factors in Computing Systems, pp. 3604–3611. ACM (2016)
42. Hiler, L., Foulk, B., Nippert-Eng, C., Shih, P.C.: Detecting biological samples using olfactory sensors. In: Animal Behavior Conference (2017)
43. Hill, C., Corbett, C., St Rose, A.: Why so few? Women in science, technology, engineering, and mathematics. ERIC (2010)
44. House, W.: President obama to announce major expansion of educate to innovate campaign to improve science, technology, engineering and math (stem) education. Office of the Press Secretary (2010)
45. Howe, J.: The rise of crowdsourcing. Wired Mag. **14**(6), 1–4 (2006)

46. Humphreys, P.: Extending ourselves: Computational science, empiricism, and scientific method. Oxford University Press (2004)
47. Hunter, J.D.: Matplotlib: a 2d graphics environment. Comput. Sci. Eng. **9**(3), 90–95 (2007)
48. Hutchins, E.L., Hollan, J.D., Norman, D.A.: Direct manipulation interfaces. Hum.-Comput. Interact. **1**(4), 311–338 (1985)
49. Ide, N., Véronis, J.: Text encoding initiative: Background and contexts, vol. 29. Springer Science and Business Media (1995)
50. Irani, L.C., Silberman, M.: Turkopticon: Interrupting worker invisibility in amazon mechanical turk. In: Proceedings of the SIGCHI Conference on Human Factors in Computing Systems, pp. 611–620. ACM (2013)
51. Irwin, A.: Citizen Science: A Study of People, Expertise and Sustainable Development. Psychology Press (1995)
52. Irwin, A.: Constructing the scientific citizen: science and democracy in the biosciences. Public Underst. Sci. **10**(1), 1–18 (2001)
53. Jang, J.Y., Han, K., Lee, D., Jia, H., Shih, P.C.: Teens engage more with fewer photos: temporal and comparative analysis on behaviors in instagram. In: Proceedings of the 27th ACM Conference on Hypertext and Social Media, pp. 71–81. ACM (2016)
54. Jang, J.Y., Han, K., Shih, P.C., Lee, D.: Generation like: comparative characteristics in instagram. In: Proceedings of the 33rd Annual ACM Conference on Human Factors in Computing Systems, pp. 4039–4042. ACM (2015)
55. Jia, Y., Shelhamer, E., Donahue, J., Karayev, S., Long, J., Girshick, R., Guadarrama, S., Darrell, T.: Caffe: Convolutional architecture for fast feature embedding. In: Proceedings of the 22nd ACM international conference on Multimedia, pp. 675–678. ACM (2014)
56. Karpathy, A., Fei-Fei, L.: Deep visual-semantic alignments for generating image descriptions. In: Proceedings of the IEEE Conference on Computer Vision and Pattern Recognition, pp. 3128–3137 (2015)
57. Kittur, A., Nickerson, J.V., Bernstein, M., Gerber, E., Shaw, A., Zimmerman, J., Lease, M., Horton, J.: The future of crowd work. In: Proceedings of the 2013 Conference on Computer Supported Cooperative Work, pp. 1301–1318. ACM (2013)
58. Koehne, B., Shih, P.C., Olson, J.S.: Remote and alone: coping with being the remote member on the team. In: Proceedings of the ACM 2012 conference on Computer Supported Cooperative Work, pp. 1257–1266. ACM (2012)
59. Kouzes, R.T., Myers, J.D., Wulf, W.A.: Collaboratories: doing science on the internet. Computer **29**(8), 40–46 (1996)
60. Le, J., Edmonds, A., Hester, V., Biewald, L.: Ensuring quality in crowdsourced search relevance evaluation: the effects of training question distribution. In: SIGIR 2010 Workshop on Crowdsourcing for Search Evaluation, vol. 2126 (2010)
61. Lease, M.: On quality control and machine learning in crowdsourcing. Hum. Comput. **11**(11) (2011)
62. Lieberman, H., Paternò, F., Klann, M., Wulf, V.: End-user development: an emerging paradigm. In: End User development, pp. 1–8. Springer (2006)
63. Liu, L.S., Shih, P.C., Hayes, G.R.: Barriers to the adoption and use of personal health record systems. In: Proceedings of the 2011 iConference, pp. 363–370. ACM (2011)
64. Maestre, J.F., MacLeod, H., Connelly, C.L., Dunbar, J.C., Beck, J., Siek, K., Shih, P.C.: Defining through expansion: conducting asynchronous remote communities (arc) research with stigmatized groups. In: ACM Conference on Human Factors in Computing Systems (2018)
65. Maestre, J.F., Shih, P.C.: Impact of initial trust on video-mediated social support. In: Australian Conference on Computer-Human Interaction. ACM Press (2017)
66. Malhotra, A., Van Alstyne, M.: The dark side of the sharing economy and how to lighten it. Commun. ACM **57**(11), 24–27 (2014)
67. McAfee, A., Brynjolfsson, E., Davenport, T.H., Patil, D., Barton, D.: Big data: the management revolution. Harv. Bus. Rev. **90**(10), 60–68 (2012)

68. McCoy, C., Shih, P.C.: Teachers as producers of data analytics: a case study of a teacher-focused educational data science program. J. Learn. Anal. **3**(3), 193–214 (2016)
69. McKinney, W., et al.: Data structures for statistical computing in python. In: Proceedings of the 9th Python in Science Conference, vol. 445, pp. 51–56. Austin, TX (2010)
70. Min, A., Lee, D., Shih, P.C.: Potentials of smart breathalyzer: an interventions for excessive drinking among college students. In: Proceedings of the iConference (2018)
71. Min, A., Shih, P.C.: Exploring new design factors for electronic interventions to prevent college students from excessive drinking by using personal breathalyzers. In: Workshop on Interactive Systems in Health Care (2017)
72. Nelson, J.K., Shih, P.C.: Companionviz: mediated platform for gauging canine health and enhancing human-pet interactions. Int. J. Hum.-Comput. Stud. **98**, 169–178 (2017)
73. Ongwere, T., Cantor, G., Martin, S.R., Shih, P.C., Clawson, J., Connelly, K.: Too many conditions, too little time: designing technological intervention for patients with type-2 diabetes and discordant chronic comorbidities. In: Workshop on Interactive Systems in Health Care (2017)
74. Oxford English Dictionary: OED Online (2015)
75. Parry-Hill, J., Shih, P.C., Mankoff, J., Ashbrook, D.: Understanding volunteer at fabricators: opportunities and challenges in diy-at for others in e-nable. In: ACM Conference on Human Factors in Computing Systems, pp. 6184–6194. ACM (2017)
76. Pena, J., Shih, P.C., Rosson, M.B.: Instructors as end-user developers: technology usage opportunities in the inverted classroom. In: Handbook of Research on Applied Learning Theory and Design in Modern Education, pp. 560–571. IGI Global (2016)
77. Peña, J., Shih, P.C., Rosson, M.B.: Scenario-based design of technology to support teaching in inverted classes. IConference 2016 Proceedings (2016)
78. Rani, P., Liu, C., Sarkar, N., Vanman, E.: An empirical study of machine learning techniques for affect recognition in human-robot interaction. Pattern Anal. Appl. **9**(1), 58–69 (2006)
79. Resnick, M., Maloney, J., Monroy-Hernández, A., Rusk, N., Eastmond, E., Brennan, K., Millner, A., Rosenbaum, E., Silver, J., Silverman, B., et al.: Scratch: programming for all. Commun. ACM **52**(11), 60–67 (2009)
80. Riesch, H., Potter, C.: Citizen science as seen by scientists: methodological, epistemological and ethical dimensions. Public Underst. Sci. **23**(1), 107–120 (2014)
81. Salehi, N., Irani, L.C., Bernstein, M.S., Alkhatib, A., Ogbe, E., Milland, K., et al.: We are dynamo: overcoming stalling and friction in collective action for crowd workers. In: Proceedings of the 33rd Annual ACM Conference on Human Factors in Computing Systems, pp. 1621–1630. ACM (2015)
82. Schirner, G., Erdogmus, D., Chowdhury, K., Padir, T.: The future of human-in-the-loop cyber-physical systems. Computer **46**(1), 36–45 (2013)
83. Schumann, J., Shih, P.C., Redmiles, D.F., Horton, G.: Supporting initial trust in distributed idea generation and idea evaluation. In: Proceedings of the 17th ACM International Conference on Supporting Group Work, pp. 199–208. ACM (2012)
84. Scriven, M., Paul, R.: Critical thinking as defined by the national council for excellence in critical thinking. In: 8th Annual International Conference on Critical Thinking and Education Reform, Rohnert Park, CA, pp. 25–30 (1987)
85. Seaborn, K., Fels, D.I.: Gamification in theory and action: a survey. Int. J. Hum.-Comput. Stud. **74**, 14–31 (2015)
86. Shih, P.C., Bellotti, V., Han, K., Carroll, J.M.: Unequal time for unequal value: implications of differing motivations for participation in timebanking. In: Proceedings of the 33rd Annual ACM Conference on Human Factors in Computing Systems, pp. 1075–1084. ACM (2015)
87. Shih, P.C., Christena, N.E.: From quantified self to quantified other: engaging the public on promoting animal well-being. In: ACM Conference on Human Factors in Computing Systems: Workshop on HCI Goes to the Zoo (2016)
88. Shih, P.C., Han, K., Carroll, J.M.: Community incident chatter: informing local incidents by aggregating local news and social media content. In: ISCRAM (2014)

89. Shih, P.C., Han, K., Carroll, J.M.: Community poll: externalizing public sentiments in social media in a local community context. In: Second AAAI Conference on Human Computation and Crowdsourcing (2014)
90. Shih, P.C., Han, K., Carroll, J.M.: Engaging community members with digitally curated social media content at an arts festival. In: Digital Heritage, 2015, vol. 1, pp. 321–324. IEEE (2015)
91. Shih, P.C., Han, K., Poole, E.S., Rosson, M.B., Carroll, J.M.: Use and adoption challenges of wearable activity trackers. IConference 2015 Proceedings (2015)
92. Shih, P.C., Nguyen, D.H., Hirano, S.H., Redmiles, D.F., Hayes, G.R.: Groupmind: supporting idea generation through a collaborative mind-mapping tool. In: Proceedings of the ACM 2009 International Conference on Supporting Group Work, pp. 139–148. ACM (2009)
93. Shih, P.C., Olson, G.M.: Using visualization to support idea generation in context. In: ACM Creativity and Cognition Conference Workshop: Creativity and Cognition in Engineering Design. ACM (2009)
94. Shih, P.C., Venolia, G., Olson, G.M.: Brainstorming under constraints: why software developers brainstorm in groups. In: Proceedings of the 25th BCS Conference on Human-computer Interaction, pp. 74–83. British Computer Society (2011)
95. Shih, P.C., Han, K., Carroll, J.M.: Using social multimedia content to inform emergency planning of recurring and cyclical events in local communities. J. Homel. Secur. Emerg. Manag. 12(3), 627–652 (2015)
96. Silvertown, J.: A new dawn for citizen science. Trends Ecol. Evol. 24(9), 467–471 (2009)
97. Su, N.M., Shih, P.C.: Virtual spectating: hearing beyond the video arcade. In: Proceedings of the 25th BCS Conference on Human-Computer Interaction, pp. 269–278. British Computer Society (2011)
98. Terveen, L., Hill, W.: Beyond recommender systems: helping people help each other. HCI New Millenn. 1(2001), 487–509 (2001)
99. Tinati, R., Van Kleek, M., Simperl, E., Luczak-Rösch, M., Simpson, R., Shadbolt, N.: Designing for citizen data analysis: A cross-sectional case study of a multi-domain citizen science platform. In: Proceedings of the 33rd Annual ACM Conference on Human Factors in Computing Systems, pp. 4069–4078. ACM (2015)
100. Tomlinson, B., Ross, J., Andre, P., Baumer, E., Patterson, D., Corneli, J., Mahaux, M., Nobarany, S., Lazzari, M., Penzenstadler, B., et al.: Massively distributed authorship of academic papers. In: CHI'12 Extended Abstracts on Human Factors in Computing Systems, pp. 11–20. ACM (2012)
101. Vaghela, S.J.D., Shih, P.C.: Walksafe: College campus safety app. In: International Conference on Information Systems for Crisis Response and Management (2018)
102. Vinyals, O., Toshev, A., Bengio, S., Erhan, D.: Show and tell: a neural image caption generator. In: Computer Vision and Pattern Recognition (CVPR), 2015 IEEE Conference on, pp. 3156–3164. IEEE (2015)
103. Walt, S.v.d., Colbert, S.C., Varoquaux, G.: The numpy array: a structure for efficient numerical computation. Comput. Sci. Eng. 13(2), 22–30 (2011)
104. Wang, J., Shih, P.C., Carroll, J.M.: Life after weight loss: design implications for community-based long-term weight management. Comput. Support. Coop. Work (CSCW) 24(4), 353–384 (2015)
105. Wang, J., Shih, P.C., Carroll, J.M.: Revisiting linuss law: benefits and challenges of open source software peer review. Int. J. Hum.-Comput. Stud. 77, 52–65 (2015)
106. Wang, J., Shih, P.C., Wu, Y., Carroll, J.M.: Comparative case studies of open source software peer review practices. Inf. Softw. Technol. 67, 1–12 (2015)
107. Ware, M., Frank, E., Holmes, G., Hall, M., Witten, I.H.: Interactive machine learning: letting users build classifiers. Int. J. Hum.-Comput. Stud. 55(3), 281–292 (2001)
108. Warschauer, M., Matuchniak, T.: New technology and digital worlds: analyzing evidence of equity in access, use, and outcomes. Rev. Res. Educ. 34(1), 179–225 (2010)
109. Wiggins, A., Crowston, K.: From conservation to crowdsourcing: a typology of citizen science. In: 2011 44th Hawaii International Conference on System Sciences (HICSS), pp. 1–10. IEEE (2011)

110. Williams, K., Li, L., Khabsa, M., Wu, J., Shih, P.C., Giles, C.L.: A web service for scholarly big data information extraction. In: 2014 IEEE International Conference on Web Services (ICWS), pp. 105–112. IEEE (2014)
111. Wing, J.: Computational thinking benefits society. 40th Anniversary Blog of Social Issues in Computing **2014** (2014)
112. Wing, J.M.: Computational thinking. Commun. ACM **49**(3), 33–35 (2006)
113. Witten, I.H., Frank, E., Hall, M.A., Pal, C.J.: Data Mining: Practical Machine Learning Tools and Techniques. Morgan Kaufmann (2016)
114. Wu, Y., Kropczynski, J., Shih, P.C., Carroll, J.M.: Exploring the ecosystem of software developers on github and other platforms. In: Proceedings of the Companion Publication of the 17th ACM Conference on Computer Supported Cooperative Work and Social Computing, pp. 265–268. ACM (2014)
115. Wu, Y., Shih, P.C., Carroll, J.M.: Design for supporting dialectical constructivist learning activities. In: EDULEARN14 Proceedings, pp. 4156–4164. IATED (2014)
116. Yang, S., Chen, P.Y., Shih, P.C., Bardzell, J., Bardzell, S.: Cross-strait frenemies: Chinese netizens vpn in to facebook taiwan. Proceedings of the ACM on Human-Computer Interaction **1**(CSCW), Article–115 (2017)
117. Zheng, S., Rosson, M.B., Shih, P.C., Carroll, J.M.: Designing moocs as interactive places for collaborative learning. In: Proceedings of the Second (2015) ACM Conference on Learning@ Scale, pp. 343–346. ACM (2015)
118. Zheng, S., Rosson, M.B., Shih, P.C., Carroll, J.M.: Understanding student motivation, behaviors and perceptions in moocs. In: Proceedings of the 18th ACM Conference on Computer Supported Cooperative Work and Social Computing, pp. 1882–1895. ACM (2015)

Chapter 4
Effective Design in Human and Machine Learning: A Cognitive Perspective

Robert Zheng and Kevin Greenberg

Abstract This chapter offers a discussion on the relations between knowledge transfer in human deep learning and machine learning. A review of cognitive theories and models related to knowledge transfer in human deep learning was made in reference to the cognitive structure of surface and deep processes in learning. This is followed by a review of the characteristics of machine learning and their unique features in terms of supporting cognitive processes in knowledge transfer. Discussions on how knowledge in human cognitive processes may assist the design and implementation of machine learning are made. A framework was proposed to advance the practice of machine learning focusing on transfer of knowledge in human deep learning with respect to the relations between human cognitive processes and machine learning.

4.1 Introduction

The growth of digital technology has significantly changed the landscape in education providing numerous opportunities for personalized and human deep learning, enabling students to engage in creative and critical thinking, and to develop skills and abilities necessary to meet the challenges in the 21st century [2, 16]. Machine learning has become a viable venue for improving learners' behaviours and cognitive processes in learning. Hildebrandt [38] points out that machine learning can "help students to improve their learning behaviours …help schools, colleges, and universities to manage, coordinate, and administrate information and communication regarding the progress of their students' performance" (p. 7). Machine learning has shown

R. Zheng (✉) · K. Greenberg
University of Utah, 1721 Campus Center Drive, SAEC Room 3220,
Salt Lake City, UT, USA
e-mail: robert.zheng@utah.edu

K. Greenberg
e-mail: kig3434@aol.com

© Springer International Publishing AG, part of Springer Nature 2018
J. Zhou and F. Chen (eds.), *Human and Machine Learning*, Human–Computer
Interaction Series, https://doi.org/10.1007/978-3-319-90403-0_4

promises in education. A review of literature reveals that machine learning has been applied in areas like domain assessment [4, 42], intelligent tutoring [41], expertise acquisition [37], educational gamification [13, 23], learner interaction [47], and curricular integration [22]. Despite its multifaceted approaches in education, the focus in machine learning research appears to be more interested in the technical aspects such as the algorithm of the expert system, the semantic functions in gamification, and so forth [6, 31, 33]. Few considerations have been given to the nature and structure of cognitive processes such as deep-level cognitive processes relating to knowledge transfer and construction. A lack of this cognitive perspective has begun to hamper the practice and application of machine learning in education. The objectives of the current chapter therefore are two-fold: First, it describes the cognitive processes in human deep learning by reviewing models and theories in research. Second, it proposes a framework that delineates the relationship between cognitive processes and machine learning. From this chapter the readers will be able to understand:

1. The role of knowledge structure and cognitive processes in learning;
2. The process of human deep learning in machine learning.

4.2   Theoretical Background

Since the second objective highlights the process of human deep learning in machine learning, it is essential that the concept of "deep learning" be defined to set the tone for the rest of the chapter. There are significant differences in the definitions of deep learning between cognitive scientists and machine learning scientists. A discussion of the differences follows. From a machine learning perspective, deep learning is part of a broader family of machine learning methods based on learning data representations. The notion of representations derives from and is loosely based on the interpretation of information processing and communication patterns in a biological nervous system, such as neural coding that attempts to define a relationship between various stimuli and associated neuronal responses in the brain. Based on the biological nervous system, machine learning researchers create architectures to explicate the data patterns from large-scale, unlabelled data sets. These architectures commonly known as deep learning architectures (also known as deep structured learning or hierarchical learning) that include deep neural networks, deep belief networks and recurrent neural networks, have been applied to fields including computer vision, speech recognition, natural language processing, audio recognition, social network filtering, machine translation, bioinformatics and drug design with results produced comparable to and in some cases superior to human experts. Differing from machine learning scientists, cognitive scientists define *deep learning* based on the processing levels of information in learning. This includes shallow learning where information is processed at lexicon and semantic level with recall and rote memorisation and deep learning where the information is processed through the connection with learners' prior knowledge and schemata that results in constructive and creative thinking, knowledge application and transfer [11, 34, 40]. In this chapter, the term *deep learning* refers to human cognitive information processing in learning as measured by their ability to thinking deeply in terms of creativity, application and transfer of knowledge.

The current study is informed by several cognitive and learning theories including Merrill's [40] component display theory, the framework on deep learning [10], and recent research on machine learning.

4.2.1   Merrill's Component Display Theory and Knowledge Process

It has been recognised that human learning activity, regardless of the learning domains and subject, can be essentially categorized into five outcomes: intellectual skills, verbal information, cognitive strategy, motor skills and attitude [19]. According to Gagne [20], intellectual skills refer to using concepts and rules to solve problems; verbal information means stating information; cognitive strategy describes the act of originating novel solutions to problems by utilizing various means for controlling one's thinking or learning processes; motor skills refer to executing bodily movements smoothly and in proper sequence; finally, attitude means choosing to behave in a particular way.

Merrill [40] further added that human learning activities in relation to their achievable outcomes interact at four levels which he described as components of knowledge. They comprise facts, concepts, procedures, and principles. Facts are the smallest units that "have no general or abstract representation" ([40], p. 288). Examples of facts include a census number or a reading from a thermometer. In contrast, concepts are general notions or ideas that combine all the characteristics of facts or particulars. Concepts can be abstract or concrete, both generalise the characteristics of individual facts. For example, the concept of car is an abstraction of the characteristics of individual cars, that is, all cars regardless of the brand and colour, have four wheels, engines, and so forth. Procedure is a particular way of carrying out an act and defines the steps of action in certain order and manner. Examples of procedure include surgical procedure, how to bake a cake, how to assemble a car, etc. Finally, principles refer to rules or beliefs that explain or control how things happen or work. For example, Newton's laws of motion explain the motion of an object or body in terms of force. The principle of diminishing returns in economics explains the point at which the level of profits or benefits gained becomes less than the amount of money or resources invested. Merrill claimed that knowledge components can be executed at three levels of cognitive processing. They are remembering, using, and finding. When learning a content, learners first memorise the facts, concepts, procedures and principles followed by using or applying the facts, concepts, procedures and principles. Finally, they find or discover concepts, procedures, and principles. Table 4.1

Table 4.1 Knowledge components with levels of cognitive processing

	Facts	Concepts	Procedures	Principles
Remember	X	X	X	X
Use	X	X	X	X
Find		X	X	X

summarises Merrill's component display theory showing the relationship between components of knowledge and levels of cognitive processing.

4.2.1.1 Shallow and Deep Processing

Research has shown that learners' processing of information can differ significantly. Some process information at a shallow or surface level by memorising and recalling information; others process information at a deeper level by making inferences about what they learn and transferring their knowledge to new learning situations [26, 34]. In Merrill's framework of knowledge components, memorisation represents a shallow cognitive processing where knowledge like facts, concepts, procedures, and principles are passively processed. Learners memorise the information verbatim without fully understanding the roles and relationship between knowledge components. For example, learners may memorise the facts of different brands of car (e.g., Ford, Honda, Mercedes, etc.) and the concept of a car (e.g., four wheels, engine, carburretor, etc.), but may never be able to tell how these cars differ in terms of air and fuel combustion ratio in relation to horse power, or compare types of wheel in terms of speed, safety and duration among different cars. In other words, if the process of learning is characterised as memorising information only, undesirable consequences associated with this process may occur. Evidence from empirical research has shown that rote memorisation and recalling lead to knowledge regurgitation and inertia, failing to meaningfully apply knowledge to new learning and application [5, 27].

In contrast, when learning focuses on application and discovery, learners begin to use the concepts, procedures and principles to understand the content thus leading them to explore and find new rules and principles. This is what Kintsch [34] describes as deep learning in his comprehension theory. According to Kintsch, the most robust learning occurs when learners integrate the content with their prior knowledge to understand rather than memorise what is being learned. This integrated comprehension approach helps promote learners' inference, application, and knowledge transfer in learning. Wilhelm [53] pointed out when learners are engaged "in the challenges of understanding and then apply what they are learning, [thus] producing important and usable meanings and actions instead of just consuming information provided from external sources" (p. 37) (See also [44]). However, Asikainen and Gijbels [3] conducted a review of 43 studies on deep learning and found no empirical evidence for the assumption that students develop deeper approaches during higher education. The finding raises some concerns in the state of student learning in regard to deep understanding. Is it due to a lack of rigour in curricular content that students are not challenged enough to engage in deep learning? Or is it due to a lack of instructional strategies that fail to properly challenge students to deep level thinking and understanding? While the curricular content can be problematic sometimes, the issue seems to lie more in the strategy than content, particularly in light of the impact of fast-paced digital technology on our information processing. The next section focuses on a theoretical framework in cognitive strategy in deep learning.

4.2.2 Deep Learning: A Two-Tier Perspective

Deep learning like knowledge transfer involves mapping between the source problem and the target problem [30] at the surface and the deep levels [10]. The source problem is the initial task presented to the learner in order for them to find the knowledge required to solve the question, while the target problem is the ensuing problem to measure the learners' transfer of the knowledge. The surface level refers to the problem state which describes what the problem is. An example would be solving the area of a triangle. The deep level refers to rules and principles underlying the problem state. For example, the formula $Area\_triangle = 1/2 * Base * Height$ is used to solve the problem at the surface structure. In complex learning like knowledge transfer, the source/target problems crisscross with the surface/deep levels to affect the outcome in knowledge transfer. In other words, transfer learning is characterised by (a) mapping between the source and target problems and (b) applying rules (deep) to the problem state (surface) (e.g., [10, 24, 30, 55]).

There are two situations associated with knowledge transfer. First, the source problem and the target problem are similar at the surface and deep levels, that is, the problem types and their underlying rules are similar (Fig. 4.1a). Second, the source problem and the target problem are dissimilar at the surface level but similar at the deep level (Fig. 4.1b). Research has shown that learners often have difficulty in applying the rules/principles to the problem state when the source problem and target

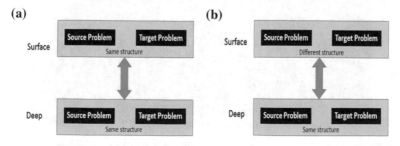

Fig. 4.1 Surface and deep structure of source and target problems

problem are dissimilar at the surface level but similar at the deep level [8, 14]. The following sections discuss the two situations in complex learning.

4.2.2.1 Similar Surface and Deep Structures Between Source and Target Problems

When surface and deep structures are similar, learners are often able to transfer knowledge from the source problem to the target problem which is defined as near transfer. Due to the structural similarity between the problem state, rules and principles, it is easy for learners to apply what they learn in the source problem to the target problem [10]. Figure 4.2 presents a situation in which the source and target problems have similar problem states (both are triangles) with the same rule ($Area\_triangle = 1/2 * Base * Height$) in problem solving. In this situation, the learner first learns to apply the formula of triangle area to solve the triangle area

Fig. 4.2 Source and target problems share the similar surface and deep structure

problem in the source problem. Then he/she applies the same formula to solve a similar problem in the target problem. There is a consistency between the source and target problems in terms of surface and deep structure. Research shows that when the surface and deep structures are similar between the source and target problems, transfer of knowledge is more likely to occur since learners can easily apply the rules and principle in the source problem to the target problem in problem solving [10].

4.2.2.2 Dissimilar Surfaces with Similar Deep Structures Between Source and Target Problems

When the source problem and the target problem are different at the surface structure level but similar at the deep structure level, transfer can be challenging. This type of knowledge transfer is often referred to as far transfer. Fig. 4.3 presents a scenario

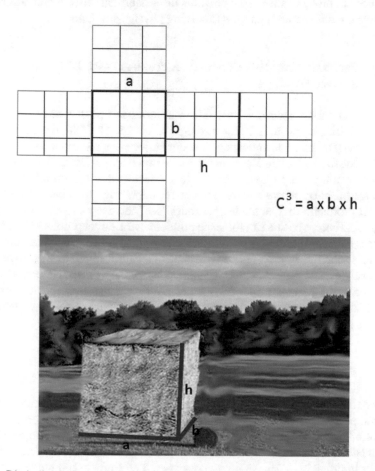

Fig. 4.3 Dissimilar surface with similar deep structure between source and target problems

where the learner transfers knowledge between different surface structures. In the source problem, the learner is given a two dimensional geometry shape consisting of six separate squares and asked to identify the height, width, and length (problem state). They then learn how to apply the cubic volume formula ($v^3 = Length * Width * Height$) to find the cubic volume (deep learning). In the target problem, the learner is presented with a three dimensional geometry figure of a hay stack and asked to identify the height, width, and length (problem state) and applies the same formula to solve the cubic volume problem (deep learning). Since the surface structures between the source and target problems are *different*, the learner could have trouble in identifying the height, width, and length and fail to transfer knowledge from source problem to target problem. Previous studies have shown that even after students have succeeded in solving a source problem, they still cannot successfully solve a target problem with the problem state different from its source problem at the surface level [9, 24, 25, 45]. The difficulty in far transfer not only lies in the differences in problem states (see previous discussion) but also in domains such as transferring mathematical concepts to solving physics problems.

4.2.2.3 Facilitate Knowledge Transfer in Problems with Different Surface Structure

As discussed earlier, students often fail in knowledge transfer when the problem states are dissimilar in surface structure [9, 10, 24, 25, 45]. Chi and VanLehn [10] point out that the failure in knowledge transfer between source and target problems is probably due to a lack of in-depth interaction between the surface and deep structures in initial learning. They suggest that the learner must have a deep interaction with the source problem before he/she can transfer knowledge to solve the problem in the target problem. That is, the learner must "see" the deep structure in the source problem first before he/she can solve the problem in the target problem [10]. Chi and VanLehn [10] noted the concept of deep structure is not limited to rules and principles. It includes schemas in problem solving research, causal relations in non-problem-solving studies, and mental models in learning studies. An indepth interaction with a deep structure (e.g., rules, principles, mental model, schema, etc.) enables learners to gain full understanding of the deep structure in initial learning which consequently facilitates transfer in target problem solving (Fig. 4.4).

4.2.2.4 Evidence of Indepth Interaction in Initial Learning

Evidence has demonstrated the effects of initial deep interaction in a source problem on knowledge transfer in a target problem [11, 25, 48, 51]. Several approaches have been introduced to solicit indepth interaction in initial learning. For example, Chi [11] conducted a study using a constructive/generative approach to foster learners' deep thinking in order to solicit knowledge transfer. The study asked students to draw a diagram that delineated the relationship among the concepts and principles and

Fig. 4.4 A two-stage knowledge transfer model for deep interaction in initial learning

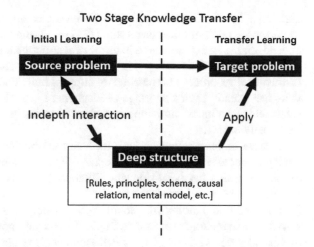

requested them to self-explain a worked-out solution to identify the deep structure principles. The results showed that the invention group developed deeper understanding that led to greater transfer than did the control group. Gick and Holyoak [25] studied student knowledge transfer by asking students to provide their own solutions to the source problem. They found providing one's own solution to initial learning led to deeper initial learning which fostered greater transfer. Schwartz et al. [48] provide two source examples and asked students to compare and contrast the two source examples so that they were able to outline the underlying abstract principles. The results showed that students who engaged in the comparing and contrasting process in initial learning performed better than did the control group in terms of knowledge transfer. VanLehn and Chi [51] studied transfer by asking students to identify, for every written step in a solution, the deep principle that generated it. They found that students gained deep understanding of the principles and were able to apply this to target problem solving.

The evidence from empirical research has demonstrated that students' initial deep interaction with learning materials "was successful enough to provide a substantive basis for them to have transferred what they learned to new contexts" ([17], p. 453).

4.2.2.5 Challenges of Deep Interaction in Initial Learning

In spite of the evidence in successful transfer by interacting deeply with the deep structure in initial learning, there are several challenges in regard to the practice of student deep interaction in initial learning. First, the challenge is related to the degree of support needed when students interact with the deep structure. For example, how much support should be provided when students try to identify deep principles in written steps in solutions in VanLehn and Chi's study [51]? What would the cognitive scaffolding look like if students fail to compare and contrast in initial learning in Schwartz et al.'s study [48]? To what extent should teachers give support to students in Gick and Holyoak's study [25] when students fail to provide a solution? Second, there is a big challenge in terms of instructional resources. Since individual students differ in their abilities to interact with deep structure, there is a need for instructional resources and teachers to support individualised deep learning. Since there has already been a shortage of teachers in schools, placing more teachers in classrooms to support individualised deep learning is practically impossible and logistically unrealistic.

Because of the challenges with the deep interaction approach, the practice of having students engaged in effective knowledge transfer through deep interaction in initial learning has been stagnant. Students basically read through the solutions provided to them and then are asked to work on new problems. Chi and VanLehn [10] pointed out "reading [the solution] is considered a passive overt engagement activity …that reading a solution example alone is not a good enough learning activity to engender deep learning" (p. 179). However, the status quo has changed with the advancement of new technology, especially artificial intelligence and machine learning. The next section discusses how machine learning can assist in deep learning.

4.3 Machine Learning as an Instructional Support in Deep Learning

Machine learning has long been considered a viable tool for education [35, 38, 43, 49]. It has been successfully used to help student learning in the form of intelligent tutoring, assessment, reading, and more recently game-based learning. Studies show that machine learning has the potential to support complex learning, adapt the content to individual students' cognitive styles, and facilitate students' deep understanding by bringing in deep representation of the subject matter [4, 13, 41, 43]. There are some unique traits of machine learning that makes it suitable for various educational purposes and goals. The next section offers a discussion of the traits associated with machine learning.

4.3.1 Individualised Performance Diagnosis

The conventional concept of performance measures in the context of education assumes that learners' behaviours can be effectively measured by quizzes, tests, examinations, and other educational assessments. Such measures often take on a global representation of the student. Subsequently, global actions are prescribed to address the issues related to the student performance. An example would be offering massive remedial courses for everyone. The approach has been proven costly and inefficient, taking a tremendous amount of time from teachers and students with little evidence of improvement. In contrast to traditional practice, machine learning provides moment-by-moment diagnosis of students' performance. It records every behaviour including hits, search paths, clicks, and answers to decide what this student needs right now in order to learn the relevant concept, fact, procedure, or principle.

The student's performance profile is determined by complex algorithms in learner analytics – a technique widely used in machine learning for educational improvement. Based on multiple sources of input (e.g., audio, video, verbal data, etc.), learner analytics provides an accurate diagnosis of the learner's performance and engenders a performance file for instructional remediation.

4.3.2 Expert Checking

When developing learners' performance profile, there are two concerns regarding learners' performance. One involves how much knowledge a learner has, the other is what a learner knows. Some researchers (e.g., [12, 43, 49]) argue that the focus should be on what a learner knows because understanding what a learner knows helps determine the learner's schema level known as prerequisite hierarchy which further assists in identifying the learner's path in learning.

In conventional learning the expert checking is often accomplished by having a domain expert (in schools it is the teacher) talk with the learner to determine what the learner already knowns so a remedial plan can be made. With machine learning, this is done by adding overlays of subject matter to the system. The overlay model breaks down the subject matter to be learned into components or prerequisites. The typical procedure of an overlay works by relating the student's performance to the prerequisite structure of the subject matter. If a student succeeds in completing a task related to the prerequisites in a subject domain, it is inferred they have acquired the knowledge items that are prerequisites for the subject domain. If they fail, it can be assumed that at least one of the prerequisites is missing in their competence. One drawback in the overlay model is that it can tell which prerequisite the student has failed but it cannot discriminate how the error was made, whether by misunderstanding or by misrepresentation.

4.3.3 Error Discrimination

Research in error diagnosis of human learning suggests that learners do not only fail to acquire the content presented to them but also misrepresent it [29, 36, 46]. Oftentimes, students acquire erroneous concepts, procedures, and false principles through various formal and informal learning environments and bring them to the classrooms when learning the subject content. In traditional classrooms explaining to students how they made an error and what type of error it is (e.g., error due to misrepresentation versus lack of knowledge) can be challenging. This is partly due to the limited instructional resources and an increasingly tight pool of teachers in schools. Machine learning provides the opportunity for supporting students in gaining an in-depth understanding of the errors they make. For example, by building an error library in machine learning, the learner will find that the error they made in assignment is due to (1) an incidental incorrect calculation (miscalculation), (2) a wrong mental model (misrepresentation), or (3) a lack of proper knowledge (inadequate schema). The error library consists of a list of possible errors. It compares the learner's errors with its list, determines type of error, and computes the best-fitting combination effectively enough to deliver a diagnosis in a reasonable time.

4.3.4 Determining Learning Path

It is believed that within a machine learning system learners' progress can be graduated to reflect the learning path of activities towards the learning goal [18, 43, 52]. Farago points out that by identifying the underlying metric, machine learning can model the system behaviour with respect to path choices. The system can monitor learners' complex learning process and observe what the learner does step by step. By installing a knowledge base consisting of several hundred problem-solving rules, which encode both correct knowledge about the domain and typical errors, the system locates the rule (or rules) that correspond with each problem-solving step the learner takes. That is, the system can represent both learners' knowledge and errors in terms of what steps the learner takes, how the goal is managed, and what mental model the learner may have to determine the optimal learning path in complex learning.

4.3.5 Limitations of Machine Learning

Despite its wide applications in general education such as curricular integration, learner interaction, and cognitive problem solving in particular [13, 22, 23, 37, 42, 47], machine learning has shown some limitations in terms of how it can promote learners' deep learning. As was discussed earlier, research in machine learning has been primarily focused on the system functions like individualised cognitive diagnosis, error detection, expert model overlay, and learning path determination. Few efforts have been directed toward understanding the role of machine learning pertaining to scaffolds of deep and surface learning. It is obvious that teaching learners to solve problems without facilitating their abilities to transfer knowledge to new learning may render the learning experience less relevant and meaningful since learners tend to repeat the problem steps without questioning the meaning of the steps and understanding their connection to new learning.

Another reason why machine learning has been slow in moving forward to deep and surface cognitive scaffolds is the technical challenges in terms of solutions to deep learning and knowledge transfer scaffolds. For example, in his discussion of algorithmic challenges in learning path metrics Farago [18] points out that significant challenges exist with respect to learning path metrics such as general non-additive metric based learning tasks. Regardless, machine learning has shown promises in automating deep learning for learners. Researchers have been exploring deep learning at a meta-structure level by studying the ontological design of teaching and learning in the digital environment [1, 21, 28, 54]. In the next section we will present a framework that focuses on the cognitive structure of deep learning and the features of machine learning.

4.4   Designing Machine Learning for Deep Learning: A Cognitive Perspective

Machine learning holds promises for deep level cognitive learning such as making inferences and transferring knowledge. Literature has shown that many of the features in machine learning such as cognitive diagnosis, error detection, expert model overlay, and learning path determination have significantly improved the diagnosis of learner performance and assist teachers in making relevant instructional and curricula decisions. However, there is a lack of attempt to marry the features of machine learning with research in deep learning, particularly the two-tie process of deep learning for knowledge transfer. In the framework we are about to propose, we will focus on the features of machine learning and how the features may enhance cognitive performance in deep learning, in this case, knowledge transfer.

4.4.1   Connecting Features of Machine Learning to Knowledge Transfer Performance

As is widely recognised, knowledge can be divided into facts, concepts, procedures and principles. Merrill [40] claimed that the actions in executing the above knowledge components should involve remembering, using and finding. The latter two are often consider deep learning whereas the first one is considered shallow or surface learning. Chi and colleagues [10, 11] proposed a constructive-generative model in deep learning by suggesting active interaction with deep learning content (i.e., rules and principles) in initial learning in order to successfully transfer knowledge to new learning. Strategies for active interaction range from students' providing their own solution [25], comparing and contrasting [48], asking students to identify deep principles [51], and asking students to draw conceptual diagrams [11]. Studies have shown that the active interaction with rules and principles deepens learners' understanding and supports both near and far transfer in learning.

While the two-tier deep learning model has demonstrated advantages in deep learning, the cognitive utility of the model can be enhanced by incorporating the features of machine learning. For example, individualised cognitive diagnosis, error detection, and expert overlay can be utilised to support learners' interaction with deep learning in initial learning and target problem solving. The individualized cognitive diagnosis monitors the learner's step by step performance and determines what the learner needs in initial and target problem solving. The error detection system has an error library which consists of a list of errors. It checks if an error exists and compares the learner's errors with its list and then determines the type of error associated with the learner's performance, i.e., error due to misrepresentation or lack of knowledge. The expert overlay, which consists of a repository of expert knowledge model, compares the learner's performance with that of expert performance simulated in the model. If the learner succeeds in completing a task in terms of the knowledge components in a subject domain, they are inferred as having acquired the knowledge for the subject domain. If they fail, it can be assumed that at least one of the knowledge components is missing in their competence. The results from individualised cognitive diagnosis, error detection, and expert overlay will be used as inputs for a higher level knowledge depository, that is, determining a learner path which compiles the data and determines how well the learner is on his/her way to target.

4.4.2   Framework for Deep Learning with Machine Learning

As discussed earlier, combining the features of machine learning with cognitive models holds a great promise for deep learning. We also argued that due to the challenges in human support with deep learning (i.e., logistical concerns, level and degree of scaffolding in problem solving), machine learning can be used as an effective support to alleviate financial and logistical constraints and release teachers from intense day-to-day effort so they can effectively engage in the design, planning, and implementation of instruction. We therefore propose a framework for deep learning with machine learning. The framework consists of two parts: activity of deep learning and infrastructure of machine learning. The activity of deep learning is built on Chi and colleagues' [10] two-tier knowledge transfer model where the interaction between surface and deep learning in initial problem solving leads to the transfer of knowledge to target problem solving. The infrastructure of machine learning consists of low and high processing databases. The low processing databases include individualised cognitive diagnosis, error detection, and expert overlay interacting directly with the learner's problem solving in the source problem, providing feedback, determining error type, and identifying missing components in the learner's knowledge structure. They also provide secondary support to the learner in his/her target problem solving where the learner applies the deep learning rules/principles to new learning situations in problem solving. In the target problem the cognitive support begins to fade away. The learner independently solves the new problem and receives limited support like hints and prompts from the system. The results from low processing databases serve as input to the high level database which determines the learner's learning path by (a) deciding whether the learner is on the right track to achieving the learning goal, and

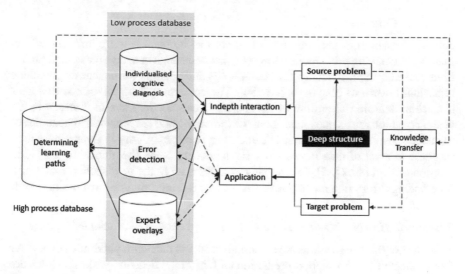

Fig. 4.5 Framework for deep learning with machine learning

(b) providing feedback, strategies, and knowledge that enable the learner to perform the transfer task successfully. Figure 4.5 presents the framework of deep learning with machine learning.

4.4.3   Implications of Cognitive Deep Learning for the Design of Machine Learning

The primary focus of this chapter is on how the characteristics of machine learning can assist and improve human cognitive processes such as knowledge application and transfer. The framework proposed (see Fig. 4.5) has both theoretical and practical significance. At the theoretical level, the framework connects the cognitive functionality of machine learning with human cognitive processes in terms of deep learning, hence bridging the gap in research on machine learning and deep cognitive processing. At the practical level, the framework identifies variables that are specific to the design of deep cognitive learning with machine learning. It delineates the relationships among the entities of cognitive processing and a machine learning based supporting system. The framework is still in its embryo form in conceptualisation and much work is needed between cognitive scientists and machine learning scientists to further flush out details of the framework at the operational levels. With that in mind, we take a flipped view to examine how the research in deep cognitive processing can inform the design of machine learning to help users understand black-box machine learning.

Black-Box Concerns

As machine learning gets smarter, it can act like humans helping inform decision making and making predictions. However, like humans, it can have biases and limitations caused by additional layers of complexity and opaqueness concerning machine behaviour known as black-box [38, 50]. The concern with black-box is that after a machine learning algorithm is developed, it can act in ways unforeseen by its designer, which raises questions about the *autonomy* and *responsibility* capacities of machine learning. Sometimes it is difficult to understand why it gives a particular response to a set of data inputs – a serious concern when the algorithm is used in mission-critical tasks [15]. Given that, our discussion in the next section focuses on how findings from human cognitive processing research may inform the design of machine learning, particularly the black-box issue.

Research in Human Cognitive Deep Learning and Design of Machine Learning

Machine Learning algorithms are essentially systems that learn patterns of behaviour from collected data to support prediction and informed decision-making, which are harnessed through two extremes:

1. Helping humans in discovering new knowledge that can be used to inform decision making;
2. Through automated predictive models that are plugged into operational systems and operate autonomously.

The above two extremes appear to be similar to what was discussed earlier in this chapter: that the purposes of researching on the mechanisms of human deep cognitive learning are to (a) inform human decision making in knowledge application and transfer and (b) predict the problem state based on prior knowledge. The human cognitive process framework (Fig. 4.5) entails elements predictable for future learner behaviour and performance. It is based on two-tier information processing derived from research in cognition. Therefore, the model has the following features: trustworthiness, interpretability, and absence of hidden rules. These are the features that machine learning scientists advocate to institute in the design of machine learning to increase transparency.

Trustworthiness. For people to use machine learning to make decisions and predictions, they must trust the model. To trust a model, they must understand how it makes its predictions, i.e., the model should be interpretable. Most current machine learning systems are operated on deep neural network principles which are not easily interpretable. Whereas in the human deep processing framework, the initial inputs (source problem, and deep structure elements: rules, principles, schema, causal relations, and mental model) are clearly defined (see Fig. 4.4). The inputs delineate the relationship between source problem and deep structure that further define the cognitive activities in the initial learning stage. As such, learning activities and paths become fully interpretable. The users can therefore trust the model to arrive at the outcomes as anticipated.

Interpretability. In the cognitive human deep learning model, the steps involved in various stages of learning (i.e., initial learning and transfer learning) are clearly laid out. The users are able to explain how knowledge can be transferred through a two stage process (Figs. 4.4 and 4.5). There are no hidden rules or principles that may deviate from the paths of learning. For the designers of machine learning, a thorough task analysis may be the initial step toward an interpretable product by examining the steps and relationships involved in a complex problem state. Depending on the nature of the problem, a proper task analysis method may be employed to unveil the relationships, complexity, as well as the depth and breadth of the problem [32].

Absence of hidden rules. Related to discussion point #2 above, machine learning that is devoid of black-box concerns should eliminate hidden rules and principles to increase its interpretability. Domingos [15] noted, "when a new technology is as pervasive and game-changing as machine learning, it's not wise to let it remain a black-box. Opacity opens the door to error and misuse." Hidden rules and principles increase the possibility of bias and errors in machine learning performance.

In conclusion, the practices and methodology in human cognitive deep learning research can inform the design of machine learning, especially in terms of the black-box issue. By observing the rules of transparency and governance in the design and development of machine learning, it is anticipated that machine learning will be a powerful tool in knowledge gathering and decision-making automation benefiting people and entities in different walks of life including economy, education, business, and so forth.

4.5   Discussion

The issue of how to nurture and develop learners' high level thinking and facilitate their knowledge transfer in deep learning has received considerable attention in cognitive research. Models and strategies related to the improvement of learners' deep learning have been proposed. While initial evidences demonstrated that transfer may occur with analogy [30], comparison and contrasting [48], think-aloud [11], and solution identification [51], the two-tier cognitive problem solving model by Chi and VanLehn [10] demonstrates a more robust path for knowledge transfer than previous practices. However, since cognitive scaffolding can be laborious and human resource intensive, there is a concern about the affordability of using a two-tier cognitive problem solving model due to a lack of teachers and instructional resources. Machine learning provides an effective alternative to the problem under study. Its automating features based on the principles of artificial intelligence opens the door for sophisticated detecting of cognitive processes in learning. Features like individualised cognitive diagnosis, error detection, expert overlay, and learning path determination have been applied in multiple areas including education [7, 39].

4.6 Conclusion

It is believed that machine learning supported by artificial intelligences and data warehouse is capable of calibrating human performance to a moment by moment level. This opens the opportunity for computing a large dataset from multiple sources of information (e.g., cognitive diagnosis, error detection and discrimination, expert checking) and making instructional and learning decisions that are uniquely adaptive to the needs of the learner. The current chapter bases its review of the literature on cognitive problem solving and knowledge transfer pertaining to learners' deep learning and the features of machine learning, particularly its adaptability to the diagnosis of cognitive information processing by proposing a framework for human deep learning with machine learning. The framework is well grounded in cognitive theories and the research in machine learning. It should be pointed out that the framework is still in its conceptual level. Further empirical studies based on evidence-based hypotheses should be conducted to understand the relationship among the variables in the framework. Research that aims at the validity and usability of the framework should be done by sampling from a wide range of population in terms of culture, ethnicity, social and economic status, as well as education level.

References

1. Abel, M.H., Benayache, A., Lenne, D., Moulin, C., Barry, C., Chaput, B.: Ontology-based organizational memory for e-learning. Educ. Technol. Soc. **7**(4), 98–111 (2004)
2. Arnab, S., Berta, R., Earp, J., Freitas, S.d., Popescu, M., Romero, M., Stanescu, I., Usart, M.: Framing the adoption of serious games in formal education. Electron. J. e-Learning **10**(2), 159–171 (2012)
3. Asikainen, H., Gijbels, D.: Do students develop towards more deep approaches to learning during studies? a systematic review on the development of students deep and surface approaches to learning in higher education. Educ. Psychol. Rev. **29**(2), 205–234 (2017)
4. Beggrow, E.P., Ha, M., Nehm, R.H., Pearl, D., Boone, W.J.: Assessing scientific practices using machine-learning methods: how closely do they match clinical interview performance? J. Sci. Educ. Technol. **23**(1), 160–182 (2014)
5. Bilican, K., Cakiroglu, J., Oztekin, C.: How contextualized learning settings enhance meaningful nature of science understanding. Sci. Educ. Int. **26**(4), 463–487 (2015)
6. Bishop, C.: Pattern Recognition and Machine Learning. Springer, New York (2006)
7. Butcher, K.R., Aleven, V.: Using student interactions to foster rule-diagram mapping during problem solving in an intelligent tutoring system. J. Educ. Psychol. **105**(4), 988–1009 (2013)
8. Case, J., Marshall, D.: Between deep and surface: procedural approaches to learning in engineering education contexts. Stud. High. Educ. **29**(5), 605–615 (2004)
9. Catrambone, R., Holyoak, K.J.: Overcoming contextual limitations on problem-solving transfer. J. Exp. Psychol. Learn. Mem. Cogn. **15**(6), 1147–1156 (1989)
10. Chi, M.T.H., VanLehn, K.A.: Seeing deep structure from the interactions of surface features. Educ. Psychol. **47**(3), 177–188 (2012)
11. Chi, M.T.H.: Active-constructive-interactive: a conceptual framework for differentiating learning activities. Top. Cogn. Sci. **1**(1), 73–105 (2009)
12. Chou, C.Y., Huang, B.H., Lin, C.J.: Complementary machine intelligence and human intelligence in virtual teaching assistant for tutoring program tracing. Comput. Educ. **57**(4), 2303–2312 (2011)

13. Conrad, S., Clarke-Midura, J., Klopfer, E.: A framework for structuring learning assessment in a massively multiplayer online educational game: experiment centered design. Int. J. Game-Based Learn. **4**(1), 37–59 (2014)
14. Diamond, N., Koernig, S.K., Iqbal, Z.: Uniting active and deep learning to teach problem-solving skills: strategic tools and the learning spiral. J. Mark. Educ. **30**(2), 116–129 (2008)
15. Domingos, P.: Why you need to understand machine learning. https://www.weforum.org/agenda/2016/05/why-you-need-to-understand-machine-learning/ (2016). Accessed 29 Oct 2017
16. Echeverri, J.F., Sadler, T.D.: Gaming as a platform for the development of innovative problem-based learning opportunities. Sci. Educ. **20**(1), 44–48 (2011)
17. Engle, R.A.: Framing interactions to foster generative learning: a situative explanation of transfer in a community of learners classroom. J. Learn. Sci. **15**(4), 451–498 (2006)
18. Farag, A.: Algorithmic challenges in learning path metrics from observed choices. Appl. Artif. Intell. **22**(7–8), 749–760 (2008)
19. Gagne, R.M., Briggs, L.: Principles of Instructional Design, 2nd edn. Holt, Rinehart, and Winston, New York (1979)
20. Gagne, R.M.: Conditions of Learning, 2nd edn. Holt, Rinehart and Winston of Canada Ltd, New York (1970)
21. Gašević, D., Hatala, M.: Ontology mappings to improve learning resource search. Br. J. Educ. Technol. **37**(3), 375–389 (2006)
22. Georgiopoulos, M., DeMara, R.F., Gonzalez, A.J., Wu, A.S., Mollaghasemi, M., Gelenbe, E., Kysilka, M., Secretan, J., Sharma, C.A., Alnsour, A.J.: A sustainable model for integrating current topics in machine learning research into the undergraduate curriculum. IEEE Trans. Educ. **52**(4), 503–512 (2009)
23. Gibson, D., Clarke-Midura, J.: Some psychometric and design implications of game based learning analytics. In: Cognition and Exploratory Learning in Digital Age (CELDA) Conference. Fort Worth, TX (2013)
24. Gick, M.L., Holyoak, K.J.: Analogical problem solving. Cogn. Psychol. **12**(3), 306–355 (1980)
25. Gick, M.L., Holyoak, K.J.: Schema induction and analogical transfer. Cogn. Psychol. **15**(1), 1–38 (1983)
26. Goldman, S.R., Braasch, J.L., Wiley, J., Graesser, A.C., Brodowinska, K.: Comprehending and learning from internet sources: processing patterns of better and poorer learners. Read. Res. Q. **47**(4), 356–381 (2012)
27. Halpin, R.: Breaking the rote memorization mindset of preservice teachers standards-based instruction: an integrated preservice teacher education model. Res. Sch. **6**(2), 45–54 (1999)
28. Henze, N., Dolog, P., Nejdl, W.: Reasoning and ontologies for personalized e-learning in the semantic web. Educ. Technol. Soc. **7**(4), 82–97 (2004)
29. Hollnagel, E.: Cognitive Reliability and Error Analysis Method. Elsevier, Oxford, UK (1998)
30. Holyoak, K.J., Thagard, P.: Analogical mapping by constraint satisfaction. Cogn. Sci. **13**(3), 295–355 (1989)
31. Jeong, J.: New methodology for measuring semantic functional similarity based on bidirectional integration. Ph.D. Thesis, University of Kansas, Lawrence, KS (2013)
32. Jonassen, D.H., Tessmer, M., Hannum, W.H.: Task Analysis Methods for Instructional Design. Taylor and Francis, Hoboken (1998)
33. Kerr, D., Mousavi, H., Iseli, M.R.: Automatic Short Essay Scoring Using Natural Language Processing to Extract Semantic Information in the Form of Propositions. Technical Report. CRESST Report 831, National Center for Research on Evaluation, Standards, and Student Testing (CRESST), UCLA, Los Angeles, CA (2013)
34. Kintsch, W.: Text comprehension, memory, and learning. Am. Psychol. **49**(4), 294–303 (1994)
35. Kirrane, D.E.: Machine learning. Train. Dev. J. **44**(12), 24–29 (1990)
36. Kroll, B.M., Schafer, J.C.: Error-analysis and the teaching of composition. College Compos. Commun. **29**(3), 242–248 (1978)
37. LaVoie, N.N., Streeter, L., Lochbaum, K., Boyce, L., Krupnick, C., Psotka, J., Wroblewski, D.: Automating expertise in collaborative learning environments. Online Learn. **14**(4), 97–119 (2010)

38. J. Learn. Anal. Learning as a machine: crossovers between humans and machines. **4**(1), 6–23 (2017)
39. Lynch, C., Ashley, K.D., Pinkwart, N., Aleven, V.: Adaptive tutoring technologies and Ill-defined domains. In: Durlach, P.J., Lesgold, A.M. (eds.) Adaptive Technologies for Training and Education, pp. 179–203. Cambridge University Press, Cambridge (2012)
40. Merrill, D.: Component display theory. In: Reigeluth, C. (ed.) Instructional design theories and models: An overview of their current status, pp. 279–334. Lawrence Erlbaum, Hillsdale, NJ (1983)
41. Nakamura, C.M., Murphy, S.K., Christel, M.G., Stevens, S.M., Zollman, D.A.: Automated analysis of short responses in an interactive synthetic tutoring system for introductory physics. Phys. Rev. Phys. Educ. Res. **12**, 010,122 (2016)
42. Nehm, R.H., Ha, M., Mayfield, E.: Transforming biology assessment with machine learning: automated scoring of written evolutionary explanations. J. Sci. Educ. Technol. **21**(1), 183–196 (2012)
43. Ohlsson, S.: Some principles of intelligent tutoring. Instr. Sci. **14**(3–4), 293–326 (1986)
44. Razzak, N.A.: Strategies for effective faculty involvement in online activities aimed at promoting critical thinking and deep learning. Educ. Inf. Technol. **21**(4), 881–896 (2016)
45. Reed, S.K., Dempster, A., Ettinger, M.: Usefulness of analogous solutions for solving algebra word problems. J. Exp. Psychol. Learn. Mem. Cogn. **11**(1), 106–125 (1985)
46. Richard, J.C. (ed.): Error Analysis: Perspectives on Second Language Acquisition, 4th edn. Routledge, New York (2014)
47. Schneider, B., Blikstein, P.: Unraveling students' interaction around a tangible interface using multimodal learning analytics. J. Educ. Data Min. **7**(3), 89–116 (2015)
48. Schwartz, D.L., Chase, C.C., Oppezzo, M.A., Chin, D.B.: Practicing versus inventing with contrasting cases: the effects of telling first on learning and transfer. J. Educ. Psychol. **103**(4), 759–775 (2011)
49. Self, J.: The application of machine learning to student modelling. Instr. Sci. **14**(3–4), 327–338 (1986)
50. Valsamis, A., Tserpes, K., Zissis, D., Anagnostopoulos, D., Varvarigou, T.: Employing traditional machine learning algorithms for big data streams analysis: the case of object trajectory prediction. J. Syst. Softw. **127**, 249–257 (2017). (Supplement C)
51. VanLehn, K., Chi, M.: Adaptive expertise as acceleration of future learning. In: Durlach, P.J., Lesgold, A.M. (eds.) Adaptive Technologies for Training and Education, pp. 28–45. Cambridge University Press, Cambridge (2012)
52. Wang, L.: Efficient regularized solution path algorithms with applications in machine learning and data mining. Ph.D. thesis, University of Michigan, Ann Arbor, MI (2009)
53. Wilhelm, J.D.: Learning to love the questions: how essential questions promote creativity and deep learning. Knowl. Quest **42**(5), 36–41 (2014)
54. Zheng, R., Dahl, L.: An ontological approach to online instructional design. In: H. Song, T.T. Kidd (eds.) Handbook of Research on Human Performance and Instructional Technology:, pp. 1–23. IGI Global, Hershey, PA (2009)
55. Zheng, R., Yang, W., Garcia, D., McCadden, E.: Effects of multimedia and schema induced analogical reasoning on science learning. J. Comput. Assist. Learn. **24**(6), 474–482 (2008)

Chapter 5
Transparency Communication for Machine Learning in Human-Automation Interaction

David V. Pynadath, Michael J. Barnes, Ning Wang and Jessie Y. C. Chen

Abstract Technological advances offer the promise of autonomous systems to form human-machine teams that are more capable than their individual members. Understanding the inner workings of the autonomous systems, especially as machine-learning (ML) methods are being widely applied to the design of such systems, has become increasingly challenging for the humans working with them. The "black-box" nature of quantitative ML approaches poses an impediment to people's *situation awareness* (SA) of these ML-based systems, often resulting in either disuse or over-reliance of autonomous systems employing such algorithms. Research in human-automation interaction has shown that transparency communication can improve teammates' SA, foster the trust relationship, and boost the human-automation team's performance. In this chapter, we will examine the implications of an agent transparency model for human interactions with ML-based agents using automated explanations. We will discuss the application of a particular ML method, reinforcement learning (RL), in Partially Observable Markov Decision Process (POMDP)-based agents, and the design of explanation algorithms for RL in POMDPs.

D. V. Pynadath · N. Wang (✉)
Institute for Creative Technologies, University of Southern California,
Los Angeles, CA, USA
e-mail: nwang@ict.usc.edu

D. V. Pynadath
e-mail: pynadath@ict.usc.edu

M. J. Barnes · J. Y. C. Chen
Human Research and Engineering Directorate, US Army Research Laboratory,
Aberdeen Proving Ground, Orlando, FL, USA
e-mail: michael.j.barnes.civ@mail.mil

J. Y. C. Chen
e-mail: yun-sheng.c.chen.civ@mail.mil

© Springer International Publishing AG, part of Springer Nature 2018
J. Zhou and F. Chen (eds.), *Human and Machine Learning*, Human–Computer
Interaction Series, https://doi.org/10.1007/978-3-319-90403-0_5

75

5.1   Introduction

As autonomous agents become prevalent in future battle spaces [11, 24], it will be increasingly difficult for humans to understand the logic and significance of an agent's purposed actions. Although machine learning (ML) techniques offer great advantages in both efficiency and adaptability, they also present a paradox. The more effective the ML algorithm, the more likely the operator is to eventually become complacent, lose attentional focus of the tasking environment, and accept erroneous outputs [21, 22]. ML processes tend to be opaque, making explainable AI necessary, but not always sufficient to achieve a synergistic relationship between humans and agents. Human partners' *situation awareness* (SA) must encompass not only their own situation, but also the agent's plans and its future implications and uncertainties. For both tactical and legal reasons, the human operator is responsible for understanding the consequences of the agent's action in a military environment [1, 9, 13].

Researchers from the U.S. Department of Defense (DoD) are investigating human-agent teaming in diverse scenarios: autonomous robots, targeting systems, assured mobility, planning, and control of aerial, ground, and ship unmanned systems, etc. [5, 7, 18, 19, 28]. It is important to develop a general framework that enables humans and agents to collaborate effectively and safely within diverse tasking environments [1]. Effective human teams are a good analogy, wherein all partners understand the objective, their respective roles, and the interaction protocols necessary for efficient collaboration [18, 32]. As an example, consider the case of an autonomous robot that moves from point A to point B carrying the infantry squad's equipment. The robotic agent must learn to recognise landmarks in order to return home, know what constitutes an anomaly, understand soldiers' intent, react to changes in the squad's mobility, and communicate with its soldier teammates [7]. That is, it must not only be aware of and signal to the operator what the agent intends, but also be aware of the changing military situation and be able to react to the actions of the other squad members [23]. While such a level of awareness does not constitute consciousness, it does require a richer shared awareness than simply understanding what the agent intends to do next.

The SA-based Agent Transparency (SAT) (Fig. 5.1) defines the essential information that a human-agent team must share for effective collaboration [7]. Section 5.2 presents the SAT model and the empirical research that supports the model's continued development. Empirical examinations of the SAT model highlight the challenges faced in trying to make ML-based autonomous systems transparent to human teammates.

In this chapter, we focus on a subset of ML that is particularly aimed at autonomous systems, namely *reinforcement learning* (RL), which has successfully applied quantitative probabilities and utilities within a variety of domains [14, 26]. RL's algorithms for computing long-term expected values can provide autonomous agents with optimal sequential decision policies. However, while RL's rich representation and complex reasoning provide useful performance guarantees for software agents, they also present a significant obstacle to human understanding.

Automatically generated explanations have provided such understanding in other areas of artificial intelligence (AI) [27]. More recent work has proposed methods for making the results of machine learning more understandable to human users [2]. However, most of these learning frameworks are unsuitable for autonomous decision-making in human-machine teams.

In contrast, *model-based* RL first learns a quantitative model in the form of Partially Observable Markov Decision Processes (POMDPs), which contain probabilistic action and sensor models, utility-based goal priorities, etc. that could facilitate explanations in human-machine interaction [15]. However, for real-world domains, the size and complexity of quantitative models like POMDPs are more likely to overwhelm human operators, rather than inform them. Existing explanation methods show potential [12], but their impact on human-machine trust and performance has not been studied.

The work described in this chapter seeks to identify the modelling content that best facilitates human comprehension. We begin by mapping the components of the POMDP model to different levels of SA in the SAT model. By developing algorithms that can generate natural-language explanations from these separate components (e.g., beliefs, observations, outcome likelihoods), we arrive at a variety of explanation content that aims to achieve different levels of team SA. By grounding these explanations in the agent's RL-based decision-making process, we can automatically generate a space of possible explanation content and measure their impact on human-machine trust and team performance.

5.2 SA-Based Agent Transparency and Trust

Trust is an important concept because it mediates between the reliability of autonomy and the operators' ability to effectively collaborate with intelligent agents (IAs) [17, 18]. Appropriate trust is not blind trust; instead, it is the ability of the operator to calibrate his or her interactions with agents to minimise disuse (failure to rely on reliable automation) and misuse (over-relying on unreliable automation) [10, 21, 22]. Calibration depends on the human partner knowing the agent's purpose, process, and performance [17]. U.S. Army Research Laboratory (ARL) researchers [9] developed the SAT model to make the agent's human partner aware of the agent's plans, reasoning, and predictions (Fig. 5.1). SAT posits three levels of information as necessary to foster insight into the IA's decision process: (L1) operator perception of the IA's actions and plans; (L2) comprehension of the IA's reasoning process; and (L3) understanding of the IA's predicted outcomes including its uncertainties about accomplishing its objectives [13].

In a series of experiments, Chen and colleagues examined the generality of SAT in a variety of military paradigms attempting to parse out what features of transparency were effective under what conditions. Two of the paradigms were part of DoD's Autonomy Research Pilot Initiative (ARPI): the use of agents for control and planning

---

- To support operator's **Level 1 SA** *(What's going on and what is the agent trying to achieve?)*

  - *Purpose*
    - · *Desire* (Goal selection)
  - *Process*
    - · *Intentions* (Planning/Execution)
    - · Progress
  - *Performance*

- To support operator's **Level 2 SA** *(Why does the agent do it?)*

  - Reasoning process *(Belief) (Purpose)*
    - · Environmental & other constraints

- To support operator's **Level 3 SA** *(What should the operator expect to happen?)*

  - Projection to Future/End State
  - Potential limitations
    - · Uncertainty: Likelihood of error
    - · History of performance

Fig. 5.1 SAT model [8]

support and an autonomous robot. Section 5.2.1 discusses these two investigations and Sect. 5.2.2 summarises the key lessons learned from these investigations.

5.2.1 Human Factors Experiments on Transparency

IMPACT (Intelligent Multi-UxV Planner with Adaptive Collaborative/Control Technologies) was a multiservice collaboration that was one of the seven ARPI research projects. IMPACT's purpose was to investigate various intelligent systems, including an intelligent planner and ML-based systems acting in concert with a human operator to send a group of unmanned vehicles (UxV) to defend various portions of a large littoral military base [5]. The transparency experiments used a simplified version of the basic paradigm, assuming that an IA planned the best route and chose the best complement of the available UxV assets to respond to an emergency [20, 25]. One experiment [20] varied SAT levels to create three conditions: Level 1 (L1: planning); Level 1 + 2 (L12: planning + reasoning information); and the final condition showing Level 1 + 2 + 3 (L123: Level 1 + 2 + predictions and uncertainties). Each of the transparency conditions received the same updated information (state of the world) ensuring that (L1, L12, L123) differed only on the transparency dimension. For each mission, the IA provided two recommended plans utilising the UxVs. Plan A was always the agent's top recommendation, and plan B was the back-up plan. About

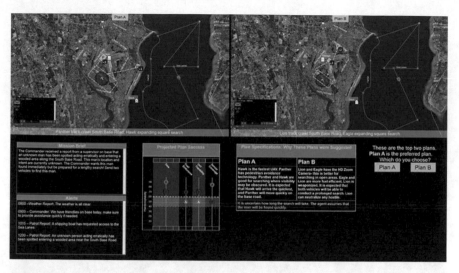

Fig. 5.2 Example of an IMPACT interface showing L123 plus uncertainty information for the second transparency experiment [25]

1/3 of the time, Plan B was actually the better option due to external information (changes in Commander's Intent, intelligence, etc.).

Results showed that L12 and L123 reduced both misuse (choosing A when B was the better option) and disuse (choosing B when A was the better option). This indicated that operators could better adapt to new information if they understood the IA's reasoning and prediction processes. Notably, participants reported greater trust in the IA in the L123 condition, which contained uncertainty information, compared to the other two transparency conditions.

Reference [25] examined 3 SAT conditions using the same basic paradigm but parsed out uncertainty information (U) to better understand its effects for the IMPACT tasks: L12, L123, and L123U. The highest level of transparency (L123U, illustrated in Fig. 5.2) resulted in the best overall performance with a slight increase in processing time (2–3 s). This suggests the utility of uncertainty information when it is added to predictions. In summary, the experiments showed the efficacy of higher levels of agent transparency to enable the operator to adjust to a changing military environment and also indicated that knowing uncertainties in the agent's planning process proved to be useful information for the operator. The IMPACT operator tasks were time constrained, but getting the right mix of UxVs and route planning was more important to mission success than the extra few seconds that processing the uncertainty information required [25].

The Autonomous Squad Member (ASM) project investigated enabling agent capabilities to support infantry squad-level performance in dynamic mission environments. The robot (ASM) behaved like a member of the squad and performed such tasks as carrying the squad's equipment. Because an infantry squad has to react instantaneously to changes in the combat situation, the ASM's operator control unit,

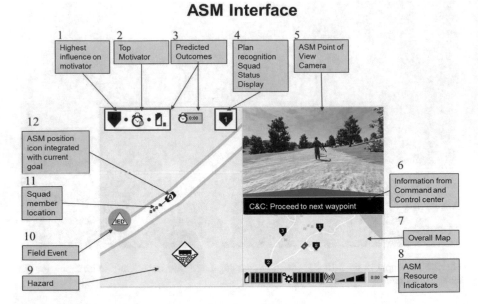

Fig. 5.3 Icons and pictorial visualisations of SAT information for the ASM experiment

a hand-held sized display, required "at a glance" status information based on a simpler icon-based visualisation interface (Fig. 5.3) The visualisation was designed based on the SAT model to enable humans to understand the agent's plan, reasoning (motivator icons), predicted outcome, and uncertainty. User studies showed that visualisations showing icons representing L123 received higher overall SA scores and subjective trust scores than displays depicting the three other SAT conditions (L1, L12, L123U). Importantly, the display with uncertainty information did not improve performance [23]. In situations (such as the ASM paradigm) where timeliness is at a premium, information that predictions were uncertain did not prove to be useful.

RoboLeader [9] is a research program investigating the human-factors aspects of a supervisory agent (RoboLeader) that is an interface between its human operators and multiple less capable semi-autonomous vehicles. In a recent experiment, RoboLeader monitored a 3-element convoy of manned and unmanned systems [31] that encountered various obstacles during its mission. Knowing RoboLeader's reasoning process decreased the human operator's misuse of erroneous agent suggestions. However, adding information about when the last intelligence update occurred (i.e., information staleness) actually caused the operator's performance to degrade compared to the reasoning-alone condition.

5.2.2   Summary of Transparency Experimentation Results

In summary, the series of transparency experiments revealed several findings that can inform how an RL-based agent can help its human teammates achieve SA. (1) Increasing SAT-level information can improve the operator performance and trust in the agent under diverse experimental conditions. (2) Adding uncertainty information was useful for paradigms that required detailed planning information (IMPACT) but less useful for paradigms that required instantaneous decisions (ASM). (3) Uncertainty is an important component of understanding the real world; currently, we have examined only a subset of uncertainty visualisation concepts [3, 8]. (4) Ultimately, success in conveying transparency will depend not only on the type of transparency information but also on the efficacy of the visualisation techniques for specific mission requirements. (5) Additionally, the type of information presented needs to be tailored to the operator's experience level and mission; too much information degrades performance. (6) Overall, the SAT researchers concluded that the underlying model needs to be expanded to include more dynamic processes and to encompass bidirectional understanding between agents and their human partners [7].

5.3   Model-Based Reinforcement Learning

These findings provide both guidance and challenges when designing an ML-based autonomous system that provides the right kind of transparency to human teammates. Using model-based RL helps address the first finding from Sect. 5.2.2 by providing the system with a declarative model that forms a potential basis for informing human teammates. Furthermore, this model includes explicit probabilities, potentially helping to address the second finding. However, the volume of quantitative information in the learned model is likely to violate the fifth finding and degrade human performance when communicated in full. We instead need to identify the most valuable subset of learned content to be made transparent to operators.

Section 5.3.1 describes the components of the modelling content built up by model-based RL. Section 5.3.2 shows how those components map to SAT levels and how they can support textual explanation content. Section 5.3.3 describes an empirical study of the impact of such content on human-machine trust and team performance.

5.3.1   POMDP Models Constructed by RL

Model-based RL can be viewed as constructing a POMDP [15], which, in precise terms, is a tuple, $\langle S, A, P, \Omega, O, R \rangle$, that we describe here in terms of an illustrative HRI scenario [28]. In it, a human teammate works with a robot in reconnaissance missions to gather intelligence in a foreign town. Each mission involves the human teammate searching buildings in the town. The robot serves as a scout, scans the buildings for potential danger, and relays its observations to the teammate. Prior to entering a building, the human teammate can choose between entering with or without putting on protective gear. If there is danger present inside the building, the human teammate will be fatally injured without the protective gear. As a result, the team will have to restart from the beginning and re-search the entire town. However, it takes time to put on and take off protective gear (e.g., 30 s each). So the human teammate is incentivised to consider the robot's observations before deciding how to enter the building. In the current implementation, the human and the robot move together as one unit through the town, with the robot scanning the building first and the human conducting a detailed search afterward. The robot has an NBC (nuclear, biological and chemical) weapon sensor, a camera that can detect armed gunmen, and a microphone that can listen to discussions in foreign language.

The state, S, consists of objective facts about the world, some of which may be hidden from the agents themselves. We use a *factored representation* [4] that decomposes these facts into individual feature-value pairs, such as the separate locations of the robots and their human teammates, as well as the presence of dangerous people or chemicals in the buildings to be searched. The state may also include feature-value pairs that represent the health level of any and all human teammates, any current commands, and the accumulated time cost so far.

The available actions, A, correspond to the possible decisions the agents can make. Given the proposed mission, each agent's first decision is where to move to next. Upon completing a search of a building, an agent can make a decision as to whether to declare a location as safe or unsafe for its human teammates. For example, if a robot believes that armed gunmen are at its current location, then it will want its teammate to take adequate preparations (e.g., put on body armour) before entering. Because there is a time cost to such preparations, the robot may instead decide to declare the location safe, so that its teammates can more quickly complete their own reconnaissance tasks.

In most RL domains, S and A are known a priori. However, the effects that the latter have on the former are typically not known. In model-based RL, the agent learns a *transition probability function*, P, to capture its action model, the possibly uncertain effects of each agent's actions on the subsequent state. For example, a robot with perfect movement may have an action model that assumes that a decision to move to a specific waypoint succeeds deterministically. More commonly, however, the robot will find a nonzero probability of failure, as is captured in more realistic robot navigation models [6, 16]. Recommendation actions by an agent can affect the health and happiness of its human teammates, although only stochastically, as a person may not follow the recommendation.

The ever-present noise when trying to sense the physical world means that realistic agents will not have perfect information about the true state of the world. The "partial observability" of a POMDP is specified through a set of possible observations, Ω (usually known a priori), that are probabilistically dependent (through the observation function, O, usually learned) on the true values of the corresponding state features.

Different observations may have different levels of noise. For example, an agent may be able to use GPS to get very accurate readings of its own location. However, it cannot detect the presence of armed gunmen or dangerous chemicals with perfect reliability or omniscience. Instead, the agent will receive local readings about the presence (or absence) of threats in the immediate vicinity. For example, if dangerous chemicals are present, then the robot's chemical sensor may detect them with a high probability. There is also a lower, but nonzero, probability that the sensor will not detect them. In addition to such a false negative, we can also model a potential false positive reading, where there is a low, but nonzero, probability that it will detect chemicals even if there are none present. By controlling the observations that the agents receive, we can manipulate their ability level in our testbed.

Partial observability gives the robot only a subjective view of the world, where it forms beliefs about what it thinks is the state of the world, computed via standard POMDP state estimation algorithms. For example, the robot's beliefs may include its subjective view on the presence of threats, in the form of a likelihood (e.g., a 33% chance that there are toxic chemicals in the farm supply store). Again, the robot would derive these beliefs from prior beliefs about the presence of such threats, updated by its more recent local sensor readings. Due to the uncertainty in its prior knowledge and sensor readings (not to mention its learning), the robot's beliefs are likely to diverge from the true state of the world. By decreasing the accuracy of the robot's observation function, O, we can decrease the accuracy of its beliefs, whether receiving correct or incorrect observations. In other words, we can also manipulate the robot's ability by allowing it to learn over- or under-estimates of its sensors' accuracy.

The human-machine team's mission objectives are captured by the reward function, R, which maps the state of the world into a real-valued evaluation of benefit for the agents. This function is also typically learned through experience. In our example domain, the robot will eventually learn that it receives the highest reward when the surveillance is complete. It will also receive higher reward values when its teammate is alive and unharmed. This reward component punishes the agents if they fail to warn their teammates of dangerous buildings. Finally, the agent will receive a slight negative reward for every epoch of time that passes. This motivates the agents to complete the mission as quickly as possible.

If we can construct such a POMDP model of the mission, the agents can autonomously generate their behaviour by determining the optimal action based on their current beliefs, b, about the state of the world [15]. Each agent uses a (possibly bounded) lookahead procedure that seeks to maximise expected reward by simulating the dynamics of the world from its current belief state across its possible action choices. It will combine these outcome likelihoods with its reward function and choose the option that has the highest expected reward.

5.3.2   POMDPs and SAT

Conventional wisdom holds that, in general, quantitative models such as POMDPs, are not readily explainable. However, the elements $\langle S, A, P, \Omega, O, R \rangle$ of a learned POMDP model correspond to concepts that teammates are likely to be familiar with. By exposing different components of an agent's learned model, we can make different aspects of its learning and decision-making transparent to human teammates. In prior work, we created static templates to translate the contents of a POMDP model into human-readable sentences. We create such templates around natural-language descriptions of each state feature and action. We then instantiate the templates at runtime with prespecified functions of the agent's current beliefs (e.g., probability of a state feature having a certain value). The following list illustrates the templates we created for each POMDP component, using specific runtime instantiations to show the final natural-language text provided to a human participant:

S: An RL-based agent can communicate its current beliefs about the state of the world, e.g., "I believe that there are no threats in the market square." Such a statement would constitute an L1 explanation within the SAT model. The agent could also use a standard POMDP probabilistic belief state to communicate its uncertainty in that belief, e.g., "I am 67% confident that the market square is safe."

A: An agent can make a decision about what route to take through its search area, e.g., "I am proceeding through the back alley to the market square." Such a statement would constitute an L1 explanation within the SAT model.

P: An agent can also reveal the relative likelihood of possible outcomes based on its learned action model, e.g., "There is a 33% probability that you will be injured if you follow this route without taking the proper precautions." With the uncertainty explicitly stated, this is an example of an L3U explanation within the SAT model.

Ω: Communicating its observation can reveal information about an agent's sensing abilities, e.g., "My NBC sensors have detected traces of dangerous chemicals." Because such a statement is meant to expose the agent's reasoning in arriving at its overall recommendation, this statement constitutes an L12 explanation within the SAT model.

O: Beyond the specific observation it received, an agent can also reveal information about the observation model it has learned so far, e.g., "My image processing will fail to detect armed gunmen 30% of the time." This elaboration on the Ω explanation is also an L12 explanation, aimed at conveying the agent's reasoning.

R: By communicating the expected reward outcome of its chosen action, an agent can reveal its benevolence (or lack thereof) contained in its current learned reward function, e.g., "I think it will be dangerous for you to enter the informant's house without putting on protective gear. The protective gear will slow you down a little." The template here relies on factored rewards, allowing the agent to compute separate expected rewards, $E[R]$, over the goals of keeping its teammate alive and achieving the mission as quickly as possible. The end result is an L123 explanation within the SAT model, as it conveys the agent's current goal, the reasoning going into the agent's decision, and what teammates can expect upon making their own subsequent decision.

5.3.3   Evaluation of Automatically Generated Explanations

We implemented an online version of our HRI scenario to study the impact of these explanation variations on trust and team performance [28]. The testbed can be accessed from a web browser through either a largely text-based interface (Fig. 5.4) or through a more immersive 3D first-person virtual environment (Fig. 5.5). The testbed's server executes the robot's POMDP to both maintain the state of the simulated mission and to generate decisions for the robot. These are displayed on the participant's web browser, which sends decisions made by the participant back to the testbed's server.

A prior study [29] used the text-based version of this online platform (Fig. 5.4) to team participants with a simulated robot with either high or low ability, and offered four classes of explanations of its decisions:

None: When the explanation condition is "None", the robot informs its teammate of only its decisions. One such communication from our scenario would be: *"I have finished surveying the Cafe. I think the place is safe."*

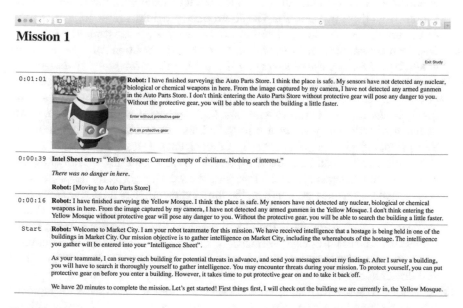

Fig. 5.4 Human robot interaction simulation testbed with HTML front-end

Fig. 5.5 Human robot interaction simulation testbed with Unity front-end

$\mathbf{\Omega^2 R}$ (L123):   When the explanation condition is $\Omega^2 R$, the robot augments the
"None" condition's decision message with non-numeric information about the
robot's sensing capability. In this case, the sensing capability is limited to the
NBC sensor and the camera–the first two sensors implemented in the testbed.
Section 5.3.2's Ω template thus provides the teammate with the robot's observations from these two sensors. The R template provides additional explanation
of the impact of the robot's decision on its teammate's subsequent behaviour.
One such communication with both decision and explanation from our scenario
would be: *"I have finished surveying the Cafe. I think the place is dangerous.
My sensors have detected traces of dangerous chemicals. From the image captured by my camera, I have not detected any armed gunmen in the Cafe. I think
it will be dangerous for you to enter the Cafe without protective gear. The protective gear will slow you down a little."*. This explanation condition provides
transparency at all three levels of the SAT model, but it does *not* provide any uncertainty information. Although these explanations can potentially actually help the
robot's teammate understand which sensors are working correctly (e.g., the NBC
sensor) and which ones are not (e.g., the faulty camera), they do not actually help
the teammate decide what to do with sensor readings from the camera. This is
because the robot, particularly the one in the Low Ability condition, has a faulty
camera that makes false-negative mistakes. This means that even when teammates
know that the robot's report of no danger found by its camera is incorrect, they
still do not know whether they should put on the protective gear or not.

$\mathbf{\Omega^3}$ (L123):   When the explanation condition is Ω^3, the explanations again augment
the "None" condition's decision message with non-numeric information about
the robot's sensing capability—in this case, all three sensors: the NBC sensor,

camera, and microphone. Section 5.3.2's Ω explanation provides the teammate with the robot's observations from these two sensors. One such communication with both decision and explanation from our scenario would be: *"I have finished surveying the Cafe. I think the place is safe. My sensors have not detected any NBC weapons in here. From the image captured by my camera, I have not detected any armed gunmen in the cafe. My microphone picked up a friendly conversation."*. Like the $\Omega^2 R$ condition, this explanation provides transparency at all three levels of the SAT model. However, unlike the $\Omega^2 R$ condition, the explanations here will potentially help the robot's teammate understand which sensors are working correctly and which ones are not, and help them decide what to do in case of camera failure. For example, even when the faulty camera is unable to detect armed gunman, the microphone would still be capable of picking up a suspicious conversation.

S (L1U):   In the S explanation condition, the confidence-level explanations augment the decision message with additional information about the robot's uncertainty in its decision. Section 5.3.2's S template incorporates the robot's probabilistic assessment of the hidden state of the world (e.g., the presence of threats) on which it bases its recommendation. One example of a confidence-level explanation would be: *"I have finished surveying the Cafe. I think the place is dangerous. I am 78% confident about this assessment."* Because the low-ability robot's one faulty sensor will lead to occasional conflicting observations, it will on those occasions have lower confidence in its erroneous decisions after incorporating that conflicting information into its beliefs. The quantitative confidence measure provides the explicit uncertainty information asked for by the SAT model (finding 2 from Sect. 5.2.2). However, there is no information provided as to Levels 2 and 3 of the SAT model. For example, the robot gives its teammate no information about what threat to expect in the building.

Consistent with the SAT model findings from Sect. 5.2.2, the results of this study showed that the robot explanations can potentially improve task performance, build transparency, and foster trust relationships [29]. However, only explanations that were designed to facilitate decision-making made much difference. Explanations that left participants unsure about how to act did not achieve such an effect and were as badly regarded as when no explanations were offered at all. This was particularly true when the robot's ability was low and made unreliable recommendations.

Additionally, the decision-facilitation explanation helped improve understanding of the robot's decision, but only in the low-ability robot and not the high-ability one. This could be due to the fact that the high-ability robot had learned a model that made correct decisions 100% of the time. Participants who interacted with this robot never needed to question the robot's decisions. Thus, these participants may have never carefully examined the robot's statement that explained its confidence level or observations. Working with a low-ability robot, on the other hand, required the teammates to pay close attention to the explanations to gauge when and when not to trust the robot's decisions.

Interestingly, this study did not find any significant differences on the measures we analyzed between the two decision-facilitating explanation conditions, Ω^3 and S. Both types of explanations are useful in helping the human teammate decide when to trust the robot. For example, a teammate in the S condition could potentially learn his/her own heuristics that if the robot's confidence level is below (for example) 75%, then do not follow the robot's decision. Similarly, a teammate in the Ω^3 condition could diagnose from the observation explanations that if the camera reports no signs of danger, but the robot's microphone picks up unfriendly conversations, then it is time to be cautious and put protective gear on, regardless of the robot's overall assessment of safety.

The positive impact of the S condition's explicit confidence-level explanation provides further validation of the SAT model's recommendation for including uncertainty information. However, it is concerning that participants in this condition also felt that they understood the robot's decision-making process, even though the explanations they received did not reveal any Level 2 or 3 information. While confidence-level explanations may help teammates make decisions just as well as with observation explanations, they will not help teammates diagnose or repair the robot (e.g., the participants will not know that it is the camera that caused the robot to make wrong decisions).

From finding 5 in Sect. 5.2.2, we should expect individual differences to exist across the robot's various human teammates. In fact, [30] identified several patterns of behaviour that the robot could use to distinguish different trust levels. Somewhat surprisingly, *compliance* with the robot's recommendation was not a strong indicator of trust. Examining our scenario's "None" and $\Omega^2 R$ conditions, although human teammates can observe the robot's mistakes in hindsight, its explanations do not help them identify them a priori. As a result, the teammates' best bet is to comply with the robot and hope for the best, leading to high compliance, but low trust.

Instead, *correctness* of teammate decisions was a better indicator of trust [30]. When teammates (usually in the Ω^3 or S conditions) could identify an incorrect robot recommendation a priori, they would ignore the robot's recommendation and successfully search the building. Even though they did not comply with the robot's recommendation, they still reported significantly higher levels of trust in it than those who were unable to correctly infer the robot's failures. In other words, higher trust was more closely tied to the success of the combined human-machine team, rather than the success of the robot's decisions in isolation. As a result, a robot should pay attention to whether its teammates make the right or wrong decision in dynamically identifying their current trust level, rather than to whether they simply obeyed or ignored its recommendation.

5.4   Conclusion

The SAT model provides a framework for examining the modelling content that needs to be made transparent to human teammates by autonomous systems in general, as well as by ML-based systems more specifically. Model-based RL provides a compatible representation of the kind of information that can be made transparent to people. However, communicating all of that potential information will most likely overwhelm people and lead to degraded performance of the human-machine team.

Fortunately, by combining the levels of the SAT model with the modelling components of a learned POMDP, we arrive at a space of possible explanation content that can reveal precisely defined subsets of the system's available information. The results presented here show promising success within even a very limited number of possible automated explanations. By systematically evaluating a wider set of these candidate explanation styles in human-machine interaction, future investigations can provide an even more comprehensive mapping of the impact that different ML-based explanation content will have on transparency and team performance.

References

1. Barnes, M.J., Chen, J.Y., Hill, S.G.: Humans and autonomy: implications of shared decision-making for military operations. Technical report ARL-TR-7919, US Army Research Laboratory (2017)
2. Biran, O., Cotton, C.: Explanation and justification in machine learning: a survey. In: Proceedings of the IJCAI Workshop on Explainable AI, pp. 8–13 (2017)
3. Bisantz, A.: Uncertainty visualization and related topics. In: Lee, J., Kirlik, A. (eds.) The Oxford Handbook of Cognitive Engineering. Oxford University Press, Oxford (2013)
4. Boutilier, C., Dearden, R., Goldszmidt, M.: Stochastic dynamic programming with factored representations. Artif. Intell. **121**(1), 49–107 (2000)
5. Calhoun, G., Ruff, H., Behymer, K., Frost, E.: Human-autonomy teaming interface design considerations for multi-unmanned vehicle control. Theoretical Issues in Ergonomics Science (in press)
6. Cassandra, A.R., Kaelbling, L.P., Kurien, J.A.: Acting under uncertainty: discrete Bayesian models for mobile-robot navigation. IROS **2**, 963–972 (1996)
7. Chen, J., Lakhmani, S., Stowers, K., Selkowitz, A., Wright, J., Barnes, M.: Situation awareness-based agent transparency and human-autonomy teaming effectiveness. Theoretical Issues in Ergonomics Science (in press)
8. Chen, J., Procci, K., Boyce, M., Wright, J., Garcia, A., Barnes, M.: Situation awareness-based agent transparency and human-autonomy teaming effectiveness. Technical report ARL-TR-6905, Army Research Laboratory (2014)
9. Chen, J.Y., Barnes, M.J.: Human-agent teaming for multirobot control: a review of human factors issues. IEEE Trans. Hum. Mach. Syst. **44**(1), 13–29 (2014)
10. de Visser, E.J., Cohen, M., Freedy, A., Parasuraman, R.: A design methodology for trust cue calibration in cognitive agents. In: Shumaker, R., Lackey, S. (eds.) Virtual, Augmented and Mixed Reality. Designing and Developing Virtual and Augmented Environments (2014)
11. Defense Science Board: Defense science board summer study on autonomy (2016)
12. Elizalde, F., Sucar, E., Reyes, A., deBuen, P.: An MDP approach for explanation generation. In: Proceedings of the AAAI Workshop on Explanation-Aware Computing, pp. 28–33 (2007)

13. Endsley, M.R.: Situation awareness misconceptions and misunderstandings. J. Cogn. Eng. Decis. Mak. **9**(1), 4–32 (2015)
14. Kaelbling, L.P., Littman, M.L., Moore, A.W.: Reinforcement learning: a survey. J. Artif. Intell. Res. **4**, 237–285 (1996)
15. Kaelbling, L.P., Littman, M.L., Cassandra, A.R.: Planning and acting in partially observable stochastic domains. Artif. Intell. **101**(1), 99–134 (1998)
16. Koenig, S., Simmons, R.: Xavier: a robot navigation architecture based on partially observable Markov decision process models. In: Kortenkamp, D., Bonasso, R.P., Murphy, R.R. (eds.) AI Based Mobile Robotics: Case Studies of Successful Robot Systems, pp. 91–122. MIT Press, Cambridge (1998)
17. Lee, J.D., See, K.A.: Trust in automation: designing for appropriate reliance. Hum. Factors **46**(1), 50–80 (2004)
18. Lyons, J.B., Havig, P.R.: Transparency in a human-machine context: approaches for fostering shared awareness/intent. In: Proceedings of the International Conference on Virtual, Augmented and Mixed Reality, pp. 181–190. Springer, Berlin (2014)
19. Marathe, A.: The privileged sensing framework: a principled approach to improved human-autonomy integration. Theoretical Issues in Ergonomics Science (in press)
20. Mercado, J., Rupp, M., Chen, J., Barnes, M., Barber, D., Procci, K.: Intelligent agent transparency in human-agent teaming for multi-UxV management. Hum. Factors **58**(3), 401–415 (2016)
21. Parasuraman, R., Riley, V.: Humans and automation: use, misuse, disuse, abuse. Hum. Factors **39**(2), 230–253 (1997)
22. Parasuraman, R., Manzey, D.H.: Complacency and bias in human use of automation: an attentional integration. Hum. Factors **52**(3), 381–410 (2010)
23. Selkowitz, A.R., Lakhmani, S.G., Larios, C.N., Chen, J.Y.: Agent transparency and the autonomous squad member. In: Proceedings of the Human Factors and Ergonomics Society Annual Meeting, pp. 1319–1323 (2016)
24. Shattuck, L.G.: Transitioning to autonomy: a human systems integration perspective. In: Transitioning to Autonomy: Changes in the Role of Humans in Air Transportation (2015). https://human-factors.arc.nasa.gov/workshop/autonomy/download/presentations/Shaddock%20.pdf
25. Stowers, K., Kasdaglis, N., Rupp, M., Newton, O., Wohleber, R., Chen, J.: Intelligent agent transparency: the design and evaluation of an interface to facilitate human and artificial agent collaboration. In: Proceedings of the Human Factors and Ergonomics Society (2016)
26. Sutton, R.S., Barto, A.G.: Reinforcement Learning: An Introduction. MIT Press, Cambridge (1998)
27. Swartout, W., Paris, C., Moore, J.: Explanations in knowledge systems: design for explainable expert systems. IEEE Expert **6**(3), 58–64 (1991)
28. Wang, N., Pynadath, D.V., Hill, S.G.: Building trust in a human-robot team. In: Interservice/Industry Training, Simulation and Education Conference (2015)
29. Wang, N., Pynadath, D.V., Hill, S.G.: The impact of POMDP-generated explanations on trust and performance in human-robot teams. In: International Conference on Autonomous Agents and Multiagent Systems (2016)
30. Wang, N., Pynadath, D.V., Hill, S.G., Merchant, C.: The dynamics of human-agent trust with POMDP-generated explanations. In: International Conference on Intelligent Virtual Agents (2017)
31. Wright, J., Chen, J., Hancock, P., Barnes, M.: The effect of agent reasoning transparency on complacent behavior: an analysis of eye movements and response performance. In: Proceedings of the Human Factors and Ergonomics Society International Annual Meeting (2017)
32. Wynn, K., Lyons, J.: An integrative model of autonomous agent teammate likeness. Theoretical Issues in Ergonomics Science (in press)

Part II
Visual Explanation of Machine Learning Process

Chapter 6
Deep Learning for Plant Diseases: Detection and Saliency Map Visualisation

**Mohammed Brahimi, Marko Arsenovic, Sohaib Laraba,
Srdjan Sladojevic, Kamel Boukhalfa and Abdelouhab Moussaoui**

Abstract Recently, many researchers have been inspired by the success of deep learning in computer vision to improve the performance of detection systems for plant diseases. Unfortunately, most of these studies did not leverage recent deep architectures and were based essentially on AlexNet, GoogleNet or similar architectures. Moreover, the research did not take advantage of deep learning visualisation methods which qualifies these deep classifiers as black boxes as they are not transparent. In this chapter, we have tested multiple state-of-the-art Convolutional Neural Network (CNN) architectures using three learning strategies on a public dataset for plant diseases classification. These new architectures outperform the state-of-the-art results of plant diseases classification with an accuracy reaching **99.76%**. Furthermore, we have proposed the use of saliency maps as a visualisation method

M. Brahimi (✉) · K. Boukhalfa
Department of Computer Science, USTHB University, Algiers, Algeria
e-mail: m_brahimi@esi.dz

K. Boukhalfa
e-mail: kboukhalfa@usthb.dz

M. Brahimi
Department of Computer Science, Mohamed El Bachir El Ibrahimi University,
Bordj Bou Arreridj, Algeria

M. Arsenovic · S. Sladojevic
Faculty of Technical Sciences, University of Novi Sad, Novi Sad, Serbia
e-mail: arsenovic@uns.ac.rs

S. Sladojevic
e-mail: sladojevic@uns.ac.rs

S. Laraba
TCTS Lab, Numediart Institute, University of Mons, Mons, Belgium
e-mail: sohaib.laraba@umons.ac.be

A. Moussaoui
Department of Computer Science, Setif 1 University, Setif, Algeria
e-mail: moussaoui.abdel@gmail.com

© Springer International Publishing AG, part of Springer Nature 2018
J. Zhou and F. Chen (eds.), *Human and Machine Learning*, Human–Computer
Interaction Series, https://doi.org/10.1007/978-3-319-90403-0_6

to understand and interpret the CNN classification mechanism. This visualisation method increases the transparency of deep learning models and gives more insight into the symptoms of plant diseases.

6.1 Introduction

Plant diseases can cause great damages to agriculture crops by significantly decreasing production [12]. Early blight is a typical example of disease that can severely decrease production [4]. Similarly, in a humid climate, late blight is another very destructive disease that affects the plant leaves, stems, and fruits [4]. Protecting plants from diseases is vital to guarantee the quality and quantity of crops [5]. A successful protection strategy should start with an early detection of the disease in order to choose the appropriate treatment at the right time to prevent it from spreading [2]. Usually, this detection is achieved by experts having an academic knowledge reinforced by practical experience on symptoms and causes of diseases [4]. Furthermore, these experts must monitor plants consistently to avoid disease spreading. This continuous monitoring represents a difficult and time-consuming task for humans, which makes the automation of the plant diseases detection and identification essential to protect plants [5]. Several studies [1, 2, 7, 26] have been proposed to detect and classify plant diseases using image processing and machine learning. These approaches try to build disease classifiers using images taken from the crops. These classifiers are based on hand-crafted features designed by experts to extract relevant information for image classification. For this reason, these classifiers suffer from the lack of automation because of the dependency on hand-crafted features [22]. Moreover, the classifier must be trained using images labelled by experts. Collecting these labelled images is very expensive because it is done manually. This difficulty of data collection has forced the previous studies to use small datasets to train and test classifiers [1, 2, 7, 26]. The use of small labelled datasets is a limiting factor in machine learning, and it can lead to overfitting. In the last few years, Deep Learning (DL) has been adopted by the computer vision community, thanks to its results that outperform the state-of-the-art in many domains. The main advantage of DL in computer vision is the direct exploitation of image without any hand-crafted features. DL classifiers are end-to-end systems that form features in a fully automated way without any intervention by human experts. In plant diseases protection, many works have proposed the use of DL to detect and classify diseases. Notably, in [15] more than 54,306 images of diseased and healthy plant leaves are collected which makes the training of DL classifier possible. This new trend produced more accurate classifiers compared to traditional machine learning approaches [5, 8, 9, 18, 24, 25, 27, 34]. Despite these good results, DL research in plant diseases remains immature and requires more attention to produce practical systems. For example, many new successful deep architectures are not tested in the context of plant diseases. Moreover, DL classifiers suffer from a lack of interpretability and transparency. These accurate classifiers are often considered as black boxes that give good results but without any explanation or details about the classification mechanism. High accuracy is not sufficient for plant disease classification. Users also need to be informed how the detection is achieved and which symptoms are present in the plant. This knowledge is very important from a practical viewpoint. For example, inexperienced farmers can gain intuition about disease and symptoms used by the classifier. Similarly, agriculture experts and experienced farmers can evaluate the classifier decision by showing its classification mechanism. Also, these experts can exploit the transparency of the classifier to discover new symptoms or to localise known symptoms that are difficult to see with the human eye. In this chapter, we will compare previous works based on DL to detect and identify diseases. Moreover, we evaluate the state-of-the-art deep architectures based on the dataset proposed in [15]. Furthermore, we investigate visualisation methods applied on deep models to increase the transparency of deep classifiers. This study presents two main contributions in plant disease classification:

- Comparison between state-of-the-art CNN architectures performance in plant diseases protection: this comparison helps researchers to choose the best deep architecture for building a practical system for plant diseases protection.
- Visualisation of symptoms used by deep classifiers: visualisation methods allow the localisation of the infected region on the plant and help the users by giving them information about the disease. Also, this biological information is extracted without the intervention of agriculture experts. In this study, we propose the saliency map as a visualisation method based on a derivative of the deep network output with respect to the image.

6.2 Related Work

Plant diseases classification can be a very complex task as it relies mainly on experts know-how. Developing a reliable system that is applicable for a large number of classes is a very challenging task. Up to now, most of the approaches for automatic plant diseases classification depended on machine learning algorithms and basic feature engineering. These approaches are usually concentrated on certain environments and are suited for a smaller number of classes, where some small changes in the system can result in a drastic fall in accuracy. In recent years, Convolutional Neural Networks (CNN) have shown great results in many image classification tasks which have given researchers the opportunity to improve classification accuracy in many fields including agriculture and plant diseases classification.

Kawasaki et al. [18] proposed the use of deep CNN to distinguish healthy cucumbers from the infected ones by using images of leaves. In this study, they used CNN to diagnose two harmful viral infections: MYSV (melon yellow spot virus) and ZYMV (zucchini yellow mosaic virus). The used dataset in this work consists of 800 images of cucumbers leaves (300 with MYSV, 200 with ZYMV and 300 non-diseased). Rotation transformations on images were used to enlarge the dataset. For this binary classification task, authors proposed CNN architecture which consists of three convolutional layers, pooling layers, and local contrast normalisation layers. The activation function used in this network is the Rectified Linear Unit (ReLU) function. The achieved accuracy of this study is 94.9% under a 4-fold cross-validation strategy.

Sladojevic et al. [34] applied deep CNN for plant diseases classification. They collected a dataset from publicly available images on the internet. This dataset contains 13 classes of plant diseases, one class of healthy leaves and one class of background images extracted from Stanford background dataset [11]. The addition of this background class is to train the classifier to distinguish the plants leaves from the background images, which is emphasised as the limitation of [25]. The obtained dataset contains 4483 original images of different sizes, qualities, and backgrounds. To increase the size of this dataset, images were pre-processed and augmented to reduce overfitting in the training stage. For the augmentation stage, affine and perspective transformation were used in addition to image rotations. Using these augmentation transformations, the produced dataset consists of 30880 images for training and 2589 images for validation. Authors proposed the transfer learning using CaffeNet architecture [17]. CaffeNet is a modified version of AlexNet architecture that switches the order of pooling and the normalisation layers. This CNN was trained with and without fine-tuning by experimental changing of hidden layers parameters and hyperparameters. Visualisation of the features in the trained classification model intuitively helped in understanding the network which aided the fine-tuning process. The overall accuracy of the best architecture was 96.3% with fine-tuning and 95.8% without fine-tuning.

Mohanty et al. [25] used the public dataset named PlantVillage [15] which consists of 38 labelled classes including 26 diseases of 14 crop species. Authors used three versions of the dataset. The first version contains colour images, the second one contains grey-scaled images, and the third one contains images of segmented leaves to assess the influence of the background information on classification. Different training-test distributions were used to measure the performance of the CNN; 80–20, 60–40, 50–50, 40–60 and 20–80%. Two standards architectures were used for classification, AlexNet and GoogLeNet. They used two training strategies for training the CNN; training from scratch and transfer learning. They used 60 experimental configurations (2 CNN architectures ×3 versions of the dataset ×2 types of training ×5 training-test distributions) to evaluate the accuracy of deep CNN for the plant diseases classification task. From all the configurations, the highest accuracy is 99.34% which was achieved by the transfer learning of GoogleNet on the colour images using 80–20 dataset distribution. However, a couple of limitations were underlined in this study. Firstly, the majority of images are captured in a controlled environment using a simple background. Secondly, the number of images is not sufficient to train a classifier that is able to generalise to images taken in an uncontrolled environment. For instance, authors achieve an evaluation of the trained model using images taken from different conditions which shows that the accuracy decreases significantly to 31%.

Nachtigall et al. [27] proposed a CNN for automatic detection and classification of nutritional deficiencies and damages on apple trees from images of leaves. To build a dataset, they collected healthy leaves, two classes of damage caused by nutritional imbalances, two classes of diseases and one class of damage caused by the herbicide. To ensure the quality of labelling, chemical analysis was conducted for symptoms caused by nutritional imbalances and herbicide damage. This well-balanced dataset of 1450 images contains 290 images in each class (15 for testing, 193 for training and 83 for validation). AlexNet was used as a CNN architecture for building a classifier. They compared shallow methods against deep CNN. For the shallow method, Multi-layer Perceptron (MLP) was chosen. Deep CNN was compared with seven volunteer experts where the final diagnoses were chosen by majority vote. The accuracy of the CNN was 97.3%, human experts had an accuracy of 96% where much less accuracy was achieved by MLP at 77.3%.

Fujita et al. [9] proposed a classifier for cucumber diseases using CNN. They used two datasets for training and validation. These datasets contain seven different types of diseases in addition to the healthy class. The first dataset consists of 7320 centred images of leaves captured under good conditions. The second dataset consists of 7520 images captured under good and bad conditions. To increase the size of this dataset, many crops from each image are used in addition to the rotated and the mirrored images. The proposed network is composed of four convolutional layers alternated with max-pooling layers and local response normalisation functions having parameters from AlexNet architecture [21]. Finally, the accuracy of the proposed system was 82.3% under a 4-fold cross validation scenario test.

Brahimi et al. [5] applied CNN for classifying tomato diseases based on images of leaves. In this study, the dataset consists of 14828 images of tomato leaves extracted from PlantVillage public dataset and divided into nine classes of diseases. For developing a classifier, the standard architectures AlexNet and GoogLeNet were trained from scratch or using transfer learning and fine-tuning. CNN models trained with fine-tuning showed a better accuracy than models trained from scratch. For GoogleNet, fine-tuning improves the accuracy from 97.71 to 99.18% and similarly for AlexNet the fine-tuning increases the accuracy from 97.35 to 98.66%. Authors have also compared the accuracy of the CNN with shallow models; SVM and Random Forest. CNN models have a better accuracy than shallow models, 94.53% for SVM and 95.46% for Random Forest. Finally, authors have proposed the use of occlusion experiments for localising and visualising the diseases regions and symptoms which can help users by giving them better insight to the diseases.

DeChant et al. [8] proposed to use the DL approach for the classification of northern leaf blight lesions on images of maize plants. 1028 images of infected leaves and 768 images of non-infected leaves were gathered on the field. From the total number of images, 70% were used for training, 15% for validation and 15% for testing. The proposed classification method in this chapter differs from the other studies presented in this chapter. In this study, instead of using only one end-to-end network in classification, the authors applied three training stages. In the first stage, several CNN models were trained to detect the presence of lesions in small parts of the images. These CNN models were used in the second stage to produce a heat map indicating the probability of infection for every image. In the last stage, the produced

Table 6.1 Comparison between deep learning studies for plant diseases classification

Paper	Year	Nbr. of classes	Nbr. of images	Image pre-processing and augmentation	CNN architecture	Transfer learning	Accuracy %
[18]	2015	3	800	Centred crop Resizing Rotation	Customised	No	94.90
[34]	2016	15	4483	Rotation Affine transformation Perspective transformation	CaffeNet	Yes	96.30
[25]	2016	38	54306	Resizing Segmentation Grey-scaling	AlexNet GoogLeNet	Yes	99.34
[27]	2016	5	1450	Resizing	AlexNet	Yes	97.30
[9]	2016	7	14840	Centred crop Resizing Rotation Shifting and Mirroring	Customised	No	82.30
[5]	2017	9	14828	Resizing	AlexNet GoogLeNet	Yes	99.18
[8]	2017	2	1796	Segmentation Rotation	Customised	No	96.70
[24]	2017	10	500	Resize Grey-scaling	AlexNet	Yes	95.48

heat map was used to classify the images. The proposed system achieved an overall accuracy of 96.7% on the test set.

Lu et al. [24] explored the use of CNN for the classification of rice diseases. They used 500 images captured in an experimental rice field to build a dataset used for training and validation purposes. AlexNet was the CNN architecture used to build a rice diseases classifier. Authors have compared the deep CNN with traditional machine learning algorithms. The overall accuracy of the deep model was 95.48% under 10-fold cross-validation. On the other side, the results of shallow models are: SVM achieved an accuracy of 91%, standard back propagation achieved 92% and Particle Swarm Optimization (PSO) achieved 88%.

Table 6.1 summarises the results of works that use DL models for plant diseases classification. We observe from Table 6.1 that most of the studies were conducted over the two last years. Also, the most used CNN architectures in these works are AlexNet, GoogleNet and similar architectures like CaffeNet.

Most of the described studies in this section focused on improving the accuracy of diseases classification without treating the interpretability challenge, by extracting insights from the classifier. There are several attempts in this direction based on visualisation methods to address this challenge. Despite these efforts, understanding and interpretation of results in the DL models is still immature and requires more attention. For example, visualisation of CNN filters as small images is used by [18,

34]. This visualisation method is applied to the first layers that interact directly with the input images. This represents a limiting factor because near-to-input layers extract only low-level feature like edges in different directions. Understanding of plant diseases still requires more abstract features like complex shapes and textures.

Visualisation of feature maps is another technique used in the classification of plant diseases [24, 25, 34]. These methods convert the internal activations to images in order to visualise the features that are activated in response to lesions and symptoms of diseases. Nevertheless, it is still difficult to localise precisely the specialised activations of these symptoms among a large number of feature maps and nodes.

The occlusion method, investigated in [5], is another method that tries to localise disease symptoms in tomato leaves. It analyses the CNN behaviour as a black box without taking into account the architecture and the internal details of CNN, such as feature maps and filters visualisations. The basic idea of this method is to apply occlusions to some parts of the images and then observe the CNN output sensitivity regarding to these occlusions. The advantage of this method is its ability to determine which image parts are important from the CNN viewpoint. However, this method is sensitive to hyperparameters like the shape, the size and the displacement stride of occlusion regions. Furthermore, a large number of occluded images are used as input of CNN which makes it computationally expensive and time-consuming.

6.3   Comparison Between Deep and Shallow Approaches

DL represents a new promising trend in the classification of plant diseases. Recently, DL algorithms have achieved the state-of-the-art in many domains, particularly in computer vision, by giving spectacular results compared to classic machine learning algorithms. For instance, the top 5 classification error achieved by the deep network called AlexNet in ImageNet dataset is 15.3% whereas the classic machine learning algorithms have a top 5 error of 26.2%. Likewise, in plant diseases classification DL outperformed shallow classifiers results and recently became a hot topic [5, 25].

These DL algorithms are different from classic machine learning algorithms in the following points:

Data Consumption: The supervised training of DL classifiers requires a large number of labelled examples, for this reason, data availability in the last decade has contributed to DL success [6]. DL classifiers require a huge training set because these classifiers contain a large number of parameters to tune. This constraint of labelled data represents a limiting factor when the labelling is expensive. For example, the biological labelled examples are expensive and difficult to collect in most cases [3]. Plant diseases classification is an example of a biological field where data collection and labelling is very expensive. In this context, each image must be labelled by an agriculture expert who should have an academic knowledge supported by practical experience in identification of disease symptoms. Also, taking a large number of images containing many diseases represents a tedious task and many years are required to cover all the existing diseases. Various approaches have been proposed to handle this data avidity. Pre-training a deep architecture with a big labelled dataset like ImageNet and fine-tuning this pretrained architecture using a small dataset is used in many studies [25]. Moreover, data augmentation can help in increasing the number of labelled examples and variations in the training set [34]. Despite that, the adaptation of DL to domains where labelling is expensive represents an active research area and requires more effort [19, 28, 31, 38].

Dedicated Hardware: The training phase of DL classifiers requires dedicated hardware like the Graphics Processing Units (GPUs) to reduce execution time [21]. These GPUs represent an essential component in DL approaches and training without GPUs leads to many further days of training. However, the testing phase of a DL classifier does not require any dedicated hardware and can be executed on small devices like mobiles or embedded systems. In plant diseases classification, a DL classifier is trained in dedicated hardware and once the training is finished, this classifier is deployed to users on mobiles to detect diseases directly in the fields.

Feature Extraction: Machine Learning algorithms contain a feature engineering phase. In this phase, experts propose the hand-crafted features to facilitate learning from examples. This phase is very important and affects the overall performance of the learning system. Unfortunately, feature engineering is a manual component in the machine learning pipeline and it is time-consuming [22]. On the other hand, in a DL pipeline, feature extraction is embedded in the learning algorithm where features are extracted in a fully automated way and without any intervention by a human expert. CNN represents a good example of automatic feature extraction in computer vision. Filters in traditional machine learning are proposed by experts of vision, where CNN filters are learned in training using a backpropagation algorithm [22]. Recently, DL features achieved better results than hand-crafted features [5, 21, 27]. Despite this superiority of DL features, they still suffer from the difficulty of interpretation. Many attempts have been made to understand the role of these features using visualisation methods. Despite these efforts, more studies are required to demystify DL features as understanding of these features is still immature [32, 39].

6.4   Deep Learning System for Plant Diseases Classification

An overview of the DL system is illustrated in Fig. 6.1. This system contains three phases presented in this section.

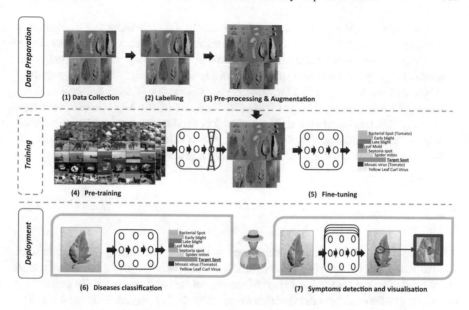

Fig. 6.1 Overview of deep learning system for plant diseases classification

6.4.1 Data Preparation

Every machine learning system starts with a data preparation phase. This data preparation phase contains the following stages:

- Data collection: is an important stage for developing any data-driven application. Particularly, deep models require a large dataset to avoid overfitting which presents a major challenge. Up to now, only a few datasets are publicly available for diseased plants. Most of the works in this area are conducted on the PlantVillage public dataset [15] or private datasets [9, 34].
- Labelling: the labelling process consists of annotating the collected images by a human expert. This expert labels images according to two possible strategies:

  - Weak labelling: where the agriculture expert identifies only the disease in each plant without any additional information about this disease.
  - Strong labelling: where the agriculture expert determines, in addition to the disease, the infected regions on the plant. This labelling strategy is expensive and time-consuming because it requires the patience of the expert where he uses the annotation software. For this reason, most of the available dataset are weakly labelled.

- Data augmentation and pre-processing: deep models like CNN are very greedy in their use of labelled data as discussed in Sect. 6.3. Unfortunately, data collection and labelling are very tedious and expensive tasks. To address this problem, data augmentation techniques are used commonly by DL researchers. Augmentation techniques aim to increase the size of the dataset and include more variations. These techniques consist of geometrical transformations (resizing, crop, rotation, horizontal flipping) and intensity transformations (contrast and brightness enhancement, colour, noise). Moreover, image pre-processing is used to normalise the images of the dataset. The most used techniques in the DL context are image resizing and mean subtraction. The resizing is used to convert input images to the size of the network input layer. However, mean subtraction is used to centre the data which accelerate the optimisation using a gradient descent algorithm.

6.4.2 Training

After the process of data preparation, deep models and particularly CNN models are trained using backpropagation algorithm. This algorithm aims to minimize a cost function that measures the total error of the model on the training set. To reduce this error, the gradient of this cost function is calculated with respect to all weights. The gradient descent algorithm is then used to find the optimum of the cost function. For more technical details about backpropagation and gradient descent algorithms, the reader is referred to [10]. As illustrated in Fig. 6.1, the training phase contains two stages:

- Pre-training: consists of training a deep CNN on a large dataset like ImageNet first, before the training on our dataset. This pre-training is carried out to prepare the CNN by the transfer learning from a big dataset to plant diseases classification. This stage is used to deal with the lack of labelled data in plant diseases classification.
- Fine-tuning: in this stage, the last layer (output layer) of the original pre-trained network is replaced with a new layer compatible with the number of classes in our dataset. The obtained network is then retrained using the backpropagation algorithm to fit our data. This method improves the results of our model because the weights have already been trained on a bigger dataset. This fine-tuning is a transfer learning method that allows the plant diseases task to take advantage of models trained on another computer vision task where a large number of labelled images is available.

6.4.3 Deployment

The trained models can be deployed to users machines (computers, mobiles...etc.) and can be used in two modes:

- Diseases classification: a captured image is used as an input of the model, then, the output of the network determines which diseases are present in the plant.

- Symptoms detection and visualisation: the user can visualise regions that characterise the identified disease. The visualisation methods used for symptoms are very useful for inexperienced users by giving them more information about the alteration to the plant made by the disease.

6.5 Evaluation of State-of-the-Art CNN Architectures for Plant Diseases Classification Task

In this section, the state-of-the-art architectures of CNN are used for plant diseases classification based on the images of the leaves. The entire procedure is divided into several steps: preparing the dataset, training and evaluating the trained models and analysis of the results discussed in detail.

6.5.1 Dataset Structure

In order to compare our results with the existing works, the evaluation process will be conducted using the PlantVillage dataset. This dataset includes 54323 images of 14 crop species with 38 classes of diseases or healthy plants, as shown in Table 6.2.

All used images in the experimental tests are randomly cropped to be $224 * 224$ or $299 * 299^1$ according to the network input size. Only colour images are used in the training stage due to the conclusion of [25] where the results show that colour images give a better accuracy than grey scale images. Moreover, a background class containing 715 images is added in order to train the classifier to distinguish between plants leaves and the surrounding environment [34]. This class is formed using colour images from Stanford public dataset of background images [11]. Finally, the size of the final dataset after adding the background class becomes 55038 divided into 39 classes.

6.5.2 Training Deep Networks for Plant Diseases Classification

In this experiment, six state-of-the-art architectures (AlexNet [21], DenseNet-169 [14], Inception v3 [37], ResNet-34 [13], SqueezeNet-1.1 [16] and VGG13 [33]) are trained on the dataset described in the previous section. To train and evaluate the performance of these state-of-the-art CNN, we use a Python deep learning framework

---

[1]Images are randomly cropped to be $299 * 299$ for Inception v3 architecture and $224 * 224$ for (AlexNet, DenseNet-169, ResNet-34, SqueezeNet-1.1 and VGG13).

Table 6.2 PlantVillage dataset details

	Name	Images no
1.	Apple Scab, Venturia inaequalis	630
2.	Apple Black Rot, Botryosphaeria obtusa	621
3.	Apple Cedar Rust, Gymnosporangium juniperi-virginianae	275
4.	Apple healthy	1645
5.	Blueberry healthy	1502
6.	Cherry healthy	854
7.	Cherry Powdery Mildew, Podoshaera clandestine	1052
8.	Corn Grey Leaf Spot, Cercospora zeae-maydis	513
9.	Corn Common Rust, Puccinia sorghi	1192
10.	Corn healthy	1162
11.	Corn Northern Leaf Blight, Exserohilum turcicum	985
12.	Grape Black Rot, Guignardia bidwellii	1180
13.	Grape Black Measles (Esca), Phaeomoniella aleophilum, Phaeomoniella chlamydospora	1383
14.	Grape Healthy	423
15.	Grape Leaf Blight, Pseudocercospora vitis	1076
16.	Orange Huanglongbing (Citrus Greening), Candidatus Liberibacter spp.	5507
17.	Peach Bacterial Spot, Xanthomonas campestris	2297
18.	Peach healthy	360
19.	Bell Pepper Bacterial Spot, Xanthomonas campestris	997
20.	Bell Pepper healthy	1478
21.	Potato Early Blight, Alternaria solani	1000
22.	Potato healthy	152
23.	Potato Late Blight, Phytophthora infestans	1000
24.	Raspberry healthy	371
25.	Soybean healthy	5090
26.	Squash Powdery Mildew, Erysiphe cichoracearum	1835
27.	Strawberry Healthy	456
28.	Strawberry Leaf Scorch, Diplocarpon earlianum	1109
29.	Tomato Bacterial Spot, Xanthomonas campestris pv. vesicatoria	2127
30.	Tomato Early Blight, Alternaria solani	1000
31.	Tomato Late Blight, Phytophthora infestans	1591
32.	Tomato Leaf Mould, Passalora fulva	1909
33.	Tomato Septoria Leaf Spot, Septoria lycopersici	952
34.	Tomato Two Spotted Spider Mite, Tetranychus urticae	1771
35.	Tomato Target Spot, Corynespora cassiicola	1676
36.	Tomato Mosaic Virus	1404
37.	Tomato Yellow Leaf Curl Virus	373
38.	Tomato healthy	5375

Table 6.3 Machine characteristics

No	Hardware and software	Characteristics
1.	Memory	16 Gb
2.	Processor (CPU)	Intel Core i7-4790 CPU @ 3.6 GHz x8
3.	Graphics (GPU)	GeForce GTX TITAN X 12 Gb
4.	Operating system	Linux Ubuntu 16.04 64 bits

called pyTorch with a GPU acceleration option[2]. Our pytorch implementation is available at https://github.com/MarkoArsenovic/DeepLearning_PlantDiseases.

These six CNN architectures are trained for the plant diseases classification task using three different strategies. Two of these strategies are based on the transfer learning from pre-trained networks. The first transfer learning approach, called shallow strategy, consists of fine-tuning only the fully connected layers, while the rest of the network is used as a feature extractor. On the other hand, the second transfer learning strategy, called deep strategy, fine-tunes all network layers and starts backpropagation optimisation from the pre-trained network. Using these two approaches, the CNN classifier tries to learn more specific features for plant diseases classification starting from pre-trained networks. Finally, the third strategy consists of training the CNN from scratch starting from a random configuration of weights.

All these 18 training configurations (6 CNN architectures × 3 strategies) use the same hyperparameters values (momentum 0.9, weight decay 0.0005, learning rate 0.001, batch sizes 20). The dataset is divided into 80% for training and 20% for evaluation. All experiments are performed on a powerful machine, having the specifications that are summarized in in Table 6.3.

6.5.3   Model Evaluation Results and Discussion

The accuracy and training time for all the six CNN architectures using the different training strategies for plant diseases classification task is displayed in Table 6.4.

The obtained results can be compared to [25], where they used the same dataset, except for the background class added in our experiments. All other works in plant diseases classification, described in related works, used only part of the PlantVillage dataset specific to particular plant species [5] or their privately collected datasets [8, 9, 18, 24, 27, 34].

In [25], authors used only two architectures AlexNet [21] and GoogLeNet (Inception v1) [36] and based on two learning strategies: training from scratch and transfer learning. In this study, the accuracy results of the training from scratch, using 80–20% train-test distribution, are (AlexNet, 97.82%) and (GoogleNet, 98.36%), while

---

[2]https://github.com/pytorch/pytorch.

Table 6.4 Experiment results

Model	Training type	Training time [h]	Accuracy
AlexNet	Shallow	0.87	0.9415
AlexNet	From scratch	1.05	0.9578
AlexNet	Deep	1.05	0.9924
DenseNet169	Shallow	1.57	0.9653
DenseNet169	From scratch	3.16	0.9886
DenseNet169	Deep	3.16	0.9972
Inception_v3	Shallow	3.63	0.9153
Inception_v3	From scratch	5.91	0.9743
Inception_v3	Deep	5.64	**0.9976**
ResNet34	Shallow	1.13	0.9475
ResNet34	From scratch	1.88	0.9848
ResNet34	Deep	1.88	0.9967
Squeezenet1_1	Shallow	**0.85**	0.9626
Squeezenet1_1	From scratch	1.05	0.9249
Squeezenet1_1	Deep	2.1	0.992
VGG13	Shallow	1.49	0.9223
VGG13	From scratch	3.55	0.9795
VGG13	Deep	3.55	0.9949

the accuracy results of training using transfer learning are (AlexNet, 99.24%) and (GoogleNet, 99.34%).

From Table 6.4, Inception v3 network (modification of GoogLeNet by introducing batch normalisation [37]) gives the best accuracy for deep training strategy, with 99.76% outperforming the results shown on [25].

From the results of Table 6.4, we observe that the most successful learning strategy in the classification of plant diseases for all CNN architectures is the deep transfer learning. Also, we can observe that DenseNet169 has a comparable accuracy to Inception-V3 with 99.72% but with less training time, followed by ResNet34 that has an accuracy of 99.67% with even less training time. Furthermore, VGG13, using deep transfer learning strategy, is ranked fourth according to accuracy with 99.49%. AlexNet and SqueezeNet have a similar accuracy of 99.2% which is smaller than the results of other architectures. DenseNet169 gave the best accuracy in the other two strategies (shallow and from scratch) with 98.86 and 96.53% respectively.

Evaluation of the performance of the models by comparing training time and accuracy is also displayed in Fig. 6.2.

A large fraction of the PlantVillage dataset are images of leaves in a controlled environment and simple background. Adding images with different qualities and complex backgrounds in the training and validation dataset could improve accuracy and produce a classifier more useful for practical usage. The PlantVillage dataset

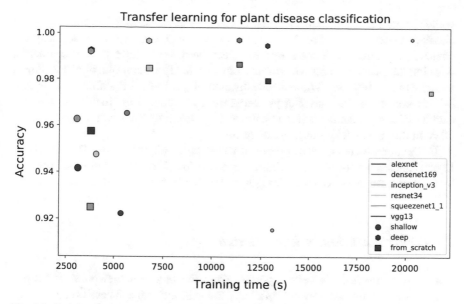

Fig. 6.2 Training time and accuracy of CNN architectures

is unbalanced, where some classes have more images than others, which could be very misleading and could lead to overfitting if not trained carefully. Augmentation techniques could help in these situations, and it is a common procedure in many classification tasks.

6.6   Deep Learning Visualisation Methods

Despite the good results of DL classifiers, they are often considered as black boxes because of their lack of interpretability. The superposition of layers and the use of nonlinear functions make the understanding of the classification difficult. Thus, DL classifiers require specialized algorithms to deal with this interpretability challenge, by extracting insights from the classifier [32, 35, 39].

These visualisation algorithms help both the designer and the user of the classifier. The classifier designer uses these algorithms to analyse the classifier behaviour to improve the performance, while the user benefits from the transparency offered by the visualisation in order to understand the classification. In many domains, classification is insufficient and requires support by an explanation of this automatic decision. Notably, plant diseases classification represents a domain where the classifiers understanding is very important. For users, a visualisation algorithm helps in disease understanding by localising the symptoms and the infected regions. Hence, biological knowledge is extracted from the classifier to help the non-expert farmers, while agriculture experts and classifier designers use visualisation to understand the classifier behaviour [5]. For example, a classifier having a good accuracy may use contextual information in the image to detect the disease and ignore symptoms. In this situation, the classifier will suffer from a generalisation problem if the subject background is different. Without visualisation algorithms, it is difficult to identify this issue based on the classifier performance. In practice, this situation of classification by background context may happen, if all training images of one disease are taken in the same background by one farmer.

In literature, there are many proposed visualisation algorithms for DL classifiers. In this chapter, we focus on algorithms proposed for CNN. This choice is motivated by the extensive use of CNN for images and particularly in plant diseases detection.

6.6.1   Visualisation in Input Image

This type of methods is very important from the practical viewpoint because it projects the features used by network back to the input image. Therefore, the image can be examined to understand how the classifier behaves [32, 35]. In plant diseases, these visualisations give valuable information about the important parts used by the network as features. If the classifier behaves correctly, these parts may represent the symptoms or the characteristics of a disease [5]. However, if the classifier uses the background or another feature unrelated to disease, then this undesirable behaviour can be detected [5].

6.6.1.1   Occlusion Experiments

Occlusion experiments aim to analyse the network sensitivity to the occlusions of image regions. Using this method, the classifier designer examines whether the network captures the characteristics of the image or not during the classification. For instance, the background of an infected leaf in a plant should not affect the diagnosis of the disease. However, the classification should be based on the symptoms of each disease in the leaf. In this specific situation, occlusion of the leaf background should not affect the classifier decision in the same way of an occlusion of a symptom region [5].

For implementing occlusion experiments, a black square is used to occlude a region in the input image. The obtained image is then classified by the network to produce an output vector. This vector is examined to understand the sensitivity of the network to this occlusion. Precisely, the node corresponding to the ground truth class of the image is checked. Naturally, if this region is important, then the value of the mentioned node decreases dramatically, in response to occlusion of this region. However, if the occluded region is not important then the node value, corresponding to ground truth class, does not fluctuate very much [39].

Fig. 6.3 Occlusion experiments in plant diseases classification. The red squares drawn in the leaves images represent the most active occluded parts in the heat map

The square of occlusion is slided by stride over the image to produce a heat map formed using the ground truth node values. This heat map visually demonstrates the influence of each region on the classification. Hotter regions are likely to be important in classification and colder regions are likely to be less important. Similarly, users of the classifier can benefit from this method to understand the disease and its symptoms by viewing the importance of each image region [39].

Figure 6.3 shows the tendency of the network to focus on lesions caused by the diseases while ignoring the healthy part of the leaf in addition to the background. Specifically, the heat map of Fig. 6.3a indicates precisely the location of grey concentric rings in the infected leaf. The occlusion of this symptom affects the classifier decision more than the leaf regions of the other samples. This result is compatible with the experts defined symptoms for early blight [20]. Similarly, for Septoria, Late Blight and Leaf Mould, active regions in the heat map match exactly the lesions that characterise these diseases. Nevertheless, the heat map visualisation misses some infected regions in the leaf. For instance, in Fig. 6.3d some yellow regions in the bottom part of the leaf are not shown on the heat map.

Occlusion experiments suffer from some problems and have many drawbacks. To produce a heat map, a large number of occluded images are used as input to the network which makes it computationally expensive and time-consuming. Considering an image of $500 * 500$ pixels resolution and an occlusion square having the size $50 * 50$ pixels and slided by a stride of 10 pixels, the size of the produced heat map is $46 * 46$ which requires 2116 occluded images. Similarly, if the stride is only one pixel, then the number of occluded images grows exponentially to $451 * 451 = 203401$ images. In addition to the computation cost, occlusion experiments are inefficient if there are several important regions in one image. In this case, the occlusion of one region among these regions does not affect so much of the network decision. This situation is likely to occur in plant diseases classification if the symptom of a disease is dispersed overall the leaf.

6.6.1.2   Saliency Map

As mentioned above, occlusion experiments are computationally expensive and time-consuming thus, another method for estimating the importance of image regions is a necessity. Notably, a saliency map is an analytical method that allows estimation of the importance of each pixel, using only one forward and one backward pass through the network [32].

The intuition behind this method is that, if one pixel is important in respect to the node corresponding to ground truth y, then changing the values of this pixel leads to a big change in this latter node. Therefore, if the value of the gradient in this pixel is big with absolute value, then this pixel is important. Conversely, if the gradient is equal or close to zero, then the pixel is not important and its variations do not affect the output node corresponding to y. The aggregation across the channels is achieved in order to estimate the overall importance of pixels rather than the importance of each pixel channel alone.

We can consider this method as an analytical version of occlusion experiments. In occlusion experiments, the saliency map matrix is estimated numerically by modifying pixels and observing the output changes. For this reason, the calculation of a saliency map is not computationally expensive like the calculation of the heat map in occlusion experiments, since the calculation of gradient in a numerically discreet way requires the modification of each pixel or region in the image in order to approximate his gradient. However, calculating gradient analytically requires only one backward pass to calculate all the derivatives with respect to all pixels.

To the best of our knowledge, the saliency map has never been used in plant disease classification. The utility of a saliency map is comparable to occlusion experiments. It helps to identify the symptoms of diseases for users. Moreover, this method is insensitive to the dispersed important regions, because the importance of pixels is calculated analytically and is not based on occluding pixels.

To calculate the saliency map, the input image x is forwarded through the network to calculate the output of network noted $f(x)$. Then, a backward pass is used to calculate the gradient of $f(x)_y$ with respect to the input image x where y is the ground truth label corresponding to the input image x. More formally, the gradient $G(x)$, using formula (6.1), is calculated to estimate the importance of each pixel in the image x. This $G(x)$ is a tensor having the same dimension of the image x. If x has a width W, height H and three channels, then $G(x)$ is a tensor having the dimension $3 * W * H$ and indexed by three indexes: i for indexing channels and j, k for indexing pixels.

$$G(x) = \frac{df(x)_y}{dx} \tag{6.1}$$

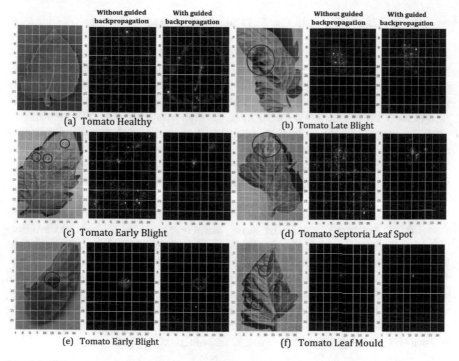

Fig. 6.4 Saliency map in plant diseases classification. For image leaves in column 1, 4 there are two types of visualisations. Images in column 2, 5 represent visualisations without guided backpropagation. Images in column 3, 6 represent a visualisation using guided backpropagation

To estimate the importance of a pixel $x(i, j)$, the maximum of the absolute values across channels is calculated. Consequently, the produced matrix having the dimension $W * H$ is called saliency map SM and calculated using the following formula:

$$SM(i, j) = Max\{|G(0, i, j)|, |G(1, i, j)|, |G(2, i, j)|\} \qquad (6.2)$$

The saliency map can localise with a good precision the infected regions in the input leaf image. Fig. 6.4b, e, f represent good examples where the visualisation of the saliency maps labels exactly the infected regions in leaves. Moreover, in Fig. 6.4f the two dispersed regions of the leaf mould disease are localised in contrast with the occlusion experiments that show only one infected region. Despite these good results, in many cases the saliency maps are not clear and suffer from noisy activations that can disturb the user. As an example, the visualisations in Fig. 6.4c, d show many activated regions in addition to the infected ones. This limitation is addressed by adding the guided backpropagation option which is described in the next section.

6.6.1.3   Saliency Map with Guided Backpropagation

The guided backpropagation method adds an additional rule during the backward pass. This rule is applied during the backpropagation through the nonlinear function called rectified linear (ReLU). In contrast with the standard backpropagation, only positive gradients are backward through ReLU [35]. This rule prevents the backward flow of negative gradients on ReLU from the higher layer in the CNN architecture [35]. This stops the gradients originated from the neurons that decrease the activation of the class node $f(x)_y$ and keeps the gradients from neurons that increase the activation of class node $f(x)_y$. Interestingly, unlike the standard backpropagation, this method produces more precise visualisations which help the user in detection of infected regions [35].

As shown in Fig. 6.4, the noisy activations on Fig. 6.4c, d are filtered and the visualisation become sharper. The three infected regions of early blight are now clear and easily distinguishable. Similarly, the main infected region of Septoria Leaf Spot is clear which gives the user a good intuition about this disease.

Furthermore, as illustrated in Fig. 6.4a, guided backpropagation produces a nice visualisation for healthy leaves. In this specific case, the network detects the contour of the leaf because no symptom is available in the leaf. This result shows the power of the network in understanding the input image by focalising only in the regions of interest and ignoring the background and non-infected regions.

6.7   Plant Diseases Classification Challenges

6.7.1   Plant Diseases Detection in Complex Images

Most studies in DL for classification of plant diseases have only focused on analysing images containing one leaf taken in a controlled environment. Although these approaches can classify a disease accurately in one image taken by a human agent, they are unable to find disease regions automatically in large fields. Obviously, a human agent is unable to monitor a large field and detects the earlier symptoms of diseases in order to take a picture. For this reason, a practical diseases detection system should automate the monitoring of fields to interact with plant diseases in due course. This automatic monitoring that leads to early detection of diseases can considerably reduce the damage on crops.

For this task, drones can fly above the field and take images for online or offline analysis. In this case, the learning system, used in data analysis, must deal with complex images containing several leaves and maybe many diseases. To achieve this, DL object detection algorithms can be used to localise and classify the affected regions in each image taken by drones. These object detection algorithms use the DL classifiers trained using simple images and adapt them to localise and classify diseases in complex images. This type of algorithm is used in literature in many contexts.

For example, in automatic driving, object detection and classification are extensively used to enhance the quality of driving. In a similar application to plant diseases classification, DL object detection algorithms are proposed in forest firefighting for detecting the fire using CNN [23]. Finally, the challenge of object detection algorithms lies in the absence of a big labelled dataset containing images taken by drones in affected crops. Efforts in this direction to collect a big dataset of labelled examples taken by drones will enhance the utility of plant diseases detection.

6.7.2   Symptoms Segmentation in Plant Diseases

DL approaches focus on diseases classification and ignores the localisation of infected regions in the leaf. This disease region identification is very important for a human expert to gain more insights into the disease and its symptoms [5]. In order to address this problem, DL segmentation algorithms can be used to divide the image into many parts in an unsupervised manner. After this segmentation, the supervised algorithm can be used to classify the disease. In this case, the user can know the diseases and the infected region at the same time. Also, more efforts in DL understanding help users to understand how classifiers classify the diseases. Visualisations algorithms should be included to enhance the user experience in understanding diseases [32, 39].

6.7.3   Labelled Images Challenge

DL algorithms require a large number of labelled images to produce a classifier not suffering from overfitting. Labelling this large number by a human expert is a real challenge and time-consuming. To address this challenge, crowdsourcing, as distributed internet framework, can produce big labelled datasets in an acceptable time. Also, crowdsourcing helps to achieve more complex labelling like the infected regions labelling [3, 30]. For example, we can divide an image using a grid of squares and ask users in crowdsourcing frameworks to select infected squares. This structured labelling can be used to evaluate automatic systems of diseases regions and symptom identification.

Crowdsourcing addresses the labelled datasets by offering an efficient tool for data collection. However, in many contexts learning algorithm must minimize the number of labelled examples and exploit unlabelled examples. Weakly and semi-supervised algorithms can be used for this objective [19, 29, 31]. This type of algorithms uses unlabelled images to improve the training of the classifier, knowing that unlabelled examples are relatively cheap and does not require human expert efforts which reduces the cost of data collection.

In addition to semi-supervised algorithms, active learning can help by choosing the examples efficiently for a labelling expert. This selective labelling improves the classifier accuracy and reduces the labelling cost at the same time [28, 38].

6.7.4 The Exploitation of Multiple Information Sources

Previous works have only focused on using images and have ignored valuable information. For example, the age of the plant is important to achieve a good disease diagnostic. Each phase in plant life has a specific set of diseases. This information can be combined with the image to avoid any incorrect decision incompatible with the age of the plant.

Climate represents an important factor for triggering plant diseases. A sudden change in temperature causes many diseases to plants. For this reason, a practical tool for protecting plants from diseases should exploit this information.

Field location is another important factor in disease detection because each region is characterised by a set of known diseases. Moreover, if one disease spreads in nearby fields, then it is likely to detect this spreading disease.

All this information can be combined with features extracted from the image to enhance the DL system performance. The fully connected layer can be combined with information from many sources and used as input of a classifier. In this case, the classifier exploits the extracted features from an image, taken directly from the field, and combines them with information that is easy to collect. Commonly, the climate state and location information can be retrieved easily from the internet on smartphones. Exploitation of this cheap information allows the detection system to adapt to the environmental factors in real time.

6.8 Conclusion

We studied in this chapter a recent trend for building a system able to detect and classify plant diseases. After analysing and comparing the previous work based on DL, we have concluded that these studies principally use two CNN architectures (AlexNet and GoogleNet). For this reason, we have evaluated the state-of-the-art CNN architectures using a public dataset of plant diseases. The results of this evaluation show clearly that we can improve the accuracy using a new CNN architecture such as inceptionV3 which achieved an accuracy of 99.76%.

In addition to this improvement in accuracy, we have investigated increasing the transparency of deep models based on visualisation techniques. In this context, the saliency map method is introduced for localising the infected regions of the plant after the identification of diseases. Despite the fact that the training images are weakly labelled, this visualisation has succeeded in the extraction of the infected regions without any expert intervention. Furthermore, this visualisation method shows a precise and sharp visualisation which helps the inexperienced users to understand the diseases.

As a limitation of this study, we can notice that visualisation method is not evaluated quantitatively using a defined measure. However, the images are assessed based on expert defined visual symptoms. This qualitative evaluation is motivated by the weak labelling of the dataset. Therefore, our future work will focus on the preparation of a strong labelled dataset, which makes it possible to measure numerically the performance of saliency maps visualisation.

References

1. Akhtar, A., Khanum, A., Khan, S.A., Shaukat, A.: Automated plant disease analysis (APDA): performance comparison of machine learning techniques. In: 2013 11th International Conference on Frontiers of Information Technology, pp. 60–65. IEEE Computer Society, Islamabad (2013)
2. Al Hiary, H., Bani Ahmad, S., Reyalat, M., Braik, M., ALRahamneh, Z.: Fast and accurate detection and classification of plant diseases. Int. J. Comput. Appl. **17**(1), 31–38 (2011)
3. Albarqouni, S., Baur, C., Achilles, F., Belagiannis, V., Demirci, S., Navab, N.: AggNet: deep learning from crowds for mitosis detection in breast cancer histology images. IEEE Trans. Med. Imaging **35**(5), 1313–1321 (2016). https://doi.org/10.1109/TMI.2016.2528120
4. Blancard, D.: 2 - Diagnosis of Parasitic and Nonparasitic Diseases. Academic Press, The Netherlands (2012)
5. Brahimi, M., Boukhalfa, K., Moussaoui, A.: Deep learning for tomato diseases: classification and symptoms visualization. Appl. Artif. Intell. **31**(4), 1–17 (2017)
6. Chen, X.W., Lin, X.: Big data deep learning: challenges and perspectives. IEEE Access **2**, 514–525 (2014). https://doi.org/10.1109/ACCESS.2014.2325029
7. Dandawate, Y., Kokare, R.: An automated approach for classification of plant diseases towards development of futuristic decision support system in Indian perspective. In: 2015 International Conference on Advances in Computing. Communications and Informatics, ICACCI 2015, pp. 794–799. IEEE, Kochi, India (2015)
8. DeChant, C., Wiesner-Hanks, T., Chen, S., Stewart, E.L., Yosinski, J., Gore, M.A., Nelson, R.J., Lipson, H.: Automated identification of northern leaf blight-infected maize plants from field imagery using deep learning. Phytopathology (2017). https://doi.org/10.1094/PHYTO-11-16-0417-R
9. Fujita, E., Kawasaki, Y., Uga, H., Kagiwada, S., Iyatomi, H.: Basic investigation on a robust and practical plant diagnostic system. In: Proceedings - 2016 15th IEEE International Conference on Machine Learning and Applications, ICMLA 2016, pp. 989–992 (2016)
10. Goodfellow, I., Bengio, Y., Courville, A.: Deep Learning. MIT Press, Cambridge (2016)
11. Gould, S., Fulton, R., Koller, D.: Decomposing a scene into geometric and semantically consistent regions. In: Proceedings of the IEEE International Conference on Computer Vision, pp. 1–8. IEEE (2009)
12. Hanssen, I.M., Lapidot, M.: Major tomato viruses in the Mediterranean basin. Adv. Virus Res. **84**, 31–66 (2012)
13. He, K., Zhang, X., Ren, S., Sun, J.: Deep residual learning for image recognition. CoRR arXiv:1512.03385 (2015)
14. Huang, G., Liu, Z., Weinberger, K.Q., van der Maaten, L.: Densely connected convolutional networks. CoRR arXiv:1608.0 (2016)
15. Hughes, D., Salathe, M.: An open access repository of images on plant health to enable the development of mobile disease diagnostics, pp. 1–13 (2015)

16. Iandola, F.N., Moskewicz, M.W., Ashraf, K., Han, S., Dally, W.J., Keutzer, K.: SqueezeNet: AlexNet-level accuracy with 50x fewer parameters and <1MB model size. CoRR arXiv:1602.07360 (2016)
17. Jia, Y., Shelhamer, E., Donahue, J., Karayev, S., Long, J., Girshick, R., Guadarrama, S., Darrell, T.: Caffe: convolutional architecture for fast feature embedding. In: Proceedings of the 22nd ACM International Conference on Multimedia, MM '14, pp. 675–678. ACM, New York, NY, USA (2014). https://doi.org/10.1145/2647868.2654889
18. Kawasaki, Y., Uga, H., Kagiwada, S., Iyatomi, H.: Basic study of automated diagnosis of viral plant diseases using convolutional neural networks. In: Advances in Visual Computing: 11th International Symposium, ISVC 2015, Las Vegas, NV, USA, 14–16 December 2015, Proceedings, Part II, pp. 638–645 (2015)
19. Kipf, T.N., Welling, M.: Semi-supervised classification with graph convolutional networks. CoRR arXiv:1609.02907 (2016)
20. Koike, S.T., Gladders, P., Paulus, A.O.: Vegetable Diseases: A Color Handbook. Academic Press, San Diego (2007)
21. Krizhevsky, A., Sutskever, I., Hinton, G.E.: ImageNet classification with deep convolutional neural networks. Commun. ACM 60(6), 84–90 (2017). https://doi.org/10.1145/3065386
22. LeCun, Y., Bengio, Y., Hinton, G.: Deep learning. Nature 521(7553), 436–444 (2015)
23. Lee, W., Kim, S., Lee, Y.T., Lee, H.W., Choi, M.: Deep neural networks for wild fire detection with unmanned aerial vehicle. In: 2017 IEEE International Conference on Consumer Electronics (ICCE), pp. 252–253 (2017)
24. Lu, Y., Yi, S., Zeng, N., Liu, Y., Zhang, Y.: Identification of rice diseases using deep convolutional neural networks. Neurocomputing 267, 378–384 (2017)
25. Mohanty, S.P., Hughes, D.P., Salathé, M.: Using deep learning for image-based plant disease detection. Front. Plant Sci. 7(September), 1–7 (2016)
26. Mokhtar, U., El-Bendary, N., Hassenian, A.E., Emary, E., Mahmoud, M.A., Hefny, H., Tolba, M.F., Mokhtar, U., Hassenian, A.E., Emary, E., Mahmoud, M.A.: SVM-Based detection of tomato leaves diseases. In: Filev, D., Jabłkowski, J., Kacprzyk, J., Krawczak, M., Popchev, I., Rutkowski, L., Sgurev, V., Sotirova, E., Szynkarczyk, P., Zadrozny, S. (eds.) Advances in Intelligent Systems and Computing, vol. 323, pp. 641–652. Springer, Cham (2015)
27. Nachtigall, L.G., Araujo, R.M., Nachtigall, G.R.: Classification of apple tree disorders using convolutional neural networks. In: 2016 IEEE 28th International Conference on Tools with Artificial Intelligence (ICTAI), pp. 472–476 (2016). https://doi.org/10.1109/ICTAI.2016.0078
28. Otálora, S., Perdomo, O., González, F., Müller, H.: Training Deep Convolutional Neural Networks with Active Learning for Exudate Classification in Eye Fundus Images, pp. 146–154. Springer International Publishing, Cham (2017)
29. Papandreou, G., Chen, L.C., Murphy, K.P., Yuille, A.L.: Weakly-and semi-supervised learning of a deep convolutional network for semantic image segmentation. In: 2015 IEEE International Conference on Computer Vision (ICCV), pp. 1742–1750 (2015)
30. Sharma, M., Saha, O., Sriraman, A., Hebbalaguppe, R., Vig, L., Karande, S.: Crowdsourcing for chromosome segmentation and deep classification. In: 2017 IEEE Conference on Computer Vision and Pattern Recognition Workshops (CVPRW), pp. 786–793 (2017). https://doi.org/10.1109/CVPRW.2017.109
31. Shinozaki, T.: Semi-supervised Learning for Convolutional Neural Networks Using Mild Supervisory Signals, pp. 381–388. Springer International Publishing, Cham (2016)
32. Simonyan, K., Vedaldi, A., Zisserman, A.: Deep Inside Convolutional Networks: Visualising Image Classification Models and Saliency Maps. CoRR arXiv:1312.6034 (2013)
33. Simonyan, K., Zisserman, A.: Very deep convolutional networks for large-scale image recognition. CoRR arXiv:1409.1556 (2014)
34. Sladojevic, S., Arsenovic, M., Anderla, A., Culibrk, D., Stefanovic, D.: Deep neural networks based recognition of plant diseases by leaf image classification. Comput. Intell. Neurosci. 2016 (2016)
35. Springenberg, J.T., Dosovitskiy, A., Brox, T., Riedmiller, M.A.: Striving for simplicity: the all convolutional net. CoRR arXiv:1412.6806 (2014)

36. Szegedy, C., Liu, W., Jia, Y., Sermanet, P., Reed, S., Anguelov, D., Erhan, D., Vanhoucke, V., Rabinovich, A.: Going deeper with convolutions. In: Proceedings of the IEEE Computer Society Conference on Computer Vision and Pattern Recognition, 07–12 June, Boston, USA, pp. 1–9 (2015). https://doi.org/10.1109/CVPR.2015.7298594
37. Szegedy, C., Vanhoucke, V., Ioffe, S., Shlens, J., Wojna, Z.: Rethinking the inception architecture for computer vision. In: 2016 IEEE Conference on Computer Vision and Pattern Recognition (CVPR), pp. 2818–2826. arXiv:1512.0 (2015)
38. Wang, K., Zhang, D., Li, Y., Zhang, R., Lin, L.: Cost-effective active learning for deep image classification. CoRR arXiv:1701.03551 (2017)
39. Zeiler, M.D., Fergus, R.: Visualizing and understanding convolutional networks. Lecture Notes in Computer Science (including subseries Lecture Notes in Artificial Intelligence and Lecture Notes in Bioinformatics. LNCS, vol. 8689 (PART 1), pp. 818–833 (2014)

Chapter 7
Critical Challenges for the Visual Representation of Deep Neural Networks

Kieran Browne, Ben Swift and Henry Gardner

Abstract Artificial neural networks have proved successful in a broad range of applications over the last decade. However, there remain significant concerns about their interpretability. Visual representation is one way researchers are attempting to make sense of these models and their behaviour. The representation of neural networks raises questions which cross disciplinary boundaries. This chapter draws on a growing collection of interdisciplinary scholarship regarding neural networks. We present six case studies in the visual representation of neural networks and examine the particular representational challenges posed by these algorithms. Finally we summarise the ideas raised in the case studies as a set of takeaways for researchers engaging in this area.

7.1 Introduction

The internal patterns and processes of artificial neural networks are notoriously difficult to interpret. The advent of deep neural networks has heightened this challenge and rendered many existing interpretive methods obsolete. This has prompted new research into methods for interpreting neural networks. One of the most fruitful areas of this research, and the focus of the present chapter, is visual representation. Central to this research is the concern that neural networks are black boxes. Growing awareness and criticism of machine learning in public discourse has transformed the explanation of these algorithms into a social and political as well as technical

K. Browne (✉) · B. Swift · H. Gardner
Australian National University, Canberra, ACT 0200, Australia
e-mail: kieran.browne@anu.edu.au

B. Swift
e-mail: ben.swift@anu.edu.au

H. Gardner
e-mail: henry.gardner@anu.edu.au

© Springer International Publishing AG, part of Springer Nature 2018
J. Zhou and F. Chen (eds.), *Human and Machine Learning*, Human–Computer
Interaction Series, https://doi.org/10.1007/978-3-319-90403-0_7

concern. Interrogating the black box is a compound problem. Its constituent parts cross disciplinary boundaries to raise questions of engineering, epistemology, aesthetics and semantics. We will argue that it is valuable for researchers aiming to explain neural networks through visual representation to become familiar with the interdisciplinary critical scholarship on this topic. We begin this chapter with a discussion of the black box problem which draws upon this research. We then situate the visual representation of deep neural networks in data visualisation and interface theory, and discuss the specific challenges it poses. In Sect. 7.2 we outline the diagrammatic representations favoured by researchers prior to 2006 and offer an explanation for their rapid obsolescence following the rise of deep neural networks. In Sect. 7.3 we present six diverse case studies in contemporary visual representation of neural networks. The case studies come from research, industry and individual makers. They have been selected for their potential to highlight critical challenges rather than their citation metrics. In the final section we summarise the ideas raised in the case studies as a list of takeaways for students or researchers engaging in this area.

7.1.1   The Black Box Problem

The term "black box" describes a system with clearly observable inputs and outputs, but with inscrutable internal processes. Neural networks are considered black boxes not because we cannot see inside as such; the relationship between input and output is observable but unintelligible. An apparently strong relationship in one layer of the network may be cancelled out or inverted in the next or simply diluted by countless other smaller relations. Like many machine learning (ML) techniques, neural networks trade interpretability for predictive power [7].

The black box problem is an ongoing concern for researchers and a growing concern for institutions and individuals who use trained models but are estranged from their development. If it is difficult to understand how neural networks make decisions, then it becomes difficult to trust the decisions they make.

The black box problem has been cited many times as a barrier to the adoption of neural networks [6, 16, 42]. This concern has proved unwarranted as the successes of deep neural networks in countless disparate fields have led to pragmatic adoption despite difficulties explaining their behaviour. Over the past decade deep neural networks have received massive investment from research councils, industry and government and have been applied to problems as broad-ranging as translation [2], gameplay [28], fine art [17], stock trading [25] and object recognition [24].

Despite some early claims to have solved the black box problem [6], concern for explainability remains. Indeed the black box has become a central metaphor for questioning how and whether neural networks can be explained. Notably, researchers have made attempts at "illuminating" [32], "coloring" [16], "opening" [39, 42] and "greying" [43] black boxes.

Since 2006, the use of deep architectures, i.e. neural networks of many layers, has become prevalent [5]. The comparatively tiny neural networks used by researchers in the 90s have been replaced by massively deep, massively multivariate networks. AlexNet [24], for example, contains 650,000 neurons and 60 million parameters. This enormous growth has rendered many existing modes of visual representation ineffective.

The invention of new types of networks has created additional challenges for explainability. Much of the recent success of neural networks has been made with alternative architectures such as convolutional neural networks and long short term memory (LSTM) networks [35]. These models augment the standard feedforward neural network with structures that enable new kinds of modelling but introduce additional behavioural complexities.

7.1.2   Interdisciplinarity

As a potentially transformative technology, ML has consequences which reach far beyond computer science. As a novel way of representing knowledge ML raises questions for epistemology [41]. Because ML is subject to human biases, anti-discrimination law must be reformed to account for it [3]. As a technology driving socially consequential mechanisms such as news trends and credit scores, the opacity of ML becomes a sociological concern [13]. There are more examples of interdisciplinary research into ML than can be enumerated here. In each case, the authors describe the critical challenges of machine learning in the nomenclature of their field. This seemingly disparate scholarship provides a useful lens with which to understand ML itself and its effects in the world. In Sect. 7.3 there are a number of cases where interdisciplinary research is leveraged to make sense of some of the particular critical challenges posed by the visual representation of neural networks.

7.2   Historical Precedents

The defining trope of pre-2006 neural network visualisation was the structure of the network itself. This was most commonly represented as a graph of nodes and edges arranged in neat layers left-to-right or bottom-to-top (Figs. 7.1 and 7.2). In these, the network's topology is central to the representation.

Craven and Shavlik's 1992 review paper [14] surveyed the contemporary cutting edge of artificial neural network visualisation. Notable amongst these were the Hinton and Bond diagrams, which have a structural focus. Curiously the authors criticise the Hinton diagram for not showing the network's "topology" despite its elements being arranged in layers that mimicked the network's structure. Although the Hinton and Bond diagrams can theoretically include any number of inputs, they are practically uninterpretable for large networks [42].

What followed was a general convergence to and then refinement of a particular representation which centred around a structural depiction of the network. We call

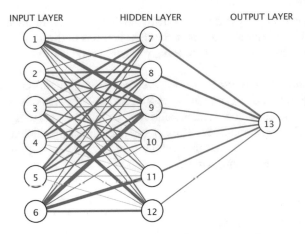

INPUT LAYER   HIDDEN LAYER   OUTPUT LAYER

Fig. 7.1 Neural interpretation diagram based on S. L. Özesmi and U. Özesmi (1999) [33] — the visual representation mirrors the structure of the schematic representation introduced by Rosenblatt (1962) [34]. The thickness of each edge is relative to the absolute value of the synapse weight. Blue edges represent positive weights and red edges represent negative weights. Source code for image available at [9]

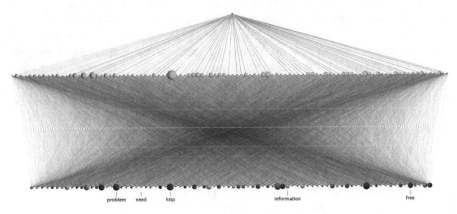

Fig. 7.2 Diagram for a large spam-classifier neural network based on Tzeng and Ma (2005) [42]. The size of nodes indicates their relative importance in identifying spam. Node colour is used to indicate the mean and standard deviation of a given node. Source code for image available at [10]

this type of image a "neural interpretation diagram" (NID) borrowing from the name used by S. L. Özesmi and Özesmi (1999) [33]. In NIDs, neurons are represented as dots or circles, and synapses are represented as lines with thickness and colour indicating value. Variations on this theme can also be seen in the work of other researchers [32, 33, 38, 42]. In their 2005 paper, Tzeng and Ma cite the Hinton and Bond diagrams as precedents to their work and note that these had failed to scale to larger networks. They go on to apply their take on the NID to a network with 8300 synapses. Although it doesn't appear to be the authors' intent, the resulting image demonstrates that NIDs share a similar scaling problem to Hinton and Bond diagrams. In the multitude of criss-crossing lines it is impossible to make sense of individual synapse values (Fig. 7.2).

The NID and its variants went out of fashion because they failed to scale to the very large, very deep networks that became the focus of research after 2006. More significantly however, these diagrams fail to target the core of the problem. Neural networks are not black boxes because we cannot see inside at all; the value of any weight, bias or activation can be easily accessed. It is clear that seeing the network does not in itself create understanding. The real challenge for explaining neural networks is untangling meaningful relationships from the multitude of connections.

By *meaningful*, we mean relating to representations for which people have concepts. It is not useful to explain how a pixel value relates to steering instructions. For self-driving cars we want our explanations in terms of semitrailers, cliffs and pedestrians. Because deep neural networks produce their own intermediate representations we require means of mapping these back to meaningful concepts and testing how robust these mappings are.

Additionally it is not possible to explain the behaviour of a network by its structure as structure does not dictate behaviour; neural networks are universal approximators [21]. Two structurally identical networks will approximate different behaviours given different data. A neural network's behaviour is latent in the dataset, not the network.

7.3 Case Studies

In this section we explore contemporary developments in visual representation of neural networks, examining six case studies drawn from research, industry and individuals. These cases have been selected for their potential to highlight critical challenges of visually representing neural networks.

7.3.1 AI Brain Scans

The *AI Brain Scans* (2016-ongoing) [19], are a collection of visualisations by Matt Fyles of Graphcore. Initially referred to as "large scale directed graph visualizations" [20], the images were dubbed "brain scans" in a report by *Wired* in early 2017 and the title stuck [12].

The *AI Brain Scans* visualise the edges and nodes of a neural network's computational graph. They are produced with Graphcore's proprietary ML framework, Poplar, and the open source graph visualisation software, Gephi [4], which is used primarily for social and biological network analysis. The "brain scans" are structural like the NID, but rather than representing the network's topology they represent the graph of computations required to train and run a neural network. Unlike other neural network graph visualisations such as those produced by TensorFlow's TensorBoard

[40], the "brain scans" do not abstract nodes into higher dimensional representations, namely tensors. The results are beautiful, but enigmatic; see [12] for images. The network is presented in its vast complexity, often containing millions of nodes and edges. These are unidentifiable in the emergent global form, making the image appear more photographic than diagrammatic. The edges of the graph are all but noise and appear as a fine grain, evocative of a micrograph.

The graph layout demonstrates patterns of growth similar to bacteria on a petri dish. Force-directed layout is used to arrange the nodes, which produces growth-like properties. There are a multitude of ways to lay out a graph visualisation, and no single "correct" way to do so. In this case as in any, the choice to use one layout over another is an aesthetic judgement. The "brain scans" revel in the complexity of deep neural networks. No longer are nodes arranged in even rows and parallel layers with neatly criss-crossing edges. Rather, the sub-structures grow radially but distort due to competition for space.

The "brain scans" appear to be a rejection of structure and clarity of contemporary visualisation which seeks to render phenomena beyond the scale of human perception accessible to our senses. Manovich (2002) [27] calls this the "anti-sublime ideal". Contrary to this, the *AI Brain Scans* are deeply sublime, they are an image of the complexity of contemporary neural networks, whose internal patterns and processes, as we have seen, are at least partially unknowable. By leveraging a biomorphic representation they present a metaphor for artificial neural networks that is complex, esoteric and uncanny.

This is not to say that the "brain scans" do not help us to understand neural networks. It is possible for example to identify convolutional and fully connected layers in the emergent structures of the images (see [19]). Importantly the *AI Brain Scans* help us to think about neural networks because they offer a visual metaphor that actually represents their complexity and obscurity rather than representing an incomplete or inconclusive visual explanation in false clarity.

7.3.2 Optimal Stimulus Images

One of the key strengths of deep neural networks over shallow ones is their capacity to build abstraction over successive layers [5]. Accordingly, one of the greatest challenges for explaining the behaviour of neural networks is interpreting these intermediate representations learned by a network and encoded in hidden layers.

Because deep neural networks are often trained on low-level representations (like pixels or characters) which have little semantic value, the use of numerical explanations such as rule extraction are undermined. Le (2013) [26] demonstrates the use of numerical optimisation to find the optimal stimulus for a given neuron in an unsupervised neural network. The author includes three instances of interpretable high-level features discovered with this method. This suggests that neural networks have the capacity to discover salient features in the pursuit of higher goals, even when these are not encoded as part of a classification. Le uses gradient descent in training,

Fig. 7.3 Optimal stimulus of interpretable neuron from Le (2013) [26]. (Copyright 2013 IEEE, reprinted by permission of IEEE)

keeping the weights and biases constant in order to to optimise the activation of a given neuron with respect to the input variable. Because the resulting optimal input data is in pixel space, it can be rendered directly as an image. Figure 7.3 is a visualisation created in this way that clearly contains a human face.

The power of this and similar methods is that they accumulate the information which encodes this representation and is distributed throughout preceding layers. In doing so, they shift the focus of explanation from network weights with no inherent semantic value to distributed high-level features.

This kind of visualisation is extraordinarily expressive. At later layers in the network it theoretically makes it possible to simplify the tangled mess of relations encoded within. Used in combination with a technique such as rule extraction, it allows us to give coefficients at the level of meaningful concepts. However, this also requires that researchers engage critically with semantics. Tun (2015) [41] problematised the epistemic status of ML, noting that statistical learning is a form of inductive inference. It is therefore subject to the problem of induction. This idea can help researchers to better understand the nature of the semantics encoded in neural networks.

Figure 7.3 shows a blurry image of a human face which is the optimal input for one of the network's neurons. The face is clearly white and clearly male. Its eyes contrast strongly with the background. Its lips are rosy and there is a hint of stubble on the upper lip. The clarity with which the face can be seen in the image led the author to claim that the tested neuron has learned "the concept of faces" [26]. However, with the problem of induction in mind, this claim becomes less certain. The image appears to represent the basic notion of a face because whiteness and maleness are unmarked categories in English. We understand the image through the lens of our preexisting linguistic categories. If the pictured face were feminine, or non-white, or that of a child we would be be less inclined to assume it represents the general concept of faces.

The optimal stimulus is an important datum but it represents an archetype not a category. Categories are defined as much by what is excluded as what is included. It is possible that this neuron activates strongly only for faces that are also white, adult and male, or even only to those that resemble the man pictured. Alternatively this really could be the generic category of "face", its features representing only an overrepresentation of white adult males in the dataset. It is not possible to know how far this representation of a face will stretch without experimentation. To test the equality of meaning between this neuron and the Anglophonic definition of a face, we need to measure how quickly the activation declines as correlates of femaleness, age and ethnicity change.

The optimal stimulus images and other methods that visualise the internal semantics of neural networks are crucial to our understanding of these systems. Nonetheless, it is necessary to take a critical approach when dealing with notions as slippery as meaning. It is valuable for researchers aiming to represent semantic encodings in neural networks to become familiar with the critical issues of semantics from philosophy and linguistics.

7.3.3 Interpretable, Long-Range LSTM Cells

Semantic relationships in recurrent neural networks are explored in Karpathy, Johnson, and Fei-Fei (2015) [23]. The authors visualise the activation of a particular neuron across a passage of text generated by an LSTM network to look for interpretable relationships between the neuron's activation and the composed content. Their visualisation highlights each character with a colour mapped to the activation of a given neuron and looks for interpretable patterns.

In Fig. 7.4 this technique was applied to an LSTM trained on Leo Tolstoy's *War and Peace*. Two interpretable neurons are shown. The first can be interpreted as relating to the carriage return which must be used approximately every 70 characters. The second turns on inside quotes, allowing the network to remember to close them. Interpreting meaningful relationships in the content of the prose itself was not achieved. It is possible that an appropriately comparative string of characters that would reveal the

Cell sensitive to position in line:

```
The sole importance of the crossing of the Berëzina lies in the fact
that it plainly and indubitably proved the fallacy of all the plans for
cutting off the enemy's retreat and the soundness of the only possible
line of action--the one Kutúzov and the general mass of the army
demanded--namely, simply to follow the enemy up. The French crowd fled
at a continually increasing speed and all its energywas directed to
reaching its goal. It fled like a wounded animal and it was impossible
to block its path. This was shown not so much by the arrangements it
made for crossing as by what took place at the bridges. When the bridges
broke down, unarmed soldiers, people from Moscow and women with children
who were with the French transport,all—carried on by vis inertiea --
pressed forward into boats and into the ice-covered water and did not,
surrender.
```

Cell that turns on inside quotes:

```
"You mean to imply that I have nothing to eat out of.... On the
contrary, I can supply you with everything even if you want to
give dinner parties," warmly replied Chichagóv, who tried by every
word he spoke to prove his own rectitude and therefore imagined
Kutúzov to be animated by the same desire.
```

```
Kutúzov, shrugging his shoulders, replied with his subtle
penetrating smile: "I meant merely to say what I said."
```

Fig. 7.4 Visualisation of interpretable activations of neurons from LSTM network trained on *War and Peace* based on Karpathy, Johnson, and Fei-Fei (2015) [23]. Text colour represents the activation of the interpretable neuron *tanh(c)*, where blue is positive and red is negative. Source code for image available at [8]

pattern simply did not emerge. It is also possible that the relationships that produce prose are more complex than the viewer can discern.

Unlike the optimal stimulus images, these visualisations engage with a softer notion of meaning. Here, meaning emerges from the consistent relation between the neuron activation and the output. The semantic meaning of a cell is inferred by the viewer in the context of real data. The visualisation exists only to service comparison.

The insight of this visualisation is to integrate neuron activation with the data it consumes or produces. By placing the abstract representation of activations in context, the viewer can discover patterns without the author's curation (Fig. 7.5).

| flower | house | computer |

Fig. 7.5 "Fooling images" produce >99% confidence predictions but are unrecognisable to humans. This process and the notion of a fooling image are introduced in Nguyen, Yosinski, and Clune (2015) [31]. The examples above were produced using a script operating on Felix Andrew's CPPN clojurescript implementation [1]. The source code is available at [11]

7.3.4 Fooling Images

The "fooling images" of Nguyen, Yosinski, and Clune (2015) [31] are a collection of images produced with genetic algorithms that are unrecognisable to humans but produce high confidence predictions from state-of-the-art deep neural networks. The works expose a significant divide between human and computer vision. Nguyen, Yosinski, and Clune (2015) [31] introduce two methods for generating "fooling images" based on evolutionary algorithms (EAs). We will focus on the second form which uses Compositional Pattern Producing Networks (CPPNs) [37] to breed images which optimise for a given fitness function, in this case a single classification of a convolutional neural network trained on ImageNet. In order to simultaneously target all 1000 classes of ImageNet the researchers used the *multi-dimensional archive of phenotypic elites* algorithm, but noted that results were unaffected for a simpler EA.

The "fooling images", unlike the previous case studies, contain no image of the network's weights, structure, training set or indeed any data about the network at all. Despite this they do foster understanding. The images probe the network with targeted experiments to seek out unusual and revelatory behaviour.

The "fooling images" are critical cases that force the viewer to reconsider assumptions about the network. The researchers found that test subjects were able to reason about why an image was classified a certain way after its class was revealed to them. It is clear however, that global coherence does not affect the network's prediction. Instead, simply having low level features from the class seems to be sufficient to predict a category with high certainty.

The "fooling images" show very clearly that despite high scores on the ImageNet benchmark, neural networks do not "see" in the same way that humans do. It is natural to assume when we see a neural network working correctly that the network perceives and reasons as we do. Critical cases such as the "fooling images" reveal glimpses of the semantic mappings that the network has learned.

The "fooling images" are powerful because they break our natural assumption that performing a complex task with low error means thinking like a human. They destabilise the default anthropocentric notion of seeing. This semantic non-equivalence is likely a property of neural networks in general and gives grounds for scepticism of any neural network that appears to be acting like a person.

7.3.5 DeepDream

DeepDream is a method for visualising the internal representations of neural networks developed by Mordvintsev, Tyka, and Olah (2015) [30]. It is also likely the best known neural network visualisation, having reached viral status.

DeepDream approaches visualisation with the same basic aim as the optimal stimulus images of Le (2013) [26]; to visualise the semantic representations encoded by

Fig. 7.6 Image produced by DeepDream — by Mordvintsev, Tyka, and Olah (2015) [30]. Used under Creative Commons Attribution 4.0 International: https://creativecommons.org/licenses/by/4.0/legalcode

"Admiral Dog!"   "The Pig-Snail"   "The Camel-Bird"   "The Dog-Fish"

Fig. 7.7 DeepDream's compound animals — by Mordvintsev, Tyka, and Olah (2015) [30]. Used under Creative Commons Attribution 4.0 International: https://creativecommons.org/licenses/by/4.0/legalcode

a network. The algorithm was modified from the research of Simonyan, Vedaldi, and Zisserman (2014) [36] and others but provides two notable variations on existing work. First, instead of maximising a single neuron or class representation, Deep-Dream reinforces whatever is activating the highest to begin with. In doing so, it can hold the representations of hundreds of classes in a single image. These need not be distinct or complete and morph seamlessly from one to another (Fig. 7.7). Second, DeepDream applies its activations at different "octaves" creating a visual repetition of self-similar forms at many scales (Fig. 7.6).

In describing their work the authors make use of the language of conscious human experience. The networks are said to be "dreaming" perhaps in reference to the Phillip K. Dick novel. Later, the process and its emergent images are described as being like children watching clouds [29].

DeepDream's emergent structures bear similarities to the drawings of MC Escher. Labyrinths grow out of thin air and form strange loops or seemingly infinite layers. Like Escher's tessellation works, representations morph from one to another, or change in scale. The eye can trace a path around the image and end up back where it started, or in a vastly different representation or a different scale. Representations morph from one to another but at every stage appear locally coherent.

The key point here is that like Escher's work, the DeepDream images are locally coherent but are globally incoherent. The images support the implication of the "fooling images", that semantic representation in neural networks does not depend on the global form.

The authors are careful to encourage the spread of their work. Alongside the published source code, readers are encouraged to make their own and share them with the hashtag #deepdream. It is also clear that the authors are cognisant of wider cultural implications of the images.

[we] wonder whether neural networks could become a tool for artists — a new way to remix visual concepts — or perhaps even shed a little light on the roots of the creative process in general. [29]

Unlike the algorithms it was based on, which visualise the representation of a single class or neuron, DeepDream combines any number of representations in the image. Because of this it is not possible to learn about particular features of a given class, or to understand how features relate to one another. DeepDream is arguably not a technical image but a cultural one. It is a picture of the strangeness and inconsistency of neural networks. Although it uses the language of conscious human experience it presents an uncanny image of neural networks that bears little resemblance to dreams or seeing.

7.3.6 Pix2Pix and FaceApp

Pix2pix (P2P) by Christopher Hesse is an online interface to a neural network that converts images of one kind to another. The work is an implementation of the Pix2Pix neural network designed by Isola et al. (2016) [22]. The interface allows for user-driven exploration of the trained network.

P2P is a behavioural visualisation like the "fooling images" in the sense that it does not directly represent information about the network itself but rather facilitates comparison between input and output. Unlike the "fooling images", it does not provide a curated list of inputs. In fact the initial state provided by the demo is rather unremarkable. It is the interaction here that is most central to the work's explanatory power. Users, over successive attempts, can test the limits of the network's semantics.

Figure 7.8 shows a P2P demo which converts an outline drawing of a cat to a photographic image based on that outline. With their outline, the user can explore representations. Users can follow their own line of inquiry to learn about the network.

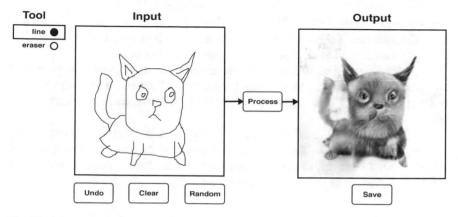

Fig. 7.8 Schematic drawing of Christopher Hesse's *edges2cats* interface https://affinelayer.com/ pixsrv/ Users are afforded simple drawing tools to produce a black and white line drawing. This is then processed by a server that uses a pix2pix network to produce an image with photographic qualities, inferring form, colour and texture from the line drawing

Can the cat have more than two eyes? How is a body distinguished from a head? What happens if I don't draw a cat at all?

The interface allows the user to intelligently explore the space of possibility of the network. Though the interface enables individual sense-making, it is on social media that the images have been most successfully interpreted. On Twitter and other social networks curious, bizarre and revelatory images are selected for. Images that create the most interest are transmitted the farthest. In comments users share discoveries and attempt to make sense of the system collectively.

A similar pattern of collective sense-making can be seen in the response to *FaceApp* [18]. The app uses neural networks to transform a face in intelligent ways. It provides filters that make the subject smile, change gender or age, and increase "attractiveness". Again, the interface allowed users to experiment with the network and seek out patterns, and again the most successful sense-making happened on social networks, which allow revelatory behaviours to spread quickly. Users of social networks quickly discovered that the filter intended to make users more attractive was turning skin white [15].

By allowing the network to infer its own semantics from the training set, it falsely equated beauty with white skin. With this unfortunate pattern in mind, it is possible to post-rationalise the existence of this bias in the training data. Datasets of this kind are labelled by people and thus imbibe the biases of the people who create them. Neural networks are not immune to this kind of bias, in fact it is almost impossible to prevent it. As universal approximators, neural networks make use of any salient patterns in data, including cultural patterns. If the application of labels such as beauty are correlated with whiteness, the network will learn to reproduce that pattern.

How is it possible that a powerful pattern of cultural bias that is completely obvious to users was invisible to those who developed the network? This pattern surprised

FaceApp because the design of a network does not produce the behaviour, the data does. Cultural biases are easily learned and repeated by neural networks when we take data uncritically; as an objective representation of what *is*.

In contrast, despite being completely estranged from the neurons and synapses of the network itself, and without requisite knowledge of how neural networks function or learn, the users of social networks were able to discover and make sense of this pattern.

Interfaces that enable exploration and socially mediated interpretation are a powerful explanatory method. There is an opportunity here for researchers to design for collective sense-making, to make it easy for users to share curious behaviours of networks and facilitate collective interpretation.

7.4 Summary

In this section, we summarise the ideas raised in the case studies as a list of takeaways for researchers engaging in this area.

7.4.1 Structure Does Not Explain Behaviour

The structure of a neural network does not explain its behaviour. The shape of a neural network is a design consideration, it has an effect on learning, but not learned behaviour. Instead, behaviour is latent in the training data and approximated by the network.

It is not true that structure is irrelevant. Thinking about structure can help researchers to design better networks, increase capacity for abstraction and restrict overfitting. But these choices do not explain a network's output.

In comparison, it is demonstrable that users can infer patterns in the network without any knowledge of the network itself or even a technical understanding of how neural networks function. Simply presenting inputs alongside outputs for comparison can allow viewers to spot patterns.

7.4.2 We Understand Better When Things Break

We learn more about how neural networks work when they fail. When neural networks do what we expect, it's easy to assume that they are thinking like a person. In the absence of a useful metaphor for how neural networks think we imagine ourselves performing the task. Given the extraordinary results achieved in benchmarks such as ImageNet, where neural networks have equalled or surpassed human accuracy, we tend to assume that the network uses the same features to identify images as we do. Indeed, it is difficult to comprehend how a system could achieve human or superhuman ability for a given task *without* thinking like a human. However, critical cases like the "fooling images" break this assumption.

Examples that break with expectations force the viewer to question their understanding of the system. By comparing input and output, the viewer can reason about which features produced the result and form a new theory for how predictions are made.

7.4.3 Interfaces for Exploration

Interfaces such as Pix2Pix and FaceApp allow users to learn about a network by experimenting with it. These interfaces allow users to control input easily and see output immediately. This is a powerful pattern because it allows users to seek out critical cases. Users are able to continually adjust their mental model of how the network behaves by testing their hypotheses immediately.

7.4.4 We Understand Better Together

The visual representations we have discussed, if created for a user at all, have been designed for individuals. Many of these, notably DeepDream, Pix2Pix and FaceApp, have been interpreted significantly on social media. Social networks enable collective sense-making, inspiring users to try similar things and add their results to the conversation. In comments users put into words their questions and theories about the system, where they can be discussed with others. Social networks also select for interesting or surprising content. This allows critical cases to be spread further.

It is possible to design for collective sense-making in neural network interfaces. An interface for collective sense-making might allow users to bookmark and share surprising behaviours and provide a place for users to discuss the content, share explanations and theories. It could also recommend recently viewed and commented bookmarks to encourage users to engage with one another.

7.5 Conclusion

The black box problem remains an ongoing challenge for researchers. Visual representation has proved to be a powerful tool with which to manage complexity and an important means of interpreting neural networks. Researchers in this space are making progress in extracting semantic encodings, developing interactive interfaces, discovering critical cases and negotiating the cultural conception of neural networks, however there is still much work to be done. The interdisciplinary interest in ML underscores the consequences of this technology beyond computer science and the importance of finding explanatory methods. The visual representation of neural networks crosses disciplinary boundaries. In this chapter we have outlined some emerging critical challenges for this research and demonstrated that they can be understood in the context of existing scholarship from disciplines considered far removed from computer science. Solving the black box problem will require critical as well as technical engagement with the neural network.

Acknowledgements We are grateful for the helpful advice of Mitchell Whitelaw throughout the development of this chapter.

References

1. Andrews, F.: CPPNX. https://floybix.github.io/cppnx/ (2017). Accessed 14 Dec 2017
2. Bahdanau, D., Cho, K., Bengio, Y.: Neural machine translation by jointly learning to align and translate. arXiv:1409.0473 (2014)
3. Barocas, S., Selbst, A.: Big data's disparate impact. Calif. Law Rev. **104**(671), 671–732 (2016). https://doi.org/10.15779/Z38BG31
4. Bastian, M., Heymann, S., Jacomy, M.: Others: Gephi: an open source software for exploring and manipulating networks. Icwsm **8**, 361–362 (2009)
5. Bengio, Y.: Learning deep architectures for AI. Found. Trends Mach. Learn. **2**(1), 1–127 (2009)
6. Benitez, J., Castro, J., Requena, I.: Are artificial neural networks black boxes? IEEE Trans. Neural Netw. **8**(5), 1156–1164 (1997)
7. Breiman, L.: Statistical modeling: the two cultures. Stat. Sci. **16**(3), 199–231 (2001)
8. Browne, K.: Interpretable long-range LSTM cells visualisation redrawn from Karpathy Johnson and Fei-Fei 2015. https://gist.github.com/kieranbrowne/70d39b2d46a2444cb64e21f38b81c578 (2017). Accessed 11 Dec 2017
9. Browne, K.: Neural interpretation diagram redrawn from özesmi and özesmi 2005. https://gist.github.com/kieranbrowne/a8d30f80484aebae796d62b85793dcc (2017). Accessed 11 Dec 2017
10. Browne, K.: Neural interpretation diagram redrawn from TZENG and MA 2005. https://gist.github.com/kieranbrowne/8ca74d07adce15f39f0c59fe7bf76f17 (2017). Accessed 18 Dec 2017
11. Browne, K.: Script for fooling images as in Nguyen Yosinski Clune (2015). https://gist.github.com/kieranbrowne/4f9fec38396e56cef88227c91283f242 (2017). Accessed 13 Dec 2017
12. Burgess, M.: Gallery: 'Brain scans' map what happens during inside machine learning. http://www.wired.co.uk/gallery/machine-learning-graphcore-pictures-inside-ai. Accessed 13 Aug 2017
13. Burrell, J.: How the machine thinks': understanding opacity in machine learning algorithms. Big Data Soc. **3**(1) (2016)
14. Craven, M.W., Shavlik, J.W.: Visualizing learning and computation in artificial neural networks. Int. J. Artif. Intell. Tools **1**(3), 399–425 (1992)
15. Cresci, E.: FaceApp apologises for 'racist' filter that lightens users' skintone. https://www.theguardian.com/technology/2017/apr/25/faceapp-apologises-for-racist-filter-which-lightens-users-skintone (2017). Accessed 30 Aug 2017
16. Duch, W.: Coloring black boxes: visualization of neural network decisions. In: Proceedings of the International Joint Conference on Neural Networks, vol. 3, pp. 1735–1740. IEEE (2003)
17. Elgammal, A., Liu, B., Elhoseiny, M., Mazzone, M.: CAN: creative adversarial networks, generating "Art" by learning about styles and deviating from style norms. arXiv:1706.07068 (2017)

18. FaceApp: Faceapp - free neural face transformation filters. https://www.faceapp.com/ (2017). Accessed 21 Dec 2017
19. Fyles, M.: Inside an AI 'brain' - What does machine learning look like? https://www.graphcore.ai/posts/what-does-machine-learning-look-like (2017). Accessed 13 Aug 2017
20. Fyles, M.: Neural network structure, MSR ResNet-50 - large directed graph visualization [OC] : dataisbeautiful. https://www.reddit.com/r/dataisbeautiful/comments/5eowv6/neural_network_structure_msr_resnet50_large/. Accessed 13 Aug 2017
21. Hornik, K., Stinchcombe, M., White, H.: Multilayer feedforward networks are universal approximators. Neural Netw. **2**(5), 359–366 (1989)
22. Isola, P., Zhu, J.Y., Zhou, T., Efros, A.A.: Image-to-image translation with conditional adversarial networks. arXiv:1611.07004 (2016)
23. Karpathy, A., Johnson, J., Li, F.: Visualizing and understanding recurrent networks. CoRR arXiv:1506.02078 (2015)
24. Krizhevsky, A., Sutskever, I., Hinton, G.E.: ImageNet classification with deep convolutional neural networks. Advances in Neural Information Processing Systems **25**(NIPS2012), 1–9 (2012)
25. Längkvist, M., Karlsson, L., Loutfi, A.: A review of unsupervised feature learning and deep learning for time-series modeling. Pattern Recognit. Lett. **42**, 11–24 (2014)
26. Le, Q.V.: Building high-level features using large scale unsupervised learning. In: 2013 IEEE International Conference on Acoustics, Speech and Signal Processing (ICASSP), pp. 8595–8598. IEEE (2013)
27. Manovich, L.: The anti-sublime ideal in data art. http://meetopia.net/virus/pdf-ps_db/LManovich_data_art.pdf (2002). Accessed 21 Dec 2017
28. Mnih, V., Kavukcuoglu, K., Silver, D., Graves, A., Antonoglou, I., Wierstra, D., Riedmiller, M.: Playing atari with deep reinforcement learning. arXiv:1312.5602 (2013)
29. Mordvintsev, A., Olah, C., Tyka, M.: Inceptionism: going deeper into neural networks. https://research.googleblog.com/2015/06/inceptionism-going-deeper-into-neural.html. Accessed 12 Aug 2017
30. Mordvintsev, A., Tyka, M., Olah, C.: Deep dreams (with Caffe). https://github.com/google/deepdream/blob/master/dream.ipynb (2017). Accessed 09 May 2017
31. Nguyen, A., Yosinski, J., Clune, J.: Deep neural networks are easily fooled: high confidence predictions for unrecognizable images. In: Proceedings of the IEEE Conference on Computer Vision and Pattern Recognition, pp. 427–436 (2015)
32. Olden, J.D., Jackson, D.A.: Illuminating the "black box": a randomization approach for understanding variable contributions in artificial neural networks. Ecol. Model. **154**(1–2), 135–150 (2002)
33. Özesmi, S.L., Özesmi, U.: An artificial neural network approach to spatial habitat modelling with interspecific interaction. Ecol. Model. **116**(1), 15–31 (1999)
34. Rosenblatt, F.: Principles of neurodynamics: perceptrons and the theory of brain mechanics. Spartan Book (1962)
35. Sainath, T.N., Vinyals, O., Senior, A., Sak, H.: Convolutional, long short-term memory, fully connected deep neural networks. In: 2015 IEEE International Conference on Acoustics, Speech and Signal Processing (ICASSP), pp. 4580–4584. IEEE (2015)
36. Simonyan, K., Vedaldi, A., Zisserman, A.: Deep inside convolutional networks: visualising image classification models and saliency maps. CoRR arXiv:1312.6034 (2013)
37. Stanley, K.O.: Compositional pattern producing networks: a novel abstraction of development. Genet. Program. Evolvable Mach. **8**(2), 131–162 (2007)
38. Streeter, M., Ward, M., Alvarez, S.A.: NVIS: an interactive visualization tool for neural networks. In: Proceedings of Visual Data Exploration and Analysis Conference (2001)
39. Sussillo, D., Barak, O.: Opening the black box: low-dimensional dynamics in high-dimensional recurrent neural networks. Neural Comput. **25**(3), 626–49 (2013)
40. Tensorflow: Tensorboard: Graph visualization. https://www.tensorflow.org/get_started/graph_viz (2017). Accessed 21 Dec 2017

41. Tunç, B.: Semantics of object representation in machine learning. Pattern Recognit. Lett. **64**, 30–36 (2015). https://doi.org/10.1016/j.patrec.2015.03.016
42. Tzeng, F.Y., Ma, K.L.: Opening the black box-data driven visualization of neural networks. Proceedings of IEEE Visualization **2005**, 383–390 (2005)
43. Zahavy, T., Ben-Zrihem, N., Mannor, S.: Graying the black box: understanding DQNS. In: International Conference on Machine Learning, pp. 1899–1908 (2016)

Part III
Algorithmic Explanation of Machine Learning Models

Chapter 8
Explaining the Predictions of an Arbitrary Prediction Model: Feature Contributions and Quasi-nomograms

Erik Štrumbelj and Igor Kononenko

Abstract Acquisition of knowledge from data is the quintessential task of machine learning. The knowledge we extract this way might not be suitable for immediate use and one or more data postprocessing methods could be applied as well. Data postprocessing includes the integration, filtering, evaluation, and explanation of acquired knowledge. Nomograms, graphical devices for approximate calculations of functions, are a useful tool for visualising and comparing prediction models. It is well known that any generalised additive model can be represented by a quasi-nomogram – a nomogram where some summation performed by the human is required. Nomograms of this type are widely used, especially in medical prognostics. Methods for constructing such a nomogram were developed for specific types of prediction models thus assuming that the structure of the model is known. In this chapter we extend our previous work on a general method for explaining arbitrary prediction models (classification or regression) to a general methodology for constructing a quasi-nomogram for a black-box prediction model. We show that for an additive model, such a quasi-nomogram is equivalent to the one we would construct if the structure of the model was known.

8.1 Introduction

The field of nomography was invented at the end of the 19th century by Maurice d'Ocagne [8]. Up to the final quarter of the 20th century, nomograms were widely used as graphical computers for tasks such as navigation, projectile trajectories, and

E. Štrumbelj (✉) · I. Kononenko
Faculty of Computer and Information Science, University of Ljubljana,
Večna pot 113, 1000 Ljubljana, Slovenia
e-mail: erik.strumbelj@fri.uni-lj.si

I. Kononenko
e-mail: igor.kononenko@fri.uni-lj.si

J. Zhou and F. Chen (eds.), *Human and Machine Learning*, Human–Computer
Interaction Series, https://doi.org/10.1007/978-3-319-90403-0_8

139

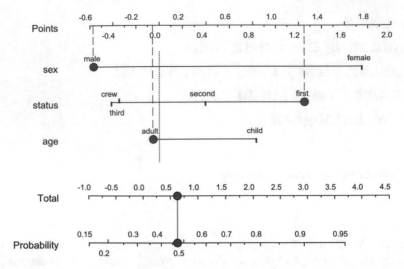

Fig. 8.1 We used the Orange data mining software [7] to produce this quasi-nomogram for the Naive Bayes model on the well known *Titanic* data set. A survival prediction for a specific instance, for example, an adult male travelling first class, is constructed in the following way. First, we mark the value of each input variable on its corresponding axis (three topmost dots) and read their points-contribution on the Points axis (vertical dashed lines). The summation of the three points-contributions is marked on the Total axis ($-0.6 - 0.05 + 1.25 \approx 0.6$). By drawing a straight vertical line, we can convert the sum into a probabilistic prediction. In this case, approximately 45%. Note that the range of the Points scale is determined by the minimum and maximum possible point contribution across all input variable values, while the range of the Total scale is determined by the minimum and maximum possible sum of point contributions across all input variables. The Points and Total axes need not be aligned, because the point summation has to be done manually

other tasks that require the computation of complex formulas. For more information see Doerfler's survey of classical nomography [9].

In this chapter we focus on a specific type of graphical representation (see Fig. 8.1). Unlike a classical nomogram, Fig. 8.1 does not facilitate graphical-only computation (using a straightedge and a pencil), but requires additional summation. In recent years there has been a resurgence of interest in such graphical representations, especially in medical diagnostics and prognostics [6, 10, 15, 16, 24].[1] Note that nearly all related publications simply refer to such graphical representations as nomograms (sometimes as Kattan nomograms), although they do not completely fit the classical definition of a nomogram. In this chapter we promote a clear distinction between the two types of graphical representations and refer to Fig. 8.1 as a quasi-nomogram - a nomogram that requires some additional (non-graphical) computation.

Quasi-nomograms serve a dual purpose. First, they are a tool for producing "offline" predictions. And second, they provide the human with information about

---

[1]www.sciencedirect.com currently lists 1393 research papers that feature the word "nomogram" in the title, keywords, or abstract and were published between 2006 and 2015. Most of them are from the medical field.

the model and the effect of the predictor variables on the target variable. As such, they are a useful tool for decision support and for providing non-experts, for example, patients in a hospital, with insight into their diagnosis and prognosis. Furthermore, quasi-nomograms can also be used by data mining practitioners as a model visualisation and inspection tool. As with other model-visualisation techniques, the informativeness and usefulness of the quasi-nomogram visualisation decreases as the number of input variables increases. However, in practical applications, such as medical prognostics, the number of input variables rarely exceeds 10.

Any generalised additive model can easily be visualised with a quasi-nomogram, which has motivated several model-specific approaches for constructing a quasi-nomogram. In this chapter, however, we show how a quasi-nomogram can be constructed for any (generalised) additive model in a uniform way and, with possible loss of prediction accuracy, for any prediction model. The main idea is to decompose the (unknown) model function into generalised additive form and then estimate each input variable's contribution function on a point-by-point basis. This is made possible by the fact that we do not need the analytical form of these functions to produce a quasi-nomogram. Instead, we only need to plot the functions in some finite resolution.

The remainder of the paper is as follows. The next Section describes our previous work and other related work in the broader area of explaining prediction models and the particular case of using nomograms to visualise models. In Sect. 8.3, we describe the construction of a nomogram for a black-box prediction model. Section 8.4 illustrates the use of the method on several data sets and models. Section 8.5 concludes the paper.

8.2 Explaining the Predictions with Feature Contributions

Prediction models are an integral part of knowledge discovery. How we choose a prediction model for a particular task strongly depends on the problem area. Sometimes we are primarily interested in prediction accuracy, on other occasions, interpretability is equally, if not more important.

Better interpretability is easily achieved by selecting a transparent model. However, more transparent models are usually less accurate than more complex models, often to an extent that we would rather consider making the latter more interpretable. As a result, numerous model-specific and general post-processing methods that provide additional explanation have been proposed (see [2, 22, 29, 35–37] and references therein).

Generating a nomogram for an arbitrary model is directly connected to developing a general (black-box) approach to explaining or increasing the interpretability of a prediction model. We illustrate this problem with a simple linear model $f(x_1, ..., x_n) = f(x) = \beta_0 + \beta_1 x_1 + ... + \beta_n x_n$. If we standardise the input features, we could interpret the coefficient β_i as the i−th feature's global importance (in statistical literature, variable importance). Note that using the features' global importance to select only a subset of features is analogous to a filter method for feature selection.

While the global importance reveals which features are more important, it does not tell us how features influence individual predictions. The difference between what the i-th feature contributes when its value is x_i and what it is expected to contribute:

$$\varphi_i(x) = f(x) - E[f(x)|i - \text{th value unknown}] =$$
$$= \beta_i x_i - \beta_i E[X_i], \qquad (8.1)$$

gives us such a local contribution. Equation (8.1) is also known as the situational importance of $X_i = x_i$ [1].

Because our model is additive, the local contribution of $X_i = x$ is the same across all instances where $X_i = x$, regardless of the values of other features.

The above illustrative example is simple, with a known model that is also additive. However, in our problem setting, we want a general method. The model has to be treated as a black-box - no assumptions are made other than that the model maps from some known input feature space to a known codomain. Therefore, we are limited to sensitivity analysis - changing the inputs and observing the outputs.

General (black-box) approaches are at a disadvantage - not being able to exploit model-specifics makes it more difficult to develop an effective and efficient method. However, being applicable to any type of model also has its advantages. It facilitates comparison of different types of models and, in practical applications, eliminates the need to replace the explanation method when the underlying model is changed or replaced.

Previously developed general approaches [21, 32, 39] tackle the problem in a similar one-feature-at-a-time way. That is, the contribution of a feature is

$$\varphi_i(x) = f(x_1, ..., x_n) - E[f(x_1, ..., X_i, ..., x_n)] \qquad (8.2)$$

Equation (8.2) is the difference between a prediction for an instance and the expected prediction for the same instance if the i-th feature is not known.

In practice, expression Eq. (8.2) can be efficiently approximated (or computed, if the feature's domain is finite). Additionally, if f is an additive model, Eq. (8.2) is equivalent to Eq. (8.1), so we do not lose any of the previously mentioned advantages associated with explaining an additive model.

However, when the features interact, as is often the case, the one-feature-at-a-time approach gives undesirable results. For example, observe the model $f(x_1, x_2) = x_1 \vee x_2$, where both features are uniformly distributed on $\{0, 1\}$. When computing the contribution of the first feature for $f(1, 1) = 1$, we see that perturbing its value does not change the prediction - the first feature's contribution is 0. The same holds for the second feature. Therefore, both features get a 0 contribution, which is clearly incorrect.

This example shows that perturbing one feature at a time gives undesirable results. All subsets have to be taken into account to avoid such issues.

In our previous work, we developed an alternative general approach that tackles the disadvantages of other general approaches described above [35–37]. To summarise the main ideas of the approach, let $\mathcal{X} = [0, 1]^n$ be our feature space and let $f : \mathcal{X} \to \mathfrak{R}$ represent the model that is used to predict the value of the target variable for an instance $x \in \mathcal{X}$. To avoid the shortcomings of other general methods, we observe the contribution of each subset of feature values. For this purpose, Eq. (8.2) is generalised to an arbitrary subset of features:

$$f_Q(x) = \mathbb{E}[f | X_i = x_i, \forall i \in Q], \tag{8.3}$$

where $Q \subseteq S = \{1, 2, ..., n\}$ represents a subset of features. This allows us to define the contribution of a subset of feature values:

$$\Delta_Q(x) = f_Q(x) - f_{\{\}}(x). \tag{8.4}$$

Equation (8.4) can be interpreted as the change in prediction caused by observing the values of a certain subset of features for some instance $x \in \mathcal{X}$.

To obtain each individual feature's local contribution, we map these 2^n terms onto n contributions, one for each feature's value. First, we implicitly define interactions by having the contribution of a subset of feature values equal the sum of all interactions across all subsets of those feature values:

$$\Delta_Q(x) = \sum_{W \subseteq Q} \mathcal{I}_W(x), \tag{8.5}$$

which, together with $\mathcal{I}_{\{\}}(x) = 0$ (an empty set of features contributes nothing), uniquely defines the interactions:

$$\mathcal{I}_Q(x) = \Delta_Q(x) - \sum_{W \subset Q} \mathcal{I}_W(x). \tag{8.6}$$

Finally, each interaction is divided among the participating feature values, which defines the $i-$th features local contribution:

$$\varphi_i(x) = \sum_{W \subseteq S \setminus \{i\}} \frac{\mathcal{I}_{W \cup \{i\}}(x)}{|W| + 1}. \tag{8.7}$$

Figure 8.2 shows two example explanations for an instance from the *monks1* data set (binary class has value 1 iff the value of the 1st feature equals the 2nd feature or the 5th feature's value is 1). The Naive Bayes model, due to its assumptions of conditional independence of input features, cannot model the importance of the equivalence between attr1 and attr2. Despite this limitation, it correctly predicts the class value, because for this instance, attr5 = 1 is sufficient. The artificial neural network correctly models both concepts.

(a)

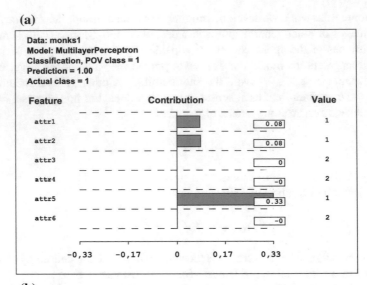

(b)

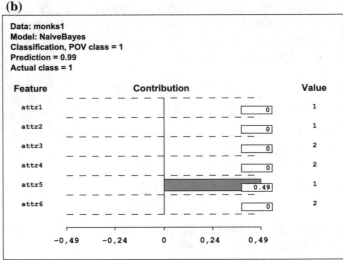

Fig. 8.2 Two visualisations of local contributions for two different models and the same instance from the *monks1* data set. The top of each visualisation shows information about the data set, model, prediction and the actual class value for this instance. The features' names and values for this instance are on the right- and left-hand side, respectively. The value of each feature's local contributions is shown in the corresponding box and visualised

The proposed method correctly reveals which features contribute. On the other hand, one-feature-at-a-time approaches would assign a 0 contribution to all features in the artificial neural network case. Perturbing just one feature does not change the model's prediction.

Equation (8.7) is shown to be equivalent to the Shapley value [33] of a coalitional game, where features are considered players and the generalised contribution is the worth of a coalition of features. This implies several desirable properties (see [35] for a more detailed and formal treatment):

- the local contributions sum up to the difference between the prediction and the expected prediction if no features are known,
- if two features have a symmetrical role in the model, they get the same contribution, and
- if a feature has no role, its contribution is 0.

This also facilitates a game-theoretic interpretation of the shortcoming of existing methods. By not correctly taking into account all interactions they violate the first property and can divide among features more (or less) than what their total worth is.

Computing the proposed local contribution has an exponential time complexity, which limits its practical usefulness. We use an alternative formulation of the Shapley value to derive an efficient sampling-based approximation, which allows us to compute the contributions in polynomial time [35]. The algorithm is extended with an online estimation of the approximation error. This provides a flexible mechanism for trade-off between running times and approximation error. The approximation algorithm is also highly parallelisable - it can be parallelised down to computing a single prediction.

We also considered two improvements that reduce running times (or approximation errors). First, the use of low-discrepancy or quasi-random sequences can improve the convergence of Monte Carlo integration [13]. We used Sobol quasi-random sequences. And second, not all features are equally important and, intuitively, less important features require fewer samples. We derive the optimal way of distributing a finite number of samples between features to minimise the expected approximation error across all n contributions. Empirical results show that non-uniform sampling substantially improves convergence, while quasi-random sampling results in a relatively small improvement. Note that the overall time complexity of generating our nomogram is $O(c \cdot n \cdot M(n))$, where n is the number of input variables, $M(n)$ is the time complexity of generating a single prediction (depends on the model), and c is a number-of-samples-per-feature constant that depends on the desired error and resolution of the nomogram lines (or number of distinct values, for features with a finite number of unique values), but not on the number of input variables n (that is, it does not increase with the number of features).

Generalised additive models are, by definition, written as a sum of the effects of individual input variables, transformed by some link function. Therefore, it is relatively straightforward to visualise any generalised additive model with a quasi-nomogram (see Sect. 8.3 for details). This has led to several model-specific methods for explaining several different types of statistical and machine learning models typically used for prediction: Support Vector Machines [5, 14, 38], the Naive Bayes classifier [20, 23], logistic regression [40]. The proposed approach, however, decomposes an individual prediction among features in a way that takes into account the other features' values. For each feature and its value, we can compute the mean local

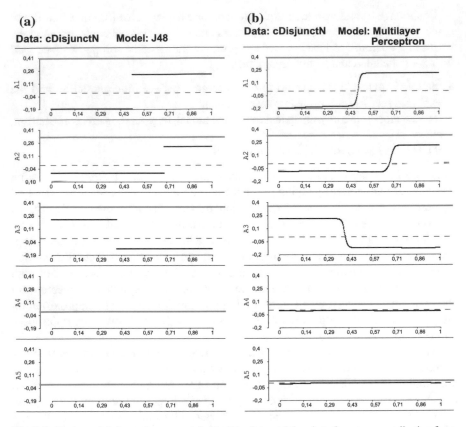

Fig. 8.3 Both models learn the concepts behind the data and the plotted average contribution functions (black) reveal where the individual features' contribution changes from negative to positive. The grey horizontal line represents the root feature importance of the feature

contribution when the feature has that value [36]. This produces, for each feature, a marginal effect function, which is similar to the marginal effect functions used in the construction of nomograms. In fact, we can show that if the underlying model is additive, this will produce equivalent results and this will be the basis for our construction of a nomogram for an arbitrary prediction model (see Sect. 8.3).

Figure 8.3 shows a pair of marginal effect visualisations for two different models on the same *cDisjunctN* data set. Out of the five features, only the first three are relevant. The class value equals 1 if (and only if) $A_1 > 0.5$ or $A_2 > 0.7$ or $A_3 < 0.4$. The visualisation reveals the difference between the step-function fit of the decision tree and smooth fit of the artificial neural network. It also reveals that the artificial neural network slightly overfits the two irrelevant features.

A feature's importance - the variance of its local contributions - can also be efficiently computed using a similar sampling-based approach. In combination with any learning algorithm the global importance can be used as a filter for feature selection. This approach is similar to the in-built feature importance of Random Forests [4] and related to the LMG variable importance method for linear regression models [11].

Note that the practical advantages of explaining model predictions with feature contributions have been established with two applications. Firstly, an application to breast cancer recurrence predictions [34], where it was shown that in 95% of the cases the oncologist agreed with both the direction and the magnitude of the contribution. Furthermore, oncologists found the explanations a beneficiary tool and helpful in increasing their trust in the model's predictions. And second, a survey which showed that providing an explanation significantly improves the humans' predictions and also increases confidence [37]. The usefulness of such an explanation method as a tool for machine learning practitioners is further supported by several documented uses by other researchers in different areas. These include maximum shear stress prediction from hemodynamic simulations [3, 28], coronary artery disease diagnosis from medical images [18, 19], businesses' economic quality prediction [27] and the use of the explanation method to explain the PRBF classification network [30, 31].

8.3 Constructing the Quasi-nomogram

Take a response random variable Y and a set of predictor variables $X_1, X_2, ..., X_n$. In a standard prediction setting, we are interested in how the response variable depends on the values of the predictor variables. We model this relationship with a model f, such that $f(x_1, x_2, ..., x_n) = \mathbb{E}(Y)$. Usually, f is trained (inferred, estimated,...) using a set of labelled training instances $\{(x_{i,1}, x_{i,2}, ..., x_{i,n}, y_i) \in [0, 1]^n \times [0, 1]\}_{i=1}^N$. Without loss of generality, we assumed that the predictor variables' domain ω is a n-dimensional unit cube.

Transparent models, such as the linear regression model $f(x_1, x_2, ..., x_n) = \beta_0 + \beta_1 x_1 + ... + \beta_n x_n$ are self-explanatory.[2] When dealing with less transparent models, we often employ explanation methods and techniques that make the model easier to understand and use. Quasi-nomograms are one such method. They make the model more transparent and can be used for the computation of the model's predictions.

Generalised additive models are a family of models that we can effectively represent with quasi-nomograms similar to one in Fig. 8.1. A generalised additive model can be written as

$$f(x_1, x_2, ..., x_n) = F^{-1}\left(\sum_{i=1}^{n} f_i(x_i) + \beta_0\right) = \mathbb{E}(Y), \tag{8.8}$$

where F is a smooth and bijective link function which relates the expectation to the predictor variables. That is, we try to fit the effect functions f_i, such that

---

[2] Linear regression is, of course, just a special case of generalised additive model with identity link function and linear effect functions

$$F(\mathbb{E}(Y)) = \sum_{i=1}^{n} f_i(x_i) + \beta_0.$$

Because a generalised additive model can be written as a sum of functions of individual predictor variables, we can plot each effect function f_i separately. To reconstruct a model's prediction for a particular instance, we read and sum the values of f_i, for each i (and β_0). Finally, we transform the sum with F^{-1}, which can be done with a simple conversion scale ("Total and Probability" in Fig. 8.1).

The described procedure is simple and effective, but assumes that the structure of the (generalised additive) model f is known. Now we describe a method that can be used to produce a nomogram for any prediction model f. Given a model f and a link function F, we define a set of functions

$$g_i(x) = \mathbb{E}\left(F(f(X_1, X_2, ..., X_i = x, ..., X_n)) - F(f(X_1, ..., X_n))\right),$$

for each $i = 1..n$. The value $g_i(x)$ can be viewed as the expected change in the model's output if the i-th predictor variable is set to x. Observe the model

$$g(x_1, ..., x_n) = F^{-1}\left(\sum_{i=1}^{n} g_i(x_i) + \mathbb{E}(F(f(X_1, ..., X_n)))\right). \tag{8.9}$$

The model in Eq. (8.9) transforms model f into a generalised additive model, without assuming the structure of f. The following useful property can be shown.

Theorem 8.1 *If f is a generalised additive model and F the corresponding link function then $g(x_1, ..., x_n) = f(x_1, ..., x_n)$, for all $(x_1, ..., x_n) \in X_1 \times ... \times X_n$.*

Proof Taking into account the theorem's assumptions:

$$g(x_1, ..., x_n) = F^{-1}\left(\sum_{i=1}^{n} g_i(x_i) + \mathbb{E}(F(f(X_1, ..., X_n)))\right) =$$

$$= F^{-1}\left(\sum_{i=1}^{n} \mathbb{E}(f_i(x_i) - f_i(X_i)) + \sum_{i=1}^{n} \mathbb{E}(f_i(X_i)) + \beta_0\right) =$$

$$= F^{-1}\left(\sum_{i=1}^{n} f_i(x_i) - \sum_{i=1}^{n} \mathbb{E}(f_i(X_i)) + \sum_{i=1}^{n} \mathbb{E}(f_i(X_i)) + \beta_0\right) =$$

$$= F^{-1}\left(\sum_{i=1}^{n} f_i(x_i) + \beta_0\right) = f(x_1, x_2, ..., x_n)$$

$$\tag{8.10}$$

That is, the predictions obtained from g will be the same as the original models' predictions, conditional to f being an additive model or a generalised additive model with known link function F.

To compute the transformed model g, we require functions g_i and

$$\mathbb{E}(F(f(X_1, ..., X_n))).$$

The latter $\mathbb{E}(F(f(X_1, ..., X_n))) = \int_\omega F(f(...))dP$ can be efficiently approximated with simple Monte Carlo integration

$$\mathbb{E}(F(f(X_1, ..., X_n))) \approx \frac{1}{M} \sum_{j=1}^{M} F(f(x_{j,1}, x_{j,2}, ..., x_{j,n})),$$

where the realisations $x_{j,k}$ are obtained by generating a sequence of random samples (that is, instances) according to some distribution P of the input variables' domain ω. Each point $g_i(x)$ can be estimated in a similar way

$$g_i(x) \approx \frac{1}{M} \sum_{j=1}^{M} (F(f(x_{j,1}, ..., x_{j,i} = x, ..., x_{j,n})) - F(f(x_{j,1}, ..., x_{j,n}))).$$

Theorem 8.1 holds for any probability distribution. Therefore, we can choose a distribution that is more convenient for sampling, such as a uniform distribution or a distribution where predictor variables X_i are independently distributed. Note that in general the estimation converges towards the actual value independently of the number of dimensions n. Furthermore, for faster convergence, quasi-random sampling can be used instead of pseudo-random sampling [25, 26]. In our experiments, we used the Sobol low-discrepancy quasi-random sequence [13].

The primary application of the proposed approach is to (generalised) additive models. However, in practice it can also be applied to a potentially non-additive model. In such cases, we are interested in how close the transformed model g is to f and how good the prediction accuracy of g is. The farther away g is from f the less useful the quasi-nomogram is in terms of providing insight into f. It is also possible that g is not close to f but has a better prediction accuracy. In such cases, we should consider using g instead of f, because it is both a better predictor and easier to interpret.

Given a set of N labelled instances, we used the root mean squared error to estimate the model's prediction accuracy

$$e_{g,y} = \sqrt{\frac{1}{N} \sum_{i=1}^{N} (f(x_{i,1}, x_{i,2}, ..., x_{i,n}) - y_i)^2}$$

and the distance between the original model f and the transformed model g

$$e_{f,g} = \sqrt{\frac{1}{N} \sum_{i=1}^{N} \left(f(x_{i,1}, x_{i,2}, ..., x_{i,n}) - g(x_{i,1}, x_{i,2}, ..., x_{i,n})\right)^2}.$$

8.4 Illustrative Examples

We start with a simple toy data set with three input variables A_1, A_2, and A_3 with continuous domains [0, 1] and uniformly distributed values. Let the relationship between the input variables and the target variable Y be linear: $Y = 0.5A_1 - 1.5A_2$. We generated 1000 instances from this data set at random, labelled each instance using the aforementioned linear relationship, and used the instances to train a *multilayer perceptron* artificial neural network model.

Let f be this multilayer perceptron model. The structure of f is unknown, but we can access its value for any point. We used the procedure described in Sect. 8.3 to generate the quasi-nomogram shown in Fig. 8.4a. The quasi-nomogram consists of three effect functions (one for each input variable) and a conversion scale. Each individual effect function graph is used to convert the input variable's value into a point-contribution. This is done by first drawing a straight vertical line that connects the input variable's value to the plotted effect function and then a horizontal line that connects this point to the vertical Points scale, where the points-contribution of this value can be read. The sum of all three variables' points is selected on the left-hand side of the conversion scale and the prediction is readily available to be read on the right-hand side of the conversion scale. Large dots and corresponding lines in Fig. 8.4a illustrate this procedure for the instance (0.6, 0.8, 0.2).

The relationship between the procedure from the previous paragraph and the equations in Sect. 8.3 (Eq. (8.9) in particular) is as follows. Each input variables' effect function is plotted separately, one point at a time. The estimated value $g_i(x)$ corresponds to the value of the i-th input variable's effect function at x. Therefore, horizontal and vertical lines are used to obtain the effect functions' values. The summation part of the procedure produces the sum in Eq. (8.9). The values on the left-hand side of the conversion scale range from the minimum to the maximum possible sum of the effect functions. What remains is to add the expectation $\mathbb{E}(F(f(X_1, ..., X_n))$ and in the case of a non-identity link function F, apply the inverse of the link function F^{-1}. Because F is a bijective and smooth function, both operations are realised simultaneously and the mapped values are written on the right-hand of the conversion scale, where the human can read the final value. Note that the Total to Probability conversion scale from the nomograms generated in Orange (see Fig. 8.1) serves the same purpose as the conversion scale.

Notice that the quasi-nomogram in Fig. 8.4a is for the *multilayer perceptron* model, which is not necessarily additive. In this case the model was close to additive and the additive transformation in Fig. 8.4a was more accurate than the original model ($e_{f,y} = 0.013$, $e_{g,y} = 0.009$, $e_{f,g} = 0.007$). For comparison, *linear regression*, which is well-suited for the linear problem, produces the following results ($e_{f,y} \approx e_{g,y} = 5.8 \times 10^{-11}$). With an additive model such as the linear regression

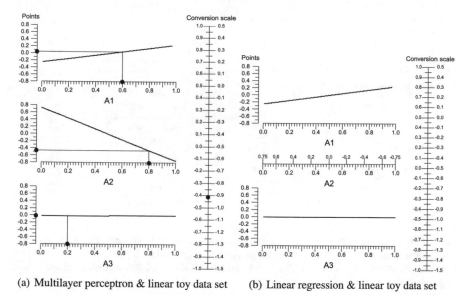

(a) Multilayer perceptron & linear toy data set   (b) Linear regression & linear toy data set

Fig. 8.4 Quasi-nomograms for two different types of models and the same linear problem data set. For this illustrative data set the input variable A_3 is irrelevant to the target variable, which is clear from its flat effect function

model, the transformation g is, at least to a practical precision, the same as the original model ($e_{f,g} = 1.1 \times 10^{-11}$). The quasi-nomogram for the *linear regression* model is shown in Fig. 8.4b and can be used to compare the two different models. Because the structure of the model is not known, A_3 is included in the nomogram, despite being irrelevant. However, the irrelevance of input variable A_3 results in a flat effect function.

Note that input variables with finite domains (see Figs. 8.1 or 8.5b) can be visualised in a more compact way. That is, listing the variable's values on a single axis, as opposed to a 2-dimensional plot. The same applies to continuous input variables for which a visual inspection reveals a linear (or monotonic) effect function (see Fig. 8.4b, input variable A_2, or Fig. 8.6, several variables). For such variables, we can reduce the visualisation by projecting the labelled values onto the x axis as it is clear how to interpolate the effect of in-between values.

Quasi-nomograms are useful even when the effect of input variables is not linear. Consider the second toy data set with two input variables A_1 and A_2 with continuous domains [0, 1] and uniformly distributed values. The target variable is defined as $Y = sin(2\pi A_1) + A_2$. Again, we generated 1000 instances from this data set and used *bagging* to train an ensemble of regression trees. The ensemble gave the following results ($e_{f,y} = 0.048$, $e_{g,y} = 0.041$, $e_{f,g} = 0.034$). For comparison, the results for linear regression were ($e_{f,y} \approx e_{g,y} = 0.43$, $e_{f,g} = 6.2 \times 10^{-16}$). Therefore, the transformed bagging model (see Fig. 8.5a) is more accurate than linear regression, while still easily represented with a quasi-nomogram.

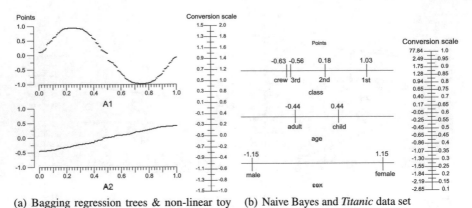

(a) Bagging regression trees & non-linear toy   (b) Naive Bayes and *Titanic* data set
data set

Fig. 8.5 Quasi-nomograms for two different types of models and data sets. The non-linear toy data set has continuous input variables and a continuous target variable. Step effect functions are a characteristic of tree-based models. The *Titanic* data set has discrete input variables and a binomial target variable

Finally, Fig. 8.5b shows the quasi-nomogram for the *Naive Bayes* classifier and the *Titanic* data set. It is equivalent to the quasi-nomogram from the introduction (see Fig. 8.1) that we produced with Orange [7]. That is, the predictions obtained from the two quasi-nomograms for the same instance are equal. For example, if we revisit the adult male travelling first class from Fig. 8.1, but use the quasi-nomogram from Fig. 8.5b instead, we obtain a sum of −0.56 (−1.15 for being male, −0.44 for an adult, and +1.03 for travelling first class). Using the conversion scale this sum converts to approximately 45%, which is the same as the prediction obtained from Fig. 8.1. The two nomograms also offer the same insight into the influence of the input variables on survival. For example, being female or travelling first class contributed more towards survival.

8.4.1 Predicting the Outcome of a Basketball Match

For a more realistic illustration of what data-mining practitioners encounter in practice, we performed the following experiment. For each basketball match of the 2007/08 NBA (National Basketball Association) season, we recorded the winner and the following three summary statistics, for both competing teams: effective field goal percentage (EFG), turnover percentage (TOV), and offensive rebounding percentage (ORB). For a more detailed description of these summary statistics see [17].

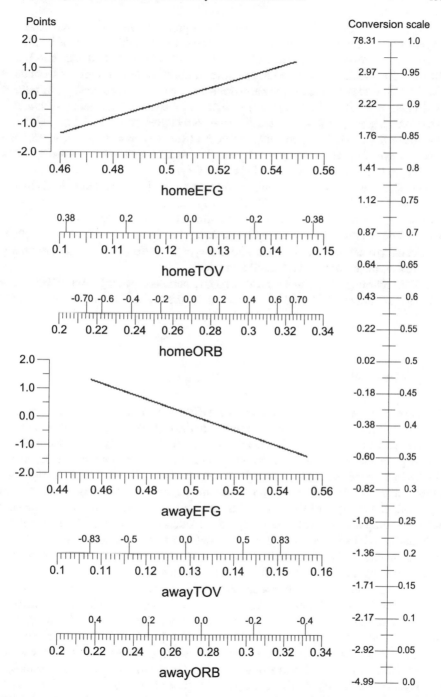

Fig. 8.6 A quasi-nomogram for predicting the win probability of the home team in an NBA basketball match. It is clear from the visualisation that the win probability of the home team increases with its shooting efficiency and decreases with the shooting efficiency of the away team. The remaining four input variables are visualised in a more compact way

This gave us a total of 958 matches with 6 predictor variables and a binomial target variable (match outcome) each. We hypothesised that this data could be used to construct a model which could predict the outcome of NBA basketball matches. Using 10-fold cross-validation, we evaluated several classification models and obtained the following results: *multilayer perceptron* ($e_{f,y} = 0.4554$, percentage of correct predictions = 68.5), *Naive Bayes* ($e_{f,y} = 0.4513$, percentage of correct predictions = 68.7), *bagging* ($e_{f,y} = 0.4565$, percentage of correct predictions = 67.3), and *logistic regression* ($e_{f,y} = 0.443$, percentage of correct predictions = 69.4). Note that the relative frequency of home team win was 0.6, so all four models outperform this default prediction for home team win probability.

Out of all the models, logistic regression gave the best results. Because this model is a generalised additive model (with a log-odds ratio link function $F(x) = ln(\frac{x}{1-x})$), its transformation g is an accurate representation of the original model ($e_{f,g} = 2.7 \times 10^{-16}$). The resulting quasi-nomogram is shown in Fig. 8.6. It can be used both to predict the winner of future matches and to inspect the effect of individual summary statistics on the outcome of a basketball match.

All the learning algorithms we used in our experiments were from the Weka data mining Java library [12], with the exception of the Naive Bayes that we used for Fig. 8.1.

8.5 Conclusion

In our previous work, which we described in Sect. 8.2, we have proposed a method for explaining an arbitrary prediction model in the form of contributions of individual features. In this chapter we extended that work by showing how such a black-box approach to explanation is closely connected to visualising the model in the form of a nomogram or quasi-nomogram. We proposed a method for constructing a quasi-nomogram for a black-box prediction model, only by changing the inputs and observing the changes of the output. This is convenient in situations when working with and comparing several different types of models, when we wish to avoid implementing a model-specific method for constructing a quasi-nomogram, or when such an implementation is not possible (only the model might be available or we want to avoid investing the time and effort necessary for modifying third-party code).

These quasi-nomograms can also be viewed as prediction curve plots (one for each variable) - plots of how the effect of the variable depends on its value. The only difference is that the values of other variables are not fixed, but varied in a way that captures interactions among all subsets of variables (see Sect. 8.2). If the prediction curve is monotonic (strictly increasing or decreasing) or the variable has only a few values, it can be collapsed onto a single axis, as was shown in some of the examples.

As shown in the illustrative examples, the procedure can be applied to classification and regression tasks, discrete and continuous input variables. For models which are known to be of the generalised additive type, the method is interchangeable with any model-specific method, as it produces equivalent quasi-nomograms, and therefore generalises them. The approach is useful for non-additive models as well, especially when the task is additive or when the resulting loss in prediction accuracy is small or outweighed by the benefits with respect to the interpretability offered by the quasi-nomogram. Additionally, non-additivity is straightforward to detect from the variability and it would be possible to visualise the most important pairwise interaction, further improving how the nomogram represents the model. Three-way or higher level interactions become problematic, however, due to the difficulties of effectively visualising, or representing in some other way, three (and higher) dimensional data and for the human to understand such representations.

References

1. Achen, C.H.: Intepreting and Using Regression. Sage Publications (1982)
2. Baehrens, D., Schroeter, T., Harmeling, S., Kawanabe, M., Hansen, K., MÃžller, K.R.: How to explain individual classification decisions. J. Mach. Learn. Res. **11**, 1803–1831 (2010)
3. Bosnić, Z., Vračar, P., Radović, M.D., Devedžić, G., Filipović, N.D., Kononenko, I.: Mining data from hemodynamic simulations for generating prediction and explanation models. IEEE Trans. Inf. Technol. Biomed. **16**(2), 248–254 (2012)
4. Breiman, L.: Random forests. Mach. Learn. J. **45**, 5–32 (2001)
5. Cho, B.H., Yu, H., Lee, J., Chee, Y.J., Kim, I.Y., Kim, S.I.: Nonlinear support vector machine visualization for risk factor analysis using nomograms and localized radial basis function kernels. IEEE Trans. Inf. Technol. Biomed. **12**(2), 247–256 (2008)
6. Chun, F.K.H., Briganti, A., Karakiewicz, P.I., Graefen, M.: Should we use nomograms to predict outcome?. Eur. Urol. Suppl. **7**(5), 396–399 (2008). Update Uro-Oncology 2008, Fifth Fall Meeting of the European Society of Oncological Urology (ESOU)
7. Demšar, J., Zupan, B., Leban, G., Curk, T.: Orange: From experimental machine learning to interactive data mining. In: PKDD'04, pp. 537–539 (2004)
8. d'Ocagne, M.: Traité de nomographie. Gauthier-Villars, Paris (1899)
9. Doerfler, R.: The lost art of nomography. UMAP J. **30**(4), 457–493 (2009)
10. Eastham, J.A., Scardino, P.T., Kattan, M.W.: Predicting an optimal outcome after radical prostatectomy: the trifecta nomogram. J. Urol. **79**(6), 2011–2207 (2008)
11. Grömping, U.: Estimators of relative importance in linear regression based on variance decomposition. Am. Stat. **61**(2), (2007)
12. Hall, M., Frank, E., Holmes, G., Pfahringer, B., Reutemann, P., Witten, I.H.: The WEKA data mining software: an update. SIGKDD Explor. Newsl. **11**(1), 10–18 (2009)
13. Jaeckel, P.: Monte Carlo Methods in Finance. Wiley, New York (2002)
14. Jakulin, A., Možina, M., Demšar, J., Bratko, I., Zupan, B.: Nomograms for visualizing support vector machines. In: KDD '05: Proceeding of the eleventh ACM SIGKDD International Conference on Knowledge Discovery In Data Mining, pp. 108–117. ACM, New York, USA (2005)
15. Kanao, K., Mizuno, R., Kikuchi, E., Miyajima, A., Nakagawa, K., Ohigashi, T., Nakashima, J., Oya, M.: Preoperative prognostic nomogram (probability table) for renal cell carcinoma based on tnm classification. J. Urol. **181**(2), 480–485 (2009)
16. Kattan, M.W., Marasco, J.: What is a real nomogram. Semin. Oncol. **37**(1), 23–26 (2010)
17. Kubatko, J., Oliver, D., Pelton, K., Rosenbaum, D.T.: A starting point for analyzing basketball statistics. J. Quantit. Anal. Sports **3**(3), 00–01 (2007)
18. Kukar, M., Grošelj, C.: Supporting diagnostics of coronary artery disease with neural networks. In: Adaptive and Natural Computing Algorithms, pp. 80–89. Springer, Berlin (2011)

19. Kukar, M., Kononenko, I., Grošelj, C.: Modern parameterization and explanation techniques in diagnostic decision support system: a case study in diagnostics of coronary artery disease. Artif. Intell. Med. **52**(2), 77–90 (2011)
20. Lee, K.M., Kim, W.J., Ryu, K.H., Lee, S.H.: A nomogram construction method using genetic algorithm and naive Bayesian technique. In: Proceedings of the 11th WSEAS International Conference on Mathematical and Computational Methods In Science And Engineering, pp. 145–149. World Scientific and Engineering Academy and Society (WSEAS), Stevens Point, Wisconsin, USA (2009)
21. Lemaire, V., Féraud, R., Voisine, N.: Contact personalization using a score understanding method. In: International Joint Conference on Neural Networks (IJCNN) (2008)
22. Lughofer, E., Richter, R., Neissl, U., Heidl, W., Eitzinger, C., Radauer, T.: Advanced linguistic explanations of classifier decisions for users' annotation support. In: 2016 IEEE 8th International Conference on Intelligent Systems (IS), pp. 421–432. IEEE, New York (2016)
23. Možina, M., Demšar, J., Kattan, M., Zupan, B.: Nomograms for visualization of naive Bayesian classifier. In: PKDD '04: Proceedings of the 8th European Conference on Principles and Practice of Knowledge Discovery in Databases, pp. 337–348. Springer, New York, USA (2004)
24. Nguyen, C.T., Stephenson, A.J., Kattan, M.W.: Are nomograms needed in the management of bladder cancer?. Urol. Oncol. Semin. Orig. Investig. **28**(1), 102 – 107 (2010). Proceedings: Midwinter Meeting of the Society of Urologic Oncology (December 2008): Updated Issues in Kidney, Bladder, Prostate, and Testis Cancer
25. Niederreiter, H.: Low-discrepancy and low-dispersion sequences. J. Number Theory **30**(1), 51–70 (1988)
26. Niederreiter, H.: Random Number Generation and Quasi-Monte Carlo Methods. Society for Industrial and Applied Mathematics, Philadelphia, PA, USA (1992)
27. Pregeljc, M., Štrumbelj, E., Mihelcic, M., Kononenko, I.: Learning and explaining the impact of enterprises organizational quality on their economic results. Intelligent Data Analysis for Real-Life Applications: Theory and Practice pp. 228–248 (2012)
28. Radović, M.D., Filipović, N.D., Bosnić, Z., Vračar, P., Kononenko, I.: Mining data from hemodynamic simulations for generating prediction and explanation models. In: 2010 10th IEEE International Conference on Information Technology and Applications in Biomedicine (ITAB), pp. 1–4. IEEE, New York (2010)
29. Robnik-Šikonja, M., Kononenko, I.: Explaining classifications for individual instances. IEEE Trans. Knowl. Data Eng. **20**(5), 589–600 (2008)
30. Robnik-Šikonja, M., Kononenko, I., Štrumbelj, E.: Quality of classification explanations with prbf. Neurocomputing **96**, 37–46 (2012)
31. Robnik-Šikonja, M., Likas, A., Constantinopoulos, C., Kononenko, I., Štrumbelj, E.: Efficiently explaining decisions of probabilistic RBF classification networks. In: Adaptive and Natural Computing Algorithms, pp. 169–179. Springer, Berlin (2011)
32. Robnik-Šikonja, M., Kononenko, I.: Explaining classifications for individual instances. IEEE TKDE **20**, 589–600 (2008)
33. Shapley, L.S.: A Value for n-person games. Contributions to the Theory of Games, vol. II. Princeton University Press, Princeton (1953)
34. Štrumbelj, E., Bosnić, Z., Zakotnik, B., Grašič-Kuhar, C., Kononenko, I.: Explanation and reliability of breast cancer recurrence predictions. Knowl. Inf. Syst. **24**(2), 305–324 (2010)
35. Štrumbelj, E., Kononenko, I.: An efficient explanation of individual classifications using game theory. J. Mach. Learn. Res. **11**, 1–18 (2010)
36. Štrumbelj, E., Kononenko, I.: A general method for visualizing and explaining black-box regression models. In: Dobnikar A., Lotric U., Ster B. (eds.) ICANNGA (2). Lecture Notes in Computer Science, vol. 6594, pp. 21–30. Springer, Berlin (2011)
37. Štrumbelj, E., Kononenko, I.: Explaining prediction models and individual predictions with feature contributions. Knowl. Inf. Syst. **41**(3), 647–665 (2014)
38. Vien, N.A., Viet, N.H., Chung, T., Yu, H., Kim, S., Cho, B.H.: Vrifa: a nonlinear SVM visualization tool using nomogram and localized radial basis function (LRBF) kernels. In: CIKM, pp. 2081–2082 (2009)

39. Zien, A., Krämer, N., Sonnenburg, S., Rätsch, G.: The feature importance ranking measure. In: ECML PKDD 2009, Part II, pp. 694–709. Springer, Berlin (2009)
40. Zlotnik, A., Abraira, V.: A general-purpose nomogram generator for predictive logistic regression models. Stata J. **15**(2), 537–546 (2015)

Chapter 9
Perturbation-Based Explanations of Prediction Models

Marko Robnik-Šikonja and Marko Bohanec

Abstract Current research into algorithmic explanation methods for predictive models can be divided into two main approaches: gradient-based approaches limited to neural networks and more general perturbation-based approaches which can be used with arbitrary prediction models. We present an overview of perturbation-based approaches, with focus on the most popular methods (EXPLAIN, IME, LIME). These methods support explanation of individual predictions but can also visualize the model as a whole. We describe their working principles, how they handle computational complexity, their visualizations as well as their advantages and disadvantages. We illustrate practical issues and challenges in applying the explanation methodology in a business context on a practical use case of B2B sales forecasting in a company. We demonstrate how explanations can be used as a what-if analysis tool to answer relevant business questions.

9.1 Introduction

Machine learning models play an increasingly large role in many applications, products, and services. Their outcomes are part of everyday life (e.g., entertainment recommendations), as well as life-changing decisions (e.g., medical diagnostics, credit scoring, or security systems). We can expect that reliance on technology and machine learning will only increase in the future. It is only natural that those affected by various automated decisions want to get feedback and understand the reason-

M. Robnik-Šikonja (✉)
Faculty of Computer and Information Science, University of Ljubljana,
Večna pot 113, 1000 Ljubljana, Slovenia
e-mail: marko.robnik@fri.uni-lj.si

M. Bohanec
Salvirt Ltd., Dunajska 136, 1000 Ljubljana, Slovenia
e-mail: marko.bohanec@salvirt.com

© Springer International Publishing AG, part of Springer Nature 2018
J. Zhou and F. Chen (eds.), *Human and Machine Learning*, Human–Computer
Interaction Series, https://doi.org/10.1007/978-3-319-90403-0_9

ing process and biases of the underlying models. Areas where model transparency is of crucial importance include public services, medicine, science, policy making, strategic planning, business intelligence, finance, marketing, insurance, etc. In these areas, users of models are just as interested to comprehend the decision process, as in the classification accuracy of prediction models. Unfortunately, most of the top performing machine learning models are black boxes in a sense that they do not offer an introspection into their decision processes or provide explanations of their predictions and biases. This is true for Artificial Neural Networks (ANN), Support Vector Machines (SVM), and all ensemble methods (for example, boosting, random forests, bagging, stacking, and multiple adaptive regression splines). Approaches that do offer an intrinsic introspection, such as decision trees or decision rules, do not perform so well or are not applicable in many cases [23].

To alleviate this problem two types of model explanation techniques have been proposed. The first type, which is not discussed in this chapter, is based on the internal working of the particular learning algorithm. The explanation methods exploit a model's representation or learning process to gain insight into the presumptions, biases and reasoning leading to final decisions. Two well-known models where such approach works well are neural networks and random forests. Recent neural networks explainers mostly rely on layer-wise relevance propagation [6] or gradients of output neurons with respect to the input [32] to visualise parts of images significant for particular prediction. The random forest visualisations mostly exploit the fact that during bootstrap sampling, which is part of this learning algorithm, some of the instances are not selected for learning and can serve as an internal validation set. With the help of this set, important features can be identified and similarity between objects can be measured.

The second type of explanation approaches are general and can be applied to any predictive model. The explanations provided by these approaches try to efficiently capture the causal relationship between inputs and outputs of the given model. To this end, they perturb the inputs in the neighbourhood of a given instance to observe effects of perturbations on the model's output. Changes in the outputs are attributed to perturbed inputs and used to estimate their importance for a particular instance. Examples of this approach are methods EXPLAIN [29], IME [35], and LIME [27]. These methods can explain the model's decision for each individual predicted instance as well as for the model as a whole. As they are efficient, offer comprehensible explanations, and can be visualised, they are the focus of this chapter. Other explanation methods are discussed in the background section.

Another aspect we try to address is how explanations of prediction models can be put into practical use. We are interested in the integration of explanations into a complex business decision process and their support of continuous organisational learning. Users of knowledge-based systems are more likely to adhere to automatic predictions, when, besides the predictive performance of models, explanations are also available [4]. In order to apply prediction models, users have to trust them first, and the model's transparency is a major factor in ensuring the trust. We illustrate an application of explanation methodology to a challenging real-world B2B sales forecasting [11]. A group of sales experts collected historical B2B sales cases to build a machine learning prediction model. The explanations of past and new cases enabled cognitive evaluation of the model. Based on the new insights, provided by the explanations, experts can update the data set, propose new features, and re-evaluate the models. We discuss several issues arising and how they can be addressed with the explanation methodology.

The objectives of the chapter are twofold. First, to explain how general perturbation-based explanation methods work, and second, to demonstrate their practical utility in a real-world scenario. The first aim is achieved through an explanation of their working principle and graphical explanation of models' decisions on a well-known data set. Two types of explanations are demonstrated, individual predictions of new unlabelled cases and functioning of the model as a whole. This allows inspection, comparison, and visualisation of otherwise opaque models. The practical utility of the methodology is demonstrated on the B2B sales forecasting problem.

The structure of the chapter is as follows. In Sect. 9.2 we present a taxonomy of explanation methodologies and present background and related work on perturbation-based approaches. In Sect. 9.3 we present methods EXPLAIN, IME, and LIME, their similarity and differences. Explanations in a business context are discussed in Sect. 9.4 through B2B sales forecasting. In Sect. 9.5 we present conclusions.

9.2 Background and Overview of Perturbation Approaches

True causal relationships between dependent and independent variables are typically hidden except in artificial domains where all the relations, as well as the probability distributions, are known in advance. Therefore only explanations of the prediction process for a particular model is of practical importance. The prediction accuracy and the correctness of explanation for a given model may be orthogonal: the correctness of the explanation is independent of the correctness of the prediction. However, empirical observations show that better models (with higher prediction accuracy) enable better explanations [35]. We discuss two types of explanations:

- **Instance explanation** explains predictions with the given model of individual instances and provides the impact of input feature values on the predictions.
- **Model explanation** is usually an aggregation of instance explanations over many (training) instances, to provide top-level explanations of features and their values. This aggregation over many instances enables identification of different roles attributes may play in the classifications of instances.

Below we list several properties of machine learning explanations. They stem from criteria for evaluation of rule extraction methods from neural networks introduced by [2] and later extended by [18]. Some items were proposed by [21, 27], and some are the result of our work.

1. *Expressive power* describes the language of extracted explanations: propositional logic (i.e. if-then rules), nonconventional logic (e.g., fuzzy logic), first-

order logic, finite state machines (deterministic, nondeterministic, stochastic), histograms, decision trees, linear models, a limited form of natural language etc.

2. *Translucency* describes the degree to which an explanation method looks inside the model. It can be decompositional (decomposes internal representation of the model, e.g., in neural networks meaning of individual neurons), pedagogical (treating the model as a black box), or eclectic (combining both compositional and pedagogical types).

3. *Portability* describes how well the technique covers the range of different models (e.g., limited to convolutional neural networks, suitable for additive models, general, etc.).

4. *Algorithmic complexity* deals with the computational complexity of algorithms producing explanations.

Quality of explanations is another very important aspect, which groups several properties of explanation methods:

5. *Accuracy*: the ability that explanation of a given decision generalises to other yet unseen instances. For example, if explanations are in the form of rules, are these rules general and do they cover unseen instances.

6. *Fidelity*: how well the explanations reflect the behaviour of the prediction model. *Local fidelity* expresses how well the explanations reflect the behaviour of the prediction model in the vicinity of predicted instances. Local fidelity does not imply general fidelity (e.g., features that are important in a local context may not be important in the global context of the model).

7. *Consistency*: the degree to which similar explanations are generated from different models trained on the same task. For example, while similar models may produce very similar predictions, the explanations of similar instances may vary due to the variance of certain explanation methods.

8. *Stability*: the degree to which similar explanations are generated for similar instances. Different to *consistency*, which covers several models, this criterion deals with explanations generated from the same model. As for consistency, while predictions of similar instances may be the same, the explanations may vary due to the variance of certain explanation methods.

9. *Comprehensibility*: readability of explanations (might depend on the audience, e.g., experts or the general public) and size of explanations (e.g., number of rules, number of items shown on a bar chart, number of words, number of factors in linear model etc.).

10. *Certainty*: are explanations reflecting certainty of a model about its predictions? For example, a classifier may be very certain of its prediction, but the explanation may or may not reflect it.

11. *Degree of importance*: are explanations reporting the degree of importance for each returned item (e.g., the importance of explained features, or importance of returned rules)?

12. *Novelty*: is a form of certainty and tells if explanations would reflect the fact that explained instance is from a new region, not contained or well represented in the training set (the model may be unreliable for such instances).

13. *Representativeness*: are explanations representative of the model? For example, a model explanation may cover behaviour of the whole model, or just a part of it.

In a typical data science problem setting, users are concerned with both prediction accuracy and the interpretability of the prediction model. Complex models have potentially higher accuracy but are more difficult to interpret. This can be alleviated either by sacrificing some prediction accuracy for a more transparent model or by using an explanation method that improves the interpretability of the model. Explaining predictions is straightforward for symbolic models such as decision trees, decision rules, and inductive logic programming, where the models give an overall transparent knowledge in a symbolic form. Therefore, to obtain the explanations of predictions, one simply has to read the rules in the corresponding model. Whether such an explanation is comprehensive in the case of large trees or large rule sets is questionable. Reference [24] developed criteria for decision trees and performed a user study, which showed that the depth of the deepest leaf that is required when answering a question about a classification tree is the most important factor influencing the comprehensibility.

For non-symbolic models, there are no intrinsic explanations. A lot of effort has been invested into increasing the interpretability of complex models. For SVM, [16] proposed an approach based on self-organising maps that groups instances then projects the groups onto a two-dimensional plane. In this plane, the topology of the groups is hopefully preserved and support vectors can be visualised. Many approaches exploit the essential property of additive classifiers to provide more comprehensible explanations and visualisations, e.g., [19, 25].

Visualisation of decision boundaries is an important aspect of model transparency. Reference [9] present a technique to visualise how the kernel embeds data into a high-dimensional feature space. With their Kelp method, they visualise how kernel choice affects neighbourhood structure and SVM decision boundaries. Reference [31] propose a general framework for visualisation of classifiers via dimensionality reduction. Reference [15] propose another useful visualisation tool for classifiers that can produce individual conditional expectation plots, graphing the functional relationship between the predicted response and the feature for individual instance.

Some explanations methods (including the ones presented in Sect. 9.3) are general in a sense that they can be used with any type of prediction model that returns a numeric score (either probability of a class or numeric prediction) [20, 27, 29, 34]. This enables their application with almost any prediction model and allows users to analyse and compare outputs of different analytical techniques. [20] applied their method to a customer relationship management system in the telecommunications industry. The method which successfully deals with high-dimensional text data is presented in [22]. Its idea is based on general explanation methods EXPLAIN and IME and offers an explanation in the form of a set of words which would change the predicted class of a given document. Reference [13] adapt the general explanation methodology to a data stream scenario and show the evolution of attribute contributions through time. This is used to explain the concept drift in their incremental model. In a real-life breast cancer recurrence prediction, [33] illustrate the usefulness of the visualisations and the advantage of using the general explanation method. Several machine learning algorithms were evaluated. Predictions were enhanced with instance explanations using the IME method. Visual inspection and evaluation showed that oncologists found the explanations useful and agreed with the computed contributions of features. Reference [26] used traditional modelling approaches together with data mining to gain insight into the connections between the quality of organisation in enterprises and the enterprises performance. The best performing models were complex and difficult to interpret, especially for non-technical users. Methods EXPLAIN and IME explained the influence of input features on the predicted economic results and provided insights with a meaningful economic interpretation. The interesting economic relationships and successful predictions come mostly from complex models such as random forests and ANN. Without proper explanation and visualisation, these models are often neglected in favour of weaker, but more transparent models. Experts from the economic-organisational field, which reviewed and interpreted the results of the study, agreed that such an explanation and visualisation is useful and facilitates comparative analysis across different types of prediction models.

Many explanation methods are related to statistical sensitivity analysis and uncertainty analysis [30]. In that methodology, the sensitivity of models is analysed with respect to models' input. A related approach, called inverse classification [1], tries to determine the minimum required change to a data point in order to reclassify it as a member of a different class. An SVM model based approach is proposed by [8]. Another sensitivity analysis-based approach explains contributions of individual features to a particular classification by observing (partial) derivatives of the classifiers' prediction function at the point of interest [7]. A limitation of this approach is that the classification function has to be first-order differentiable. For classifiers not satisfying this criterion (for example, decision trees) the original classifier is first fitted with a Parzen window-based classifier that mimics the original one and then the explanation method is applied to this fitted classifier. The method was used in practice with kernel-based classification method to predict molecular features [17].

Due to recent successes of deep neural networks in image recognition and natural language processing, several explanation methods specific to these two application areas emerged. Methods working on images try to visualise parts of images (i.e., groups of pixels) significant for a particular prediction. These methods mostly rely on the propagation of relevance within the network, e.g., layer-wise relevance propagation [6], or computation of gradients of output neurons with respect to the input [32]. In language processing, [5] applied layer-wise relevance propagation to a convolutional neural network and a bag-of-words SVM classifier trained on a topic categorisation task. The explanations indicate how much individual words contribute to the overall classification decision.

9.3   Methods EXPLAIN, IME, and LIME

General explanation methods can be applied to any classification model which makes them a useful tool both for interpreting models (and their predictions) and comparing different types of models. By modification of feature values of interest, what-if analysis is also supported. Such methods cannot exploit any model-specific properties (e.g., gradients in ANN) and are limited to perturbing the inputs of the model and observing changes in the model's output [20, 29, 34].

The three presented general explanation methods provide two types of explanations for prediction models: instance explanations and model explanations (see Sect. 9.2). Model explanations work by summarising a representative sample of instance explanations. All three methods estimate the impact of a particular feature on the prediction of a given instance by perturbing similar instances.

The key idea of EXPLAIN and IME is that the contribution of a particular input value (or set of values) can be captured by "hiding" the input value (set of values) and observing how the output of the model changes. As such, the key component of general explanation methods is the expected conditional prediction - the prediction where only a subset of the input variables is known. Let Q be a subset of the set of input variables $Q \subseteq S = \{X_1, \ldots, X_a\}$. Let $p_Q(y_k|x)$ be the expected prediction for x, conditional to knowing only the input variables represented in Q:

$$p_Q(y_k|x) = \mathbb{E}(p(y_k)|X_i = x_{(i)}, \forall X_i \in Q). \tag{9.1}$$

Therefore, $p_S(y_k|x) = p(y_k|x)$. The difference between $p_S(y_k|x)$ and $p_Q(y_k|x)$ is a basis for explanations. In practical settings, the classification function of the model is not known - one can only access its prediction for any vector of input values. Therefore, an exact computation of $p_Q(y_k|x)$ is not possible and sampling-based approximations are used.

In model explanations, to avoid loss of information due to summarisation of instance level explanations, in the presented visualisation the evidence for and against each class is collected separately. In this way, one can, for example, see that a particular value of an attribute supports specific class but not in every context.

9.3.1   EXPLAIN, One-Variable-at-a-Time Approach

The EXPLAIN method computes the influence of a feature value by observing its impact on the model's output. The EXPLAIN method assumes that the larger the changes in the output, the more important role the feature value plays in the model. The shortcoming of this approach is that it takes into account only a single feature at a time, therefore it cannot detect certain higher order dependencies (in particular disjunctions) and redundancies in the model. The EXPLAIN method assumes that the characterisation of the i-th input variable's importance for the prediction of the instance x is the difference between the model's prediction for that instance and the model's prediction if the value of the i-th variable was not known, namely: $p(y_k|x) - p_{S\setminus\{i\}}(y_k|x)$. If this difference is large then the i-th variable is important. If it is small then the variable is less important. The sign of the difference reveals whether the value contributes towards or against class value y_k. This approach was extended in [29] to use log-odds ratios (or weight of evidence) instead of the difference in predicted class probabilities.

To demonstrate behaviour of the method, an example of an explanation is given. We use a binary classification problem with three important (A_1, A_2, and A_3) and one irrelevant attribute (A_4), so the set of attributes is $S = \{1, 2, 3, 4\}$. Let us assume that the learned model correctly expresses the class value as the parity (xor) relation of three attributes $C = A_1 \oplus A_2 \oplus A_3$. The correct model would classify an instance $x = (A_1 = 1, A_2 = 0, A_3 = 1, A_4 = 1)$ to class $C = 0$, and assigns it probability $p(C = 0|x) = 1$. When explaining classification for this particular instance $p(C = 0|x)$, method EXPLAIN simulates the lack of knowledge of a single attribute at a time, so one has to estimate $p_{S-\{1\}}(C = 0|x)$, $p_{S-\{2\}}(C = 0|x)$, $p_{S-\{3\}}(C = 0|x)$, and $p_{S-\{4\}}(C = 0|x)$. Without the knowledge about the values of each of the attributes A_1, A_2, and A_3, the model cannot correctly determine the class value, so the correct estimates of class probabilities are $p_{S-\{1\}}(C = 0|x) = p_{S-\{2\}}(C = 0|x) = p_{S-\{3\}}(C = 0|x) = 0.5$ The differences of probabilities $p_S(y_k|x) - p_{S-\{i\}}(y_k|x)$ therefore equal 0.5 for each of the three important attributes, which indicate that these attributes have positive impact on classification to class 0 for the particular instance x. The irrelevant attribute A4 does not influence the classification, so the classification probability remain unchanged $p_{S-\{4\}}(C = 0|x) = 1$. The difference of probabilities $p_S(C = 0|x) - p_{S-\{4\}}(C = 0|x) = 0$ so the explanation of the irrelevant attributes impact is zero.

The produced explanations, i.e. conditional probabilities of Eq. (9.1) computed for each feature separately with EXPLAIN method can be visualised with a form of quasi-nomograms. The positive and negative impacts of each feature for a given class value are presented separately. We present an example of this visualisation in Sect. 9.3.4.

9.3.2 IME, All-Subsets Approach

The one-variable-at-a-time approach is simple and computationally less-intensive but has some disadvantages. The main disadvantage is that disjunctive concepts or redundancies between input variables may result in unintuitive contributions for variables [35]. A solution was proposed in [34], where all subsets of values are observed. Such procedure demands 2^a steps, where a is the number of attributes, and results in the exponential time complexity. However, the contribution of each variable corresponds to the Shapley value for the coalitional game of a players. This allows an efficient approximation based on sampling.

9.3.3 LIME, Optimisation of Explanations

LIME (Local Interpretable Model-agnostic Explanations) [27] efficiently calculates explanations also for very large data sets in terms of a number of instances and number of features. It uses perturbations in the locality of an explained instance to produce explanations (e.g., in a fashion of locally weighted regression). It defines explanations as an optimisation problem and tries to find a trade-off between local fidelity of explanation and its interpretability. The search space is over explanations generated by interpretable models $g \in G$, where G is a class of interpretable models. These are not necessary input features but can be linear models, decision trees, or rule lists. Interpretability is quantified with the complexity of explanations $\Omega(g)$, where complexity measure Ω can be the depth of tree for decision trees or the number of non-zero weights for linear models. The model f being explained has to return numeric values $f : \Re^d \to \Re$, for example probability scores in classification. Locality is defined using a proximity measure π between the explained instance x and perturbed points z in its neighbourhood. Local fidelity $L(f, g, \pi)$ is a measure of how unfaithful the explanation model g is in approximating the prediction model f in the locality defined by $\pi(x, z)$. The chosen explanation then minimises the sum of local infidelity L and complexity Ω:

$$e(x) = \arg\min_{g \in G} L(f, g, \pi) + \Omega(g) \qquad (9.2)$$

The approach uses sampling around explanation instance x to draw samples z weighted by the distance $\pi(x, z)$. The samples form a training set for a model g from an interpretable model class, e.g., a linear model. Due to locality enforced by π, the model g is hopefully a faithful approximation of f. In practice, [27] use linear models as a class of interpretable models G, the squared loss as a local infidelity measure, number of non-zero weights as complexity measure Ω, and choose sample points in the neighbourhood of explanation instance x according to the Gaussian distribution of distance between x and sampled point z.

To explain text classification tasks, LIME uses bag-of-words representation to output a limited number of the most locally influential words. In image classification, it returns a list of the most influential image areas (super-pixels) for particular prediction.

By presenting explanation as an optimisation problem, LIME avoids the exponential search space of all feature combinations which is solved by game-theory based sampling in IME. However, LIME offers no guarantees that the explanations are faithful and stable. Using neighbourhood around explanation instance, it may fall into a curse of dimensionality trap, which is fatal for neighbourhood-based methods like kNN in high dimensional spaces. The problem of feature interactions is seemingly avoided by using approximating function from a class of interpretable explanation but the problem is just swept under the carpet, as the interpretable explanation class may not be able to detect them (e.g., linear functions). Further investigation of this question is needed and we suggest a combination of IME and LIME components as a further work. An idea worth pursuing seems to be integration of game theory based sampling from IME and explanations as optimisation used in LIME.

9.3.4 Presenting Explanations

The explanations produced by EXPLAIN and their visualisation are illustrated on the well-known Titanic data set (we used the version accompanying the Orange toolkit [14]). The task is to classify survival of passengers in the disaster of the HMS Titanic ship. The three input variables report the passengers' status during travel (first, second, third class, or crew), age (adult or child), and gender (male or female). We have chosen this data set due to its simplicity but note the similarity of the problem with many business decision problems, such as churn prediction, mail response, insurance fraud, etc. As an example of an opaque prediction model, we use random forest (rf) classifier. This is an ensemble of many (typically hundreds), almost random, tree models. While this approach typically produces models with good predictive performance (on the Titanic problem the classification accuracy is 78%), the models are incomprehensible.

We demonstrate explanations extracted from the random forest model. Figure 9.1a shows an example of an instance explanation for the prediction of the instance with id 583 (a second class adult female passenger). The text at the top includes the predicted value ("survived = yes"), instance id (583), and model name (rf). Below the graph, there is information on the explanation method (EXPLAIN, using the weight of evidence), the model's prediction (P("survived = yes") = 0.86), and the actual class value of the instance ("survived = no"). The input variables' names are shown on the left-hand side (sex, age, and class) and their values for the particular instance are on the right-hand side (female, adult, and second class). The thick dark shaded bars going from the centre to the right or left indicate the contributions of the instance's values for each corresponding input variable towards or against the class value "survived = yes", respectively. The longer the bars the stronger the contributions of the corresponding feature values. The scale of the horizontal axis depends on the explanation method. For the EXPLAIN method and weight of evidence (WE) shown in Fig. 9.1a, the horizontal axis shows the log-odds transformed difference of probabilities (see Sect. 9.3.1). The thinner and lighter bars above the thick dark bars indicate average contributions of these values across all training instances. For the given instance, one can observe that both "sex = female" and "status = second class" speaks in favour of survival (therefore the model is pretty sure of survival with probability 86%), while being an adult has a tiny negative influence. Thinner average bars above them reveal that being a female is on average beneficial, while a second class can have both positive and negative impact. Being an adult has on average a tiny negative impact. Note that the same visualisation can be used even if some other classification method is applied.

A more general view of the model is provided by averaging the explanations over all training set instances. This summary form visualisation shows the average impor-

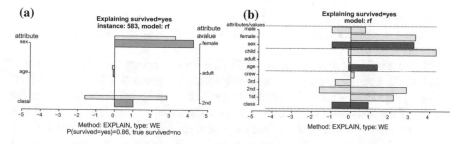

Fig. 9.1 An instance explanation (on the left-hand side) and a model explanation (on the right-hand side) for the random forest model classifying the Titanic data set

tance of each input variable and its values. An example of such model explanation for the Titanic data set is presented in Fig. 9.1b. On the left-hand side, the input variables and their values are shown. For each value, the average negative and the average positive contributions across all instances is displayed. Note that negative and positive contributions would cancel each other out if summed together, so it is important to keep them separate. The lighter bars shown are equivalent to the lighter bars in the instance explanation on Fig. 9.1a. For each input variable, the average positive and negative contributions for all values and instances are shown (darker bars). The visualisation reveals that travelling in first class or being a child or female has a strong positive contribution towards survival, travelling in third class has a predominately negative contribution, while other statuses have smaller or mixed effect in the random forest model. For more complex data sets with many attributes the visualisation of model explanation may become cluttered, so we can set the threshold and only visualise the most important values.

The presented visualisations are produced by the function explainVis from R package ExplainPrediction [28], which has many parameters controlling the computation of explanations and their visualisation. The most important parameters controlling computation of explanations are the type of explanation (EXPLAIN, IME), which class value shall be explained, and parameters specific for EXPLAIN (how the lack of information about certain feature is simulated) and IME (allowed error and the maximal number of iterations). The parameters controlling visualisation are the type of graphical output (e.g., jpg, eps, or png), the selection of attributes to be shown, the threshold of importance for displayed attributes, text shown on the graph, colours, etc.

9.4 Explanation in Business Context: A Case of B2B Sales Forecasting

Reference [3] reviewed the academic work in the field of sales forecasting and concluded that due to sophisticated statistical procedures and despite major advances in forecasting methods, the forecasting practice has seen little improvement. Our practical use case demonstrates that this need not be the case. We show that explanations can successfully support data-based decision process in a real-world business context [11, 12].

We use a publicly available real-world data set describing the sales history of a medium-sized company providing software solutions to clients in international B2B markets [10]. The data set consists of 22 predictive attributes describing different aspects of the B2B sales process (e.g., a type of offered product, the authority of a contact person at the client, size of the company, seller's id, etc.). The class variable is boolean indicating if a deal was won or lost. The data set promotes research in understanding factors impacting the outcome of the sales process. To construct the dataset, the sales team analysed 448 open opportunities with the help of an external consultant. The predictions, as well as the final outcomes, were recorded and analysed with machine learning prediction models. To gain knowledge about the properties of the decision process, the sales team used general explanation methods EXPLAIN and IME. The analysis included explanations of individual decisions as well as the whole model. For new (open) cases, decision makers were supported with the explanations to assess various scenarios with explanatory what-if analysis. We discuss two interesting use cases, the effect of updates as a result of new information and adaptation of the model to the specifics of new customers.

Figure 9.2a shows instance explanation for a new sale opportunity, with values of all 22 attributes shown (the importance threshold is not set). The prediction model explained is a random forest. During the sales team's discussion, it was observed that value of the attribute *Competitors* was recorded incorrectly and should be corrected to "No". Furthermore, the sales managers wanted to assess the impact of assigning a different seller with more expertise in Product D. This is reflected in the change for the attribute (note the change of *Seller* from "Seller 2" to "Seller 10"). The team could immediately investigate the effect of these two updates, which is visible in Fig. 9.2b, where the likelihood of a successful outcome increases from 0.52 to 0.68. We show only the most relevant attributes by setting the appropriate importance threshold (to value 3).

The participating company wanted to get insight into how to address a slowdown in the acquisition of new clients. To respond to this request, from the initial business data set, only instances related to new clients were selected (158 instances). This new data set was assessed with the same approach as the initial, complete business data set. By selecting only instances involving new clients, the learning outcome was intentionally biased. The resulting model and its explanations are not generally applicable but can help in distinguishing successful and unsuccessful deals involving new clients.

The model explanation is presented in Fig. 9.3. We applied the importance threshold (value of 3) to discard features with low impact. The strongest positive impact comes from the attribute *Partnership* with value "Yes", which indicates a recommendation to form partnerships with companies when bidding for new business. Positive statements about the vendor have a positive impact, as well as when sales opportunities stem from participation in an event (e.g., booth at a conference). For this specific segment of new clients, some attributes have marginal or no impact

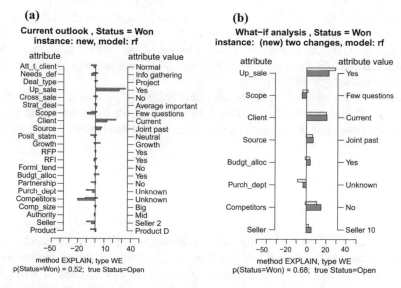

Fig. 9.2 Initial explanation **a** and explanation after updates **b**

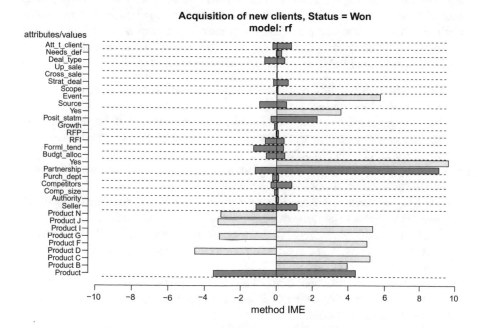

Fig. 9.3 Explanation of drivers for the acquisition of new clients

(e.g. *Up_sale, Cross_sale*). This is in-line with reality – only existing clients qualify for *up sale* or *cross sale*. We can observe different impacts of products; some have positive and other have a negative impact. The rest of the values have impact below the set threshold of 3. Such a compact view enables a more targeted discussion when building a company's sales strategy.

One can conclude that the explanation methodology presented is a useful tool for many different problems. It is especially important for problems where prediction performance has to be supplemented with models transparency or knowledge discovery.

9.5   Conclusion

We presented three general methods for explanations of prediction models. The methods allow explanation of individual decisions as well as the prediction model as a whole. The methods can be efficiently computed and visualised, EXPLAIN and LIME work efficiently even for very large data sets. The explanations reveal how the individual input variables influence the outcome of otherwise completely opaque models, thus making them transparent and comprehensible. The general methods allow users to compare different types of models or replace their existing model without having to replace the explanation method. The explanation methods EXPLAIN, IME, and LIME exhibit the following properties:

- *Instance dependency*: different instances are predicted differently, so the explanations will also be different.
- *Class dependency*: explanations for different classes are different, different attributes may have a different influence on different classes (for two-class problems, the effect is complementary).
- *Model dependency*: the methods explain a given model, so if the model is wrong for a given instance, the produced explanations will reflect that.
- *Capability to detect strong conditional dependencies*: if the model captures strong conditional dependencies, the explanations will also reflect that.
- *Visualisation ability*: the generated explanations can be graphically presented in terms of the positive/negative effect each attribute and its values have on the classification of a given instance.
- *Local fidelity*: the perturbation based approaches perturb instances in the neighbourhood of explanation instance, therefore they are sensitive to the model's functioning in the local context.
- *Efficiency*: methods EXPLAIN and LIME can be efficiently used with a large number of instances and features, while current implementation of IME is limited to a relatively low number of features (up to 100).
- *Fair contributions*: only for the IME method, the explanations in the form of attribute-value contributions have a theoretical guarantee that the computed con-

tributions to the final prediction are fair in the sense that they represent Shapley values from coalitional game theory.
- *Availability*: the software implementation of the explanation methodology is available as the open-source R package *ExplainPrediction* [28]. Furthermore, the real-world B2B sales forecasting data set is publicly accessible [10].

We can list the following limitations which can spur further improvements:

- EXPLAIN method is unable to detect and correctly evaluate the utility of attributes' values in instances where the change in more than one attribute value at once is needed to affect the predicted value. IME method samples the space of feature interactions and therefore avoids this problem.
- IME suffers from relatively large computational load required to reach probabilistic guarantees of its performance. The explanations would have to be pre-computed in order to be used interactively in a discussion session and computations may be too slow for high dimensional problems.
- While efficient in high dimensional spaces, LIME offers no guarantees that the explanations are faithful, and ignores the required number and nature of obtained samples. By using uniform sampling in the proximity of explanation instance, it may be susceptible to problems of neighbourhood-based methods like kNN in high dimensional spaces. The problem of possible feature interactions is also not adequately solved.
- The interactions between attributes are captured but not expressed explicitly in the visualisations; therefore, the user has to manually discover the type of interdependencies with interactive analysis.

In a business context, we presented an extract from the successful grounded application of machine learning models coupled with general explanation methodology. On the complex real-world business problem of B2B sales forecasting, we show how powerful black-box ML models can be made transparent and help domain experts to iteratively evaluate and update their beliefs. For new (open) cases, we demonstrated interactive support for decision makers, assessing various scenarios with explanatory what-if analysis. We presented flexibility of the methodology to address a specific business request (weak performance in one segment). The explanations of the prediction models and what-if analysis proved to be an effective support for B2B sales predictions. The presented methodology enhanced the team's internal communication and improved reflection on the team's implicit knowledge.

The simplicity and elegance of the perturbation-based explanations coupled with efficient implementations and visualisation of instance- and model-based explanations allow application of general explanation approaches to many areas. We expect that broader practical use will spur additional research into explanation mechanisms and improvements in the visual design of explanations. Machine learning based automatic decisions have already spread to many areas of life and attracted attention of the general public and law-makers, who demand its better transparency. This makes model explanation a much needed and attractive research and application topic.

Acknowledgements We are grateful to the company Salvirt, ltd., for funding a part of the research and development presented in this paper. Marko Robnik-Šikonja was supported by the Slovenian Research Agency, ARRS, through research programme P2-0209.

References

1. Aggarwal, C.C., Chen, C., Han, J.: The inverse classification problem. J. Comput. Sci. Technol. **25**(3), 458–468 (2010)
2. Andrews, R., Diederich, J., Tickle, A.B.: Survey and critique of techniques for extracting rules from trained artificial neural networks. Knowl.-Based Syst. **8**(6), 373–384 (1995)
3. Armstrong, J.S., Green, K.C., Graefe, A.: Golden rule of forecasting: be conservative. J. Bus. Res. **68**(8), 1717–1731 (2015)
4. Arnold, V., Clark, N., Collier, P.A., Leech, S.A., Sutton, S.G.: The differential use and effect of knowledge-based system explanations in novice and expert judgment decisions. MIS Q. **30**(1), 79–97 (2006)
5. Arras, L., Horn, F., Montavon, G., Müller, K.R., Samek, W.: What is relevant in a text document?: An interpretable machine learning approach. PloS ONE **12**(8), e0181142 (2017)
6. Bach, S., Binder, A., Montavon, G., Klauschen, F., Müller, K.R., Samek, W.: On pixel-wise explanations for non-linear classifier decisions by layer-wise relevance propagation. PloS ONE **10**(7), e0130140 (2015)
7. Baehrens, D., Schroeter, T., Harmeling, S., Kawanabe, M., Hansen, K., Müller, K.R.: How to explain individual classification decisions. J. Mach. Learn. Res. **11**, 1803–1831 (2010)
8. Barbella, D., Benzaid, S., Christensen, J.M., Jackson, B., Qin, X.V., Musicant, D.R.: Understanding support vector machine classifications via a recommender system-like approach. In: Stahlbock R., Crone S.F., Lessmann S. (eds.) Proceedings of International Conference on Data Mining, pp. 305–311 (2009)
9. Barbosa, A., Paulovich, F., Paiva, A., Goldenstein, S., Petronetto, F., Nonato, L.: Visualizing and interacting with kernelized data. IEEE Trans. Vis. Comput. Graph. **22**(3), 1314–1325 (2016)
10. Bohanec, M.: Anonymized B2B sales forecasting data set (2016). http://www.salvirt.com/research/b2bdataset
11. Bohanec, M., Borštnar Kljajić, M., Robnik-Šikonja, M.: Explaining machine learning models in sales predictions. Expert Syst. Appl. **71**, 416–428 (2017)
12. Bohanec, M., Robnik-Šikonja, M., Kljajić Borštnar, M.: Decision-making framework with double-loop learning through interpretable black-box machine learning models. Ind. Manag. Data Syst. **117**(7), 1389–1406 (2017)
13. Bosnić, Z., Demšar, J., Kešpret, G., Rodrigues, P.P., Gama, J., Kononenko, I.: Enhancing data stream predictions with reliability estimators and explanation. Eng. Appl. Artif. Intell. **34**, 178–192 (2014)
14. Demšar, J., Curk, T., Erjavec, A.: Črt Gorup, Hočevar, T., Milutinovič, M., Možina, M., Polajnar, M., Toplak, M., Starič, A., Štajdohar, M., Umek, L., Žagar, L., Žbontar, J., Žitnik, M., Zupan, B.: Orange: Data mining toolbox in python. J. Mach. Learn. Res. **14**, 2349–2353 (2013)
15. Goldstein, A., Kapelner, A., Bleich, J., Pitkin, E.: Peeking inside the black box: visualizing statistical learning with plots of individual conditional expectation. J. Comput. Graph. Stat. **24**(1), 44–65 (2015)
16. Hamel, L.: Visualization of support vector machines with unsupervised learning. In: Proceedings of 2006 IEEE Symposium on Computational Intelligence in Bioinformatics and Computational Biology (2006)
17. Hansen, K., Baehrens, D., Schroeter, T., Rupp, M., Müller, K.R.: Visual interpretation of Kernel-based prediction models. Mol. Inf. **30**(9), 817–826 (2011)
18. Jacobsson, H.: Rule extraction from recurrent neural networks: a taxonomy and review. Neural Comput. **17**(6), 1223–1263 (2005)

19. Jakulin, A., Možina, M., Demšar, J., Bratko, I., Zupan, B.: Nomograms for visualizing support vector machines. In: Grossman R., Bayardo R., Bennett K.P. (eds.) Proceedings of the Eleventh ACM SIGKDD International Conference on Knowledge Discovery and Data Mining, pp. 108–117. ACM (2005)
20. Lemaire, V., Féraud, R., Voisine, N.: Contact personalization using a score understanding method. In: Proceedings of International Joint Conference on Neural Networks (IJCNN) (2008)
21. Lughofer, E., Richter, R., Neissl, U., Heidl, W., Eitzinger, C., Radauer, T.: Explaining classifier decisions linguistically for stimulating and improving operators labeling behavior. Inf. Sci. **420**, 16–36 (2017)
22. Martens, D., Provost, F.: Explaining documents' classifications. Tech. rep., Center for Digital Economy Research, New York University, Stern School of Business (2011). Working paper CeDER-11-01
23. Meyer, D., Leisch, F., Hornik, K.: The support vector machine under test. Neurocomputing **55**, 169–186 (2003)
24. Piltaver, R., Luštrek, M., Gams, M., Martinčić-Ipšić, S.: What makes classification trees comprehensible? Expert Syst. Appl. **62**, 333–346 (2016)
25. Poulin, B., Eisner, R., Szafron, D., Lu, P., Greiner, R., Wishart, D.S., Fyshe, A., Pearcy, B., Macdonell, C., Anvik, J.: Visual explanation of evidence with additive classifiers. In: Proceedings of AAAI'06. AAAI Press (2006)
26. Pregeljc, M., Štrumbelj, E., Mihelčič, M., Kononenko, I.: Learning and explaining the impact of enterprises organizational quality on their economic results. In: Magdalena-Benedito, R., Martínez-Sober, M., Martínez-Martínez, J.M., Escandell-Moreno, P., Vila-Francés, J. (eds.) Intelligent Data Analysis for Real-Life Applications: Theory and Practice, pp. 228–248. Information Science Reference, IGI Global (2012)
27. Ribeiro, M.T., Singh, S., Guestrin, C.: Why should I trust you?: Explaining the predictions of any classifier. In: Proceedings of the 22nd ACM SIGKDD International Conference on Knowledge Discovery and Data Mining, pp. 1135–1144. ACM (2016)
28. Robnik-Šikonja, M.: ExplainPrediction: Explanation of predictions for classification and regression (2017). http://cran.r-project.org/package=ExplainPrediction. R package version 1.1.9
29. Robnik-Šikonja, M., Kononenko, I.: Explaining classifications for individual instances. IEEE Trans. Knowl. Data Eng. **20**(5), 589–600 (2008)
30. Saltelli, A., Chan, K., Scott, E.M.: Sensitivity Analysis. Wiley, Chichester; New York (2000)
31. Schulz, A., Gisbrecht, A., Hammer, B.: Using discriminative dimensionality reduction to visualize classifiers. Neural Process. Lett. **42**(1), 27–54 (2015)
32. Simonyan, K., Vedaldi, A., Zisserman, A.: Deep inside convolutional networks: visualising image classification models and saliency maps. arXiv preprint arXiv:1312.6034 (2013)
33. Štrumbelj, E., Bosnić, Z., Kononenko, I., Zakotnik, B., Kuhar, C.G.: Explanation and reliability of prediction models: the case of breast cancer recurrence. Knowl. Inf. Syst. **24**(2), 305–324 (2010)
34. Štrumbelj, E., Kononenko, I.: An efficient explanation of individual classifications using game theory. J. Mach. Learn. Res. **11**, 1–18 (2010)
35. Štrumbelj, E., Kononenko, I., Robnik-Šikonja, M.: Explaining instance classifications with interactions of subsets of feature values. Data Knowl. Eng. **68**(10), 886–904 (2009)

Chapter 10
Model Explanation and Interpretation Concepts for Stimulating Advanced Human-Machine Interaction with "Expert-in-the-Loop"

Edwin Lughofer

Abstract We propose two directions for stimulating advanced human-machine interaction in machine learning systems. The first direction acts on a *local level* by suggesting a reasoning process why certain model decisions/predictions have been made for current sample queries. It may help to better understand how the model behaves and to support humans for providing more consistent and certain feedbacks. A practical example from visual inspection of production items underlines higher human labeling consistency. The second direction acts on a *global level* by addressing several criteria which are necessary for a good interpretability of the *whole model*. By meeting the criteria, the likelihood increases (1) of gaining more funded insights into the behavior of the system, and (2) of stimulating advanced expert/operators feedback in form of active manipulations of the model structure. Possibilities how to best integrate different types of advanced feedback in combination with (on-line) data using incremental model updates will be discussed. This leads to a new, *hybrid interactive model building* paradigm, which is based on subjective knowledge versus objective data and thus integrates the *"expert-in-the-loop"* aspect.

10.1 Introduction

Machine learning and soft computing models are essential components in today's supervision, prediction and decision support systems for highly automatised industrial and biomedical (engineering) processes — see, for instance, [25, 47, 60, 67] for various concrete applications in the fields of web mining [126], supervision of human's behaviour, predictive maintenance [68], healthcare systems, texture perception modeling [32] and visual inspection systems [36, 122]. Unlike "old-school" fixed

E. Lughofer (✉)
Department of Knowledge-Based Mathematical Systems,
Johannes Kepler University Linz, Linz, Austria
e-mail: edwin.lughofer@jku.at

© Springer International Publishing AG, part of Springer Nature 2018   177
J. Zhou and F. Chen (eds.), *Human and Machine Learning*, Human–Computer
Interaction Series, https://doi.org/10.1007/978-3-319-90403-0_10

coded decision rules [50], either obtained through analytical laws and mathematical derivation or by explicitly formulated expert knowledge, resulting in so-called *expert systems* [2], machine learning models are typically established more or less automatically based on data recorded at the system [123]. This leads to a significant reduction in development time of the decision, prediction and supervision models [95], thus saving human expert/operator effort and costs for companies and industrial facilities, see recent newsletters.[1,2]

In many applications, machine learning models are nowadays used as embedded, in-line or on-line component(s). *Embedded* means that they are operating fully autonomously without any interaction with humans and provide their outputs directly to the neighbouring components, environments etc. on machine level (in-line usage). Typical examples are (i) intelligent and smart sensors [13, 105], where compact machine learning models are deployed for their in-line execution within restricted resources, (ii) production process lines or factories of the future,[3] where ML models are used for predictive and proactive maintenance [27] towards full process optimisation [100, 127] with some self-healing capabilities[4] [31].

In some cases, the machine learning models need to be updated based on newly recorded on-line data, in order to account for dynamically changing system behaviours, new operation modes not included in the initial batch data set from which the models have been learnt. In other cases non-stationary environmental changes occur [110], which may arise even unexpectedly. In other fields of applications, such as health-care systems or social media platforms, the patient's or agent's behaviour may change due to different moods and daily constitutions (small, abrupt changes) [30, 47] or due to a shift in the mainstream fashion and communication style (bigger, gradual long-term changes) [48, 97]. This also requires the update of embedded data stream models or decision support systems [45].

Techniques from the fields of evolving intelligent systems [10, 53], incremental machine learning methods [29, 110] and adaptive soft computing and control [61, 69] can be applied to guarantee fast updates to these changes. This is accomplished and realised through the following concepts, which are ideally operated in single-pass manner (no past data revisited) to keep computation time for model updates on a low level:

- Recursive parameter adaptation to adapt to permanent process changes and to increase model significance and accuracy.
- Evolution of new model components on the fly in order to account for variations in the process such as new operations modes, system states, [10, 110] which requires an expansion of the knowledge of the model to new territories in the feature space.
- Deletion of obsolete and merging of redundant model components to assure compactness of the models, thus to prevent over-fitting and to reduce computation times

---

[1]https://mapr.com/blog/reduce-costs-and-improve-health-care-with-big-data/.

[2]https://arimo.com/machine-learning/2016/manufacturing-downtime-cost-reduction-predictive-maintenance/.

[3]http://ec.europa.eu/research/industrial_technologies/factories-of-the-future_en.html.

[4]http://whatis.techtarget.com/definition/self-healing.

for model updates — the latter is especially important in the case of high-speed processes.

- Increasing the model flexibility for (quickly) drifting system behavior [54] through down-weighing older learned relations.

Central questions then arise in the following directions:

- Are the updated models still trustful? can we guarantee fully automatic model updates with high performance and no quality deterioration over time?
- How can the humans be persuaded that updated models are still valid by still representing valid interrelations between inputs and outputs from a physical, chemical and/or biological point of view?
- How can the humans benefit from the models and the models benefit from the humans (knowledge)? - this raises the question what may stimulate an enhanced communication between humans and machines which may furthermore bring knowledge gains for humans as well as performance boosts for the machines likewise?

Such challenges have been generically formalised and addressed under the umbrella of the *human-inspired evolving machines (HIEM)* concept [70] and are also discussed in the research communities under the umbrella of *expert-in-the-loop (EIL)* [33] or *human-in-the-loop* paradigms [40]. However, they have been only loosely realized in particular fields of real-world applications so far [17, 81, 121].

Mostly, the current situation is that humans communicate with machine learning tools either on a pure monitoring level or in minimal form on a good-bad reward level, qualifying the model outputs so that the model can improve itself. Communication on a deeper, structural level, for instance, enabling human manipulation of structural components or decision boundaries, is currently (almost) missing. Such communication, however, may also help us to achieve a deeper, evidence-based understanding of how people can interact with machine learning systems in different contexts and to enrich models by combining objective data with subjective experience. Figure 10.1 shows a generic work-flow for a possible *human-inspired evolving machines* concept with some more advanced components stimulating advanced interaction rather than naive feedbacks.

An essential point of such communication-based machine learning tools is the establishment of models which can be interpreted and whose outputs can be explained linguistically, eye-catching and plausible to the human. Otherwise, humans may become incurious, distracted or not really motivated to communicate with the system. Thus, this chapter is dedicated to this particular issue: under this scope, it will propose and describe several concepts for

1. Model explanation on a local level, i.e. reasons for model outputs (in the form of classification statements, predictions, quantifications) are provided to humans in a readable and understandable form (handled in Sect. 10.2) — this may be intrinsically important for providing a feedback on the quality of the outputs (in the form of good/bad rewards, for instance) or for the purpose of on-line,

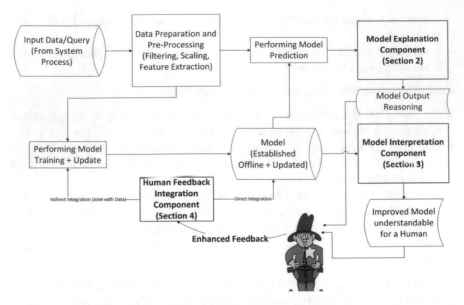

Fig. 10.1 Framework for enhanced human-machine interaction based on machine learning models (*human-inspired evolving machines (HIEM)*) with the integration of Expert-in-the-Loop (EIL, denoted by the sheriff); the components highlighted in bold font are addressed in this chapter

interactive sample annotation and labelling (to improve model significance on-the-fly) [86].

2. Model interpretation on a global level, i.e. models are prepared in a way such that their components can be linguistically interpreted easily towards the complete understanding of what the model represents and actually does (Sect. 10.3) — this may be intrinsically important for supervision purposes in industrial installations, i.e., that humans can check whether the model is still plausible and reliable (e.g., in a physical, chemical or biological sense) after being autonomously updated with on-line samples [7].

Additionally, the chapter will address the continuation of model learning and teaching in the context of enriched human-machine interaction and expert-in-the-loop. Thus, methods will be suggested how to integrate enhanced human feedback in various forms and how to properly handle human-defined model components or changes in the model structure in the context of further data-driven model adaptation (Sect. 10.4).

Choice of Appropriate Model Architecture

According to these ambitious goals discussed above, it is essential to focus on machine learning model architecture(s) which support per se any form of interpretation and component explanation, and therefore offer the possibility of an enhanced communication with the human (user) in a 'natural way'. This makes, for instance, (deep learning) neural networks, support vector machines and/or various forms of evolutionary algorithms less attractive than any form of rule-based models such as decision trees [104], patterns trees [111] or fuzzy systems [99], see [46] for a detailed discussion about the comprehensibility of rule-based model types.

Fuzzy systems offer linguistically readable rules in IF-THEN form and also allow uncertainty feedback in the model decision through the concepts of conflict and ignorance, which they can resolve in a natural way [43]. So, they have the natural capability to offer enhanced model output explanation, which cannot be so easily established for decision and pattern trees. The inherent fuzziness in their rules allows their knowledge to be expressed in the form of vague statements using linguistic terms [119], which may accord with a human's experience. Furthermore, they are able to provide a reasonable tradeoff between readability and accuracy due to their universal approximation capability [20], especially when being equipped with specific compactness and transparency improvements techniques during or after model learning from data [18, 28, 75] — which we will also partially discuss in Sect. 10.3. Due to all these nice properties, fuzzy systems are tendentially the most prominent candidate (and hence our focus) for a comprehensible rule-based model architecture, to meet model explanation and interpretation issues and thus enriched interactions with humans as discussed above.

General Notation and Definition of Fuzzy Rule Bases

In a general context, linguistically readable rules have the form [62]:

IF (a set of conditions is satisfied) THEN (the set of consequences can be inferred)

The consequences are typically some actions which are performed based on the fulfillment (degree) of the antecedents comprised by a set of conditions, connected through AND and OR operators. These conditions often describe the characteristics of objects, events, systems states and behaviours etc.

In real-world applications, several types of uncertainty may arise during modeling, e.g. due to noisy data and/or uncertain knowledge of humans about process behaviours, which leads to vagueness in their feedback or knowledge formulation [112, 119]. Usually, the antecedents can then no longer be defined as crisp statements, and using fuzzy instead of Boolean rules for describing the class space relations becomes more promising. A fuzzy rule can be defined as:

$$\text{Rule}_i : \text{IF } x_1 \text{ IS } \mu_{i1} \text{ AND} \ldots \text{AND } x_p \text{ IS } \mu_{ip} \text{ THEN } l_i(\mathbf{x}) = \Phi_i. \quad (10.1)$$

where p is the dimensionality of the feature space and $\mu_{i1}, \ldots, \mu_{ip}$ are the linguistic terms (such as, e.g., HIGH, INTENSE, WARM), formally represented by fuzzy sets [125]. These terms provide a coarse granulation of the input features into different local regions, where each region is represented by a membership function associated with a *fuzzy set*.

Fuzzy sets are thus assigning arguments from a corresponding range of some input feature to a membership degree, which may take any value in [0, 1]. A fuzzy

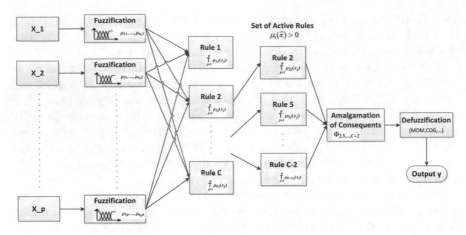

Fig. 10.2 Topology of a fuzzy rule base with C rules and how the inference of new queries is conducted

set is usually described by a modal value (its centre **c**), where its membership degree receives 1, a core range of influence (σ) (subject to an α-cut level [51]), a concrete shape and a linguistic term typically assigned by the expert. It is usual that several fuzzy sets, each one referring to a different linguistic term, are assigned to a single input feature (variable). Those fuzzy sets together form a so-called fuzzy partition of the input feature. The fuzzy partitions of all input variables are the core components of a fuzzy system in order to express uncertainty (e.g., due to noise) and vagueness (e.g., due to human thinking, perception, feelings) in a possibilistic manner [99]. In particular, according to the rule definition in (10.1), each antecedent part describes a fuzzy condition containing a linguistic term, which is activated for new query instances subject to a certain degree (0 if not activated at all).

Φ_i denotes the consequent functions and can be of different forms: fuzzy sets as in the case of Mamdani fuzzy systems [91], hyper-planes or higher-order polynomials as in the case of Takagi–Sugeno(–Kang) fuzzy systems [116], multi-dimensional Mercer kernels, wavelet or even auto-regressive functions [1]. In case of classification, Φ is either represented by a singleton class label (classical case) [58] or by a whole confidence vector with confidence levels for each class [9].

A collection of $i = 1, \ldots, C$ fuzzy rules as defined in (10.1) forms a so-called *fuzzy rule base F*. Based on this fuzzy rule base, an overall output is inferred for new query points, e.g., in the form of a classification or regression statements, by using the topology as shown in Fig. 10.2. The following steps are carried out:

1. Fuzzification of the p-dimensional input vector $\mathbf{x} = \{x_1, \ldots, x_p\}$: this is done by sending each single vector entry into the corresponding fuzzy partitions and evaluating the membership degrees to all fuzzy sets: $\mu_{n_j}(x_j)$ for $j = 1, \ldots, p$, with n_j the number of fuzzy sets defined for the jth input x_j.
2. Eliciting the firing levels of all rules by combining the membership degrees μ_{ij} for all C rules, i.e. for $i = 1, \ldots, C$, with A_{ij} the fuzzy set appearing in the

jth antecedent part ($j \in n_j$) of the ith rule and μ_{ij} its activation degree for the current sample. The combination is achieved through a t-norm (default: product or minimum) [55].

3. Eliciting the set of active rules, i.e. those ones with activation level $\mu_i > 0$.
4. Amalgamation of the consequents of the active rules through a t-conorm [34] (default: maximum).
5. Defuzzification of the amalgamated consequents in order to obtain a crisp value.

The last step depends on the concrete consequent type functions chosen, see [101] for possibilities, and produces a numerical output value (classification, prediction statement). Typically, a kind of weighted average or a centre (maximum) of gravity is used.

Hierarchical rule bases may help to reduce the length of the rules which may become unreadable in case of a higher number of inputs [107], where also rule explosion takes place when considering most of the fuzzy set combinations as proper rule antecedents. In hierarchical rule bases, smaller rule bases are constructed based on subsets of features, and their outputs used as inputs for subsequent rule bases, leading to a chain of rule bases. Each smaller rule base is easier to interpret for its own, and the output connections can be interpreted on a more global level, achieving some insights into feature links etc.

10.2 Model Explanation Concepts (On Local Level)

Model explanation concepts on the local level, means that for each new query instance x passing through the fuzzy rule base not only the output (in the form of a classification or prediction statement) is inferred, but also an advanced explanation is provided as to why this output has been produced, and the certainty and intrinsic reason behind it. Uncertain output can be treated with more care by humans and not trusted so easily. The explanation of model decisions may become an essential aspect to stimulate human feedback, especially when reasons are provided for the decisions [14] and features most influencing the decisions are highlighted [115]. Then, when the model seems to be wrong from human users' first glance, by looking at the reason and induced features, she/he may be persuaded to change her/his opinion or she/he may be confirmed in her/his first intuition. In the latter case, she/he can directly associate the rule leading to the reason shown and thus may change or even discard it. This in turn means that the model is enriched with knowledge provided by the human and thus can benefit from it (becoming more accurate, more precise in certain regimes, parts).

The following concepts are addressed in this section to make (fuzzy) model outputs understandable to humans:

- The *reason for model decisions* in linguistic form (addressed in Sect. 10.2.1): the most active fuzzy rule(s) for current query instances is (are) prepared in transparent form and shown to the human as reason.

- The *certainty of model decisions* in relation to the final output and possible alternative suggestions (Sect. 10.2.2). This indicates the degree of ambiguity, i.e. the 'clearness' of a model output.
- The *feature importance levels* for the current model decision (Sect. 10.2.4) are provided: (1) to reduce the length of the rules (=reasons) to show only the most essential premises and thus to increase their readability, (2) to get a better feeling about which features and corresponding conditions in the rules' antecedents strongly influenced the decision.
- The *coverage degree* of the current instance to be predicted/classified (Sect. 10.2.3): this is another form of certainty, which tells the human how novel the content in the current sample is. In the case of high novelty content (equivalent to a low coverage), the human may pay additional attention to provide his feedback, which may be in some cases even highly recommended (e.g., to encourage her/him to define new fault types, new classes or new operation modes).

In sum, such an advanced explanation of models' decisions should help the humans to better understand them and also allow them to provide more consistent feedback, e.g. in form of good/bad rewards, definition of new event types (e.g., fault classes) and description of local behaviour, or sample annotations. The latter will be addressed in a concrete case study (Sect. 10.2.6) within the context of an image-based event classification system for surface inspection problems: it will be shown that advanced (linguistic) explanations of model decisions can improve the consistency and certainty of sample labellings.

10.2.1 Reasons for Model Decisions

The reasons for model decisions can be best explained when taking into account the geometric and linguistic interpretation of fuzzy rules. In the case of data-driven extraction of fuzzy models, the fuzzy rules represent possibilistic distribution models for the local data clouds in the feature space. The form of the rule shapes depends on the functions chosen for modelling the fuzzy sets in the partitions or, in the case of generalised rules [84], on the chosen high-dimensional kernel functions.

Once the fuzzy rules have been learned from data by any type of clustering or machine learning techniques [69, 99], the rules typically represent partial dependencies of variables/features within local regions of the feature space — e.g., local correlations and partial local trends (regression case) or local descriptors for shapes of class clouds (classification case). A concrete example of a geometric interpretation for a two-dimensional classification case (with three classes) is shown in Fig. 10.3.

There, the rules have ellipsoidal contours which result from multi-dimensional Gaussian kernels for achieving arbitrarily rotated positions. The fuzzy sets shown along the axes (HIGH, MEDIUM, LOW) can be obtained by projection of the higher-dimensional rule contours onto the single axes, see, e.g., [84].

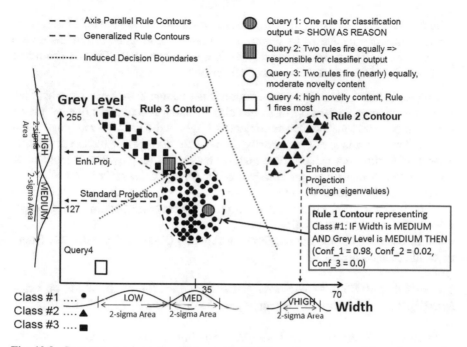

Fig. 10.3 Geometric interpretation of fuzzy classification rules as extracted from data samples containing three classes (their contours shown as dotted ellipsoids)

Also shown in Fig. 10.3 are four query point cases whose classification interpretation can be seen as follows:

- *Query 1 (circle, shaded)*: In the case of this sample, only one rule (Rule (1) fires significantly, and it is therefore sufficient to show this rule to the human (operator/user) (in IF-THEN form) as a reason for the final model output. In our example, Rule 1 reads as:
  Rule 1: IF Width is MEDIUM AND Grey Level is MEDIUM, THEN Class #1 with ($conf_1 = 0.98$, $conf_2 = 0.02$, $conf_3 = 0.0$).
  Thus, the reason why Class #1 has been returned is that the width of the object is MEDIUM (around 35 units) and its (average) grey level is MEDIUM (i.e., somewhere around 127 when assuming a range of $[0, 255]$).
- *Query 2 (rectangular, shaded)*: Rule 3 fires most actively, but also Rule 1 fires significantly, so the induced linguistic IF-THEN forms of both are to be shown to the human, as the classification response will depend mainly on the weighted scoring of these two rules.
- *Query 3 (circle, non-shaded)*: this query point lies in between Rules 1, 2 and 3, but it is significantly closer to Rules 1 and 3; thus, their induced linguistic IF-THEN forms are to be shown to the human; the novelty content of this query is moderate.
- *Query 4 (rectangular, non-shaded)*: this query point indicates high novelty content, as it lies far away from all extracted rules; since Rule 1 is by far the closest,

its induced linguistic IF-THEN form will be shown to the human. This type of uncertainty is not covered by the weighted output scoring, as it remains on the "safe" side of the decision boundary, shown as a dotted line. Thus, it should be separately handled by the concept of *coverage*.

Linguistic terms can only be understood if the human knows exactly what they mean: for instance, in the case of image classification, it is obvious that a "VERY HIGH Grey Level" means that the object is bright and thus "eye-catching" in an image. However, this is not necessarily the case for all types of feature in general real-world applications, where some features may be less expressive. In such cases, it may be beneficial to show the core part of the (firing) fuzzy set in terms of $c \pm \sigma$, with c being the centre value and σ the *core range of influence*. This provides a more concrete indication of the local region within which the corresponding input feature value of the current sample falls.

In the case of the rule example above in Fig. 10.3 (Rule 1), the reason for Query #1 would then become:

The reason why Class #1 has been returned is that the width of the object is MEDIUM (35 ± 10) and its (average) grey level is MEDIUM (127 ± 25).

In the case of regression problems, the reasoning can be constructed in a similar manner, with the major difference that rules represent partial local trends of the whole approximation (regression) surface — also termed as piecewise local predictors [76], which can be exploited for local stability analysis of controllers and models [63]. Such trends can be expressed well with the usage of hyper-planes or higher order polynomials in the consequents [116]. Then, each rule describes the local correlation between variables represented through the hyper-plane (or higher-order polynomials), whereas 'locality' is yielded by the range of the rule defined through the rule's antecedent (e.g., ellipsoid contours). Figure 10.4 provides a geometric interpretation example for the regression case.

Each of the three local trends contained in the approximation curve (shown as a solid regression line going through the samples) is represented by one rule (contours as ellipsoids), whereas the certainty of the curve varies from rule to rule due to varying local noise levels (spreads) of the samples — the certainty is thereby expressed by so-called error bars modelling confidence intervals which are shown as red dotted lines surrounding the approximation curve.

According to the positioning of the two queries, the reason for the two queries adopted to the regression case then becomes:

Query 1: The reason why a prediction value for Energy of 38.5 has been returned is that the temperature is LOW (around 10 ± 4).
Query 2: The reason why a prediction value for Energy of 90.7 has been returned is that the temperature is HIGH (around 30 ± 5).

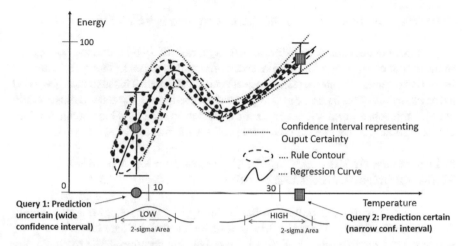

Fig. 10.4 Geometric interpretation of rules in fuzzy regression models as extracted from data samples containing three partial local trends of the approximation curve; their contours shown as dotted ellipsoids, the regression curve as a solid dark line; surrounding confidence intervals (error bars) are shown as red dotted lines, indicating the uncertainty in model outputs due to noise in the data

10.2.2 Certainty of Model Decisions

According to the rule representation as demonstrated in Sect. 10.2.1, certainties in relation to classifier responses can be directly associated with the class confidence levels in the most active rule(s), i.e. rules with highest membership degrees $\mu.(\mathbf{x})$, where $\mu.(\mathbf{x}) = \mathsf{T}_{j=1}^{P} \mu._{j}(\mathbf{x})$ or $\mu.(\mathbf{x}) = K.(\mathbf{x})$ in case of generalised rules. If it is a single rule (i.e., obtained by $argmax_{i=1,\ldots,C}\mu_i(\mathbf{x})$), it corresponds to the winner-takes-all classification strategy widely used in the fuzzy community [58, 94]. If more rules are taken into consideration for producing the classification statements, advanced concepts such as the inverse gravitation concept [85] or the weighted voting concept [49] can help to improve classification accuracy. In both cases, class confidence levels can be embedded in the rule consequents Φ_i (see (10.1)) by

$$\Phi_i = [\text{Class}_i = 1(conf_{i1}), \text{Class}_i = 2(conf_{i2}), \ldots, \text{Class}_i = K(conf_{iK})], \quad (10.2)$$

and thus amalgamated when producing the classification statement [85]. $conf_{ik}$ represent the confidence of the ith rule in the kth class, with K classes in sum. In case of winner-take-it-all classification, the certainty for output class L is calculated by

$$\text{certainty}_L = \max_{j=1,\ldots,K} (conf_{i*j}) \quad i* = \text{argmax}_{i=1,\ldots,C}\mu_i(\mathbf{x}). \quad (10.3)$$

According to the example shown in Fig. 10.3, Query #1 can be safely classified as belonging to Class #1. Thus, the explanatory text about the certainty of the classifier decision reads as

"The sample is classified as 'Class 1'. The certainty is VERY HIGH ($\approx 100\%$)".

In contrast, the decision is less clear-cut for Queries #2 and #3, and the confidence in the output class is therefore similar to that in another class. In this case, it may be helpful to offer an alternative class suggestion to the human. This also then gives rise to the *clearness of the decision* in one particular class among the second most certain class. In this sense, an additional linguistic explanation for a possible alternative class can be foreseen. In the case of Query #3 in Fig. 10.3, this reads as:

"The sample is classified as 'Class 3'. The certainty is LOW ($\approx 55\%$).
The sample might also be 'Class 1' with a LOW certainty ($\approx 45\%$)".

In the case of regression problems, the certainty of fuzzy model outputs heavily depends on the density, the model bias and noise level of the data in the local parts where the most active rules are defined. Error bars are an appropriate methodology to track the uncertainty of model output. These are shown as surrounding red dashed lines around the real functional trends in Fig. 10.4. The wider the error bars become, the higher the uncertainty in the model output, as a larger band of responses is statistically possible. This means predictions have to be taken with more care in case of large error bars and the human may be motivated to sharpen the most active rule(s) per manual input or even delete the rule(s) if no reasonable conclusion from the prediction can be drawn at all.

Typically, error bars serving as confidence intervals are calculated based on estimations of the parameter uncertainty, which arose during the regression fit. The most prominent choice is the Fisher information matrix I, whose cell (i, j) includes the derivative of the model with respect to the parameter pair (i, j) in the current sample. In the case of linear (regression) models, the Fisher information matrix becomes equivalent to the Hessian matrix $X^T X$, thus the fit quality falls together with the parameter sensitivity of the model. In case of hyper-planes in the consequents, each rule can be seen as a local linear model, modelling local correlations between the input variables and the output. Thus, error bars $conf_y$ for model outputs y, have been defined by using $X^T Q_i X$ with Q_i the membership degrees of the samples to the ith rule and amalgamating these over all C rules through weighted averaging [78] and/or quantization through student's distribution and associated quantiles [114]. In all cases, they define the statistical significance interval of a model output y for a query instance $\mathbf{x}$:

$$y \pm conf_y(\mathbf{x}), \tag{10.4}$$

with $conf_y(\mathbf{x}) = g(X^T Q_i X, \mathbf{x}) \in [min_y, max_y]$ as a function g of weighted Fisher information matrix. Hence, certainty can be percentually expressed by dividing $conf_y$ through the range (or interquartile range) of y:

$$\text{certainty}_y = 1 - \frac{conf_y}{(\text{inter})\text{range}_y}. \tag{10.5}$$

This can be embedded in the linguistic description and shown to the human similarly as in the case of classification, but in relation to the range of the target ($100-\%$ of the range covered by the error bar) thus:

Query 1: the sample is predicted as 38.5. **The certainty is LOW% (approx 50%).**
Query 2: the sample is predicted as 90.7. **The certainty is HIGH% (approx 85%).**

10.2.3 Query Coverage

Another viewpoint on model prediction certainty is to consider how well the current sample is covered by the current model, that is, how close it is to the past training samples and to the rules they induced. For instance, in Fig. 10.3, Query #1 is well covered by the contour of Rule #1, and can thus be safely classified as belonging to Class #1, whereas Query #4 falls within an "empty" space, i.e., an *extrapolation region*. Such situations should be handled with care by humans, as the model has no real definition space where the sample occurs and these may produce any output. A human feedback in such cases would be even more desirable than in safe cases (safely predicted outputs), especially when taking into account that such samples may denote anomalies, outliers or in extreme cases failure modes, which should not be included in subsequent model adaptation cycles [77].

In the context of fuzzy models, the concept of *coverage* was developed in [44] for the batch and in [73] for the on-line case (there within the context of *ignorance*). It can be expressed in a natural way, because the fuzzy rules represent local models of local regions by partitioning the feature space into local granules. The distance of a query point to the local regions can then be directly associated with the degrees of membership of the corresponding fuzzy rules describing the local regions, which are always normalised to [0, 1]: 1 denotes full coverage and 0 no coverage. Obviously, the maximum membership degree over all fuzzy rules is a reliable indicator of the coverage of the current query $\mathbf{x}$:

$$\text{coverage} = \max_{i=1,\ldots,C} \mu_i(\mathbf{x}), \tag{10.6}$$

with C being the number of fuzzy rules in the model and μ_i the membership of the ith rule in $\mathbf{x}$. A linguistic term can be assigned to this value according to a fuzzy partition for 'coverage' pre-defined over the range [0, 1] to retrieve a linguistic explanation text, for instance, in the form (e.g. cf. Query #4 in Fig. 10.3):

"The coverage of the sample by the current classifier is BAD (around 5%)".

10.2.4 Feature Importance Levels (Instance-Based)

The rule antecedent parts forming the reason for model decisions can become lengthy if a high number of input features is used to explain the classification problem/process (resulting in many AND-connections). This yields reasons (rules) which are incomprehensible, i.e., cannot be described in a compact form. Lengthy explanations may lead to human frustration rather than stimulating feedback and input. Furthermore, a sorting of the rule antecedent parts would be favourable for humans, where the parts closer to the IF-statement can be seen as having a higher impact on the final model output than parts occurring in latter conjunctions. A cutoff threshold can then be established to show only the M most important antecedents to the humans. This threshold may be user-defined or based on percentual feature contributions to the final model output.

Feature contributions can be established through the design and calculation of so-called *feature importance levels*. Such levels indicate how important each of the features is for obtaining the current model output. The most prominent way in current literature to do this is to realise how sensitive the model output becomes whenever a specific feature changes its value around the actual value in the current instance, see, e.g. [12, 86, 106, 115]. This is because the sensitivity reflects the degree of change of the model output with respect to changing feature values: e.g., in a case when changing a feature over its complete range, always the same (or very similar) output is obtained, then it means that the model behaves pretty constantly with respect to this feature. Hence, the feature does not have any influence on the output, and thus can be seen as unimportant. On the other hand, whenever there is a significant change in model output when a single feature changes its value slightly, it means that the feature highly impacts the model output, thus can be seen as highly responsible for the actual output.

The basic idea in [86] is that the prediction of the current query instance $L = f(\mathbf{x})$ (i.e, the final class output by the model) containing the values of p features ($\mathbf{x} = [x_1, x_2, \ldots, x_p]$) is compared with the prediction without the knowledge of x_i (for all $i = 1, \ldots, p$ features):

$$imp_L(x_i) = pD_i(\mathbf{x}) = |f(\mathbf{x}) - f(\mathbf{x}/x_i)|. \tag{10.7}$$

If this value is >0, the feature is important, because without it another class would be predicted; in other words, the probability/certainty in relation to the output class L decreases significantly when feature x_i is ignored. Thus, pD_i can be directly associated with the local feature importance $imp_L(x_i)$ on the output class L. $pD_i(\mathbf{x})$ can be calculated by a certainty estimate for the output (winning) class in case of the current full sample $\mathbf{x}$ and by an average certainty estimate in the case when x_i is varied over its complete range (as a simulation of $f(\mathbf{x}/x_i)$), see [86] for full formulas. In the regression case, this idea can be adopted by using the absolute value of $f(\mathbf{x}) - f(\mathbf{x}/x_i)$ as an approximation of the overall change in output when omitting variable x_i. The importance degree of variable x_i should be normalised by the sum of the importance degrees of all features to retrieve a relative importance for all features lying in [0, 1], thus:

$$imp_i = \frac{|f(\mathbf{x}) - f(\mathbf{x}/x_i)|}{\sum_{j=1}^{p} |f(\mathbf{x}) - f(\mathbf{x}/x_j)|}.$$
(10.8)

The importance degree of each feature can be reported to a human both, on instance level and over time based on development plots of feature importance levels — as e.g. suggested in [14]. In the latter approach, the feature contributions are calculated by a random sub-sampling approach, i.e. exchanging some coordinates of $\mathbf{x}$ randomly chosen with corresponding values from other samples drawn from the data set, one time including x_j (thus substituting it with a random value), the other time using the actual value contained in $\mathbf{x}$.

The approach in [12] is based on local explanation vectors as local gradients of the probability function $p(x) = P(L = 1|X = \mathbf{x})$ of the learned model for the positive class (Class #1). The sign of each of the individual entries of the gradient vector (achieved through the derivative in each direction) indicates whether the prediction would increase or decrease when the corresponding feature of $\mathbf{x}$ is increased locally and each entries absolute value gives the amount of influence in the change in prediction. This idea could be also easily adopted to fuzzy models in the following way:

- For the classification case, each multivariate rule kernel K, obtained through combining the antecedent parts (most typically by t-norms [55]), represents a particular class. Depending on the classification scheme to produce the final model output, local gradients of the influencing rules need to be respected. For instance, in winner-takes-all classification, only the most active rule $i*$ is responsible for the final output class L, thus the local gradient in x_j becomes:

$$grad_j = \frac{\partial K_i *}{\partial x_j}.$$
(10.9)

In the case when there is a weighted voting among different rules $c < C$ to produce the final output class L, with weights $w_1, \ldots, w_c$, then the local gradient in each $x_j, j = 1, \ldots, p$ is the weighted summand of the gradient term in (10.9) over all c rules:

$$grad_j(\mathbf{x}) = \sum_{i=1}^{c} w_i \frac{\partial K_i(\mathbf{x})}{\partial x_j}.$$
(10.10)

Again, each of the gradients should be normalised by the sum over all gradients, similarly as done in (10.8) in order to obtain relative importance values imp_j in [0, 1].

- For the regression case, the local gradient is influenced by both, the multidimensional kernels in the rule antecedents and the associated rule consequents (defined through hyper-planes, polynomials or more complex structures). In any

case of rule consequent functions, the defuzzified output is usually obtained by
[69, 101]:

$$f(\mathbf{x}) = \sum_{i=1}^{C} l_i(\mathbf{x}) \Psi_i(\mathbf{x}) \quad \Psi_i(\mathbf{x}) = \frac{K_i(\mathbf{x})}{\sum_{j=1}^{C} K_j(\mathbf{x})}, \tag{10.11}$$

thus respecting all C rules in the rule base. Hence, the local gradient in $\mathbf{x}$ after x_j
is calculated after the product chain rule as

$$grad_j(\mathbf{x}) = \sum_{i=1}^{C} \left(l_i(\mathbf{x}) \frac{\partial \Psi_i(\mathbf{x})}{\partial x_j} + \Psi_i(\mathbf{x}) \frac{\partial l_i(\mathbf{x})}{\partial x_j} \right), \tag{10.12}$$

where $\partial \Psi_i(\mathbf{x})$ is obtained through the quotient rule for derivatives applied on the
multi-dimensional rule kernel defined through $K_i(\mathbf{x}) = \mu_i(\mathbf{x})$.

Finally, sorting the values of $imp(x_i) = pD_i(\mathbf{x})$ across all features $i = 1, \ldots, p$
and using only the M highest, leads to a reduced as well as sorted representation of
AND-connections in the rules and associated reasons.

Other types of feature importance level calculations (such as LIME, DeepLIFT
etc.) can be found in the recent article [89], where the authors favoured expected
Shapley (ES) values in combination with functions in additive form (and showed
some unique determination of several important factors/parameters).

10.2.5 Rule-Based Similarity and Expected Change Visualisation

So far, the advanced model explanation concepts were rooted in and based on the
components embedded in the current model — from these, the necessary information has been extracted and polished up for humans as users. Additionally, in certain
applications it may be interesting to confirm or overrule model outputs by showing
the human past similar query samples which were classified into the same class resp.
which produced similar prediction values. This may be probably most helpful in the
case of (human-understandable) context-based data such as image, videos or audio
signals. Then, the reasoning text would receive another cute touch in the form of:

**The reason why Prediction X has been returned is that there appeared sev-
eral very similar samples before for which the same prediction was produced
by the model, namely X1, X2, ...**

(and then visually show the context-based data of X1, X2, ..., also in comparison
with the current query).

This indeed requires the usage of a history sample buffer which may slow down the on-line model adaptation process, but could be omitted when using representatives of the most active rules (e.g., their centres) for current queries (compressed information).

Expected change visualisation addresses the important issue to still guarantee human confidence in the model, also in the case when the model may change significantly its parameters/components/structure, most often due to significant novelty content contained in new data (requiring a knowledge expansion of the model). Based on our experience when working with several company partners and industrial installations, often the human operators/experts working with the on-line (ML) system may wish to get a feeling about the extent of the model change expressed by its *expected change in performance* — this is because they are already used to a particular performance and behaviour of the model ('humans are creatures of habit'). Assuming that all stream samples have been stored in a history buffer $Hist$ together with their real target values, then such a buffer can be used for re-calculating model accuracy, to observe how it develops whenever the model structure/components change or are evolved, see [85] for a fast stream-based solution in the case of integrating new classes.

10.2.6 A Case Study on the Impact of Explaining Model Decisions on Human's Annotation Behavior

Here, we present a case study in the context of an image vision based surface inspection system for micro-fluidic chips used for sample preparation in DNA sequencing [86]. The inspection of the quality of the chip is indispensable in order to avoid non-functioning chips and thus complaints by customers to whom the chips are sold. Several different event types (10 classes) may occur on chips and may reduce the quality. The original classifier for the existing inspection system was based on a rudimentary hard-coded rule base which is established manually and operates on features extracted from the regions of interest.

In order to establish machine learning classifiers for a fully automated inspection, a significant amount of real-world recorded sample images must be annotated and labelled by experts in order to guarantee a high performance of the classifier [42, 81] — especially, in the case of a significant system dynamics, human feedback in the form of labels have to be provided from time to time, ideally during on-line usage of the classifier. Based on this feedback, the classifier is able to update its parameters and structures and thus to keep pace with (intended) changes and drifts in the system [54]. The annotation and labeling process is time-intensive and typically affected by concentration problems due to fatigue, boredom, tiredness of the humans; this typically leads to inconsistent and uncertain labelings, which affect the classifier performance when being used in its update. Therefore, the aim was to support the humans with linguistic model explanations in order to reduce this undesired effect [86].

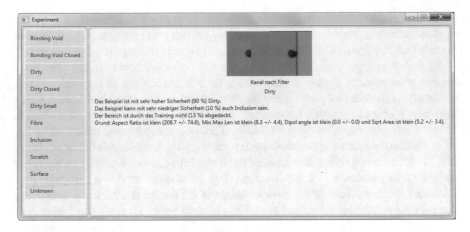

Fig. 10.5 GUI for labeling events with linguistic explanation: four lines of text below the event image and the basic information, following the concepts discussed throughout Sects. 2.1–2.4

For (off-line and on-line) sample annotation purposes, a graphical user interface (GUI) was designed, that is able to visualise the current events (objects) as well as the output information provided by the current classifier. As shown in Fig. 10.5, the GUI consists of two main panels:

- On the left-hand side, the possible class labels for the current application are presented in a list: there are nine types of potential defects; the human user may also provide a label if the event cannot be recognised (termed as 'Unknown').
- In the middle part, the human user can find the next event to be labelled. This event is represented by the image of the event, the event information and — if configured — the linguistic explanation of the classifier prediction, provided by the classifier instance.

The basic event information underneath the image includes two lines of text. The first line is coded in the feature vector and represents the position of the event on the micro-fluidic chip. The second event information is the actual classifier prediction for the event shown. The third event information shows 4 lines of advanced model explanations in the form as discussed earlier sections (reasoning, certainty, alternative suggestions, feature importance due to sorting and coverage). It can be configured in an ini-file to be switched on or off.

6 people were asked to provide their labellings on the same larger stream comprising several thousands of image samples, as taken directly from the real on-line production process: 3 people were obliged to perform the labellings without any advanced model explanations in two consecutive runs, 3 other people performed the labellings in the second run with the advanced model explanations. Thus, we were able to check whether better labellings and thus higher performant classifiers (or not) could be really achieved because of the advanced explanations and not just because the people saw the same stream of samples a second time. An initial set of

Table 10.1 Statistical preference analysis using the results from all-pairs fuzzy classifier (**Fuzzy AP**), '0' indicates no preference for the human operator's run listed in the row over that one mentioned in the column; '+' means a preference with a significance level of $0.95 = 1 - 0.05$ and '++' a stronger preference with a significance level of $0.975 = 1 - 0.025$; the diagonal entries underlined are the most important, as they compare the two runs from one operator

	Op A/1	Op B/1	Op F/1
Op A/2	<u>++</u>	++(+)	++
Op B/2	0	<u>±</u>	0
Op F/2	+	++	<u>±</u>
	Op C/1	Op D/1	Op E/1
Op C/2	<u>0</u>	+	+
Op D/2	0	<u>0</u>	0
Op E/2	−	0	<u>0</u>

200 samples has been labelled by a 'super-operator' with extraordinary experience, based on which an initial fuzzy classifier was trained to start with.

The main interest layed in the change in the degree of uncertainty of the human operators in relation to their labellings between two consecutive runs. In the context of a multi-class classification problem, human certainty can be estimated using the accuracies of the classifiers that were extracted based on the human's labelling, because the feature vectors were the same for all human operators and thus appeared at the same positions in the high-dimensional feature space. Hence, higher classifier accuracies indicate a better ability to distinguish between the classes (i.e., a smaller class overlap), which in turn points to a greater consistency and thus higher certainty of a human's labelling. A reliable estimator of the expected accuracy of a classifier is the 10-fold cross-validation (CV) procedure, see also Chap. 7 of [35] for a detailed analysis. Thus, it was applied to all labelled sets from all 6 human operators achieved in the two runs, and this by using different types of classifiers such as support vector machines [118], decision trees (CART approach) [15], and an all-pairs fuzzy classifier approach (fuzzy-AP) [80] among other famous approaches [86]. These three delivered the best CV accuracies on average over all human operators. A statistical significance analysis was carried out in order to obtain whether there is a preference of classifier accuracy achieved through human labels obtained in the second run over those obtained in the first run.

Table 10.1 shows the results in the case using Fuzzy AP, the first and second parts show the matrices for human operators (A, B, F) with and for human operators (C, D, E) without linguistic explanation support, respectively; the diagonal entries are the most important ones, as they compare the two runs from one operator. Obviously, there is a clear preference of all second over the first runs in the case when linguistic explanation is switched on (human operators A, B and F), whereas this is not the case when it is not switched on.

Similar pictures with similar preference levels in the diagonal entries could be obtained in case of SVMs and decisions trees. Summarising the preference analysis

Table 10.2 The numbers of non-fulfillments (before the slashes) versus fulfillments (after the slashes) of the helpfulness (NH/H), compatibility (NC/C) and understanding (NU/U) of the explanations mentioned in questions Q2, Q3 and Q5 of the interview sheet

Human/Ling./Question	Q2 (NH/H)	Q3 (NC/C)	Q5 (NU/U)
Human A Run 1 (wo)	3/0	3/0	3/0
Human A Run 2 (with)	0/3	0/3	2/1
Human B Run 1 (wo)	6/0	5/1	6/0
Human B Run 2 (with)	3/1	3/1	3/1
Human C Run 1 (wo)	0/2	0/2	0/2
Human C Run 2 (wo)	0/2	0/2	0/2
Human D Run 1 (wo)	0/2	2/0	0/2
Human D Run 2 (wo)	0/2	0/2	0/2
Human E Run 1 (wo)	2/0	2/0	0/2
Human E Run 2 (wo)	1/1	2/0	0/2
Human F Run 1 (wo)	4/0	4/0	0/4
Human F Run 2 (with)	2/2	0/4	0/4
Human A, B, F Run 1 (wo)	11/0	12/1	9/4
Human A, B, F Run 2 (with)	5/6	3/8	5/6
Human C, D, E Run 1 (wo)	2/4	4/2	0/6
Human C, D, E Run 2 (wo)	1/5	2/4	0/6

results over all methods, there finally could be recognised a 7:2 ($\approx$80%) chance to improve labelling certainty in a second run with and only a 1:8 ($\approx$10%) chance to improve it without linguistic explanations (thus by only seeing the samples a second time). As these numbers are underlined by a statistical preference analysis, it can be concluded that a significant overall difference in terms of about *80 versus about 10 percentage chance for improvement of the humans' labelling behaviour* takes place.

Another interesting analysis was the human subjective perception of model explanations on a cognitive level. Therefore, the humans were asked to fill out an interview sheet with some essential questions about the helpfulness, compatibility with the shown image and understanding of the explanations after each labelling cycle comprising 200 samples. They should subjectively make crosses whether these properties were fulfilled 'hardly ever', 'sometimes', 'often' or 'almost always'. The evaluation of the sheets led to the picture as shown in Table 10.2. Remarkably, from the first to the second run, the helpfulness (H), the compatibility with the shown image (C) and the understanding of the explanations (U), improved significantly when model explanations were used (human operators A, B, F), but much more marginally when they were not used. The exception is the property 'understanding': the human operators of the second group already had a good understanding from the plain classifier feedback (in form of model outputs) alone.

10.3   Model Interpretation Concepts (On a Global Level)

Improved transparency and interpretability of machine learning models on a global level, i.e. to make the whole model understandable as such and especially to express in a better way to humans what it really does and which interrelations and dependencies in the system it describes, is typically very challenging in real-world applications — especially in those,

1. where the humans intend to gain a deeper understanding of the interrelations and dependencies in the system — e.g., for improving automatisation, productivity and efficiency in the future design of hard- or software components [21] or for being able to properly react in case of system failures and product quality downtrends [88, 98], i.e. as a support of predictive maintenance actions [66]; and,
2. where the encouragement of richer human-machine interactions is a central goal for increasing productivity, knowledge exchange and quality [23, 57, 81].

In the latter case, improved transparency and interpretability is necessary, because only by understanding the model components and model behaviour, can the humans provide reliable, meaningful and contradiction-free enhanced feedback; e.g., in the form of defining shapes and outlooks of new upcoming classes, behaviour of new operation modes and system dynamics or even changes or add-ons in the decision boundaries or approximation surfaces — as will be discussed in Sect. 10.4.

Fuzzy systems (EFS) and rule-based models are a powerful tool of addressing these demands as they offer fuzzy logic model architectures and systems that include components with a clear, linguistically interpretable meaning [18, 28] — unlike many other machine learning and soft computing models which rely on black box model architectures such as neural networks or support vector machines and are thus un-interpretable per se. This is also the reason, apart from several advantages over these architectures regarding model explanation (see previous section), why we have chosen fuzzy models as a basis for stimulating advanced humans' feedback. However, when fuzzy systems are trained with data (as is the case in a machine learning system), they may loose some of their interpretability [5], especially in a case where learning is conducted in an incremental, evolving manner based on stream samples: rules and fuzzy sets, originally necessary for an appropriate partitioning of the feature space, may move together, thus becoming overlapping and finally redundant due to the nature of streams (samples in the future are not really foreseeable); this goes against the simple and compact nature for understanding a fuzzy rule base, and sometimes may even lead to contradictory rules, which in turn may lead to the loss of human trust.

The loss in interpretability can be diminished by applying specific improvement and assurance techniques, either already during the training stages or in an a posteriori manner with post-processing techniques [75, 128]. Here, we provide a summarised

description of the basic criteria for guiding fuzzy models to a higher level of interpretability and especially consider the applicability of these criteria during on-line
(stream-based) processes. According to the position paper in [75], there are the following central aspects responsible for a readable and understandable rule base:

- Distinguishability and Simplicity
- Consistency
- Coverage (global) and Completeness
- Feature and Rule Importance Levels (global)
- Interpretation of Consequents
- Interpretability of Input-Output Behaviour
- Model-Based Reliability
- Knowledge Expansion

including both, high-level (rule-based) and low-level (fuzzy-set) interpretation spirits
[28, 128]. In the subsequent paragraphs, we will discuss the most important ones in
the context of stimulating enhanced human communication with the model.

Distinguishability and Simplicity

While *distinguishability* requires structural components (rules, fuzzy sets) that are
clearly separable as non-overlapping and non-redundant, *simplicity* goes a step further and expects models with a trade-off between low complexity and high accuracy.
From the mathematical point of view, *distinguishability* can be defined as follows:

Definition 10.1 Distinguishability is guaranteed whenever

$$\nexists_{i,j,k} \quad (S(R_i, R_j) > thr) \vee (S(A_{ik}, A_{jk}) > thr), \tag{10.13}$$

with S the similarity $\in [0, 1]$ between two rules R_i and R_j resp. two fuzzy sets A_{ik}
and A_{jk} appearing in the same antecedent part of rules R_i and R_j ($k = 1, \ldots, p$ with
p the input dimensionality of the feature space).

In literature, there exist several similarity measures S between two fuzzy sets or
rules, ranging from inclusion measures through geometric aspects to kernel-based
metrics, see [24, 65, 93]. The threshold thr governs the degree of similarity allowed
between two components and may depend on the chosen similarity measure. Generally, without loss of generality we can say that a value of S close to 1 points to a
high similarity, whereas a value of S close to 0 points to a low similarity.

From a practical viewpoint, *distinguishability* ensures that rules and fuzzy sets
are not becoming significantly overlapping and thus redundant. In the case of
two- or three non-distinguishable rules or fuzzy sets, the whole rule base or fuzzy
partition may indeed be still comprehensible, but when this number increases, the
interpretability for humans typically severely suffers. An example for highly overlapping, redundant fuzzy sets is shown in Fig. 10.6a. In this example, it is obviously
very hard (or impossible) to provide a semantic meaning and unique linguistic terms
to all these sets: this leaves the antecedent parts of some rules unreadable for human
experts and users, which also negatively affects the reasoning process based on model

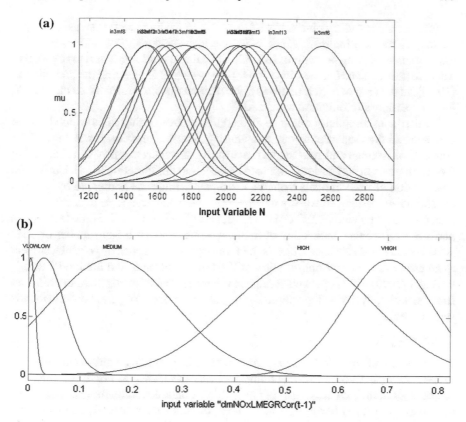

Fig. 10.6 **a** weird fuzzy partition for rotation speed at an engine modelling task, the fuzzy sets are not distinguishable, thus no clear semantic meaning in the form of linguistic terms can be assigned to them; **b** interpretable fuzzy partition with 5 distinct entities (fuzzy sets)

explanations (see previous section). Figure 10.6b demonstrates how a fuzzy partition should ideally look like: here, it is possible to assign linguistic terms (from very low to very high), thus to assure readability of the AND-connections in the rule antecedent parts.

From the mathematical point of view, *simplicity* can be defined as follows:

Definition 10.2 Let F_1 be a fuzzy system fully evolved from a data stream. Then, maximum simplicity of this system meets the following criterion:

$$\min\{|F| | (|F_1| > |F|) \wedge (acc(F) \geq acc(F_1) - \varepsilon)\}, \qquad (10.14)$$

with acc the accuracy of the fuzzy system and $|F|$ the number of components (rules, fuzzy sets) in the simplest possible, yet accurate enough model F. ε is expressing the allowed loss in accuracy and is application dependent, i.e. usually set by the human according to a maximal allowed model error.

From a practical viewpoint, various forms of complexity reduction steps are proper techniques for assuring *distinguishability* and increasing *simplicity*. They typically employ some merging procedures [65, 82, 113]: if two rules may (start to) overlap to a degree greater than thr, merging is conducted as a way of assuring the condition in (10.13); in the case of high redundancy, the merged system F usually meets (10.14) (only superfluous information is discarded).

Furthermore, simplicity might be also addressed by deleting rules which became obsolete and thus superfluous due to changing system dynamics, for instance. The concepts of rule age and rule support, measuring the addressability of rules during the recent process(ing) period, offer nice strategies in this direction [6, 8]. During the construction of fuzzy models from data, simplicity might be addressed by specific constraints or learning constructs which emphasize simpler models over more complex ones, also by tending to keep the model error on a low level. Some techniques perform a top-down construction of fuzzy systems, where a larger number of rules is initialized in the rule base which is then 'out-sparsed' as much as possible, subject to an error criteria (joint optimisation of the number of rules and the model error), see e.g. [87, 90]. Others put constraints on the movement of focal and knot points on fuzzy sets directly during the optimisation cycles to omit overlaps and out-of-bounds sets [16, 26].

Consistency

Inconsistency of the rule base may arise whenever two rules significantly overlap in their antecedents (due to overlapping fuzzy sets as shown in Fig. 10.6), but little or not at all in their consequents. In fact, within a data-driven learning context, this case may point to either a high noise level or to an inconsistently learnt output behaviour. Apart from a low interpretability level, different consequents of equally firing rules may lead to highly blurred outputs, thus even affecting the accuracy of the predictions. From a practical point of view, such inconsistencies should be resolved as the human may get confused when such rules are shown to him: in fact, mostly both rules would be shown to her/him as both are almost equally firing, but both are pointing to different predictions or class outputs — so, which rule (and associated reason for the model output) should she/he trust?

Formally, the inconsistency between the two rules R_1 and R_2 can be defined in the following way:

Definition 10.3 Rule R_1 is inconsistent to Rule R_2 if and only if $S_{ante}(R_1, R_2) \geq S_{cons}(R_1, R_2)$ with $S_{ante}(R_1, R_2) \geq thr$.

with S_{ante} the similarity degree in the antecedent parts and S_{cons} the similarity degree in the consequent parts. No matter which similarity measure is used, a value of S_{ante} close to 1 always can be assumed to point to a high similarity and of S_{ante} close to 0 to a low similarity. This is obviously an extension to the inconsistency condition for crisp rules.

In [79], in order to resolve inconsistencies among two rules, a merging concept of rule consequents is proposed. It respects the inconsistency level between two overlapping contradictory rules, which is measured in terms of an exponential function:

$$Cons(R_1, R_2) = e^{ -\frac{\left(\frac{S_{ante}(R_1, R_2)}{S_{cons}(R_1, R_2)} - 1 \right)^2}{\left(\frac{1}{S_{ante}} \right)^7} } \tag{10.15}$$

and assures that a low value of S_{ante} (<0.4) always achieves a high consistency close to 1, as the denominator in the exponential function gets overly high. This is natural as the antecedent parts do overlap only a little in this case. The merging to one joint consistent rule (consequent) is achieved by following the idea of participatory learning [124], which results in the following formula:

$$\mathbf{w}_{new} = \mathbf{w}_{R_1} + \alpha \cdot Cons(R_1, R_2) \cdot (\mathbf{w}_{R_2} - \mathbf{w}_{R_1}), \tag{10.16}$$

where $\alpha = k_{R_2}/(k_{R_1} + k_{R_2})$ and k_{R_1} the support (=significance) of rule R_1 (e.g., based on data samples forming this rule in the past). In this sense, the consequent vector of the merged rule is more influenced by the more supported rule R_1 when the consistency degree is lower, thus increasing the belief in the more supported rule R_1. Interestingly, this approach can be easily applied in a posteriori manner without requiring external input or data. A successful application of this measure leading to contradictory-free and transparent rule bases for two real-world application scenarios has been carried out in [82].

Coverage (Global) and Completeness

Coverage on a global level is a generalisation of the local (per query) coverage handled in Sect. 10.2.3 to the overall model definition space. Thus, coverage refers to the specific characteristics of a machine learning model that does not allow undefined input states, i.e. it is well-defined over the complete range of the feature space. In the case of fuzzy models, this means that sufficient fuzzy partitions and rules should be ideally extracted from data, covering the whole feature space well. In a data-driven learning context, coverage may, however, suffer as usually rules are only extracted in regions of the feature space where samples actually appear.

Humans may be interested in the model coverage to get a glance of the expected trustworthiness of model outputs for query instances appearing within the ranges of the input features: if the coverage is (too) low, the inclusion of additional knowledge (data, user-defined rules) in the model is indispensable to guarantee a model with sufficient performance. This is because typically fuzzy models and machine learning models in general tend to produce incorrect and uncertain outputs in extrapolation regions (=regions with low or no coverage) [41]. Thus, human input, e.g., in the form of expert-based rules or additional data based on which the model can be expanded to regions uncovered so far, is urgently requested in low coverage cases. Figure 10.7 exemplarily shows two rule bases, where the left one induces a low coverage of the samples space (many holes appear there) and the right one a high coverage (only a few small holes appear).

The overall model coverage degree of the input space can be objectively measured (and reported to humans) by calculating the maximal membership degrees to all rules

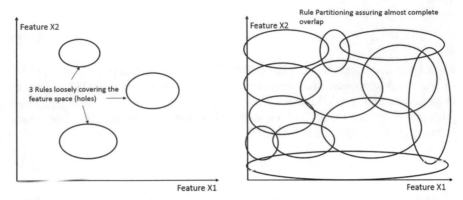

Fig. 10.7 Left: loose rule partitioning with low coverage of the feature space; right: crowded partitioning with almost perfect coverage

for a collection of representative samples in the feature space (according to (10.6)) and performing some statistics on these degrees (mean, variance, number of samples below a certain degree of maximal membership, etc.). As this space is often a high-dimensional one, statistical sample generation techniques such as Latin hypercube sampling [92] are of great help to guarantee a widely spread and well-covering data set. A good idea is to calculate coverage degrees over various partial regions of the input feature space — then the human becomes an impression in which regions additional knowledge is required.

Completeness in fuzzy systems is also often referred to as ε-completeness with $\varepsilon \in]0, 1]$ [75, 108]. It can be seen as a specification of coverage by guaranteeing a minimal coverage with degree ε over the entire feature space. The definition on fuzzy set level is as follows:

Definition 10.4 A fuzzy partition for feature X_i containing the fuzzy sets $A_1, \ldots,$ A_M is said to be ε-complete whenever there is no point $x \in [min(X_i), max(X_i)]$ such that $\mu_{A_i}(x) < \varepsilon$, with $\varepsilon > 0$ a small positive number.

Extending this to rule level, requires a rule base $\mu_1, \ldots, \mu_C$ such that $\max_{i=1,\ldots,C} \mu_i$ $(\mathbf{x}) > \varepsilon$ for all points $\mathbf{x}$ in the input feature space, i.e. for all points (samples) at least one rule fires with a significant degree. Taking into account that each fuzzy set is used in at least one rule, the ε-completeness of rules can be directly associated with the ε-completeness of sets through the applied t-norm T: as $\mathsf{T}(x_1, x_2, \ldots, x_p) \leq min(x_1, x_2, \ldots, x_p)$, the following holds

$$\left(\forall \mathbf{x} \; \exists i \; \left(\mu_i = \mathop{\mathsf{T}}_{j=1,\ldots,p} (\mu_{ij}) > \varepsilon\right)\right) \Rightarrow \left(\forall \mathbf{x} \; \exists i \; (\forall j \; \mu_{ij} \geq \mathop{\mathsf{T}}_{j=1,\ldots,p} (\mu_{ij}) > \varepsilon)\right),$$

(10.17)

with μ_{ij} the membership degree of fuzzy set A_j appearing in the jth antecedent part of the ith rule and p the rule length. In this sense, assuring ε-completeness on rule level automatically ensures ε-completeness on fuzzy set level.

In [75], two approaches for approaching ε-completeness in fuzzy models are demonstrated:

- The first acts on the fuzzy partition level and is based on heuristic adjustments of the ranges of influence of those fuzzy sets which were updated during the last incremental learning step(s). The adjustment should not be too large in order to stay within the model error limits.
- The second one acts on the rule level and employs an enhanced incremental optimisation procedure for non-linear antecedent parameters in rules. Thereby, a term representing model coverage degree is embedded into the least squares objective function in order to trigger synchronous optimisation of both. This has been realised within a top-down sparse fuzzy model training procedure (termed Sparse-FIS) [87] and successfully tested on various real-world data sets, outperforming various SoA fuzzy modelling methods in terms of improved coverage degrees while achieving similar model errors.

Nevertheless, in both approaches, ε-completeness is only approached, but cannot be assured, such that checking the whole model coverage and reporting it to the human (as described above) is still important.

Feature and Rule Importance Levels (Global)

The role of *feature importance* (on model predictions) has been discussed in Sect. 10.2.4 on a per query instance (local) level. On a global model level, it serves three purposes: (i) to provide the human with the information as to which features are more important than others over the entire range of the model definition space; (ii) to reduce the lengths of *all* rules contained in the rule base, thus to increase the readability of the whole rule base and (iii) to reduce the curse of dimensionality effect in subsequent model updates (based on incremental learning with new samples).

(i) and (ii) are essential aspects for humans to understand which features are important for modeling the process (problem), and to ensure compact rule bases. In order to address the global feature of importance problematic, approaches in [71, 103] (for classification) and [4, 84] (for regression) have proposed the concepts of (incrementally) calculating so-called *feature weights*, which denote how much they contribute to the (i) discriminatory power of the model in the classification case and (ii) how much they contribute to the model output (error) in the regression case. The sample-wise update mechanisms of feature weights in these approaches guarantee a smooth, continuous change of feature importance over time. Thus, features may become down-weighted at an earlier stage and then reactivated at a later stage of the on-line (modelling) process without 'disturbing' or abruptly changing the (convergence of the) model structure and parameters. Furthermore, the feature weights are integrated into the model adaptation process in order to diminish the effect of unimportant features in the rule evolution criteria. This decreases the likelihood that unnecessary rules are evolved due to the violation of the stability condition caused by unimportant features, which in turn decreases over-fitting. The output of all these methods is a feature weight vector, which can be visualised as a bar chart and shown to the human.

Rule importance levels, representable in the form of rule weights, may serve as important corner stones for a smooth rule reduction during learning procedures. Rules with low weights can be seen as unimportant and may be pruned or even re-activated at a later stage in an on-line learning process. This strategy may be beneficial when, e.g., starting with an expert-based system, where originally all rules are fully interpretable (as designed by human experts/users), however some may turn out to be superfluous over time for the modelling problem at hand. Rule weights can be integrated into the fuzzy model inference process shown in (10.11) by

$$f(\mathbf{x}) - \sum_{i=1}^{C} l_i(\mathbf{x}) \Psi_i(\mathbf{x}) \quad \Psi_i(\mathbf{x}) = \frac{\rho_i K_i(\mathbf{x})}{\sum_{j=1}^{C} \rho_j K_j(\mathbf{x})}. \tag{10.18}$$

Thus, rules with low weights ρ also contribute little to the overall model output. In this sense, the rule weights are appearing as additional non-linear parameters, which may be optimised and updated within incremental data-driven procedures such as recursive gradient descent (RGD) [96], recursive Levenberg–Marquardt (RLM) [120] or recursive Gauss-Newton as applied in [52].

Rules receiving low weights ρ_i may then be ignored in an interpretation stage when the human expert/user inspects the fuzzy model, subject to having contributed in a low manner to the final model outputs (prediction) on the stream samples seen so far. The connection with a low contribution is necessary, as hidden rules (due to low weights) could have a reduced effect but still be perceived by an expert. The relative contribution level of a rule R_i to the model output over N past data samples can be calculated as:

$$\text{contrib}_i = \frac{1}{N} \sum_{k=1}^{N} \Psi_i(\mathbf{x}_k). \tag{10.19}$$

Thus, those rules can be ignored when showing the fuzzy system to the human, for which $contrib_i < \varepsilon \ \wedge \ \rho_i < \varepsilon$.

Rule Chains for Tracking the Changing Behaviour of Fuzzy Systems over Time:

Visual interpretability refers to an interesting alternative to *linguistic interpretability* (as discussed above), namely to the representation of a model in a graphical form. In our context, this approach could be especially useful if models evolve quickly, since monitoring a visual representation might then be easier than following a frequently changing linguistic description. Under this scope, alternative "interpretability criteria" may then become interesting to discover which are more dedicated to the timely development of the evolving fuzzy model — for instance, a trajectory of rule centres showing their movement over time, or trace paths showing birth, growth, pruning and merging of rules. The first pioneering attempts in this direction have been conducted in [37], employing the concept of *rule chains*. These have been significantly extended in [38] by setting up a visualisation framework with a grown-up user fron-tend (GUI), integrating various similarity, coverage and overlap measures as well

Fig. 10.8 An example of a rule chain system as occurred for a specific data stream: each rule is arranged in a separate row, its progress over time shown horizontally; each vertical (circular) marker denotes a data chunk. We can see that in the second data chunk a new rule is born, which died out later in the 9th data chunk

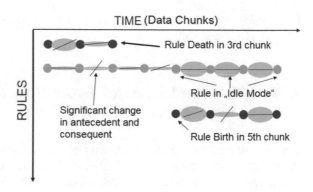

as specific techniques for an appropriate catchy representation of high-dimensional rule antecedents and consequents. Internally, it uses the FLEXFIS++ approach [72] as an incremental learning engine for evolving a fuzzy rule base.

An example of a typical rule chain system is provided in Fig. 10.8. The size of the ellipsoids indicates the similarity of the rules' antecedent parts between two consecutive time instances (marked as 'circles'), the rotation degree of the small lines indicates the similarity of the rules' consequent parts in terms of their angle between two consecutive time instances: a high angle indicates a larger change between two time instances, thus the rule has been intensively updated during the last chunk. This may provide the human with an idea about the dynamics of the system. Also, when several rules die out or are born within a few chunks, the human may gain some insight into the system dynamics and this may stimulate her/him to react properly. Furthermore, rules which are highly fluctuating, thus changing their antecedents and consequents much with back-and-forth, may be taken with care and even removed by a human.

An example of a **successful application of some interpretation and assurance concepts** discussed throughout this section can be found in [83]. This has been achieved within a real-world application scenario of premise price prediction, especially with the usage of simplicity and distinguishability assurance concepts, but also with the support of consistency assurance and out-sparsing the initial rule base in a top-down manner. Compact fuzzy partitions (containing maximal 4 fuzzy sets in each dimension) and nine transparent and consistent rules could be finally achieved.

10.4 Enhanced Human Feedback and Integration Concepts

We will discuss several possibilities of human feedback to transparent and explainable ML models. We realised these as the most widely accepted ones according to our long-term experience in various industrial installations. Each feedback variant will be described in a single section, and an appropriate integration in the form of a homogenization with ongoing data-driven model update schemes will be discussed along the feedback variants.

10.4.1 Plain Feedback Based on Good/Bad Rewards and/or Sample Annotation

The most naive feedback the human may give is in the form of a plain feedback on the outputs produced by the model. This feedback may either comprise a good/bad reward, indicating whether the model output was plausible for her/him or in a more extended version with a more detailed value, e.g., in the form of a concrete annotation response. The latter case has been discussed within the case study of classifying events in a visual inspection system included in Sect. 10.2.6. There, it could be demonstrated that advanced model explanations discussed throughout Sect. 10.2 in fact can improve the feedback annotation (=class label) quality and consistency, where appropriate visualisation of the explanations to the user in a GUI frontend was essential.

Now, the question arises how this plain humans' feedback can be ideally integrated into the model. This is especially important in a case when the model output is not confirmed. Then, ideally the model should be improved in order to increase its prediction quality on new samples which are similar to the current (badly predicted) one. The improvement can be established by an *incremental adaptation of the model* with such new sample(s). Two typical cases which may arise in the case of classification problems are visualised in Fig. 10.9 for a simple 2-D example. The upper row shows the case when the decision boundary between new classes requires an adjustment in order to correctly classify the new sample (lying on the wrong side of the boundary and thus having been wrongly classified) and further samples lying close to it. Such a case can also be seen as a *refinement of model's response surfaces*. The upper right image shows the updated model based on human feedback (overruled class), leading to an expansion/deformation of the rule representing the circular class (indicated by the dotted ellipsoid). The lower row shows the case when the model requires an expansion to a new region of the feature space so far unexplored — induced by three new samples. Such a case can also be seen as a *knowledge expansion of the model*. The lower right image shows the expanded model based on human feedback on the three new samples, leading to the generation of a new rule representing the rectangular class (indicated by an ellipsoid). This also induces a significant change in the decision boundary.

Techniques from the field of incremental (machine) learning [29, 110] are able to update the model (parameters) in a single-pass, stream-wise manner in order to induce changes in the model response surfaces as shown in the upper right image. Techniques from the field of evolving (intelligent) systems [10, 53] are additionally able to change their structure and thus to perform real expansion of the model and its knowledge to new (undiscovered) regions of the feature space — as shown in the lower right image

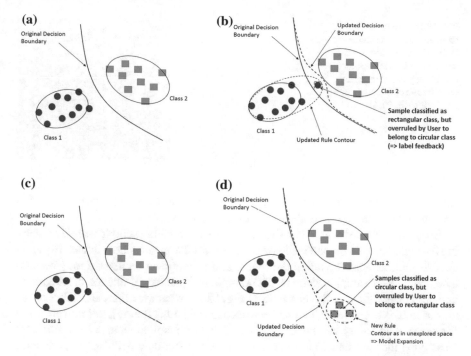

Fig. 10.9 a Original class distribution, decision boundary and rule contours (solid ellipsoids); **b** incorrectly classified sample (to rectangular class) overruled by a human to belong to the circular class → updated decision boundary and updated rule contour based on human's feedback shown in dashed lines; **c** same as in **a**; **d** three new samples incorrectly classified, overruled by a human to belong to the circular class → evolution of a new rule (shown as dotted ellipsoid) required in order to extend the decision boundary and to reduce the *version space* (the concept version space has been proposed in [44])

in Fig. 10.9. In the concrete case of fuzzy systems and classifiers, a large collection and comparison of more than 40 EFS (evolving fuzzy systems) approaches can be found in [69, 76]. Principally, almost all of the techniques include the following single-pass learning concepts as mentioned on p. 3 (itemisation points). EFS have been successfully applied in many real-world application and on-line processes whenever real target values have been made available (either through automatic measurements or human's feedback), see [76].

Human input may be handled differently when interacting with the same machine learning systems, based on the level of expertise and past experience of the humans. Intuitively, feedback by humans with lower expertise may be handled with more care, and thus less weight when integrating it into the model, than feedback by long term experts. In some other cases, the same human may be more or less confident about his feedback (and thus may choose a confidence level between [0, 1], e.g., by button press, as feedback in addition to the sample annotation — see Fig. 10.10 which shows an example from a GUI (in one of our past projects) [81] where humans

Fig. 10.10 An example
from an image classification
GUI, where the human can
specialise his feedback in the
form of good/bad rewards
with certain confidence
levels (20, 40, 60, 80 and
100%)

can give feedback on classified images in the form of good/bad rewards, together
with their belief in their confidences of the chosen reward.

Both cases can be treated with the integration of so-called *sample weights* reflecting the uncertainty in human feedbacks: experienced users may be reflected in higher
sample weights when updating the model and unconfident feedbacks may be pun-
ished with lower samples weights. The sample weights then influence the degree of
update. For instance, in the example in Fig. 10.9b, whenever the class label of the
new sample is overruled with a low confidence (high uncertainty), the movement of
the decision boundary will be less intense. This may result in an updated model still
classifying the new sample to the rectangular class, but now with lower confidence
than before. Then when a new similar sample (lying close to this sample) comes
in and the classifier response is overruled again with low confidence, the decision
boundary will be again moved slightly, and so on. This finally has the desired effect
that low confidences in human feedback require more confirmations to have an actual
effect on the model responses.

Although the uncertainty in human feedback can be easily parameterised within
an interaction frontend (see Fig. 10.10) and appropriately handled in adequate model
update schemes, it would be more efficient to influence the human's cognition in a
way to 'make' her/him more certain about his feedback. A strategy to accomplish
this is to show the human samples similar to the current query, collected and stored
in a history buffer which have been used for annotation during past (on-line) learning
cycles or which are available in an external historic data base from which information
can be gathered [36, 122]. This is only reliably accomplishable whenever the samples
have contextual, understandable meaning for humans, e.g., images or textures, for
instance. The similar samples may help the human user to provide a more certain
feedback on new queries (e.g., confirmation of class labels she/he had already in
mind). The similarity can be expressed by employing similarity measures [11], where
usually a similarity value of 0 indicates no similarity at all and a similarity measure
of 1 full equivalency.

10.4.2   Structural Feedback by Human-Defined Rules

Depending on the human's experience and knowledge, she/he may also go a step further and not only provide her/his plain feedback on model output level, but may specify a more detailed description about specific relations and dependencies within the system she/he is aware of. This can have its motivation due to the following situations:

- The human sees some model components (in our case fuzzy rules and sets) misplaced or embedding inadequate consequences — these can arise due to insufficient data, high noise levels in the data or inexperienced humans defining erroneous rules [75].
- New operations modes [22, 64] or new events (expressed by new classes [39, 85]) may arise on the fly of which the model so far unaware.

The former can be only stimulated when employing advanced concepts for improving model interpretability and understandability, as intrinsically discussed throughout Sect. 10.3 (otherwise, the human may not be able to realise 'misplaced' rules etc.). In the latter case, human input is very welcome for the early increase of the significance of new modes/events in the model, thus avoiding any deteriorating performance. Decision boundaries and approximation surfaces can thus be extended and sharpened much earlier and predictions for the new modes/event can be made more accurate and reliable. Often, such human knowledge is available in the form of a linguistic description provided by the domain expert [56, 117]. More specifically, by using the natural language to express the required knowledge, the expert uses a number of IF/THEN rules. If she/he does not explicitly state the rules in such forms, mostly her/his linguistic description can be transferred and coded in the form of rules [2] (see also Sect. 10.4.4). This was one major reason for building the model explanation and interpretation concepts on the basis of fuzzy systems as model architecture, as these naturally express IF-THEN constructs.

The open question is then, how to continue the update of the model with newly arriving samples, whenever human-defined or human-changed rules have been integrated. This also belongs to the case where a whole expert system has been designed comprising a larger set of rules — as established during interviews, for instance, see Sect. 10.4.4. In order to underline this problematic issue, we exemplarily show a two-dimensional example (Fig. 10.11) in a case where a human defines a new event class in the form of a rule, either by linguistically defining it through AND-conjunctions of fuzzy sets (see text in the image) or by drawing the rule contour directly into the feature space using an appropriate interacting frontend. The human-defined rule for a new class is shown as a solid ellipsoid, whereas new arising data samples belonging to the new class (dark circular dots) turn out to be shifted away from the human-defined rule. So, there is a conflicting situation between subjectively defined positioning of a new class and the objectively measured (real occurring) positioning.

So, the question arises as to which type of input should the ML system trust more, resp. how should both input types (human knowledge and data) be fused in

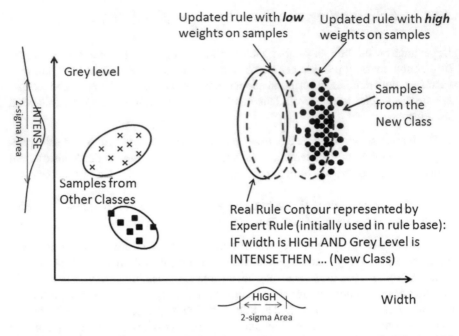

Fig. 10.11 A human-defined rule (solid ellipsoid in black colour) for a new class (dark dots), which appears to be misplaced subject to the data defining the new class; possible weighting strategies for updating the human-defined class are shown by dashed red ellipsoids — note that, depending on the preferred human's choice, the rule for the new class can be either defined by linguistically formulating the IF-THEN conditions, by drawing the ellipsoidal contour directly in the feature space or by prototypical specification of the new class (based on which the rule contour can be shaped out)

an appropriate way to assure a consistent model? An approach which tackles this problematic issue is presented in [74] for the case of updating a complete fuzzy expert system with new data collected during post parcel services (in order to assess the dispatch risk of parcels). The authors suggest a weighted update scheme of human defined rules with those new samples lying closest to a rule. This means that for each sample $\mathbf{x}_j$, $j = 1, \ldots, M$ in a new data chunk containing M samples, the closest rule subject to a distance metric d, i.e. $i* = argmin_{i=1,\ldots,C} d(R_i, \mathbf{x}_j)$ (respecting the type of rule shape), is elicited and the sample stored into the buffer B_{i*}. Then, the update of the centre $\mathbf{c}_i$ of the human-defined rule R_i (=the focal point where the membership degree is maximal (1) is conducted by a weighted averaging:

$$\mathbf{c}_i(new) = \frac{w_{\text{data}}\mu_i + w_{\text{human}}\mathbf{c}_i}{w_{\text{data}} + w_{\text{human}}}, \tag{10.20}$$

with μ_i the mean value of the samples in B_i (those which are closest to the human-defined rule). w_{data} and w_{human} represent the weights for the sample-based mean and the human-based rule centre, respectively. A promising option would be to include the uncertainty of the human feedback into the weights, which can either stem from her/his experience level or by her/his active confidence feedback (see previous section). Then, $w_{\text{data}} = 1 - w_{\text{human}}$ with $w_{\text{human}} = conf_{\text{human}}$. Another important factor uses the number of samples for 'forming' μ_i: a higher number increases the certainty that the human-defined rule is misplaced and thus w_{data} should be increased, no matter how confident the human was when defining his rule or changing an already available one. The update of the range of influence σ_i of the human-defined rule R_i along each direction (dimension) with the samples rule range $\sigma*_i$ can be conducted with the usage of recursive variance formula including rank-1 modification (see also [74] for motivation), thus:

$$
\sigma_i(new) = \sqrt{\frac{w_{\text{human}}\sigma_i}{w_{\text{human}} + w_{\text{data}}} + (\mathbf{c}_i - \mathbf{c}_i(new))^2 + \frac{(\mathbf{c}_i(new) - \mu_i)^2}{w_{\text{human}} + w_{\text{data}}} + \frac{w_{\text{data}}\sigma*_i}{w_{\text{human}} + w_{\text{data}}}}.
$$

$$(10.21)$$

Another form of structural human input could be that she/he extends one or more of the current fuzzy partitions in order to increase their granularity level (for input explanation) or to expand their definition ranges. For instance, in the context of the example shown in Fig. 10.11, a partitioning of the grey level into INTENSE (close to 255) and WEAK (close to 0) may be too insufficient in order to characterise (object/image) classes which may only occur at a medium grey level (around 127) — then, a fuzzy set describing the range of influence of a MEDIUM grey level would be a preferred human input. On the other hand, due to weak expertise, the human may not be able or may not dare to formulate whole rules including the new fuzzy set MEDIUM. In this case, such rules have to be automatically constructed by data (either off-line stored or new on-line data). The difference in a regular data-driven rule construction, however, is that they should not be 'shaped out' from scratch, but by respecting the human-defined fuzzy set(s) input.

An idea to accomplish this is to set up all possible combinations of a newly defined fuzzy set with existing fuzzy sets in other input partitions in order to form various rule antecedents (all fuzzy sets are connected by AND), leading to a so-called *all-coverage* approach. This procedure follows the spirit that every possible fuzzy set combination could in principle form a valuable relation for explaining the dependencies between inputs and the output. However, this usually leads to an explosion of the number of rules, especially when the number of inputs is not very small. This is because the increase of the number of rules with the number of inputs is exponential. Hence, in a second step, the idea is to perform a kind of rule out-sparsing concept. Based on available data, rule weights $\in [0, 1]$ denoting the importance levels of rules, are configured within a numerical optimisation procedure. In other words, those rules (fuzzy set combinations) which are not required are out-sparsed, i.e. their weights decreased towards 0, over multiple iterations of the optimisation process. In order to keep the rule base compact, it is favourable to out-sparse as many rules as possible. Thus, the optimisation criterion is ideally defined as a combination of the least squares error (accounting for the quality of the predictions) and the number of rules with a significant weight $\rho > 0$ (accounting for model complexity):

$$\min_{\rho,\mathbf{w}} J(\mathbf{w}, \mathbf{c}, \sigma, \rho) \quad \text{such that } \sum_{i=1}^{N} |\rho_i| \leq K, \tag{10.22}$$

with

$$J(\mathbf{w}, \mathbf{c}, \sigma, \rho) = \sum_{k=1}^{N} (y_k - \sum_{i=1}^{C} l_i(\mathbf{x}_k) \Psi_i(\mathbf{x}_k))^2 \tag{10.23}$$

and Ψ_i the normalised membership degree as defined in (10.18). Interestingly, the rule weights play a similar role here to those discussed in Sect. 10.3, Paragraph 'Feature and Rule Importance Levels' — there, the focus layed on providing compact rule bases to humans (by omitting the rules with low weights), here the focus is to again establish a rule base as compact as possible. The difference is that here rules are enforced to be outweighed and thus omitted during the optimisation process. The optimisation problem in (10.22) can be solved by an iterative projected gradient descent algorithm including regularized Lagrange multipliers; this can even be achieved by respecting a minimal coverage ε of the feature space [87], meeting the coverage demands discussed in Sect. 10.3, paragraph 'Coverage (global) and Completeness'.

10.4.3 Extensions/Change of Model Boundaries by Human-Defined Limits

In some cases, the human is neither able to define a vague description of a new operation mode nor a rule defining the relation/dependency among features in certain classes and/or local regions. However, often humans are aware of minimal and maximal bounds in which certain events or modes may occur and vary. For instance, in [36] various types of fault occurrences on die-cast parts have been specialised through the definition of upper and lower bounds on the input features; or in [64], human operators define fault modes in control valves for servo motors by specifying border constructs on the features.

Such hard boundaries can be integrated in fuzzy rule bases by defining crisp sets over the input features most responsible for the mode/event from the human's perspective. For instance, in the context post parcel management and services [74], the human may define for a new class ('very save parcels') that the country as well as the dispatch risk to lie inbetween 0 and 0.2; or, she/he may define that an inacceptable post parcel happens when the country risk is above 0.9. Both occurrences lead to rectangles (in the generalised high-dimensional case hyper-boxes) as shown striped in Fig. 10.12. And which can be represented easily by the following rules:

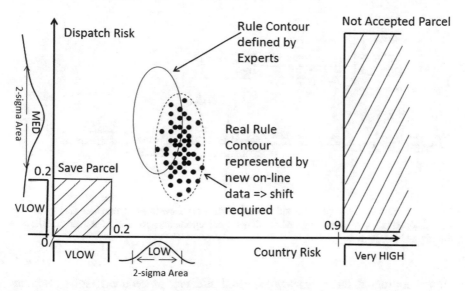

Fig. 10.12 Human defined rules and data samples in the case of post parcel services; the two shaded rectangles describe rules according to the definition of upper and lower limits of humans to characterise not accepted parcels (right most area) and very safe parcels (lower left area); another ellipsoidal rule has been defined in the middle by drawing, which however requires adjustment due to new data samples a bit shifted from this ellipsoid (see previous section how to handle such occurrences)

- IF Country Risk is Very LOW AND Dispatch Risk is Very LOW THEN Parcel is Very SAFE.
- IF Country Risk is Very HIGH AND Dispatch Risk Don't Care THEN Parcel is INACCEPTABLE.

Then, upon receiving new incoming data, such (boundary-based) rules can be adapted with the same concepts as discussed in the previous section, also respecting possible contradictions between the data and the human-defined rules.

10.4.4   Relational Feedback Based on Humans Experience/Knowledge

In an advanced knowledge exchange context, the human may also provide input in the form of her/his long-term expertise working with the system, rather than giving a response in the form of ad-hoc rules according to the current situation at the system. The advanced exchange typically leads to broader design, formulation and coding phases of human knowledge into so-called *expert systems* [19], usually conducted within off-line backstage cycles as requiring deep knowledge acquisition cycles (e.g., interviews, discussions, …). An expert system can be inspected as an 'intelligent

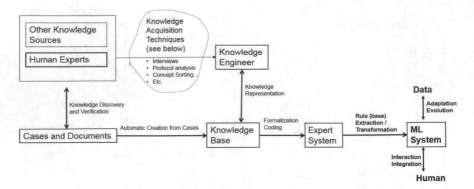

Fig. 10.13 Knowledge acquisition and formalisation work-flow from experts to expert systems to be embedded in machine learning (ML) systems; interaction concepts with the human and the data highlighted in bold font

computer program that uses knowledge and inference procedures to solve problems that are difficult enough to require significant human expertise for their solution' [3]. It is also imaginable that the funded human knowledge serves as a starting point for establishing a (initial) model, which is then further updated with machine learning techniques (again in a kind of hybrid modelling scheme).

According to [2], there exist three basic components of human knowledge:

- **Facts**: they represent sets of raw observation, alphabets, symbols or statements: e.g., 'every crane has a ladder stage'.
- **Rules**: they encompass conditions and actions, which are also known as antecedents and consequences. These basically follow the same structure as linguistically readable rules used in fuzzy systems and handled in several examples above.
- **Heuristics in a more general, arbitrary form**: they are the way to represent problem-solving experiences within the knowledge base, typically solutions which humans employed in a similar situation. Thus, they are often stored in the minds of humans (in the form of 'past experience').

The picture in Fig. 10.13 shows an overview on the basic activities which may be taken into account during a knowledge acquisition design phase in communication with humans (expert's view). Knowledge acquisition techniques may range from (structured and unstructured) interviews and discussions, through protocols (interviews with loud thinking included), observations (what the human does during his work, how he communicates with the system, which form of knowledge he brings in etc.) and concrete questionnaires to diagram-based techniques (e.g., conceptual maps). No matter which knowledge acquisition technique is used, an appropriate knowledge representation and coding and formulation phase is requested by experts, which finally results in a kind of expert system.

The expert system can then be embedded within a machine-learning oriented system upon the extraction of a (core) rule base. This is usually possible, because human knowledge can be expected to be mostly available in some linguistically expressible form [56, 117]. There are three possible ways to integrate a knowledge-based fuzzy rule base into a ML system:

- Initial rule base: no model is available so far and the predictions and classifications are started with the initial rule base which may be further updated with new data.
- Additional rule base: a rule base has already been established, either by data or through the expertise and past experience from a different human user/expert working with the system; the new rule base established can be used in parallel to the current rule base, standing as a model for its own, to improve its prediction within a kind of ensembling scheme, or to overrule predictions produced by the other rule base.
- Merger with an existing rule base: similarly as in the previous point, a rule base has already been established, but here the new rule base is directly merged with the old one to form a new homogenous rule base. In this sense, it is an extended form of defining one or two additional rules (in the current model) for specific circumstances such as new events and operation modes (as discussed in Sect. 10.4.2).

An initial rule base is the case where the expert does not want to start with a pure data-driven model from scratch, but she/he feels experienced enough to provide her/his knowledge in advance — or, in the case when an initial knowledge-based model is already present (e.g., within an historic data base), such that its exploitation is probably beneficial for the system, to start already with good quality predictions.

An additional rule base becomes apparent when the human is disappointed by the current ML system, feels that it does not work properly etc., or also when there are different viewpoints from different humans, each one telling her/his own 'story' based on past experiences. In the latter case, a fusion technique within a model (rule base) ensembling concept is required to appropriately resolve contradictory or inconsistent outputs among them, see e.g., [59, 102, 109].

Merger is the most conventional one, as it can be seen as an extension of the on the fly component and plain feedback integration discussed throughout the previous sections. So, the human simply feels very motivated to provide more of her/his knowledge to the ML system (than is actually necessary) — so, she/he probably likes the system, but sees some necessary extension to improve predictive quality and to expand the model to new system states she/he is aware of, but which have not been embedded into the model so far. Merging can be achieved by direct integration of the rules with the application of consistency and distinguishability checks as discussed in Sect. 10.3, to again assure a transparent and interpretable rule base, or by specific merging operations on the model level. The latter has been, to our best knowledge, not addressed so far in literature and would thus be a promising future research topic.

10.5   Conclusion

The idea of this chapter was to demonstrate several concepts for improved model output explanation and model component interpretation, such that humans feel stimulated and motivated to provide enhanced feedback to the machine learning system. The concepts range from output reasoning via feature contributions to the assurance of simplicity and consistency of machine learning models, basically with the usage of fuzzy systems architecture. Several possible directions for integrating various forms of enhanced user feedback have been outlined, showing how machine learning models and humans can benefit from each others' knowledge.

Case studies indeed show strong potential of the concepts demonstrated to be applied in on-line application scenarios. However, still, there are some open research challenges regarding how humans and machines can interact in a more automatised and economic way, i.e. more on a cognitive context by recording and interpreting human thoughts or even feelings about ML systems and their outputs (rather than requiring active manipulations), and translating these to become "understandable" and thus further processible for machines.

Acknowledgements The author acknowledges the Austrian research funding association (FFG) within the scope of the 'IKT of the future' programme, project 'Generating process feedback from heterogeneous data sources in quality control (mvControl)' (contract # 849962) and the Upper Austrian Technology and Research Promotion.

References

1. Abonyi, J.: Fuzzy Model Identification for Control. Birkhäuser, Boston (2003)
2. Akerkar, R., Sajja, P.: Knowledge-Based Systems. Jones & Bartlett Learning, Sudbury (2009)
3. Al-Taani, A.: An expert system for car failure diagnosis. Eng. Technol. **1**, 445–458 (2007)
4. Alizadeh, S., Kalhor, A., Jamalabadi, H., Araabi, B., Ahmadabadi, M.: Online local input selection through evolving heterogeneous fuzzy inference system. IEEE Trans. Fuzzy Syst. **24**(6), 1364–1377 (2016)
5. Alonso, J., Magdalena, L.: Special issue on interpretable fuzzy systems. Inf. Sci. **181**, 4331–4339 (2011)
6. Angelov, P.: Evolving Takagi-Sugeno fuzzy systems from streaming data, eTS+. In: Angelov, P., Filev, D., Kasabov, N. (eds.) Evolving Intelligent Systems: Methodology and Applications, pp. 21–50. Wiley, New York (2010)
7. Angelov, P.: Autonomous Learning Systems: From Data Streams to Knowledge in Real-time. Wiley, New York (2012)
8. Angelov, P., Filev, D.: Simpl_eTS: A simplified method for learning evolving Takagi-Sugeno fuzzy models. In: Proceedings of FUZZ-IEEE 2005, pp. 1068–1073. Reno, Nevada, U.S.A. (2005)
9. Angelov, P., Lughofer, E., Zhou, X.: Evolving fuzzy classifiers using different model architectures. Fuzzy Sets Syst. **159**(23), 3160–3182 (2008)
10. Angelov, P., Filev, D., Kasabov, N.: Evolving Intelligent Systems – Methodology and Applications. Wiley, New York (2010)
11. Ashby, F., Ennis, D.: Similarity measures. Scholarpedia **2**(12), 4116 (2007)

12. Baerhens, D., Schroeter, T., Harmeling, S., Kawanabe, M., Hansen, K., Müller, K.: How to explain individual classification decisions. J. Mach. Learn. Res. **11**, 1803–1831 (2010)
13. Boltryk, P., Harris, C.J., White, N.M.: Intelligent sensors - a generic software approach. J. Phys: Conf. Ser. **15**, 155–160 (2005)
14. Bosnić, Z., Demšar, J., Kešpret, G., Rodrigues, P., Gama, J., Kononenko, I.: Enhancing data stream predictions with reliability estimators and explanation. Eng. Appl. Artif. Intell. **34**, 178–192 (2014)
15. Breiman, L., Friedman, J., Stone, C., Olshen, R.: Classification and Regression Trees. Chapman and Hall, Boca Raton (1993)
16. Burger, M., Haslinger, J., Bodenhofer, U., Engl, H.W.: Regularized data-driven construction of fuzzy controllers. J. Inverse Ill-Posed Probl. **10**(4), 319–344 (2002)
17. Caleb-Solly, P., Smith, J.: Adaptive surface inspection via interactive evolution. Image Vis. Comput. **25**(7), 1058–1072 (2007)
18. Casillas, J., Cordon, O., Herrera, F., Magdalena, L.: Interpretability Issues in Fuzzy Modeling. Springer, Berlin (2003)
19. Castillo, E., Alvarez, E.: Expert Systems: Uncertainty and Learning. Computational Mechanics Publications, Southampton (2007)
20. Castro, J., Delgado, M.: Fuzzy systems with defuzzification are universal approximators. IEEE Trans. Syst. Man Cybern. B Cybern. **26**(1), 149–152 (1996)
21. Chin, K.S., Chan, A., Yang, J.B.: Development of a fuzzy FMEA based product design system. Int. J. Adv. Manuf. Technol. **36**(7–8), 633–649 (2008)
22. Costa, B., Angelov, P., Guedes, L.: Fully unsupervised fault detection and identification based on recursive density estimation and self-evolving cloud-based classifier. Neurocomputing **150**(A), 289–303 (2015)
23. Costabile, M., Fogli, D., Mussion, P., Piccinno, A.: Visual interactive systems for end-user development: a model-based design methodology. IEEE Trans. Syst. Man Cybern. part A: Cybern. **37**(6), 1029–1046 (2007)
24. Cross, V.V., Sudkamp, T.A.: Similarity and Compatibility in Fuzzy Set Theory: Assessment and Applications. Springer, Physica, Heidelberg (2010)
25. Dua, S., Acharya, U., Dua, P.: Machine Learning in Healthcare Informatics. Intelligent Systems Reference Library. Springer, Berlin (2014)
26. Fiordaliso, A.: A constrained Takagi-Sugeno fuzzy system that allows for better interpretation and analysis. Fuzzy Sets Syst. **118**(2), 281–296 (2001)
27. Fitch, E.: Proactive Maintenance for Mechanical Systems. Elsevier Science Publishers, Amsterdam (1992)
28. Gacto, M., Alcala, R., Herrera, F.: Interpretability of linguistic fuzzy rule-based systems: an overview of interpretability measures. Inf. Sci. **181**(20), 4340–4360 (2011)
29. Gama, J.: Knowledge Discovery from Data Streams. Chapman & Hall/CRC, Boca Raton (2010)
30. Greene, J., Hibbard, J., Alvarez, C., Overton, V.: Supporting patient behavior change: approaches used by primary care clinicians whose patients have an increase in activation levels. Ann. Fam. Med. **14**(2), 148–154 (2016)
31. Grizzard, J.: Towards self-healing systems: re-establishing trust in compromised systems. Ph.D. thesis, Georgia Institute of Technology Atlanta (2006). Georgia, U.S.A
32. Groissboeck, W., Lughofer, E., Thumfart, S.: Associating visual textures with human perceptions using genetic algorithms. Inf. Sci. **180**(11), 2065–2084 (2010)
33. Guo, x., Yu, Q., Li, R., Alm, C., Calvelli, C., Shi, P., Haake, A.: An expert-in-the-loop paradigm for learning medical image grouping. In: Proceedings of the Pacific-Asia Conference on Knowledge Discovery and Data Mining, Lecture Notes in Computer Science, vol. 9651, pp. 477–488 (2016)
34. Hájek, P.: Metamathematics of Fuzzy Logic. Kluwer Academic Publishers, Dordrecht (1998)
35. Hastie, T., Tibshirani, R., Friedman, J.: The Elements of Statistical Learning: Data Mining, Inference and Prediction, 2nd edn. Springer, New York (2009)

36. Heidl, W., Thumfart, S., Lughofer, E., Eitzinger, C., Klement, E.: Machine learning based analysis of gender differences in visual inspection decision making. Inf. Sci. **224**, 62–76 (2013)
37. Henzgen, S., Strickert, M., Hüllermeier, E.: Rule chains for visualizing evolving fuzzy rule-based systems. Advances in Intelligent Systems and Computing. In: Proceedings of the 8th International Conference on Computer Recognition Systems CORES 2013, vol. 226, pp. 279–288. Springer, Cambridge, MA (2013)
38. Henzgen, S., Strickert, M., Hüellermeier, E.: Visualization of evolving fuzzy rule-based systems. Evol. Syst. **5**(3), 175–191 (2014)
39. Hisada, M., Ozawa, S., Zhang, K., Kasabov, N.: Incremental linear discriminant analysis for evolving feature spaces in multitask pattern recognition problems. Evol. Syst. **1**(1), 17–27 (2010)
40. Holzinger, A.: Interactive machine learning for health informatics: when do we need the human-in-the-loop? Brain Inform. **3**(2), 118–131 (2016)
41. Hooker, G.: Diagnostics and extrapolation in machine learning. Ph.D. thesis, Department of Statistics, Stanford University (2004). Stanford, U.S.A
42. Hu, R., Namee, B., Delany, S.: Active learning for text classification with reusability. Expert Syst. Appl. **45**, 4388–449 (2016)
43. Hühn, J., Hüllermeier, E.: FR3: a fuzzy rule learner for inducing reliable classifiers. IEEE Trans. Fuzzy Syst. **17**(1), 138–149 (2009)
44. Hüllermeier, E., Brinker, K.: Learning valued preference structures for solving classification problems. Fuzzy Sets Syst. **159**(18), 2337–2352 (2008)
45. Hunink, M.M., Weinstein, M., Wittenberg, E.: Decision Making in Health and Medicine: Integrating Evidence and Values. Cambridge University Press, Cambridge (2014)
46. Huysmans, J., Dejaeger, K., Mues, C., Vanthienen, J., Baesens, B.: An empirical evaluation of the comprehensibility of decision table, tree and rule based predictive models. Decis. Support Syst. **51**(1), 141–154 (2011)
47. Iglesias, J., Angelov, P., Ledezma, A., Sanchis, A.: Evolving classification of agent's behaviors: a general approach. Evol. Syst. **1**(3), 161–172 (2010)
48. Iglesias, J., Angelov, P., Ledezma, A., Sanchis, A.: Creating evolving user behavior profiles automatically. IEEE Trans. Knowl. Data Eng. **24**(5), 854–867 (2012)
49. Ishibuchi, H., Nakashima, T.: Effect of rule weights in fuzzy rule-based classification systems. IEEE Trans. Fuzzy Syst. **9**(4), 506–515 (2001)
50. Jackson, P.: Introduction to Expert Systems. Addison Wesley Pub Co Inc., Edinburgh Gate (1999)
51. Jin, Y.: Advanced Fuzzy Systems Design and Applications. Springer, Berlin (2003)
52. Kalhor, A., Araabi, B., Lucas, C.: An online predictor model as adaptive habitually linear and transiently nonlinear model. Evolv. Syst. **1**(1), 29–41 (2010)
53. Kasabov, N.: Evolving Connectionist Systems: The Knowledge Engineering Approach, 2nd edn. Springer, London (2007)
54. Khamassi, I., Sayed-Mouchaweh, M., Hammami, M., Ghedira, K.: Discussion and review on evolving data streams and concept drift adapting. In: Evolving Systems (2016). https://doi.org/10.1007/s12530-016-9168-2
55. Klement, E., Mesiar, R., Pap, E.: Triangular Norms. Kluwer Academic Publishers, Dordrecht (2000)
56. Kosko, B.: Fuzzy Thinking: The New Science of Fuzzy Logic. Flamingo, New York (1994)
57. Kraiss, K.: Advanced Man-Machine Interaction: Fundamentals and Implementation (Signals and Communication Technology). Springer, Berlin (2014)
58. Kuncheva, L.: Fuzzy Classifier Design. Physica, Heidelberg (2000)
59. Kuncheva, L.: Combining Pattern Classifiers: Methods and Algorithms. Wiley-Interscience (Wiley), Southern Gate (2004)
60. Last, M., Sinaiski, A., Subramania, H.: Predictive maintenance with multi-target classification models. In: Proceedings of the Intelligent Information and Database Systems, Lecture Notes in Computer Science, vol. 5991, pp. 368–377. Springer, Berlin (2010)

61. Lavretsky, E., Wise, K.: Robust Adaptive Control. Springer, London (2013)
62. Lee, C.: Fuzzy logic in control systems: fuzzy logic controller - part i and ii. IEEE Trans. Syst. Man Cybern. **20**(2), 404–435 (1990)
63. Lee, D., Hu, J.: Local model predictive control for ts fuzzy systems. IEEE Trans. Cybern. **47**(9), 2556–2567 (2017)
64. Lemos, A., Caminhas, W., Gomide, F.: Adaptive fault detection and diagnosis using an evolving fuzzy classifier. Inf. Sci. **220**, 64–85 (2013)
65. Leng, G., Zeng, X.J., Keane, J.: An improved approach of self-organising fuzzy neural network based on similarity measures. Evol. Syst. **3**(1), 19–30 (2012)
66. Levitt, J.: Complete Guide to Preventive and Predictive Maintenance. Industrial Press Inc., New York (2011)
67. Liu, B.: Web Data Mining (Data-Centric Systems and Applications). Springer, Heidelberg (2013)
68. Liu, Y.: Predictive modeling for intelligent maintenance in complex semi-conductor manufacturing processes. Ph.D. thesis, University of Michigan, Ann Arbor (2008)
69. Lughofer, E.: Evolving Fuzzy Systems – Methodologies, Advanced Concepts and Applications. Springer, Berlin (2011)
70. Lughofer, E.: Human-inspired evolving machines — the next generation of evolving intelligent systems? SMC Newsletter **36** (2011)
71. Lughofer, E.: On-line incremental feature weighting in evolving fuzzy classifiers. Fuzzy Sets Syst. **163**(1), 1–23 (2011)
72. Lughofer, E.: Flexible evolving fuzzy inference systems from data streams (FLEXFIS++). In: Sayed-Mouchaweh, M., Lughofer, E. (eds.) Learning in Non-Stationary Environments: Methods and Applications, pp. 205–246. Springer, New York (2012)
73. Lughofer, E.: Single-pass active learning with conflict and ignorance. Evol. Syst. **3**(4), 251–271 (2012)
74. Lughofer, E.: Expert-based, hybrid and data-driven design of fuzzy systems for risk management of post parcels. Technical Report FLLL-TR-1301, Department of Knowledge-Based Mathematical Systems, Johannes Kepler University Linz, Austria (2013)
75. Lughofer, E.: On-line assurance of interpretability criteria in evolving fuzzy systems – achievements, new concepts and open issues. Inf. Sci. **251**, 22–46 (2013)
76. Lughofer, E.: Evolving fuzzy systems – fundamentals, reliability, interpretability and useability. In: Angelov, P. (ed.) Handbook of Computational Intelligence, pp. 67–135. World Scientific, New York (2016)
77. Lughofer, E.: Robust data-driven fault detection in dynamic process environments using discrete event systems. In: Sayed-Mouchaweh, M. (ed.) Diagnosis and Diagnosability of Hybrid Dynamic Systems. Springer, New York (2018)
78. Lughofer, E., Guardiola, C.: On-line fault detection with data-driven evolving fuzzy models. J. Control Intell. Syst. **36**(4), 307–317 (2008)
79. Lughofer, E., Hüllermeier, E.: On-line redundancy elimination in evolving fuzzy regression models using a fuzzy inclusion measure. In: Proceedings of the EUSFLAT 2011 Conference, pp. 380–387. Elsevier, Aix-Les-Bains, France (2011)
80. Lughofer, E., Buchtala, O.: Reliable all-pairs evolving fuzzy classifiers. IEEE Trans. Fuzzy Syst. **21**(4), 625–641 (2013)
81. Lughofer, E., Smith, J.E., Caleb-Solly, P., Tahir, M., Eitzinger, C., Sannen, D., Nuttin, M.: Human-machine interaction issues in quality control based on on-line image classification. IEEE Trans. Syst. Man Cybern. Part A Syst. Hum. **39**(5), 960–971 (2009)
82. Lughofer, E., Bouchot, J.L., Shaker, A.: On-line elimination of local redundancies in evolving fuzzy systems. Evol. Syst. **2**(3), 165–187 (2011)
83. Lughofer, E., Trawinski, B., Trawinski, K., Kempa, O., Lasota, T.: On employing fuzzy modeling algorithms for the valuation of residential premises. Inf. Sci. **181**(23), 5123–5142 (2011)
84. Lughofer, E., Cernuda, C., Kindermann, S., Pratama, M.: Generalized smart evolving fuzzy systems. Evol. Syst. **6**(4), 269–292 (2015)

85. Lughofer, E., Weigl, E., Heidl, W., Eitzinger, C., Radauer, T.: Integrating new classes on the fly in evolving fuzzy classifier designs and its application in visual inspection. Appl. Soft Comput. **35**, 558–582 (2015)
86. Lughofer, E., Richter, R., Neissl, U., Heidl, W., Eitzinger, C., Radauer, T.: Advanced linguistic explanations of classifier decisions for users annotation support. In: Proceedings of the IEEE Intelligent Systems Conference 2016, pp. 421–432. Sofia, Bulgaria (2016)
87. Lughofer, E., Kindermann, S., Pratama, M., Rubio, J.: Top-down sparse fuzzy regression modeling from data with improved coverage. Int. J. Fuzzy Syst. **19**(5), 1645–1658 (2017)
88. Lughofer, E., Zavoianu, A.C., Pollak, R., Pratama, M., Meyer-Heye, P., Zörrer, H., Eitzinger, C., Haim, J., Radauer, T.: Self-adaptive evolving forecast models with incremental PLS space update for on-line predicting quality of micro-fluidic chips. Eng. Appl. Artif. Intell **68**, 131–151 (2018)
89. Lundberg, S., Lee, S.: An unexpected unity among methods for interpreting model predictions. In: Proceedings of the 29th Conference on Neural Information Processing Systems (NIPS 2016). Barcelona, Spain (2016)
90. Luo, M., Sun, F., Liu, H.: Hierarchical structured sparse representation for ts fuzzy systems identification. IEEE Trans. Fuzzy Syst. **21**(6), 1032–1043 (2013)
91. Mamdani, E.: Application of fuzzy logic to approximate reasoning using linguistic systems. Fuzzy Sets Syst. **26**(12), 1182–1191 (1977)
92. McKay, M., Beckman, R., Conover, W.: A comparison of three methods for selecting values of input variables in the analysis of output from a computer code. Technometrics (JSTOR Abstract) **21**(2), 239–245 (1979)
93. Mencar, C., Castellano, G., Fanelli, A.: Distinguishability quantification of fuzzy sets. Inf. Sci. **177**, 130–149 (2007)
94. Nakashima, T., Schaefer, G., Yokota, Y., Ishibuchi, H.: A weighted fuzzy classifier and its application to image processing tasks. Fuzzy Sets Syst. **158**(3), 284–294 (2006)
95. Nelles, O.: Nonlinear System Identification. Springer, Berlin (2001)
96. Ngia, L., Sjöberg, J.: Efficient training of neural nets for nonlinear adaptive filtering using a recursive Levenberg-Marquardt algorithm. IEEE Trans. Signal Process. **48**(7), 1915–1926 (2000)
97. Ordonez, J., Iglesias, J., de Toledo, P., Ledezma, A., Sanchis, A.: Online activity recognition using evolving classifiers. Expert Syst. Appl. **40**(4), 1248–1255 (2013)
98. Park, C., Moon, D., Do, N., Bae, S.: A predictive maintenance approach based on real-time internal parameter monitoring. Int. J. Adv. Manuf. Technol. **85**(1), 623–632 (2016)
99. Pedrycz, W., Gomide, F.: Fuzzy Systems Engineering: Toward Human-Centric Computing. Wiley, Hoboken (2007)
100. Permin, E., Bertelsmeier, F., Blum, M., Bützler, J., Haag, S., Kuz, S., Özdemir, D., Stemmler, S., Thombansen, U., Schmitt, R., Brecher, C., Schlick, C., Abel, D., Popraw, R., Loosen, P., Schulz, W., Schuh, G.: Self-optimizing production systems. Procedia CIRP **41**, 417–422 (2016)
101. Piegat, A.: Fuzzy Modeling and Control. Physica, Springer, Heidelberg (2001)
102. Polikar, R.: Ensemble based systems in decision making. IEEE Circuits Syst. Mag. **6**(3), 21–45 (2006)
103. Pratama, M., Lu, J., Lughofer, E., Zhang, G., Anavatti, S.: Scaffolding type-2 classifier for incremental learning under concept drifts. Neurocomputing **191**(304–329) (2016)
104. Quinlan, J.R.: C4.5: Programs for Machine Learning. Morgan Kaufmann Publishers, San Francisco (1993)
105. Rallo, R., Ferre-Gine, J., Arena, A., Girault, F.: Neural virtual sensor for the inferential prediction of product quality from process variables. Comput. Chem. Eng. **26**(12), 1735–1754 (2004)
106. Robnik-Sikonja, M., Kononenko, I.: Explaining classifications for individual instances. IEEE Trans. Knowl. Data Eng. **20**, 589–600 (2008)
107. Ronald, R.: On the construction of hierarchical fuzzy systems models. IEEE Trans. Syst. Man Cybern. **28**(1), 55–66 (1998)

108. Rong, H.J., Sundararajan, N., Huang, G.B., Saratchandran, P.: Sequential adaptive fuzzy inference system (SAFIS) for nonlinear system identification and prediction. Fuzzy Sets Syst. **157**(9), 1260–1275 (2006)
109. Sannen, D., Lughofer, E., Brussel, H.V.: Towards incremental classifier fusion. Intell. Data Anal. **14**(1), 3–30 (2010)
110. Sayed-Mouchaweh, M., Lughofer, E.: Learning in Non-Stationary Environments: Methods and Applications. Springer, New York (2012)
111. Senge, R., Huellermeier, E.: Top-down induction of fuzzy pattern trees. IEEE Trans. Fuzzy Syst. **19**(2), 241–252 (2011)
112. Serdio, F., Muoz-Garca, M., Saminger-Platz, S.: Detecting clipping in photovoltaic solar plants using fuzzy systems on the feature space. Sol. Energy **132**, 345–356 (2016)
113. Setnes, M.: Simplification and reduction of fuzzy rules. In: Casillas, J., Cordón, O., Herrera, F., Magdalena, L. (eds.) Interpretability Issues in Fuzzy Modeling, pp. 278–302. Springer, Berlin (2003)
114. Skrjanc, I.: Confidence interval of fuzzy models: an example using a waste-water treatment plant. Chemometr. Intell. Lab. Syst. **96**, 182–187 (2009)
115. Strumbelj, E., Kononenko, I.: Explaining prediction models and individual predictions with feature contributions. Knowl. Inf. Syst. **41**(3), 647–665 (2014)
116. Takagi, T., Sugeno, M.: Fuzzy identification of systems and its applications to modeling and control. IEEE Trans. Syst. Man Cybern. **15**(1), 116–132 (1985)
117. Tsoukalas, L., Uhrig, R.: Fuzzy and Neural Approaches in Engineering. Wiley, New York (1997)
118. Vapnik, V.: Statistical Learning Theory. Wiley, New York (1998)
119. Vetterlein, T.: Vagueness: where degree-based approaches are useful, and where we can do without. Soft. Comput. **16**(11), 1833–1844 (2012)
120. Wang, W., Vrbanek, J.: An evolving fuzzy predictor for industrial applications. IEEE Trans. Fuzzy Syst. **16**(6), 1439–1449 (2008)
121. Ware, M., Frank, E., Holmes, G., Hall, M., Witten, I.: Interactive machine learning: letting users build classifiers. Int. J. Hum Comput Stud. **55**(3), 281–292 (2001)
122. Weigl, E., Heidl, W., Lughofer, E., Eitzinger, C., Radauer, T.: On improving performance of surface inspection systems by on-line active learning and flexible classifier updates. Mach. Vis. Appl. **27**(1), 103–127 (2016)
123. Witten, I., Frank, E., Hall, M.: Data Mining: Practical Machine Learning Tools and Techniques. Morgan Kaufmann Series in Data Management Systems. Morgan Kaufmann, Bulrington (2011)
124. Yager, R.R.: A model of participatory learning. IEEE Trans. Syst. Man Cybern. **20**(5), 1229–1234 (1990)
125. Zadeh, L.: Fuzzy sets. Inf. Control **8**(3), 338–353 (1965)
126. Zain, C., Pratama, M., Lughofer, E., Anavatti, S.: Evolving type-2 web news mining. Appl. Soft Comput. **54**, 200–220 (2017)
127. Zavoianu, A.C., Lughofer, E., Pollak, R., Meyer-Heye, P., Eitzinger, C., Radauer, T.: Multi-objective knowledge-based strategy for process parameter optimization in micro-fluidic chip production. In: Proceedings of the SSCI 2017 Conference (CIES Workshop), 1927–1934, Honolulu, Hawaii (2017)
128. Zhou, S., Gan, J.: Low-level interpretability and high-level interpretability: a unified view of data-driven interpretable fuzzy systems modelling. Fuzzy Sets Syst. **159**(23), 3091–3131 (2008)

Part IV
User Cognitive Responses in ML-Based Decision Making

Chapter 11
Revealing User Confidence in Machine Learning-Based Decision Making

Jianlong Zhou, Kun Yu and Fang Chen

Abstract This chapter demonstrates the link between human cognition states and Machine Learning (ML) with a multimodal interface. A framework of informed decision making called *DecisionMind* is proposed to show how human's behaviour and physiological signals are used to reveal human cognition states in ML-based decision making. The chapter takes the revealing of user confidence in ML-based decision making as an example to demonstrate the effectiveness of the proposed approach. Based on the revealing of human cognition states during ML-based decision making, the chapter presents a concept of adaptive measurable decision making to show how the revealing of human cognition states are integrated into ML-based decision making to make ML transparent. On the one hand, human cognition states could help understand to what degree humans accept innovative technologies. On the other hand, through understanding human cognition states during ML-based decision making, ML-based decision attributes/factors and even ML models can be adaptively refined in order to make ML transparent.

11.1 Introduction

With the rapid advancement of "Big Data" and data science technologies, we are continuously coming across different intelligent systems that seem to work (or have worked) surprisingly well in practical scenarios (e.g. AlphaGO's beating with professional GO players in 2016 and 2017, and the self-driving cars for deciding to

J. Zhou (✉) · K. Yu · F. Chen
DATA61, CSIRO, 13 Garden Street, Eveleigh, NSW 2015, Australia
e-mail: jianlong.zhou@data61.csiro.au

K. Yu
e-mail: kun.yu@data61.csiro.au

F. Chen
e-mail: fang.chen@data61.csiro.au

© Crown 2018
J. Zhou and F. Chen (eds.), *Human and Machine Learning*, Human–Computer Interaction Series, https://doi.org/10.1007/978-3-319-90403-0_11

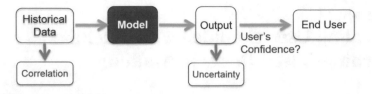

Fig. 11.1 ML-based data analysis pipeline

choose among different road conditions). Much of Machine Learning (ML) research is driven by such intelligent systems. Despite the recognised value of ML techniques, ML technologies are currently still facing prolonged challenges with user acceptance of delivered solutions as well as seeing system misuse, disuse, or even failure. Furthermore, in most cases data science applications are implemented as an aid to human decision making, such as in intelligent systems [41]. Such intelligent systems are inherently about humans — providing information to humans and getting feedback from humans. Therefore, the human factors play significant roles in the success of the intelligent system, and thus also are indispensable components of data science solutions. Scantamburlo [41] suggested that by considering the outline of some potential risks underlying the ML process, the ML method requires an in-depth analysis of the human factors involved throughout the whole implementation of the system. Watanabe [48] suggested that the judgement of ML resulting as "right" or "wrong" is an activity that comes after apprehension, and which needs a very human intervention [41]. As a result, human-in-the-loop Machine Learning (ML) is getting increasing attention from both the technical and business communities [5, 6].

For many non-technical users, an ML-based intelligent system is like a "black-box" (see Fig. 11.1), to which they simply provide their input data and (after selecting some menu options on screen) colourful viewgraphs and/or recommendations are displayed as output. This "black-box" approach has obvious drawbacks: it is difficult for the user to understand the complicated ML models, such as what is going on inside the ML models, and how to accomplish the learning problem [56]. It is neither clear nor well understood how trustworthy is this output, or how uncertainties are handled/manipulated by underlying algorithmic procedures. The user is more or less unconfident in the ML model output when making predictive decisions, and thus also unconfident in the ML methods themselves. In a word, significant barriers to widespread adoption of ML approaches still exist in the areas of trust (of ML results), comprehension (of ML processes), as well as confidence (in recommended courses of action or decision making) by users. As a result, the User Experience involved in real world ML applications has been more recently identified as an area requiring research and development (innovation) [47, 53, 54].

Moreover, decision making is an active research topic in Human-Computer Interaction (HCI) with the fast growing use of intelligent systems. Making decisions is one of the most complex cognitive processes and much work has been done on the relations between human neural activities and decision making. Nonverbal information such as physiological information and human behaviours is increasingly parsed and interpreted by computers to interactively construct models of humans' cognition states in order to understand the decision making process [13, 14, 44, 55]. Physiological signals are also interpreted allowing users to perceive the quality of their decisions [57]. Besides neurophysiological information, research found that human behaviour can also reflect humans mental state, such as cognitive load and trust [8].

These motivate us to investigate the revealing and modeling of human cognition states during ML-based decision making based on physiological and behavioural responses. By modelling human cognition states, it is possible to automatically adapt ML parameters and even ML models for optimal decision performance. Therefore, we strongly argue that the revealing of human cognition states during ML-based decision making could provide a rich view for both ML researchers and domain experts to learn the effectiveness of ML-based intelligent systems. On the one hand, human cognition states could help understand in what degree a human accepts innovative technologies. On the other hand, through understanding human cognition states during data analytics-driven decision making, ML-based decision attributes and even ML models can be adaptively refined in order to make ML understandable and transparent. The current ML-based decision making systems do not take the human cognition states into consideration, which significantly affects the impact of ML technologies in real-world applications.

This chapter demonstrates the link between human cognition states and ML technologies with a multimodal interface during ML-based decision making. A framework of informed decision making called *DecisionMind* is proposed to demonstrate how humans' behaviour and physiological signals are used to reveal human cognition states in ML-based decision making. Based on the framework, the chapter takes the revealing of user confidence in ML-based decision making as an example to demonstrate the effectiveness of the proposed approach in making ML transparent.

11.2 Related Work

This section first investigates the relations between human physiological/behavioural signals and human cognition states. Decision making especially the physiological and behavioural indicators for decision making are then reviewed. Such investigations motivate the informed decision making afterwards.

11.2.1 Human Cognition States

Extensive research has found the physiological correlations to human cognition states. Moll et al. [32] reviewed evidence on brain regions identified during functional imaging of cognition activities irrespective of task constraints. It was demonstrated that the investigation of mechanisms of cognition-emotion interaction and of the neural bases is critical for understanding of human cognition. van Gog et al. [15] used an interdisciplinary approach combining evolutionary biological theory and neuroscience within a cognitive load theory framework to explain human's behaviour during observational learning. Different human physiological signals are used to measure cognitive load, e.g. heart rate and heart rate variability, brain activity (e.g. changes in oxygenation and blood volume, Electroencephalography (EEG)), Galvanic Skin Response (GSR), and eyes [8]. Besides cognitive load, Aimone et al. [1] investigated the neural signature of trust. The results showed that the anterior insula modulates trusting decisions that involve the possibility of betrayal. Hahn et al. [18] showed that a person's initial level of trust is determined by brain electrical activity acquired with EEG.

Besides physiological correlations, much work has been done on the investigation of human behaviours as indicators of human cognition states. For instance, Gütl et al. [16] used eye tracking to observe subjects' learning activities in real-time by monitoring their eye movements for adaptive learning purposes. Others have used mouse clicking and keyboard key-pressing behaviour to make inferences about their emotional state and adapt the system's response accordingly [2]. In addition, features of mouse movement behaviour such as movement distance, slope, and movement count also show different patterns under different trust conditions during a task [27]. Research also suggested that eye movements such as duration, sequence, and frequency of fixations can be used as indicators of trust [24].

These works suggest that human cognition states can be effectively communicated with physiological and behavioural signals. Based on such communications, it is possible to adapt cognitive task options for optimal human cognition states.

11.2.2   Decision Making

Making decisions is one of the most complex cognitive processes and there is a long history of investigation in different domain areas. For example, Morgado et al. [34] reviewed the impact of stress in decision making and found that this complex cognitive process involves several sequential steps including analysis of internal and external states, evaluation of different options available and action selection. Making good decisions implies an estimate not only of the value and the likelihood of each option but also of the costs and efforts implied in obtaining it. Kahneman et al. [25, 46] suggested that people make a variety of errors when making decisions (or solving problems) involving probability. The Subjective Expected Utility (SEU) model suggests that the decision weights people attach to events are their beliefs about the likelihood of events [26].

Researches have been investigated to find connections between physiological responses and decision making. Heekeren et al. [19] reviewed findings from human neuroimaging studies in conjunction with data analysis methods that can directly link decision making and signals in the human brain. Smith et al. [42] used functional Magnetic Resonance Imaging (fMRI) to investigate the neural substrates of moral cognition in health resource allocation decision making. White et al. [49] investigated the physiological correlates of confidence and uncertainty by means of fMRI. It was found that different brain regions correlate to confidence and uncertainty. Much work has also been done on using physiological responses such as pupil dilation and skin conductance to understand humans decision making process. For example, an investigation [14] shows that the pupil dilation increases over the course of the decision making. Pupil dilation and GSR are also used to index confidence and decision quality in decision making [57].

Much work has also been done on using behavioural information such as eye movement to understand humans' decision making process [38]. Fiedler and Glockner [12] utilised eye-tracking to analyse dynamics of decision making in risk conditions. It shows that attention to an outcome of a gamble increases with its probability and its value and that attention shifts toward the subsequently favoured gamble after two thirds of the decision process, indicating a gaze-cascade effect.

These observations motivate us to investigate human cognition states during ML-based predictive decision making. Such investigations not only help to understand the effectiveness of ML approaches from human responses, but also motivate ML researchers to refine ML models to improve human attitudes to ML based decision making.

11.3   A Framework of Informed Decision Making

The review in the previous section shows that human physiological and behavioural signals closely correlate to both decision making and human cognition states. This section proposes *DecisionMind* as a framework of informed decision making to incorporate human cognition states into an ML-based decision making scenario. In this framework, human cognition states in ML-based predictive decision making are revealed with physiological and behavioural signals. Through revealing human cognition states, a feedback loop is set up to adaptively improve both effectiveness of ML approaches and human attitudes to ML approaches.

A typical ML-based decision making process can be illustrated as a loop as shown in Fig. 11.2. As shown in this figure, when an ML-based intelligent system is used for decision making, a human usually has a mental model on decisions firstly. The human then makes decisions based on different cues including different decision alternatives. At the same time, human cognition during decision making is evaluated and is used as feedback in order to refine the decision making.

Based on this decision loop shown in Fig. 11.2, we present a framework of informed decision making — *DecisionMind* (see Fig. 11.3). In this framework, when a human makes decisions with an ML model-based intelligent system, signals related to human cognition states are recorded at the same time with different modalities. Human cognition states during decision making are then derived from the recorded signals. If the human's cognition is not in an acceptable state and the human is not satisfied with the decision quality, feedback is sent to the decision system to refine decision attributes and even ML models and a new decision process is started until the

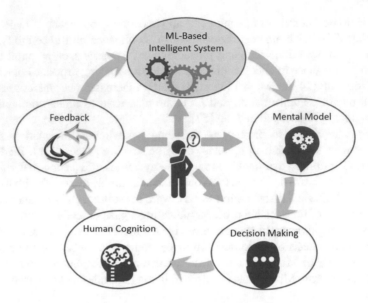

Fig. 11.2 A typical ML-based decision making process in a feedback loop

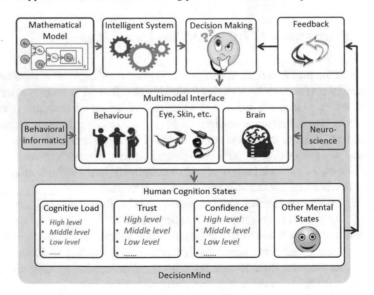

Fig. 11.3 Framework of informed decision making – DecisionMind

human is satisfied with the decision performance with appropriate cognition states. During this informed decision making process, human's cognition states are tracked and revealed explicitly to help the human refine decisions. DecisionMind therefore evaluates human cognition and allows human cognition to be quantitatively visible during ML-based decision making, imagining that a human perceives his/her cognition states during decision making, and further imagining that the decision attributes and even ML models could be adaptively refined based on the estimated cognition states. The examples of human cognition states include cognitive load, trust, confidence, etc. They are revealed with multimodalities such as skin conductance with GSR sensors, eye activity with eye-tracker, etc.

Based on this framework, the following sections demonstrate the effectiveness of the proposed framework by revealing user confidence and factors affecting user confidence.

11.4 User Confidence in ML-Based Decision Making

As reviewed in the previous sections, user confidence is one of the significant human cognition states during ML-based decision making. It is generally described as a state of being certain that a chosen course of action is the best or most effective during decision making. Lee and Dry [30] showed that user confidence in decision making does not depend solely on the accuracy of the advice, it is also influenced by the frequency of the advice. Considering that decisions are often made based on probability evaluations of which users are not entirely sure, Hill [20] developed a decision rule incorporating users' confidence in probability judgments. A formal representation of the decision maker's confidence is also presented in [20]. Moran et al. [33] argued that a critical property of decision confidence is its positive correlation between confidence and decision correctness. In other words, with greater confidence the decider is more likely to be correct in his or her decision. In a typical decision making scenario, once the problem scenario along with supplementary material is presented, several other factors can come into play as well. One such group of factors is individual differences that were investigated by Pallier et al. [35]. Differences in experience, motivation, attitudinal predispositions etc. can have an impact on the decision making process.

In an ML-based decision making scenario, different factors may affect user confidence in decision making, for example, ML performance, uncertainty of ML results, correlation between attributes of data set. However, it is important to learn what are the factors and how these factors benefit user confidence in ML-based decision making. While decision making has become an important topic in various areas of HCI research in recent years [43], this section firstly understands ML-based decision making from an HCI perspective and then demonstrates how different factors affect user confidence in ML-based decision making.

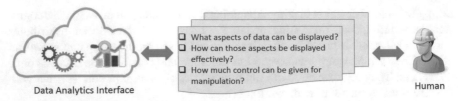

Fig. 11.4 Interactive data analytics: an HCI perspective

11.4.1 Interactive Data Analytics from An HCI Perspective

The multimodal interface trend in HCI [8] tries to build interfaces intelligent enough to actively incorporate a human's intuitions and load. In hte case of ML-based inter-active data analytics, the key HCI research questions would be (see Fig. 11.4): (1) what aspects of data would humans like to see on screen? (2) how could the desired data aspects be best visualised? and (3) how much control can be transferred for the human to adequately manipulate the visualised data? This section is concerned mainly with the first two questions. More specifically, the effects of uncertainty and correlation on user confidence in ML-based decision making are investigated in this section.

11.4.2 Effects of Uncertainty on User Confidence

As shown in Fig. 11.1, "uncertainty" is inherent in an ML-based data analytics pipeline. It can be defined in many ways. For a user, uncertainty can be a psy-chological state in which the decision maker lacks knowledge about what outcome will follow from which choice, where uncertainty is considered as "risk". Risk refers to situations with a known distribution of possible outcomes (probabilities) [37]. "Ambiguity" is the other kind of uncertainty, where outcomes have unknown prob-abilities and research in neurosciences [22] indicates that decision making under ambiguity does not represent a special, more complex case of risky decision making. Decision making under uncertainty is widely investigated in decision theory [45], where uncertainty is usually considered as probabilities in utility functions. Beller et al. [4] showed that the presentation of automation uncertainty helped the automation system receive higher trust ratings and increase acceptance. When humans make decisions under uncertainty, it was thought that they prefer to bet on events they know more about, even when their beliefs are held constant, i.e. they are averse to ambiguity [7]. However, this was shown to be otherwise by [21] in their study responding to degrees of uncertainty. Their experiments and corresponding neuro-logical observations showed that humans are more willing to bet on risky outcomes than ambiguous ones.

Furthermore, uncertainty information is typically presented to users visually, most commonly in graphical format [23]. Edwards et al. [10] compared different graphical methods from presenting quantitative uncertainty in decision making tasks. The representation of uncertainty can have a significant impact on human performance. It was shown that when the representation of uncertainty for a spatial task better matches the expert's preferred representation of the problem even a non-expert can show expert-like performance [28].

These findings motivate us to account for both risk (i.e. uncertainty due to known probabilities) and ambiguity (i.e. uncertainty due to unknown probabilities) while investigating variations in user confidence due to uncertainty in ML-based decision making. In a case study of ML-based decision making scenario, Zhou et al. [51] introduced three uncertainty conditions (without uncertainty, risk, and ambiguity)

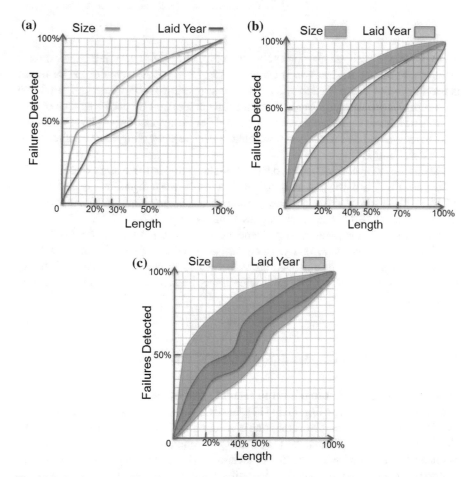

Fig. 11.5 Performance of predictive models: **a** without uncertainty, **b** with non-overlapping uncertainty (risk), **c** with overlapping uncertainty (ambiguity)

Fig. 11.6 Average
subjective ratings of user
confidence in decision
making tasks under different
uncertainty conditions
(Control: without
uncertainty, OLUT:
overlapping uncertainty
(ambiguity), Non-OLUT:
non-overlapping uncertainty
(risk))

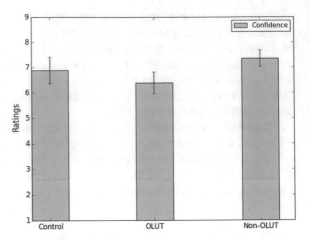

into a predictive decision making as shown in Fig. 11.5, and investigated their effects
on user confidence in decision making. In Fig. 11.5, the ML model performance
is presented as a curve, which is the functional relationship between the input and
its successful predictions. Fig. 11.5 shows the comparison of performances of two
models which are represented with green and purple respectively. The tasks in the
case study were to ask participants to make a decision targeting for a smaller input
and a higher output.

Regarding user confidence in decision making under three uncertainty conditions (see Fig. 11.6) [51], it was found that users were significantly more confident in tasks under risk uncertainty than in tasks under ambiguity uncertainty
($Z = 79.0$, $p < .001$). The result suggests that when uncertainty was presented to
users, non-overlapping uncertainty made users more confident in decision making than overlapping uncertainty. However, there were no significant differences
found between tasks without uncertainty presentation and tasks under ambiguity
uncertainty or between tasks without uncertainty presentation and tasks under risk
uncertainty.

11.4.3 Effects of Correlation on User Confidence

Statistical correlation is often used in feature selection and plays significant roles
in data analytics (also see Fig. 11.1) [17]. Furthermore, good decision-making often
requires a human to perceive and handle a myriad of statistical correlations [11].
However, Eyster and Weizsacker [11] found that humans have limited attention and
often neglect correlations in financial decision making. Ye [50] used the weighted
correlation coefficients to rank the alternatives and get the best alternative in multi-
attribute decision making. Liao et al. [31] used correlation coefficients of hesitant
fuzzy linguistic terms set in the process of qualitative decision making in traditional

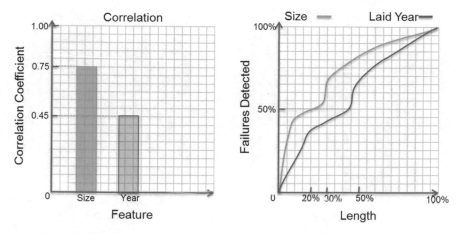

Fig. 11.7   Correlation and performance of model output share the same trend

Chinese medical diagnosis. All these motivate us to investigate the roles of correlation in user confidence in ML-based decision making. Moreover, domain experts are usually good at utilising experiences in their decision making, while correlation from input data reflects statistic summaries of historical facts. We strongly argue that the revealing of a correlation between features and target values would significantly affect user confidence in decision making.

As shown in Fig. 11.1, from the input data perspective in an ML-based data analytics pipeline, correlation can describe how much target values are related to features in input data of the model. The correlation may affect humans' decision making based on their domain experiences, e.g. domain experts may have experiences that the older the pipes are, the higher the failure rate is. In the same case study as shown in Sect. 11.4.2, the correlation is introduced to investigate its effect on user confidence in ML-based decision making.

As shown in Fig. 11.1, correlation is not associated with a model, but associated with input data. Correlation in this case study refers to the correlation between one feature and the target variable in historical records. The correlation is often described by a correlation coefficient. Correlation coefficient illustrates a quantitative measure of correlation and dependence, meaning statistical relationships between two or more random variables or observed data values. The correlation can be displayed as 2D bar charts with the horizontal axis being features and the vertical axis being the correlation coefficients (e.g. Fig. 11.7 left). For example, in Fig. 11.7 left, the feature "Size" and "Laid Year" (Year) have a correlation coefficient of 0.75 and 0.45 respectively with the target variable (failure rate), meaning that "Size" is more related to the failure rate than "Laid Year". The relations between model performance and correlation can be divided into two groups:

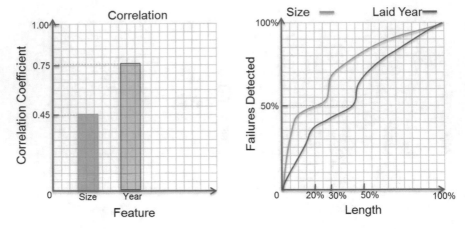

Fig. 11.8 Correlation and performance of model output do not share the same trend

- Correlation and performance of model output share the same trend (see Fig. 11.7). That is, the correlation between a feature and the target variable is high and the associated model performance is also high, or the contrary.
- Correlation and performance of model output do not share the same trend (see Fig. 11.8). That is, the correlation between a feature and the target variable is high, but the associated model performance is low, or the contrary.

Regarding user confidence in decision making under different correlation conditions (see Fig. 11.9) [52], it was found that there was a significant difference between tasks without correlation presentation and Same Trend tasks ($Z = 167.5$, $p = .008$). It suggests that revealing correlation between features and target values helped users be more confident in predictive decision making. However, there was no significant difference found between tasks without correlation presentation and Non-Same Trend tasks. Such results suggest that the pattern between correlation and performance of model output affected user confidence in predictive decision making. It was also found that participants were significantly more confident in Same Trend tasks than in Non-Same Trend tasks ($Z = 105.0$, $p < .001$). It suggests that when correlation and performance of model output shared the same trend (i.e. the correlation between a feature and the target variable was high and the associated model performance was also high, or the contrary), users were more confident in predictive decision making. This was maybe because of the "grounding communication" referred to by psychologists [9]. Because of grounding, confidence in decision making was resolved through a drive towards a mutual understanding or common ground (correlation has the same trend with the performance) in the process.

Fig. 11.9 Average
subjective ratings of users'
confidence in decision
making under different
correlation conditions
(Control: without correlation
presentation, Non-Same
Trend: correlation and model
performance do not share the
same trend, Same Trend:
correlation and model
performance share the same
trend)

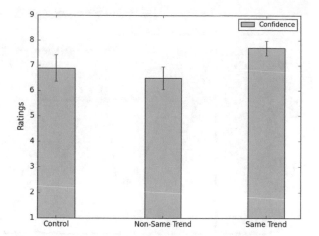

11.5   User Confidence and Human Physiological Responses

As reviewed in Sect. 11.2, human physiological and behavioural responses have close relations with decision making. This section investigates the connection between human physiological responses and predictive decision making. In the same case study as shown in Sect. 11.4.2, GSR and Blood Volume Pulse (BVP) devices from Pro-Comp Infiniti of Thought Technology Ltd were used to collect skin conductance responses and BVP signals of subjects respectively. BVP measures the blood volume in the skin capillary bed in the finger with photoplethysmography (PPG) in BVP sensors [36], which reflects the emotional state of humans. Both GSR and BVP are often used as indicators of affective processes and emotional arousal. Figs. 11.10 and 11.11 show examples of GSR signal and BVP signal during a decision making task.

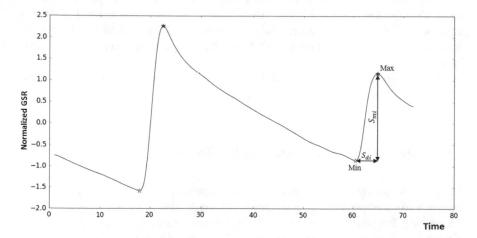

Fig. 11.10   An example of GSR signal during an ML-based decision making task

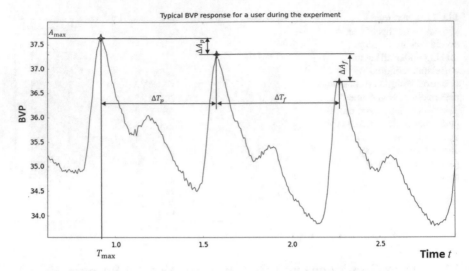

Fig. 11.11 An example of BVP signal during an ML-based decision making task

By analysing GSR features during decision making, it was found that ambiguity uncertainty made GSR features such as GSR sum of duration S_d ($S_d = \sum S_{di}$, the duration S_{di} is defined as in Fig. 11.10) values increased significantly. Therefore, lower confidence level tasks made a GSR feature such as GSR S_d values significantly higher.

Similarly, it was also found that ambiguity uncertainty made BVP features such as ΔT_p (delta time precedent, see Fig. 11.11) and ΔT_f (delta time following, see Fig. 11.11) values increased significantly. However, both ambiguity uncertainty and risk uncertainty made BVP max features such as T_{max} (time at the extrema point with the maximum amplitude, see Fig. 11.11) and A_{max} (maximum amplitude at the extrema point, see Fig. 11.11) values decreased significantly. As a result, BVP features show significant differences among tasks with different confidence levels, e.g. lower confidence level tasks made BVP features of ΔT_p and ΔT_f values significantly higher.

These findings suggest that both GSR and BVP features can be used as indicators of user confidence in decision making tasks.

11.6 Decision Performance in ML-Based Decision Making

In addition to user confidence, decision performance also plays significant roles in the human's attitude to an intelligent system of ML-based decision making. Decision performance refers to the measurement of whether humans choose the most favourable alternative among multiple alternatives. Various approaches for evaluating decision performances were proposed [3, 39]. For example, decision performance is defined as the degree of confirmation to specifications of activities in relation to one or more of their desired values [39].

In an ML-based travel route decision making study, Zhou et al. [57] evaluated ML-based decision performance with the use of decision utility widely investigated in decision theory [29, 40]. In [57], the user's decision performance is measured based on the following steps: (1) Compute utility U_i of each decision alternative; (2) Decide the best alternative which has the highest utility. This can be regarded as the ground-truth of decisions; (3) Compare the user's decision with the best alternative. If the user's decision matches the best alternative, the user's decision performance is marked as 1. Otherwise, it is marked as 0. This value is defined as decision quality score. The decisions which have high scores are defined as high quality decisions.

The investigation in [57] found that when more ML-based decision factors were introduced into decision making, the decision quality was increased significantly. This result suggests that it is necessary to control the number of decision factors in decision making in order to get decisions of high quality. It was also found that different types of ML-based decision factors (e.g. predicted congestion rate and predicted incident rate in travel route decision making) affected decision quality differently. [57] also demonstrates that decision qualities can be indexed with human physiological and behavioural signals.

11.7 Adaptive Measurable Decision Making

As reviewed in the previous sections, different factors affect user confidence as well as decision performance in ML-based decision making and these effects can be indexed with physiological and behavioural signals. In order to incorporate these findings in real-world applications, the user interface for an ML-based decision making application may include the following components from the HCI perspective:

- Components which collect users' physiological and behavioural signals unobtrusively during decision making;
- Components which allow updating of different factors (e.g. uncertainty, decision factors) automatically based on user confidence and decision performance;
- Present user confidence and decision quality in real-time.

Such a user interface can help users make higher quality decisions confidently. By using physiological and behavioural sensors such as GSR devices during decision making, the user confidence and quality of each decision may be measured and displayed in real-time. The real-time feedback of user confidence and quality of decisions allows the users or system to adjust factors impacting their decisions adaptively, in order to balance the user confidence and decision quality during the decision making process. Such a framework is called adaptive measurable decision making.

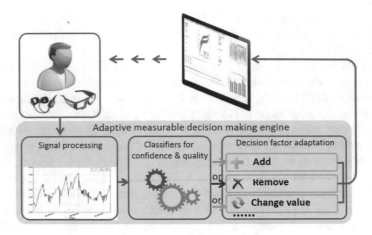

Fig. 11.12 The framework of adaptive measurable decision making

Figure 11.12 illustrates the loop of using adaptive measurable decision making in an application. In this loop, the adaptive measurable decision making engine is mainly composed of the physiological and behavioural signal processing component, classifiers for user confidence and decision quality, as well as decision factor adaptation. Raw physiological and behavioural signals from the user are input into the adaptive measurable decision making engine. The user confidence levels and decision quality are derived from the signals. If the user is not satisfied with the user confidence levels and decision quality, the decision factors are refined (e.g. add/remove some decision factors, change uncertainty information) and a new decision process is performed based on the updated decision factors. This process is iteratively performed until the user is confidently satisfied with the decision performance.

The proposed framework integrated parsing and interpretation of physiological and behavioural information of humans with computational algorithms that, in turn, fed into processes that adapt the interface for ML-based decision factors to enhance the user performance in decision making. The examples of interface adaptations in an intelligent interface that one may consider include: (1) addition or deletion of decision factors; (2) changing values of decision factors; (3) changing the visualisation of uncertainty or correlation; (4) addition or deletion of signal channels used to measure user's physiological and behavioural information.

Following the framework of adaptive measurable decision making, users are aware of which ML models produce ML results for confident higher decision quality. As a result, ML models can be evaluated not based on ML results directly, but based on user confidence and decision quality which are more acceptable by both ML researchers and domain experts. Therefore, this framework provides an applicable approach to make ML transparent for both ML researchers and domain experts by revealing user's confidence. More generally, human's other cognition states such as trust and cognitive load can be revealed in real-time during the ML-based decision making to make ML transparent.

11.8   Conclusion

Despite the recognised value of machine learning techniques and high expectation of applying ML techniques within various applications, significant barriers to widespread adoption and local implementation of ML approaches still exist in the areas of trust (of ML results), comprehension (of ML processes) and related workload, as well as confidence (in decision making based on ML results) by humans. This chapter proposed that the revealing of human cognition states with a multimodal interface during ML-based decision making could provide a rich view for both ML researchers and domain experts to learn the effectiveness of ML technologies in applications. On the one hand, human cognition states could help understand to what degree users accept innovative technologies. On the other hand, through understanding human cognition states during ML-based decision making, ML-based decision attributes/factors and even ML models can be adaptively refined in order to make ML transparent. Based on the revealing of human cognition states, this chapter presented a framework of adaptive measurable decision making to show how the revealing of human cognition states are integrated into an ML-based decision making to make ML transparent.

Acknowledgements This work was supported in part by AOARD under grant No. FA2386-14-1-0022 AOARD 134131.

References

1. Aimone, J.A., Houser, D., Weber, B.: Neural signatures of betrayal aversion: an fMRI study of trust. Proc. Biol. Sci. / Royal Soc. **281**(1782), 20132127 (2014)
2. Arshad, S., Wang, Y., Chen, F.: Interactive mouse stream as real-time indicator of user's cognitive load. In: Proceedings of the 33rd Annual ACM Conference Extended Abstracts on Human Factors in Computing Systems, pp. 1025–1030 (2015)
3. Azizi, H., Ajirlu, S.F.: Measurement of overall performances of decision-making units using ideal and anti-ideal decision-making units. Comput. Ind. Eng. **59**(3), 411–418 (2010)
4. Beller, J., Heesen, M., Vollrath, M.: Improving the drivercautomation interaction an approach using automation uncertainty. Hum. Factors J. Human Factors Ergon. Soc. **55**(6), 1130–1141 (2013)
5. Biewald, L.: Why human-in-the-loop computing is the future of machine learning. http://www.computerworld.com/article/3004013/robotics/why-human-in-the-loop-computing-is-the-future-of-machine-learning.html (2015). [Online; Accessed 4 June 2017]
6. Bridgwater, A.: Machine learning needs a human-in-the-loop. https://www.forbes.com/sites/adrianbridgwater/2016/03/07/machine-learning-needs-a-human-in-the-loop/#2bbb379f4cab (2016). [Online; Accessed 4 June 2017]
7. Camerer, C., Weber, M.: Recent developments in modeling preferences: uncertainty and ambiguity. J. Risk Uncertain. **5**(4), 325–370 (1992)
8. Chen, F., Zhou, J., Wang, Y., Yu, K., Arshad, S.Z., Khawaji, A., Conway, D.: Robust Multimodal Cognitive Load Measurement, 1st edn. Springer, Berlin (2016)
9. Clark, H.H., Brennan, S.E.: Grounding in communication. In: Perspectives on Socially Shared Cognition, pp. 127–149. American Psychological Association (1991)

10. Edwards, J.A., Snyder, F.J., Allen, P.M., Makinson, K.A., Hamby, D.M.: Decision making for risk management: a comparison of graphical methods for presenting quantitative uncertainty. Risk Anal. Off. Publ. Soc. Risk Anal. **32**(12), 2055–2070 (2012)
11. Eyster, E., Weizsacker, G.: Correlation Neglect in Financial Decision-Making. DIW Berlin Discussion Paper No. 1104 (2010). https://doi.org/10.2139/ssrn.1735339
12. Fiedler, S., Glockner, A.: The dynamics of decision making in risky choice: an eye-tracking analysis. Front. Psychol. **3** (2012)
13. Figner, B., Murphy, R.O.: Using skin conductance in judgment and decision making research. In: A Handbook of Process Tracing Methods for Decision Research: A critical Review and User's Guide, pp. 163–184 (2010)
14. Franco-Watkins, A.M., Johnson, J.G.: Applying the decision moving window to risky choice: Comparison of eye-tracking and mouse-tracing methods. Judgm. Decis. Mak. **6**(8), 740–749 (2011)
15. Gog, T.V., Paas, F., Marcus, N., Ayres, P., Sweller, J.: The mirror neuron system and observational learning: implications for the effectiveness of dynamic visualizations. Educ. Psychol. Rev. **21**(1), 21–30 (2008)
16. Gütl, C., Pivec, M., Trummer, C., Garcabarrios, V.M., Mdritscher, F., Pripfl, J., Umgeher, M.: ADELE (adaptive e-learning with eye-tracking): theoretical background, system architecture and application scenarios. Eur. J. Open Distance E-Learn. **2** (2005)
17. Guyon, I., Elisseeff, A.: An introduction to variable and feature selection. J. Mach. Learn. Res. **3**, 1157–1182 (2003)
18. Hahn, T., Notebaert, K., Anderl, C., Teckentrup, V., Kaßecker, A., Windmann, S.: How to trust a perfect stranger: predicting initial trust behavior from resting-state brain-electrical connectivity. Soc. Cogn. Affect. Neurosci. **10**(6), 809–813 (2015)
19. Heekeren, H.R., Marrett, S., Ungerleider, L.G.: The neural systems that mediate human perceptual decision making. Nature Rev. Neurosci. **9**(6), 467–479 (2008)
20. Hill, B.: Confidence and decision. Games Econ. Behav. **82**(C), 675–692 (2013)
21. Hsu, M.: Neural systems responding to degrees of uncertainty in human decision-making. Science **310**(5754), 1680–1683 (2005)
22. Huettel, S.A., Stowe, C.J., Gordon, E.M., Warner, B.T., Platt, M.L.: Neural signatures of economic preferences for risk and ambiguity. Neuron **49**(5), 765–775 (2006)
23. Ibrekk, H., Morgan, M.G.: Graphical communication of uncertain quantities to nontechnical people. Risk Anal. **7**(4), 519–529 (1987)
24. Jenkins, Q., Jiang, X.: Measuring trust and application of eye tracking in human robotic interaction. In: Proceedings of the 2010 Industrial Engineering Research Conference (2010)
25. Kahneman, D., Tversky, A.: Prospect theory: an analysis of decision under risk. Econometrica **47**(2), 263–91 (1979)
26. Kelsey, D.: Maxmin expected utility and weight of evidence. Oxf. Econ. Pap. **46**(3), 425–444 (1994)
27. Khawaji, A., Chen, F., Zhou, J., Marcus, N.: Trust and cognitive load in the text-chat environment: the role of mouse movement. In: Proceedings of the 26th Australian Computer-Human Interaction Conference on Designing Futures: The Future of Design, OzCHI '14, pp. 324–327 (2014)
28. Kirschenbaum, S.S., Trafton, J.G., Schunn, C.D., Trickett, S.B.: Visualizing uncertainty: the impact on performance. Hum. Factors **56**(3), 509–520 (2014)
29. Köbberling, V.: Strength of preference and cardinal utility. Econ. Theory **27**(2), 375–391 (2006)
30. Lee, M.D., Dry, M.J.: Decision making and confidence given uncertain advice. Cogn. Sci. **30**(6), 1081–1095 (2006)
31. Liao, H., Xu, Z., Zeng, X.J., Merigó, J.M.: Qualitative decision making with correlation coefficients of hesitant fuzzy linguistic term sets. Knowl.-Based Syst. **76**, 127–138 (2015)
32. Moll, J., De Oliveira-Souza, R., Zahn, R.: The neural basis of moral cognition: sentiments, concepts, and values. Ann. N. Y. Acad. Sci. **1124**, 161–180 (2008)
33. Moran, R., Teodorescu, A.R., Usher, M.: Post choice information integration as a causal determinant of confidence: novel data and a computational account. Cogn. Psychol. **78**, 99–147 (2015)

34. Morgado, P., Sousa, N., Cerqueira, J.J.: The impact of stress in decision making in the context of uncertainty. J. Neurosci. Res. **93**(6), 839–847 (2015)
35. Pallier, G., Wilkinson, R., Danthiir, V., Kleitman, S., Knezevic, G., Stankov, L., Roberts, R.D.: The role of individual differences in the accuracy of confidence judgments. J. Gen. Psychol. **129**(3), 257–299 (2002)
36. Peper, E., Harvey, R., Lin, I.M., Tylova, H., Moss, D.: Is there more to blood volume pulse than heart rate variability respiratory sinus arrhythmia, and cardiorespiratory synchrony? Biofeedback **35**(2), 54–61 (2007)
37. Platt, M.L., Huettel, S.A.: Risky business: the neuroeconomics of decision making under uncertainty. Nature Neurosci. **11**(4), 398–403 (2008)
38. Preuschoff, K., 't Hart, B.M., Einhäuser, W.: Pupil dilation signals surprise: evidence for noradrenaline's role in decision making. Front. Neurosci. **5**, 115 (2011)
39. Ray, P.K., Sahu, S.: Productivity measurement through multi-criteria decision making. Eng. Costs Prod. Econ. **20**(2), 151–163 (1990)
40. Rothbard, M.N.: Toward a reconstruction of utility and welfare economics. Cent. Lib. Stud. (1977)
41. Scantamburlo, T.: Machine learning in decisional process: a philosophical perspective. ACM SIGCAS Comput. Soc. **45**(3), 218–224 (2015)
42. Smith, L.J., Anand, P., Benattayallah, A., Hodgson, T.L.: An fMRI investigation of moral cognition in healthcare decision making. J. Neurosci. Psychol. Econ. **8**(2), 116–133 (2015)
43. Smith, P.J., Geddes, N.D., Beatty, R.: Human-centered design of decision-support systems. In: Sears, A., Jacko, J.A. (eds.) Human-Computer Interaction: Design Issues, Solutions, and Applications. CRC Press (2009)
44. Stickel, C., Ebner, M., Steinbach-Nordmann, S., Searle, G., Holzinger, A.: Emotion detection: application of the valence arousal space for rapid biological usability testing to enhance universal access. In: Stephanidis, C. (ed.) Universal Access in Human-Computer Interaction. Addressing Diversity. Lecture Notes in Computer Science, vol. 5614, pp. 615–624. Springer, Berlin (2009)
45. Taghavifard, M.T., Damghani, K.K., Moghaddam, R.T.: Decision Making Under Uncertain and Risky Situations. Enterprise Risk Management Symposium Monograph Society of Actuaries, Schaumburg, Illinois, Tech. rep (2009)
46. Tversky, A., Kahneman, D.: Judgment under uncertainty: heuristics and biases. Science **185**(4157), 1124–1131 (1974)
47. Wagstaff, K.: Machine learning that matters. In: Proceedings of ICML2012, pp. 529–536 (2012)
48. Watanabe, S.: Pattern Recognition: Human and Mechanical. John Wiley & Sons Inc, New York, USA (1985)
49. White, T.P., Engen, N.H., Sørensen, S., Overgaard, M., Shergill, S.S.: Uncertainty and confidence from the triple-network perspective: voxel-based meta-analyses. Brain Cogn. **85**, 191–200 (2014)
50. Ye, J.: Multicriteria decision-making method using the correlation coefficient under single-valued neutrosophic environment. Int. J. Gen. Syst. **42**(4), 386–394 (2013)
51. Zhou, J., Arshad, S.Z., Wang, X., Li, Z., Feng, D., Chen, F.: End-user development for interactive data analytics: uncertainty, correlation and user confidence. IEEE Trans. Affect. Comput. (2017)
52. Zhou, J., Arshad, S.Z., Yu, K., Chen, F.: Correlation for user confidence in predictive decision making. In: Proceedings of the 28th Australian Conference on Computer-Human Interaction, OzCHI'16, pp. 252–256 (2016)
53. Zhou, J., Bridon, C., Chen, F., Khawaji, A., Wang, Y.: Be informed and be involved: effects of uncertainty and correlation on user's confidence in decision making. In: Proceedings of the 33rd Annual ACM Conference Extended Abstracts on Human Factors in Computing Systems, pp. 923–928 (2015)
54. Zhou, J., Chen, F.: Making machine learning useable. Int. J. Intell. Syst. Tech. Appl. **14**(2), 91 (2015)

55. Zhou, J., Jung, J.Y., Chen, F.: Dynamic workload adjustments in human-machine systems based on GSR features. In: Human-Computer Interaction – INTERACT 2015. Lecture Notes in Computer Science, pp. 550–558. Springer, Berlin (2015)
56. Zhou, J., Khawaja, M.A., Li, Z., Sun, J., Wang, Y., Chen, F.: Making machine learning useable by revealing internal states update & #45; a transparent approach. Int. J. Comput. Sci. Eng. 13(4), 378–389 (2016)
57. Zhou, J., Sun, J., Chen, F., Wang, Y., Taib, R., Khawaji, A., Li, Z.: Measurable decision making with GSR and pupillary analysis for intelligent user interface. ACM Trans. Comput. Hum. Interact. 21(6), 33:1–33:23 (2015)

Chapter 12
Do I Trust a Machine? Differences in User Trust Based on System Performance

Kun Yu, Shlomo Berkovsky, Dan Conway, Ronnie Taib, Jianlong Zhou and Fang Chen

Abstract Trust plays an important role in various user-facing systems and applications. It is particularly important in the context of decision support systems, where the system's output serves as one of the inputs for the users' decision making processes. In this chapter, we study the dynamics of explicit and implicit user trust in a simulated automated quality monitoring system, as a function of the system accuracy. We establish that users correctly perceive the accuracy of the system and adjust their trust accordingly. The results also show notable differences between two groups of users and indicate a possible threshold in the acceptance of the system. This important learning can be leveraged by designers of practical systems for sustaining the desired level of user trust.

K. Yu (✉) · S. Berkovsky · D. Conway · R. Taib · J. Zhou · F. Chen
DATA61, CSIRO, 13 Garden St, Eveleigh, NSW 2015, Australia
e-mail: Kun.Yu@data61.csiro.au

S. Berkovsky
e-mail: Shlomo.Berkovsky@data61.csiro.au

D. Conway
e-mail: Dan.Conway@data61.csiro.au

R. Taib
e-mail: Ronnie.Taib@data61.csiro.au

J. Zhou
e-mail: Jianlong.Zhou@data61.csiro.au

F. Chen
e-mail: Fang.Chen@data61.csiro.au

© Springer International Publishing AG, part of Springer Nature 2018
J. Zhou and F. Chen (eds.), *Human and Machine Learning*, Human–Computer
Interaction Series, https://doi.org/10.1007/978-3-319-90403-0_12

12.1 Introduction

Trust is a critical factor that impacts interpersonal relationship, and it used to be established via face-to-face communications between people until technologies made human-machine communications possible. The extensive usage of internet everywhere in the world has boosted the information revolution, under which circumstance the human alone is not capable of processing the vast amount of information which is booming exponentially over time, so people may resort to computers for help now and then. However, switching from a smiling colleague to a cold emotionless machine, the human does need time and experience to build up trust with the new partner, although it can conduct many tasks that are beyond the capability of a human. In this context, it is particularly important for systems where users are required to make decisions based, at least partially, on machine recommendations. For instance, consider a medical decision support system or an e-commerce recommender system. In both cases, a user decides on the course of actions — be it medical treatment for a patient or product to purchase — in uncertain conditions and based (in part) on the system's suggestions. Since in both cases there is something at stake, i.e., there are possible negative implications for incorrect decisions, the lack of user trust may deter the user from following these suggestions and be detrimental to the uptake of the system.

Trust in automation, and, in particular, in decision support information technologies, has been the focus of many studies over the last decades [5, 7]. It has mainly been studied in the context of task automation and industrial machinery. In one of the seminal works in this field, Muir et al. [13] found a positive correlation between the level of user trust and the degree to which the user delegated control to the system. Furthermore, McGuirl and Sarter [11] found similar responses specifically within an automated decision support system. Note that both works highlighted the impact of establishing and maintaining trust on user reliance on system suggestions, and, indirectly, on the uptake of the system.

Although much work has been devoted to the impact of system performance [18] and transparency [21] on user trust, less attention has been paid to the temporal variations of trust, and to individual differences of such dynamic aspects. In this chapter, we discuss our investigations on the fine-grained dynamics of trust in an experiment that simulates an Automated Quality Monitoring (AQM) system that alerts users to the existence of faulty items, in a fictional factory production line scenario. In the experiment, every one of the 22 participants interacted with four AQM systems each exhibiting a different level of accuracy. After each trial (30 per AQM system), the users reported their perceived level of trust in the system, which we refer to as explicit trust. In addition, we also measured implicit trust through reliance, quantified through the proportion of times the user followed the AQM's suggestion. It should be noted that for any decision made by the user, reliance for a single task is a binary feature, since it captures whether the user followed (or not) the system's advice.

Three hypotheses guided our examinations:

- H1: Learned trust, i.e. the trust gained after some experience and collaboration, would stabilise over time to a level correlated with the systems' accuracy;
- H2: Users would exhibit thresholds of acceptable accuracy for a system, under which reliance would drop;
- H3: Differences would exist for acceptable accuracy in terms of trust and stereotypical user profiles will still be able to be constructed.

This chapter will address our work which experimentally validates these hypotheses and draws practical conclusions that can help system designers maintain user trust in systems. In the following sections, we first present related work on user-system trust, followed by a detailed description of the experimental protocol. We then present and discuss the results, and finally conclude with a discussion on practical steps that might be taken to sustain user trust.

12.2   Background

Human-machine trust has generated an extensive body of literature since it was originally investigated within the context of industrial automation systems in the 1990s. Although multiple definitions, frameworks and decompositions of trust exist, there is convergent evidence about its central characteristics. We adopt the definition proposed by Lee and See [8] where trust can be defined as *the attitude that an agent will help achieve an individual's goals in a situation characterised by uncertainty and vulnerability.* This succinctly encapsulates the primary sources of variance (the user, the system, the context) and identifies a key aspect of this relationship, that of vulnerability. Similar definitions exist by Rousseau et al. [15], Mayer et al. [10] and Hoff and Bashir [5]. Trust is a hypothesised variable that has been shown to be a key mitigating factor in system use/disuse (reliance) [7, 20]. It can be inferred from both self-report and behavioural measures [10], and importantly, is dynamic, with acquisition and extinction curves, subject to the users' experience of system performance.

Trust has been proposed to be a multi-dimensional construct with a number of models existing in the current literature, each with slightly different proposed component subscales. We have adopted Hoff and Bashir's model [2], which he based on an empirical research overview of existing literature in the area. This model is also nicely applicable to our research focus in that it includes variables important to HCI contexts such as 'design features' as well as encompassing a number of important situational factors and individual differences such as culture, age, gender and personality. Hoff and Bashir also base their work on the Lee and See's definition of trust as mentioned above.

In specific, this model proposes that three conceptual types of factors influence user-system trust. Dispositional trust reflects the user's natural tendency to trust machines and encompasses cultural, demographic, and personality factors. Situational trust refers, to more specific factors, such as the task to be performed, the complexity and type of system, user's workload, perceived risks and benefits, and even mood. Lastly, learned trust encapsulates the experiential aspects of the construct which are directly related to the system itself. This variable is further decomposed into two components. One is initial learned trust, which consists of any knowledge of the system acquired before interaction, such as reputation or brand awareness. This initial state of learnt trust is then also affected by dynamic learned trust which develops as the user interacts with the system and begins to develop experiential knowledge of its performance characteristics such as reliability, predictability, and usefulness. The relationships and interaction between these different factors influencing trust are complicated and subject to much discussion within the literature. In our work we focus on how trust changes through human-machine interaction and therefore seek to manipulate experimental variables thought to influence dynamic learned trust, whilst keeping situational (and initial learned) variables static, and allowing for variation in individual differences via factors affecting dispositional trust.

Individual differences in trust response are a key focus of our research. In the original body of work on human-human trust, Rotter [14] established that trust (human-human) was a stable character trait and developed an instrument that detected variations in propensity to trust between people. Extending this, Scott [16] demonstrated that trust was composed of at least two factors, one being situational, and the other being a stable, trait based factor (equivalent to Hoff's dispositional trust). When extending the original human constructs into the realm of humans and machines, Singh et al. [17] operationalised the construct of 'complacency' in automation, which included a subscale on 'trust' and found reliable, and stable variations between people. Lee and Moray [7] found differences between people's likelihood in using automation when error rates are held constant.

When comparing human-human to human-machine trust, Madhavan and Wiegmann's [9] review outlines a number of important differences. Jian et al. [6] found that people's ratings are less extreme towards other humans than towards machines. Earley [4] found that people evaluated system estimations as more trustworthy than human equivalents, but in contrast, Dietvorst et al. [2] found that people were more likely to under-rely on an automated aid in decision making even when shown that the machine performed more accurately than their own efforts and even when there was a financial stake involved. On the other hand, Dzindolet et al. [3] notes that human machine trust sometimes begins at a higher level than human-human trust and is characterised by more dramatic collapses when trust is proven to be misplaced. To explain this phenomena he suggested that some individuals harbour a 'Perfect automation schema' where expectations of system performance are unrealistically high. Such expectations result in differential reactions to system-failures, where those who possess this schema exhibit higher loss of trust on system failure than those who do not.

However, as Lee and See [8] and Hoff et al. [5] have claimed, individual differences are likely to be overcome by the experiential effects of steady state machine behaviour resulting in less variance between users after exposure to the machine. The experiment we outline below contradicts this finding to some extent. We have found that clustering users into two groups uncovers two patterns of trust behaviour where one group exhibits greater variance in trust ratings than the other. We use this finding to single out users, whose trust in the system may be at risk and take proactive steps to sustain their trust.

12.3 Methodology

12.3.1 Context

The scenario of the experiment was a typical production factory quality control task. This simulated task consisted of checking the quality of drinking glasses on a production line, with the assistance of a decision support system called an Automatic Quality Monitor (AQM). However, the AQM was not always correct, i.e., it would occasionally exhibit false positives (suggesting failing a good glass) and misses (suggesting passing a faulty glass).

12.3.2 Trials

Each trial required the participant to make a decision about whether to pass or fail a glass, with no other information about the glass other than the AQM's suggestion. Trials were presented sequentially, providing a time-based history of interaction with a given AQM. At each trial, the participant could trust the AQM or override it and make their own decision. A simple graphical user interface coded in Python and running on a 64-bit Windows operating system was used, as shown in Fig. 12.1.

Each trial starts with the AQM providing a suggestion for a new glass, by illuminating a red warning light-bulb if it predicts the glass to be faulty. Otherwise the warning light remains off. It should be noted that the status of the AQM light and the possible quality of the glass are both binary features to help generalise results, as mentioned above.

The participant must then decide whether to pass the glass by clicking the Pass button, or conversely to fail the glass by clicking the Examine button. The actual glass is then displayed, so the participant receives direct feedback on their decision, as shown in Figs. 12.2 and 12.3. Furthermore, we gamified the experiment in an attempt to increase motivation and attention: each time the participant made a correct decision, i.e., examined a faulty glass or passed a good glass, they earned a fictional $100 reward. However, each incorrect decision cost them a fictional $100 loss. The total earnings were updated after each decision and displayed within the user interface. The rewards and the fines were used for gamification purposes only, and no

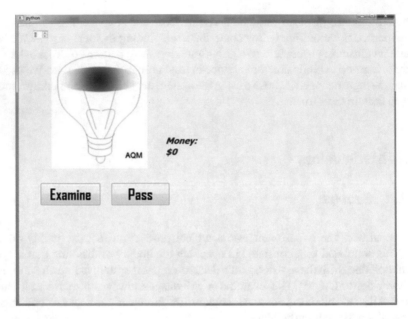

Fig. 12.1 The trial starts with an AQM recommendation, with two buttons (examine/pass) for users to make a decision

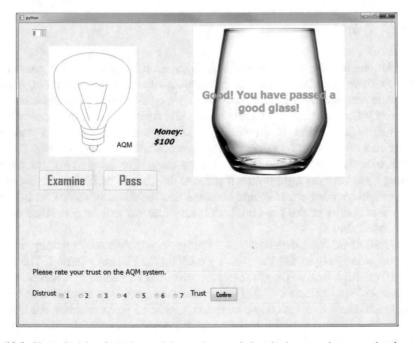

Fig. 12.2 Upon decision from the participant, the actual glass is shown and score updated

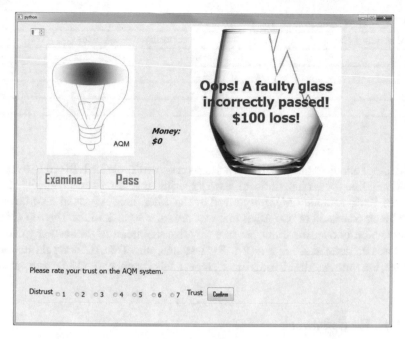

Fig. 12.3 A wrong decision leads to decreased score, and red text indicating the outcome of a glass

actual remuneration was offered to the participants. Exemplary interfaces showing that the user has made correct and incorrect decisions are shown in Figs. 12.2 and 12.3 respectively.

We operationalised a binary decision making task in our experiment for two reasons. Firstly, any complex decision process can be arguably decomposed into a series of binary decisions. The decision-trust relationship thus can be easily generalised to complicated decision-making problems. Secondly, the simplified decision making protocol we implemented, similar in effect to the 'micro-worlds' discussed by Lee and See [8], makes it convenient to map trust levels to decisions without the interference of other parameters [19].

12.3.3   AQM Accuracy and Blocks

The experiment session was separated into four blocks, and participants were instructed that a different AQM was used for each block. The accuracy of each of the four AQMs presented was manipulated by varying the average rate of false positives and false negatives exhibited by each system. These errors were presented in a randomised order within the 30 trials presented for each participants and each AQM.

Table 12.1 AQM accuracies

AQM accuracy (%)	False positives + negatives (%)
100	0
90	10
80	20
70	30

We used four different AQM accuracies, as shown in Table 12.1. In order to capture a trust baseline for each participant, each experiment session systematically started with the 100% accuracy AQM, followed by the other three AQMs in random order. Each block consisted of one AQM that was used for 30 task trials. The AQM made errors randomly over the trials, but in a way that the mean AQM accuracy over the block was as defined for that AQM. For instance, the 80% AQM would make, on average, 6 errors over the 30 trials (on average, 3 false positives and 3 false negatives).

12.3.4 Participants

Twenty-two participants took part in the 45 minute experiment. Twenty of the participants were university students and the remaining two were IT professionals. No specific background or requirements were required to complete the task. Recruitment and participation were conducted in accordance with the University-approved ethics plan for this study. No reward or compensation was offered for taking part in the experiment.

12.3.5 Information logging

For each trial, we collected:

- The participant's binary decision (pass or examine);
- The AQM suggestion (light on or light off);
- The actual glass condition (good or faulty);
- The time required to make the decision, i.e., the time elapsed between the AQM light being presented to the participant and the Pass/Examine button being clicked;
- The subjective trust rating, collected after the actual state of the glass is revealed. This rating is collected using a 7-point Likert scale ranging from 1: distrust to 7: trust. In the instructions issued at the outset of the experiment we explained that a rating of 4 meant neutral, or no disposition in either direction.

One of the participants consistently rated the trust at extreme levels (either 1 or 7) of the 7-point scale across the four sessions, and hence his data was excluded from the examination. Considering the individual differences, the trust data was normalised to the range of 0–1 on an individual basis, for all the trials conducted on the four AQMs. The binary decision of the participants was further quantified in terms of a reliance score R_s, i.e. the ratio between the number of decisions consistent with the AQM recommendation and the total decisions for a set number of consecutive trials, and thus the value of the reliance score falls between 0 and 1.

$$R_s = \frac{N_r}{N_r + N_n} \tag{12.1}$$

where N_r and N_n refer to the number of decisions consistent and inconsistent with the AQM recommendation respectively for all the previous trials on it.

12.4 Results

In this section we present and discuss the results of our user study in the light of our hypotheses.

12.4.1 Trust Correlation to System Accuracy

We start with the investigation of acquisition and extinction of trust, as observed over the course of user interactions with the AQMs. The level of trust is measured subjectively after each trial, as described earlier. Since the AQM errors were randomised over the 30 trials for each AQM, and given the number of participants, trust variations for each trial exhibit a number of local variations. We address this issue by applying a simple low-pass filter, specifically a 5-trial sliding window, reducing our data to 25 points per AQM. That is, T_n, the level of trust after trial n, was computed as the average trust across the last 5 trials $(n\text{-}4\text{-}n)$. Figure 12.4 shows the aggregated normalised trust for all 21 participants, for all four AQMs.

$$T_n = \frac{\sum_{i=0}^{4} t_{n-i}}{5} \tag{12.2}$$

where t_n is the trust rating for trial n.

At first, trust in all AQMs seems uniform as would be expected since participants know that each new AQM is different from the others they may have encountered, and the order is randomised. Trust in the 100% AQM appears to be above the other AQMs.

Fig. 12.4 Mean trust for all
participants, all AQMs

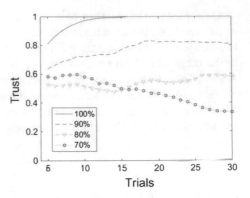

An analysis of variance showed that the effect of the AQM accuracy on the first trust point (trust mean over the first five trials) was significant for all participants, $F(3, 80) = 6.463$, $p < 0.001$. Post hoc Tuckey tests showed there was a significant difference between the 100% AQM and both the 80 and 70% AQMs. We think this may be linked to two possible factors. Firstly, since we use a sliding window to capture trust, the participants will have started to form a preliminary trust judgement on each AQM by the time of the first trust point (recall that the first point is actually after 5 trials). Secondly, it is possible that individual differences between participants combine in a way that creates such a wide initial variation in trust. We investigate this second possibility in later sections of this chapter, by grouping participants and then revisiting their initial trust assessment.

As a side note, the test of homogeneity (Levene's) for the first reliance point was significant, hence violating ANOVA's assumption of equal variances. However, the sample sizes being equal, this statistic should be robust. Hence, we accept the results.

Looking at the temporal fluctuations of the trust values, we observe that these stabilise with important differences between the AQMs. As expected, trust in the 100% AQM stabilises at 1 after only 13 trials. Also the 90% AQM converges to reasonably high levels of trust from trial 19. The 80% AQM is initially stable but exhibits a slight increase in trust starting from trial 15, while the trust in the 70% AQM steadily declines after fewer than 10 trials and eventually drops as low as 0.33.

An analysis of variance showed that the effect of the AQM accuracy on the last trust point (trust mean over the last five trials) was significant for all the participants, $F(3, 80) = 27.03$, $p < 0.001$. Post hoc Tuckey tests show there is a significant difference between the 100% AQM and both the 80 and 70% AQMs, as well as between the 90% AQM and the 70% AQM, and again between the 80% AQM and the 70% AQM.

It should be noted that the final order of the trust ratings corresponds to that of the AQM accuracies. That is, the 100% AQM stabilises at the highest trust level, followed by the 90, 80, and 70% AQM, in this order. This finding supports our H1 hypothesis that learned trust would stabilise over time to a level correlated with the

Fig. 12.5 Mean reliance for
all participants, all AQMs

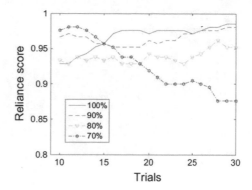

systems' accuracy. However, we will later examine what role individual differences
may play in this process.

In addition, since we only selected a small set of discrete accuracies for our AQMs,
it can be interesting to analyse our results from the perspective of a rank-ordering
problem. Indeed, this would provide an indication of whether the reported trust ranking aligns to such discrete accuracy levels. A Friedman's test shows significant differences between the trust levels (Friedman's $\chi^2(20, 3) = 45.31$, $p < 0.001$), with
mean ranks of 3.8, 2.9, 2.0 and 1.3 for AQMs of accuracy 100, 90, 80 and 70%
respectively. These statistics suggest that trust ratings correlate with increased levels
of AQM accuracy, when considered as discrete values (here 10% increments), again
supporting our H1 hypothesis.

12.4.2   Acceptable Accuracy and Reliance

We now examine the dynamics of reliance, which we regard as an objective measure
of trust. Recall that reliance is measured implicitly during each trial, as described
earlier. Again, we apply a simple low-pass filter, but this time we use a 10-trial sliding
window, reducing our data to 20 points per AQM. The reason for this larger window
is mainly because reliance is a binary feature (at every trial the participant either did
or did not follow the system suggestion). Hence, local variations tend to add weight
to the reading for a small window size. Figure 12.5 shows the aggregated reliance
for all the 21 participants and all four AQMs.

We observe that despite the larger sliding window of 10 interactions, the reliance
curves are less stable than the trust curves. We believe that the reason for this observation is two-fold. Firstly, the effect of a binary feature on smoothing is strong and
could require a wider sliding window size, but this would mean losing temporal accuracy in our analysis of reliance dynamics. Secondly, we think that while participants
exhibit relatively uniform trust trends, they have different strategies to deal with it,

Fig. 12.6 First reliance
point variance for all
participants

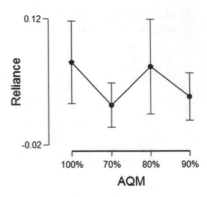

as per our H3 hypothesis of individual differences. We will explore this aspect in the
next sections.

Qualitatively, the AQMs exhibit different reliance patterns. These differences are
not linked to the order in which AQMs are presented to the participant, because
it is randomised. It is possible that, by way of randomisation, the AQMs in each
subset behaved similarly over the first few trials, which would then be picked up
as different levels by the sliding window. However, this explanation seems unlikely
given the number of participants.

All curves, except for the 70% AQM, demonstrate slight (and often unstable)
increases and their final levels are in the range of 0.95–0.98. The 100 and 90%
AQMs seem to converge strongly, while the 70% AQM exhibits a steady decline
in reliance. The 80% AQM seems close to the 100% AQM baseline. This could
indicate that the acceptable level of accuracy for a system is around 80%, possibly a
bit above since the AQM 80% is slightly lower. An analysis of variance showed that
the effect of the AQM accuracy on the first reliance point was not significant for all
participants, $F(3, 80) = 1.597$, $p = 0.197$ n.s. That is, the apparent reliance pairs
observed are not significant in view of the variance, further demonstrated by Fig. 12.6.
This means that the participants interacted with all four AQMs with a comparable
level of dispositional trust, as comes through the implicit reliance measure.

Focussing on the last reliance observed after 30 trials, an analysis of variance
showed that the effect of the AQM accuracy on the last reliance point was significant for all participants, $F(3, 80) = 4.182$, $p = 0.008$. The test of homogeneity
(Levene's) was significant, but again the sample sizes are equal. Due to the binary
notion of reliance, we can test our hypothesis of acceptable level of accuracy by
comparing all the AQMs to the 100% AQM baseline, in order to determine where
the threshold for accuracy may lay. To do so, we applied a simple contrast in the
ANOVA for the last reliance point, and obtained significance only for the pair 100%
AQM versus 70% AQM. This means that the 80% AQM, while being visually apart
from the 100 and 90% AQMs, is actually not significantly different. However, the
AQM 70% is significantly different from the other three AQMs. These results support
our hypothesis H2 that users have thresholds of acceptable accuracy for a system,

under which the reliance drops. Since there is no significant difference between the AQMs in terms of the initial reliance levels, participants start interacting with the AQMs free of pre-disposition. But later on we observe a specific behaviour only for the 70% AQM, whereby the reliance of the participants on that AQM declines significantly compared to other AQMs. This indicates that a threshold of acceptable accuracy in our AQM for the cohort of our participants lies somewhere between 70 and 80%. Having said that, the high values and narrow range of reliance values should be highlighted. Over the course of the whole experiment, reliance curves of all the four AQMs remain fairly compact and above the 0.9 mark. This behaviour is not surprising, however, and can be explained by the relatively high accuracies chosen for all the AQMs. Even the poorest AQM operating at 70% accuracy can correctly classify a glass 7 times out of 10, which is well above chance. We believe that the participants rightfully perceived this benefit of the AQM over pure random choice. Hence they decided to follow the AQM's suggestions, leading to very high levels of reliance. However, examining individual differences and grouping users can help understand the substantial reliance drop observed for the 70% AQM.

12.4.3   Clustering of Participants

While individual user profiles can be appealing for high-precision applications, it may not be justifiable in the context of trust, which as a construct has broadly defined metrics. In addition, the number of participants in our experiment would not allow us to generate fine grain profiles, if they were to exist. So, we endeavoured to partition the participants into two groups using clustering.

The participants were clustered using the reported trust for the last five trials of each AQM, with a K-means method. The trust ratings for the last five trials of each AQM were used because most participants approached stable trust during these trials. We clustered the participants into two groups due to the limited number of participants involved in this study, and ended up with Group 1 including 13 participants and Group 2 with the remaining 8 participants.

Initially, we set out to examine the stability of the clusters. For this, we considered the final clustering produced after the 30 trials as the ground truth and evaluated the relative accuracy of the clusters as they could have been generated at earlier stages of interaction. That is, we executed the above clustering method after a smaller number of trials, say 20, and measured the proportion of users that are correctly mapped to their ground truth cluster. The results of this analysis are shown in Fig. 12.7. Since the clustering is based on the trust levels calculated with a 5-trial sliding window, no clustering can be done for the first 5 trials. The relative accuracy of the clustering increases between trials 5 and 11, as more user information becomes available, and stabilises thereafter above the 0.9 mark. That is, the clusters become stable after 11 trials, after which less than 10% of users are incorrectly mapped to the other cluster.

The curves marked Group1 or Group2 error provide details about users mapped to the incorrect cluster. We observe that the majority of these come from Group 2 users

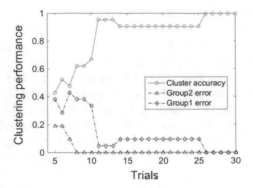

Fig. 12.7 Clustering performance. The Group2 error indicates the participants that belong to Group 1 but are incorrectly clustered to Group 2, and the Group1 error indicates the participants that belong to Group 2 but are incorrectly clustered to Group 1. The clustering accuracy indicates the overall rate of participants correctly assigned to the final two groups

mistakenly mapped to Group 1. Beyond several initial incorrect mappings, Group 1 users were reliably identified and mapped to the right cluster.

Having clustered the participants, we repeated the above analyses of trust and reliance dynamics, but this time for each group separately. The trust curves for the four AQMs observed for Group 1 and Group 2 are shown in Figs. 12.8 and 12.9 respectively. Since clustering was based on trust levels, we expect to find differences in trust between the two groups. Notably, the curves for the 100% AQM are similar in both groups, which can be expected based on H2, since a 100% accuracy AQM is very likely to be acceptable to all users, regardless of their sensitivity. Therefore, we focus the rest of the analysis on differences between groups with regards to the other three AQMs.

Qualitatively, the Group 1 curves are much more spread out than those of Group 2. The initial trust levels of the 90, 80, and 70% AQM in Group 1 are in the range of 0.5–0.63, whereas in Group 2 they are in the range of 0.55–0.77. Despite this, the range of final trust is fairly different: it ranges 0.08–0.73 for Group 1 versus 0.70–0.94 for Group 2. It should also be highlighted that the three trust curves are clearly separable for Group 1, while the differences are less pronounced for Group 2. Also note that the order of the curves for Group 2 does not correspond to the accuracy levels of the AQMs.

An analysis of variance showed that the effect of the AQM accuracy on the first trust point was significant for Group 1, $F(3, 48) = 7.267$, $p < 0.001$. Post hoc Tukey tests have identified the significant difference between Group 1's trust on the 100% AQM and all the remaining AQMs. For Group 2, no significant difference has been found for the first trust point $F(3,28) = 0.820$, $p = 0.494$. The test of homogeneity (Levene's) for the two groups' first reliance point was not significant.

Examining the last trust point now, an analysis of variance showed that the effect of the AQM accuracy on the last trust point was significant for Group 1, $F(3, 48) = 48.51$, $p < 0.001$ and also for Group 2, $F(3, 28) = 7.510$, $p < 0.001$.

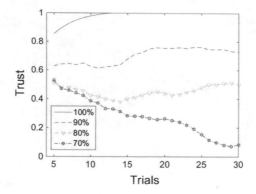

Fig. 12.8 Mean trust for Group 1, all AQMs

Fig. 12.9 Mean trust for
Group 2, all AQMs

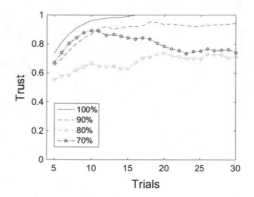

In terms of pairwise post hoc comparison, Group 1 showed significantly different trust for any pair of AQMs, while for Group 2, significant difference was observed between three pairs of AQMs, i.e. 100 and 80%, 100 and 70%, 90 and 80%. The test of homogeneity (Levene's) for both groups last reliance point was significant, but can be ignored because of the equal sample sizes.

In order to address hypotheses H2 and H3 of acceptable levels of accuracy, it is necessary to compare all the AQMs to the baseline 100% AQM. To do so, we applied a simple contrast in the ANOVA for the last trust point for Group 1, and obtained significance only for the pair 100% AQM versus 70% AQM. This finding means that the 80% AQM, while being slightly apart is not significantly different. However, the 70% AQM was indeed found to be significantly different from the other AQMs, and we argue that this AQM falls below the threshold of acceptable accuracy postulated in our hypothesis.

These results support the hypothesis H3 that individual differences exist for acceptable accuracy, but typical user groups may be constructed, where Group 1 demonstrates significant difference in terms of trust on different AQMs, however Group 2 doesn't show significant trust difference.

Fig. 12.10 Mean reliance
for Group 1, all AQMs

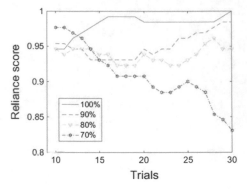

Fig. 12.11 Mean reliance
for Group 2, all AQMs

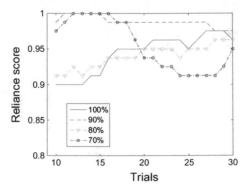

As observed earlier, the differences between the AQMs in terms of reliance level are less clear than the differences in trust. The reliance curves of the four AQMs observed for Group 1 and Group 2 are shown in Figs. 12.10 and 12.11 respectively.

Qualitatively, the two groups exhibit distinct patterns. Group 1 starts with a fairly uniform level of reliance across the AQMs, which can be expected, since the accuracy of each AQM is not known to the participants at the start. Conversely, the reliance in Group 2 is initially split into two ranges: the 90 and 70% AQMs hover above the 0.95 mark, while the 100 and 80% are much closer to 0.9. This result is in line with our earlier observations of reliance using all the participants. An analysis of variance showed that the effect of the AQM accuracy on the first reliance point was not significant for Group 1, $F(3, 48) = 0.441, p = 0.725$ n.s. and also not significant for Group 2, $F(3, 28) = 1.584, p = 0.215$ n.s. This means that the apparent subsets observed for Group 2 are not significant in view of the variance, as demonstrated by Fig. 12.12.

Examining the last reliance point, we observe that the reliance levels in Group 1 correctly reflect the order of the AQM accuracies. Also note that the curves of the 100, 90, and 80% AQM obtain high reliance scores of almost 0.95 or greater than this, while the 70% AQM is clearly placed below the others. This indicates that in Group 1 the acceptable level of accuracy for a system is around 80% (possibly a bit

Fig. 12.12 First reliance
point variance for Group 2

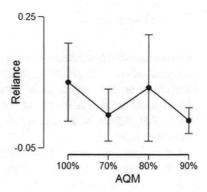

above that), since the reliance on the 80% AQM is slightly lower than on the 100 and 90% AQM. For Group 2, all the curves converge around the 0.95 mark, although the 70% AQM is slightly lower than the others. An analysis of variance showed that the effect of the AQM accuracy on the last reliance point was significant for Group 1, $F(3, 48) = 4.532, p = 0.007$ and not significant for Group 2, $F(3, 28) = 0.153$, $p = 0.927$, n.s. The test of homogeneity (Levene's) for the last reliance point in Group 1 was significant, but the variances were equal for all the other analyses above.

Again, we applied a simple contrast in the ANOVA for the last reliance point for Group 1, and obtained significance only for the pair 100% AQM versus 70% AQM. Just as for trust in Group 1, this means that the 80% AQM while being slightly apart is not significantly different from the 100 and 90% AQMs. However, the 70% AQM is significantly different from the other levels, arguably because it is under the threshold of acceptable accuracy postulated in our hypothesis. Similarly to subjective trust, these results support our hypothesis H3 that Individual differences exist for acceptable accuracy, but typical user profiles may be constructed. Both groups start interacting with the AQMs free of pre-disposition, but Group 1 later on exhibits a threshold of acceptable accuracy in the range of 70–80%. Group 2 again seems to be more resilient or have a lower threshold of acceptable accuracy.

Seen from a rational behaviour perspective, the behaviour of Group 1 is not optimal, since adhering to the AQM's recommendations would provide a 20% better than chance outcome. We conjecture that one possible explanation for this may be that the AQM accuracy perceived by the participants is lower than the actual AQM accuracy, i.e., participants in Group 1 may perceive the 70% AQM as being worse than chance. It should be noted, however, that our experiment does not allow us to establish the exact cause of the observed behaviour, as this would require a substantially different experimental set-up.

12.5 Discussion

In this chapter we discussed the fine-grained dynamics of user-system trust, an important construct of human interaction with a decision support system. We specifically focused on an automated quality monitoring (AQM) simulation, which provided indication of faulty glasses being produced. In our study, each user interacted with four AQMs and out of these interactions we populated the explicit trust and implicit reliance scores.

We analysed the temporal dynamics of both trust and reliance, as well as their dependence on the accuracy exhibited by the AQM. It was found that the reported trust levels aggregated across the entire cohort of users, stabilised over time and, at large, corresponded to the accuracy of the AQMs. Somewhat surprisingly, we discovered that the implicit reliance levels were very high and comparable across the four AQMs. We attribute this finding to the relatively high accuracy of the AQMs in our experiment. Following this, we conducted an additional analysis of individual user differences in trust and reliance. For this, we split the users into two clusters and compared the trust and reliance scores obtained in these clusters. This analysis discovered differences in the dynamics of user trust in the two clusters and also some differences in user reliance on the low-accuracy AQMs. Hence, the obtained experimental results support the hypotheses raised at the beginning of this chapter. Firstly, we observe that the learned user-system trust stabilised over time and generally correlated with the level of accuracy exhibited by the system. Secondly, our findings indicate that at reasonably high levels of system accuracy, user reliance is high, whereas once the system accuracy falls below an acceptance threshold, the reliance may deteriorate as well. Thirdly, we show that these acceptance thresholds are dynamic and user-dependent, and we successfully manage to separate users into two groups with different trust profiles and reliance patterns.

These observations brought to the surface an important practical question referring to the implications of our work on the sustainability of user-system trust. Due to the low transparency but complex structure of most machine learning systems, users are mostly unable to understand their internal working mechanism or parameters, however there is a possibility to improve the users' performance, based on their interaction history. Once the system recognises that certain users are in the 'risk group' and the performance exhibited by the system is not up to their expectations, additional steps may need to be taken in order to sustain the trust of these users. For instance, the system may show its historical performance to these users, thus increasing the experience of these users, or revealing some details of the internal machine algorithm which allows for further understanding of the users. Alternatively, system designers may want to enrich the interactions of these users, e.g., through additional explanations of the suggested actions or through implanting persuasive messages strengthening user trust [1].

Another intriguing question refers to identifying the users at risk. In our study, we conduct a posterior clustering of the participants and split them into two groups. However, a more relevant task would be to identify the type of users and their system acceptance at the beginning of the interaction or, even, before the interaction. The analysis of our clustering shows that the clusters were stable and little changes of cluster were observed at late stages of interaction, possibly indicating stable acceptance preferences. One possible predictor of this preference could potentially be the user's personality or behavioural traits, which can be derived, for example, from the user's past interactions with other systems. Prior research shows that trust correlates to some personality characteristics [12], and this information can be extracted and leveraged in order to sustain user trust. This research is beyond the scope of our work.

In addition, we should note that our findings are based on a fairly limited cohort of participants, all of which had reasonably short interactions with the system. Validating our findings with a larger set of users (and, possibly, with a different target system) is a natural future extension of our work. Also, we would like to increase the length of interactions on the account of reducing the frequency of users reporting their explicit trust. For example, we could collect the explicit trust level every second interaction, allowing us to double the length of interactions without over-burdening the users. This would allow us to collect a more solid empirical evidence and better support our hypotheses.

Finally, more work is needed to address the fine-grained dynamics of trust acquisition and extinction. In our work, we assumed a stable level of accuracy of every system. This, however, may vary over the course of user interaction. Hence, it is important to validate the evolution of user trust as a function of the user's initial trust disposition, observed system performance, and temporal aspects of this performance (e.g., initial failures vs. failures when the trust was already formed). We highlight the importance of these research questions, but leave this work for the future.

12.6 Conclusion

This chapter examines the relationship between system performance, a user trust and reliance on the system. We observe that users correctly perceive the accuracy of the system and adjust their trust and reliance accordingly. We have successfully segmented the users into two groups who showed different patterns in trust dynamics and reliance with different AQM systems. This important learning can be leveraged by designers of practical systems for group-focused interaction systems. Furthermore, we have established a possible threshold in the acceptance of the system. These findings taken together, have dramatic implications for general system design and implementation, by predicting how trust and reliance change as human-machine interaction occurs, as well as providing new knowledge regarding system performance that is necessary for maintaining a user's trust.

Acknowledgements This work was supported in part by AOARD under grant No. FA2386-14-1-0022 AOARD 134131.

References

1. Berkovsky, S., Freyne, J., Oinas-Kukkonen, H.: Influencing individually: fusing personalization and persuasion. ACM Trans. Interact. Intell. Syst. (TiiS) **2**(2), 9 (2012)
2. Dietvorst, B.J., Simmons, J.P., Massey, C.: Algorithm aversion: people erroneously avoid algorithms after seeing them err. J. Exp. Psychol. Gen. **144**(1), 114 (2015)
3. Dzindolet, M.T., Pierce, L.G., Beck, H.P., Dawe, L.A.: The perceived utility of human and automated aids in a visual detection task. Hum. Factors **44**(1), 79–94 (2002)
4. Earley, P.C.: Computer-generated performance feedback in the magazine-subscription industry. Organ. Behav. Human Decis. Process. **41**(1), 50–64 (1988)
5. Hoff, K.A., Bashir, M.: Trust in automation: integrating empirical evidence on factors that influence trust. Human Factors **57**(3), 407–434 (2015)
6. Jian, J.Y., Bisantz, A.M., Drury, C.G.: Foundations for an empirically determined scale of trust in automated systems. Intern. J. Cogn. Ergon. **4**(1), 53–71 (2000)
7. Lee, J.D., Moray, N.: Trust, self-confidence, and operators' adaptation to automation. Int. J. Human Comput. Stud. **40**(1), 153–184 (1994)
8. Lee, J.D., See, K.A.: Trust in automation: designing for appropriate reliance. Human Factors **46**(1), 50–80 (2004)
9. Madhavan, P., Wiegmann, D.A.: Similarities and differences between human-human and human-automation trust: an integrative review. Theor. Issues Ergon. Sci. **8**(4), 277–301 (2007)
10. Mayer, R.C., Davis, J.H., Schoorman, F.D.: An integrative model of organizational trust. Acad. Manag. Rev. **20**(3), 709–734 (1995)
11. McGuirl, J.M., Sarter, N.B.: Supporting trust calibration and the effective use of decision aids by presenting dynamic system confidence information. Human Factors **48**(4), 656–665 (2006)
12. Merritt, S.M., Ilgen, D.R.: Not all trust is created equal: dispositional and history-based trust in human-automation interactions. Human Factors **50**(2), 194–210 (2008)
13. Muir, B.M.: Trust in automation: part i. theoretical issues in the study of trust and human intervention in automated systems. Ergonomics **37**(11), 1905–1922 (1994)
14. Rotter, J.B.: A new scale for the measurement of interpersonal trust. J. Pers. **35**(4), 651–665 (1967)
15. Rousseau, D.M., Sitkin, S.B., Burt, R.S., Camerer, C.: Not so different after all: a cross-discipline view of trust. Acad. Manag. Rev. **23**(3), 393–404 (1998)
16. Scott III, C.L.: Interpersonal trust: a comparison of attitudinal and situational factors. Human Relat. **33**(11), 805–812 (1980)
17. Singh, I.L., Molloy, R., Parasuraman, R.: Automation-induced "complacency": development of the complacency-potential rating scale. Int. J. Aviat. Psychol. **3**(2), 111–122 (1993)
18. Wang, W., Benbasat, I.: Attributions of trust in decision support technologies: a study of recommendation agents for e-commerce. J. Manag. Inf. Syst. **24**(4), 249–273 (2008)
19. Yu, K., Berkovsky, S., Conway, D., Taib, R., Zhou, J., Chen, F.: Trust and reliance based on system accuracy. In: Proceedings of the 2016 Conference on User Modeling Adaptation and Personalization, pp. 223–227. ACM (2016)
20. Yu, K., Berkovsky, S., Taib, R., Conway, D., Zhou, J., Chen, F.: User trust dynamics: An investigation driven by differences in system performance. In: Proceedings of the 22nd International Conference on Intelligent User Interfaces, pp. 307–317. ACM (2017)
21. Zhou, J., Li, Z., Wang, Y., Chen, F.: Transparent machine learning—revealing internal states of machine learning. In: Proceedings of IUI2013 Workshop on Interactive Machine Learning, pp. 1–3 (2013)

Chapter 13
Trust of Learning Systems: Considerations for Code, Algorithms, and Affordances for Learning

Joseph Lyons, Nhut Ho, Jeremy Friedman, Gene Alarcon
and Svyatoslav Guznov

Abstract This chapter provides a synthesis on the literature for Machine Learning (ML), trust in automation, trust in code, and transparency. The chapter introduces the concept of ML and discusses three drivers of trust in ML-based systems: code structure; algorithm performance, transparency, and error management – algorithm factors; and affordances for learning. Code structure offers a static affordance for trustworthiness evaluations that can be both deep and peripheral. The overall performance of the algorithms and the transparency of the inputs, process, and outputs provide an opportunity for dynamic and experiential trustworthiness evaluations. Predictability and understanding are the foundations of trust and must be considered in ML applications. Many ML paradigms neglect the notion of environmental affordances for learning, which from a trust perspective, may in fact be the most important differentiator between ML systems and traditional automation. The learning affordances provide contextualised pedigree for trust considerations. In combination, the trustworthiness aspects of the code, dynamic performance and transparency, and learning affordances offer structural, evidenced performance and understanding, as well as pedigree information from which ML approaches can be evaluated.

J. Lyons (✉) · G. Alarcon · S. Guznov
Air Force Research Laboratory, Airman Systems Directorate, 2215 1st St., Bldg. 33,
Wright-Patterson AFB, OH 45433, USA
e-mail: joseph.lyons.6@us.af.mil

G. Alarcon
e-mail: gene.alarcon.1@us.af.mil

S. Guznov
e-mail: svyatoslav.guznov.1@us.af.mil

N. Ho · J. Friedman
California State University, Northridge, CA, USA
e-mail: nhut.ho.51@csun.edu

J. Friedman
e-mail: jeremy.friedman.583@my.csun.edu

J. Zhou and F. Chen (eds.), *Human and Machine Learning*, Human–Computer
Interaction Series, https://doi.org/10.1007/978-3-319-90403-0_13

13.1 Introduction

With the advent of autonomous (and semi-autonomous) cars, big data analytics, and sophisticated tools for speech recognition, Artificial Intelligence (also known as AI) has anecdotally become both panacea and scapegoat in discussions of future technology's promise. It's true, just ask Alexa, Siri, Cortana, or Google Home. AI is evident when we search Amazon or Netflix, when we search for romance online, and even when programming our thermostats thanks to the Nest system. AI is already part of our lives, yet many of the pundits of AI have suggested that it has yet to really make an impact on society. In fact, AI has a long way to go before it reaches its full potential. How will it get there one might ask? Two words – machine learning. Machine learning offers a mechanism for advanced technology to do what it does best ingest, process, and learn from data. Machine learning offers great promise in terms of technology innovation and performance, yet it also offers a parallel problem that may eventually lead to its demise in that the more complex (and potentially useful) machine learning can become, the less understandable, and hence less palatable, it can become for humans who will choose to use it or not. This chapter will examine the domain of machine learning and propose methods for infusing user understanding into the inevitable complexity that comprises machine learning techniques. User understanding can arise from structural features of the code, evidenced performance and understanding, and pedigree.

As noted by [8] there are several challenges that learning systems pose to human acceptance:

1. The behaviour of the learning system may be difficult to anticipate or predict.
2. Errors by the system may be difficult to detect (or actions may be erroneously interpreted as erroneous when they are not) due to the human's lack of understanding of how the technology works.

The subtle simplicity and yet omnipresent nature of change that humans experience in every interaction is a challenging concept when applied to machines. Machines are believed to be constant, reliable and invariable, yet the concept of learning injects the idea that machines encountered at one point in time will be different than that at a future time. As such, the AI community needs to seek ways to make AI more predictable.

Explainability will be a key to the future of AI [23]. "Just as society is built upon a contract of expected behaviour, we will need to design AI systems to respect and fit with our social norms. If we are to create robot tanks and other killing machines, it is important that their decision-making be consistent with our ethical judgment" [23]. As humans, we need to understand the AI in order to accept it. The current chapter will discuss three methods for enhancing the predictability of machine learning by shaping the structure of code, the interactive features of the algorithm, and by considering additive transparency features to include an understanding of the learning affordances from which the algorithm is based. We first begin with a brief review of the machine learning literature.

13.2 Machine Learning Background

Machine Learning is the process by which an automated system uses data from past experiences to make predictions about the future or to improve some measure of future performance. This is done algorithmically and sometimes it does not rely on human interaction or assistance [11, 34]. The creation and optimisation of these algorithms has become a popular field of theoretical and applied research, joining together fields of computer science and statistical mathematics [11].

Machine learning is closely related to both data mining and AI. With the former, it shares methods of interpreting data as well as recognising ingrained patterns and correlations. With the latter, it shares the goal of facilitating machine-driven problem solving without the need of human intervention. Machine learning builds on these fields by adding the capability for a machine to train itself from existing datasets to more effectively solve problems [45]. Research in machine learning also draws from cognitive sciences, such as neuroscience and psychology, which examine how humans learn and make decisions; and from social and behavioural sciences, which attempt to apply human theories of explanation and attribution to design more transparent algorithms [33]. Some machine learning techniques have also been derived through bio-inspired concepts such as neural networks.

In addition to receiving interest in the research sphere, machine learning has found its way into several highly impactful applications. Websites have been designed to learn from their users' behaviours to customise marketing experience, categorise search results, and identify credit card fraud [6, 9]. Email clients have used algorithms that learn to block spam [9]. Robots have been trained to utilise cameras and computer vision to develop increasingly accurate visual identification and visual simultaneous localisation and mapping (SLAM) capabilities [22, 37]. In general, machine learning has been proven to be a powerful tool for applications in which massive amounts of data can be used to make accurate predictions [43, 44].

There have been numerous works on machine learning detailing algorithms spanning multiple decades of research. Though not all can be covered here, the following paragraph will provide an overview of different styles of machine learning and examples of some of the most popular algorithms being used.

Supervised learning is a style which involves training using a labeled set of data [4]. Support Vector Machines (SVM) are a broad category of supervised learning algorithm which uses decision planes to locate decision boundaries within classified and labeled data [10]. Regression Algorithms are a type of supervised learning algorithm which uses the statistical relationships between dependent and independent variables for prediction. Examples include Linear Regression, Logistic Regression, Stepwise Regression, Ordinary Least Squares Regression (OLSR), and Multivariate Adaptive Regression Splines (MARS) [11]. Instance-based Algorithms are a type of supervised learning algorithm which stores instances of training data and replace them with better fits as more data is acquired. Each new problem encountered is analysed against the existing instances to try and make a prediction. Examples include Learning Vector Quantization (LVQ), and Locally Weighted Learning (LWL) [11].

Unsupervised learning is a style for which the data used for training is unlabeled. This algorithm deduces existing patterns in the data and determines relationships between data [4]. Clustering Algorithms are a type of unsupervised learning algorithm which use existing patterns, or clusters, in data to classify and label new data. Examples include K-Means, K-Medians, Affinity propagation, and Spectral Clustering [11].

Semi-supervised learning is similar to both unsupervised and supervised learning, in that it deduces clusters in data, then uses those patterns to label the data, as well as for prediction [4, 11]. Decision Tree Algorithms are a type of supervised or semi-supervised learning algorithm which solves problems and makes predictions based on branched decision trees which represent multiple possible solutions and constraints. Examples include Classification and Regression Tree (CART) and Chi-squared Automatic Interaction Detection (CHAID) [11].

Reinforcement learning involves training to find the action or value which maximises a reward function, allowing learning through trial-and-error [4, 11]. Greedy algorithms choose actions based on achieving the highest reward per action. Examples include the interval exploration method, exploration bonus method, and curiosity-driven exploration method. Randomised algorithms are similar to greedy algorithms but include the possibility of random choices to expand the algorithm's knowledge of different action rewards. Interval-based algorithms further encourage exploration of possible actions by storing statistics about each previous action's reward and making choices using confidence ratings [20].

Several popular algorithms can utilise different learning styles or utilise multiple styles of learning concurrently. Bayesian Algorithms use Bayes' Theorem of Conditional Probability to classify data. Examples include Nave Bayes, Gaussian Nave Bayes, and Bayesian Belief Network (BBN) [11]. Artificial Neural Network Algorithms (ANN) utilise non-linear models based on human and animal neural networks to identify relationships between data sets. They often utilise supervised, unsupervised, and reinforcement learning. Examples include Perceptron, Back-Propagation, and Radial Basis Function Network (RBFN) [11]. Deep Learning Algorithms are similar to Artificial Neural Network Algorithms, but they make use of the abundance of big data available today. They have been shown to have groundbreaking results, however, they are some of the most opaque algorithms in use. Examples include Deep Boltzmann Machine (DBM), Deep Belief Networks (DBN), and Convolutional Neural Networks (CNN) [37]. Ironically, it is with some of these most sophisticated techniques that show great promise that significant user resistance may be experienced due to the lack of understanding of the complex algorithms. Unfortunately, when it comes to many contemporary machine learning techniques "You just can't look inside a deep neural network to see how it works." [23]. The same holds true for many other modern day machine learning paradigms, they are simply too complex for humans to dissect, and hence, fully understand. Herein lies the problem.

13.3 Trust Considerations for Learning Systems: Code Structure, Algorithm Performance, and Affordances for Learning

While machine learning algorithms have been applied widely and successfully, there are still numerous unsolved problems in the field of machine learning. From a technical perspective, as mentioned, machine learning requires availability of massive amounts of data, which are not always obtainable. Further, many types of algorithms require that the data be pre-labeled to be effective. This means that extensive preprocessing, often employing multiple machine learning algorithms at once, can make solving certain problems very difficult [7, 47]. Further, machine learning can be biased by the data set that it learns from, leading to instances of demographic bias in systems designed to generate advertising, which is concerning considering the growing responsibilities being given to machine learning systems [44]. From a human factors perspective, many of the most powerful machine learning algorithms have outputs that are opaque to human observers and this lack of transparency can lead to disuse or misuse, especially in situations where humans and automations are needed to make decisions collaboratively [6]. Although it is expected that the development of machine learning systems which can explain themselves will help alleviate this problem, it is not yet clear what such an explanation ought to contain [6, 13]. These problems are some of the reasons that the World Economic Forum Global Risks Report lists AI as "the emerging technology with the greatest potential for negative consequences over the coming decade" [44]. Thus, it is the goal of researchers across machine learning-related fields to develop methods for learning and problem solving in the most efficient, responsible, and safest way.

With rising technology advancements, researchers have witnessed a concomitant increase in research on the concept of trust. This is logical given an increased role of the machine in making judgements, taking actions, and filtering information for humans in contexts spanning the gamut from benign to dangerous. In such cases, it is critical that humans evaluate whether or not to rely on the technology. Trust represents one's willingness to be vulnerable to the actions and intent of another entity [31]. A key ingredient in this notion is the idea that higher trust results in increased reliance on technology in situations of heightened vulnerability [25, 27]. In other words, trust is most important in the context of risk, where humans must decide whether or not to rely on technology. This is a significant research issue because as humans we may fail to adopt appropriate reliance strategies, and as such, research has shown that technologies with the highest levels of automation pose the greatest risks to performance degradations when they err [35]. There are at least three trust-relevant domains to consider for the use of learning systems: code structure, algorithm performance, and transparency of learning affordances (see Fig. 13.1). These three domains provide a non-orthogonal set of factors that interact when considering trust of learning systems. Further, the domains offer a set of features for gauging trustworthiness using structural components, evidenced performance and understanding components and environmental components that allow users to understand the

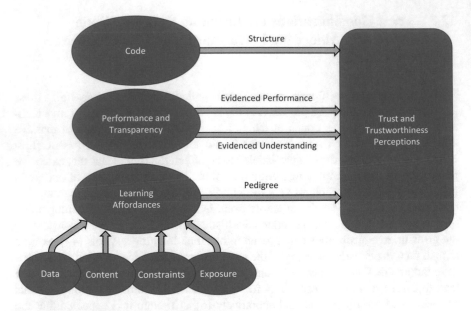

Fig. 13.1 Trust factors for machine learning systems

pedigree of the algorithms. Each of the domain areas will be discussed in the following sections.

13.3.1 Code Structure

The cognitive processes behind how programmers perceive software code has been increasing in interest across disciplines. In the computer science field eye tracking has been used to determine how programmers perceive code [42]. The trust domain has also been expanded to computer code in recent years. A recent cognitive task analysis identified reputation, transparency, and performance as key factors that influence perceptions of code trustworthiness [3]. Reputation is information obtained via professional networks and research. Transparency is the comprehensiveness of the code by viewing it. Lastly, performance is the capability of the code to meet project requirements. In addition, environmental factors are posited to moderate the relationship of the factors with perceived trustworthiness [1, 3]. For example, software utilised in high risk environments will be scrutinized more than software utilised in low risk environments due to the consequences of failure being greater in the former. Indeed, Alarcon et al. [2] found programmers trusted server code less if it was from an unknown source and spent less time reviewing the code.

The transparency construct has been reviewed the most in regards to trust in code. Walter et al. [46] explored readability, organization and source as influences on perceptions of code trustworthiness. They found code that was degraded in readability led to decreased trustworthiness assessments and less time was spent reviewing the code. In contrast, highly organised code led to lower trustworthiness assessments, but longer time spent on the code. Alarcon et al. [2] replicated the main effects of [46] and also explored the interaction effects to determine why code that was less organised was trusted more. The three-way interactions indicated if code was from a reputable source but degraded in organisation participants were willing to spend more time on the code, which in turn made the participants more familiar with the code and thus increased trustworthiness. In contrast, if the code was from an unknown source when organisation was degraded, programmers distrusted the code and spent less time on the code as they abandoned the code. Similar processing results were found for comments in code.

Commenting is another aspect of code that influences transparency. Comments are a description of the code that does not influence the operation of the code. Comments are placed in the code file to act as headers to describe the overall functional expectations of code [19] or decompose the code into logical segments [48]. Research has demonstrated commenting influences the perceptions of the code, even if the source code has not been changed [2]. Specifically, they manipulated comment placement, style and validity. Validity led to increased trustworthiness and less time spent on the code. In contrast, placement had a reverse effect leading to less trust and less time spent on the code, as organisation did in the study mentioned above. If comments were improperly placed but valid, programmers spent more time on the code and became more familiar with the code, leading to higher trustworthiness. However, if comments were not valid and improperly placed, programmers abandoned the code quickly. The results of these studies indicate transparency is an important factor in how programmers perceive computer code. However, the relationship is not as straightforward as one might expect.

Machine generated code offers unique research areas for trust and particularly trust of system-generated code like that of a learning system. Computer generated code has been available for some time, however programmers are reticent to use computer-generated code due to the lack of transparency [3]. The cognitive task analysis discussed above only referred to computer generated code that was static, i.e. not autonomous. However, current research is exploring how to implement autonomous code that changes itself or a larger architecture without the human in the loop (e.g., [15]. Future issues with autonomous programs will focus on transparency as the types of changes made by the autonomous program are not intuitive to programmers due to the algorithms the programs use to make changes. Rather than changing the algorithms of the autonomous system, human factors engineers will be faced with attempting to make the program changes more transparent for software engineers reviewing the changes.

With regard to learning systems, the technology may begin to "write" code on its own. Based on the above literature, it will be important for that output to be structured in ways to foster both human engagement with the code (i.e., organised code from reputable sources) and trust (transparent code). Engineers of learning systems need to provide opportunities for humans to feasibly review code, particularly code that is system-generated. This code will need to be structured in a way that fosters understanding of the code and traceability between actions and decisions. Learning systems will pose novel challenges to software engineers not just from a coding creation perspective but also from the perspective that the code must be interpretable to humans to facilitate understanding, and hence predictability of the learning system. Software engineers should develop a commenting template structure/architecture for the learning system to convey things like decisions, rationale, goals, which may manifest as a signal for "intent" from the code perspective. Research has shown that added rationale for automated system recommendations can improve trust [28], thus improving the organisation, transparency, and commenting features of code may enable better understanding of learning systems from a structural perspective.

13.3.2 Algorithm Performance

Despite the best efforts of the designers, machines can make errors or have imperfect reliability; the same will be true of learning systems hence they will have the "opportunity" to learn. As noted above, it is critical for a human working as a team with learning systems to have appropriate trust and reliance. In fact, previous research suggests that machine error is a major factor affecting trust (e.g., [39]). If the machine makes an error, a human teammate might either under-trust or over-trust its capabilities (i.e., trust miscalibration) depending on whether the error is noticed and, if noticed, how it is perceived. The resulting trust miscalibration can lead to reliance miscalibration and, consequently, misuse or disuse of the machine [36].

The effects of error types on trust can be grouped into three major categories including error rates, error types, and error severity. An error rate is defined as frequency of errors committed by the machine during a fixed performance period. Previous research suggests that error rates are negatively correlated with trust and reliance (e.g., [5]. Moreover, even a single error can negatively impact trust resulting in under-trust [38]. While error rates have a somewhat straightforward effect on trust, error type effects are more contradictory and appear to be asymmetrical. Dixon and Wickens [12] suggest that false alarms (FA) and misses differentially affect human behaviour. In their study, the participants showed more of verification behaviour when interacting with a FA prone system and reacted more to a miss prone system. Additionally, [14, 40] showed that FAs committed by an automated system are more detrimental to trust when compared to misses, although the number of errors was equated. On the other hand, [16] found that misses decreased reliance (which is thought of as a behavioural outcome of trust) more when compared to FAs. Finally, in addition to the error rate and error type, error severity has shown an impact on trust. For example, [16, 21] showed that more severe errors decreased trust more than less severe errors. Additionally, a system committing "easy" errors was found to produce a larger decrement in trust and reliance [30]. Overall, isolated errors (e.g., false alarms) in laboratory tasks produce somewhat predictable effects on trust. However, in realistic task environments a machine might commit, for example, in one situation a single false alarm and in another situation multiple misses requiring more research focused on exploring interactions between error categories.

The implications of algorithm performance for learning systems are the following. First, designers need to be ready for users to reject learning systems if they make easy errors, particularly if they occur earlier in the interactive process. System performance remains the most robust predictor of trust in robotic systems [17] and automation [41]. Learning systems will need to ensure that users experience reliable performance if they are to be trusted by users. Second, designers also should understand errors that occur in one facet of the system may be attributed to other aspects of the technology as specified in system-wide trust theory [14]. This is important since learning systems may apply knowledge acquired from one domain to applications in a different domain. Users of these systems may apply distrust of a system acquired through an error experienced in one domain to an application in another domain. In contrast, users may apply trust earned in one domain to another domain albeit, perhaps inappropriately. Third, designers should understand that different kinds of errors (e.g., FAs or misses; severe and not severe) have different impacts on user interactions and these effects may not be symmetrical. In fact, leveraging a novel model of Situation awareness-based Agent Transparency (see [32]) designers of learning systems may explain errors such that the systems provide (a) awareness of errors, (b) understanding for why they occurred, and (c) projection of why these errors will not be encountered in the future. Finally, given the above issues, users should be given the opportunity to experience the learning in a variety of contexts which vary in complexity. This will ensure that the user has experienced multiple domains in relation to the learning system, and hopefully, will be armed with more accurate trustworthiness information from which to base future reliance decisions.

13.3.3 Affordances for Learning

Educational institutions represent opportunities for learning, yet not all such institutions are equal nor do they each provide the same degree of opportunity for learning. While AI systems will not be attending Harvard or Yale, it is important to consider the types of learning opportunities they have encountered as a means for better trust calibration. This information can be used to evaluate the pedigree of the algorithms. Learning is only as good as the constraints from which we learn from - in other words what opportunities for learning exist in our training environments. For example, Machine A can perform left hand turns with 100% accuracy and right hand turns only with 30% accuracy. The reason for this was because Machine A's training course had nine left-hand turns and only one right hand turn, so is that the fault of the algorithm or the limitation of the structure of the learning environment for the system? Machine A simply had greater affordances for learning left-hand turns relative to right-hand turns. The above example is a very simplified idea of the impact of learning affordances but if one endorses the latter as a probable cause of performance differences, then researchers should be called to emphasise the role of environmental affordances as a key influence on trust of learning systems. The following section will attempt to flip existing ML paradigms into greater consideration of the role of learning affordances in terms of data, content, and environmental constraints when making trust attributions of learning systems.

When considering the impact of learning affordances on trust for learning systems, the following factors may be relevant: the types of data used in training, the types of content used in training, the types of environmental constraints the system is exposed to during training, and the frequency of exposure. These features become one aspect of the transparency information provided to the user about the technology to help the user establish shared awareness and shared intent with the technology [26]. This added transparency will help the user in judging the suitability of the learning system in future situations. While logical and perhaps an intuitive aspect of learning systems, highlighting the learning affordances provided to the system is not currently viewed as a key transparency feature for learning systems.

13.3.3.1 Types of Data

Many machine learning systems are dependent on labelled training data as in the case for supervised learning techniques, and these cases the data used for training matter. Users of these systems need to understand the assumptions of using one kind of data over another. What are the limitations of the data, what are their intended uses, where are they valid or invalid. These are important questions that users of learning systems may need to consider. Sometimes data are artificially injected or replaced as in the case of instance-based algorithms and users need to understand what data were replaced and why. As a recommendation, designers of learning systems need to provide a way for users to understand the following: (1) the type of data used for training, (2) the limitations of the data, (3) the desired application domains for that data, (4) if data were artificially introduced and why, (5) the amount of data used. While this is only a piece of the larger picture of learning affordances it is an important feature particularly for machine learning techniques such as supervised learning.

13.3.3.2 Types of Content

Humans train in specific areas, such as medicine, law, psychology, education, to name a few. Knowledge acquired in one domain may carry little utility when applied to a novel domain. For instance, one might not expect a well-trained doctor to fully understand the intricacies of the law profession. Vice versa, one would likely not want a lawyer to perform a life threatening surgical procedure. In this sense, the domain in which one has trained matters. Yet, with machine learning there is some level of assumption that the system will need to extrapolate knowledge acquired in one domain and apply it in novel situations. In the case of statistical machine translation, machine learning techniques may utilise content from one domain that is readily available with the explicit intent to apply the learning to a novel domain [18, 24]. The very utility of learning systems is contingent on the ability of the system to apply knowledge acquired from one domain into a novel domain, this is the essence of learning and the pinnacle of an AI enthusiasts. As such, knowing the pool of potential knowledge that the system's extant capabilities are derived from is a useful piece of information for a user when making reliance decisions on the learning system.

Greater variety of content used in the training phase may help to create a more robust learning system. Returning to the case of the statistical machine translation system, the greater the domain diversity used to train the system should lead to greater robustness when the system is applied to a novel domain. Users would benefit from knowing the system had trained with more versus fewer domain areas, yet this kind of information may reside predominantly with the engineers who built and trained the system. For instance, users may favour a machine translation system that had trained using data from the domains of news, baseball, hockey, and literature when making inferences about its capabilities for translating golf content. Whereas if the system had only trained on hockey, users may be less inclined to trust the system due to the limited domain training. The key point in this section is that users may benefit from this information as it will make the behaviour, performance, and robustness of the system more predictable.

13.3.3.3   Environmental Constraints

The difficult and complexity of the conditions through which machine learning systems are trained is also very relevant and should be conveyed to users of the systems. SLAM algorithms that are trained on nominal terrain should be juxtaposed against those trained on austere terrain. This becomes a piece of information that a user can evaluate when making reliance decisions. As discussed in [29], instructional scaffolding could be used as a technique to modify the conditions under which the technology is exposed varying difficulty and complexity. As systems demonstrate successful performance in one level of difficulty, the stakes and complexity could be raised in an iterative fashion. Learning systems may need to be subjected to an accreditation/certification process to demonstrate achievement to some threshold [29]. When systems use techniques such as reinforcement learning, users should fully understand the conditions under which the system's behaviour has been shaped. In other words, what features were used as the conditions for rewards/punishment? Once users begin to understand the conditions through which a system was trained, and there is an understanding of how robust those conditions were, the user will be better armed to make informed reliance decisions. The same principles hold true when making reliance decisions on humans. Many professionals are granted swift trust due to their credentials, as humans infer both competence and intent from the prior experiences of the individual.

13.3.3.4 Frequency of Exposure

Generally more training is better. In the case of machine learning, users need to have an understanding of the extent to which training has occurred, the length [or quantity] of training, and the number of different scenarios used. Many extant policies regarding activities such as verification and validation require that systems evidence deterministic behaviour [29], yet for learning systems this invariance is a certainty. Instead, what the field may need is "assurance" that the system will operate predictably [29] and this assurance should emerge through repeated tests of the system in a variety of situations. Users should be made aware of the breadth, or lack thereof, from which the learning system has been tested.

13.4 Conclusion

Machine learning will be an important driver of the success of failure of AI systems. Yet, the nature of learning, and hence change, creates challenges for user acceptance of such systems. As noted in [29], humans and learning systems should comprise a team where one backs up the other yet this is only possible given predictability of each team member. The current chapter discussed three ways to help to foster appropriate trust of learning systems with implications for code structure, algorithm performance, and making affordances for learning more transparent to the users. These domains offer structural, evidenced performance and understanding, and pedigree mechanisms for gauging trustworthiness of machine learning approaches.

References

1. Alarcon, G.M., Ryan, T.J.: Trustworthiness perceptions of computer code: a heuristic-systematic processing model. In: Proceedings of the Hawaii International Conference on System Sciences, Hawaii, USA (2018)
2. Alarcon, G.M., Gamble, R.F., Ryan, T.J., Walter, C., Jessup, S.A., Wood, D.W.: The influence of commenting validity, placement, and style on perceptions of computer code trustworthiness: a heuristic-systematic processing approach. Cogent Psychology (2017)
3. Alarcon, G.M., Militello, L.G., Ryan, P., Jessup, S.A., Calhoun, C.S., Lyons, J.B.: A descriptive model of computer code trustworthiness. J. Cogn. Eng. Decis. Mak. **11**(2), 107–121 (2017)
4. Ayodele, T.O.: Types of machine learning algorithms. In: Zhang, Y. (ed.) New Advances in Machine Learning. InTech (2010)
5. Bailey, N.R., Scerbo, M.W.: Automation-induced complacency for monitoring highly reliable systems: the role of task complexity, system experience, and operator trust. Theor. Issues Ergon. Sci. **8**(4), 321–348 (2007)
6. Brinton, C.: A Framework for explanation of machine learning decisions. In: Proceedings of the IJCAI 2017 Workshop on Explainable Artificial Intelligence (XAI), Melbourne, Australia (2017)
7. Chapelle, O., Sindhwani, V., Keerthi, S.S.: Optimization techniques for semi-supervised support vector machines. J. Mach. Learn. Res. **9**, 203–233 (2008)

8. Christensen, J.C., Lyons, J.B.: Trust between humans and learning machines: developing the gray box. In: American Society of Mechanical Engineers (ASME) Dynamic Systems and Control (DSC) Magazine, pp. 9–13 (2017)
9. Clos, J., Wiratunga, N., Massie, S.: towards explainable text classification by jointly learning lexicon and modifier terms. In: Proceedings of the IJCAI 2017 Workshop on Explainable Artificial Intelligence (XAI), Melbourne, Australia (2017)
10. Cristianini, N., Shawe-Taylor, J.: An Introduction to Support Vector Machines: And Other Kernel-based Learning Methods. Cambridge University Press, New York (2000)
11. Das, K., Behera, R.: A survey on machine learning: concept, algorithms and applications. Int. J. Innov. Res. Comput. Commun. Eng. **5**(2), 1301–1309 (2017)
12. Dixon, S.R., Wickens, C.D.: Automation reliability in unmanned aerial vehicle control: a reliance-compliance model of automation dependence in high workload. Hum. Factors **48**(3), 474–486 (2006)
13. Fox, M., Long, D., Magazzeni, D.: Explainable planning. In: Proceedings of the IJCAI 2017 Workshop on Explainable Artificial Intelligence (XAI), Melbourne, Australia (2017)
14. Geels-Blair, K., Rice, S., Schwark, J.: Using system-wide trust theory to reveal the contagion effects of automation false alarms and misses on compliance and reliance in a simulated aviation task. Int. J. Aviat. Psychol. **23**(3), 245–266 (2013)
15. Goues, C.L., Nguyen, T., Forrest, S., Weimer, W.: GenProg: a generic method for automatic software repair. IEEE Trans. Softw. Eng. **38**(1), 54–72 (2012)
16. Guznov, S., Lyons, J., Nelson, A., Woolley, M.: The effects of automation error types on operators trust and reliance. In: Proceedings of International Conference on Virtual, Augmented and Mixed Reality. Lecture Notes in Computer Science, pp. 116–124. Springer, Cham (2016)
17. Hancock, P.A., Billings, D.R., Schaefer, K.E., Chen, J.Y.C., de Visser, E.J., Parasuraman, R.: A meta-analysis of factors affecting trust in human-robot interaction. Hum. Factors **53**(5), 517–527 (2011)
18. Hildebrand, A.S., Eck, M., Vogel, S., Waibel, A.: Adaptation of the translation model for statistical machine translation based on information retrieval. In: Proceedings of the 10th Conference of the European Association for Machine Translation (EAMT) (2005)
19. Johnfx: 5 best practices for commenting your code. https://improvingsoftware.com/2011/06/27/5-best-practices-for-commenting-your-code/ (2011). Accessed 10 Nov 2017
20. Kaelbling, L.P., Littman, M.L., Moore, A.W.: Reinforcement learning: a survey. J. Artif. Intell. Res. **4**, 237–285 (1996)
21. Khasawneh, M.T., Bowling, S.R., Jiang, X., Gramopadhye, A.K., Melloy, B.J.: Effect of error severity on human trust in hybrid systems. In: Proceedings of the Human Factors and Ergonomics Society Annual Meeting, vol. 48, pp. 439–443. SAGE Publications, Los Angeles, CA (2004)
22. Kim, A., Eustice, R.M.: Active visual SLAM for robotic area coverage: theory and experiment. Int. J. Robotics Res. **34**(4–5), 457–475 (2015)
23. Knight, W.: The dark secret at the heart of AI. MIT Technology Review (2017)
24. Koehn, P., Schroeder, J.: Experiments in domain adaptation for statistical machine translation. In: Proceedings of the Second Workshop on Statistical Machine Translation, StatMT '07, pp. 224–227. Association for Computational Linguistics, Stroudsburg, PA, USA (2007)
25. Lee, J.D., Seppelt, B.D.: In: Nof, S. (ed.) Human Factors in Automation Design. Springer Handbook of Automation, pp. 417–436. Springer, Berlin (2009)
26. Lyons, J.: Being transparent about transparency: a model for human-robot interaction. In: Sofge, D., Kruijff, G.J., Lawless, W.F. (eds.) Trust and Autonomous Systems: Papers from the AAAI Spring Symposium (Technical Report SS-13-07), pp. 48–53. AAAI Press, Menlo Park, CA (2013)
27. Lyons, J.B., Stokes, C.K.: Human-human reliance in the context of automation. Hum. Factors **54**(1), 112–121 (2012)
28. Lyons, J.B., Koltai, K.S., Ho, N.T., Johnson, W.B., Smith, D.E., Shively, R.J.: Engineering trust in complex automated systems. Ergon. Design **24**(1), 13–17 (2016)

29. Lyons, J.B., Clark, M.A., Wagner, A.R., Schuelke, M.J.: Certifiable trust in autonomous systems: making the intractable tangible. AI Mag. **38**, 37–49 (2017)
30. Madhavan, P., Wiegmann, D.A., Lacson, F.C.: Automation failures on tasks easily performed by operators undermine trust in automated aids. Hum. Factors **48**(2), 241–256 (2006)
31. Mayer, R.C., Davis, J.H., Schoorman, F.D.: An integrative model of organizational trust. Acad. Manag. Rev. **20**(3), 709–734 (1995)
32. Mercado, J.E., Rupp, M.A., Chen, J.Y.C., Barnes, M.J., Barber, D., Procci, K.: Intelligent agent transparency in human-agent teaming for multi-UxV management. Hum. Factors **58**(3), 401–415 (2016)
33. Miller, T., Piers, P., Sonenberg, L.: Explainable AI: beware of inmates running the Asylum. Or: how i learnt to stop worrying and love the social and behavioural sciences. In: Proceedings of the IJCAI 2017 Workshop on Explainable Artificial Intelligence (XAI), Melbourne, Australia (2017)
34. Mitchell, T.: Machine Learning. McGraw-Hill International (1997)
35. Onnasch, L., Wickens, C.D., Li, H., Manzey, D.: Human performance consequences of stages and levels of automation: an integrated meta-analysis. Hum. Factors **56**(3), 476–488 (2014)
36. Parasuraman, R., Riley, V.: Humans and automation: use, misuse, disuse, abuse. Hum. Factors **39**(2), 230–253 (1997)
37. Rajani, N.F., Mooney, R.J.: Using explanations to improve ensembling of visual question answering systems. In: Proceedings of the IJCAI 2017 Workshop on Explainable Artificial Intelligence (XAI), Melbourne, Australia (2017)
38. Robinette, P., Wagner, A.R., Howard, A.M.: The effect of robot performance on human-robot trust in time-critical situations. Technical report, Georgia Institute of Technology, Georgia, USA (2015)
39. Salem, M., Lakatos, G., Amirabdollahian, F., Dautenhahn, K.: Would you trust a (faulty) robot?: effects of error, task type and personality on human-robot cooperation and trust. In: Proceedings of the Tenth Annual ACM/IEEE International Conference on Human-Robot Interaction, HRI '15, pp. 141–148 (2015)
40. Sanchez, J., Rogers, W.A., Fisk, A.D., Rovira, E.: Understanding reliance on automation: effects of error type, error distribution, age and experience. Theor. Issues Ergon. Sci. **15**(2), 134–160 (2014)
41. Schaefer, K.E., Chen, J.Y.C., Szalma, J.L., Hancock, P.A.: A meta-analysis of factors influencing the development of trust in automation: implications for understanding autonomy in future systems. Hum. Factors **58**(3), 377–400 (2016)
42. Sharif, B., Falcone, M., Maletic, J.I.: An eye-tracking study on the role of scan time in finding source code defects. In: Proceedings of the Symposium on Eye Tracking Research and Applications, pp. 381–384. ACM, New York, NY, USA (2012)
43. Sliwinski, J., Strobel, M., Zick, Y.: A characterization of monotone influence measures for data classification (2017). arXiv:1708.02153 [cs]
44. Thelisson, E., Padh, K., Celis, L.E.: Regulatory mechanisms and algorithms towards trust in AI/ML. In: Proceedings of the IJCAI 2017 Workshop on Explainable Artificial Intelligence (XAI), Melbourne, Australia (2017)
45. Vapnik, V.N.: Statistical Learning Theory, 1st edn. Wiley-Interscience, New York (1998)
46. Walter, C., Gamble, R., Alarcon, G., Jessup, S., Calhoun, C.: Developing a mechanism to study code trustworthiness. In: Proceedings of the 50th Hawaii International Conference on System Sciences, Hawaii, USA, pp. 5817–5826 (2017)
47. Wang, J., Jebara, T., Chang, S.F.: Semi-supervised learning using greedy max-cut. J. Mach. Learn. Res. **14**(1), 771–800 (2013)
48. Wikipedia: Comment (computer programming). https://en.wikipedia.org/wiki/Comment

Chapter 14
Trust and Transparency in Machine Learning-Based Clinical Decision Support

Cosima Gretton

Abstract Machine learning and other statistical pattern recognition techniques have the potential to improve diagnosis in medicine and reduce medical error. But technology can be both a solution to and a source of errors. Machine learning-based clinical decision support systems may cause new errors due to automation bias and automation complacency which arise from inappropriate trust in the technology. Transparency into a systems internal logic can improve trust in automation, but is hard to achieve in practice. This chapter discusses the clinical and technology related factors that influence clinician trust in automated systems, and can affect the need for transparency when developing machine learning-based clinical decision support systems.

14.1 Introduction

The recent realisation of Machine Learning (ML) techniques such as Artificial Neural Networks (ANNs) as a viable technology outside academia has opened new areas of human activity to automation. In healthcare, where human error is a significant cause of morbidity and mortality, these new approaches have revived interest in building intelligent Clinical Decision Support Systems (CDSS). Intelligent CDSS is intended as an advanced cognitive or perceptual tool to support clinicians in making sense of large amounts of data, or detecting abnormalities in complex images.

The potential applications for Machine Learning-based Clinical Decision Support (ML-CDSS) are manifold: studies have shown ANNs perform above clinicians at tasks involving interpretation of clinical data, such as diagnosing pulmonary emboli or predicting which patients are at high risk for oral cancer [23, 40]. ANNs are particularly effective in image recognition and have been applied to several radiological imaging methodologies, such as early detection of breast cancer in mammograms,

C. Gretton (✉)
University College London, School of Management, Level 38, 1 Canada Square,
London E14 5AA, UK
e-mail: cosima.gretton@ucl.ac.uk

© Springer International Publishing AG, part of Springer Nature 2018
J. Zhou and F. Chen (eds.), *Human and Machine Learning*, Human–Computer
Interaction Series, https://doi.org/10.1007/978-3-319-90403-0_14

with accuracy as high as 97% [35]. Humans perform particularly poorly at this task, making it ideal for automated support: some studies estimate human error rates in radiological image interpretation to be as high as 30% [4].

But technology plays a role both in preventing and unfortunately contributing to medical error [3]. New technologies impact the user and the entire system of care by altering workflows, processes, and team interactions [10]. In fast-paced inpatient environments, where multiple teams visit and give opinions on a patient, a false diagnosis by a decision support system can take on *diagnostic momentum*. Subsequent teams are less likely to question the information and will continue an already initiated treatment course [8]. This is particularly true of technologies that fully or partly automate human tasks, inducing phenomena in human operators known as automation bias and automation complacency [17]. This is the propensity for the human operator to favour the decision made by the system over their own internal judgement, or the presence of contradictory information.

ML-CDSS may be particularly at risk for inducing automation bias, posing the threat of new, unintended errors. In part this is because these models often lack transparency into their internal logic, rendering them impervious to inspection or understanding of root cause. Second, such models often find new insights and patterns in super-human amounts of data, which may prevent clinicians from evaluating the veracity of their output because the insights are novel. This has meant that despite hubris from industry there is much hesitation amongst clinicians to adopt these systems [23].

Given the current scale of medical error this is hardly surprising. In the US estimates range from 44,000 to as high as 251,454 deaths per year [25, 33], placing medical error as the third leading cause of death in the US. There is much controversy surrounding these estimates, and the lack of clarity only serves to highlight the inadequate reporting of errors in clinical medicine [49, 52]. In a system of such complexity and risk, the introduction of new technologies must be carefully considered.

There are several clinical and technology factors that can increase the likelihood of automation bias, including lack of transparency. But transparency is hard to achieve with some ML approaches and may lead to more confusion in a non-technical user. Given the challenges in developing transparent ML, optimising other clinical and technology factors may reduce the risk of automation errors and thereby the degree of transparency needed. This chapter discusses automation bias and complacency and proposes a conceptual model for the factors influencing the appropriate use of an ML-CDSS as a basis for further research.

When discussing CDSS, this chapter focusses on point-of-care systems defined as *"computer systems designed to impact clinician decision making about individual patients at the point in time that these decisions are made"*[6]. Machine learning approaches have great potential in public health and reimbursement applications but these are not considered in this chapter since they do not drive point-of-care decision-making.

14.2 Learning from History: Trends in Clinical Decision Support

Attempts to build clinical decision support systems date back half a century and provide rich insight into contextual constraints facing new ML-CDSS. The first paper on mathematical models for medical diagnosis was published in 1959 and since then attempts to automate aspects of clinical practice have followed summers and winters of artificial intelligence research [28].

Initial approaches focused on developing 'expert' diagnostic systems. These systems provided only one suggestion that the clinician was expected to follow. They focused on providing the right information at the right time: such as drug allergy alerts, guideline suggestions or diagnostic screening reminders. The rules on which they were based were relatively simple and human-understandable. For example, a colon cancer screening reminder generated when consulting a patient over a specified age [43]. The systems comprised of a knowledge base with IF/THEN rules, an inference engine with which to combine the knowledge base with patient specific data and a communication mechanism to relay the output to the clinician [50].

But in the early 1980s developers realised physicians were not interested in using these Greek oracle-like expert systems: they valued their own expertise and autonomy as decision makers. From this emerged decision support, a more collaborative approach in which a list of options is presented to the clinician. This remains the dominant approach today [38].

The decision support systems of the last century relied on an internal knowledge base. These have since evolved into non-knowledge based systems that employ machine learning or other statistical pattern recognition techniques [6, 36]. These new approaches have several advantages. Decisions in clinical practice are often made based on incomplete information. Previous knowledge-based systems perform poorly with incomplete data, but based on their training machine learning algorithms can infer missing data points and perform under uncertainty [34]. Additionally, rather than having a knowledge base derived from medical literature in need of constant updating, such systems derive associations from patient data to generate a diagnosis [6]. While this is clearly an advantage these approaches can be subject to their own unique performance limitations, which can present interpretation challenges for the clinician.

14.3 Over-Reliance and Under-Reliance in Automated Systems

As all humans, clinicians are not often aware of their own propensity for thinking errors known as cognitive biases, and have been shown to suffer from over-confidence in their abilities [5].

Table 14.1 Interaction between system performance and user response

User response	System performance			
	True positive	False positive	True negative	False negative
Agree	Appropriate reliance	Commission errors	Appropriate reliance	Omission errors
Disagree	Under-reliance	Appropriate reliance	Under-reliance	Appropriate reliance

As much as clinicians fail to recognise their own internal thinking errors, they also fail to detect the influence that technology or system design can have upon their behaviour. Technology can change behavior and induce error by occupying valuable cognitive resources through poor user interface design, poor adaptation to the clinician's workflow, or inducing automation bias [12].

Of specific relevance to ML-CDSS is automation over-reliance, a phenomenon that occurs when a human places inappropriate trust in an automated system. This takes two forms: a commission error known as *automation bias*, where the human acts upon a system's incorrect diagnosis, and an omission error known as *automation complacency*, where the system fails to make a diagnosis, and the clinician fails to spot the miss [12]. Automation bias and complacency result from the interaction of system performance and user response (see Table 14.1). There are several examples from traditional CDSS in the literature. Lyell and colleagues found that even simple e-prescribing decision-support led to automation bias. Although a correct suggestion by the CDSS reduced omission errors by 38.3%, when incorrect it increased omission errors by 33.3% [32]. Similar results were found in a study of Computer-Aided Detection (CAD) of breast cancers in mammograms: human sensitivity was significantly lower in the CAD supported condition due to errors of omission [1].

Automation under-reliance, where the human fails to trust a reliable system is also a source of error. What is clear is that for optimal human-machine performance, the human must know when to trust and when not to trust the system. Transparency influences the appropriate attribution of trust by providing insight into how the system arrived at its decision. An expert human can then evaluate the decision against their own internal knowledge [20, 46]. Evidence from other industries shows trust in recommender systems and decision support systems is increased when the system provides an explanation for its recommendation [13]. But transparency is only one factor to influence appropriate attribution of trust, and the degree to which it is needed varies depending on the context. The successful adoption of ML-CDSS in clinical practice will depend upon designing the system to elicit appropriate trust, either through transparency or other means.

14.4   Clinical and Technology Factors in Human-Machine Performance

Transparency influences trust and appropriate system use by providing insight into how the machine arrived at a decision. But full transparency is unlikely to be useful or understandable and may worsen human-machine performance. Clinicians may not be familiar with the statistical techniques underlying the technology and must use these systems under time pressure and high cognitive load. Given the heterogeneity of clinical practice transparency may also mean different things in different contexts and should be tailored to the specific goals of the human at that time. This section describes clinical and technology factors important in designing ML-CDSS for appropriate trust, and proposes a conceptual model as the basis for further research. These factors will influence trust in the system, the degree to which transparency will be important, and shape the ultimate product requirements for optimal human-machine performance.

14.4.1   Clinical Considerations for ML-CDSS

When designing point-of-care ML-CDSS there are two important clinical factors to consider that will affect the degree of transparency needed: clinical risk and the availability of expert evaluation.

14.4.1.1   Clinical Risk

The clinical risk presented by an ML-CDSS decision may influence the level of transparency needed. The United Kingdom's National Patient Safety Agency defines clinical risk as *"the chance of an adverse outcome resulting from clinical investigation, treatment or patient care."* Clinical risk can be understood in terms of severity of a healthcare hazard multiplied by the probability that it will occur [41]. For example, consider an ML-CDSS that takes real-time physiological data from a patient under anaesthesia to support the anaesthetist in titrating sedation. The impact of an error is clearly significant (high severity). Given the time pressure and operator cognitive load the probability that an error will go unidentified by the clinician and ultimately impact the patient is potentially high (high probability). In this context, system transparency around performance and the inputs on which it is basing its decision are important to enable the clinician to evaluate its output and mitigate the risk.

Contrast this with an algorithm that uses health record data to predict which members of a primary care physician's patient cohort might develop diabetes in the next five years. The clinical risk presented by an error in this example is lower: immediate interventions based on the information are minor and errors would have a low impact (low severity). The clinician also has ample time to evaluate the validity of the decision, check orthogonal data or discuss with her colleagues. The probability that errors will go unidentified and impact the patient is lower, the clinical risk is lower and transparency may be less of a critical requirement.

Assessing the impact and probability of an error is important in defining the requirements for ML-CDSS systems. Doing so requires close collaboration with the clinicians who will ultimately be using the technology.

14.4.1.2   Expert Evaluation

The clinician plays an important role in verifying the output of an ML-CDSS and in doing so, mitigating the risk. There are several factors, including transparency that influence a clinician's ability to evaluate the output of an ML-CDSS: experience with CDSS, time pressure, interruptions, the availability of orthogonal data, familiarity with the subject matter and task complexity [17, 20, 29, 53]. Given the constraints on achieving transparency with some ML approaches such as ANNs, designers and developers may be able to optimise for other factors to elicit appropriate trust in their systems.

Experience with CDSS

In a meta-analysis of effect modifiers of automation bias, experience with a CDSS was found to decrease automation bias [20]. Repeated use of a CDSS allows a user to understand the limits of its performance and know when to place appropriate trust. Trust is one of the most extensively studied and strongest factors to affect automation bias [17]. But one of the challenges inherent in healthcare as opposed to other industries such as aviation, is the lack of reliable feedback loops. When an error occurs it might have no immediate consequences, significant time can elapse before it is discovered, or news of the error may never get back to the decision-maker [14]. In human diagnostic performance, this results in a cognitive bias called the *feedback sanction* and subsequent over-confidence in diagnostic performance [14]. In the context of human-machine interaction lack of feedback makes it hard for the user to assess the performance of a system, and thereby calibrate their trust. Feedback may vary depending on the context: in the examples above, the anaesthesiologist has immediate feedback from the physiology of the patient. The primary care physician, however, may not know if the system is correct for several years, meaning experience may not improve human-machine performance.

Experience and training also help users generate correct conceptual models of the way the system works. A conceptual model is a mental model of how a system or device works. In the absence of correct conceptual models humans form their own often erroneous conceptual models, leading to errors in using the device [42]. Even a highly simplified conceptual model can improve trust and appropriate use of a technology.

Subject matter expertise and task complexity

Familiarity with the subject matter also affects a clinician's ability to evaluate the output of a system: those less confident in their own abilities are more likely to be subject to automation bias [15]. This is closely related to task complexity and work load, which was found to be associated with automation over-reliance [21]. More experienced clinicians are likely to cope well with more complex work-loads, and potentially be better at evaluating the output of a CDSS.

The attraction of ML-CDSS lies in the potential to take large data sets and identify novel associations or predictions. For example, a 2015 paper by researchers at the Icahn School of Medicine at Mount Sinai applied a clustering algorithm to medical record and genotype data from 11,210 individuals. They identified three sub-types of type 2 diabetes, each susceptible to different complications of the disease [31]. But before use in clinical practice these novel associations will need to be validated, and will continue to be unfamiliar to clinicians. This is a critical consideration when building ML-CDSS: is the system automating current medical practice or discovering new associations? The former will be easier to implement and transparency not as essential; the clinician can compare the output with their own internal knowledge. The latter, in addition to rigorous clinical validation, may require greater transparency to elicit trust and gain adoption. As more domains are supported by CDSS there is a risk of de-skilling, and as a result a reduction in the ability of clinicians to evaluate the performance of their systems [7, 18, 19]. As an example, some electrocardiogram (ECG) machines currently provide a suggested diagnosis, written at the top of the printed page. But doctors are encouraged to ignore the decision-support and come up with their own conclusions to ensure the skill of ECG interpretation is maintained.

Time pressure

Urgency and frequent interruptions are major barriers to proper evaluation of a decision [12]. They are also universal characteristics of inpatient working conditions: a review of the literature found that nurses can be interrupted from a task over 13 times an hour [39]. Transparent ML-CDSS in such environments must be highly context specific, provide simple, task relevant information to reduce cognitive load and make it easy to return to the task after a distraction.

High urgency also removes the opportunity to consult with colleagues or assess orthogonal data. Insufficient sampling of information has been shown to be associated with increased rates of commission errors [2]. Transparency matters too: in high pressure situations the degree to which the CDSS can provide an explanation for its decisions will impact the appropriate attribution of trust in the system [37]. The primary care physician described above has ample opportunity to discuss the output of the algorithm with colleagues and decide whether to act upon its recommendations. The anaesthesiologist does not have that opportunity: the system must be sufficiently transparent for her to decide whether to trust its output without additional data or team support.

Individual differences

While not specific to clinical practice, individual differences in cognition and personality can also affect a clinician's propensity for automation bias and therefore the level of transparency that might be required [20]. Some users have a predisposition to trust an automated system, while others are more likely to distrust it [17]. In designing systems to scale across multiple clinical contexts it is hard to account for individual differences, but it is important to consider this when interpreting user feedback. Each physician may respond differently to an ML-CDSS, making it helpful to work with several different users.

14.4.2   Technical Considerations for ML-CDSS

In addition to clinical and contextual factors the design and performance of the technology itself influences trust and the likelihood of error. There is an interaction between user interface design and system performance: poor system performance and poor user interface design create a perfect storm for the inappropriate attribution of trust. The system performs poorly and the user is unable to identify the error [30]. But even a system with excellent performance can facilitate errors or bias physician behaviour if the user interface design is inadequate.

14.4.2.1   User Interface Design

Human-machine interaction errors due to user interface design are likely to be more common in healthcare than is currently known. A study of errors over a four-year period in a tertiary care hospital in Hong Kong found that 17.1% of all incidents reported were technology related, and of those 98.1% were socio-technological. The errors were not due to a technology failure, but due to how the system was operated by the user [48].

   User interface design is essential for communicating system performance. Consider the following example from a device designed to deliver radiation therapy, the Therac-25, used between 1985 and 1987. It was discovered that the user interface made it possible for a technician to enter erroneous data, but despite appearing to correct it on the display the system would continue to deliver the wrong level of radiation. The only indication the dose being delivered was incorrect was an ambiguous 'Malfunction 54' code [30]. During the two years that the fault remained undiscovered multiple patients received lethal levels of radiation. Further software problems were found, each alerting the clinician by similar ambiguous malfunction codes. One technician reported 40 codes in a day, none of which enabled the clinician to understand the underlying issue [30]. Clear communication in the user interface as to the nature of the error would have avoided the continued use of this device, and continued patient harm.

User interface and information design can not only be a cause of error, but also greatly influence clinician decision-making behaviour, for better or worse. Torsvik and colleagues found that different data visualisations influenced medical students' interpretation of identical clinical chemistry results, to the extent that for one of the visualisations the results were more likely to be interpreted as within range [51]. Another study found that user interface design can directly affect treatment decisions. Persil and colleagues showed that simple grouping of antibiotic options could influence whether the clinicians chose a conservative versus an aggressive treatment for a patient with pneumonia [44]. This is important when considering how to present the output of an ML-CDSS to a clinician. Care must be taken not to inadvertently bias clinician decision-making.

14.4.2.2   System Performance

One path to reducing errors of omission and commission and improving human-machine performance is to improve system performance. As shown in Table 14.1 automation bias and complacency both occur when a system under-performs. Developers and clinicians should be aware of errors particular to statistical pattern recognition techniques that may impact performance. *Data leakage* is a phenomenon that occurs when a variable included in the training/test set contains more information than one would have access to in practice. The model exploits the variable, resulting in good performance on the test set but poor performance in practice [24]. As an example, a 2008 ML competition for detecting cancer in mammograms involved training a model on a data set which contained amongst other data points, patient IDs. The patient IDs had been assigned consecutively in the data sets, which meant the IDs were relied upon to determine the source of the data and thereby increased predictive power. But in practice, patient IDs are random and by relying on this data in training the algorithm would perform sub-optimally in the wild [47].

A similar example is that of *dataset shift*: this refers to when the conditions under which the model is trained differ from the conditions under which it is deployed. An image recognition model trained on a set of images under controlled light conditions, might fail when deployed in practice on images under varying light conditions [45]. To mitigate automation bias and complacency, systems should state performance characteristics, population demographics on which the algorithm was trained, and the conditions under which the system performs poorly [6].

14.5   The Interaction of Clinical and Technology Factors in the Attribution of Appropriate Trust

Figure 14.1 outlines a proposed conceptual model for understanding the factors that influence appropriate system use. This model is by no means exhaustive and serves to structure further discussion and investigation. Both an understanding of system

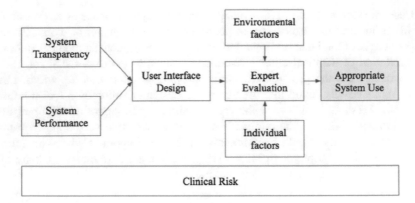

Fig. 14.1 Clinical and technology factors impacting appropriate system use

performance and transparency into the system's internal logic will help users place appropriate trust in an ML-CDSS. Both, however, depend upon good user interface design to communicate effectively to the user.

Clear communication of this information will enable expert evaluation. Expert evaluation is itself determined by individual (e.g. training) and environmental (e.g. time pressure) factors. Clinical risk is important throughout, influencing every consideration from acceptable performance characteristics to the need for regular reviews of appropriate utilisation once the system is in routine use.

14.6 Adoption of ML-CDSS: Legal, Ethical and Policy Implications Beyond Point-of-Care

Designing point-of-care systems with attention to the factors described may improve system design and reduce the risk of error. But transparency into an ML-CDSS's internal logic is important beyond the bedside.

One of the major concerns regarding the lack of transparency, which cannot be addressed through other means, lies in the attribution of blame in situations of medical error. Technology developers often place the burden of responsibility on the clinician [26]. The clinician must use the device within the bounds of their medical knowledge and interpret the information in the context of the patient. The Therac-75 case highlights how poor communication and lack of transparency limits the information available, meaning the user cannot make an informed decision [16, 30]. To justifiably defer responsibility, the technology must equip the clinician with sufficient information to make an informed decision. Further, transparency is essential for identifying root cause and attributing blame. This concern is reflected in a recent directive from the European Union states that by 2018, companies deploying algorithms that influence the public must provide explanations for their models' internal logic [22].

Second, from an ethical and legal standpoint transparency is needed to support clinicians in gaining informed consent. If the physician does not understand the logic behind a certain treatment recommendation they cannot reasonably inform the patient and obtain consent.

Finally, true adoption in medicine depends on obtaining clinical utility data and updating medical guidelines. For algorithms that generate novel associations transparency may be needed in order for policy makers and medical societies to trust the findings and invest in costly clinical trials or health economic studies.

14.7   Conclusion

Clinical decision support in medicine has a rich history and is undergoing a renaissance with the advent of new machine learning techniques. But new technologies face the same challenges as the previous approaches. The inappropriate attribution of trust is one of the major barriers to widespread adoption and leads to medical error in the form of omission and commission errors. Lack of transparency is an issue for clinical practice as it prevents physicians from evaluating decision-support outputs against their own internal knowledge base. But full transparency, given the conditions under which clinicians work, is hard to achieve and may negatively impact trust. Different degrees of transparency may be needed depending on clinical risk and the ability of the expert to evaluate the decision. Designing with an appreciation of real-world practice constraints such as time pressure, combined with good user interface design to enable expert evaluation can facilitate appropriate use. Early engagement with clinicians in the design, development and implementation of new technologies will reduce risks and improve system adoption [27]. Given the potential for new errors and work-arounds, continued monitoring of technologies as they enter common use is important to ensure patient safety [9].

These practical, ethical and legal constraints on ML-CDSS may mean that developers are forced to take different approaches if ML-techniques are unable to provide the required transparency [11]. But medicine is highly heterogeneous and local collaborations between clinicians and technologists will identify niche areas where risk, transparency and utility align and ML-based approaches can provide value.

References

1. Alberdi, E., Povyakalo, A., Strigini, L., Ayton, P.: Effects of incorrect computer-aided detection (CAD) output on human decision-making in mammography. Academic Radiology **11**(8), 909–918 (2004)
2. Bahner, J.E., Hüper, A.D., Manzey, D.: Misuse of automated decision aids: Complacency, automation bias and the impact of training experience. International Journal of Human Computer Studies **66**(9), 688–699 (2008)
3. Battles, J.B., Keyes, M.A.: Technology and patient safety: A two-edged sword (2002)

4. Berlin, L.: Radiologic errors, past, present and future. Diagnosis 1(1), 79–84 (2014)
5. Berner, E.S., Graber, M.L.: Overconfidence as a Cause of Diagnostic Error in Medicine. American Journal of Medicine (2008)
6. Berner, E.S., La Lande, T.J.: Overview of Clinical Decision Support Systems. In: Clinical Decision Support Systems, pp. 1–17. Springer, Cham (2016)
7. Berner, E.S., Maisiak, R.S., Heudebert, G., Young, K.: Clinician performance and prominence of diagnoses displayed by a clinical diagnostic decision support system (2003)
8. Campbell, S.G., Croskerry, P., Bond, W.F.: Profiles in Patient Safety: A "Perfect Storm" in the Emergency Department. Academic Emergency Medicine 14(8), 743–749 (2007)
9. Carayon, P., Kianfar, S., Li, Y., Xie, A., Alyousef, B., Wooldridge, A.: A systematic review of mixed methods research on human factors and ergonomics in health care (2015)
10. Carayon, P., Schoofs Hundt, A., Karsh, B.T., Gurses, A.P., Alvarado, C.J., Smith, M., Flatley Brennan, P.: Work system design for patient safety: the SEIPS model. Quality and Safety in Health Care 15(suppl–1), i50–i58 (2006)
11. Castelvecchi, D.: Can we open the black box of AI? Nature 538(7623), 20–23 (2016)
12. Coiera, E.: Technology, cognition and error. BMJ Quality & Safety 24(7), 417–422 (2015)
13. Cramer, H., Evers, V., Ramlal, S., Van Someren, M., Rutledge, L., Stash, N., Aroyo, L., Wielinga, B.: The effects of transparency on trust in and acceptance of a content-based art recommender. User Modeling and User-Adapted Interaction 18(5), 455–496 (2008)
14. Croskerry, P.: The feedback sanction. Academic Emergency Medicine 7(11), 1232–8 (2000)
15. Dreiseitl, S., Binder, M.: Do physicians value decision support? A look at the effect of decision support systems on physician opinion. Artificial Intelligence in Medicine 33(1), 25–30 (2005)
16. Dworkin: Autonomy and informed consent. President's Commission for the Study of Ethical Problems in Medicine and Biomedical and Behavioral Research Making Health Care Decisions. Federal Register 3(226), 52,880–52,930 (1982)
17. Dzindolet, M.T., Peterson, S.A., Pomranky, R.A., Pierce, L.G., Beck, H.P.: The role of trust in automation reliance. International Journal of Human Computer Studies 58(6), 697–718 (2003)
18. Friedman, C.P., Elstein, A.S., Wolf, F.M., Murphy, G.C., Franz, T.M., Heckerling, P.S., Fine, P.L., Miller, T.M., Abraham, V.: Enhancement of Clinicians' Diagnostic Reasoning by Computer-Based Consultation: A Multisite Study of 2 Systems. JAMA 282(19), 1851–1856 (1999)
19. Friedman, C.P., Gatti, G.G., Franz, T.M., Murphy, G.C., Wolf, F.M., Heckerling, P.S., Fine, P.L., Miller, T.M., Elstein, A.S.: Do physicians know when their diagnoses are correct? Implications for decision support and error reduction. Journal of General Internal Medicine 20(4), 334–339 (2005)
20. Goddard, K., Roudsari, A., Wyatt, J.C.: Automation bias: a systematic review of frequency, effect mediators, and mitigators. Journal of the American Medical Informatics Association 19(1), 121–127 (2012)
21. Goddard, K., Roudsari, A., Wyatt, J.C.: Automation bias: Empirical results assessing influencing factors. International Journal of Medical Informatics (2014)
22. Goodman, B., Flaxman, S.: EU regulations on algorithmic decision-making and a "right to explanation". 2016 ICML Workshop on Human Interpretability in Machine Learning (WHI 2016) (Whi), 26–30 (2016)
23. Holst, H., Aström, K., Järund, A., Palmer, J., Heyden, A., Kahl, F., Tägil, K., Evander, E., Sparr, G., Edenbrandt, L.: Automated interpretation of ventilation-perfusion lung scintigrams for the diagnosis of pulmonary embolism using artificial neural networks. European journal of nuclear medicine 27(4), 400–406 (2000)
24. Kaufman, S., Rosset, S.: Leakage in data mining: Formulation, detection, and avoidance. Proceedings of the 17th ACM SIGKDD international conference on Knowledge discovery and data mining pp. 556–563 (2012)
25. Kohn, Linda T.; Corrigan, Janet M.; Donaldson, M.S.: [To err is human: building a safer health system]., vol. 21 (2002)
26. Koppel, R., Kreda, D.: Health Care Information Technology Vendors' Hold Harmless Clause. JAMA 301(12), 1276–1278 (2009)

27. Korunka, C., Weiss, A., Karetta, B.: Effects of new technologies with special regard for the implementation process per se. Journal of Organizational Behavior **14**(4), 331–348 (1993)
28. Ledley, R.S., Lusted, L.B.: Reasoning foundations of medical diagnosis; symbolic logic, probability, and value theory aid our understanding of how physicians reason. Science (New York, N.Y.) **130**(3366), 9–21 (1959)
29. Lee, C.S., Nagy, P.G., Weaver, S.J., Newman-Toker, D.E.: Cognitive and system factors contributing to diagnostic errors in radiology (2013)
30. Leveson, N.G., Turner, C.S.: An Investigation of the Therac-25 Accidents. Computer **26**(7), 18–41 (1993)
31. Li, L., Cheng, W.Y., Glicksberg, B.S., Gottesman, O., Tamler, R., Chen, R., Bottinger, E.P., Dudley, J.T.: Identification of type 2 diabetes subgroups through topological analysis of patient similarity. Science Translational Medicine **7**(311), 311ra174–311ra174 (2015)
32. Lyell, D., Magrabi, F., Raban, M.Z., Pont, L., Baysari, M.T., Day, R.O., Coiera, E.: Automation bias in electronic prescribing. BMC Medical Informatics and Decision Making **17**(1), 28 (2017)
33. Makary, M.A., Daniel, M.: Medical error the third leading cause of death in the US. BMJ p. i2139 (2016)
34. Marakas, G.: Decision Support Systems in The 21st Century. Prentice Hall (1999)
35. Mehdy, M.M., Ng, P.Y., Shair, E.F., Saleh, N.I.M., Gomes, C.: Artificial Neural Networks in Image Processing for Early Detection of Breast Cancer. Computational and Mathematical Methods in Medicine **2017**, 1–15 (2017)
36. Metzger, J., MacDonald, K.: Clinical decision support for the independent physician practice. October (2002)
37. Miller, R.A., Gardner, R.M.: Summary recommendations for responsible monitoring and regulation of clinical software systems. Annals of Internal Medicine **127**(9), 842–845 (1997)
38. Miller, R.A., Masarie, F.E.: The demise of the 'Greek Oracle' model for medical diagnostic systems. Methods of Information in Medicine **29**(1), 1–2 (1990)
39. Monteiro, C., Avelar, A.F.M.: Pedreira, M.d.L.G.: Interruptions of nurses' activities and patient safety: an integrative literature review. Revista Latino-Americana de Enfermagem **23**(1), 169–179 (2015)
40. Naguib, R.N.G., Sherbet, G.V.: Artificial neural networks in cancer diagnosis, prognosis, and patient management (2001)
41. National Patient Safety Agency: Healthcare risk assessment made easy. National Patient Safety Agency **3**(March) (2007)
42. Norman, D.a.: The Design of Everyday Things: Revised and Expanded Edition (1988)
43. Osheroff, J.A.: Improving Medication Use and Outcomes with Clinical Decision Support:: A Step by Step Guide. HIMSS (2009)
44. Persell, S., Friedberg, M., Meeker, D., Linder, J., Fox, C., Goldstein, N., Shah, P., Doctor, J., Knight, T.: Use of behavioral economics and social psychology to improve treatment of acute respiratory infections (BEARI): rationale and design of a cluster randomized controlled trial [1RC4AG039115-01] - study protocol and baseline practice and provider characteris. BMC infectious diseases **13**, 290 (2013)
45. Quionero-Candela, J., Sugiyama, M., Schwaighofer, A., Lawrence, N.: Dataset Shift in Machine Learning. MIT Press (2008)
46. Rogers, Y., Rogers, Y: A brief introduction to Distributed Cognition. Cognitive Science (1997)
47. Rosset, S., Perlich, C., Świrszcz, G., Melville, P., Liu, Y.: Medical data mining: Insights from winning two competitions. Data Mining and Knowledge Discovery **20**(3), 439–468 (2010)
48. Samaranayake, N.R., Cheung, S.T., Chui, W.C., Cheung, B.M.: Technology-related medication errors in a tertiary hospital: A 5-year analysis of reported medication incidents. International Journal of Medical Informatics **81**(12), 828–833 (2012)
49. Shojania, K.G., Dixon-Woods, M.: Estimating deaths due to medical error: the ongoing controversy and why it matters: Table1. BMJ Quality & Safety pp. bmjqs–2016–006,144 (2016)
50. Tan, J., Sheps, S.: Health decision support systems (1998)
51. Torsvik, T., Lillebo, B., Mikkelsen, G.: Presentation of clinical laboratory results: an experimental comparison of four visualization techniques. Journal of the American Medical Informatics Association **20**(2), 325–331 (2013)

52. Weingart, S.N.: McL Wilson R, R.M., Gibberd, R.W., Harrison, B.: Epidemiology of medical error. The. Western journal of medicine **172**(6), 390–3 (2000)
53. Westbrook, J.I.: Association of Interruptions With an Increased Risk and Severity of Medication Administration Errors. Archives of Internal Medicine **170**(8), 683 (2010)

Chapter 15
Group Cognition and Collaborative AI

Janin Koch and Antti Oulasvirta

Abstract Significant advances in artificial intelligence suggest that we will be using intelligent agents on a regular basis in the near future. This chapter discusses group cognition as a principle for designing collaborative AI. Group cognition is the ability to relate to other group members' decisions, abilities, and beliefs. It thereby allows participants to adapt their understanding and actions to reach common objectives. Hence, it underpins collaboration. We review two concepts in the context of group cognition that could inform the development of AI and automation in pursuit of natural collaboration with humans: conversational grounding and theory of mind. These concepts are somewhat different from those already discussed in AI research. We outline some new implications for collaborative AI, aimed at extending skills and solution spaces and at improving joint cognitive and creative capacity.

15.1 Introduction

The word 'collaboration' is derived from the Latin *col-* ('together') and *laborare* ('to work'). The idea of a machine that collaborates with humans has fired the imagination of computer scientists and engineers for decades. Already J.R. Licklider wrote about machines and humans operating on equal footing and being able to 'perform intellectual operations much more effectively than a man alone' [60].

If there is a shared tenet among the visionaries, it is that the more complex the activities become – consider, for example, planning, decision-making, idea generation, creativity, or problem-solving – the more beneficial collaboration is. However,

J. Koch (✉) · A. Oulasvirta
Department of Communications and Networking, School of Electrical Engineering,
Aalto University, Espoo, Finland
e-mail: janin.koch@aalto.fi

A. Oulasvirta
e-mail: antti.oulasvirta@aalto.fi

© Springer International Publishing AG, part of Springer Nature 2018   293
J. Zhou and F. Chen (eds.), *Human and Machine Learning*, Human–Computer
Interaction Series, https://doi.org/10.1007/978-3-319-90403-0_15

although collaboration has received attention from research on automation, robotics, Artificial Intelligence (AI), and Human-Computer Interaction (HCI), it can be safely said that most technology is not yet collaborative in the strong sense of the term. Humans are mainly in a commanding role or probed for feedback, rather than parties to a mutually beneficial partnership. There is much that could be done to better use human abilities in computational processes, and vice versa.

The topic of this chapter is group cognition: the ability to bring about a common understanding among agents; relate to other agents' decisions, abilities, and beliefs; and adapt one's own understanding toward a common objective [82]. This goes beyond the common notion of a computer 'understanding' human intents and actions, and highlights the necessity of contextual awareness, the ability of communicating reasoning behind actions to enable valuable contributions [51]. This, we argue, would result in human–machine collaboration that not only is more efficient but also is more equal and trustworthy.

We find group cognition particularly promising for re-envisioning what AI might need to achieve for collaboration, because it meshes with a strong sense of the concept of collaboration. Group cognition emerges in interaction when the group members involved, humans or computers, share knowledge and objectives and also dynamically and progressively update their understanding for better joint performance. This captures one aspect of the essence of machines that can be called collaborative.

Group cognition points towards various abilities necessary for collaboration. In this chapter we ask which of these abilities are needed for collaborative AI's. Among the many fields one might consider in the context of collaborative behaviour, management psychology presents an extensive body of research on how team members collaborate to solve common problems together [46], while developmental psychology has looked more closely at collaboration as an evolving behaviour in humans [32]. By comparison, AI and HCI research has looked at collaboration from the principal–agent perspective [65], in terms of dialogue and initiative [5], and as computer-mediated human–human collaboration [35]. Perhaps the most significant advances related to algorithmic principles of collaboration in the field of computer science have been made in the field of interactive intelligent systems [9, 81] and human–robot interaction [77]. However, on account of its roots in psychology and education, the concept of group cognition is rarely referred to within computational and engineering sciences.

To this end, we provide definitions, examples, and discussion of implications of the design of such an AI, where 'AI' refers mainly to machine learning-based intelligent systems though not being limited to that sense. We further discuss two key aspects of group cognition, by borrowing the concepts of conversational grounding and theory of mind. Even though these concepts overlap somewhat with each other, their use in combination does not map onto any existing concept in AI research.

Recent advances in AI have shown capabilities that are clearly relevant for group cognition, such as intent recognition [59], human-level performance in problem-solving [23], and cognitive artificial intelligences [90]. However, these capabilities do not trivially 'add up to' a capability of group cognition. In contrast to previous thought, wherein machines have often been described as extended minds or 'assistants', we hold that a system capable of group cognition would better understand human actions as part of a joint effort, align its actions and interpretations with the interpretation of the group, and update them as the activity evolves. A sense of dependability and common cause would emerge, which would improve the trustworthiness of such collaboration. In this way, a system capable of group cognition could participate in more open-ended, or ill-defined, activities than currently possible.

15.2 Definitions of Collaboration

We start by charting some definitions of collaboration. This groundwork serves as a basis for reflecting on group cognition as a theory of social behaviour. In social sciences and philosophy, the key phenomenon in collaboration is called *intersubjectivity*. Intersubjectivity refers to how two or more minds interrelate: understand each other and work together from their individual cognitive positions [83]. Some well-known social theories related to intersubjectivity are *mediated cognition* [87], *situated learning* [56], *knowledge building* [45], and *distributed cognition* [42]; D.J. Wood and B. Gray present an overview of differences among these perspectives [91]. We illustrate these differences with reference to a small selection of commonly accepted definitions.

Collaborative work has been defined within the domain of organisational work as 'a mutually beneficial relationship between two or more parties who work toward common goals by sharing responsibility, authority, and accountability for achieving results' [18]. This definition is used to understand collaboration in companies and other organisations, and the focus has been mainly on the outcome and values of team collaboration. Knowledge discovery in problem-solving is emphasised in the definition of collaboration as 'a continued and conjoined effort towards elaborating a "joint problem space" of shared representations of the problem to be solved' [7]. A third definition we wish to highlight focuses on differences among the contributing actors. Here, collaboration is 'a process through which parties who see different aspects of a problem can constructively explore their differences and search for solutions that go beyond their own limited vision of what is possible' [38].

In this chapter, we build on a fourth definition, from Roschelle et al., who define collaboration as 'a coordinated, synchronous activity that is the result of a continued attempt to construct and maintain a shared conception of a problem' [72]. This definition builds on the notion of collaboration as a cognitive action but also includes aspects of the previously mentioned definitions. The latter definition originated in the field of collaborative learning. Some empirical evidence exists that such collaborative learning enhances the cognitive capabilities of the people involved, allowing them as a team to reach a level of cognitive performance that exceeds the sum of the individuals' [7].

Collaboration also has to be distinguished from co-operation, a notion that is at times used to characterise intelligent agents. Roschelle et al. suggest that co-operative work is 'accomplished by the division of labour among participants, as an activity where each person is responsible for a portion of the problem-solving' [72], whereas collaborative learning involves the 'mutual engagement of participants in a coordinated effort to solve the problem together' [72]. Co-operation and collaboration differ also in respect of the knowledge involved and the distribution of labour. To co-operate means at least to share a common goal, towards whose achievement each participant in the group will strive. But this is compatible with dividing the task into subtasks and assigning a specific individual (or subgroup) responsibility for completing each of these. We can conclude, then, that 'to collaborate' has a stronger meaning than 'to co-operate' (in the sense of pursuing a goal that is assumed to be shared). The former involves working together in a more or less synchronous way, in order to gain a shared understanding of the task. In this sense, co-operation is a more general concept and phenomenon than collaboration.

Collaboration is a specific form of co-operation: co-operation works on the level of tasks and actions, while collaboration operates on the plane of ideas, understanding, and representations. In light of these definitions, research on group cognition can be viewed as an attempt to identify a necessary mechanism behind humans' ability to collaborate.

15.3   Group Cognition: A Unifying View of Collaboration

The core research goal on group cognition has been to shed light on cognitive abilities and social phenomena that together enable what is called 'collaboration'. The widely cited definition of group cognition alluded to above points out three qualities: (1) an ability to converge to a common understanding among agents; (2) an ability to relate to other agents' decisions, abilities, and beliefs; and (3) an ability to adapt one's own understanding toward a common objective during collaboration [82].

Research on group cognition has focused mostly on learning and ideation tasks in small groups (of people). A group's shared knowledge is claimed to be constructed through a process of negotiating and interrelating diverse views of members. Participants learn from each other's perspectives and knowledge only by accepting the legitimate role of each within the collaboration. This distinguishes group cognition from concepts such as extended cognition [36], wherein other participants are vehicles for improving or augmenting the individual's cognition rather than legitimate partners. The implication for AI is that, while a system for extended cognition would allow a person to complete work more efficiently by lessening the cognitive load or augmenting cognitive abilities, a 'group-cognitive system' would complement a human partner and take initiative by constructing its own solutions, negotiating, and learning with and for the person. It would not only improve the cognitive abilities of the human but enhance the overall quality of joint outcomes.

In group cognition, participants construct not only their own interpretations but interpretations of other participants' beliefs [82]. This distinguishes group cognition from previous concepts of collaboration such as conversational grounding [20]. Group cognition is not so much the aggregation of single cognitions as the outcome of synchronisation and coordination of cognitive abilities among the participants, cohering via interpretations of each other's meanings [86]. It has been argued that groups that achieve this level feel more ownership of the joint activity [24, 63]. This observation has encouraged studies of group cognition in childhood development, work, and learning contexts [3, 13].

In contrast to isolated concepts traditionally used in HCI and AI today, group cognition may offer a theoretical and practical framing of cognitive processes underpinning human-with-human collaboration. For machines to become collaborative participants, their abilities must be extended toward the requirements following from attributes of group cognition. This would allow machines to expand their role from the current one of cognitive tools toward that of actual collaborating agents, enabling the construction of knowledge and solutions that go beyond the cognition of each individual participant.

In this chapter, though, we consider mainly dyadic collaboration, involving a human–machine pair. Even though this restricts our scope to a subset of the phenomena encompassed by group cognition, larger groups require additional co-ordination, which is not addressed within the constraints of this chapter.

Taking the definition of group cognition as a foundation for our analysis, we can identify two main aspects of successful human–machine collaboration: (1) the ability of recurrently constructing mutual understanding and meaning of the common goal and interaction context and (2) the ability to interpret not only one's own reasoning but also the reasoning of other participants. In order to discuss these requirements in more detail, we make use of recognised theories from cognitive science and collaborative learning – namely, *conversational grounding* and *theory of mind*. Both theories contribute to a comprehensive view of group cognition. Though the two have considerable overlap, both are necessary if we are to cover the fundamental aspects of group cognition [7, 82].

In the following discussion, we briefly introduce these theories and explain their relation to group cognition. Proceeding from this knowledge, we then present key requirements and explain their potential resolution. Then, in Sect. 15.6, we present current realisations of systems addressing these requirements, identify limitations, and present ideas for future research.

15.4 Conversational Grounding

'Grounding' refers to the ability to create a shared base of knowledge, beliefs, or assumptions surrounding a goal striven toward [8]. Whilst taking grounding to be a complete explanation of collaborative behaviour has been questioned, the concept's explanatory power for constructing meaning in small-scale, dyadic collaboration has been demonstrated in several studies [82].

The term is used in the sense employed by Clark et al. within the tradition of conversational analysis [20]. They argue that common ground and its establishment are the basis for collaboration, communication, and other kinds of joint activity.

Especially within dyadic interactions, it has informed various theoretical frameworks, even in AI. Among the most prominent are the collaborative model [19], the Mixed-Initiative (MI) framework [5], and theories of collaborative learning [8]. Grounding highlights the necessity for efficient communication to ground the collective understanding by ensuring not only clear expression of the contributions to the collaboration but also correct reception by the addressees. It is thus a basic constitutive activity in human–human communication and collaboration.

It has been claimed that two factors influence success in grounding: purpose and medium [20]. *Purpose* refers to the objective, desire, or emotion that should be conveyed within a collaborative undertaking. The *medium* is the technique to express the current purpose, which includes the cost its application requires. Clark et al. introduce the concept of the 'least collaborative effort' [20], according to which participants often try to communicate as little as possible – but as much as necessary – with the most effective medium to allow correct reception. From this perspective, work on mixed-initiative interaction has addressed mainly the co-ordination of communication, *when* to communicate. Grounding could inform MI and other AI frameworks with regard to how reciprocal understanding among participants could be achieved. To this end, we can identify four key requirements:

(1) Expressing one's own objectives: Grounding is based on successful expression of one's objectives, requirements, and intents that define the purpose of the conversation in the collaborative activity [20]. Achieving this with a computer is not trivial. In a manner depending on the medium, a system has to divide information into sub-elements, which can then be presented to other group members (e.g., a concept into sufficiently descriptive words). Among examples that already exist are dialogue systems applying Belief–Desire–Intention models [48] and theoretical models for purposeful generation of speech acts [21] to construct meaningful expressions of objectives. Also, there is a growing body of research exploring the potentials of concept learning [25, 53], which would enable a machine to combine objectives and communicate or associate them with existing concepts.

(2) Selecting the most effective medium: To collaborate, a participant has to select the medium that can best convey the purposes of the conversation. In human-to-human conversation, a purpose can be expressed in various ways, including verbal and non-verbal communication. The choice of medium depends on the availability of tools, the effort it requires to use the medium, and the predicted ability of the collaborator to perceive the purpose correctly. Tools in this context are all of the means that help to convey the purpose – e.g., speech, pointing, body language, and extended media such as writing or drawing. The effort of using a medium depends on skills and the ability to apply them. In the case of drawing, the effort would include getting a pencil and paper as well as having the ability to draw the intended purpose. Finally, the selection of the medium depends also on the ability of other participants to perceive it correctly. This is related to the ability to physically perceive the medium (for example, hand gestures' unavailability during a phone call) and to the predicted ability to understand the medium. The ability of an intelligent system to select a medium is obviously limited by its physical requirements. While embodied robots share the same space and the same media as a human and can engage in pointing,

eye movement, or use of voice [62], virtual agents possess limitations in addressing physical elements when referring. On the other hand, virtual agents' enhanced skills with visual, animated, or written representations of information can be exploited as a comparatively strong expressive medium.

(3) Evaluating the effort of an action: H.H. Clark and D. Wilkes-Gibbs introduce the principle of least collaborative effort as a trade-off between the initial effort of making oneself understood and the effort of rephrasing the initial expression upon negative acknowledgement, as in the case of misunderstanding [19]. Previous work on least effort has examined short and precise communication efforts, which favour unique wording as optimal strategy. In contrast, Clark and Wilkes-Gibbs show that least *collaborative* effort does not necessarily follow the same pattern. On account of the joint effort of understanding within collaboration, the interpretation of least effort can be relaxed and groups can also accept wordings with internal references that are not necessarily unique to the given context. This presents both an opportunity and a challenge for machines. The conversation structure of most conversational agents, such as Siri [47], follows the least effort principle, by providing short and specific answers. Extending this to a least-collaborative-effort strategy would imply the ability to connect knowledge with previous and general expressions. N. Mavridis presents 'situated language' to overcome these issues and enable a machine to extend its communication ability to time- and place-dependent references [62].

(4) Confirming the reception of the initial objective: For successful conversational grounding, the group member expressing knowledge not only must find the right medium and dimension for expression but also has to verify correct reception by other members through evidence [20]. This allows the group to create mutual understanding within the process. Evidence for understanding may be positive, indicating that the receiving participant understood, or negative. People often strive for positive evidence of correct reception of their expression, which can be provided either through positive acknowledgement, such as nodding or 'mmm-hmm', or via a relevant next-turn response, which may be an action or expression building on the previous turn(s). Naturally, the reaction to the expression might differ with the medium used. Enabling a machine to evaluate understanding by other group members, therefore, entails new research into not just natural-language processing in relation to natural interaction [11] but also handling of non-verbal behaviour [29].

While grounding refers to the ability to communicate and receive knowledge to find 'common ground', group cognition goes beyond that. It additionally requires reciprocal interpretation of thoughts and intentions, for relation to other group members' decisions and beliefs [7]. In order to highlight this, we borrow from theory of mind as a basis for our analysis in the next part of the chapter.

15.5 Theory of Mind

The ability of interpreting one's own knowledge and understanding as well as interpreting other collaborators' understanding is crucial for successful collaboration in group cognition [31]. Theory of mind is a topic originating from research on cognitive development. It focuses on the ability to attribute mental states to oneself and others and to recognise that these mental states may differ [15]. Mental states may be beliefs, intentions, knowledge, desires, emotions, or perspectives, and understanding of these builds the basis for grounding. The ability to interpret others' mental states allows humans to predict the subsequent behaviour of their collaborators, and it thereby enables inferring the others' aims and understandings.

While most research on theory of mind has focused on developmental psychology, a growing body of literature backs up its importance for group behaviour [2] and group cognition [83], suggesting the importance of the concept for human–machine collaboration [15]. Human–machine interaction nevertheless is often limited by the level of ability to interpret the 'mind' of machines, on account of their different, sometimes unexpected, behaviour. People still approach new encounters with technology similarly to approaching other human beings, and attribute their own preconceptions and social structures to them [15, 34]. For reason of machines' inability to interpret their own mental state and that of others, prediction of the behaviour of humans in line with preconceptions often fails.

Three abilities stand out as vital for the development of collaborative AI in this context:

(1) Interpreting one's own mental states: Enabling an intelligent machine to interpret its own mental states requires a computational notion of and access to intentions, desires, beliefs, knowledge, and perspectives. At any point during collaboration, a mental state with regard to another group member may depend on the content of the discourse, the situation, and the information about the current objective.

Most AI applications have been limited to specific tasks, to reduce the complexity of the solution space by decreasing the number of objectives, requirements, and intents involved. However, this also reduces the machine's ability to adapt to changing contexts as found in a discourse, wherein it is necessary to extend the predefined belief space. Recent approaches in collaborative machine learning have constituted attempts to overcome the limitation of single-purpose systems [55]. These allow various information sources, such as sensors, to be integrated into a larger system, for broader knowledge. However, these sources have to be well integrated with each other if they are to create coherent knowledge about a situation [36].

(2) Interpreting others' mental states: Humans constantly strive to attribute mental states to other collaboration participants, to enable prediction of the others' subsequent reactions and behaviours [15]. Such reasoning enables conversations to be incremental. Incremental conversation refers to the ability to follow a common chain of thoughts and forms the basis of any argumentation and subsequent discussion (as in brainstorming). A large body of work on machine learning and AI is related to identifying and predicting human intention [28, 66] and actions [29, 88, 89]. However, this requirement is reciprocal and implies the same needs related to human understanding of the AI mind.

(3) Predicting subsequent behaviour: Similarly to interpretation of another's mental state, prediction of later behaviour can be considered from two sides: Humans apply a certain set of underlying preconceptions to interactions with intelligent

systems, which often leads to disrupted experiences that arise from unexpected behaviour of the system [15, 77]. Scholars are attempting to identify the information needed for predicting behaviour of machines. In A. Chandrasekaran et al.'s study of human perception of AI minds [15], humans were not able to predict the subsequent behaviour of the AI even when information about the inner mental states, like certainty and attention, of the machine was presented. In contrast, research into machines' prediction of human behaviour has a long history and has already yielded promising results [67, 73].

Group cognition is an interactive process among group members and requires participants to reason about decisions and actions taken by others in order to find common, agreeable ground for progress in the collaboration. While theory of mind explains the former underlying cognitive principles well, it does not explain how this common ground is built. For this reason, we have combined the two theories for our discussion, to elaborate a more comprehensive list of abilities necessary for AIs' engagement in collaboration.

15.6 Challenges for Collaborative AI

The group cognition angle may pinpoint mechanisms necessary for collaborative interaction between humans and artificial agents. In this context, we have highlighted two key concepts – conversational grounding and theory of mind. In summary, group cognition requires both the ability to internalise and constantly update knowledge in line with one's interpretation, as described in theory of mind, and a mutual understanding of the collaboration's purpose, provided through grounding. In the following discussion, we reflect on how these two concepts tie in with current research on AI, highlighting which capabilities may already be achievable by means of existing methods and which still stand out as challenges for future research.

15.6.1 Identify One's Own Mental States

Human–human collaboration is based on the assumption that participants are able to identify their own objectives, knowledge, and intents – in other words, their mental states. Extrapolating intentions from one's own knowledge based on the collaboration interaction and the mutual understanding of the goal is crucial.

Two limitations stand out. Firstly, although there is increasing interest in self-aware AI, most work on the inference of mental states has considered inference of people's mental states while ignoring the necessity of interpreting the machines' 'mental states' [15]. Secondly, because 'common sense' is still out of reach for AI, most (interactive) machine learning and AI systems address only narrow-scoped tasks. This limits their ability to form a complete picture of the situation, inferring and constructing human-relatable intents.

15.6.2 Select the Communication Medium and Express Objectives

If it is to express objectives and intents, a machine has to select the most efficient way to express them, as suggested in our discussion of grounding. There is a trade-off between the effort it takes for the machine to use a certain communication medium and the chances of the communication being received incorrectly.

The medium of choice for most interactive virtual agents is text. Examples include interactive health interfaces [33, 71] and industrial workflows [39], along with dialogue systems such as chat bots [41] and virtual personal assistants [57]. In recent virtual assistants, text is often transformed into spoken expression. However, the systems usually apply stimulus–response or stimulus–state–response paradigms, which does not suffice for natural speech planning or dialogue generation [62]. Another medium is visual representation via, for example, drawing, sketching, and/or presenting related images. Even if it requires further effort to translate the objectives of a conversation to visual representation, people are especially good at understanding drawings of concepts, even when these are abstract [19]. While virtual agents are starting to use graphics such as emoji or more complex images to convey emotions [30], communication through visual representations, overall, represents an under-researched opportunity in human–machine collaboration. The field of human–robot interaction, meanwhile, has looked at more natural conversational media for expressing objectives or intents [62]. Here, verbal communication is combined with non-verbal communication, such as gaze-based interaction [93], nodding [79], pointing [74], and facial gestures.

However, more studies are needed before we will be able to exploit the potential of gestural and gaze behaviour, along with more graphical representations at different abstraction levels. That work could result in a more efficient medium for communication to humans than is observable in human interaction today.

15.6.3 Confirm the Reception and Interpretation of Objectives

Communication, according to the grounding theory, is successful when a mutual understanding is created. This requires successful reception of the objective expressed. Reception – and acknowledgement of it to the communication partner – is necessary for understanding of mental states and objectives within a group. We can borrow the principle of evidence for reception [20] to state that machines should expect and work with the notion of positive or negative evidence.

Here, negative and positive evidence have a more specific meaning than in the sense of negative and positive feedback familiar from machine learning. Clark et al. identify two possible ways of giving positive evidence, next-turn responses and positive acknowledgement [20]. Next-turn responses are evaluated by looking at the coherence between one's own inference and the group member's next-turn responses as well as the initial objectives of the conversation. A.C. Graesser et al., for example, present an intelligent tutoring system that emphasises the importance of next-turn response that is based on learning expectations instead of predefined questions [37]. When interacting with a student, it 'monitors different levels of discourse structure and functions of dialogue moves' [37]. After every answer, it compares the response with the objectives by applying latent semantic analysis, then chooses its communication strategy accordingly. This allows the system to reformulate the question or objective when it perceives that the response does not match expectations. Further examples of such systems are presented by B.P. Woolf [92].

In open-ended tasks such as brainstorming, however, the next-turn response might not have to do with the initial objective so much as with extension or rejection of the intent behind it. In such contexts, humans often fall back to positive and negative acknowledgements. Recognising social signals such as nodding, gaze, or back-channel words of the 'uh-huh' type as positive acknowledgement plays an important role in human interaction and hence is an important ability for a fully collaborative machine. Within the field of human–robot interaction, recognising these signals has been an active research topic for some time [69, 94]. D. Lala et al. have presented a social signal recognition system based on hierarchical Bayesian models that consider nodding, gaze, laughing, and back-channelling as social signals for engagements and acknowledgement [54] with promising results. This approach allows determining which social cues are relevant on the basis of judgements of multiple third-party observers and includes the latent character of an observer as a simulation of personality. The detection of social signals, acknowledgements, would allow a machine to adapt its behaviour and reactions to the other group members.

15.6.4   Interpret the Reasoning of Others

If they are to contribute efficiently to a collaborative effort, group members have to understand the reasoning of the other participants. We use 'reasoning' to mean not merely mental states but also the logic and heuristics a partner uses to move from one state to another. This is necessary for the inclusion and convergence of thoughts, intentions, and perspectives in group cognition. While there is a large body of research on human intent recognition [50, 64] and cognitive state recognition [10], researchers have only recently acknowledged the importance of the *reciprocal* position, that humans need to understand the computer's reasoning. We review the topic only briefly here and refer the interested reader to chapters of this book that deal with it more directly.

Transparent or explainable machine learning is a topic of increasing interest. Stemming mainly from the need to support people who apply machine learning in, for example, health care [14] or finance [96], the need for understanding the internal states of machines is relevant also with regard to collaborative machines. Z.C. Lipton [61] points out, in opposition to popular claims, that simple models – such as linear models – are not strictly more interpretable than deep neural networks, because it depends on the notion of interpretability employed. The complexity of neural networks through different acting layers and raw input data increases the realism of presented results relative to human expectations; this supports interpretability of the machine's actions. In contrast, linear models rely on hand-engineered features, which can increase the algorithmic predictability but can render unexpected results, which are less expressible themselves.

T. Lei et al.'s approach of rationalising neural networks provides insight into the explainability of internal states on the basis of text analysis [58]. By training a separate neural network on subsections of the text, they highlighted those parts likely to have caused the decision of the main network. Another example of explaining deep neural networks is presented by L.A. Hendricks et al. [40]. They used a convolutional neural network to analyse image features and trained a separate recurrent neural network to generate words associated with the decision-relevant features. While this method provided good results, the explanatory power is tied to the structure of the network. In a third example, M.T. Ribeiro contributed his LIME framework, a technique to explain any classifier prediction, by learning a proxy interpretable model for certain locally limited predictions [68]. While the above-mentioned work focuses on the explainability of machine learning and AI output, a promising framework presented by T. Kulesza et al. describes some tenets for self-explainable machines [52]. In their work, a system was able to explain how each prediction was made and allowed the user to explain any necessary corrections back to the system, which then learned and updated in line with that input.

Most of today's approaches rely on separate training or manually added information, which limits the scope of these systems to carefully selected and limited tasks. In contrast, with more open-ended tasks, the potential context to be considered might not be manually pre-determined. We note that for group cognition it may not be necessary to explain to the user the reasoning that produced the outcome as opposed to a selected set of belief states. Their relevance is determined, in contrast, by the collaboration situation and the mental state of the communication partner. That poses a challenge for future work.

15.6.5 Predict Collaborative Actions of Others

Proceeding from their own knowledge and the reasoning of other group members, participants can predict others' behaviour. Again, this should be interpreted as a reciprocal process including *all* members of the group. While previous research has focused primarily on the prediction of human behaviour [67, 73], some recent work has looked at prediction of machine actions by a human [15].

Chandrasekaran et al. evaluated the modalities necessary to enable humans to create a 'Theory of AI Mind' [15]. In their study, participants were asked to infer the AI's answer with regard to a given image for questions such as 'How many people are in this image?', with or without additional information presented alongside the AI's response for the previous item. The users' answers could be seen as the behaviour expected of the AI. The modalities tested were a confidence barchart of the five best predictions; and an implicit and explicit attention map provided as a heatmap for the image. After the prediction, users were provided with instant feedback in the form of the system's answers. Users who had been presented with additional modalities too were shown to have results with equal or lower accuracy in comparison to users who received only the instant feedback. However, an increase in prediction accuracy after only a few trials indicates that users learned to predict the machine's behaviour better through familiarisation than via additional information about internal processes. The additional information seemed to encourage users to overadapt to system failures, which resulted in worse overall prediction. Further studies are needed to evaluate other potential sources of improved behaviour prediction. However, these first results might indicate that, to understand and predict AI, humans may need more information than that referring to reasoning alone.

The concept of group cognition comes from the discipline of collaborative learning, which has emphasised the necessity of each participant continuously learning and updating said participant's knowledge, concepts, and ideas. Having their origins in psychology, the notions behind collaborative learning assume human-level understanding, communication, and learning capabilities. In the context of collaborative *machines*, these traits do not exist yet and will have to be explicitly implemented. We will next consider some opportunities for such implementations.

15.6.6 Update Knowledge for Social Inference

During collaboration, the group members must integrate inferences of other participants with their existing knowledge. An extensive set of methods exists that may achieve this. Among these are inverse reinforcement learning [1], Bayesian belief networks [17], and variants of deep neural networks [22]. Results have been presented for social inference in special tasks, as language learning [17] and learning through presentation [1, 6]. However, these approaches assume for the most part that the human provides input for the machine to learn from, and they do not integrate the human more deeply into the loop.

Interactive machine learning adds the human to the loop but has mainly been applied for purposes of enriching data or boosting unsupervised or supervised learning [70]. P. Sinard et al. define interactive machine learning as machine learning wherein the user can provide information to the machine during the interaction process [80]. Meanwhile, A. Holzinger [43] considers interactive machine learning as a type of collaboration between algorithm and human [70]. He points out that not all input presented to a machine can be trained for, and that the machine has to be able to adapt to such situations. He presents an approach using an ant-colony algorithm to solve a travelling-salesman problem [44]. The algorithm presents the optimal path found thus far and allows the user to alter this path, in line with the contextual knowledge he possesses. Holzinger's results illustrate that this approach speeds up the discovery of the optimal path in terms of iteration when compared to machine-only optimisation. Even though this approach allows the machine and the human to work on a mutual goal, the common objective is fixed at the outset of the task.

Another line of research relevant in this context is that into multi-agent systems [84]. Work on multi-agent systems often refers to critical tasks such as disaster-response control systems [75] or autonomous cars [27], wherein the aim is of 'a mixture of humans performing high level decision-making, intelligent agents coordinating the response and humans and robots performing key physical tasks' [75]. For a review of multi-agent systems, we direct the reader to Y. Shoham and K. Leyton-Brown [78]. In general, research on human-in-the-loop multi-agent systems has focused on the task, the activity, and the role each agent should have in order to contribute to reaching the defined goal [12]. For example, A. Campbell and A.S. Wu highlight the criticality of role allocation, where a role is 'the task assigned to a specific individual within a set of responsibilities given to a group of individuals', for designing, implementing, and analysing multi-agent systems [12]. They further present computational models for various role-allocation procedures in accordance with a recent review of multi-agent methods. Role allocation, according to them, grows 'more important as agents become more sophisticated, multi-agent solutions become more ubiquitous, and the problems that the agents are required to solve become more difficult' [12]. While most multi-agent research looks at machine agents, as found in sensor–networks [4], some concepts and principles for the co-ordination of collaboration and for how roles within a group can be allocated in the most efficient way could be used for collaborative AI. However, in the strong sense of the word 'collaboration', most of the multi-agent methods do not foster interactive behaviour on common ground so much as favour individual task allocation. Nevertheless, experiences from these models can aid in understanding how roles influence this interaction.

15.6.7 Apply New Types of Initiative in Turn-Taking

While learning in groups is a shared task with a common goal, in open-ended interaction the goal depends on the current topics and can change as soon as new ideas start being explored. Hence, there is a need for understanding which knowledge most efficiently contributes to the current collaboration, and when. J. Allen et al.'s [5] well-known mixed-initiative interaction framework provides a method for inferring when to take initiative. Since Allen proposed it, this framework has been applied in various contexts of interactive systems, among them intelligent tutoring systems [37], interactive machine learning [16], and creative tools [26].

On the other hand, the decision on *what* to contribute presents a trade-off between context-aligned recommendations (following the current chain of thoughts) and exploratory recommendation (diversion from the current ideas). Contextually aligned reactions, analogously with value-aligned interactions [76], may take less effort to communicate and react to, for reason of existing context and already shared references. While these reactions are more likely to be understood by other group members, they do not necessarily explore new possible solution spaces. What could be called 'exploratory initiatives', on the other hand, bring with them the problem that future topics are partly unknown and that, accordingly, selection of the 'right' idea path to follow can be a thorny problem. This unknown solution space presents a challenge for selection, encouraging, and elaboration of new ideas. Perhaps the trade-off of initiatives that explore versus exploit new topics could be modelled in a manner paralleling that in optimisation. However, the first solutions for acting and learning in partly non-observable environments, known mainly as a partially observable Markov decision process (POMDP), are promising. Already, POMDPs are being used for decision-making and selection in human–robot interaction [49, 85, 95]. In T. Taha et al.'s work, for example, a POMDP guides the communication layer, which facilitates the flow and interpretation of information between the human and the robot [85]. Applying this information, the robot makes its action plan, while the current task, status, observed intention, and satisfaction are used to model the interaction within the POMDP. The paper's authors highlight that with a minimum amount of input the system was able to change the action plan or add corrective actions at any time.

While current research on interactive systems offer various approaches to coordinate, engage in, and facilitate interactions, none of them cover all the necessities for collaborative behaviour in the sense of group cognition. However, these approaches do present the prerequisites for future developments of such systems.

15.7 Conclusion

We have discussed cognitive abilities necessary for collaborative AI by building on the concept of group cognition. We reviewed some promising current approaches, which reflect that some aspects of these abilities are already identifiable and partially addressed. However, more research needs to be done. The main topics we have identified for future research are related to the expressiveness of machines, the ability to understand human interaction, and inherent traits of the behaviour of machines. We have highlighted in this context the necessity of extending and enhancing potential communication media of machines for purposes of more human-like communication, including social signal recognition within collaborative processes. Scholars researching collaborative machines could draw from previous experiences of human-robot interaction and adapt the findings to the particular context at hand. Another limitation of current approaches is related to the explainability of machine reasoning. In order to construct a 'Theory of AI Mind', as framed by Chandrasekaran et al. [15], a human has to be able to understand the reasoning behind an action, so as to recognise the machine's intent and most probable behaviour. We have presented several approaches to resolving this issue; however, the question of what best explains the reasoning of a machine remains. Finally, we must reiterate the necessity of extending current approaches in machine learning and interactive machine learning to act under the uncertainty conditions typical of human collaboration. This would enable machines to make suggestions and act in open-ended collaboration such as discussions and brainstorming, for which the idea space is not defined beforehand.

Acknowledgements The project has received funding from the European Research Council (ERC) under the European Union's Horizon 2020 research and innovation programme (grant agreement 637991).

References

1. Abbeel, P., Ng, A.Y.: Apprenticeship learning via inverse reinforcement learning. In: Proceedings of the twenty-first international conference on Machine learning, p. 1. ACM (2004)
2. Abrams, D., Rutland, A., Palmer, S.B., Pelletier, J., Ferrell, J., Lee, S.: The role of cognitive abilities in children's inferences about social atypicality and peer exclusion and inclusion in intergroup contexts. Br. J. Dev. Psychol. **32**(3), 233–247 (2014)
3. Akkerman, S., Van den Bossche, P., Admiraal, W., Gijselaers, W., Segers, M., Simons, R.J., Kirschner, P.: Reconsidering group cognition: from conceptual confusion to a boundary area between cognitive and socio-cultural perspectives? Educ. Res. Rev. **2**(1), 39–63 (2007)
4. Alexakos, C., Kalogeras, A.P.: Internet of things integration to a multi agent system based manufacturing environment. In: 2015 IEEE 20th Conference on Emerging Technologies and Factory Automation (ETFA), pp. 1–8. IEEE (2015)
5. Allen, J., Guinn, C.I., Horvitz, E.: Mixed-initiative interaction. IEEE Intell. Syst. Appl. **14**(5), 14–23 (1999)
6. Argall, B.D., Chernova, S., Veloso, M., Browning, B.: A survey of robot learning from demonstration. Robot. Auton. Syst. **57**(5), 469–483 (2009)
7. Baker, M.J.: Collaboration in collaborative learning. Interact. Stud. **16**(3), 451–473 (2015)
8. Baker, M., Hansen, T., Joiner, R., Traum, D.: The role of grounding in collaborative learning tasks. Collab. Learn. Cogn. Comput. Approach. **31**, 63 (1999)
9. Bradáč, V., Kostolányová, K.: Intelligent tutoring systems. In: E-Learning, E-Education, and Online Training: Third International Conference, eLEOT 2016, Dublin, Ireland, August 31–September 2, 2016, Revised Selected Papers, pp. 71–78. Springer (2017)
10. Cai, Z., Wu, Q., Huang, D., Ding, L., Yu, B., Law, R., Huang, J., Fu, S.: Cognitive state recognition using wavelet singular entropy and arma entropy with afpa optimized gp classification. Neurocomputing **197**, 29–44 (2016)
11. Cambria, E., White, B.: Jumping nlp curves: a review of natural language processing research. IEEE Comput. Intell. Mag. **9**(2), 48–57 (2014)
12. Campbell, A., Wu, A.S.: Multi-agent role allocation: issues, approaches, and multiple perspectives. Auton. Agent. Multi-Agent Syst. **22**(2), 317–355 (2011)
13. Cannon-Bowers, J.A., Salas, E.: Reflections on shared cognition. J. Organ. Behav. **22**(2), 195–202 (2001)
14. Caruana, R., Lou, Y., Gehrke, J., Koch, P., Sturm, M., Elhadad, N.: Intelligible models for healthcare: Predicting pneumonia risk and hospital 30-day readmission. In: Proceedings of the 21th ACM SIGKDD International Conference on Knowledge Discovery and Data Mining, pp. 1721–1730. ACM (2015)
15. Chandrasekaran, A., Yadav, D., Chattopadhyay, P., Prabhu, V., Parikh, D.: It takes two to tango: towards theory of ai's mind (2017). arXiv:1704.00717
16. Chau, D.H., Kittur, A., Hong, J.I., Faloutsos, C.: Apolo: making sense of large network data by combining rich user interaction and machine learning. In: Proceedings of the SIGCHI Conference on Human Factors in Computing Systems, pp. 167–176. ACM (2011)

17. Cheng, J., Greiner, R.: Learning bayesian belief network classifiers: algorithms and system. In: Advances in artificial intelligence, pp. 141–151 (2001)
18. Chrislip, D.D., Larson, C.E.: Collaborative leadership: how citizens and civic leaders can make a difference, vol. 24. Jossey-Bass Inc Pub (1994)
19. Clark, H.H., Wilkes-Gibbs, D.: Referring as a collaborative process. Cognition 22(1), 1–39 (1986)
20. Clark, H.H., Brennan, S.E., et al.: Grounding in communication. Perspect. Soc. Shar. Cogn. 13(1991), 127–149 (1991)
21. Cohen, P.R., Perrault, C.R.: Elements of a plan-based theory of speech acts. Cogn. Sci. 3(3), 177–212 (1979)
22. Dahl, G.E., Yu, D., Deng, L., Acero, A.: Context-dependent pre-trained deep neural networks for large-vocabulary speech recognition. IEEE Trans. Audio Speech Lang. Process. 20(1), 30–42 (2012)
23. Dartnall, T.: Artificial intelligence and creativity: an interdisciplinary approach, vol. 17. Springer Science & Business Media (2013)
24. de Haan, M.: Intersubjectivity in models of learning and teaching: reflections from a study of teaching and learning in a mexican mazahua community. In: The theory and practice of cultural-historical psychology, pp. 174–199 (2001)
25. De Jong, K.A., Spears, W.M., Gordon, D.F.: Using genetic algorithms for concept learning. Mach. Learn. 13(2–3), 161–188 (1993)
26. Deterding, C.S., Hook, J.D., Fiebrink, R., Gow, J., Akten, M., Smith, G., Liapis, A., Compton, K.: Mixed-initiative creative interfaces (2017)
27. Dresner, K., Stone, P.: A multiagent approach to autonomous intersection management. J. Artif. Intell. Res. 31, 591–656 (2008)
28. El Kaliouby, R., Robinson, P.: Mind reading machines: automated inference of cognitive mental states from video. In: 2004 IEEE International Conference on Systems, Man and Cybernetics, vol. 1, pp. 682–688. IEEE (2004)
29. El Kaliouby, R., Robinson, P.: Real-time inference of complex mental states from facial expressions and head gestures. In: Real-Time Vision for Human-Computer Interaction, pp. 181–200. Springer (2005)
30. Emojis as content within chatbots and nlps (2016). https://www.smalltalk.ai/blog/2016/12/9/how-to-use-emojis-as-content-within-chatbots-and-nlps
31. Engel, D., Woolley, A.W., Jing, L.X., Chabris, C.F., Malone, T.W.: Reading the mind in the eyes or reading between the lines? Theory of mind predicts collective intelligence equally well online and face-to-face. PloS one 9(12), e115,212 (2014)
32. Flavell, J.H.: Theory-of-mind development: retrospect and prospect. Merrill-Palmer Q. 50(3), 274–290 (2004)
33. Fotheringham, M.J., Owies, D., Leslie, E., Owen, N.: Interactive health communication in preventive medicine: internet-based strategies in teaching and research. Am. J. Prev. Med. 19(2), 113–120 (2000)
34. Fussell, S.R., Kiesler, S., Setlock, L.D., Yew, V.: How people anthropomorphize robots. In: 2008 3rd ACM/IEEE International Conference on Human-Robot Interaction (HRI), pp. 145–152. IEEE (2008)
35. Galegher, J., Kraut, R.E., Egido, C.: Intellectual Teamwork: Social and Technological Foundations of Cooperative Work. Psychology Press (2014)
36. Goldstone, R.L., Theiner, G.: The multiple, interacting levels of cognitive systems (milcs) perspective on group cognition. Philos. Psychol. 30(3), 334–368 (2017)
37. Graesser, A.C., VanLehn, K., Rosé, C.P., Jordan, P.W., Harter, D.: Intelligent tutoring systems with conversational dialogue. AI Mag. 22(4), 39 (2001)
38. Gray, B.: Collaborating: Finding Common Ground for Multiparty Problems (1989)
39. Guzman, A.L.: The messages of mute machines: human-machine communication with industrial technologies. Communication+ 1 5(1), 1–30 (2016)
40. Hendricks, L.A., Akata, Z., Rohrbach, M., Donahue, J., Schiele, B., Darrell, T.: Generating visual explanations. In: European Conference on Computer Vision, pp. 3–19. Springer (2016)

41. Hill, J., Ford, W.R., Farreras, I.G.: Real conversations with artificial intelligence: a comparison between human-human online conversations and human-chatbot conversations. Comput. Hum. Behav. **49**, 245–250 (2015)
42. Hollan, J., Hutchins, E., Kirsh, D.: Distributed cognition: toward a new foundation for human-computer interaction research. ACM Trans. Comput.-Hum. Interact. (TOCHI) **7**(2), 174–196 (2000)
43. Holzinger, A.: Interactive machine learning for health informatics: when do we need the human-in-the-loop? Brain Inform. **3**(2), 119–131 (2016)
44. Holzinger, A., Plass, M., Holzinger, K., Crişan, G.C., Pintea, C.M., Palade, V.: Towards interactive machine learning (iml): applying ant colony algorithms to solve the traveling salesman problem with the human-in-the-loop approach. In: International Conference on Availability, Reliability, and Security, pp. 81–95. Springer (2016)
45. Hong, H.Y., Chen, F.C., Chai, C.S., Chan, W.C.: Teacher-education students views about knowledge building theory and practice. Instr. Sci. **39**(4), 467–482 (2011)
46. Huber, G.P., Lewis, K.: Cross-understanding: implications for group cognition and performance. Acad. Manag. Rev. **35**(1), 6–26 (2010)
47. iOS Siri, A.: Apple (2013)
48. Jurafsky, D., Martin, J.H.: Speech and Language Processing: An Introduction to Natural Language Processing, Computational Linguistics, and Speech Recognition (2014)
49. Karami, A.B., Jeanpierre, L., Mouaddib, A.I.: Human-robot collaboration for a shared mission. In: Proceedings of the 5th ACM/IEEE international conference on Human-robot interaction, pp. 155–156. IEEE Press (2010)
50. Kelley, R., Wigand, L., Hamilton, B., Browne, K., Nicolescu, M., Nicolescu, M.: Deep networks for predicting human intent with respect to objects. In: Proceedings of the seventh annual ACM/IEEE international conference on Human-Robot Interaction, pp. 171–172. ACM (2012)
51. Koch, J.: Design implications for designing with a collaborative ai. In: AAAI Spring Symposium Series, Designing the User Experience of Machine Learning Systems (2017)
52. Kulesza, T., Burnett, M., Wong, W.K., Stumpf, S.: Principles of explanatory debugging to personalize interactive machine learning. In: Proceedings of the 20th International Conference on Intelligent User Interfaces, pp. 126–137. ACM (2015)
53. Lake, B.M., Salakhutdinov, R., Tenenbaum, J.B.: Human-level concept learning through probabilistic program induction. Science **350**(6266), 1332–1338 (2015)
54. Lala, D., Inoue, K., Milhorat, P., Kawahara, T.: Detection of social signals for recognizing engagement in human-robot interaction (2017). arXiv:1709.10257 [cs.HC]
55. Lang, F., Fink, A.: Collaborative machine scheduling: challenges of individually optimizing behavior. Concurr. Comput. Pract. Exp. **27**(11), 2869–2888 (2015)
56. Lave, J., Wenger, E.: Situated Learning: Legitimate Peripheral Participation. Cambridge university press, Cambridge (1991)
57. Lee, D., Lee, J., Kim, E.K., Lee, J.: Dialog act modeling for virtual personal assistant applications using a small volume of labeled data and domain knowledge. In: Sixteenth Annual Conference of the International Speech Communication Association (2015)
58. Lei, T., Barzilay, R., Jaakkola, T.: Rationalizing neural predictions (2016). arXiv:1606.04155
59. Levine, S.J., Williams, B.C.: Concurrent plan recognition and execution for human-robot teams. In: ICAPS (2014)
60. Licklider, J.C.: Man-computer symbiosis. IRE Trans. Hum. Factors Electron. **1**, 4–11 (1960)
61. Lipton, Z.C.: The mythos of model interpretability (2016). arXiv:1606.03490
62. Mavridis, N.: A review of verbal and non-verbal human-robot interactive communication. Robot. Auton. Syst. **63**, 22–35 (2015)
63. Mohammed, S., Ringseis, E.: Cognitive diversity and consensus in group decision making: the role of inputs, processes, and outcomes. Organ. Behav. Hum. Decis. Process. **85**(2), 310–335 (2001)
64. Nehaniv, C.L., Dautenhahn, K., Kubacki, J., Haegele, M., Parlitz, C., Alami, R.: A methodological approach relating the classification of gesture to identification of human intent in the context of human-robot interaction. In: ROMAN 2005. IEEE International Workshop on Robot and Human Interactive Communication, 2005, pp. 371–377. IEEE (2005)

65. Novak, J.: Mine, yours... ours? Designing for principal-agent collaboration in interactive value creation. Wirtschaftsinformatik **1**, 305–314 (2009)
66. Oliver, N.M., Rosario, B., Pentland, A.P.: A bayesian computer vision system for modeling human interactions. IEEE Trans. Pattern Anal. Mach. Intell. **22**(8), 831–843 (2000)
67. Pantic, M., Pentland, A., Nijholt, A., Huang, T.S.: Human computing and machine understanding of human behavior: a survey. In: Artifical Intelligence for Human Computing, pp. 47–71. Springer (2007)
68. Ribeiro, M.T., Singh, S., Guestrin, C.: Why should i trust you?: Explaining the predictions of any classifier. In: Proceedings of the 22nd ACM SIGKDD International Conference on Knowledge Discovery and Data Mining, pp. 1135–1144. ACM (2016)
69. Rich, C., Ponsler, B., Holroyd, A., Sidner, C.L.: Recognizing engagement in human-robot interaction. In: 2010 5th ACM/IEEE International Conference on Human-Robot Interaction (HRI), pp. 375–382. IEEE (2010)
70. Robert, S., Büttner, S., Röcker, C., Holzinger, A.: Reasoning under uncertainty: towards collaborative interactive machine learning. In: Machine Learning for Health Informatics, pp. 357–376. Springer (2016)
71. Robinson, T.N., Patrick, K., Eng, T.R., Gustafson, D., et al.: An evidence-based approach to interactive health communication: a challenge to medicine in the information age. JAMA **280**(14), 1264–1269 (1998)
72. Roschelle, J., Teasley, S.D., et al.: The construction of shared knowledge in collaborative problem solving. Comput.-Support. Collab. Learn. **128**, 69–197 (1995)
73. Ruttkay, Z., Reidsma, D., Nijholt, A.: Human computing, virtual humans and artificial imperfection. In: Proceedings of the 8th international conference on Multimodal interfaces, pp. 179–184. ACM (2006)
74. Sato, E., Yamaguchi, T., Harashima, F.: Natural interface using pointing behavior for human-robot gestural interaction. IEEE Trans. Industr. Electron. **54**(2), 1105–1112 (2007)
75. Schurr, N., Marecki, J., Tambe, M., Scerri, P., Kasinadhuni, N., Lewis, J.P.: The future of disaster response: humans working with multiagent teams using defacto. In: AAAI Spring Symposium: AI Technologies for Homeland Security, pp. 9–16 (2005)
76. Shapiro, D., Shachter, R.: User-agent value alignment. In: Proceedings of The 18th National Conference on Artificial Intelligence AAAI (2002)
77. Sheridan, T.B.: Human-robot interaction: status and challenges. Hum. Factors **58**(4), 525–532 (2016)
78. Shoham, Y., Leyton-Brown, K.: Multiagent systems: Algorithmic, game-theoretic, and logical foundations. Cambridge University Press, Cambridge (2008)
79. Sidner, C.L., Lee, C., Morency, L.P., Forlines, C.: The effect of head-nod recognition in human-robot conversation. In: Proceedings of the 1st ACM SIGCHI/SIGART conference on Human-robot interaction, pp. 290–296. ACM (2006)
80. Simard, P., Chickering, D., Lakshmiratan, A., Charles, D., Bottou, L., Suarez, C.G.J., Grangier, D., Amershi, S., Verwey, J., Suh, J.: Ice: enabling non-experts to build models interactively for large-scale lopsided problems (2014). arXiv:1409.4814
81. Soller, A.: Supporting social interaction in an intelligent collaborative learning system. Int. J. Artif. Intell. Educ. (IJAIED) **12**, 40–62 (2001)
82. Stahl, G.: Shared meaning, common ground, group cognition. In: Group Cognition: Computer Support for Building Collaborative Knowledge, pp. 347–360 (2006)
83. Stahl, G.: From intersubjectivity to group cognition. Comput. Support. Coop. Work (CSCW) **25**(4–5), 355–384 (2016)
84. Stone, P., Veloso, M.: Multiagent systems: a survey from a machine learning perspective. Auton. Robots **8**(3), 345–383 (2000)
85. Taha, T., Miró, J.V., Dissanayake, G.: A pomdp framework for modelling human interaction with assistive robots. In: 2011 IEEE International Conference on Robotics and Automation (ICRA), pp. 544–549. IEEE (2011)
86. Theiner, G., Allen, C., Goldstone, R.L.: Recognizing group cognition. Cogn. Syst. Res. **11**(4), 378–395 (2010)

87. Turner, P.: Mediated Cognition. Springer International Publishing, Cham (2016)
88. Vondrick, C., Oktay, D., Pirsiavash, H., Torralba, A.: Predicting motivations of actions by leveraging text. In: Proceedings of the IEEE Conference on Computer Vision and Pattern Recognition, pp. 2997–3005 (2016)
89. Vondrick, C., Pirsiavash, H., Torralba, A.: Anticipating visual representations from unlabeled video. In: Proceedings of the IEEE Conference on Computer Vision and Pattern Recognition, pp. 98–106 (2016)
90. Wenger, E.: Artificial Intelligence and Tutoring Systems: Computational and Cognitive Approaches to the Communication of Knowledge. Morgan Kaufmann (2014)
91. Wood, D.J., Gray, B.: Toward a comprehensive theory of collaboration. J. Appl. Behav. Sci. **27**(2), 139–162 (1991)
92. Woolf, B.P.: Building Intelligent Interactive Tutors: Student-Centered Strategies for Revolutionizing e-Learning. Morgan Kaufmann (2010)
93. Yoshikawa, Y., Shinozawa, K., Ishiguro, H., Hagita, N., Miyamoto, T.: Responsive robot gaze to interaction partner. In: Robotics: Science and Systems (2006)
94. Yu, Z., Ramanarayanan, V., Lange, P., Suendermann-Oeft, D.: An open-source dialog system with real-time engagement tracking for job interview training applications. In: Proceedings of IWSDS (2017)
95. Zhang, S., Sridharan, M.: Active visual sensing and collaboration on mobile robots using hierarchical pomdps. In: Proceedings of the 11th International Conference on Autonomous Agents and Multiagent Systems-Volume 1, pp. 181–188. International Foundation for Autonomous Agents and Multiagent Systems (2012)
96. Zhou, J., Chen, F.: Making machine learning useable. Int. J. Intell. Syst. Technol. Appl. **14**(2), 91–109 (2015)

Part V
Human and Evaluation of Machine Learning

Chapter 16
User-Centred Evaluation for Machine Learning

Scott Allen Cambo and Darren Gergle

Abstract Activity tracking wearables like Fitbit or mobile applications like Moves have seen immense growth in recent years. However, users often experience errors that occur in unexpected and inconsistent ways making it difficult for them to find a workaround and ultimately leading them to abandon the system. This is not too surprising given that intelligent systems typically design the modelling algorithm independent of the overall user experience. Furthermore, the user experience often takes a seamless design approach which hides nuanced aspects of the model leaving only the model's prediction for the user to see. This prediction is presented optimistically meaning that the user is expected to assume that it is correct. To better align the design of the user experience with the development of the underlying algorithms we propose a validation pipeline based on user-centred design principles and usability standards for use in model optimisation, selection and validation. Specifically, we show how available user experience research can highlight the need for new evaluation criteria for models of activity and we demonstrate the use of a user-centred validation pipeline to select a modelling approach which best addresses the user experience as a whole.

16.1 Introduction

Activity tracking systems such as wearable devices like Fitbit and Jawbone or mobile applications like Moves and Google Fit have seen extraordinary growth in commercial activity over the past several years. Yet, a common problem with these systems is early user abandonment – shortly after initial adoption many users stop

S. A. Cambo (✉) · D. Gergle
Northwestern University, 2240 Campus Drive, Evanston, IL 60208, USA
e-mail: cambo@u.northwestern.edu

D. Gergle
e-mail: dgergle@northwestern.edu

© Springer International Publishing AG, part of Springer Nature 2018   315
J. Zhou and F. Chen (eds.), *Human and Machine Learning*, Human–Computer
Interaction Series, https://doi.org/10.1007/978-3-319-90403-0_16

engaging with the tracked information or even stop using the system entirely. To better understand why this is happening, researchers have begun to survey users of activity trackers [10, 27], conduct detailed user interviews [23], and synthesise feedback from online product reviews [27]. Across these studies, users often report that inaccuracy and errors play a big role in their decision to abandon their activity trackers [10, 23, 27] and that they are uncomfortable with activity tracking performance, system behaviour and overall user experience.

To address these challenges, user experience researchers have recommended integrating interactive elements into activity tracking systems that permit the users to better understand errors and play a more active role in calibrating the system. Some health tracking systems researchers have gone a step further to argue that manual calibration could actually aid the user to better understand their tracked and inferred data [7, 10, 23, 27]. However, there is a gap in our understanding that exists between the design of these interactive aspects of the user-experience and the performance of underlying algorithms and models of activity tracking systems. In particular, computational techniques such as model personalisation and active learning—which are inherently suited to the integration of user interaction—tend to be developed and evaluated with a focus on model accuracy instead of considering the broader implications of performance and how it relates to the user experience and interaction with the activity tracking system.

In this chapter, we show how a user-centred approach to the evaluation of model personalisation techniques could help bridge the gap that exists between the way we research and develop the user interaction and the way we research and develop the underlying model. User-centred evaluations like those we describe in this chapter can lead to designs and technical implementations that better enable users to have a richer and more fulfilling interactive experience with their activity tracking systems. In Sect. 16.2, we contrast the technical performance perspective of model evaluation with the user experience perspective derived from research on why people abandon activity trackers. We use research in health technology design and health behavior change to motivate the need to identify *seamful design* opportunities in the system's underlying algorithms. In Sect. 16.3, we use these principles to define a validation algorithm that provides an individualised view of model performance and demonstrate how it can be used in model optimisation, validation, and selection. Then we identify seamful design presentations of model confidence which can help address the user challenges described in Sect. 16.2. Finally, in Sect. 16.4, we describe how these principles of usability along with the user-centred validation process help us make model selection decisions that address the whole user experience and not just the model validation. Throughout this chapter we discuss approaches that may support better visibility by making model behaviour more salient to the user and better transparency by aiding the user's understanding of model behavior. We further see visibility and transparency as prerequisites for users to gain the trust needed to use systems for sustained behavioural change.

16.2   Background

16.2.1   A Technical Performance Perspective on Evaluation

A common evaluation approach used in much of the technical literature examining activity tracking systems is to treat model performance as a binary construct (i.e., correct or incorrect) and to minimise errors at the aggregate level in an effort to optimise activity tracking performance for the user base as a whole. Consider the case of a wearable device used to infer activity from a stream of motion sensor (accelerometer) data. In building such a system, researchers collect examples of accelerometer data associated with the activities they are interested in and then build a model using a supervised machine learning technique. In order to measure how well the resulting model recognises the correct activity from the accelerometer data, each incorrect prediction is recorded as an error. Researchers then assess model performance by examining the overall error rate or its inverse, accuracy. Using this measure, they can decide between competing modelling approaches and determine which will work best for their given activity recognition application. Subsequent iterations and refinements of these algorithms may be optimised based on this same measure – but a question exists as to whether this binary and aggregate view of errors is descriptive enough when considering the entire user experience.

16.2.2   A User Experience Perspective on Evaluation

While many technically oriented approaches to errors in the context of activity recognition focus on minimising errors and optimising accuracy, it's important to keep in mind that the larger goal of these systems is often to help users track their behavior in such a way that patterns will emerge to help them make better decisions concerning their activities and health related behaviors. One way to focus model evaluation on this more user-centred goal is to go beyond the simple binary treatment of errors and consider more graded measurements such as prediction likelihoods for individual users and corresponding confidence measures. These metrics can serve a dual purpose which is to provide more detail about model performance and to provide more clarity to the users about how or why a given model prediction may be off.

It's also important to go beyond a single aggregate measure of performance and think carefully about the distribution of performance scores and how a given model affects individuals or groups of users. As an example, consider two models with similar accuracies - the first with an overall accuracy of 80% and the second with an overall accuracy of 70%. The first model may seem the easy choice based on aggregate performance. However, if the distribution in the first model is unimodal and falls within a narrow range (e.g., [77–83%]), and the second model is bi-modal with two narrow ranges (e.g., [43–47%] and [93–97%]), the decision becomes much more complex. Other aspects of the performance distribution may also affect what is considered "the best" model depending on the user goals. Should researchers pick the model that does the best (on average) for everyone or one that ensures the worst performance for an individual is still above a certain threshold? The correct answer to such questions requires looking closely at the distribution and likely depends on the particular application and the user's intended goals and tasks. Once the technology moves beyond proving that an algorithm is capable of learning the target concept to proving that it can help humans improve their health, errors become more complex than a simple binary construct of correct or incorrect and optimisation isn't as simple as choosing the best aggregate performance measure.

User Expectations and Perceptions of Errors

In addition to the ways in which we measure errors and consider model performance, it's also important to consider users' expectations and their perception of errors when using activity tracking systems. Users begin forming their expectations from activity tracking systems with marketing and advertisement materials such as Fitbit's slogan "Every Beat Counts" and as a result they often initially expect near perfect accuracy. As soon as users begin interacting with their activity trackers, they begin developing a mental model of the underlying algorithm formed by both correct predictions and errors [10, 23, 27]. These errors do not immediately cause users to abandon their activity trackers; instead, users take this to be a limit of the technology's capabilities and consider new behaviours or workarounds, which allow them to continue getting value from the activity tracker. One example of a workaround comes from a participant in Harrison et al.'s interview study [10], *"I was trying to figure out where I could put my Fitbit to get what I thought was a good amount of steps. I was yknow, putting it in my sock, putting it in my pants pocket, tying it to the cuff of my pants [...] I was also pedalling backwards whilst going down hills"*.

Users also test their understanding of the system by trying to replicate correct and incorrect predictions which should align with their understanding of the boundaries of the model [23, 27]. When the performance of the system continues to violate expectations that it will perform consistently, as advertised, or as designed, users begin disengaging from the system until they eventually abandon it [27]. Another way to think of this is that each violation of expectation erodes the trustworthiness of the model. As previously alluded to, one way to help the users set better expectations is to provide them with richer details regarding the predictions and model confidence – a design decision that involves consideration of technical components such as model selection. These details can provide greater model transparency that help the user to understand what they can and cannot expect from their activity trackers.

User expectations and experiences are also highly variable. Variations in individual lifestyle, physical characteristics and values for the tracked information can lead users to different conclusions about whether the accuracy of the activity tracker is adequate for them to derive meaningful use from it. A common conclusion users make when they encounter errors is that the system was designed for someone else. This point is well captured by an interviewee from Yang et al.'s study [27]: *"The [FitBit] Flex does not count steps if you are pushing a stroller or cart. This may not be an issue to some, but it is to me b/c I have stroller age children. Then I noticed it was logging hundreds of steps while I was rocking my baby. Maybe something else out there will be more accurate for my lifestyle.*" In such cases, the ability of a model to learn personal idiosyncrasies or adequately present the likelihood of being correct or incorrect is likely to be an important evaluation criteria.

The Burden of Interaction or the Benefit of Engagement?

Up until this point in the chapter, we have mainly discussed the challenges that errors present. However, some researchers argue that engagement with errors may actually be beneficial for the end-users of activity tracking systems [7]. An original vision of many ubiquitous computing technologies, such as activity tracking, focused on ways to make the technology fade into the background, helping the user to increase focus on the task at hand and decrease focus on the tool designed to help with that task. To achieve this, research has pushed the boundary of what we can infer automatically about user context from passively collected sensor data using machine learning and artificial intelligence. In the initial vision of ubiquitous computing environments, this is referred to as a *seamless design* approach in which particular technical nuances of a tool (or model) are made invisible to the user [25]. In [17], we see this design philosophy in action as the authors recommend a fully-automated approach to the personalisation of an activity recognition model (semi-supervised learning) over a semi-automated and interactive approach (active learning), even though model performances were comparable stating that it would be too burdensome for the user to interact with such a system.

Other researchers [10, 23, 27] have argued that the way in which users fail to develop a working understanding of the underlying algorithms, and the way in which users attempt to find workarounds that make the system more useful, imply that the design of activity tracking systems should make the underlying model more visible and include more interactive features that allow the user to calibrate the system to their personal idiosyncrasies and requirements. Choe et al. [7] state that fully automated tracking is not only difficult (or impossible) to achieve in some scenarios, it ignores the potential for synergies between the user's goal (understand and change health related behaviour) and the goal of the activity recognition model (accurately predict the appropriate activity label from the user's smartphone motion sensors). In contrast to seamless design approaches, *seamful design* has been proposed as a design philosophy which aims to strategically build "seams" into the user interface. These seams represent aspects of the model that the user can utilise to get a better sense of the underlying algorithms. Activity trackers employing seamless design can fail silently such that the user has no way of knowing that the knowledge generated by the system is no longer valid until it becomes evident when the output displayed is outside the boundaries of the user's expectations. While seamful design complicates the design and interaction process, it has the potential to make errors more visible making the limitations of the system salient such that corrections can be easily made to the tracked information. These additional opportunities for awareness and engagement are likely to have the positive side effect of continued use and lasting health change as observed by [19].

Seamful design of intelligent systems such as activity trackers requires a user-centred approach to *align the underlying mechanics* used to derive the "intelligence" of the system *with the user interface and experience*. In the next section, we'll discuss different algorithms that have been proposed for future activity tracking systems, how they are likely to affect the overall user experience and how we can better validate them with respect to the user experience before implementing the entire activity tracking system.

16.2.3   How Model Selection Affects the User Experience

To understand how seamful design may be achieved in activity recognition technologies, we discuss how the user experience research described in the previous section can help guide us in the research and development process at the stage of algorithm development and model selection. To help structure how to do this, we consider various facets of common usability and user-centred design principles in the context of model development and algorithm selection. Then, we describe the potential modelling approaches in terms of what they afford the design of the user interface and user experience.

User-Centred Design for Machine Learning

One of the goals of this chapter is to motivate and highlight a user-centred design process for developing ML-driven technology in which there is more of a focus on the final user experience at the earliest stages of research and development. We draw inspiration from the following principles of user-centred design as specified in the International Usability Standard, ISO 13407 and consider them in the context of model selection and algorithm design for activity tracking:

1. The design is based upon an explicit understanding of users, task and environments.
2. Users are involved throughout the design and development.
3. The design is driven and refined by user-centred evaluation.
4. The process is iterative.
5. The design addresses the whole user experience.
6. The design team includes multidisciplinary skills and perspectives.

These principles suggest a process by which we iteratively incorporate knowledge of and by the user into the design of the underlying learning algorithms and models. The first principle encourages an initiative to understand the user's relationship to the technology by answering questions like: *"Why will someone use this technology?"*, *"What will they use it for?"* and *"In what context will they use it?"*. For activity recognition, we can begin to answer these questions by drawing on research into how people use and abandon activity tracking systems as well as research on why tracking desirable and undesirable behavior is expected to have a positive impact on the user's health. The second principle aims to directly include feedback from the user during all stages of design and development. Doing this at the algorithm development and model selection stage is challenging, because these components are generally decoupled from the user interface. However, we can use knowledge of users, their tasks and their environment to develop user stories which can help direct the development of algorithm evaluation metrics such that they better reflect the expected model performance and user experience.[1] For example, one of the users we quoted in the previous section tells a story about how she feels that the activity tracker was not intended for someone like her because it demonstrated that it could not recognize the steps she took while pushing a baby stroller. This story should indicate to the algorithm developer that the model has likely learned to distinguish activities based on arm movement and that this arm movement is not always present in cases of everyday walking. By looking at model accuracy from the perspective of accuracy for an individual, we can begin to see how the model might address this aspect of the user experience.

16.3   Experiments in User-Centred Machine Learning for Activity Recognition

In this section, we describe how we can apply user-centred design principles to the algorithm design and model selection stage of development even when this stage is decoupled from the end user. Here, we demonstrate two experiments which were designed to help us refine the modelling approach from a more user-centred perspective. For each experiment, we first describe the expected effect each modelling approach will have on the user experience and what potential there is for seamful design. Then we define an evaluation algorithm which allows us to compare modelling approaches with respect to the expected individual model performance and user experience. To reflect the current research in activity recognition, which proposes individual models of activity rather than a single general impersonal model for all, the evaluation algorithms we define are designed so that we can analyse distributions of model performance as opposed to aggregate measures.

---

[1] In user-centred design, the term "user stories" refers to a set of scenarios (sometimes fictional) that best reflect common experiences of the target user in the context of their task and environment.

16.3.1   Experiment 1: Impersonal, Personal and Hybrid Models

For an activity tracking system to understand when a user is performing a particular activity, it must have some model of how the sensor data relates to that activity. Typically this model is constructed in a supervised approach where sensor data is collected in a controlled setting so that the ground truth label can be easily observed and recorded. The motivation for this approach is that by collecting data in the lab for many different people, the model might learn characteristics of the relationship between the sensor data and the activity that can be applied generally to data from new users who were not observed in the initial data collection process. In activity recognition, this is referred to as an *impersonal model*.

In contrast, *personal models* use only training data representing an individual end-user obtained through manual interaction. While personal models often perform with better accuracy than impersonal models, researchers are often reluctant to recommend the approach since the labelling task could be considered burdensome by the user [4]. Furthermore, the models can be brittle if the user hasn't labelled activity cases in varying contexts or environments. Personalised or *hybrid models* (sometimes called mixed models) have been proposed as a compromise in which the system is initially deployed with an impersonal model that becomes increasingly personalised by incorporating observations of new data that better represent the end-user.

The *impersonal*, *personal* and *hybrid* modelling approaches each present different possibilities for the user interaction design. Since impersonal models are the current commercial standard, use by consumers of the commercial product can be studied to understand how impersonal models affect the user experience [10, 23, 27]. From this research, we can expect that users are reasoning about errors in ways that make it difficult for them to apply the information from activity tracking systems. Increasing the sophistication of the learning algorithm may increase prediction accuracy from a traditional validation perspective, but this does not necessarily result in a better understanding of personal health behaviour that can be used to make better health decisions.[2] Alternatively, most personal and hybrid modelling approaches require that the user manually label recorded activity data. This could take place in an initial calibration phase or as an ongoing and dynamic process integrated with user interface features that are designed for the continued engagement and awareness that leads to better health outcomes as described by [7]. In experiment 1, we aim to recreate the experiment described in [15] and extend the analysis to achieve the following:

---

[2]There are also reasons to believe that there may be a ceiling to the accuracy of impersonal model performance. Yang et al. suggest that one barrier to better impersonal model accuracy is inherent in the translation of medical grade tracking equipment to the consumer market which prioritises ergonomics, size, fashionability and many other factors over accuracy [27]. Lockhart et al. suggest that as the number of individuals represented in the impersonal training dataset approaches 200, the increased accuracy gained from each individual decreases and plateaus around 85% accuracy [15].

1. Understand the distribution of expected model performance for individuals represented in the dataset instead of a single aggregate measure of model performance.
2. Compare the expected benefits (increased model performance) and expected burden (increased user interaction) exhibited by either a personal or hybrid model.

A User-Centred Validation Pipeline for Experiment 1

Algorithm 1 User-Centred Validation for Experiment 1

```
Let D be all the labelled activity recognition data
    we have available to study
D_personal will represent the subset of data representing a user, u

for all u in the set of users in D
    Let D_personal be all data in D where D_personal == u
    Let D_impersonal be all data in D where D_personal != u

    Let T_personal be the subset of D_personal
        which was sampled through some sampling function,
        s(D_personal) for training the personal model

    Let T_impersonal = D_impersonal to use all
        available impersonal data

    Let T_hybrid be the training set which combines data from both
        T_personal and T_impersonal by joining the sets
        through some function j(personal, impersonal)

    Let V_personal be the subset of D_personal
        which was sampled through some sampling function,
        s(D_personal) for testing or validating all models

    Let θ_personal be the model trained on T_personal
    Let θ_impersonal be the model trained on T_impersonal
    Let θ_hybrid be the model trained on T_hybrid

    Make predictions on V_personal using θ_personal and record for analysis.
    Make predictions on V_personal using θ_impersonal and record for analysis.
    Make predictions on V_personal using θ_hybrid and record for analysis.
```

Algorithm 1 begins by iterating through a set of validation users. This set of validation users can be the same as the training set as long as the user is held out as would be done in a leave-one-user-out validation process. For each iteration, we separate the personal data, $D_{personal}$, from the impersonal data, $D_{impersonal}$. $D_{personal}$ is then sampled through some sampling function, $s(D_{personal})$, to create independent training, $T_{personal}$ and validation, $V_{personal}$ datasets. To put a user-centred perspective on this, $T_{personal}$ is attempting to represent the data that the user might have labelled during an initial calibration phase while T_{hybrid} is attempting to represent the data

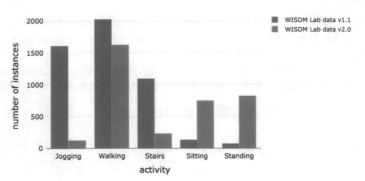

Fig. 16.1 This figure represents the number of labels of each activity class we have in each WISDM dataset

that the user might have labelled during an ongoing data collection interaction. The sampling function, $s(D_{personal})$, should be a representation of the process by which the user discloses the label for a particular activity. A first validation approach might use a random sampling function to approximate which personal training instances get disclosed. Using the validation pipeline with enough iterations to generate stable metrics for a stochastic process like random sampling, we can start to approximate how the model building process affects performance for various individuals.

To demonstrate the utility of our pipeline we use it to assess the importance of hybrid and personalised models as described by Lockhart and Weiss [15]. Specifically, we want to evaluate Lockhart and Weiss's idea that a model, $\theta_{personal}$ where the amount of personal data, $T_{personal}$, is much smaller than $T_{impersonal}$, is preferable to both, $\theta_{impersonal}$, and, θ_{hybrid}, when the sampling function, $s(D_{personal})$, is a function that samples at random and tries to preserve the overall class distribution in $D_{personal}$. For this part of the experiment, we iterate on the sampling of the personal data, training of the models and testing on the validation sample four times and report the mean accuracy for each user (Figs 16.3, 16.4 and 16.5).

The Data and Modelling Approach

We use publicly available datasets by WISDM lab (Wireless Sensor Data Mining) to perform our analysis. The first dataset, v1.1, represents a study in which data was labelled by asking participants to perform various activities with a smartphone in their front pocket recording all movement with a tri-axial accelerometer sampling at 20 hertz [12]. In this study, the data were labelled by a research assistant while the participant performed the activity. The second dataset, v2.0, represents a study in which a modestly interactive system called ActiTracker was developed to allow users to label their activity data in the wild using pre-determined activity labels [16, 26] in order to create personalised activity recognition models. Fig. 16.1 shows the distribution of labels for each class by dataset. WISDM v1.1 includes 35 users who have labelled more than one activity type while v2.0 includes 25. For more information on the WISDM datasets we used refer to [15, 16, 26].

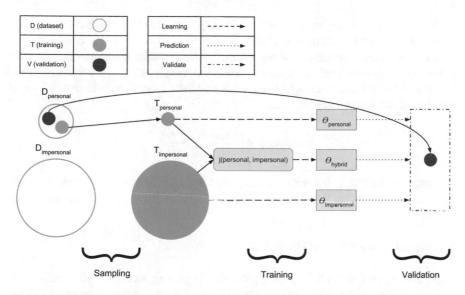

Fig. 16.2 This figure visualises the sampling, training and validation process

In the development of activity tracker systems, we need to consider how developers should go about curating the data for the impersonal dataset (Figs. 16.1 and 16.2). Many context-aware systems will do this by paying participants to perform the activities in a setting where the ground truth activity can be easily labelled with the intention of using the model trained on the data from an initial set of paid users to provide a working model for the first set of unpaid users. We reflect this in these experiments by using the WISDM v1.1 dataset as the impersonal dataset while iterating through v2.0 as the personal dataset. While both datasets included the activities "jogging", "walking", "sitting", "standing" and "stairs", the v1.1 dataset differentiated "stairs" into "up stairs" and "down stairs", while the v2.0 dataset included a "lying down" activity label. To resolve these differences, we removed the instances labelled with "lying down" from the v2.0 dataset and consolidated the "up stairs" and "down stairs" classes into a "stairs" class similar to the first dataset. The final class distribution for each dataset can be seen in Fig. 16.1.

To best replicate the work of Lockhart and Weiss, we used the Random Forest classifier as implemented in the Scikit Learn module for machine learning in Python [20]. For all the experiments presented in this paper, we use the parameters described in [15] unless stated otherwise. However, Random Forest models randomly sample the training instances to create simple decision trees (shallower depth, fewer features to consider at each split) and then average the results to maximise predictive accuracy while mitigating over-fitting. This means that the predictions can be inconsistent with the exact same input data. To ensure more consistent results we use 1000 decision trees or more.

In assessing accuracy we take our modelling process to be a multi-class classification task in which each label is assumed to be mutually exclusive. To validate the expected prediction accuracy for each user, we simply take the number of prediction errors, e, from a model on a user's validation sample, $V_{personal}$, subtract it from the size of the validation sample $|V_{personal}|$, and finally normalize the result by the number of validation samples.

$$accuracy = \frac{|V_{personal}| - e}{|V_{personal}|}$$

Since the sampling for both $V_{personal}$ and $T_{personal}$ is randomly sampled with replacement, we repeat the modelling process 10 times for each user and report the mean.

Experiment 1 Results and Discussion

Figures 16.3, 16.4 and 16.5 are box plots that represent the distribution of model accuracies among different users on the y-axis and the number of personal training samples along the x-axis. The red, blue and green boxes represent the impersonal, personal and hybrid models respectively with dots representing mean accuracy across random sampling iterations for each user. Similar to Lockhart and Weiss, Fig. 16.3 shows that the impersonal model has the lowest accuracy in nearly all scenarios. A closer look on an individual basis reveals that the user receiving the best performance is at 79% accuracy, while the modal user performance is 45% and the worst individual performance is at 3%. The hybrid and personal models each considerably outperform the impersonal model even with only 5 samples from the end-user's labelled data

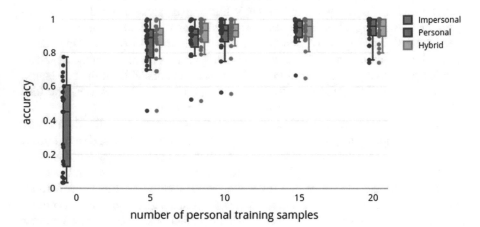

Fig. 16.3 These box plots represent the distribution of accuracy measurements across participants given a Random Forest Classifier, when trained with an impersonal, personal and hybrid dataset

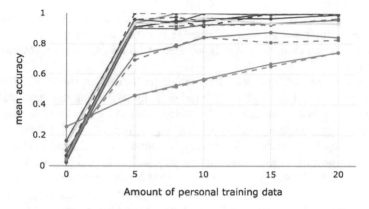

Fig. 16.4 Similar to Fig. 16.3 this plot highlights those whose expected impersonal accuracies were lowest and shows how this accuracy progresses as we increase the number of personal training samples for a particular user. The solid lines represents the personal model and the dashed lines represents the hybrid model. Each color represents a different user

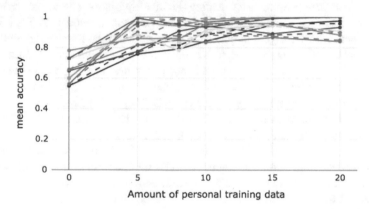

Fig. 16.5 Similar to Fig. 16.4 but with those whose expected impersonal accuracies were highest. The solid lines represents the personal model and the dashed lines represents the hybrid model. Each color represents a different user

with which to use for training. With each sample being equivalent to 10 s of activity being labelled, 5 samples equates to 50 s of labelled activity.

In comparing the personal and hybrid models, we see some differences when the model is trained with 5 or 8 personal samples with a higher inner quartile range for the hybrid model in both cases and a tighter inner quartile range (85–95%) for the hybrid model with only 5 training samples. However, what differences there might be between the personal and hybrid models appear to go away as the number of samples increases beyond 10. This translates to approximately 100 s of user labelling – which may or may not be burdensome for the user depending on the overall fitness level and demographic characteristics of the users. For example, a minute and a half of jogging for a relatively fit undergraduate student may not be very burdensome at all. However, the same amount of required labelling activity may be excessively burdensome for an older adult that is not used to exercising and is recovering from knee surgery.

The distribution *within* a modelling technique is another aspect of model performance that should be explored. By individually evaluating the expected model performance for users, we can see that there seem to be two clusters concerning impersonal model accuracy with one achieving higher than 40% accuracy and the other achieving lower than 25% accuracy. To understand how individuals in each of these groups may benefit from either a personal or hybrid model, we highlight the eight individuals who get the worst expected performance from the impersonal model in Fig. 16.4 and the eight individuals who get the best performance from the impersonal model in Fig. 16.5. In Fig. 16.4 we can see that seven out of these eight participants would have found that the model is nearly always incorrect. We also see that whether we incorporate impersonal data or not (i.e., creating a hybrid or personal model), the accuracy of a model quickly exceeds 90% for all but two users with only 5 labelled instances from the user making the labelling indispensable for those who would have had terrible performance using the impersonal model. In Fig. 16.5, we find that users who were getting better performance with the impersonal model will likely get less of an increase in performance as they label their activity data.

Often when we discuss the potential benefit of hybrid models, it is in the context of reducing the burden of labelling. In our experiment, we do not observe evidence that hybrid models substantially reduce the labelling effort presented by personal models which would present itself in Figs. 16.4 and 16.5 as a datapoint higher than its counterpart of the same colour on the dashed line.

To quantify the concepts of "burden" and "benefit" for the purpose of algorithm optimisation, we might consider "benefit" to be the increase in model performance and "burden" to be the amount of additional interaction or labelled instances required. This "benefit-to-burden" ratio for a particular personal or hybrid model should help us make decisions at the level of algorithm design with a user-centred perspective. It is important to note that "burden" and "benefit" as we define them here are not fully representative of how these concepts play out in the user experience. As we mentioned in Sect. 16.2.2, these interactions can help the user achieve the goal of changing their health related behaviour. Rather we make this naïve reduction in order to present a tractable algorithm optimisation metric to aid the algorithm design process. To fully understand the dynamic between burdensome and beneficial interactions in intelligent systems, additional user experience research is required with working prototypes in the context of a final user interface and interaction design. Furthermore, richer aspects of burden (e.g., those that account for physical exertion as it relates to the intended user population and demographics) could be integrated into a notion or measure of burden in a way that better matches the user experience goals of the system.

16.3.2 Experiment 2: Model Confidence for Seamful Design and Model Personalisation

Seamful design, as described in Sect. 16.2, requires that appropriate affordances of the underlying algorithms and models are identified as a potential "seam". This means that there exists the possibility for a user interface design which exposes this aspect of the model such that it can be appropriated by the user for their task without the need for expert technical knowledge of the system. In experiment 1, we see that a small amount of labelled personal data yields a great improvement in model performance compared to impersonal models when these labels are chosen at random. However, users are likely not choosing which moments to label at random. From [27] we see that users typically begin thinking about interactions which will improve the model performance when they observe errors in the system. In experiment 2, we aim to demonstrate a way in which model confidence, the model's ability to assess the likelihood that its prediction is correct, can help guide both the user's understanding of the system and the user's manual tracking behaviour. Specifically, we design experiment 2 with the following objectives:

1. To understand the potential for model confidence to be used in the seamful design of activity tracking.
2. To understand the potential for model confidence to aid model personalisation through either an active learning or semi-supervised learning approach.

In integrating the concept of seamful design to algorithm evaluation, we can draw insight from work by Chalmers et al. that has explored seamful design in the context of presentation approaches to model certainty along the following facets [5, 6]:

- *optimistic*: show everything as if it were correct.
- *pessimistic*: show everything that is known to be correct.
- *cautious*: explicitly present uncertainty.
- *opportunistic*: exploit uncertainty.

Currently available activity trackers use an *optimistic* approach to the presentation of model confidence. *Pessimistic* and *cautious* approaches can help users understand the limitations and strengths of the model. Additionally, these approaches can give the user a sense of moments when they should rely on their own accounting of their activity instead of the system's.

Opportunistic presentation of model confidence lends itself to a research topic within machine learning called *active learning* in which the system attempts to select unlabelled observations that would be most beneficial to model performance if they were to be labelled. We can think of this as selecting the samples which present the best benefit-to-burden ratio. One of the most common ways of deciding which sensor observations should be labelled is *least confident sampling*. In theory, least confident sampling helps the user to know which instances increase model performance the most by informing the user when the likelihood of predicting a sensor observation correctly is low. This is done by notifying the user of model

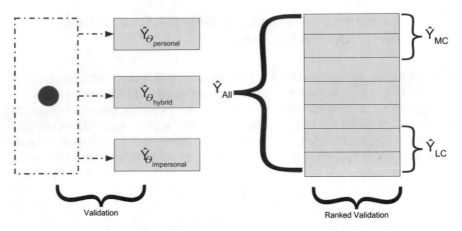

Fig. 16.6 This figure shows how the confidence ranked predictions are partitioned in order to best assess the model's ability to be accurate when considering its most confident (MC) and least confident (LC) predictions

confusion and a labelling opportunity. One point of caution in using least confident sampling is that a model that does not represent the target concept (activity) well can have the unintended consequence of performing worse than it would have using random sampling. This can happen when the model has not learned the target concept well enough to accurately assess the confidence of its predictions. A bad model can steer the active sampling procedure away from the kinds of observations which are likely to be wrong (i.e., the observations we assume will improve the model the most), because the model is overconfident. From an information retrieval point of view, this means that the model should have high recall with regard to selecting which instances it will likely get wrong in order to address the areas of the feature space which result in the most confusion for the model. For more information on theory and application of active learning, we recommend reading [21].

Semi-supervised learning approaches can also leverage model confidence, but they do not explicitly lend themselves to interactivity. The *self-training* algorithm uses an initial model learned using all available labelled data to make predictions on the unlabelled data. The predicted labels of instances with the highest prediction confidence, or likelihood of having a correct prediction, are assumed to be equivalent to ground truth. In theory, incorporating these observations and their predicted labels into the training set and retraining the model will yield higher model performance. With this approach, it is not the recall of the selected samples that matters, but rather the precision. Incorrect predictions will "pollute" the training set if selected. For more information on the theory and application of semi-supervised learning methods we suggest [29]. One potential caveat of using this approach in activity recognition is that each self-training iteration is likely to result in new model behaviours where the patterns of correct and incorrect predictions that the user has come to expect may no longer be valid (Fig. 16.6).

User-Centred Validation Algorithm for Experiment 2

We can modify the validation algorithm in experiment 1 to better understand how we might leverage model confidence for the benefit of an activity recognition system. In algorithm 2, we specifically seek to analyse accuracy across users, among a model's 30 most confident (MC) predictions and 30 least confident (LC) predictions in order to help us make system and user interaction design decisions with regard to active learning, semi-supervised learning, or seamful design approaches.

The purpose of algorithm 2 is to help us understand the expected quality of model confidence for each user using either a personal, hybrid, or impersonal model. Algorithm 2 differs from algorithm 1 in two ways. First, with each user, all data that is not part of the personal training set, $D_{personal}$, is added to a pool of unlabelled personal data, $U_{personal}$. We then record predictions and their respective model confidence on all observations in the $U_{personal}$ dataset with the impersonal, personal and hybrid models. The second difference is that the predictions are now ordered from most confident to least confident predictions. Model confidence in the SciKit-Learn python module is calculated as the mean predicted class probabilities of all decision trees in the forest. For each decision tree, the class probability is the fraction of samples of the same class in a leaf [20].[3] We can think of model confidence as a rough approximation of the probability that our prediction is true or $p(\hat{y} = y)$ where $\hat{y}$ is our activity prediction and y is the actual activity label. With the confidence ranked predictions for a user's unlabelled data, $\hat{Y}_{\theta,user} = \text{argsort}_y\, p(\hat{y} = y)$, we can now assess accuracy with respect to seamful designs which emphasise predictions that are most likely to be correct, $\hat{Y}_{MC} = (y_0, \ldots, y_i)$ (pessimistic presentation) or seamful designs which emphasise predictions that are most likely to be incorrect, $\hat{Y}_{LC} = (y_{n-j}, \ldots, y_n)$ (cautious or opportunistic presentation). Here, i is the cutoff in the confidence ranked predictions where predictions indexed greater than i are no longer trusted to be correct and j is the index where all values indexed greater than j represent the least confident samples that we are interested in evaluating.[4]

Experiment 2: Results and Discussion

In Fig. 16.7, we see that the inner quartile range and mode for accuracy of all models across users shifts upward when we select only the 30 most confident examples and downward for the 30 least confident predictions for each user. As seen in the top panel of Fig. 16.7 while the modal accuracy for the impersonal model shifts up to 83% from 45%, there are still many cases of poor accuracy among these most confident predictions. When considering the results in the context of a pessimistic

---

[3]The way in which model confidence is assessed can vary in many ways. It can vary depending on how we determine class probability from the model. For example, a K-nearest neighbors algorithm might assess confidence as the average distance to the neighbors of a new observation while an SVM approach might assess confidence as the distance from a new observation to the hyperplane used to separate classes. Model confidence can vary depending on utility functions as described in the second chapter of [21]. It can also vary depending on whether or not evidence is taken into account [22].

[4]In our experiment we take $i = j = 30$ for ease of comparison and exposition, but in practice these cutoff points can vary and be optimised for recall or precision as mentioned earlier in this section.

Algorithm 2 User-Centred Validation Pipeline for Model Confidence in Activity Recognition

---

```
Let D be all the labelled activity recognition data
    we have available to study
Dpersonal will represent the subset of data representing a user, u

for all u in the set of users in D
    Let Dpersonal be all data in D where Dpersonal == u
    Let Dimpersonal be all data in D where Dpersonal != u

    Let Tpersonal be the subset of Dpersonal
        which was sampled through some sampling function,
        s(Dpersonal)

    Let Upersonal be the subset of Dpersonal
        where all x in Upersonal is not in Tpersonal to serve as
        the unlabelled dataset.

    Let Thybrid be the training set which combines data from both
        Tpersonal and Timpersonal by joining the sets
        through some function j(personal, impersonal)

    Let θpersonal be the model trained on Tpersonal
    Let θhybrid be the model trained on Thybrid
    Let θimpersonal be the model trained on Timpersonal

    Using θpersonal record predictions ranked by model confidence,
        Ŷθpersonal,user for each instance in Upersonal.
    Using θhybrid record predictions ranked by model confidence,
        Ŷθhybrid,user for each instance in Upersonal.
    Using θimpersonal record predictions ranked by model confidence,
        Ŷθimpersonal,user for each instance in Upersonal.
```

---

seamful design where we use impersonal model confidence as a way of signaling to the user when they should trust the system, some users will likely benefit, but many others will still find incorrect predictions among even the most confident examples. A self-training approach can also yield poor results considering that many (sometimes all) of the most confident predictions are incorrect for a user. Selecting only the least confident examples, as a system might do in an active learning approach, or to highlight moments of system confusion in a cautious seamful design approach, appears to yield mostly instances which are likely to be wrong, but it is difficult to resolve this with the overall likelihood of the model to make mistakes.

Table 16.1 focuses on likely experiences for individual users and shows those who get the least accuracy from the 30 least confident predictions each model makes. The users represented in rows 1, 4 and 5 of the impersonal model do not get any reasonable accuracy overall or within the most confident examples meaning that the low accuracy

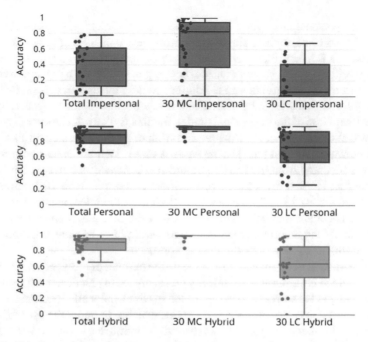

Fig. 16.7 This figure shows model accuracy for impersonal (top), personal (middle) and hybrid (bottom) approaches when we select only 30 most confident (MC) or 30 least confident (LC) and compare them to the model's overall accuracy. Similar to previous graphs, each data point represents a single user. The hybrid and personal models were each trained using 5 personal samples using the same sampling function described in experiment 1

Table 16.1 Impersonal, personal and hybrid model accuracies for all predictions, 30 most confident (MC) predictions and 30 least confident (LC) predictions, among the 5 who received the worst accuracy from the least confident predictions of that particular model

Impersonal			Personal			Hybrid		
All	30 MC	30 LC	All	30 MC	30 LC	All	30 MC	30 LC
0.00	0.00	0.00	0.66	1.00	0.26	0.94	1.00	0.00
0.45	0.82	0.00	0.50	0.80	0.29	0.66	1.00	0.20
0.55	1.00	0.00	0.69	1.00	0.36	0.79	0.99	0.21
0.027	0.50	0.00	0.74	1.00	0.38	0.49	0.83	0.27
0.14	0.20	0.00	0.71	0.86	0.50	0.93	1.00	0.47

is likely due to the model's inability to generalize to this user. However, those users represented in rows 2 and 3 can at least benefit from self-training or by integrating model confidence as pessimistic or cautious seamful design. With a user-centred perspective, we can further explore the cases that stand out to understand whether there is potential for a system design that can at least provide model confidence before requiring manual input from the user.

For both personal and hybrid models, the most confident predictions are highly accurate across users, with no single user getting less than 80% accuracy from these predictions. This means that after a user has done about 50 s of activity labelling, an activity tracking system should consider leveraging self-training to improve accuracy or pessimistic seamful design techniques to help the user understand when the inferred information is most reliable. The least certain examples are generally more accurate than those of the impersonal model, but this is likely due to overall accuracy of the model meaning that even the least confident predictions are still likely to be correct. However, this isn't always the case. A closer look at the user who received the lowest accuracy from the least confident predictions of the hybrid model (also represented in the first row of the hybrid model column in Table 16.1) reveals that this user also received 100% accuracy from their most confident predictions and that overall the accuracy was 94%. This means that the 30 least confident predictions represent all of the incorrect predictions and would have been very helpful for an active learning or cautious seamful design approach.

It's important to note that we chose 30 to be the number of most and least confident examples somewhat arbitrarily to simplify our analysis. In practice, these models will need to be adapted to a stream-based approach in which unlabelled personal instances are observed one-by-one and a decision about whether to query the user for a label will need to be made before the user becomes unaware of exactly what activity they were doing during the 10-second window of time that the unlabelled instance represents. The pool based approach we demonstrate here is representative of some of the earlier approaches to understanding whether active learning is theoretically possible in an activity tracking system [3, 14, 17, 24].

16.4 Discussion

User-centred evaluation has long been a central component of user interface and user experience design. Intelligent systems which aim to provide users with new information that can be used to make better decisions rely on complex and sophisticated machine learning algorithms. These algorithms need to observe human behaviour in order to model it, making them inherently dependent on the human experience even though the algorithms themselves do not directly face the user. To evaluate an algorithm in machine learning, we often have to reduce the expected context of the system (many users with many different and unique styles of activity behaviour) to a problem which is easier to evaluate and optimise. We believe user-centred evaluation can be integrated into the algorithm design process by adapting principles from the International Usability Standard as stated in Sect. 16.2.3 and illustrated in experiments 1 and 2.

During the stage of system development concerning the learning algorithm and a model representation of activity, we can incorporate an understanding of the users, their goals and tasks and their environments to show that not only can the concept of activity be learned using machine learning algorithms, but that the technology can help users in achieving their broader goals that stem from activity tracking. To help guide our understanding of the design challenges facing the development of activity tracking technology, we studied the research regarding current commercial activity trackers from the user perspective. Researchers observe that people have varying motivations for using the technology including maintaining a healthy exercise routine or finding opportunities to build better health habits [10, 23, 27]. Similarly, user lifestyles range from amateur athletes looking to challenge themselves to recent mothers who may be pushing a stroller while exercising. When the users begin to witness the first incorrect predictions, their task shifts from leveraging tracked information to testing the boundaries of the system's capabilities by creating ad-hoc folk tests [27]. These prior studies provide detailed insight into the way users interact with the technology, their purpose for interacting with the technology and the context and environments in which they employ it to best understand the appropriateness of an approach.

This enriched understanding of variability in users guided our development of an extension to a standard leave-one-user-out algorithm that allows us to better understand the variability in user experience from the model perspective. In experiment 1, we saw that users of a system with an impersonal model fall into one of two clusters: one which experiences less than 25% accuracy and one which experiences between 45 and 79% accuracy. With uniform probability across five potential activity classes, the former group will experience performance that is, at best, slightly better than a random guess. These users have the highest benefit-to-burden ratio - meaning that they have the most to gain from their labelling interactions with the system. For the latter group, the model performs better than chance meaning that while it may have learned something about activity as it relates to these users, they will frequently experience incorrect predictions making it difficult for them to utilise the information to make decisions regarding their health. These users will still have a positive benefit-to-burden ratio, but will experience lower gains for each label contributed than users in the first group. In experiment 2, when we look at the group of users with the lowest accuracy in the set of the least confident predictions, we can see two users with 45 and 55% overall impersonal model accuracy who get 82 and 100% accuracy among the 30 most confident predictions made by the model. What this means is that while the impersonal model may present a low benefit-to-burden ratio for a labelling interaction for some users, it can leverage model confidence to lower burden or increase benefit. For example, this model can lower burden by using the self-training algorithm which is likely to increase model accuracy making manual interaction less necessary or increase benefit by leveraging seamful design approaches like the pessimistic presentation of model confidence which fosters greater understanding of the model's behaviour in the user. By simply validating with respect to individual users we can derive much greater insight at the level of algorithm design than we can when validation is agnostic to the individual users who are represented in the test data.

A better understanding of users also helps to address the whole user experience (the third usability standards principle) while making decisions about the underlying algorithmic components of the system. Impersonal models have not only shown that they provide suboptimal accuracy, they also lack the interactivity that users need to calibrate the model to their personal needs, test their understanding of the model's behaviours, and foster the engagement and awareness of tracked information that help users to make better health decisions. These interactive capabilities can be thought of in the context of a calibration phase or in the context of ongoing manual intervention. An initial calibration phase is a necessity of a personal model and would set the expectation that the system will likely not understand scenarios where the user has not provided examples. A hybrid model may also require an initial calibration phase though there is the possibility that for some people the model is at least modestly capable of making predictions without it. Continued model personalisation that leverages model confidence could "unlock" after the system has reason to believe that the model will perform at least adequately for the user. For example, the data labelled during the calibration phase could first be used as a personal test set. If the model fails to meet a certain threshold of accuracy for the calibration data, then the data can be incorporated into the training set so that the model can be retrained and a notification for new calibration data can be made randomly at some point in the near future. If the model exceeds a threshold for accuracy in predicting the calibration data, then the model confidence features can be unlocked since it can at least be confident in its ability to select observations that it is likely to predict correctly or incorrectly.

16.5 Future Directions

While we know that users are interested in interactive design components, designing interactions and interfaces for intelligent systems is complicated by the behaviour of the underlying model given the way it handles input from varying users. Furthermore, dynamic models, such as those used in model personalisation which continue to learn after being deployed to the user, will learn new discriminative patterns over time. How users will feel about this learning process remains an open question that will be difficult yet important to study empirically. Patterns of model behaviour that the user noticed early in their use of the system may no longer hold after the model further adapts to the user's personal behaviour. Studies of intelligent user interfaces have shown how interactive features allowing the user to do things like roll back model changes can give the user the level of control they need to maintain a reasonably working system [11].

From a modelling perspective, we know that physical activity tends to be fairly consistent over short periods of time meaning that the likelihood of walking at time, t, is heavily dependent on whether we were walking at time $t - 1$. Much of the research that we cite and conduct in this paper does not take this into consideration and this is mostly because of the added level of complication it adds to analysis. That said, it is an important aspect of activity recognition that should be studied in context with model personalisation and interactive approaches to activity tracking system design.

[1, 2, 18] are examples of research that we know of in activity recognition that are studying active learning in a stream-based temporal context.[5]

To address the shortcomings of impersonal models, some researchers are studying the "population diversity" problem in which impersonal datasets can include a wide variety of activity behaviour, much of which is irrelevant to the activity behaviour of many individual users. With a better understanding of the *population diversity* of impersonal datasets and how the data can better complement personal data, we may be able to better utilise the impersonal data when combining it with personal data for a hybrid model. For example, [13] have devised methods for comparing an individual end-user's data to the individuals in the impersonal dataset in an effort to filter other users who have data which is likely to be beneficial to the end-user's hybrid model. [9] aim to address population diversity by combining the instances of a particular class from the impersonal and personal datasets which were found to be similar through a clustering approach. This can also be thought of as a transfer learning task in which some of the knowledge learned from training a model on impersonal data (e.g., clusterings of which users have similar activity behaviors can be *transferred* to a *personal* model). Future work should consider using neural network algorithms for transfer learning which learn lower level features that are more likely to generalise accurately to new users in a transfer learning task [28]. For a comprehensive survey of transfer learning research in the activity recognition space refer to [8].

Additionally, we can expect a kind of "concept drift" where activity behaviour changes either suddenly due to injury or slowly due to aging causing the discriminatory patterns learned by the model at one point in time to lose its predictive accuracy. Whether adaptive modelling approaches alleviate or exacerbate this effect is an open question. Future work should seek to apply user-centred evaluation to understand how models of activity recognition which are adaptive, temporal and stream-based could be used in interactive and seamfully designed activity tracker systems and how they will behave over extended periods of time.

16.6   Conclusion

Designing intelligent systems often begins with the most novel component, the learning algorithm, independent from other components like the user interface. As a result, the objective when optimising the algorithm (e.g., to minimise errors as much as possible) is often misaligned with the user's goal (e.g., to understand patterns in active behaviour in the case of activity trackers). We demonstrate how user experience research can help inform model optimisation and selection so that evaluation processes which are more user-centred can be developed and integrated into the development process. These user-centred evaluation methods can highlight problematic patterns which help with selecting a model which addresses the whole user experi-

---

[5]The temporal component also introduces the added complexities addressed by the online learning and incremental learning research within machine learning.

ence. User-centred evaluation can also highlight opportunities for seamful design. Using this process we found impersonal models for activity recognition to be problematic because they present poor model accuracy (<25%) for many and mediocre model accuracy (45–79%) for the rest. Additionally, we define a benefit-to-burden ratio metric as the ratio of the amount of expected benefit to the user and their system (mostly, but not exclusively with respect to model performance) to the amount of expected burden to the user (mostly, but not exclusively with respect to the amount of interaction). Using this, we find that most models for activity recognition (based on random forest regression trees) which perform with better than 45% accuracy are capable of leveraging model confidence, appear capable of selecting predictions which are likely to be incorrect and predictions which are likely to be correct. This representation of model confidence can be leveraged for model personalisation approaches such as self-training and active learning as well as seamful design features such as those that present predictions pessimistically (only those which are likely to be correct) or cautiously (only those which are likely to be incorrect).

References

1. Abdallah, Z.S., Gaber, M.M., Srinivasan, B., Krishnaswamy, S.: StreamAR: incremental and active learning with evolving sensory data for activity recognition. In: 2012 IEEE 24th International Conference on Tools with Artificial Intelligence, vol. 1, pp. 1163–1170 (2012)
2. Abdallah, Z.S., Gaber, M.M., Srinivasan, B., Krishnaswamy, S.: Adaptive mobile activity recognition system with evolving data streams. Neurocomputing **150**, 304–317 (2015)
3. Alemdar, H., van Kasteren, T., Ersoy, C.: Using active learning to allow activity recognition on a large scale. In: Ambient Intelligence, pp. 105–114 (2011)
4. Bao, L., Intille, S.: Activity recognition from user-annotated acceleration data. In: Pervasive Computing, pp. 1–17 (2004)
5. Chalmers, M.: Seamful design: showing the seams in wearable computing. In: Proceedings of IEE Eurowearable'03, vol. 2003, pp. 11–16. IEE (2003)
6. Chalmers, M., MacColl, I.: Seamful and seamless design in ubiquitous computing. In: Workshop at the Crossroads: The Interaction of HCI and Systems Issues in UbiComp, vol. 8 (2003)
7. Choe, E.K., Abdullah, S., Rabbi, M., Thomaz, E., Epstein, D.A., Cordeiro, F., Kay, M., Abowd, G.D., Choudhury, T., Fogarty, J., Lee, B., Matthews, M., Kientz, J.A.: Semi-automated tracking: a balanced approach for self-monitoring applications. IEEE Pervasive Comput. **16**(1), 74–84 (2017)
8. Cook, D., Feuz, K.D., Krishnan, N.C.: Transfer learning for activity recognition: a survey. Knowl. Inf. Syst. **36**(3), 537–556 (2013)
9. Garcia-Ceja, E., Brena, R.: Building personalized activity recognition models with scarce labeled data based on class similarities. Ubiquitous Computing and Ambient Intelligence. Sensing, Processing, and Using Environmental Information. Lecture Notes in Computer Science, pp. 265–276. Springer, Cham (2015)
10. Harrison, D., Marshall, P., Bianchi-Berthouze, N., Bird, J.: Activity tracking: barriers, workarounds and customisation. In: Proceedings of the 2015 ACM International Joint Conference on Pervasive and Ubiquitous Computing, UbiComp '15, pp. 617–621. New York, NY, USA (2015)
11. Kulesza, T., Burnett, M., Wong, W.K., Stumpf, S.: Principles of explanatory debugging to personalize interactive machine learning. In: Proceedings of the 20th International Conference on Intelligent User Interfaces, IUI '15, pp. 126–137. ACM Press, New York (2015)

12. Kwapisz, J.R., Weiss, G.M., Moore, S.A.: Activity recognition using cell phone accelerometers. ACM SigKDD Explor. Newsl. **12**(2), 74–82 (2011)
13. Lane, N.D., Xu, Y., Lu, H., Hu, S., Choudhury, T., Campbell, A.T., Zhao, F.: Enabling large-scale human activity inference on smartphones using community similarity networks (csn). In: Proceedings of the 13th International Conference on Ubiquitous Computing, pp. 355–364. ACM, New York (2011)
14. Liu, R., Chen, T., Huang, L.: Research on human activity recognition based on active learning. In: 2010 International Conference on Machine Learning and Cybernetics, vol. 1, pp. 285–290 (2010)
15. Lockhart, J.W., Weiss, G.M.: The benefits of personalized smartphone-based activity recognition models. In: Proceedings of the 2014 SIAM International Conference on Data Mining, pp. 614–622. SIAM (2014)
16. Lockhart, J.W., Weiss, G.M., Xue, J.C., Gallagher, S.T., Grosner, A.B., Pulickal, T.T.: Design considerations for the WISDM smart phone-based sensor mining architecture. In: Proceedings of the Fifth International Workshop on Knowledge Discovery from Sensor Data, pp. 25–33 (2011)
17. Longstaff, B., Reddy, S., Estrin, D.: Improving activity classification for health applications on mobile devices using active and semi-supervised learning. In: 2010 4th International Conference on Pervasive Computing Technologies for Healthcare, pp. 1–7 (2010)
18. Miu, T., Missier, P., Pltz, T.: Bootstrapping personalised human activity recognition models using online active learning. In: 2015 IEEE International Conference on Computer and Information Technology; Ubiquitous Computing and Communications; Dependable, Autonomic and Secure Computing; Pervasive Intelligence and Computing (CIT/IUCC/DASC/PICOM), pp. 1138–1147. IEEE (2015)
19. Patel, M.S., Asch, D.A., Volpp, K.G.: Wearable devices as facilitators, not drivers, of health behavior change. JAMA **313**(5), 459–460 (2015)
20. Pedregosa, F., Varoquaux, G., Gramfort, A., Michel, V., Thirion, B., Grisel, O., Blondel, M., Prettenhofer, P., Weiss, R., Dubourg, V., others: Scikit-learn: machine learning in Python. J. Mach. Learn. Res. **12**, 2825–2830 (2011)
21. Settles, B.: Active learning literature survey. University of Wisconsin, Madison, vol. 52(55–66), p. 11 (2010)
22. Sharma, M., Bilgic, M.: Evidence-based uncertainty sampling for active learning. Data Min. Knowl. Discov. **31**(1), 164–202 (2017)
23. Shih, P.C., Han, K., Poole, E.S., Rosson, M.B., Carroll, J.M.: Use and adoption challenges of wearable activity trackers. In: iConference 2015 Proceedings (2015)
24. Stikic, M., Van Laerhoven, K., Schiele, B.: Exploring semi-supervised and active learning for activity recognition. In: 12th IEEE International Symposium on Wearable Computers (ISWC2008), pp. 81–88 (2008)
25. Weiser, M.: Some computer science issues in ubiquitous computing. Commun. ACM **36**(7), 75–84 (1993)
26. Weiss, G.M., Lockhart, J.W.: The impact of personalization on smartphone-based activity recognition. In: AAAI Workshop on Activity Context Representation: Techniques and Languages, pp. 98–104 (2012)
27. Yang, R., Shin, E., Newman, M.W., Ackerman, M.S.: When fitness trackers don't 'fit': end-user difficulties in the assessment of personal tracking device accuracy. In: Proceedings of the 2015 ACM International Joint Conference on Pervasive and Ubiquitous Computing, UbiComp '15, pp. 623–634. New York, NY, USA (2015)
28. Yosinski, J., Clune, J., Bengio, Y., Lipson, H.: How transferable are features in deep neural networks? In: Advances in Neural Information Processing Systems, pp. 3320–3328 (2014)
29. Zhu, X., Goldberg, A.B.: Introduction to semi-supervised learning. Synth. Lect. Artif. Intell. Mach. Learn. **3**(1), 1–130 (2009)

Chapter 17
Evaluation of Interactive Machine Learning Systems

Nadia Boukhelifa, Anastasia Bezerianos and Evelyne Lutton

Abstract The evaluation of interactive machine learning systems remains a difficult task. These systems learn from and adapt to the human, but at the same time, the human receives feedback and adapts to the system. Getting a clear understanding of these subtle mechanisms of co-operation and co-adaptation is challenging. In this chapter, we report on our experience in designing and evaluating various interactive machine learning applications from different domains. We argue for coupling two types of validation: *algorithm-centred* analysis, to study the computational behaviour of the system; and *human-centred* evaluation, to observe the utility and effectiveness of the application for end-users. We use a visual analytics application for guided search, built using an interactive evolutionary approach, as an exemplar of our work. Our observation is that human-centred design and evaluation complement algorithmic analysis, and can play an important role in addressing the "black-box" effect of machine learning. Finally, we discuss research opportunities that require human-computer interaction methodologies, in order to support both the visible and hidden roles that humans play in interactive machine learning.

17.1 Introduction

In interactive Machine Learning (iML), a human operator and a machine collaborate to achieve a task, whether this is to classify or cluster a set of data points [1, 11], to find interesting data projections [5, 9, 13], or to design creative art works [36, 43]. The underlying assumption is that the human-machine co-operation yields better results than a fully automated or manual system. An interactive machine learning

N. Boukhelifa (✉) · E. Lutton
INRA, Université Paris-Saclay, 1 av. Brétignières, 78850 Thiverval-Grignon, France
e-mail: nadia.boukhelifa@inra.fr

E. Lutton
e-mail: evelyne.lutton@inra.fr

A. Bezerianos
Univ Paris-Sud, CNRS, INRIA, Université Paris-Saclay, Orsay 91405, France
e-mail: anab@lri.fr

© Springer International Publishing AG, part of Springer Nature 2018   341
J. Zhou and F. Chen (eds.), *Human and Machine Learning*, Human–Computer
Interaction Series, https://doi.org/10.1007/978-3-319-90403-0_17

system comprises an automated service, a user interface, and a learning component. A human interacts with the automated component via the user interface and provides iterative feedback to a learning algorithm. This feedback may be explicit or inferred from human behaviour and interactions. Likewise, the system may provide implicit or explicit feedback to communicate its status and the knowledge it has learnt.

The interactive approach to machine learning is appealing for many reasons including:

- to integrate valuable experts knowledge that may be hard to encode directly into mathematical or computational models;
- to help resolve existing uncertainties as a result of, for example, bias and error that may arise from automatic machine learning;
- to build trust by making humans involved in the modelling or learning processes;
- to cater for individual human differences and subjective assessments such as in art and creative applications.

Recent work in interactive machine learning has focused on developing working prototypes, but less on methods to evaluate iML systems and their various components. The question of how to effectively evaluate such systems is challenging. Indeed, human-in-the-loop approaches to machine learning bring forth not only numerous intelligibility and usability issues, but also open questions with respect to the evaluation of the various facets of the iML system, both as separate components and as a holistic entity [40]. Holzinger [28] argued that conducting methodically correct experiments and of iML systems is difficult, time-consuming, and hard to replicate due to the subjective nature of the "human agents" involved. Cortellessa and Cesta [19] found that the quantitative evaluation of mixed-initiative systems tended to focus either on problem-solving performance of the human and what they call the artificial solver, or the quality of interaction looking at user requirements and judgment of the system. This statement also applies to iML systems, where current evaluations tend to be either *algorithm-centred* to study the computational behaviour of the system, or *human-centred* focusing on the utility and effectiveness of the application for end-users [7–9].

The aim of this chapter is to review existing evaluation methods for iML systems, and to reflect upon our own experience in designing and evaluating such applications over a number of years [3, 6, 32, 34, 36, 46, 47]. The chapter is organised as follows: First we provide a review of recent work on the evaluation of iML systems focusing on types of human and system feedback, and the evaluation methods and metrics deployed in these studies. We then illustrate our evaluation method through a case study on an interactive machine learning system for guided visual search, covering both algorithm-centred and human-centred evaluations. Finally, we discuss research opportunities requiring human-computer interaction methodologies in order to support both the visible and hidden roles that humans play in machine learning.

17.2 Related Work

In this section, we review recent work that evaluates interactive machine learning systems. We consider both qualitative and quantitative evaluations. Our aim is not to provide an exhaustive survey, but rather to illustrate the broad range of existing methods and evaluation metrics.

17.2.1 Method

We systematically reviewed papers published between 2012–2017 from the following venues: IEEE VIS, ACM CHI, EG EuroVis, HILDA workshop, and CHI HCML workshop. We downloaded then filtered the proceedings to include papers having the following keywords: "learn AND algorithm AND interact AND (user OR human OR expert) AND (evaluation OR study OR experiment)". We then drilled down to find papers that describe an actual iML system (as defined in the introduction) with an evaluation section. In this chapter, we focus on studies from the fields of visualisation and human-computer interaction. Our hypothesis was that papers from these domains are likely to go beyond algorithm-centred evaluations. In total, we reviewed 19 recent papers (Table 17.1), from various application domains including multidimensional data exploration [5, 9, 20, 26, 48], data integration [2], knowledge base construction [21], text document retrieval [27], photo enhancement [31], audio source separation [12], social network access control [1], and category exploration and refinement [35]. We examined these evaluations in terms of the machine learning tasks they support, the types of user feedback, the nature of system feedback, and their evaluation methods and metrics.

17.2.2 Human Feedback

Broadly speaking, human feedback to machine learning algorithms can be either *explicit* or *implicit*. The difference between these two mechanisms stems from the field of Information Retrieval (IR). In the case of implicit feedback, humans do not assess relevance for the benefit of the IR system, but rather to fulfil their own task. Besides, they are not necessarily aware that their assessment is being used for relevance feedback [30]. In contrast, for explicit feedback, humans indicate their assessment via a suitable interface, and are aware that their feedback is interpreted for relevance judgment. Whereas implicit feedback is *inferred* from human interactions with the system, explicit feedback is directly provided by humans.

The systems we reviewed either use implicit (7 papers), explicit (8 papers), or mixed (4 papers) human feedback. In the case of mixed feedback, the system tries to infer information from user interactions to complement the explicit feedback.

Implicit Human Feedback

Endert et al. [22, 38] developed *semantic interaction* for visual analytics where the analytical reasoning of the user is inferred from their interactions, which in turn helps steer a dimension reduction model. Their system ForceSpire learns from human input, e.g., moving objects, to improve an underlying model and to produce an improved layout for text documents. Similarly, UTOPIAN [18] supports what the authors describe as a "semantically meaningful set of user interactions" to improve topic modelling. These interactions include keyword refinement, and topic splitting and merging. Implicit feedback may also be gathered from user interactions with raw data. For example, Azuan et al. [2] developed a tool where manual data corrections, such as adding or removing tuples from a data table, are leveraged to improve data integration and cleaning.

Interactive machine learning systems may infer other types of information such as attribute salience or class membership. Wenskovitch and North implemented the Observation-Level Interaction technique (OLI) [48], where the importance of data attributes is inferred from user manipulations of nodes and clusters, and is used to improve a layout algorithm. The ReGroup tool [1] learns from user interactions and a faceted search on online social networks, to create custom on-demand groups of actors in the network.

In the previous examples, the system learns from individual users. In contrast, Dabek and Caban [20] developed an iML system that learns from crowd interactions with data to generate a user model capable of assisting analysts during data exploration.

Explicit Human Feedback

Often explicit human feedback is provided through annotations and labels. This feedback can be either binary or graduated. The View Space Explorer [5] for instance, allows users to choose and annotate relevant or irrelevant example scatter plots. Gao et al. [23] proposed an interactive approach to 3D model repository exploration, where a human assigns "like" or "dislike" labels to parts of a model or its entirety. RCLens [35] supports user guided exploration of rare categories through labels provided by a human. In a text document retrieval application [27], humans decide to accept, reject or label search query results. Similarly, but for a video search system [33], users can either accept or reject sketched query results.

A richer and more nuanced approach to human feedback is proposed by Brown et al. in their Dis-function system [11], where selections of scatterplot points can be dragged and dropped to reflect human understanding of the structure of a text document collection. In this case, the closer the data points in the projected 2D space, the more similar they are. Ehrenberg et al. [21] proposed the "data programming" paradigm, where humans encode their domain expertise using simple rules, as opposed to the traditional method of hand-labelling training data. This allows the generation of a large amount of noisy training labels, which the machine learning algorithm then tries to de-noise and model. Bryan et al. [12] implemented an audio source separation system where humans annotate data and errors, or directly paint on a time-frequency or spectrogram display. In each of these cases, human feedback and choices are taken into consideration to update a machine learning model.

Mixed Human Feedback

To guide user exploration of large search spaces, EvoGraphDice [6, 9] combines explicit human feedback regarding the pertinence of evolved 2D data projections, and an implicit method based on past human interactions with a scatterplot matrix. For the explicit feedback, the user ranks scatterplots from one to five using a slider. The system also infers view relevance by looking at the visual motifs [49] in the ranked scatterplots. For example, if the user tends to rank linear point distributions highly, then this motif will be favoured to produce the next generation of scatterplots. Importantly, the weights of these feedback channels are set to equal by default, but the user can choose to change the importance of each at any time during the exploration.

Healey and Dennis [26] developed interest-driven navigation in visualisation, based on both implicit and explicit human feedback. The implicit feedback is gathered from human interactions with the visualisation system, and from eye tracking to infer preferences based on where the human is looking. Their argument is that data gathered through implicit feedback is noisy. To overcome this, they built a preference statement interface, where humans provide a subject, a classification, and a certainty. This preference interface allows the human to define rules to identify known elements of interest.

Another example is the SelPH system [31], which learns implicitly from a photo editing history, and explicitly from the direct interaction of a human with an optimisation slider. Together, these two feedback channels help to exclude what the authors call the "uninteresting" or "meaningless" design spaces.

17.2.3 System Feedback

System feedback goes beyond showing the results of the co-operation between the human and the machine. It seeks to inform humans about the state of the machine learning algorithm, and the provenance of system suggestions, especially in the case of implicit user feedback.

System feedback can be *visual*: Boukhelifa et al. [6] used colour intensity and a designated flag to visualise the system's interpretation of the mixed user feedback regarding the pertinence of 2D projections. Heimerl et al. [27] implemented a visual method and text labels to show the classifier's state, and the relevance of the selected documents to a search query. Legg et al. [33] visualised the similarity metrics they used to compute a visual search.

System feedback can be *uncertain*: Koyama at al. [31] indicated the system's confidence in the estimation of humans' preferences with respect to colour enhancement. Behrisch et al. [5] provided a feature histogram and an incremental decision tree. These meta visualisations also communicate the classifier's uncertainty. Lin et al. [35] showed visualisation of rare categories using their "category view", and a glyph-based visualisation to show classification features as well as confidence.

System feedback can be *progressive*: Dabek and Caban [20] discussed the importance of choosing when to propose something to the human. Their approach consisted in providing feedback when the human is in need of guidance. They established a number of rules to detect when this occurs. UTOPIA [18] visualises intermediate output even before algorithmic convergence. Ehrenberg et al. [21] showed "on-the-spot" performance feedback using plots and tables. They claimed that this allows the user to iterate more quickly on system design and helps navigate the key decision points in their data programming workflow.

For the majority of the iML systems we reviewed, system feedback was provided. It appears that this feedback is an important feature, perhaps because it helps humans better interpret the results, and allows them to correct any mistakes or areas of uncertainty in the inferred user model. The challenge, however, is to find the right level of feedback without having to fully expose the inner workings of the underlying models and their parameters.

17.2.4 Evaluation Methods and Metrics

In total, for the systems we reviewed, there were nine papers with case studies and usage scenarios [5, 18, 21–23, 26, 33, 35, 48], ten user studies [1, 2, 9, 11, 12, 20, 23, 27, 31, 33] and two observational studies [6, 38], in addition to surveys, questionnaires and interviews (seven papers). Although a number of papers included some form of a controlled user study, it was however acknowledged that this type of evaluation is generally difficult to conduct due to the various potential confounding factors such as previous knowledge [33]. Indeed, evaluating accuracy of an iML system is not always possible as ground truth does not always exist [1].

Objective Performance Evaluations

One way to evaluate how well the human-machine co-operation performs to achieve a task is to compare the iML system with its non-interactive counterpart, i.e. no human feedback, or to an established baseline system. Legg at al. [33] conducted a small-scale empirical evaluation with three participants using three metrics inspired from content-based information retrieval: time, precision and recall. The idea was to manually identify five video clips as the ground truth, then to compare an iML video search system with a baseline system (a standard video tool with fast-forward) for a video search task. They found that participants performed better in the iML condition for this task. In a user study with twelve participants, Amerish et al. [1] compared a traditional manual search to add people to groups on online social networks (using an alphabetical list or searching by name), to an interactive machine learning approach called ReGroup. They looked at the overall time it took participants to create groups, final group sizes, and speed of selecting group members. Their results show that the traditional method works well for small groups, whereas the iML method works best for larger and more varied groups.

Another way to objectively evaluate the success of the human-machine co-operation is to look at insights. In the context of exploratory data visualisation, Endert et al. [22] and Boukhelifa et al. [6] found that with the help of user feedback, their respective iML systems were able to confirm known knowledge and this led to new insights.

Other evaluations in this category compared the iML application with and without system feedback. Dabek et al. [20] proposed a grammar-based approach to model user interactions with data, which is then used to assist other users during data analysis. They conducted a crowdsourced formal evaluation with 300 participants to assess how well their grammar-based model captures user interactions. The task was to explore a census dataset and answer twelve open-ended questions that required looking for combinations of variables and axis ranges using a parallel coordinates visualisation. When comparing their tool with and without system feedback, they found that system suggestions significantly improved user performance for all their data analysis tasks, although questions remain with regards to the optimal number of suggestions to display to the user.

A number of studies looked at algorithmic performance when user feedback was implicit versus explicit. Azuan et al. [2] who used a "pay-as-you-go" approach to solicit user feedback during data integration and cleaning, compared the two human feedback methods for a data integration task. They found that user performance under the implicit condition was better than for the explicit feedback in terms of number of errors. However, the authors noted some difficulties in separating usability issues related to the explicit feedback interface from the performance results.

Finally, some authors focused on algorithm-centred evaluations, where two or more machine learning methods are compared. For instance, in the context of topic modelling, Choo et al. [18] compared latent Dirichlet allocation and non-negative matrix factorisation algorithms, from the practical viewpoints of consistency of multiple runs and empirical convergence. Another example is by Bryan et al. [12] who chose objective separation quality metrics defined by industry standards, as objective measures of algorithmic performance for audio source separation.

Subjective Performance Evaluations

The subjective evaluations described in Table 17.1 were carried out using surveys, questionnaires, interviews, and informal user feedback. They included evaluation metrics related to these aspects of user experience: happiness, easiness, quickness, favourite, best helped, satisfaction, task load, trust, confidence in user and system feedback, and distractedness. Moreover, the observational studies [6, 38] that we reviewed provided rich subjective user feedback on iML system performance. Endert et al. [38] looked at semantic interaction usage, to assess whether the latter aids the sensemaking process. They state that one sign of success of iML systems is when humans forget that they are feeding information to an algorithm, and rather focus on "synthesising information relevant to their task".

Table 17.1 Summary of reviewed interactive machine learning systems, characterised by the types of human feedback (implicit, explicit, or both, i.e. mixed), system feedback, the evaluation methods (case study, user study, observational study, survey), and evaluation metrics (objective or subjective). These systems are ordered in terms of the machine learning tasks they each support: classification, clustering, density estimation or dimensionality reduction

Paper	Classification	Clustering	Density estimation	Dimensionality reduction	Implicit user feedback	Explicit user feedback	System feedback	Case study	User study	Observational study	Survey	Objective metrics	Subjective metrics
Co-integration [2]	✓				✓				✓			✓	
DDLite [21]	✓					✓	✓	✓				✓	✓
Interest driven navigation [26]	✓				✓	✓	✓	✓					✓
ISSE [12]	✓					✓	✓	✓	✓		✓	✓	✓
RCLens [35]	✓					✓	✓	✓			✓	✓	✓
ReGroup [1]	✓				✓	✓	✓		✓		✓	✓	✓
View space explorer [5]	✓											✓	
Visual classifier [27]	✓				✓	✓	✓		✓		✓	✓	✓
OLI [48]		✓		✓	✓			✓				✓	
ForceSPIRE [22]		✓			✓			✓				✓	
ForceSPIRE [38]		✓			✓	✓	✓			✓		✓	
RugbyVAST [33]		✓				✓	✓	✓	✓			✓	✓
3D model repository explorer [23]		✓				✓		✓	✓			✓	
User interaction model [20]		✓			✓		✓		✓		✓	✓	✓
SelPh [31]			✓	✓	✓	✓	✓		✓		✓	✓	✓
EvoGraphDice [9]				✓	✓	✓	✓		✓			✓	
EvoGraphDice [6]				✓	✓	✓	✓			✓	✓	✓	✓
Dis-function [11]				✓		✓	✓		✓			✓	✓
UTOPIAN [18]				✓	✓		✓	✓				✓	

Other evaluations looked at human behavioural variations with regards to different iML interfaces. Amerish et al. [1] compared two interfaces for adding people to online social networks, with and without the interactive component of iML. They looked at behavioural discrepancies in terms of how people used the different interfaces and how they felt. They found that participants were frustrated when model learning was not accurate.

Koyama et al. [31] compared their adaptive photo enhancement system with the same tool stripped of advanced capabilities, namely the visual system feedback, the optimisation slider functions, and the ordering of search results in terms of similarity. Because photo enhancement quality can be subjective, performance of the iML system was rated by the study participants. In this case, they were satisfied with the iML system and preferred it over more traditional workflows.

In summary, there are many aspects of interactive machine learning systems that are being evaluated. Sometimes authors focus on the quality of the user interaction with the iML system (*human-centred evaluations*), or the robustness of the algorithms that are deployed (*algorithm-centred evaluations*), and only in a few cases is detailed attention drawn to the quality of human-machine co-operation and learning. These studies use a variety of evaluation methods, as well as objective and subjective metrics. Perhaps our main observation from this literature review, is that for the majority of the reviewed papers, only a single aspect of the iML system is evaluated. We need more evaluation studies that examine the different aspects of iML systems, not only as separate components but also from an integrative point of view.

In the next section, we introduce an interactive machine learning system for guided exploratory visualisation and describe our *multi-faceted* evaluation approach to study the effectiveness and usefulness of this tool for end users.

17.3 Case Study: Interactive Machine Learning For Guided Visual Exploration

Exploratory visualisation is a dynamic process of discovery that is relatively unpredictable due to the absence of a priori knowledge of what the user is searching for [25]. The focus in this case is on organisation, testing, developing concepts, finding patterns and definition of assumptions [25]. When the search space is large, as is often the case for multi-dimensional datasets, the task of exploring and finding interesting patterns in data becomes tedious. Automatic dimension reduction techniques, such as principal component analysis and multidimensional scaling, reduce the search space, but often are difficult to understand [42], or require the specification of objective criteria to filter views before exploration. Other techniques guide the exploration towards the most interesting areas of the search space based on information learned during the exploration, which appears to be more adapted to the free nature of exploration [9, 11].

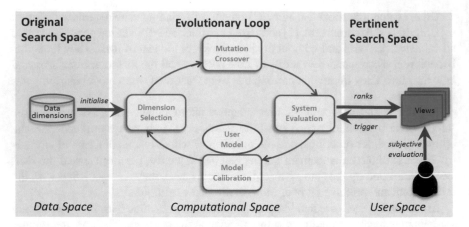

Fig. 17.1 The Evolutionary Visual Exploration Framework (EVE). Raw data dimensions (from the data space) are fed into an evolutionary loop in order to progressively evolve new interesting views to the user. The criteria for deciding on the pertinence of the new views is specified through a combination of automatically calculated metrics (from the computational space) and user interactions (at the user space)

In our previous work on guided exploratory visualisation [6, 7, 9, 13, 14], we tried to address the problem of how to efficiently explore multidimensional datasets characterised by a large number of projections. We proposed a framework for Evolutionary Visual Exploration (EVE, Fig. 17.1) that combines visual analytics with stochastic optimisation by means of an Interactive Evolutionary Algorithm (IEA). Our goal was to guide users to interesting projections, where the notion of "interestingness" is defined *implicitly* by automatic indicators such as the amount of visual pattern in the two-dimensional views visited by the user, and *explicitly* via subjective human assessment.

In this section, we report on our experience in building and evaluating an interactive machine learning system called EvoGraphDice (Fig. 17.3) using the EVE framework. We note that existing evaluations of interactive evolutionary systems tend to be algorithm-centred. Through this case study, we argue for a *multi-faceted* evaluation approach that takes into account all components of an iML system. Similar recommendations can be found for evaluating interactive visualisation systems. For example, Carpendale [15] advocates for adopting a variety of evaluative methodologies that together may start to approach the kind of answers sought.

17.3.1 Background on Interactive Evolutionary Computation IEC

There are many machine learning approaches, including artificial neural networks, support vector machines and Bayesian networks. Moreover, many machine learning problems can be modelled as optimisation problems where the aim is to find a trade-off between an adequate representation of the training set and a generalisation capability on unknown samples. In contrast to traditional local optimisation methods, Evolutionary Algorithms (EAs) have been widely used as a successful stochastic optimisation tool in the field of machine learning in recent years [44]. In this sense, machine learning and the field of Evolutionary Computation (EC), that encompasses EAs, are tightly coupled.

Evolutionary Algorithms (EAs) are stochastic optimisation heuristics that copy, in a very abstract manner, the principles of natural evolution that let a population of individuals be adapted to its environment [24]. They have the major advantage over other optimisation techniques of making only few assumptions on the function to be optimised. An EA considers populations of potential solutions exactly like a natural population of individuals that live, fight, and reproduce, but the natural environment pressure is replaced by an "optimisation" pressure. In this way, individuals that reproduce are the best ones with respect to the problem to be solved. Reproduction (see Fig. 17.2) consists of generating new solutions via variation schemes (the genetic operators), that, by analogy with nature, are called mutation if they involve one individual, or crossover if they involve two parent solutions. A *fitness function*, computed for each individual, is used to drive the selection process, and is thus optimised by the EA. Evolutionary optimisation techniques are particularly efficient to address complex problems (irregular, discontinuous) where classical deterministic methods fail [4, 39], but they can also deal with varying environments [50], or non computable quantities [45].

Interactive Evolutionary Computation (IEC) describes evolutionary computational models where humans, via suitable user interfaces, play an active role, *implicitly* or *explicitly*, in evaluating the outputs evolved by the evolutionary computation (Fig. 17.2). IEC lends itself very well to art applications such as for melody or graphic art generation where creativity is essential, due to the subjective nature of the fitness evaluation function. For scientific and engineering applications, IEC is interesting when the exact form of a more generalised fitness function is not known or is difficult to compute, say for producing a visual pattern that would interest a human observer. Here, the human visual system, together with their emotional and psychological responses are far superior to any automatic pattern detection or learning algorithm.

Whereas current IEC research has focused on improving the robustness of the underlying algorithms, much work is still needed to tackle human-factors in systems where adaptation between users and systems is likely to occur [37].

Fig. 17.2 The evolutionary loop: user interactions can occur at any stage including the selection and evaluation of individuals and the genetic operators

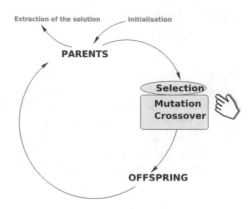

17.3.2   The Visible and Hidden Roles of Humans in IEC

The role of humans in IEC can be characterised by the evolutionary component at which they operate, namely: initialisation, evolution, selection, genetic operators, constraints, local optimisation, genome structure variation, and parameters tuning. This may or may not be desirable from a usability perspective, especially for non-technical users. The general approach when humans are involved, especially for parameter tuning, is mostly by trial-and-error and by reducing the number of parameters. Such tasks are often visible, in that they are facilitated by the user interface. However, there exists a hidden role of humans in IEC that has often been neglected. Algorithm and system designers play a central role in deciding the details of the fitness function to be optimised and in setting the default values of system parameters, and thus contributing to the "black-box" effect of IEC systems. Such tasks are influenced by the designer's previous experience and end-user task requirements.

Besides this hidden role in the design stage, there is a major impact of the "human-in-the-loop" on the IEC. This problem is known as the "user bottleneck", i.e. human fatigue due to the fact that the human and the machine do not live and react at the same rate. Various solutions have been considered in order to avoid systematic and repetitive or tedious interactions, and the authors themselves have considered several of them, such as: (i) reducing the size of the population and the number of generations; (ii) choosing specific models to constrain the exploration in a priori "interesting" areas of the search space; and (iii) performing an automatic learning (based on a limited number of characteristic quantities) in order to assist the user and only present interesting individuals of the population, with respect to previous votes or feedback from the user. These solutions require considerable computational effort. A different approach and new ideas to tackle the same issue could come from Human Computer Interaction (HCI) and usability research, as discussed later in this chapter.

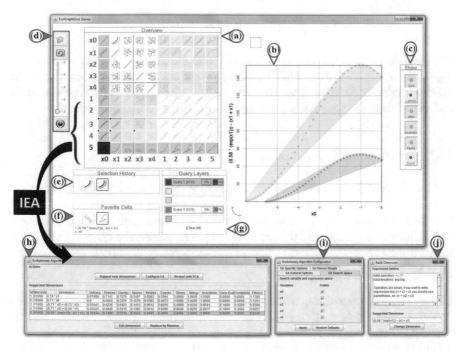

Fig. 17.3 EvoGraphDice prototype showing an exploration session of a synthetic dataset. Widgets: **a** an overview scatterplot matrix showing the original data set of 5 dimensions (x0..x4) and the new dimensions (1..5) as suggested by the evolutionary algorithm. **b** main plot view. **c** tool bar for main plot view. **d** a tool bar with (top to bottom) favourite toggle button, evolve button , a slider to evaluate cells and a restart (PCA) button. **e** the selection history tool. **f** the favourite cells window. **g** the selection query window. **h** IEA main control window. **i** window to limit the search space. **j** dimension editor operators

17.3.3   EvoGraphDice Prototype

EvoGraphDice [6, 7, 9, 13] was designed to aid the exploration of multidimensional datasets characterised by a large space of 2D projections (Fig. 17.3). Starting from dimensions whose values are automatically calculated by a Principle Component Analysis (PCA), an IEA progressively builds non-trivial viewpoints in the form of linear and non-linear dimension combinations, to help users discover new interesting views and relationships in their data. The criteria for evolving new dimensions is not known a priori and is partially specified by the user via an interactive interface. Pertinence of views is modelled using a fitness function that plays the role of a predictor: (i) users select views with meaningful or interesting visual patterns and provide a satisfaction score; (ii) the system calibrates the fitness function optimised by the evolutionary algorithm to incorporate user's input, and then calculates new views. A learning algorithm was implemented to provide pertinent projections to the user based on their past interactions.

17.3.4 Multi-faceted Evaluation of EvoGraphDice

We evaluated EvoGraphDice quantitatively and qualitatively following a mixed-approach, where on the one hand we analysed the computational behaviour of the system (algorithm-centred approach), and on the other hand we observed the utility and effectiveness of the system for the end-user (human-centred approach).

17.3.4.1 Quantitative Evaluation

For this study [9], we synthesised a 5D dataset with an embedded curvilinear relationship between two dimensions and noise for the rest of the dimensions. The task was to find a data projection that shows a derived visual pattern. We logged user interactions with the tool and the state of the system at each algorithm iteration. For log data analysis, we used both statistical and exploratory visualisation techniques.

Algorithm-Centred Evaluation

This evaluation focused on two aspects of our iML system: the *robustness* of the underlying algorithm, and the *quality of machine learning*. To study robustness, we conducted two types of analyses: (a) *convergence analysis* to assess the algorithms ability to steer the exploration toward a focused area of the search space, and (b) *diversity analysis* to assess the richness and variability of solutions provided by the algorithm. These two analyses are relevant because they relate to two important mechanisms in evolutionary algorithms, *exploitation* and *exploration* [4], where on the one hand users want to visit new regions of the search space, and on the other hand they also want to explore solutions close to one region of the search space. In terms of objective metrics, we used the number of generations and task outcome to measure algorithmic performance and mean visual pattern differences (using scagnostics [49]) to assess diversity. To evaluate the quality of learning, we used the rate of concordance between user evaluation scores, and the "predicted" values as calculated by the algorithm.

Our analysis showed that on average the interactive evolutionary algorithm followed the order of user ranking of scatterplots fairly consistently, even though users seemed to take different search and evaluation strategies. For example, some participants tended to lump evaluation scores into fewer levels, others used the five provided score levels, whereas the rest alternated between the two strategies at different stages of the exploration. Moreover, these results indicated a possible link between user evaluation strategy, and outcome of exploration and speed of convergence, where users taking a more consistent approach converged more quickly. The diversity analysis showed that, in terms of visual pattern, the IEA provided more diverse solutions at the beginning of the exploration session before slowly converging to a more focused search space.

Human-Centred Evaluation

The user-centred evaluation of EvoGraphDice focused on two different aspects related to human interactions with the iML system. First we performed a *user strategy analysis* to understand the different approaches users took to solve a data exploration task. The evaluation metrics we used here were the type of searched visual pattern, and stability of the exploration strategy. Second, we looked at *user focus* to highlight hot spots in the user interface and assess user evaluation strategies. In this case, our evaluation metrics were related to the user view visitation and evaluation patterns.

In terms of results, the user strategies analysis showed that EvoGraphDice allows for different types of exploration strategies that appear to be relevant for the study task. In the case of a two-curve separation task, these strategies centred around three dominant types of scagnostics: skinny, convex and sparse. We also found that the stability of the exploration strategy may be an important factor for determining the outcome of the exploration task and the speed of convergence, since successful exploration sessions had a more consistent strategy when compared to the unsuccessful ones, and they converged more quickly on average.

From the user visitation and evaluation analyses, we found that users were more likely to visit scatterplots showing dimensions relevant to their task. Moreover, these plots were on average ranked highly by the user. Since for this game task, the main dimensions relevant to the task appeared on the top left side of the proposed cells, users intuitively started navigating that way. What we saw in these results was probably a mixture of task-relevance and intuitive-navigation, as the relevant original dimensions are placed in a prominent position in the matrix.

17.3.4.2 Qualitative Evaluation

To assess the usability and utility of EVE, we conducted another user study [6] where we tried to answer these three questions: is our tool understandable and can it be learnt; are experts able to confirm known insights in their data; and are they able to discover new insight and generate new hypotheses. We designed three tasks: (a) a game-task (similar to the task in the quantitative evaluation above) with varying levels of difficulty to assess participants abilities to operate the tool; (b) we asked participants to show in the tool what they already knew about their data; and (c) to explore their data in light of a hypothesis or research question that they prepared. This sequence of tasks assured that experts became familiar with the tool and understood how to concretely leverage it by looking for known facts, before looking for new insights. This evaluation approach sits between an observational study and an insight-based evaluation, such as the one proposed by Saraiya et al. [41].

The study led to interesting findings such as the ability of our tool to support experts in better formulating their research questions and building new hypotheses. For insight evaluation studies such as ours, reproducing the actual findings across subjects is not possible as each participant provided their own dataset and research questions. However, reproducing testing methodologies and coding for the analysis is. Although we ran multiple field studies with domain experts from different domains, with sessions that were internally very different, the high-level tasks, their order and the insight-based coding were common. Training expert users on simple specific tasks that are not necessarily "theirs" also seemed to help experts become confident with the system, but of course comes at a time cost.

17.4   Discussion

We conducted qualitative and quantitative user studies to evaluate EVE which helped us validate our framework of guided visual exploration. While the observational study showed that using EVE, domain experts were able to formulate interesting hypothesis and reach new insights when exploring freely, the quantitative evaluation indicated that users, guided by the interactive evolutionary algorithm, are able to converge quickly to an interesting view of their data when a clear task is specified. Importantly, the quantitative study allowed us to accurately describe the relationship between user behaviour and algorithms response.

Besides interactive machine learning, guided visualisation systems such as EVE fall under the wider arena of knowledge-assisted visualisation and mixed-initiative systems [29]. In such cases, where the system is learning, it is crucial that users understand what the system is proposing or why changes are happening. Thus, when evaluating iML systems with users, we need to specifically test if the automatic state changes and their provenance are understood. It would be interesting, for example, to also consider evolving or progressive revealing of the provenance of system suggestions. This way, as the user becomes more expert, more aspects of the underlying mechanics are revealed. When creativity and serendipity are important aspects, as is the case in artistic domains and data exploration, new evaluation methodologies are required.

Research from the field of mixed initiative systems describes a set of design principles that try to address systematic problems with the use of automatic services within direct manipulation interfaces. These principles include considering uncertainty about a user's goal, transparency, and considering the status of users' attention [29]. We can be inspired by the extensive experience and past work from HCI, to also consider how user behaviour can in turn adapt to fit our systems [37].

During the design, development and evaluation of EVE, we worked with domain experts at different levels. For the observational study, we worked with data experts from various disciplines, which allowed us to assess the usefulness, usability and effectiveness of our system in different contexts. In particular, we largely benefited from having one domain expert as part of the design and evaluation team. This expert explored multidimensional datasets as part of her daily work, using both algorithmic and visual tools. Involving end-users in the design team is a long-time tradition in the field of HCI as part of the user-centred design methodology. This is a recommendation we should consider more, both as a design and as a system validation approach. While HCI researchers acknowledge the challenges of forming partnerships with domain experts, their past experiences (e.g., [17]) can inform us on how to proceed with the evaluation of iML systems.

17.5 Research Prospects

We report on observations and lessons learnt from working with application users both for the design and the evaluation of our interactive machine learning system, as well as the results of experimental analyses. We discuss these below as research opportunities aiming to facilitate and support the different roles humans play in iML, i.e. in the design, interaction and evaluation of these systems.

Human-centred Design: during the design, development and evaluation of many of our tools, we worked with domain experts at different levels. For EvoGraphDice, for instance, we largely benefited from having a domain expert as part of the design and evaluation team. However, this was carried out in an informal way. Involving end-users in the design team is a long-time tradition in the field of HCI as part of the user-centred design methodology. Participatory design, for instance, could be conducted with iML end-users to incorporate their expertise in the design of, for example, learning algorithms and user models. This is a recommendation we should consider in a more systematic way, both as a design and as a system validation approach.

Interaction and visualisation: often the solutions proposed by the iML systems are puzzling to end-users. This is because the inner workings of machine learning algorithms, and the user exploration and feedback strategies that lead to system suggestions are often not available to the user. This "black-box" effect is challenging to address as there is a fine balance to find between the richness of a transparent interface and the simplicity of a more obscure one. Finding the tipping point requires an understanding of evolving user expertise in manipulating the system, and the task requirements. Whereas HCI and user-centred design can help elicit these requirements and tailor tools to user needs over time, visualisation techniques can make the provenance of views and the system status more accessible.

At the interaction level, HCI can contribute techniques to capture rich user feedback without straining the user, that are either implicit (e.g., using eye-tracking); or explicit such as using simple gestures or interactions mediated by tangible objects to indicate user subjective assessment of a given solution. Here, our recommendation is to investigate rich and varied interaction techniques to facilitate user feedback, and to develop robust user models that try to learn from the provided input.

Multifaceted Evaluation: the evaluation of iML systems remains a difficult task as often the system adapts to user preferences but also the user interprets and adapts to system feedback. Getting a clear understanding of the subtle mechanisms of this co-adaptation [37], especially in the presence of different types and sources of uncertainty [10], is challenging and requires consideration of evaluation criteria other than speed of algorithm convergence and the usability of the interface.

In the context of exploration, both for scientific and artistic applications, creativity is sought and can be characterised by lateral thinking, surprising findings, and the way users learn how to operate the interactive system and construct their own way to use it. For IEC, our observation is that augmented creativity can be achieved with the right balance between randomness and user-guided search. What is important to consider for evaluating iML systems in the context of creativity, are the exploration components. Our recommendation in this respect is two-fold: first, to work towards creating tools that support creativity (something that the HCI community is already looking into [16]); and second, to investigate objective and subjective metrics to study creativity within iML (e.g., to identify impacting factors such as optimisation constraints, user engagement and the presence or absence of direct manipulation). Some of these measures may only be identifiable through longitudinal observations of this co-adaptation process.

17.6 Conclusion

User-driven machine learning processes such as the ones described in this chapter, rely on systems that adapt their behaviour based on user feedback, while users themselves adapt their goals and strategies based on the solutions proposed by the system. In this chapter, we focused on the evaluation of interactive machine learning systems, drawing from related work, and our own experience in developing and evaluating such systems. We showed through a focused literature review that despite the multifaceted nature of iML systems, current evaluations tend to focus on single isolated components such as the robustness of the algorithm, or the utility of the interface. Through a visual analytics case study, we showed how coupling algorithm-centred and user-centred evaluations can bring forth insights on the underlying co-operation and co-adaptation mechanisms between the algorithm and the human. Interactive machine learning presents interesting challenges and prospects to conduct future research not only in terms of designing robust algorithms and interaction techniques, but also in terms of coherent evaluation methodologies.

References

1. Amershi, S., Fogarty, J., Weld, D.: Regroup: interactive machine learning for on-demand group creation in social networks. In: Proceedings of the SIGCHI Conference on Human Factors in Computing Systems, CHI '12, pp. 21–30. ACM, New York, NY, USA (2012)
2. Azuan, N., Embury, S., Paton, N.: Observing the data scientist: Using manual corrections as implicit feedback. In: Proceedings of the 2nd Workshop on Human-In-the-Loop Data Analytics, HILDA'17, pp. 13:1–13:6. ACM, New York, NY, USA (2017)
3. Bach, B., Spritzer, A., Lutton, E., Fekete, J.D.: Interactive random graph generation with evolutionary algorithms. In: Graph Drawing. Lecture Notes in Computer Science. Springer, Berlin (2012)
4. Banzhaf, W.: Handbook of Evolutionary Computation. Oxford University Press, Oxford (1997)
5. Behrisch, M., Korkmaz, F., Shao, L., Schreck, T.: Feedback-driven interactive exploration of large multidimensional data supported by visual classifier. In: 2014 IEEE Conference on Visual Analytics Science and Technology (VAST), pp. 43–52 (2014)
6. Boukhelifa, N., Cancino, W., Bezerianos, A., Lutton, E.: Evolutionary visual exploration: evaluation with expert users. Comput. Graph. Forum **32**(3), 31–40 (2013)

7. Boukhelifa, N., Bezerianos, A., Lutton, E.: A mixed approach for the evaluation of a guided exploratory visualization system. In: Aigner, W., Rosenthal, P., Scheidegger, C. (eds.) EuroVis Workshop on Reproducibility, Verification, and Validation in Visualization (EuroRV3). The Eurographics Association, Spain (2015)

8. Boukhelifa, N., Bezerianos, A., Tonda, A., Lutton, E.: Research prospects in the design and evaluation of interactive evolutionary systems for art and science. In: CHI Workshop on Human Centred Machine Learning. San Jose, United States (2016)

9. Boukhelifa, N., Bezerianos, A., Cancino, W., Lutton, E.: Evolutionary visual exploration: evaluation of an iec framework for guided visual search. Evol. Comput. **25**(1), 55–86 (2017)

10. Boukhelifa, N., Perrin, M.E., Huron, S., Eagan, J.: How data workers cope with uncertainty: a task characterisation study. In: Proceedings of the 2017 CHI Conference on Human Factors in Computing Systems, CHI '17, pp. 3645–3656. ACM, New York, NY, USA (2017)

11. Brown, E., Liu, J., Brodley, C., Chang, R.: Dis-function: Learning distance functions interactively. In: 2012 IEEE Conference on Visual Analytics Science and Technology (VAST), pp. 83–92 (2012)

12. Bryan, N., Mysore, G., Wang, G.: ISSE: an interactive source separation editor. In: Proceedings of the SIGCHI Conference on Human Factors in Computing Systems, CHI '14, pp. 257–266. ACM, New York, NY, USA (2014)

13. Cancino, W., Boukhelifa, N., Lutton, E.: Evographdice: interactive evolution for visual analytics. In: IEEE Congress on Evolutionary Computation, pp. 1–8. IEEE (2012)

14. Cancino, W., Boukhelifa, N., Bezerianos, A., Lutton, E.: Evolutionary visual exploration: experimental analysis of algorithm behaviour. In: Blum, C., Alba, E. (eds.) GECCO (Companion), pp. 1373–1380. ACM (2013)

15. Carpendale, S.: Information visualization. Evaluating Information Visualizations, pp. 19–45. Springer, Berlin (2008)

16. Cherry, E., Latulipe, C.: Quantifying the creativity support of digital tools through the creativity support index. ACM Trans. Comput.-Hum. Interact. **21**(4), 21:1–21:25 (2014)

17. Chilana, P., Wobbrock, J., Andrew, J.: Understanding usability practices in complex domains. In: Proceedings of the SIGCHI Conference on Human Factors in Computing Systems, CHI '10, pp. 2337–2346. ACM, New York, NY, USA (2010)

18. Choo, J., Lee, C., Reddy, C., Park, H.: Utopian: user-driven topic modeling based on interactive nonnegative matrix factorization. IEEE Trans. Vis. Comput. Graph. **19**(12), 1992–2001 (2013)

19. Cortellessa, G., Cesta, A.: Evaluating mixed-initiative systems: an experimental approach. ICAPS **6**, 172–181 (2006)

20. Dabek, F., Caban, J.: A grammar-based approach for modeling user interactions and generating suggestions during the data exploration process. IEEE Trans. Vis. Comput. Graph. **23**(1), 41–50 (2017)

21. Ehrenberg, H., Shin, J., Ratner, A., Fries, J., Ré, C.: Data programming with DDLite: putting humans in a different part of the loop. In: Proceedings of the Workshop on Human-In-the-Loop Data Analytics, HILDA '16, pp. 13:1–13:6. ACM, New York, NY, USA (2016)

22. Endert, A., Fiaux, P., North, C.: Semantic interaction for visual text analytics. In: Proceedings of the SIGCHI Conference on Human Factors in Computing Systems, CHI '12, pp. 473–482. ACM, New York, NY, USA (2012)

23. Gao, L., Cao, Y., Lai, Y., Huang, H., Kobbelt, L., Hu, S.: Active exploration of large 3d model repositories. IEEE Trans. Vis. Comput. Graph. **21**(12), 1390–1402 (2015)

24. Goldberg, D.: Genetic Algorithms in Search, Optimization and Machine Learning, 1st edn. Addison-Wesley Longman Publishing Co., Inc., Boston (1989)

25. Grinstein, G.: Harnessing the human in knowledge discovery. In: Simoudis, E., Han, J., Fayyad, U.M. (eds.) KDD, pp. 384–385. AAAI Press (1996)

26. Healey, C., Dennis, B.: Interest driven navigation in visualization. IEEE Trans. Vis. Comput. Graph. **18**(10), 1744–1756 (2012)

27. Heimerl, F., Koch, S., Bosch, H., Ertl, T.: Visual classifier training for text document retrieval. IEEE Trans. Vis. Comput. Graph. **18**(12), 2839–2848 (2012)

28. Holzinger, A.: Interactive machine learning for health informatics: when do we need the human-in-the-loop? Brain Inform. **3**(2), 119–131 (2016)
29. Horvitz, E.: Principles of mixed-initiative user interfaces. In: Proceedings of the SIGCHI Conference on Human Factors in Computing Systems, CHI '99, pp. 159–166. ACM, New York, NY, USA (1999)
30. Kelly, D., Teevan, J.: Implicit feedback for inferring user preference: a bibliography. SIGIR Forum **37**(2), 18–28 (2003)
31. Koyama, Y., Sakamoto, D., Igarashi, T.: Selph: Progressive learning and support of manual photo color enhancement. In: Proceedings of the 2016 CHI Conference on Human Factors in Computing Systems, CHI '16, pp. 2520–2532. ACM, New York, NY, USA (2016)
32. Landrin-Schweitzer, Y., Collet, P., Lutton, E.: Introducing lateral thinking in search engines. Genet. Program. Evolvable Hardw. J. **1**(7), 9–31 (2006)
33. Legg, P., Chung, D., Parry, M., Bown, R., Jones, M., Griffiths, I., Chen, M.: Transformation of an uncertain video search pipeline to a sketch-based visual analytics loop. IEEE Trans. Vis. Comput. Graph. **19**(12), 2109–2118 (2013)
34. Legrand, P., Bourgeois-Republique, C., Pean, V., Harboun-Cohen, E., Lévy Véhel, J., Frachet, B., Lutton, E., Collet, P.: Interactive evolution for cochlear implants fitting. GPEM **8**(4), 319–354 (2007)
35. Lin, H., Gao, S., Gotz, D., Du, F., He, J., Cao, N.: RCLens: interactive rare category exploration and identification. IEEE Trans. Vis. Comput. Graph. **PP**(99), 1–1 (2017)
36. Lutton, E.: Evolution of fractal shapes for artists and designers. IJAIT Int. J. Artif. Intell. Tools **15**(4), 651–672 (2006) (Special Issue on AI in Music and Art)
37. Mackay, W.: Responding to cognitive overhead: co-adaptation between users and technology. Intellectica **30**(1), 177–193 (2000)
38. North, C., Endert, A., Fiaux, P.: Semantic interaction for sensemaking: inferring analytical reasoning for model steering. IEEE Trans. Vis. Comput. Graph. **18**, 2879–2888 (2012)
39. Poli, R., Cagnoni, S.: Genetic programming with user-driven selection: experiments on the evolution of algorithms for image enhancement. In: Genetic Programming Conference, pp. 269–277. Morgan Kaufmann (1997)
40. Sacha, D., Sedlmair, M., Zhang, L., Lee, J., Weiskopf, D., North, S., Keim, D.: Human-centered machine learning through interactive visualization. ESANN (2016)
41. Saraiya, P., North, C., Duca, K.: An insight-based methodology for evaluating bioinformatics visualizations. IEEE Trans. Vis. Comput. Graph. **11**(4), 443–456 (2005)
42. Sedlmair, M., Brehmer, M., Ingram, S., Munzner, T.: Dimensionality reduction in the wild: Gaps and guidance. Department of Computer Science, University British Columbia, Vancouver, BC, Canada, Technical Report TR-2012-03 (2012)
43. Song, Y., Pickup, D., Li, C., Rosin, P., Hall, P.: Abstract art by shape classification. IEEE Trans. Vis. Comput. Graph. **19**(8), 1252–1263 (2013)
44. Stanley, K., Miikkulainen, R.: Evolving neural networks through augmenting topologies. Evolut. Comput. **10**(2), 99–127 (2002)
45. Takagi, H.: Interactive evolutionary computation: system optimisation based on human subjective evaluation. In: Proceedings of Intelligent Engineering Systems (INES'98). IEEE (1998)
46. Tonda, A., Spritzer, A., Lutton, E.: Balancing user interaction and control in Bayesian network structure learning. In: Artificial Evolution Conference. LNCS, vol. 8752. Springer, Berlin (2013)
47. Valigiani, G., Lutton, E., Jamont, Y., Biojout, R., Collet, P.: Automatic rating process to audit a man-hill. WSEAS Trans. Adv. Eng. Educ. **3**(1), 1–7 (2006)
48. Wenskovitch, J., North, C.: Observation-level interaction with clustering and dimension reduction algorithms. In: Proceedings of the 2Nd Workshop on Human-In-the-Loop Data Analytics, HILDA'17, pp. 14:1–14:6. ACM, New York, NY, USA (2017)
49. Wilkinson, L., Anand, A., Grossman, R.: Graph-theoretic scagnostics (2005)
50. Yaochu, J., Branke, J.: Evolutionary optimization in uncertain environments-a survey. IEEE Trans. Evolut. Comput. **9**(3), 303–317 (2005)

Part VI
Domain Knowledge in Transparent Machine Learning Applications

Chapter 18
Water Pipe Failure Prediction: A Machine Learning Approach Enhanced By Domain Knowledge

Bang Zhang, Ting Guo, Lelin Zhang, Peng Lin, Yang Wang, Jianlong Zhou and Fang Chen

Abstract Drinking water pipe and waste water pipe networks are valuable urban infrastructure assets that are responsible for reliable water resource distributions and waste water collection. However, due to fast growing demand and aging assets, water utilities find it increasingly difficult to efficiently maintain their pipe networks. Pipe failures - drinking water pipe breaks and waste water pipe blockages - can cause significant economic and social costs, and hence have become the primary challenge to water utilities. Identifying key influential factors, e.g., pipes' physical attributes, environmental features, is critical for understanding pipe failure behaviours. The domain knowledge plays a significant role in this aspect. In this work, we propose a Bayesian nonparametric machine learning model with the support of domain knowledge for pipe failure prediction. It can forecast future high-risk pipes for physical condition assessment, thereby proactively preventing disastrous failures. Moreover, compared with traditional machine learning approaches, the proposed model considers domain expert knowledge and experience, which helps avoid the limit of traditional machine

B. Zhang (✉) · T. Guo · L. Zhang · P. Lin · Y. Wang · J. Zhou · F. Chen
DATA61, CSIRO, 13 Garden Street, Eveleigh, NSW 2015, Australia
e-mail: mattbang.zhang@data61.csiro.au

T. Guo
e-mail: Ting.Guo@data61.csiro.au

L. Zhang
e-mail: Lelin.Zhang@data61.csiro.au

P. Lin
e-mail: peng.lin.c@gmail.com

Y. Wang
e-mail: Yang.Wang@data61.csiro.au

J. Zhou
e-mail: Jianlong.Zhou@data61.csiro.au

F. Chen
e-mail: Fang.Chen@data61.csiro.au

© Springer International Publishing AG, part of Springer Nature 2018
J. Zhou and F. Chen (eds.), *Human and Machine Learning*, Human–Computer Interaction Series, https://doi.org/10.1007/978-3-319-90403-0_18

learning approaches - learning only from what it sees - and improves prediction performance.

18.1 Introduction

Pipe networks are valuable urban infrastructure assets that are responsible for reliable water resource distributions and waste water collection. However, as urbanisation trends continue and urban populations rise, water utilities find it increasingly difficult to meet growing water demand with ageing and failing water pipe networks. Water pipe failures, which can cause tremendous economic and social costs have become the primary challenge to water utilities. In order to tackle the problem in a financially viable way, preventative risk management strategies are widely adopted by water utilities to prevent disastrous failures. The basic idea of the strategies is to proactively identify high-risk pipes and renew them in time to avoid potential failures. Meanwhile, replacement of pipes that are still in healthy condition is to be avoided. Accordingly, the strategies consist of two main steps: (1) high-risk pipe prioritisation, in which pipes are ranked based on their risk of failure, and (2) physical condition assessment, in which physical inspections are conducted on highly rated pipes to confirm their actual condition for replacements. The pipes, which are not identified as high-risk pipes at the prioritisation step, will only be renewed reactively. Hence, the success of the strategies relies heavily on the prioritisation step. To make accurate selections of high-risk pipes, the prioritisation step requires a failure prediction method that can give a precise estimation of pipe failure likelihood, based on which the estimated failure cost and renewal cost can be readily obtained.

The problem of estimating water pipe failure risk has been studied for many decades. There are two main methodologies for tackling the problem, namely data-driven modelling and domain knowledge-driven modelling.

For domain knowledge-driven physical modelling, a variety of models has been proposed for explaining and predicting the deterioration processes of water pipes. They usually consider an individual aspect of the problem based on the domain knowledge in the related area, such as pipe-soil interaction analysis, residual structural resistance, or hydraulic characteristics modelling. A comprehensive review can be found in [14]. For data-driven statistical machine learning-based modelling, it assumes that pipes with similar intrinsic attributes share similar failure patterns, and that failure patterns which have appeared before are likely to reappear in the future. The patterns can be learnt from the available factors and data sets.

Both methodologies have limitations. For domain knowledge-based physical models, they often just consider one aspect of the problem, e.g., corrosion, and lack the ability to learn knowledge from heterogeneous features. While, for data-driven statistical machine learning-based models, they usually learn from what they see, i.e., learning from the provided basic features, and lack the ability to identify and include the informative features that only domain experts are aware of, e.g., a significant proportion of the waste water pipe failures (blockages) are caused by tree

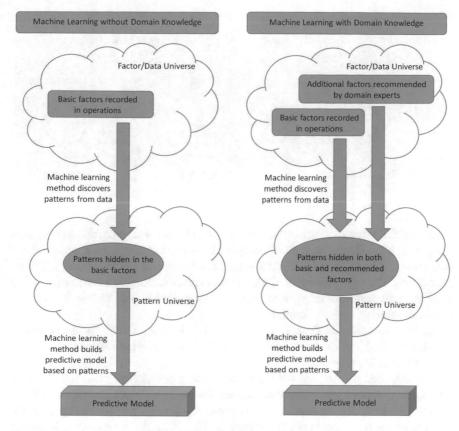

Fig. 18.1 Traditional machine learning versus machine learning with domain knowledge. Traditional machine learning methods suffer the limit of learning only from what they see. Domain knowledge can help avoid such limit via transferring the knowledge into machine learning models

root penetration. Therefore, in this work, we suggest and demonstrate that the incorporation of domain knowledge into machine learning methods could significantly improve the model performance. Figure 18.1 illustrates the difference between traditional machine learning methods and the machine learning methods considering domain knowledge.

For the modelling perspective, in order to improve high-risk pipe prioritisation for large-scale metropolitan pipe networks, we propose a Bayesian nonparametric statistical approach, namely the Dirichlet process mixture of hierarchical beta process model, for water pipe failure prediction. Unlike parametric approaches, the structure and complexity of the proposed model can grow as the amount of observed data increases. It makes the model invulnerable to faulty assumptions of model forms and adaptable to various failure patterns, thereby leading to more accurate predictions for different application scenarios.

It is worth noting that water pipe failure data is extremely sparse in reality. Very few pipes have failure records during the observation period. Such sparsity makes

Fig. 18.2 Water supply networks in the selected regions

traditional failure prediction methods incompetent for accurate pipe failure prediction since most pipes do not have failure data for training. The proposed approach deals with this issue by sharing failure data via a flexible hierarchical modelling of failure behaviours. The key component of the hierarchical modelling is a flexible grouping scheme. It clusters similar pipes together for modelling so that failure data can be shared by similar pipes for training.

Additionally, domain experts' experience, i.e., helping identify potential useful features for building the model and rejecting false correlated features, also helps tackle the data sparsity challenge.

The proposed method has been applied to the pipe network of an international metropolis that has a total population of near five million people. In this work, three representative regions are selected from the metropolis for comparison experiments. The regions and the networks are shown in Fig. 18.2. As we can see, the water supply network is constituted of two main categories of water pipes, critical water main (CWM) indicated by red lines and reticulation water main (RWM) indicated by blue lines. CWMs have larger diameters (300 mm and above), and RWMs have smaller diameters (smaller than 300 mm). Each water pipe is composed of a set of pipe segments connected in series. Failure records can be precisely matched with pipe segments, allowing the proposed method to model failure behaviours of pipe segments.

The rest of the chapter is organised as follows. Section 18.2 reviews the related work. Section 18.3 describes the details of the proposed method. Empirical studies and the importance of the domain knowledge are shown in Sect. 18.4. The conclusions are drawn in Sect. 18.5.

18.2 Related Work

In the past decades, a large number of statistical approaches have been proposed for water pipe failure prediction with significant success. However, most of them need to pre-define the form of the model, hence lack the flexibility of modelling complex situations, where the recent Bayesian nonparametric machine learning strategy can readily solve the model selection problem. In this section, we briefly review the related work on statistical water pipe failure prediction methods and Bayesian nonparametric approaches.

18.2.1   Statistical Failure Prediction Methods

In recent decades, many statistical models have been proposed for water pipe failure prediction. In the early stages, various methods were developed for modelling the relationship between pipe age and pipe failure rate. For instance, the work in [15] proposed a time-exponential model, which formulates the number of failures per unit length per year as an exponential function of pipe age. Similarly, time-power model [12] and time-linear model [9] were developed with comparable performances.

Later, multivariate probabilistic models were suggested. They make predictions based on a variety of pipe attributes, such as age, material, length and diameter. One of the most popular multivariate approaches is the Cox proportional hazards model [3]. It is a semi-parametric method, in which the baseline hazard function has an arbitrary form and the pipe attributes alter the baseline hazard function via an exponential function multiplicatively. The Weibull model and its variants [2, 8] are also widely adopted in practice. They utilise either a Weibull distribution or a Weibull process for modelling pipe failure behaviours.

Recently, a ranking-based method [18] was proposed for predicting water pipe failures. It treats failure prediction as a ranking problem. Pipes are ranked based on their failure risk. The method performs failure prediction via a real-valued ranking function rather than an estimation of failure probability.

18.2.2   Bayesian Nonparametric Approaches

All the aforementioned methods are parametric or semi-parametric, which means the forms of the methods are predefined and fixed during the training process. If the assumptions made on the model form are not satisfied, accurate predictions cannot be achieved. In contrast, Bayesian nonparametric approaches do not make assumptions about the model structure. Instead, their model complexities grow as the amount of observed data increases, endowing Bayesian nonparametric approaches with flexibility for modelling complex real-world data.

The Beta process [5] and the Dirichlet process [4] are two Bayesian nonparametric approaches that were developed recently with tremendous success in a variety of domains. They have become the cornerstones for building more sophisticated Bayesian nonparametric models.

The Beta process was originally developed for survival analysis on life history data. It was utilised as a prior distribution over the space of cumulative hazard function. Later, the work in [17] extended the Beta process to more general spaces for different applications, such as factor analysis [13], image reconstruction [20, 21], image interpolation and document analysis [17]. One of its variants was also applied to water pipe failure prediction [10, 11].

The Dirichlet process [4] is a flexible Bayesian nonparametric prior for data clustering. It does not set any assumptions on the number of clusters. Instead, it allows the number of clusters to grow as the number of data points increases. It is the foundation of many nonparametric mixture models, and has been widely adopted in various applications, such as document analysis [16], musical similarity analysis [6] image annotation [19] and DNA sequence analysis [7].

18.3   The Proposed Method

The proposed Dirichlet process mixture of an hierarchical beta process model consists of two main components working with each other interactively: a hierarchical representation of water pipe failure behaviours and a flexible pipe grouping scheme. The grouping scheme generates a set of groups, on each of which the hierarchical representation can be constructed. The hierarchical representation provides a precise modelling of each group's failure behaviours, hence acts as the basis of grouping.

The two main components are described in Sects. 18.3.1 and 18.3.2 respectively. The details of the proposed model are given in Sect. 18.3.3.

18.3.1   Hierarchical Modelling of Water Pipe Failure Behaviours

The hierarchical beta process is adopted in this work as the hierarchical modelling of water pipe failure behaviours. We first briefly introduce the beta-Bernoulli process for modelling failure event and failure probability in Sects. 18.3.1.1 and 18.3.1.2. Then the details of the hierarchical modeling are given in Sect. 18.3.1.3.

18.3.1.1   Beta Process

On a measurable space Ω, a beta process H is defined as a positive Levy process, a positive random measure whose masses on disjoint subsets of Ω are independent. It is parameterised by a positive concentration function c and a base measure H_0, which is also defined on space Ω. In simplified cases, where function $c(\omega_i)$ becomes a constant, we call c concentration parameter.

For disjoint infinitesimal partitions of Ω, the beta process can be generated as:

$$H(B_k) \sim Beta(cH_0(B_k), c(1 - H_0(B_k))), \qquad (18.1)$$

where B_k indicates a partition, and $k \in \{1, \cdots, K\}$ is the index. The process can be denoted as $H \sim BP(c, H_0)$.

When the base measure H_0 is discrete and has a set function form of $H_0 = \sum_i p_i \delta_{\omega_i}$, H turns to have atoms at the same locations as H_0's and can be written in a set function form accordingly as:

$$H(\omega) = \sum_i \pi_i \delta_{\omega_i}(\omega)$$
$$\pi_i \sim Beta(cq_i, c(1 - q_i)) \qquad (18.2)$$

where $\delta_{\omega_i}(\omega) = 1$ when $\omega = \omega_i$ and 0 otherwise.

As defined in a general space Ω, the Beta process provides us a flexible Bayesian nonparametric prior for water pipe failure events which themselves can be modelled by the Bernoulli process.

18.3.1.2   Bernoulli Process

For a Bernoulli process $BeP(H)$, each of its draws X_j is again a measure on space Ω. j represents the draw index. H indicates a beta process on Ω, as defined before. It acts as the prior of the Bernoulli process. A draw of the Bernoulli process can also be represented via a set function form as:

$$X_j(\omega) = \sum_i x_{ij} \delta_{\omega_i}(\omega)$$
$$x_{i,j} \sim Bernoulli(\pi_i) \qquad (18.3)$$

where δ_{ω_i} corresponds to the same atom location of H. The random variable x_{ij} is generated from a Bernoulli distribution parameterised by π_i which is defined as Eq. 18.2. With x_{ij} as its elements, an infinite binary column vector, also denoted by X_j, can be used for representing a draw of the Bernoulli process. Then the draws of the Bernoulli process can form an infinite binary matrix X, with X_j representing a column and j representing the column index. Each row of the matrix corresponds to an atom location δ_{ω_i}. We can see that the beta process appears to be a proper Bayesian nonparametric prior for such infinite binary matrices.

It is worth noting that the Beta process is a conjugate prior of the Bernoulli process. Given a beta process prior $H \sim BP(c, H_0)$, and a set of m observations drawn from a Bernoulli process $X_j \sim BeP(H)$, the posterior is again a beta process, with parameters updated as follow:

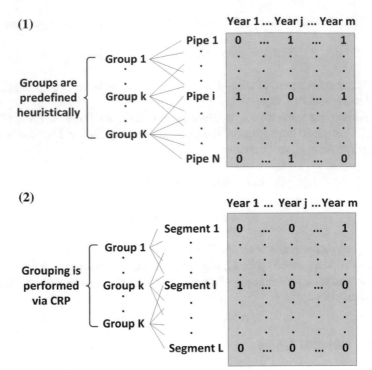

Fig. 18.3 Binary failure matrices for pipes and pipe segments

$$H|X_{1,\cdots,m} \backsim BP\left(c+m, \frac{c}{c+m}H_0 + \frac{1}{c+m}\sum_{j=1}^{m}X_j\right) \qquad (18.4)$$

The conjugacy significantly simplifies the inference procedure for parameter estimation.

18.3.1.3 Hierarchical Modelling

With the aid of a Beta-Bernoulli process, a hierarchical representation can be developed for modelling water pipe failure behaviours. Firstly, failure events can be modelled by a Bernoulli process $BeP(H)$. Let an infinite binary matrix X, as illustrated in Fig. 18.3 (1), represent failure records of pipes. Each of its columns, X_j, can be treated as a draw from the Bernoulli process $BeP(H)$. It is an infinite binary column vector with the i-th element $x_{i,j}$ generated from $x_{i,j} \backsim Bernoulli(\pi_i)$. $x_{i,j} = 1$ means pipe i failed in year j, and $x_{i,j} = 0$ otherwise. Then the beta process, $H \backsim BP(c, H_0)$, defined as a positive Levy process on pipe space Ω, can be used as a prior of failure events, namely failure probability. Its set function form is defined as Eq. 18.3.

With beta process H as a prior, each row of the matrix X corresponds to an atom location δ_{ω_i} in the pipe space Ω, which can be infinitely large. We assume that two pipes share the same failure patterns if they have the same intrinsic attributes and environmental factors. Hence, we treat such two pipes as the same in the pipe space Ω. Considering all the possible combinations of pipe attributes and environmental factors, the number of "unique" pipes in the pipe space becomes infinite. Therefore, each column of the matrix X is an infinite binary vector that is drawn from a Bernoulli process. The beta process H is then a conjugate prior of the infinite binary matrix X. It models the failure probabilities of pipes via π_i.

While the Beta-Bernoulli process is capable of modelling failure behaviours as described above, there are two issues of adopting it in practice. Firstly, the number of failures is extremely small compared with the number of pipes, especially for CWMs. Only a small portion of CWMs have failure records since most of the CWMs did not fail during the observation period. Thus, the majority of CWMs have no failure data for model training. Secondly, in addition to pipe failure histories, pipe attributes and environmental factors are also crucial for estimating failure probabilities. However, they are not properly considered in the Beta-Bernoulli process. The fact that the pipes with similar intrinsic attributes and environmental factors often share similar failure patterns is ignored by the Beta-Bernoulli process.

In order to address these issues, the hierarchical beta process (HBP) model [11, 17] can be adopted as a hierarchical modelling of water pipe failure behaviours. Given a water pipe grouping, e.g., grouping by intrinsic attributes, one more beta process can be added into the model hierarchy for modelling the failure behaviours of groups. The new beta process is on top of the existing beta process, serving as the prior of its mean parameter. The graphical model in Fig. 18.4 (1) illustrates the HBP model. It can also be described as the followings:

$$q_k \backsim Beta(c_0 q_0, c_0(1 - q_0)), \ k \in [1, \cdots, K],$$
$$\pi_i \backsim Beta(c_k q_k, c_k(1 - q_k)), \ i \in [1, \cdots, N], \qquad (18.5)$$
$$x_{i,j} \backsim Bernoulli(\pi_i), \qquad j \in [1, \cdots, m_i],$$

where π_i and x_{ij} are defined as before, modelling the failure probability of pipe i and failure history of pipe i in year j respectively. q_k and c_k are the mean and concentration parameters for group k. q_k can be regarded as modeling the failure rate of group k. q_0 and c_0 are the hyper parameters.

By adding one more hierarchy level, the HBP model estimates failure probabilities through the inferences on both group level and pipe level. Group level inference estimates the group failure rate q_k, and pipe level inference estimates the pipe failure probability π_i. Failure data can be shared by the same group of pipes for estimating group failure rate q_k. It helps to solve the failure data sparsity problem. The failure patterns that are shared by similar pipes are captured at the group level since the pipes within the same group share the same q_k. At the pipe level, the pipe failure probability π_i is estimated by considering not only the failure observations x_{ij}, but also the group similarity through the group failure rate q_k.

18.3.2   Flexible Water Pipe Grouping

Real world data is complicated and often demonstrates multi-modality property, which is the case for water pipe failures. Consequently, single-modality models become insufficient in such circumstances for modelling the whole data corpora. Mixture model is a widely adopted probabilistic approach for modelling the data arising from different modalities. It assumes that the final model consists of a set of mixture components, each of which can accurately model a portion of data.

For conventional parametric mixture models, the number of mixture components is required to be known in advance, which is unrealistic for many real world applications, such as water pipe grouping. Therefore, we adopt the Dirichlet process (DP), a nonparametric approach, for pipe grouping. It serves as a flexible prior for data partitioning and sets no assumptions on the number of partitions. Correspondingly, the Dirichlet process mixture model, which is built based on the Dirichlet process, can comprise a countably infinite number of components and adjust itself for fitting observed data.

In order to adopt DP as the prior of pipe grouping, we use the Chinese restaurant process (CRP) [1] as the constructive representation of DP. It exhibits the clustering property of DP via the following metaphor. Suppose there is a Chinese restaurant that has an infinite number of tables. A sequence of customers enters and select a table to sit. The first customer sits at the first table. The following customers sit at tables with a guide:

$$p(z_l = r | z_{-l}, \alpha) \propto \begin{cases} \frac{n_r}{n-1+\alpha} & \text{if } r \leqslant k \\ \frac{\alpha}{n-1+\alpha} & \text{if } r = k + 1. \end{cases} \qquad (18.6)$$

z_l indicates a customer, z_{-l} denotes all the customers that appeared before z_l, r indicates a cluster index, and k represents the current number of clusters. n_r is the number of customers in cluster r and α is the concentration parameter for CRP, controlling the probability that a customer is assigned to an unoccupied table.

The CRP offers an exchangeable distribution over the table assignments z_l. The joint distribution is invariant to the order of customers. The procedure of assigning a table for a customer can be performed as he or she is the last customer entering the restaurant. As described by Eq. 18.6, the i-th customer sits at an occupied table with a probability proportional to the number of customers who are already sitting at that table. He or she sits at an unoccupied table with a probability proportional to the concentration parameter α. In this metaphor, customers correspond to data points and tables correspond to clusters. Fig. 18.4 (2) shows the Dirichlet process mixture model with the CRP as the constructive definition. Each data point x_i is drawn from a component of the mixture model. z_i is the component indicator for x_i. θ_k represents the parameter for component k.

With the aid of the CRP, we can group pipes adaptively for fitting data observations. As a result, pipes with similar failure behaviours are grouped together. Moreover, the CRP helps to integrate the grouping process and the failure modeling process for achieving accurate performance.

18.3.3 Dirichlet Process Mixture of Hierarchical Beta Process

In this section, we give the detailed description of the proposed Dirichlet process mixture of the hierarchical Beta process (DPMHBP) model for water pipe failure prediction.

For the proposed DPMHBP model, a water pipe is treated as a set of pipe segments that are connected in series. The failure probability of a pipe segment is modelled by a beta process. It is different from the HBP model [11] where the Beta process is used for modelling failure probabilities of pipes.

Pipe length is an important attribute for estimating failure probability. The intuition is that longer pipes tend to have higher failure probabilities if other attributes and external factors are the same. However, the HBP model ignores the impact of the length attribute when estimating failure probabilities. It only focuses on pipe age attribute and failure histories. The significant variance of pipe lengths is neglected. In order to tackle the problem, the proposed approach suggests modelling the failure probabilities of pipe segments whose lengths are relatively constant with a very small variance.

Another difference between the HBP model and the proposed DPMHBP model is that the HBP model groups pipes based on heuristic domain information e.g., pipe age. Its grouping is predefined and fixed during the inference process. The number of the groups is also required to be set beforehand, which can be heuristic. In contrast, for the proposed DPMHBP method, the grouping process is integrated with the inference process via the DP mixture model. They interact with each other to achieve an optimal model. The number of groups is not fixed and can grow as the size of the training data increases.

Considering all the issues mentioned above, the DPMHBP model can finally be given as follows:

$$
\begin{aligned}
q_k &\sim Beta(c_0 q_0, c_0(1 - q_0)), \quad k \in [1, \cdots, K], \\
z_l &\sim CRP(\alpha), \qquad\qquad\quad z_l \in [1, \cdots, K], \\
\rho_l &\sim Beta(c_{z_l} q_{z_l}, c_{z_l}(1 - q_{z_l})), \, l \in [1, \cdots, L], \\
y_{l,j} &\sim Bernoulli(\rho_l), \qquad\quad j \in [1, \cdots, m_l], \\
\pi_i &= 1 - \prod_{l=1}^{s_i}(1 - \rho_l), \qquad l \in [1, \cdots, s_i].
\end{aligned}
\tag{18.7}
$$

The failure probability estimation is conducted on three levels: segment group level, segment level and pipe level. The failure events are recorded for segments rather than pipes. The grouping is performed on segments via the CRP, as illustrated by Fig. 18.3 (2). At segment group level, q_k denotes the failure rate of segment group k. z_l represents the group index for segment l. At segment level, ρ_l indicates the failure probability of segment l. Once the segment level estimation is obtained, pipe failure probability π_i can be readily computed via the failure probability of a series of connected segments. Figure 18.4 (3) shows the graphical model of the DPMHBP model.

It is worth noting that the Bernoulli process is more suitable for modelling segment failures than modelling pipe failures because it is very rare for a segment to fail twice in a year.

Regarding the inference of the model parameters from the training data, since no analytical solution is available for the proposed model, we use a Markov chain Monte Carlo (MCMC) sampling algorithm for inference. Gibbs sampling is the MCMC-based method that has been widely used for DP mixture models when conjugacy exists between prior and likelihood. However, for the DPMHBP model, such conjugacy is broken by the extra hierarchy of the HBP model. Therefore, we choose to utilise a Metropolis-within-Gibbs sampling method for inference.

18.4 Experiments

In this section, we conduct comparison experiments on the metropolitan water supply network data to demonstrate the superiority of the proposed DPMHBP model. We first introduce the pipe network data and the failure data in Sect. 18.4.1. The features that are suggested by domain experts and used in the experiments are explained in Sect. 18.4.2. Then the compared methods are listed in Sect. 18.4.3. Finally, we give the comparison results and discuss the impact of the proposed method in Sect. 18.4.4.

18.4.1 Data Collection

Three representative regions from the metropolis are selected to perform the experiments. Region A is a local government area with a population around 210,000, which is one of the most populous local government areas in its state. Its population density is 629 people per km². Region B is a local government area with a high population density of 2,374 people per km². Its population is about 182,000. Region C is a low density suburban local government area, which has a population of 205,000 and a population density of 300 people per km².

For each region, both network data and failure data are collected. Network data consists of pipe IDs, pipe attributes, pipe locations and environmental factors. Pipe location is represented as a set of connected line segments, each of which corresponds to a pipe segment. Failure data contains pipe IDs, failure dates and failure locations.

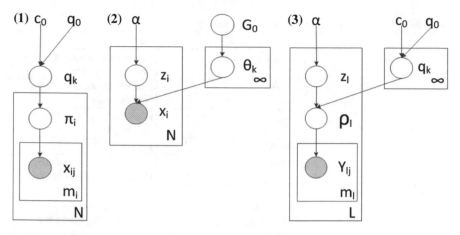

Fig. 18.4 Graphical models for **1** Hierarchical Beta process, **2** Dirichlet process mixture model (with Chinese restaurant process as the constructive definition), **3** Dirichlet process mixture of hierarchical beta process

Table 18.1 Summary of pipe network data and pipe failure data

		# Pipes	# Failures	Laid years	Observation period
Region A	All	15189	4093	1930–1997	1998–2009
	CWM	3793	520	1930–1997	1998–2009
Region B	All	11836	3694	1888–1997	1998–2009
	CWM	2457	432	1888–1997	1998–2009
Region C	All	18001	4421	1913–1997	1998–2009
	CWM	5041	563	1913–1997	1998–2009

Pipe amount, failure amount, laid year range and observation period are sum-marised for different pipe types in Table 18.1. As we can see, CWMs only take a small portion of the network, 24.97% for region A, 20.76% for region B, and 28.00% for region C. The ratio between CWM failures and all the failures is even smaller, 12.71% for region A, 11.70% for region B, and 12.74% for region C.

The observation period covers 12 years, spanning from 1998 to 2009. It is short compared with pipe life span which can be more than 100 years as shown in Table 18.1. The majority of the pipes did not fail or just failed once during the observation period. If considering pipe segment failures, the failure events are even more sparse. Hence, the sparsity assumption holds for the proposed approximated sampling algorithm.

Failure locations are used for matching failures with pipe segments. It enables the proposed DPHBP model to work on pipe segment level for estimating failure probabilities.

Table 18.2 Pipe attributes and environmental factors

	Property and factors	Description
Pipe attributes	Protective coating	Categorical value indicating the type of coating
	Diameter	Continuous value indicating pipe diameter
	Length	Continuous value indicating pipe length
	Laid date	Laid date for pipe
	Material	Categorical value indicating the type of pipe material
Environmental factors	Soil corrosiveness Soil expansiveness Soil geology Soil map	Categorical value indicating soil property for the corresponding soil factor
	Distance to traffic intersection	Continuous value indicating the distance between pipe segment and the closest traffic intersection

As mentioned before, we focus on CWMs for comparison experiments since both physical condition assessment and proactive replacement are conducted for CWMs. For comparing the performances of different approaches, we use the first 11 years' failure records as training data and the last year's failure records as testing data. All the compared methods have the same setting for fair comparison.

18.4.2 Considered Features - The Importance of Domain Knowledge

In this section, we describe the pipe attributes and the environmental factors that we used in the experiments. As mentioned before, by considering the domain experts' knowledge, informative features can be readily identified and considered in the model. Without the support of domain knowledge, important features could be ignored by the model and false correlated features could be incorporated into the model, in which case, the model performance would be significantly reduced.

For drinking water pipe, there are five pipe attributes utilised in the experiments including protective coating, diameter, length, laid date, and material. Two types of environmental factors are considered in the experiments. One is the surrounding soil condition, and the other is the distance between pipe segment and its closest traffic intersection. These features are summarised in Table 18.2.

For pipe attributes, protective coating and material are categorical features indicating the type of coating and material. Typical protective coatings are a polyethylene sleeve and tar coating. Typical materials are cast iron cement lined (CICL) and polyvinyl chloride (PVC). Diameter, length, and laid date are continuous features.

Surrounding soil condition is one of the most complex and important environmental factors for water pipe failure prediction. It directly impacts on the pipe degradation process. In the experiments, four different soil features are considered including soil corrosiveness, soil expansiveness, soil geology and soil map. They depict different perspectives of soil characteristics.

Soil corrosiveness describes the risk of pipe pitting (metal corrosion) which is essentially an electrical phenomenon and can be measured by a linear polarisation resistance test. Soil expansiveness describes the a shrinking and swelling of expansive clays in response to moisture content change. It is a phenomenon that affects clay soil and can be measured by shrink swell test. Soil geology depicts the information of rocks, e.g., sandstone and shale. A soil map represents the landscape information, e.g., fluvial, colluvial and erosional. It also includes information on the soil types that are associated with different landscapes.

Each soil factor is a categorical feature containing several distinct values. The selected local government areas are partitioned into small regions according to the distinct values of soil factors. Pipe segments falling into the same region share the same soil factor value.

A large portion of CWMs are buried underneath roads. It makes the change of road surface pressure another important environmental factor for estimating water pipe failures. It has been shown that frequent pressure changes can lead to high failure rate. One of the main sources causing road surface pressure change comes from traffic intersections due to the frequent vehicle starting and stopping. In order to measure the impact of road surface pressure change, we calculate the distance between each pipe segment and its closest traffic intersection. The obtained continuous value is regarded as a feature of the pipe segment for predicting its failure probability.

For the waste water pipes, tree root coverage percentage, soil evaporation and soil moisture are also considered based on domain experts' knowledge. A key cause of waste water pipe failures is the intrusion of tree roots. Roots have three basic functions; they anchor the plant and hold it upright, store food, and absorb water and nutrients. The extent of the tree root system is dependent on the species, the age of the tree, the nutrient availability from surrounding decaying organic matter and the physical limitations of the surrounding soil (soil depth, soil density/pore size, oxygen and moisture content). A constant soil temperature and adequate moisture availability lead to horizontal growing roots, in day soil condition tends to lead to vertical growing roots. In temperate conditions, tree root growth is most active during spring and autumn. In this work, we use tree canopy area (obtained by satellite image recognition) as the estimation of the tree root area. Figure 18.5 illustrates the relationship between tree root canopy coverage and the waste water pipe failures. Figure 18.6 demonstrates the relationship between soil moisture and waste water pipe failures.

As we can see in Figs. 18.5 and 18.6, both tree canopy coverage and soil moisture have a strong positive correlation with waste water pipe blockage. It demonstrates

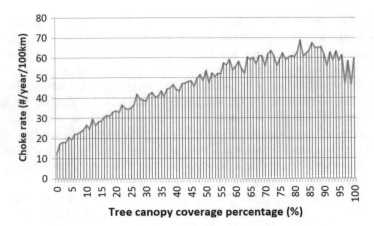

Fig. 18.5 The relationship between tree canopy coverage and waste water pipe failure (choke)

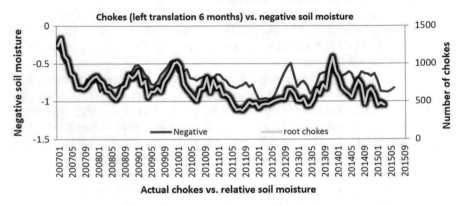

Fig. 18.6 The relationship between soil moisture and waste water pipe failure (choke)

that domain experts' knowledge can help identify important factors and later improve model performance.

18.4.3 *Compared Approaches*

In order to evaluate the proposed approach, four state-of-the-art methods are compared in the experiments including the Cox proportional hazard model, the Weibull model, the HBP model and a support vector machine (SVM) based ranking method. Additionally, different grouping methods are used with the HBP model as comparisons for demonstrating the advantage of the grouping scheme of the proposed approach.

The Cox proportional hazard model [3] is one of the most popular approaches for survival analysis. It is a semi-parametric approach, in which the form of the baseline hazard function can be arbitrary, and the explanatory features put impacts on the baseline hazard function via an exponential function multiplicatively. Formally, the Cox proportional hazard model can be described as:

$$h(t, z) = h_0(t)e^{b^T z},$$ (18.8)

where h_0 indicates the baseline hazard function, z indicates the explanatory features of water pipe, and b is the parameter vector that can be learned from training data via a partial likelihood maximisation procedure.

For the Weibull model [2, 8], water pipe failures are modelled as a set of stochastic events governed by a time dependent stochastic process, namely the Weibull process. It can be regarded as a nonhomogeneous Poisson process whose intensity varies as time changes. The intensity function can be formally given as:

$$\lambda(t) = \alpha \beta t^{\beta-1},$$ (18.9)

where t represents pipe age, α and β are parameters that need to be learned from training data. Similar to the Cox proportional hazard model, the explanatory features can also be utilised via an exponential function multiplicatively.

Analogous to the method proposed in [18], an SVM-based ranking approach is compared. This approach formulates pipe failure prediction as a ranking problem. It ranks pipes according to their failure risks without estimating their actual failure probability. It learns a real-valued ranking function H that maximises the objective function:

$$\sum_{z \in P, z' \in N} \frac{I(H(z) > H(z'))}{|P| \cdot |N|},$$ (18.10)

where P and N represent the positive class dataset (failure dataset) and negative class dataset respectively. $I(\cdot)$ is the indicator function. $|P|$ and $|N|$ indicate the numbers of data points in the positive and negative class datasets respectively.

The HBP model proposed by [11] is also compared. In order to evaluate the grouping scheme of the proposed approach, three different grouping methods are integrated with the HBP model for comparison. They group pipes based on pipe attributes according to domain expert suggestions. Specifically, pipes are grouped based on material, diameter and laid year.

For fair comparison, the features described in the previous section are used for all the compared methods. For HBP and DPMHBP, the features are applied multiplicatively similar to the Cox proportional hazard model and the Weibull model. A linear kernel is used for the SVM-based ranking approach.

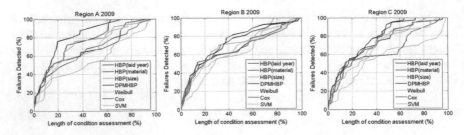

Fig. 18.7 Failure prediction results for the selected regions by different models

Table 18.3 AUC of different approaches. The second row shows the AUC when 100% of CWMs are inspected. The third row shows the AUC when 1% of CWMs are inspected

	Region A			Region B			Region C		
	DPM HBP Cox	HBP SVM	Weibull	DPM HBP Cox	HBP SVM	Weibull	DPM HBP Cox	HBP SVM	Weibull
AUC (100%)	82.67% 66.91%	77.05% 56.45%	68.44%	74.51% 65.53%	72.56% 61.90%	65.20%	78.37% 64.50%	73.54% 69.48%	55.84%
AUC (1%)	8.09‰ 4.67‰	5.64‰ 4.32‰	5.84‰	4.21‰ 2.46‰	3.60‰ 3.41‰	2.70‰	5.11‰ 2.50‰	2.48‰ 1.73‰	2.98‰

18.4.4 Prediction Results and Real Life Impact

In this section, we compare the prediction results to demonstrate the superiority of the proposed approach. As mentioned before, the historical failure data from 1998 to 2008 is used for training and the failures which occurred in 2009 are used for testing. Water pipes are ranked by different methods based on their estimated failure risks. The failure prediction results are shown in Fig. 18.7. The x-axis represents the cumulative percentage of the inspected water pipes, and the y-axis indicates the percentage of the detected pipe failures.

Additionally, we calculate AUC for measuring the performances of different approaches. The results are shown in Table 18.3. Statistical significance tests, particularly the one-sided paired t-test at 5% level of significance, are performed on AUC to evaluate the significance of the performance differences. The results are shown in Table 18.4. For Tables 18.3 and 18.4, only the results from the best groupings are shown for the HBP model.

As we can see from Fig. 18.7 and Table 18.3, the proposed DPMHBP model consistently gives the most accurate prediction for all the three regions, whereas the other methods only perform accurately for some of the regions. It demonstrates the adaptability of the proposed approach to the diversity of failure patterns. The significance test results, listed in Table 18.4, show that the proposed model significantly outperforms the other methods.

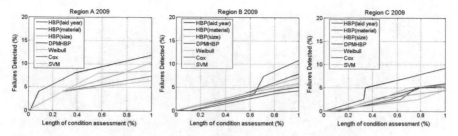

Fig. 18.8 The detection results with 1% of pipe network length inspected

Table 18.4 Statistical significance test (t-test) results for the proposed method and the others. The second row shows the results when 100% of CWMs are inspected. The third row shows the results when 1% of CWMs are inspected

	Region A		Region B		Region C	
	versus HBP	versus Weibull	versus HBP	versus Weibull	versus HBP	versus Weibull
	versus Cox	versus SVM	versus Cox	versus SVM	versus Cox	versus SVM
AUC	2.56(= 0.08)	9.37(<0.05)	3.12(= 0.05)	22.01(<0.05)	7.83(<0.05)	43.55(<0.05)
(100%)	10.58(<0.05)	18.88(<0.05)	21.17(<0.05)	30.11(<0.05)	26.08(<0.05)	15.63(<0.05)
AUC	44.29(<0.05)	40.46(<0.05)	1.26(<0.05)	4.64(<0.05)	65.90(<0.05)	53.43(<0.05)
(1%)	62.44(<0.05)	69.01(<0.05)	5.53(<0.05)	1.99(<0.05)	65.43(<0.05)	61.72(<0.05)

In addition to the comparison studies shown above, we also demonstrate the real-life impact of the proposed method by showing its improvements in its real-world application. Different from the standard performance measurement, domain experts often adopt evaluation criteria that can reflect the constraints encountered in reality. In the context of water pipe failure prediction, as mentioned before, only a small portion of the pipes can be physically inspected each year. Specifically, due to budget constraint, only 1% of the total CWMs can be inspected every year. Therefore, we show the performance curves with 1% of CWMs inspected in Fig. 18.8. AUC and significance test results are also given in Tables 18.3 and 18.4 for the situation of inspecting 1% of CWMs. As we can see, the proposed approach significantly outperforms the other methods for all the three regions. In region C, the proposed approach nearly doubles the number of detected failures compared with the second best method.

A risk map, as shown in Fig. 18.9, is another widely used method for visualising real-life impact. As illustrated in the figure, the prioritisation of pipes is coded by different colours. For instance, red lines indicate the top 10% high-risk pipes predicted by our method. Black stars in the figure denote the failures which occurred in the testing year. As we can see, many failures could be prevented and significant economic and social savings could be brought to the water utility if the proposed method were applied.

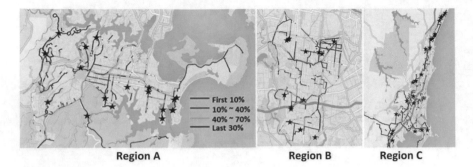

Region A   Region B   Region C

Fig. 18.9 Risk maps for the selected three regions

18.5 Conclusion

In this work, we present the Dirichlet process mixture of the hierarchical beta process model for water pipe failure prediction. The model demonstrates high adaptability to the diversity of failure patterns. Its structure and complexity can grow as the number of data points increases. It tackles the sparse failure data problem by sharing failure data through pipe grouping. An efficient Metropolis-within-Gibbs sampling algorithm is also proposed for handling large-scale datasets. The empirical studies conducted on the real water pipe data verify the superiority of the proposed approach. The domain expert knowledge also gave significant impact on the model development and the informative factor identification. It would be extremely difficult, if not impossible, to discover the key informative factors without the support of domain knowledge. Besides, the incorporation of domain experts' knowledge and experience can help enhance domain users' trust in the model as it improves their understanding of the model and makes them trust the basis of the model development.

References

1. Aldous, D.J.: Exchangeability and Related Topics. Springer, Berlin (1985)
2. Constantine, A.G.: Pipeline reliability: Stochastic Models in Engineering Technology and Management. World Scientific, Singapore (1996)
3. Cox, D.R.: Regression models and life-tables. In: Journal of the Royal Statistical Society. Series B Methodological, pp. 187–220. (1972)
4. Ferguson, T.S.: A bayesian analysis of some nonparametric problems. Ann. Stat. **1**, 209–230 (1973)
5. Hjort, N.L.: Nonparametric bayes estimators based on beta processes in models for life history data. Ann. Stat. **18**, 1259–1294 (1990)
6. Hoffman, M.D., Blei, D.M., Cook, P.R.: Content-based musical similarity computation using the hierarchical dirichlet process. In: ISMIR, pp. 349–354 (2008)
7. Huelsenbeck, J.P., Jain, S., Frost, S.W., Pond, S.L.K.: A dirichlet process model for detecting positive selection in protein-coding dna sequences. Proc. Natl. Acad. Sci. **103**(16), 6263–6268 (2006)

8. Ibrahim, J.G., Chen, M.H., Sinha, D.: Bayesian Survival Analysis. Wiley Online Library (2005)
9. Kettler, A., Goulter, I.: An analysis of pipe breakage in urban water distribution networks. Can. J. Civil Eng. **12**(2), 286–293 (1985)
10. Li, B., Zhang, B., Li, Z., Wang, Y., Chen, F., Vitanage, D.: Prioritising water pipes for condition assessment with data analytics. OzWater (2015)
11. Li, Z., Zhang, B., Wang, Y., Chen, F., Taib, R., Whiffin, V., Wang, Y.: Water pipe condition assessment: a hierarchical beta process approach for sparse incident data. Mach. Learn. **95**(1), 11–26 (2014)
12. Mavin, K.: Predicting the failure performance of individual water mains. Urban Water Research Association of Australia (114) (1996)
13. Paisley, J., Carin, L.: Nonparametric factor analysis with beta process priors. In: Proceedings of the 26th Annual International Conference on Machine Learning, pp. 777–784. ACM (2009)
14. Rajani, B., Kleiner, Y.: Comprehensive review of structural deterioration of water mains: physically based models. Urban Water **3**(3), 151–164 (2001)
15. Shamir, U., Howard, C.: An analytic approach to scheduling pipe replacement. Am. Water Works Assoc. **71**(5), 248–258 (1979)
16. Teh, Y.W., Jordan, M.I., Beal, M.J., Blei, D.M.: Hierarchical dirichlet processes. J. Am. Stat. Assoc. **101**(476), a (2006)
17. Thibaux, R., Jordan, M.I.: Hierarchical beta processes and the Indian buffet process. In: International Conference on Artificial Intelligence and Statistics, pp. 564–571 (2007)
18. Wang, R., Dong, W., Wang, Y., Tang, K., Yao, X.: Pipe failure prediction: a data mining method. In: 2013 IEEE 29th International Conference on Data Engineering (ICDE), pp. 1208–1218. IEEE (2013)
19. Yakhnenko, O., Honavar, V.: Annotating images and image objects using a hierarchical dirichlet process model. In: Proceedings of the 9th International Workshop on Multimedia Data Mining: Held in Conjunction with the ACM SIGKDD 2008, pp. 1–7. ACM (2008)
20. Zhou, M., Chen, H., Ren, L., Sapiro, G., Carin, L., Paisley, J.W.: Non-parametric bayesian dictionary learning for sparse image representations. In: Advances in Neural Information Processing Systems, pp. 2295–2303 (2009)
21. Zhou, M., Yang, H., Sapiro, G., Dunson, D.B., Carin, L.: Dependent hierarchical beta process for image interpolation and denoising. In: International Conference on Artificial Intelligence and Statistics, pp. 883–891 (2011)

Chapter 19
Analytical Modelling of Point Process and Application to Transportation

Le Minh Kieu

Abstract This chapter aims to explain the inference mechanisms of the expected number of passengers arriving at transit stops. These questions are crucial in tactical planning and operational control of public transport to estimate the impact and effectiveness of different planning and control strategies. The existing literature offers a limited number of approaches for these problems, which mainly focus more on the prediction of aggregated passenger counts. We propose two analytical models to model the arrival of passengers: The first model is a non-homogeneous Poisson Process (NHPP); the second model is a time-varying Poisson Regression (TPR) model. Finally, numerical experiments and a case study show the performance of the proposed models using simulated data. The analysis of the estimated model's parameters using domain knowledge also provides good insights into the factors that impact the patronage level of buses in New South Wales, Australia.

19.1 Introduction

Passenger demand plays an essential role in tactical planning and operational control in transportation, especially in public transport, because transit vehicles have to stop for passengers boarding and alighting. Transit tactical planning and operational control, as defined in [9], concerns the decisions to design the exact transit services, e.g. frequency of services and timetables; and the decisions to control the operating service, especially in real time. The questions of modelling the expected number of passengers arrival at transit stops are essential for these studies. For instance, the total or mean waiting time is often used as the main objective function for public transport tactical planning and operation studies [3, 8–10], which in turn is estimated using a knowledge of passenger demand.

L. M. Kieu (✉)
DATA61, CSIRO, 13 Garden Street, Eveleigh, NSW 2015, Australia
e-mail: leminh.kieu@data61.csiro.au

© Springer International Publishing AG, part of Springer Nature 2018   385
J. Zhou and F. Chen (eds.), *Human and Machine Learning*, Human–Computer
Interaction Series, https://doi.org/10.1007/978-3-319-90403-0_19

The expected number of passenger arrivals can be explicitly linked to the estimation of aggregated passenger counts within a time period. Literature currently offers two major lines of research for this problem, one for long-term and the other for short-term passenger demand estimation. Long-term demand estimation models aim to complement long-term transit planning practice, such as in four-step demand modelling [19], route planning and frequency setting [9]. These models are developed to anticipate the approximation of passenger demand in the long-term for transit strategic planning, rather than the tactical planning and operational control problem discussed in this chapter. The other line of research, a short-term demand estimation model, that favours the use of data-driven and black-box methods, mainly aims for predictions. Examples of them include Neural Network [4, 20], Support Vector Machine [23] and the time-series analysis models [18]. While these methods showed their accuracy and robustness, the majority of them aim to provide predictions rather than an analytical connection between passenger demand and explanatory variables. For transit tactical planning and operational studies, data-driven models for short-term prediction may not be as useful as analytical models, because analytical models can be a part of an holistic framework, where researchers can estimate the passenger demand given the changes in explanatory variables. Existing data-driven methods generally use aggregated counts at previous time steps to predict the count at the next time step by relying on the underlying dynamic relationship between adjacent time steps.

One question which is of interest is *how* passengers arrive at transit stops. Transport researchers are generally interested in modelling and simulating the exact passenger arrival times at transit stops. This information is helpful for various purposes, for instance, to estimate the total travel time for passengers from the moment of arrival at transit stops to the moment of alighting from a transit vehicle. Existing studies in transit planning and operational control usually assume a known passenger arrival rate, which is the number of passengers arriving at a transit stop per time unit. The arrival rate allows a convenient simulation of passenger arrivals under one of two approaches: (a) deterministic or (b) stochastic point process. The deterministic approach assumes that passengers arrive uniformly to transit stops, so that the number of boarding/arrived passengers is simply the product of the passenger arrival rate and the time headway between consecutive vehicles. The approach has been used in many earlier studies such as [10, 13]. References [6, 7] also use a variation of this approach, where a dimensionless parameter is used to represent the marginal increase in vehicle delay resulted from a unit increase in headway. The stochastic point process approach assumes that passengers arrive randomly at stops with a stable arrival rate. In the majority of existing studies, this point process is an Homogeneous Poisson Process (HPP), which aims to model the passenger arrival times using only the arrival rate and the time interval between consecutive arrivals, regardless of the interval starting time. HPP is widely used to model systems with stochastic events, such as modelling the presence of connected vehicle in traffic [25] or traffic incidents [1]. An emerging number of existing studies in public transport have also adopted this stochastic approach, such as [12, 17, 24]. There is considerable evidence that assumptions of stochastic HPP process for passenger arrivals is reasonable for high-frequency services, such as those with scheduled headway to 10–15 min [9]. At longer headways, there is another line of research concerning passengers who time their arrivals with the schedule and service reliability [2, 11]. In this study, we assume that passengers do not consult the schedule prior to arrival at transit stops, thus the use of a stochastic point process such as HPP remains valid.

In literature, existing stochastic processes of public transport assume a stable passenger arrival rate or an intensity that does not change over time. A common approach to include time into consideration is to define exogenous time intervals. In each interval, the passenger arrival rate is constant. This approach has limited accuracy, because the passenger arrival process is not fully continuous time-dependent, but rather multiple independent HPP superimposed [22]. The non-homogeneous Poisson Process (NHPP), which allows the arrival rate to be continuous time-dependent, is a substantial advance from the HPP in terms of versatility and accuracy to the model passenger arrival process. NHPP models are not popular in public transit studies, but have been used elsewhere, such as software reliability [14] and finance [5].

This chapter proposes two analytical methods to model expected arrival rate of passengers arriving at transit stops. After the literature review, the first part of the chapter concerns the modelling of exact passenger arrival times using a time-varying Point Process model. Another aspect of the chapter concerns that of the modelling of aggregated counts of passenger demand, using a time-varying Poisson Regression model. This model aims to count *how many* passengers will be at a stop in a specific time period under certain conditions. Only aggregated counts of passenger demand are required to train this model. Finally, we also show the model calibration process using synthetic simulated data.

19.2 Modelling Exact Arrival Times with Point Process

In this section, we briefly recap the fundamentals of point processes and the celebrated *Poisson process*, which would be used to 'count' and further evaluate the passenger demands. The following section serves as the building block for realistic modelling of passenger demands in later sections, to include periodicities in demands.

19.2.1 A Representation of Point Processes

A point process is a mathematical construct to record times at which event happens, which we shall denote by $T_1, T_2, \ldots$. For example T_1 represents the time when passenger 1 arrives at a bus stop, T_2, represents the following passenger arrival and so on. T_k can usually be interpreted as the time of occurrence of the kth event, in this case - the kth arrival. In this chapter, we refer to T_i as event times. Formally, we define a counting process N_t as a random function defined on time $t \geq 0$, and taking integer values $1, 2, \ldots$. We define $N_0 = 0$. N_t is piecewise constant and has jump size of 1 at the event times T_i. The Poisson process can be defined as follows:

Definition 19.1 (*Poisson process*) Let $(Q_k)_{k \geq 1}$ be a sequence of independent and identically distributed Exponential random variables with parameter λ and event times $T_n = \sum_{k=1}^{n} Q_i$. The process $(N_t, t \geq 0)$ defined by $N_t := \sum_{k \geq 1} \mathbb{1}_{\{t \geq T_k\}}$ is called a *Poisson process* with intensity λ.

Memoryless Property

Note that the sequence of Q_k are known as the *inter-arrival times*, and it can be interpreted as follows in terms our modelling context: the first passenger arrives at time Q_1, the second arrives at Q_2 after the first, so on and so forth. One can show that this construct means that each passenger arrives at an average rate of λ per unit time, since the expected time between event times is $\frac{1}{\lambda}$. Suppose we were waiting for an arrival of an event, say another bus passenger arrival to a bus stop, the inter-arrival times of which follow an Exponential distribution with parameter λ. Assume that r time units have elapsed and during this period no events have arrived, i.e. there are no events during the time interval $[0, r]$. The probability that we will have to wait a further t time units is given by

$$
\begin{aligned}
p(Q > t + r \mid Q > r) &= \frac{p(Q > t + r, \, Q > r)}{p(Q > r)} \\
&= \frac{p(Q > t + r)}{p(Q > r)} = \frac{\exp(-\lambda(t + r))}{\exp(-\lambda r)} \\
&= \exp(-\lambda t) = p(Q > t).
\end{aligned}
\tag{19.1}
$$

Equation (19.1) is said to have no memory and it is one of the special properties of the Poisson process. Usually memorylessness is a property of certain distribution rather than a process. It usually refers to the waiting time distribution until a certain event; and does not depend on how much time has elapsed already.

Moment Generating Functions

We now look at a particular kind of transformed average. The moment generating function φ of a random variable X, is defined as $\varphi_X(s) := E[e^{sX}]$. We now compute the moment generating function of a Poisson distribution $X \sim Pois(\lambda)$:

$$
\varphi_X(s) = E[e^{sX}] = \sum_{k=0}^{\infty} e^{sk} p(X = k) = \sum_{k=0}^{\infty} \frac{e^{sk} e^{-\lambda} \lambda^k}{k!} = e^{-\lambda} \sum_{k=0}^{\infty} \frac{(\lambda e^s)^k}{k!} = e^{\lambda(e^s - 1)}.
\tag{19.2}
$$

The moment generating functions are important because each distribution possesses a unique moment generating function. This means that we can infer the distribution from the moment generating function. In addition, the moment generating function of a sum of independent random variables is the product of the moment generating function of the individual random variables.

19.2.2 Non-homogeneous Poisson Process

The Poisson process, as we defined it so far, is simply characterised by a *constant* arrival rate λ. It is equivalent to an assumption, for example, that public transport passengers arrival rate to stops is the same regardless of the time being mid-night or peak periods. It is more useful to extend the Poisson process to a more general point process in which the arrival rate varies as a function of time. Note that the intensity usually depends on the arrival time, not just on the interarrival time. We can define this type of process as non-homogeneous Poisson process (NHPP).

Definition 19.2 The point process N is said to be an inhomogeneous Poisson process with intensity function $\lambda(t) \geq 0$ with $t \geq 0$, if

$$
\begin{aligned}
p(N_{t+h} = n + m \mid N_t = n) &= \lambda(t)h + o(h) & &\text{if} \quad m = 1, \\
p(N_{t+h} = n + m \mid N_t = n) &= o(h) & &\text{if} \quad m > 1, \\
p(N_{t+h} = n + m \mid N_t = n) &= 1 - \lambda(t)h + o(h) & &\text{if} \quad m = 0. \quad (19.3)
\end{aligned}
$$

Note that if the point process N be a NHPP with intensity function $\lambda(t)$, then $N(t)$ follows a Poisson distribution with parameter $\int_0^t \lambda_u \, du$, i.e. $p(N_t = n) = \frac{1}{n!} \exp\left(-\int_0^t \lambda_u \, du\right) \left(\int_0^t \lambda_u du\right)^n$. One can also show that the number of points in the interval $[s, t]$ follows a Poisson distribution with parameter $\int_s^t \lambda_u \, du$, i.e. $p(N_t - N_s = n) = \frac{1}{n!} \cdot \exp\left(-\int_s^t \lambda_u \, du\right) \left(\int_s^t \lambda_u du\right)^n$.

We can see that the exact event times are needed to calculate moments in the NHPP setting. This next section proposes a public transport demand model and aims to simulate the dynamic and stochastic arrival process of public transport passengers.

19.2.3 The Proposed Time-Varying Intensity Function for Dynamic and Stochastic Passenger Arrival Process

We propose a parametric form for the rate of demand of passengers:

$$
\lambda_t = pc^p \, t^{p-1} + \varepsilon, \tag{19.4}
$$

where $c > 0$ and $p \in \mathbb{R}$. The parameter ε is usually taken to be fixed and acts as a parameter such that the rate never goes negative (bounded away from zero), since a negative rate of demand is non-sensical. Note that this function is rich enough for several reasons. When the parameter is $p = 1$, it reduces to a constant and we know from above that this specifies the parameter for the Exponential random variables. If this is respected then the data follows a Poisson process. If on the other hand, under the case that $p < 1$, this gives a decreasing curve (see plot). We interpret this as a decreasing rate of demand. Finally, our choice of intensity function can also

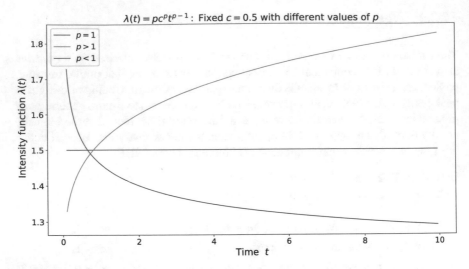

Fig. 19.1 A proposed NHPP model with time-varying intensity function

handle the case when $p > 1$ - this corresponds to the increasing rate of demand. We summarise the following description below:

- it reduces to a constant when $p = 1$, and hence is able to recover Poisson process should the data respects this,
- when $p < 1$, the rate of demand is decreasing,
- when $p > 1$, the rate of demand is increasing.

Figure 19.1 shows a plot of this intensity. It can be easily noted that this is a generalisation of the HPP, where the rate can be constant (similar to HPP) or varies over time.

19.2.4 Likelihood Function for Nonhomogeneous Poisson Process

One of the main problems in modelling a nonhomogeneous Poisson process is inferring its parameters given data so that we have a calibrated model for the demand of passenger arrivals. Let N_t be a counting process on $[0, T]$ for $T < \infty$ and let $\{T_1, T_2, \ldots, T_n\}$ denote a set of event times of N_t over the period $[0, T]$. Then the data likelihood L (see [21] for instance) is a function of parameter set θ:

$$L(\theta) = \prod_{j=1}^{n} \lambda(T_j) e^{-\int_0^T \lambda_x \, dx}. \tag{19.5}$$

Let Θ be the set of parameters of the modulating of the nonhomogeneous Poisson process. The maximum likelihood estimate can be found by maximising the likelihood function in Eq. 19.5 with respect to the space of $\theta \in \Theta$. Concretely, the maximum likelihood estimate $\hat{\theta}$ is defined to be $\hat{\theta} = \arg\max_{\theta \in \Theta} l(\theta)$. It is customary to maximise the log of the likelihood function:

$$l(\theta) = \log L(\theta) = -\int_0^T \lambda_x \, dx + \sum_{j=1}^{N(T)} \log \lambda(T_i) \qquad (19.6)$$

This negative log-likelihood can then be minimised with standard optimisation packages.

19.3 Modelling Aggregated Passenger Demand with Time-Varying Poisson Regression

In this section, we argue that a *collective* point process framework can also be formulated as a time-varying Poisson Regression model to estimate the count of arriving passengers to public transport stops. Aggregated counts of passengers are assumed to follow a Poisson distribution, which is consistent with the collective assumption in a Poisson Process (Definition 19.2). We then further propose a time-varying formulation of Poisson Regression to model the aggregated passenger counts at different time of the day.

19.3.1 A Representation of a Generalised Linear Model: Poisson Regression

One of the most common type of regression, the ordinary least squares assumes that the dependent variable Y is normally distributed around the expected value, and can take any real value, even negative values. Another type of regression, the Logistic Regression assumes a binary 0-or-1 dependent variable. These models are often unsuitable for count data, such as aggregated passenger counts, where the data is intrinsically non-negative integer-valued.

Poisson Regression is widely considered as the benchmark model for count data. It assumes the dependent variable Y has a Poisson distribution, and assumes the logarithm of Y can be modelled by a linear combination of X. It is a type of Generalized Linear Model (GLM). Let k be the number of independent variables (regressors). X is a 1-dimension vector $X = (X_1, X_2, X_k)$, which can be both continuous or categorical variables. Poisson Regression can be written as a GLM for counts:

$$\log(\mu) = \beta_0 + \beta_1 x_1 + \beta_2 x_2 + \cdots + \beta_k x_k = x^T \beta \qquad (19.7)$$

The dependent variable Y has a Poisson distribution, that is $y_i \sim Poisson(\mu_i)$ for $i = 1, \ldots, N$. The Poisson distribution has only one parameter μ that decides both conditional mean and variance. The conditional mean $\mathbb{E}(y|x)$ and conditional variance $Var(y|x)$ are equal in the Poisson regression model. The following exponential mean function can be written:

$$\mathbb{E}(y|x) = \mu = \exp(x^T \beta) \qquad (19.8)$$

Under the GLM framework and assuming an n independent sample of pairs of observations (y_i, x_i), the regression coefficient β_j can be estimated using Maximum Likelihood Estimation (MLE). It is worth reiterating that MLE aims to find parameters that maximise the probability that the specified model has generated the observed sample. Given the observed data, we can define the joint probability distribution of the sample as the product of individual conditional probability distributions.

$$f(y_1, \ldots, y_N | x_1, \ldots, x_N; \beta) = \prod_{i=1}^{N} f(y_i | x_i; \beta) \qquad (19.9)$$

As per the previous section, Eq. 19.9 is often called *likelihood function*, which is often written in a shorter form:

$$L = L(\beta; y_1, \ldots, y_N, x_1, \ldots, x_N) \qquad (19.10)$$

MLE aims to maximise this likelihood function with regard to parameters $\hat{\beta}$:

$$\hat{\beta} = \arg_\beta \max L(\beta; y_1, \ldots, y_N, x_1, \ldots, x_N) \qquad (19.11)$$

It is often more convenient to maximise the logarithmic transformation of this likelihood function, as it replaces products by sums and allows the use of the central limit theorem. We define the log-likelihood function of Poisson Regression as:

$$\ell(\beta; Y, X) = \log \prod_{i=1}^{N} f(y_i | x_i; \beta)$$

$$= \sum_{i=1}^{N} \log f(y_i | x_i; \beta) \qquad (19.12)$$

$$= \sum_{i=1}^{N} -\exp(x_i' \beta) + y_i x_i' \beta - \log(y_i !)$$

The estimated regression coefficient β_j that maximizes the value of the log-likelihood function, is found by computing the k first derivatives of the log-likelihood function with respect to $\beta_1, \beta_2, \ldots, \beta_k$ and setting them equal to zero.

$$s_N(\beta; y, x) = \frac{\partial \ell(\beta; y, x)}{\partial \beta} = \sum_{i=1}^{N} [y_i - \exp(x_i'\beta)]x_i \qquad (19.13)$$

We define $\hat{\beta}$ as the value of β that solves the first order conditions:

$$s_N(\hat{\beta}; y, x) = 0 \qquad (19.14)$$

The system of k equations in Eq. 19.13 has to be solved using a numerical iterative algorithm due to the non-linearity of β. There are a number of existing algorithms in literature that have been well implemented in various statistical packages, such as Newton-Raphson, Broyden-Fletcher-Goldfarb-Shanno (BFGS), Nelder-Mead and Simulated Annealing method.

19.3.2 Time-Varying Poisson Regression Model

As we are concerned with the time dimension in the passenger arrival process, the arrival patterns can be considered as a time series Y_t. Autoregressive-based approaches for time-series, such as [18], or Neural Network based [4] approaches show high accuracy and robustness, but focus on short-term demand prediction, rather than developing an analytical formulation which is more useful for statistical studies. This section focuses on proposing an analytical model for public transport planning and operational control. Thus we introduce here a time-varying formulation of Poisson Regression to capture the variations of passenger arrivals to transit stops. We call this model the Time-varying Poisson Regression (TPR) model.

We are interested in modelling the counts of passenger demand throughout the time of the day. One can observe from aggregated passenger demand data that this count variable has a periodic sinusoidal pattern with two demand peaks at AM and PM rush hours, while gradually reducing to a plateau during off-peak periods. This bimodality distribution of passenger demand is well observed and analysed in literature [15]. A natural modelling approach to capture this sinusoidal pattern is to use a Fourier series:

$$f(x) = \frac{1}{2}a_0 + \sum_{n=1}^{\infty} a_n \cos(nx) + \sum_{n=1}^{\infty} b_n \sin(nx), \qquad (19.15)$$

where

$$a_0 = \frac{1}{\pi} \int_{-\pi}^{\pi} f(x)dx, \qquad (19.16)$$

$$a_n = \frac{1}{\pi} \int_{-\pi}^{\pi} f(x) \cos(nx) dx, \tag{19.17}$$

$$b_n = \frac{1}{\pi} \int_{-\pi}^{\pi} f(x) \sin(nx) dx. \tag{19.18}$$

Here we assume the dependent variable Y is both Poisson distributed and time dependent, that is $y_t \sim Poisson(\mu_t)$ where $t = 1, \ldots, N$ are a time-of-day variable. The time-varying formulation of our Poisson Regression model can be written as:

$$\log(\lambda_t) = \alpha_0 + \sum_{k=1}^{K} \left[\beta_h \cos\left(k\frac{2\pi}{T}t\right) + \gamma_h \sin\left(k\frac{2\pi}{T}t\right) \right] \tag{19.19}$$

The harmonic terms $\sin(k\frac{2\pi}{T}t)$ and $\cos(k\frac{2\pi}{T}t)$ are added to capture the daily demand patterns. K is the number of harmonics, in which larger K would generally increase the accuracy, but also the complexity of the model. If t is in minutes, T equals 24*60 min.

We further increase the adaptability of the model to observed passenger demand data by adding time-invariant independent variables into the model in Eq. 19.19. These variables do not have a time-varying formulation. Many variables in practice can be classified into this group, such as weather, day-of-the-week, events or travel cost. For generality, The TPR model can be formulated as:

$$\log(\mu_t) = \alpha_0 + \sum_{h=1}^{H} \left[\beta_h \cos\left(k\frac{2\pi}{T}t\right) + \gamma_h \sin\left(k\frac{2\pi}{T}t\right) \right] + \sum_{v=1}^{V} \xi_v x_v \tag{19.20}$$

where V is the number of time-invariant independent variables. Larger V would generally increase the model complexity. The question whether a time-invariant variable x_i is used in the model is to be decided by considering its correlation to other variables, and its contribution to the prediction of the dependent variable $\log(\mu_t)$.

The TPR model in Eq. 19.20 has both time-varying and time-invariant independent variables. The next section will discuss the parameter estimation procedure of this model using MLE.

19.4 Simulated Experiments

In this section, we describe the numerical experiments of NHPP and TPR models using synthetic simulated data. We first generate the synthetic data using predefined parameters, and then fit this simulated data to the proposed NHPP models. The models perform well if they can get back the predefined parameters.

19.4.1   Non-homogeneous Poisson Process (NHPP)

This subsection discusses the simulation of data from NHPP with predefined parameters as well as the parameter estimation process for NHPP.

Simulation of a Nonhomogeneous Poisson Process Using Predefined Parameters

Given predefined parameters, we briefly explain how we can apply the thinning method [21] to simulate a NHPP. Thinning is a method to imitate the trajectory of the counting process over time. Given a NHPP with time-dependent intensity function λ_t, we choose a constant λ^* such that

$$\lambda_t \leq \lambda^*, \quad \text{for all } t, \quad 0 \leq T, \tag{19.21}$$

for some maturity $T < \infty$. We then simulate a homogeneous Point process with the designated rate λ^* through a sequence of independent and identically distributed exponential distributed random variables, each having a theoretical mean of $(\lambda^*)^{-1}$. We then look at simulated event times of the homogeneous Poisson process and assign some of these to be the event times of the nonhomogeneous Poisson process with intensity function λ_t. We let an event time at a particular time t in the homogeneous Poisson process be also an event time in the nonhomogeneous Poisson process with probability $\frac{\lambda(t)}{\lambda^*}$, independent of the history up to and including time t, and assign no event time otherwise. Hence, the set of event times of the nonhomogeneous Poisson process constructed is a subset of the event times from the homogeneous Poisson process. The resulting pseudo-algorithm reads as follows:

1. Set $T_0 \leftarrow 0$ and $T^* \leftarrow 0$ where T^* denotes the event times of homogeneous Poisson process with intensity λ^*
2. For $j = 1, 2, \ldots, n$: generate an exponential random variable $\mathscr{E}$ with mean $(\lambda^*)^{-1}$ and set $T^* = T^* + \mathscr{E}(\lambda^*)$. We then generate a unit uniform random variable and accept the event time $(T_i = T^*)$ if $U < \frac{\lambda(T^*)}{\lambda^*}$, and reject otherwise. The sequence T_i generated from this algorithm is the event times from a nonhomogeneous Poisson process with rate λ_t.

Numerical Experiments

We set our parameters for the NHPP model in Eq. 19.4 as in Table 19.1 as follows:

The aforementioned thinning simulation is therefore performed for the intensity function $\lambda_t = 0.304 \cdot t^{-0.25} + \varepsilon$. The simulated arrival times are then used to estimate the parameters for the proposed NHPP model in Eq. 19.4. The calibrated

Table 19.1 Parameters for NHPP

Variables	Value
p	0.75
c	0.3

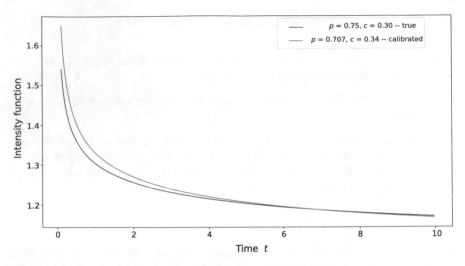

Fig. 19.2 Calibrated and true trajectory of the proposed NHPP intensity function

parameters should be as close as possible to the predefined parameters in Table 19.1. Figure 19.2 shows the calibration results. The calibrated parameters are very similar to the predefined parameters.

19.4.2 Time-Varying Poisson Regression (TPR)

This sub-section describes the generation of synthetic simulated data and the parameter estimation process for time-varying Poisson Regression model

Data Generation Process

The TPR model has $1 + 2 \times K + V$ parameters, where K is the number of harmonics and V is the number of time-invariant independent variables. The complexity of the model depends on the values of K and V. In this section, we generate the synthetic data using 3 harmonics ($K = 3$) and 3 time-invariant variables ($V = 3$). The time-invariant variables x_i are normally distributed with zero mean, and standard deviation of 0.1, 0.2 and 0.3, respectively. Table 19.2 shows the chosen parameters for the synthetic simulation.

We simulate 100 days of data, with the time varying from 4 AM to 10 PM everyday and each sample is an aggregated passenger count for a 15-min interval. Figure 19.3 shows the simulated passenger demand for the first 3 days. The x-axis is the passenger count and the y-axis is the every time window for the first 3 days of the dataset.

We use this synthetic simulated data to estimate the parameters for 4 TPR models, from simple to complex model. The details for each model are as follows:

Table 19.2 Parameters for synthetic simulation data

Variables	Value	Note
α_0	1	Intercept
β_1	-1	Harmonic 1
γ_1	1	Harmonic 1
β_2	-1	Harmonic 2
γ_2	1	Harmonic 2
β_3	1	Harmonic 3
γ_3	-1	Harmonic 3
ξ_1	0.5	$x_1 \sim \mathcal{N}(0, 0.1)$
ξ_2	0.5	$x_2 \sim \mathcal{N}(0, 0.2)$
ξ_3	0.5	$x_3 \sim \mathcal{N}(0, 0.3)$

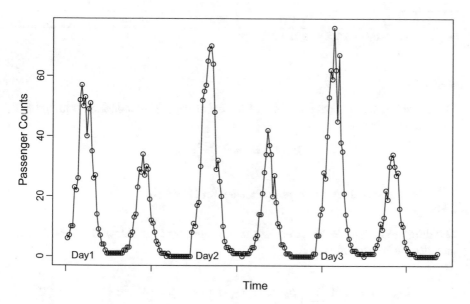

Fig. 19.3 Synthetic simulated data of passenger demand

- **H1V1**

The first model is a simple model with 1 level of harmonic and 1 time-invariant variable.

$$\log(\lambda_t) = \alpha_0 + \beta_1 \cos\left(\frac{2\pi}{T}t\right) + \gamma_1 \sin\left(\frac{2\pi}{T}t\right) + \xi_1 x_1 \qquad (19.22)$$

Table 19.3 shows the parameter estimates for Model 1.

Table 19.3 Estimated parameters for Model 1

Coefficients	Estimate	Std. error	z value	$Pr(>|z|)$	
α_0	2.4169	0.0043	564.761	<2E-16	***a
β_1	−0.0316	0.0062	−5.139	2E-07	***
γ_1	0.8776	0.0047	185.005	<2E-16	***
ξ_1	0.4064	0.0322	12.628	<2E-16	***

a Significant codes: *** 0.001 ** 0.01 * 0.05

Table 19.4 Estimated parameters for H0V3

Coefficients	Estimate	Std. error	z value	$Pr(>|z|)$	
α_0	2.5691	0.0033	787.4	<2E-16	***a
ξ_1	0.2484	0.0321	7.739	1E-14	***
ξ_2	0.5940	0.0161	36.824	<2E-16	***
ξ_3	0.4111	0.0106	38.607	<2E-16	***

a Significant codes: *** 0.001 ** 0.01 * 0.05

• **H0V3**

The second model ignores the effect of the harmonics. This model only includes 3 time-invariant variables.

$$\log(\lambda_t) = \alpha_0 + \sum_{v=1}^{3} \xi_v \, x_v \tag{19.23}$$

Table 19.4 shows the parameter estimates for H0V3.

• **H3V0**

The third model ignores the effect of the time-invariant variables. This model only includes the 3 harmonic levels.

$$\log(\lambda_t) = \alpha_0 + \sum_{h=1}^{H} \left[\beta_h \, \cos\left(k\frac{2\pi}{T}t\right) + \gamma_h \, \sin\left(k\frac{2\pi}{T}t\right) \right] \tag{19.24}$$

Table 19.5 shows the parameter estimates for H3V0.

• **H3V3**

The last model includes 3 harmonic levels and 3 time-invariant variables.

$$\log(\lambda_t) = \alpha_0 + \sum_{h=1}^{H} \left[\beta_h \, \cos\left(k\frac{2\pi}{T}t\right) + \gamma_h \, \sin\left(k\frac{2\pi}{T}t\right) \right] + \sum_{v=1}^{V} \xi_v \, x_v \tag{19.25}$$

Table 19.6 shows the parameter estimates for Model H3V3.

Table 19.5 Estimated parameters for H3V0

Coefficients	Estimate	Std. error	z value	$Pr(>|z|)$	
α_0	0.63622	0.03264	19.5	<2e-16	***a
β_1	−1.65975	0.05754	−28.84	<2e-16	***
γ_1	1.26252	0.0208	60.7	<2e-16	***
β_2	−1.27614	0.03227	−39.55	<2e-16	***
γ_2	1.27385	0.02118	60.15	<2e-16	***
β_3	0.92572	0.01676	55.22	<2e-16	***
γ_3	−0.83519	0.01336	−62.54	<2e-16	***

[a]Significant codes: *** 0.001 ** 0.01 * 0.05

Table 19.6 Estimated parameters for H3V3

Coefficients	Estimate	Std. error	z value	$Pr(>|z|)$	
α_0	0.64099	0.03144	20.39	<2e-16	***a
β_1	−1.61123	0.05556	−29	<2e-16	***
γ_1	1.24552	0.02028	61.43	<2e-16	***
β_2	−1.25812	0.03142	−40.04	<2e-16	***
γ_2	1.24861	0.02058	60.67	<2e-16	***
β_3	0.93607	0.01662	56.34	<2e-16	***
γ_3	−0.85728	0.01304	−65.73	<2e-16	***
ξ_1	0.50175	0.03191	15.72	<2e-16	***
ξ_2	0.50383	0.01596	31.56	<2e-16	***
ξ_3	0.50248	0.01076	46.68	<2e-16	***

[a]Significant codes: *** 0.001 ** 0.01 * 0.05

Table 19.7 Goodness-of-fit of the proposed models

Model	Degree of freedom	AIC
H1V1	4	135816.44
H0V3	4	173589.48
H3V0	7	26920.61
H3V3	10	23441.78

Model Comparison

The results from Table 19.3, 19.4, 19.5 and 19.6 show the model performance. It is clear that H3V3 has the closest parameters to the actual parameters for synthetic simulation. We further evaluate the goodness-of-fit of each model by comparing their Akaike Information Criterion (AIC) statistics in Table 19.7.

As expected, H3V3 shows the best fit among the proposed models. This is because the model incorporates all the determinants in the data, including 3 harmonics and 3 time-invariant variables. H1V1 and H0V3 have significantly lower fits due to the lack of harmonic variables, in which H1V1 has a slightly better fit compared to H0V3 due

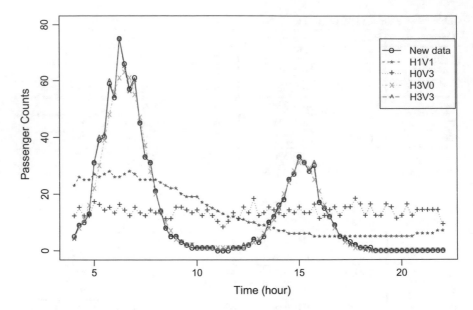

Fig. 19.4 Comparison of different Poisson Regression model performance on simulation data

to the inclusion of one harmonic. The time-invariant variables further increase the goodness-of-fit of modelling. One can see this fact by comparing the AIC statistic of H3V0 and H3V3 because the only difference between them is the time-invariant variables.

We also simulate one day's worth of new aggregated data to evaluate the performance of each Poisson Regression model. The data is simulated using the same parameters in Table 19.2 for 73 time periods of 15 min each. The new simulated data is used in H1V1 to H3V3 to predict the value of Counts. Figure 19.4 shows the new data and the estimation results from H1V1 to H3V3. One can easily see that H0V3 does not capture the sinusoidal pattern of the data. Model 1 captures some pattern with limited accuracy, such as the fact that the demand in earlier time periods are larger than those in later time periods. H3V0 captures the sinusoidal pattern of the data, even the difference between two peaks periods around 8:00 and 16:00. Only H3V3 captures both the sinusoidal pattern and the deviation of the sinusoidal pattern introduced by time-invariant variables. In fact, H3V3 provides a very close estimation to the simulated data.

19.5 Case Study

This section describes a case study where the proposed models are implemented using an observed dataset. We use domain knowledge in Transportation to decide the explanatory variables and to process the data for the models.

19.5.1   Case Study Site and Dataset

This chapter uses an aggregated Smart Card data from New South Wales (NSW), Australia for the case study. Smart Card is a microchip card, typically the size of a credit card, which has been widely used for ticketing purposes around the world. Examples of Smart Card in public transport are the Oyster Card in London, Opal Card in Sydney, or Myki Card in Melbourne. This chapter uses a 14-day Smart Card data. The data consists of over 2.4 million Smart Card transactions over large metropolitan areas in NSW, including Sydney, Newcastle and Wollongong City from February to March 2017. The data consists of all bus transactions in the aforementioned metropolitan areas. Each data record contains the following fields:

- $Card_{ID}$: the unique Smart Card ID, which has been hashed into a unique number
- T_{on}: the time when the passenger with $Card_{ID}$ boards a bus
- T_{off}: the time when the passenger with $CardID$ alight from a bus
- S_{on}: the stop/station ID of T_{on}
- S_{off}: the stop/station ID of T_{off}.

We only focus our case study on estimating aggregated passenger counts using the Time-varying Poisson Regression (TPR) model proposed in Sect. 19.3 because the timestamps in the Smart Card are the boarding and alighting times of a passenger to a bus, rather than the passenger arrival times that are required for the model in Sect. 19.2. The objective is to estimate an aggregated count of passengers per time period for each travel choice between a pair of origin and destination. Transit providers can use this proposed TPR model to estimate the change in passenger demand given the changes in explanatory variables such as travel time or transfer time.

The next few subsections describe the required steps to process the input data for the proposed TPR model.

19.5.2   Journey Reconstruction Algorithm

For each Smart Card record from each individual passenger, the first step is to reconstruct the full public transport journey with transfers from origin to destination from individual Opal card transactions. This step is essential because Smart Card data only includes the tap-on and tap-off, while we are interested in modelling a completed journey between an origin and a destination. A completed journey would naturally give us the following explanatory variables for the TPR model:

- Travel time tt: the time gap between the first tap-on and the last tap-off of a journey
- Transfer time tf: the time gap between a tap-off from a bus to a tap-on to another bus to continue the journey
- Travel distance d: the Euclidean distance between the first tap-on and the last tap-off

- Distance from the origin to CBD d_o: the Euclidean distance from the origin to the Sydney CBD
- Distance from the destination to CBD d_d: the Euclidean distance from the destination to the Sydney CBD

The journey reconstruction algorithm is based on the time and distance gap between individual tap-on and tap-off. Figure 19.5 shows the proposed journey reconstructing algorithm that is based on [16]. We revise the algorithm proposed in [16] by adding the distance gap Δd, which is set to be 500 m. Δd is added to ensure that the transfer time will only be spent on walking and waiting, rather than any other side activity using a private vehicle.

The time gap Δt is defined to be less than 60 min, because in Sydney passengers will receive a discount if they make a transfer within 60 min from the last tap-off, so the majority of passengers would continue their journeys within this time frame. The following steps describes the trip reconstruction process.

- Step 1: Query all the Opal transactions of an individual passenger i. A binary indicator *RID* is assigned as zero.
- Step 2: For each transaction in the above database, the corresponding transaction is discarded if it is a tap-on reversal, where tap-on and tap-off are at the same location
- Step 3: If *RID* equals zero, a variable *Origin Location* is defined and set as equal to the current tap-on. We also assign a new unique *Journey ID*, change *RID* to one and move to the next transaction. Otherwise we move to Step 4.
- Step 4: Now with *RID* equals one, the current transaction will be assigned the current *Journey ID* if it satisfies three conditions: (1) time gap between the current tap-on and the last tap-off δt is less than 60 minutes, (2) the distance gap δd is less than 500 m, and (3) the current tap-off is different to *Origin Location*. Otherwise, we assign a new *Journey ID* and set *RID* equals zero.
- Step 5: The journey reconstruction process for the passenger i is finished after the last transaction of the day, otherwise we move to the next transaction.

19.5.3 Data Processing

After journey reconstruction, the remaining data processing in preparation for the inputs for TPR is self-explanatory. Variables tt, tf, d, d_o and d_d are directly calculated from each completed journey. We then aggregate the completed journeys according to their start time and their *Alternative ID* to produce passenger demand counts. The *Alternative ID* is an indicator of the route choice. It has been defined in a way such that passengers from the same area who make similar choices will have the same *Alternative ID*. Table 19.8 shows an example of the data used for the case study.

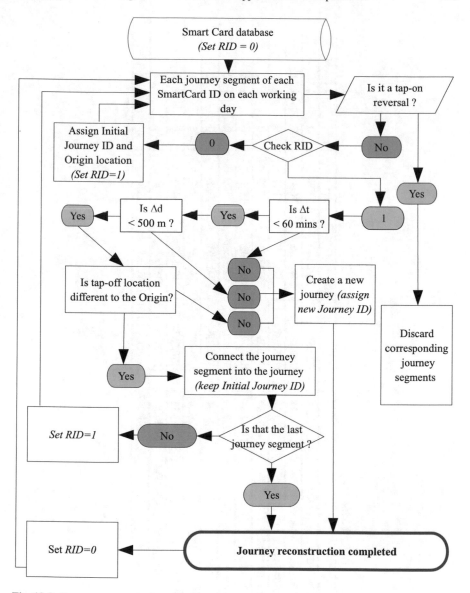

Fig. 19.5 Journey reconstruction algorithm

The *AlternativeID*, as shown in Table 19.8, has been coded in the format: [Origin Zone ID, Destination Zone ID, Mode, Route of the first tap-on, Zone of the first tap-on, Zone of the first tap-off, Route of the last tap-on, Zone of the last tap-on, Zone of the last tap-off]. The Count is total number of passengers who travelled within the same time period, and made the same travel decision as shown in *AlternativeID*.

Table 19.8 Examples of processed data for the case study

Time	AlternativeID	d	d_o	d_d	tt	tf	Count
2:45:00	205_1306_B.N60.205.1306	15947.24	327.688	16223.4	2379	0	20
2:45:00	1701_971_B.N90.1701.83_B.N80.96.971	13963.24	15291.12	10497.86	3660	240	1
2:45:00	2764_144_B.N10.2764.144	9810.014	9865.593	291.957	1104	0	10
2:45:00	1059_1306_B.N60.1059.1306	4439.947	19943.25	16223.4	720	0	3
2:45:00	105_1571_B.520.105.1571	11487.84	1140.505	11981.43	1370	0	6
17:00:00	247_301_B.428.247.301	2319.39	2582.726	4866.599	520	0	12
17:00:00	81_4579_B.616X.81.4579	19921.91	1559.606	20985.03	2298	0	19
17:00:00	242_183_B.428.242.140_B.333.107.183	3738.204	2334.387	1408.359	1740	300	1
17:00:00	305_321_B.428.305.321	1560.36	4570.752	4835.734	450	0	2
17:00:00	81_4568_B.616X.81.3903_B.617X.3903.4568	29567.6	1559.606	30539.1	3750	150	2
17:00:00	6414_6344_B.320.6414.6344	6342.787	111994.2	116865.5	1350	0	6

19.5.4   Case Study Modelling Results

We use the five explanatory variables, as described in Sect. 19.5.1, as the time invariant variables of the TPR model, as described in Sect. 19.3. The dataset is randomly divided into the training dataset, which includes 90% of data points, and the testing dataset, which includes the remaining 10%. We develop TPR models with 3, 4, 5 harmonics and 5 time-invariant variables. Thus the models are named H3V5, H4V5 and H5V5, similar to Sect. 19.4.2. We then compare them using Root Mean Square Error (RMSE) as the criteria, which can be calculated as follows:

$$RMSE = \sqrt{\frac{1}{D} \sum_{i=1}^{D} (c_i - \bar{c}_i)^2} \tag{19.26}$$

where c_i and $\bar{c}_i$ are the actual and estimated count, respectively. D is the total number of data points in the testing dataset. Thus RMSE measures the mean error of our prediction compared to the observed value. The models are trained using the training dataset, and then tested using the testing dataset (Table 19.9).

H5V5 shows better performance than H3V5 and H4V5. Table 19.10 shows the estimated parameters of H5V5. Most of the parameters are significant.

The values and especially the signs of the explanatory variables d_o, d_d, d, tt and tf provide insights into the bus passenger demand in NSW, Australia. The positive sign of d_o and d show that the further passengers are from the Sydney CBD and the longer the travel distance, the more likely that a journey by bus will be made. Similarly, the negative sign of d_d shows that if the journey ends near the CBD, the less likely that a journey by bus will be made. This is because the Sydney CBD is well serviced by other public transport modes such as train, light rail and ferry, so bus travels are more for distant areas. The negative signs of travel time tt and transfer time tf show that passengers care about these factors. If transit providers can provide services with shorter travel time and transfer time, bus patronage will be increased. Passengers are concerned most about distance of travel and transfer time, which is shown by the fact that the estimated coefficients d and tf are significantly larger than others.

Table 19.9 Estimation errors with different TPR models

Model	RMSE
H3V5	7.29
H4V5	6.84
H5V5	6.67

Table 19.10 Estimated parameters for H5V5

Coefficients	Estimate	Std. error	z value	Pr(> |z|)	
α_0	1.6030	0.0038	418.9300	<2e-16	***a
β_1	−0.2198	0.0059	−37.3720	<2e-16	***
γ_1	−0.0262	0.0038	−6.9340	<2e-16	***
β_2	−0.1925	0.0027	−72.6250	<2e-16	***
γ_2	−0.0043	0.0054	−0.7850	0.4330	
β_3	0.1262	0.0025	50.9330	<2e-16	***
γ_3	0.1108	0.0049	22.7230	<2e-16	***
β_4	−0.0882	0.0027	−33.2090	<2e-16	***
γ_4	0.2382	0.0032	75.6170	<2e-16	***
β_5	−0.0938	0.0016	−57.8180	<2e-16	***
γ_5	0.0456	0.0015	30.2900	<2e-16	***
d_o	0.0017	0.0001	24.0960	<2e-16	***
d_d	−0.0015	0.0001	−22.2250	<2e-16	***
d	0.0365	0.0001	281.0640	<2e-16	***
tt	−0.0071	0.0000	−147.7890	<2e-16	***
tf	−0.0226	0.0001	−194.6990	<2e-16	***

[a]Significant codes: *** 0.001 ** 0.01 * 0.05

19.6 Conclusion

The inference of the expected number of passengers arrivals at transit stops are essentially important for transit tactical planning and operation control studies. We propose a non-homogeneous Poisson Process (NHPP) framework to model the exact records of passenger arrival times. Simulation and calibration for this model are discussed. To estimate the aggregated count of passengers arriving at transit stops, this chapter proposes a time-varying Poisson Regression (TPR) model, given the time and other explanatory variables. This model uses aggregated counts of passenger demand within a time period and several other variables to estimate the passenger counts. The numerical experiments using synthetic simulated data show the calibration process for parameters of both NHPP and TPR.

We also use domain knowledge to implement the TPR model on a case study using observed Smart Card data in New South Wales, Australia. The transportation domain knowledge is used to define the important explanatory variables for the TPR model, and to process the data. The variables of travel time, transfer time, and distance are the most important to explain bus passenger demand. Domain knowledge has also been used to obtain great insights into the factors that impact the patronage level of buses in NSW, Australia. By analysing the values and signs of variables d_o, d_d, d, tt and tf, we have found that passengers are more likely to use a bus when the journey is long, and starts further from the Sydney CBD. They are less likely to use a bus if the travel time or transfer time are large; and if the journey is also serviced by other modes of transport such as train, light rail or ferry.

The proposed analytical models are useful as a part of a transit tactical planning and operational control framework to estimate the passenger demand at transit stops. Future work includes the use of observed data, a more involved formulation for NHPP model and possibly an inclusion of the autoregressive term for the TPR model.

Acknowledgements This study is supported by Strategic Research Funding at the DATA61, CSIRO, Australia and partly by the NSW Premier's Innovation Initiatives Project. The author is grateful for invaluable contributions from Young Lee, Yuming Ou and Chen Cai at DATA61, CSIRO on earlier drafts of this chapter. The data used in this study is provided by the Transport for NSW, the transport operator of NSW, Australia. The conclusions in this paper reflect the understandings of the authors, who are responsible for the accuracy of the data.

References

1. Baykal-Gürsoy, M., Xiao, W., Ozbay, K.: Modeling traffic flow interrupted by incidents. Eur. J. Op. Res. **195**(1), 127–138 (2009)
2. Bowman, L.A., Turnquist, M.A.: Service frequency, schedule reliability and passenger wait times at transit stops. Transp. Res. Part A: Gen. **15**(6), 465–471 (1981)
3. Cats, O., Larijani, A., Koutsopoulos, H., Burghout, W.: Impacts of holding control strategies on transit performance: bus simulation model analysis. Transp. Res. Rec.: J. Transp. Res. Board **2216**, 51–58 (2011)
4. Celikoglu, H.B., Cigizoglu, H.K.: Public transportation trip flow modeling with generalized regression neural networks. Adv. Eng. Softw. **38**(2), 71–79 (2007)
5. Cizek, P., Härdle, W.K., Weron, R.: Statistical Tools for Finance and Insurance. Springer Science & Business Media, Berlin (2005)
6. Daganzo, C.F.: A headway-based approach to eliminate bus bunching: systematic analysis and comparisons. Transp. Res. Part B: Methodol. **43**(10), 913–921 (2009)
7. Daganzo, C.F., Pilachowski, J.: Reducing bunching with bus-to-bus cooperation. Transp. Res. Part B: Methodol. **45**(1), 267–277 (2011)
8. Delgado, F., Muñoz, J., Giesen, R., Cipriano, A.: Real-time control of buses in a transit corridor based on vehicle holding and boarding limits. Transp. Res. Rec.: J. Transp. Res. Board **2090**, 59–67 (2009)
9. Desaulniers, G., Hickman, M.D.: Public transit. Handb. Op. Res. Manag. Sci. **14**, 69–127 (2007)
10. Eberlein, X.J., Wilson, N.H., Barnhart, C., Bernstein, D.: The real-time deadheading problem in transit operations control. Transp. Res. Part B: Methodol. **32**(2), 77–100 (1998)
11. Fonzone, A., Schmöcker, J.D., Liu, R.: A model of bus bunching under reliability-based passenger arrival patterns. Transp. Res. Part C: Emerg. Technol. **59**, 164–182 (2015)
12. Fu, L., Yang, X.: Design and implementation of bus-holding control strategies with real-time information. Transp. Res. Rec.: J. Transp. Res. Board **1791**, 6–12 (2002)
13. Fu, L., Liu, Q., Calamai, P.: Real-time optimization model for dynamic scheduling of transit operations. Transp. Res. Rec.: J. Transp. Res. Board **1857**, 48–55 (2003)
14. Hossain, S.A., Dahiya, R.C.: Estimating the parameters of a non-homogeneous poisson-process model for software reliability. IEEE Trans. Reliab. **42**(4), 604–612 (1993)
15. Kieu, L.M., Bhaskar, A., Chung, E.: Public transport travel-time variability definitions and monitoring. J. Transp. Eng. **141**(1), 04014,068 (2014)
16. Kieu, L.M., Bhaskar, A., Chung, E.: Passenger segmentation using smart card data. IEEE Trans. Intell. Transp. Syst. **16**(3), 1537–1548 (2015)
17. Kieu, L.M., Bhaskar, A., Cools, M., Chung, E.: An investigation of timed transfer coordination using event-based multi agent simulation. Transp. Res. Part C: Emerg. Technol. **81**, 363–378 (2017)

18. Ma, Z., Xing, J., Mesbah, M., Ferreira, L.: Predicting short-term bus passenger demand using a pattern hybrid approach. Transp. Res. Part C: Emerg. Technol. **39**, 148–163 (2014)
19. McNally, M.G.: The four-step model. In: Handbook of Transport Modelling, 2nd edn., pp. 35–53. Emerald Group Publishing Limited (2007)
20. Pekel, E., Soner Kara, S.: Passenger flow prediction based on newly adopted algorithms. Appl. Artif. Intell. **31**(1), 64–79 (2017)
21. Ross, S.M.: Introduction to Probability Models, 6th edn. Academic Press, San Diego (1997)
22. Sayarshad, H.R., Chow, J.Y.: Survey and empirical evaluation of nonhomogeneous arrival process models with taxi data. J. Adv. Transp. **50**(7), 1275–1294 (2016)
23. Sun, Y., Leng, B., Guan, W.: A novel wavelet-svm short-time passenger flow prediction in beijing subway system. Neurocomputing **166**, 109–121 (2015)
24. Toledo, T., Cats, O., Burghout, W., Koutsopoulos, H.N.: Mesoscopic simulation for transit operations. Transp. Res. Part C: Emerg. Technol. **18**(6), 896–908 (2010)
25. Wang, X.: Modeling the process of information relay through inter-vehicle communication. Transp. Res. Part B: Methodol. **41**(6), 684–700 (2007)

Chapter 20
Structural Health Monitoring Using Machine Learning Techniques and Domain Knowledge Based Features

Nguyen Lu Dang Khoa, Mehrisadat Makki Alamdari, Thierry Rakotoarivelo, Ali Anaissi and Yang Wang

Abstract Structural Health Monitoring (SHM) is a condition-based maintenance technology using sensing systems. In SHM, the use of domain knowledge is essential: it motivates the use of machine learning approaches; it can be used to extract damage sensitive features and interpret the results by machine learning. This work focuses on two SHM problems: damage identification and substructure clustering. Our solutions to address them are based on machine learning techniques and robust feature extraction using domain knowledge. In the first problem, damage sensitive features were extracted using a frequency domain decomposition, followed by a robust one-class support vector machine for damage detection. In the second problem, a novel clustering technique and spectral moment feature were utilised for substructure grouping and anomaly detection. These methods were evaluated using data from lab-based structures and data collected from the Sydney Harbour Bridge. We obtained high damage detection accuracies and were able to assess damage severity. Furthermore, the clustering technique was able to group substructures of similar behaviour and detect spatial anomalies.

N. L. D. Khoa (✉) · T. Rakotoarivelo · Y. Wang
DATA61, CSIRO, 13 Garden Street, Eveleigh, NSW 2015, Australia
e-mail: khoa.nguyen@data61.csiro.au

T. Rakotoarivelo
e-mail: thierry.rakotoarivelo@data61.csiro.au

Y. Wang
e-mail: yang.wang@data61.csiro.au

M. Makki Alamdari
School of Civil and Environmental Engineering, University of New South Wales,
Kensington, NSW 2052, Australia
e-mail: m.makkialamdari@unsw.edu.au

A. Anaissi
School of IT, The University of Sydney, Sydney, NSW 2006, Australia
e-mail: ali.anaissi@sydney.edu.au

© Springer International Publishing AG, part of Springer Nature 2018
J. Zhou and F. Chen (eds.), *Human and Machine Learning*, Human–Computer
Interaction Series, https://doi.org/10.1007/978-3-319-90403-0_20

409

20.1 Introduction

Most structural and mechanical system maintenance is time-based, i.e. an inspection is carried out after a predefined amount of time. Structural health monitoring (SHM) is a condition-based approach to monitor infrastructure using sensing systems. SHM systems promise significant safety and economic benefits [21], and thus they have been the focus of several studies and activities with sometime real-world deployments [21, 24, 62].

One of the key problems in SHM is damage identification, which can be classified into different levels of complexity [49]:

- Level 1 (Detection): to detect if damage is present in the structure.
- Level 2 (Localisation): to locate the position of the damage.
- Level 3 (Assessment): to estimate the extent of the damage.
- Level 4 (Prediction): to give information about the safety of the structure, e.g. remaining life estimation. This level requires an understanding of the physical damage progression in the structure.

A typical engineering approach in SHM adopts a physic-based model of the structure, usually based on finite element analysis. The differences between measured data and the data generated by the model are used to identify any damage [18]. However, a numerical model may not always be available in practice and does not cater well to uncertainties due to changes in environmental and operational conditions. This challenge motivates the use of a data-driven approach which establishes a model by learning from measured data and then makes a comparison between the data model and new measured responses to detect damage. This approach normally uses techniques in machine learning [62].

Farrar and Worden defined the SHM process in terms of a four-step statistical pattern recognition paradigm [21]: (1) operational evaluation; (2) data acquisition, normalisation and cleansing; (3) feature extraction and information condensation; (4) statistical model development. Among the four, feature extraction and information condensation in Step 3 is an important step to help the statistical modelling using machine learning in Step 4 to identify damage.

Feature extraction is a process of extracting meaningful indicative information from the measured response to determine the structural health state of the system and identify the presence, location and severity of any possible damage. Features may or may not have explicit physical meaning. However, the features that represent the underlying structural physic are preferred for SHM from the point of view that they can provide more effective insight into the condition of the structure. An ideal feature should be sensitive to damage and correlated with the severity of damage but insensitive to environmental and operational effects. The reason is that in real-world SHM applications the effect of environmental and operational changes on features might camouflage damage-related changes and also alter the correlation between the magnitude of changes in the features and associated damage levels [51], and this is one of the main challenges in SHM [21].

All the aforementioned challenges highlight the role of domain experts in solving SHM problems and in this chapter domain knowledge is used in all stages of the data analysis. First, domain knowledge shows data-driven machine learning approaches are suitable for forming an SHM problem. Second, it shows robust feature extraction techniques using domain knowledge are essential in order to extract damage sensitive features. Last, domain knowledge is also used to explain the results found by machine learning techniques.

This work is part of our ongoing efforts to apply data driven SHM to the Sydney Harbour Bridge (SHB), one of the iconic structures in Australia. We tackle two different problems faced by a civil infrastructure: damage detection and substructure clustering. Our approaches to these problems are based on machine learning techniques and robust feature extraction using domain knowledge. The first problem is identifying damage in components of a structure over time. In this case, we fused and extracted damage sensitive features from multiple sensors using a frequency domain decomposition (FDD), and then applied a novel self-tuning one-class support vector machine (SVM) for damage detection. The second problem is detecting similar characteristics of a structure's components by comparing and grouping them across locations. In this case, we extended a robust clustering technique and utilised a novel spectral moment feature for substructure grouping and anomaly detection. These methods were evaluated using data from controlled lab-based structures and data collected from a real world deployment on the SHB.

The remainder of this chapter is organised as follows. Section 20.2 provides information about the SHM system of the SHB. Section 20.3 presents a review on feature extraction and fusion in SHM, which is based on domain knowledge. Then the proposed approaches to extract features, to identify damage and to group substructures are introduced in Sect. 20.4. Section 20.5 presents the results of our proposed techniques in two case studies. Finally, there are concluding remarks in Sect. 20.6.

20.2 A Large Scale SHM on the Sydney Harbour Bridge

The SHB supports eight lanes of road traffic and two railway lines. Lane 7 on its eastern side is dedicated to buses and taxis. This lane is supported by 800 concrete and steel jack arches, which may develop cracks due to the ageing of the structure and traffic loadings on the lane. It is critical to detect such a deterioration as early as possible. However, they are currently visually inspected once every two years and some locations are difficult to access.

We have developed and deployed a SHM system on the SHB which acquires, integrates, and analyses a large amount of data from about 2400 sensors distributed underneath Lane 7 of the infrastructure [48]. Our SHB system is composed of four layers, as described in Fig. 20.1. First at the Sensing and Data Acquisition layer, we have deployed three tri-axial accelerometers on each of the 800 jack arches. These

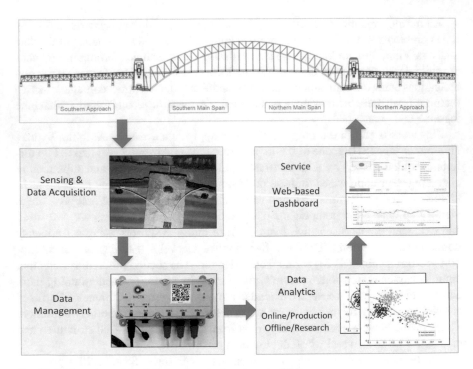

Fig. 20.1 Overview of the SHM system deployed on the SHB

sensors are low-cost MEMS (Microelectromechanical systems) and they record the vibrations of the structure.

At the Data Management layer, we have smart nodes and gateways, which concentrate the data from the sensors. Vibration data are captured at 250 Hz from the three sensors on a given jack arch, when a vehicle drives over it. Each node also collects continuous ambient vibration at midnight for 10 min at 1500 Hz. The data are transmitted and used by the next Data Analytics layer.

At the third Data Analytics layer, we can deploy several algorithms to derive actionable information from the data. Some algorithms are online and in production, i.e. they operate on real-time data to produce information for the bridge manager and engineers. Other algorithms are offline and in research phase, i.e. they operate on past collected data for a research purpose.

Finally at the Service layer, we developed a secure web-based visualisation dashboard, which allows the bridge manager and engineers to monitor all the jack arches in real time so that they can optimise the maintenance schedule.

20.3 Feature Extraction Using Domain Knowledge: A Review

As a result of damage occurrence in the structure, the physical characteristics of the structure (e.g. stiffness, mass or damping) change, which consequently induces a change to the dynamic response [39]. Therefore, one of the key factors in a successful implementation of any vibration-based SHM technique is an appropriate selection of damage sensitive feature from the measured vibration response of the structure [55]. The efforts of previous researchers have been directed to damage sensitive features in modal domain [20], frequency domain [38], time domain [11] and time-frequency domain [43].

Examples of the early features introduced and adopted for SHM applications are modal parameters (e.g. natural frequencies [50], damping [14], and mode shapes), and their derivatives such as modal strain energy [53] and flexibility matrix [44]. Although successful applications of these features have been widely reported in the literature (as discussed in [7]), the use of modal-based features to identify damage in real-world applications has been highly debated in the last few years. Modal-based features are suffering from several problems. Firstly, they are not broadband data and they only provide information at limited frequency resonances. Secondly, they are error prone by nature as they are not directly-measured data and thus complicated modal analysis should be carried out to extract these features from the measured time responses, which may lead to computational errors [40]. Moreover, in real-world applications, it is not possible to capture a complete set of modal parameters from the measurements because only a limited number of lower modes are measured and the information related to higher modes, which is more sensitive to minor changes in the structural integrity, is missed. Finally, it has been demonstrated that modal parameters and in particular natural frequencies are quite sensitive to environmental changes, which is not desirable [45]. These major shortcomings make modal-based approaches less suitable for practical applications.

SHM schemes based on time-domain features have also attracted attention in recent years since no domain transformation is required, which leads to faster monitoring applications [11]. In such a case, damage identification is directly sought based on discrepancies of the measured responses in time domain. Basically, time domain-based features can be treated as data-based features rather than physics-based features and the adopted features might not have an explicit physical meaning. Damage is identified by comparison of a current characteristic quantity with its baseline in a statistical sense. Statistical properties of a time series (e.g. mean and variance) were amongst the earliest statistical frameworks employed for monitoring the acceleration measurements in order to identify data that are inconsistent with the past data (e.g. undamaged state) [22]. Features based on autoregressive models have also been adopted in various SHM applications [54]. In this regard, features are either based on the residues between the prediction from an autoregressive model and the actual measured time history at each time interval, or they are simply based on autoregressive model coefficients [63].

Frequency-based features such as power spectral density (PSD) [34], frequency response functions and their derivatives [33] can be derived from the response in the frequency domain. Unlike modal parameters, frequency data are broadband data which contain a wide range of frequencies [2]. Spectral-based methods in the frequency domain have become another alternative to extract features in mechanical components under stochastic loadings [8]. Applications of spectral methods in the context of damage detection have been found in the literature [5]. Spectral-based methods use spectral moments which can be evaluated directly from the PSD of time responses. Spectral moments represent some major statistical properties of a stochastic process; for example, the variance of a random process is the zero-order spectral moment of that observation [46]. Spectral moments are useful for characterisation of non-Gaussian signals buried in a Gaussian background such as noisy environment [59]. The early efforts in this field were conducted by Vanmarcke to estimate modal parameters (natural frequency and damping) from ambient response measurements of dynamically excited structures [60]. Zero, first and second moments were applied to identify modal parameters. Later on, some researchers used spectral moments to predict the fatigue damage evaluation and estimate the rate of damage accumulation in structures subjected to random processes [8]. Several researchers have applied higher order spectral moments such as spectral kurtosis of the time series data for health assessment of rotary structures [5].

Further, features can be extracted by time-frequency analysis of the measured response using wavelet analysis [43]. Wavelet transform has emerged as a powerful tool for capturing changes in structural properties induced by damage. Wavelet analysis allows the study of local data with a "zoom lens having an adjustable focus" to provide multiple levels of details and approximations of the original signals. Therefore, transient behaviour of the data can be retained [23]. Wavelet analysis not only can detect any subtle differences in the signals but also can localise them in time, and therefore it is quite useful for studying non-stationary systems. Promising applications of wavelet transform approaches to SHM have been reported in the literature [32, 58].

In addition to feature extraction from one single sensor, data fusion which is the process of integrating information from multiple sensors, needs to be considered. An appropriate fusion process can reduce imprecision, uncertainties and incompleteness and achieve more robust and reliable results than a single source approach [26, 57]. Various data fusion methods have been used in SHM [37, 56]. Fusion can be executed in three levels: data-level fusion, feature-level fusion, and decision-level fusion [35]. In data-level, raw data from multiple sensors are combined to produce new raw data that are expected to be more informative than data from a single sensor. In feature-level, features obtained from individual sensors are fused to obtain more relevant information [26]. Data fusion in feature-level can be performed in an unsophisticated manner by simply concatenating features obtained from different sensors. However, more advanced methods including Principle Component Analysis (PCA), neural networks and Bayesian methods have been adopted at this level. Fusion at decision-level can be achieved through various techniques such as voting or fuzzy logic to obtain an ultimate decision based on each decision obtained from individual sensors.

In this study, we adopt a spectral-based approach using the concept of spectral moment to extract the damage sensitive feature from the measured acceleration response. Spectral moment correlates to the energy of the signal in the frequency domain and is computed from the PSD of a signal. Moreover, we also adopt a feature extraction and data fusion approach using FDD to integrate frequency data from multiple sensors. The next section describes in detail our feature extraction and fusion methods.

20.4 Damage Identification and Substructure Grouping

In this section, we discuss how domain knowledge is used to phrase a general SHM problem as a machine learning problem and the importance of domain knowledge for feature extraction. Then two typical problems faced by a civil infrastructure are presented: damage detection and substructure clustering. We propose solutions for these two problems which utilise machine learning techniques and robust features extracted using domain knowledge. Specifically, FDD is used with a self-tuning one-class SVM for damage identification; and a spectral moment feature is used with k-means$--$ for substructure grouping.

20.4.1 Machine Learning Approach for SHM Using Domain Knowledge

Any change in the structural integrity reflects the vibration characteristic, e.g. natural frequency of the structure. In the context of vibration-based SHM, the main objective is thus to identify any change in these characteristics with respect to a benchmark state. To achieve this, either a physics-based model of the structure or a statistical-based model of the system under study is developed to build a representative model of the structure in the benchmark state. In the first approach, finite element method and optimisation techniques are adopted to establish and calibrate a numerical model of the structure. Future measured response of the structure is then compared with the numerical model prediction to identify any potential change in the system. Although this approach is capable of providing additional useful information about any potential change in the structure, e.g. location and severity, its capability is quite limited to small scale structures in a controlled environment. The main reason is that obtaining a detailed, reliable and calibrated model of the structure is not straightforward, especially in the case of large infrastructures and in the presence of practical uncertainties.

In contrast, a data-based or machine learning model relies solely on measured data. The massive data obtained from monitoring are transformed into meaningful information using domain knowledge as reviewed in Sect. 20.3. It is a more promising alternative for real-world SHM applications. Not only is establishing the model more straightforward, but also it is capable of overcoming problems associated with environmental and operational variability in SHM since the measured data from many different conditions can be employed for learning the model, which is not the case for a physics-based approach.

Most of the vibration-based SHM techniques require both input and output signals in order to identify possible structural damage. This technique is applied only to small and moderate sized structures and often requires disruption of traffic and human activities for structures under in-service condition. These drawbacks make this approach less practical, specifically in the case of large infrastructures. In contrast, methods based on output-only dynamic test where the structure is excited by natural or randomly varying environmental excitations such as traffic, winds, waves or human movements are more practical for SHM applications. In this approach, structural integrity assessment is performed based on only response measurement data without any knowledge of the input driving forces. Hence, a smaller number of operators and equipment is required, which makes this approach more attractive over measured input vibration. In order to extract the vibration characteristics of the structure, a special procedure named output-only modal identification needs to be considered [41]. It highlights the role of domain knowledge experts in extracting the most characteristic features from the measured response. In the following sections, two different features have been employed based on the domain knowledge about output-only modal identification.

20.4.2 Damage Identification

This section presents an approach to identifying damage in components of a structure over time. A flowchart of the approach is shown in Fig. 20.2. First, damage sensitive features are extracted using FDD followed by a dimensionality reduction using random projection. Then an adaptive (self-tuning) one-class SVM is used on the reduced dimensional space for damage detection.

20.4.2.1 Data Fusion and Feature Extraction: Frequency Domain Decomposition

FDD was used in this study to fuse data from a sensor network in a data-level. FDD assumes that the vibration responses from l distinct locations within the structure are available. From a probabilistic point of view, the response process at locations p and q (p and $q \in [1 : l]$) can be characterised through a correlation function, R_{pq}, in the time domain as [10],

$$R_{pq}(\tau) = E[x_p(t)x_q(t + \tau)] \tag{20.1}$$

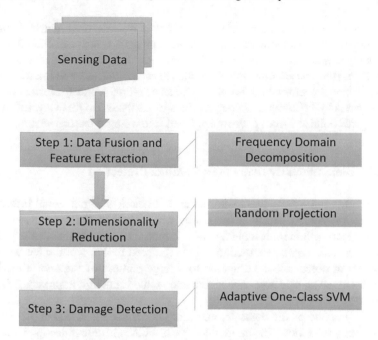

Fig. 20.2 The flowchart of the proposed damage detection and severity assessment

where $E[]$ and τ are, respectively, the probabilistic expected value operator and the lag operator. $R_{pq}(\tau)$ function defines how a signal is correlated with the other, with a time separation τ.

The frequency characterisation of such a random stationary process can be computed using the PSD function which is calculated by taking the Fourier transform as,

$$S_{pq}(\omega) = \int_{-\infty}^{+\infty} R_{pq}(\tau) \exp^{-i\omega\tau} d\tau \tag{20.2}$$

where $S_{pq}(\omega)$ is the cross PSD of the response at locations p and q, and frequency ω. Once $p = q$, $S_{pq}(\omega)$ is referred to as the auto-power, otherwise it is called cross-power.

At each frequency spectra, a symmetric matrix of $S_{l \times l}(\omega)$ can be populated using an auto and cross power information obtained earlier for different pair-wise locations. Matrix S can be decomposed using the singular value decomposition (SVD) as,

$$S(\omega) = U \sum U^H \tag{20.3}$$

where U and $\sum$ are $l \times l$ matrix of singular vectors and diagonal matrix of singular values, respectively, and superscript H is the conjugate transpose. Singular values are typically in a descending order and the first singular value is the highest one.

Combining the first singular value obtained at each frequency spectra will result in an m dimensional vector which is considered as a feature vector for further analysis, where m refers to the number of spectral lines or attributes. In this way, information from l signals obtained from l sensors is fused into a single feature vector.

20.4.2.2 Dimensionality Reduction: Random Projection

Dimensionality reduction aims to extract an intrinsic low dimensional information from a high dimensional dataset. It transforms a high-dimensional data set into a lower dimensional one which represents the most important variables that can explain the original data. This feature extraction step is required in this work since we have a low number of observations compared to a large number of features. In [31], the authors discussed an effectiveness of dimensionality reduction approaches in SHM applications.

PCA [29] is one of the most popular and widely used techniques proposed for dimensionality reduction. The main objective of PCA is to calculate eigenvalues and eigenvectors of a covariance matrix computed from a given dataset to determine the components where the data have a maximum variance. However, PCA has a complexity of $O(m^3)$ due to the eigen decomposition of the covariance matrix where m is the dimension of data. This makes it impractical to use for very high dimensional datasets, a common issue in SHM sensing data. Moreover, its performance is sensitive to the number of the selected components.

Random projection is an alternative and less expensive method to reduce the dimensionality of extremely high dimensional data [1]. Using random projection, the dimension of the projected space only depends on the number of data points n, no matter how high the original dimension m of the data is. It is an effective and efficient dimensionality reduction method for high-dimensional data [9]. The rational idea of random projection is to preserve the pairwise Euclidean distances between data points which is achieved by projecting the high-dimensional data into a random subspace spanned by $O(\log n)$ columns [28]. Further study, carried out by Achlioptas [1], shows that the number of dimensions required for random projection can be calculated using:

$$k = \log n / \xi^2 \tag{20.4}$$

where k is the number of dimensions in the low-dimensional space and ξ is a small positive number.

Given $X \in \mathbf{R}^{n \times m}$, $\xi > 0$, and $k = \log n / \xi^2$. Let $R_{m \times k}$ be a random matrix where each entry r_{ij} can be drawn from the following probability distribution [1]:

$$r_{ij} = \begin{cases} +1 & \text{with probability} \quad \frac{1}{2s} \\ 0 & \text{with probability} \quad 1 - \frac{1}{2s} \\ -1 & \text{with probability} \quad \frac{1}{2s} \end{cases} \tag{20.5}$$

where s represents the projection sparsity. With probability at least $1 - \frac{1}{n}$, the projection, $Y = XR$ approximately preserves the pairwise Euclidean distances for all data points in X.

In practice, k is usually a small number. Venkatasubramanian and Wang [61] suggested that $k_{RP} = 2 \ln n / 0.25^2$.

20.4.2.3 Damage Detection: Self-tuning One-Class Support Vector Machine

In practice, events corresponding to damaged states of structures are often unavailable for a supervised learning approach. Therefore, a one-class approach using only data from a healthy structure is more practical. In this work, we use one-class SVM [52] as an anomaly detection method.

Given a set of data $X = \{x_i\}_{i=1}^{n}$ extracted from the original sensor data (feature vector) collected from a healthy structure and where n is the number of training samples, one-class SVM maps these samples into a high dimensional feature space using a function ϕ through the kernel $K(x_i, x_j) = \phi(x_i)^T \phi(x_j)$. Then one-class SVM learns a hyperplane that separates these data points from the origin with a maximum margin. A feature vector is defined as a vector of m elements, and each element is called an attribute.

The classification model is a function described by $f : \mathbf{R}^m \rightarrow \{-1, +1\}$ and is written in the form of

$$f(x) = sgn(w \cdot \phi(x) - \rho) \tag{20.6}$$

where '.' is the dot product. w and ρ are the parameters of the model and can be learned from the training data. $f(x) = +1$, if $(w \cdot \phi(x) - \rho) > 0$ which indicates that the structure is healthy; otherwise $f(x) = -1$ which means that the state of the structure has changed.

Using the data samples, $X = \{x_i\}_{i=1}^{n}$, the training process determines the model parameters w and ρ by minimising the classification error on the training set while still maximizing the margin. Mathematically, it is equivalent to the following minimisation problem,

$$\min_{w, \xi, \rho} \frac{1}{2} \|w\|^2 + \frac{1}{vn} \sum_{i=1}^{n} \xi_i - \rho \tag{20.7}$$

$$s.t \quad w \cdot \phi(x_i) \geq \rho - \xi_i, \quad \xi_i \geq 0, \quad i = 1, \ldots, n.$$

where ξ_i is a slack variable for controlling the amount of training error allowed and $\nu \in [0, 1]$ is a user-specified variable for controlling the balance between ξ_i (the training error) and w (the margin). The problem can be transformed to a dual form using Lagrangian multiplier as,

$$\min_{\alpha_1, \alpha_2, \ldots, \alpha_n} \sum_{i,j}^{n} \alpha_i \alpha_j K(x_i, x_j) \tag{20.8}$$

$$s.t \quad 0 \leq \alpha_i \leq \frac{1}{\nu n}, \quad \sum_{i=1}^{n} \alpha_i = 1.$$

This problem can then be solved using quadratic programming [27]. Having obtained a learned model, the decision values for a new data instance x_{new} can be computed as,

$$f(x) = sgn(\sum_{i=1}^{n} \alpha_i K(x_i, x_{new}) - \rho) \tag{20.9}$$

A negative decision value indicates an anomaly, which likely corresponds to a structural damage.

Self-tuning Gaussian Kernel:

Gaussian kernel defined in Eq. 20.10 has gained much popularity in the area of machine learning and it turned out to be an appropriate setting for one-class SVM [13, 30, 36]. It has a parameter denoted σ which may severely affect the performance of a one-class SVM. An inappropriate choice of σ may lead to overfitting or underfitting.

$$K(x_i, x_j) = \exp(-\frac{\|x_i - x_j\|^2}{2\sigma^2}) \tag{20.10}$$

where $\sigma \in \mathbf{R}$ is the kernel parameter.

K-fold cross validation is often used at a training stage in order to tune σ. However, in case of a one-class learning, this technique is not possible because it selects σ that works only on the training class data and thus it is lack of generalisation capability (overfitting problem). Therefore, alternative approaches have been proposed for tuning σ in one-class SVM. The Appropriate Distance to the Enclosing Surface (ADES) algorithm [4] is our recent proposed method for tuning σ based on inspecting the spatial locations of the edge and interior samples, and their distances to the enclosing surface of one-class SVM. ADES showed successful performances on several datasets and thus was adopted for tuning σ in this work.

Following the objective function $f(\sigma_i)$ described in Eq. 20.11, the ADES algorithm selects the optimal value of $\hat{\sigma} = argmax_{\sigma_i}(f(\sigma_i))$, which generates a hyperplane that is the furthest from the interior samples and the closest to the edge samples, using a normalised distance function.

$$f(\sigma_i) = mean(d_N(x_n)_{x_n \in \Omega_{IN}}) - mean(d_N(x_n)_{x_n \in \Omega_{ED}}) \quad (20.11)$$

where Ω_{IN} and Ω_{ED}, respectively, represent sets of interior and edge samples in the healthy training data points identified using a hard margin linear SVM, and d_N is the normalized distance from these samples to the hyperplane. It is defined as:

$$d_N(x_n) = \frac{d(x_n)}{1 - d_\pi} \quad (20.12)$$

where d_π is the distance of a hyperplane to the origin described as $d_\pi = \frac{\rho}{\|w\|}$, and $d(x_n)$ is the distance of the sample x_n to the hyperplane. It is calculated using:

$$d(x_n) = \frac{f(x_n)}{\|w\|} = \frac{\sum_{i=1}^{n} \alpha_i K(x_i, x_n) - \rho.}{\sqrt{\sum_{ij}^{n} \alpha_i \alpha_j K(x_i, x_j)}} \quad (20.13)$$

where w is a perpendicular vector to the decision boundary, α_i are the Lagrange multipliers, and ρ is the bias term. More details on the ADES method can be found in [4].

20.4.3   Substructure Grouping

This section proposes a robust clustering technique, which uses spectral moment features for substructure grouping and anomaly detection. The proposed approach follows the following steps, which are further detailed in the remainder of this section:

- a structurally meaningful feature is extracted using spectral moment from the measured acceleration for each jack arch for many time windows,
- a modified k-means$--$ clustering algorithm is applied to this feature data to identify groups of similar substructures and potential anomalies,
- a multi-indices criterion is used to select the best grouping outcome,
- under the assumption that near-by substructures should have similar behaviours and thus should belong to the same cluster groups, any substructure which is identified as an outlier or which belongs to a one-member group, is then marked as an anomaly.

20.4.3.1   Feature Extraction Using Spectral Moment

In this study, a frequency-based feature using spectral moments of the measured acceleration responses is adopted as a damage sensitive feature. PSD of the response signal is required to calculate spectral moment. For a stationary random process,

PSD contains some major characteristics of the system that can be extracted. In a classical Fourier analysis, the power of a signal can be obtained by integrating the PSD, i.e., the square of the absolute value of the Fourier-transform coefficients [15].

The energy contents of a signal within a frequency band of interest can also be quantified using PSD. The calculation of PSD is computationally efficient, as it has a low processing cost compared to modal analysis. Moreover unlike modal data, PSD does not suffer the lack of information and provides an abundance of information in a wider frequency range.

The spectral moment of a random stationary signal provides some important information about its statistical properties. They explicitly depend on the frequency content of the original signal, which makes them suitable to SHM applications. Spectral moment captures information from entire spectra and hence they can distinguish any subtle difference between normal and distorted signals.

As described in Sect. 20.4.2.1, the frequency characterisation of a random stationary process can be computed using the PSD function as,

$$S_{xx}(\omega) = \int\limits_{-\infty}^{\infty} R_{xx}(\tau)e^{-iw\tau}\,d\tau \tag{20.14}$$

For a given PSD, the nth-order spectral moment can be then computed as,

$$\lambda_x^n = \int\limits_{-\infty}^{\infty} |\omega|^n S_{xx}(\omega)\,d\omega \tag{20.15}$$

where n is the order of spectral moment. Finally, for a discretised signal x, the nth-order spectral moment λ_x^n can be obtained using,

$$\lambda_x^n = \frac{2}{N^{n+1}} \sum_{0}^{\lfloor N/2 \rfloor} S_{xx}(j) \left(\frac{j}{\Delta t}\right)^n \qquad j \in [1 : N/2] \tag{20.16}$$

where S_{xx} and Δt are, respectively, the discrete spectral density and the sampling period.

The zero-th order moment refers to the area under the spectral curve which represents the significance of the response. Higher order moments assign more weight to frequency components. Past research studies have concluded that spectral moments with orders 1–4 provide useful information about the system, whereas higher order moments usually do not provide further information as they are highly masked by noise [17].

20.4.3.2   *k*-means– Clustering

Clustering is a popular method in data mining applications [25]. The goal of clustering is to partition a set of data objects into groups of similar objects based on a given set of features. k-means is a widely used clustering algorithm, which groups data into k clusters $C = \{C_1, ..., C_k\}$ with the goal of minimising the within-cluster sum of squares, i.e.

$$\arg\min_{C} \sum_{i=1}^{k} \sum_{x \in C_i} ||x - \mu_i||^2 \tag{20.17}$$

where μ_i is the centre of cluster i (mean of data points in C_i). This optimisation function can be solved in an iterative manner, which converges after no further assignment changes between iterations.

However, the k-means method may converge to a sub-optimal partitioning, as it is sensitive to the initial selection of cluster centres. The k-means++ algorithm [6] is an alternative method, which uses a specific mechanism to select the initial set of centres, before applying the original k-means steps. k-means++ only selects one initial centre uniformly at random from all data points (as opposed to all the initial centres for k-means). Each subsequent cluster centre is then selected from the remaining data points with a probability proportional to its squared distance to the closest existing centre.

Outliers in the data can skew the selection of cluster centres and thus can lead both k-means and k-means++ to sub-optimal solutions. The recent k-means-- alternative [12] proposes a mechanism to detect such outliers (e.g. potential anomalies). In the previous methods, such anomalies were likely located in significantly small clusters as a by-product of the iterative process. In contrast, in k-means--, these anomalies are explicitly detected and isolated before the iterative cluster update process.

We propose the following extension to the original k-means-- algorithm. When convergence is achieved, any group with a single member is removed from the cluster set and its data point is added to the set of anomalies. This additional step prevents biases when selecting the best cluster result, as described in the next subsection. Our extended k-means-- is described in Algorithm 3. It follows the iterative steps of k-means, but first selects o anomalies in the data before assigning the remaining points into k clusters. Thus, these o data points that are furthest from their closet centres are isolated and are not used to recompute the centres in the update step and subsequent iterations.

20.4.3.3   Selection of the Best Clustering Result

Due to the random choice of the initial first centres in Algorithm 3, multiple runs over the same data set will produce different clustering results. This can be addressed by using a high number of replications, such as 50. However, different settings of

---

Algorithm 3 A modified k-means$--$ clustering.

Input: Matrix of X data points, number of clusters k, number of anomalies o
Output: o anomalies in L, cluster ID for each data point in $X - L$

1: **Initialisation**: using k-means$++$ to find k initial centres
2: **Assignment**: assign each data point to the nearest centre, and set their cluster ID accordingly
3: **Anomaly detection**: find the o points, which are furthest from their cluster centres (i.e. anomalies), and assign them to L
4: **Update**: recompute the centre for each cluster (excluding the found anomalies)
5: **Iterate**: repeat steps 2 to 4 until the algorithm converges, i.e. no further changes in the data point assignments
6: **Finalise**: convert clusters with only one data point to anomalies

---

k and o will also produce different clustering results. To address this issue, we limit the choice for k to a fixed maximum arbitrary value. In practice, this selection of the maximum k should be guided by domain knowledge of the application at hand. In the case of SHM such as the application of our scheme to a bridge, the maximum k value could be set equal to the number of structural spans of a bridge. For example, k could be set to 6 for a bridge which has 6 different structural spans. The o parameter may remain arbitrarily low, such as less than 5.

We then propose the following mechanism to select the most informative clustering and anomaly detection results. For each pair of input parameters (k, o), we compute the values of the Silhouette [47], the Davies-Bouldin [16], and the Dunn [19] indices over the resulting cluster set. Each index measures a specific characteristic of such a resulting cluster set. Indeed, the Silhouette index measures the averaged dissimilarity of each point against its assigned cluster, and then compares these measurements against the dissimilarity of the points within their nearest neighbouring clusters. On the other hand, the Davies-Bouldin index reports on the compactness and separation of the clusters, through the ratio between the similarities within a group and the differences between groups. The Dunn index computes the ratio between the closest points across different groups and the furthest points within groups.

We then select the (k, o) results which have extremum values for each of the computed indices, i.e. maximum value for Silhouette and Dunn; and minimum value for Davies-Bouldin. Within this set of results, we select the logical intersection of all identified anomalies as the final set of anomalies, i.e. points which have instrumentation issues or indicate structural damage. Any empty set of identified anomalies is treated as the identity element for this operation (i.e. does not influence the outcome). As the three indices report on different aspects of the cluster groups, using their intersection may lead to a more accurate set of anomalies. This is confirmed through experimental results in the next Sect. 20.5.

20.5 Case Studies and Results

20.5.1 Damage Identification

20.5.1.1 Case Study: The Sydney Harbour Bridge Specimen

A concrete cantilever beam, which has an arch section with a similar geometry to those on the SHB, was manufactured and tested, as shown in Fig. 20.3. The beam consists of a 200UB18 steel I-Beam with a 50 mm concrete cover on both ends. The length of the specimen is 2 m, the width is 1 m and the depth is 0.375 m. The specimen was fixed at one end using a steel bollard to form a cantilever, where 400 mm along the length of the beam were fully clamped. In addition, a support was placed at 1200 mm away from the tip to avoid any cracking occurring in the specimen under its self-weight [42].

Ten PCB 352C34 accelerometers were mounted on the specimen to measure the vibration response resulting from impact hammer excitation. Accelerometers were mounted on the front face of the beam. The cross-section of the beam and locations of the accelerometers are shown in Fig. 20.3. The structure was excited using an impact hammer with steel tip, which was applied on the top surface of the specimen and just above the location of sensor A9. The acceleration response of the structure was collected over a time period of 2 s at a sampling rate of 8 kHz, resulting in 16000 samples for each event (i.e. a single excitation). A total of 190 impact tests were collected from a healthy condition of the specimen.

A crack was introduced into the specimen in the location marked in Fig. 20.3 using a cutting saw. The crack is located between sensor locations A2 and A3 and progressively increases towards sensor location A9. The length of the cut was increased gradually from 75 to 150 mm, 225 and 270 mm, and the depth of the cut was fixed to 50 mm. After introducing each damage case, a total of 190 impact tests were performed on the structure in the location described earlier.

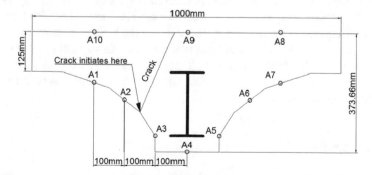

Fig. 20.3 A laboratory specimen with cracking

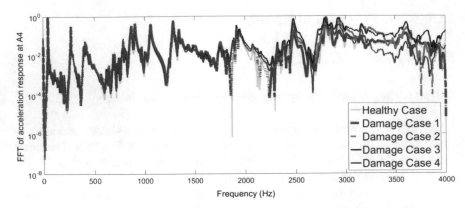

Fig. 20.4 Comparison of the frequency response function (inertance) between the healthy state and the four damage cases for sensor location A4

Table 20.1 Comparison of the first three modes of the structure in the healthy state and the four damage cases

Natural Fre-quency (Hz)	Healthy		Damage case 1		Damage case 2		Damage case 3		Damage case 4	
	ω	Δ %	ω	Δ %	ω	Δ %	ω	Δ %	ω	Δ %
$\omega 1$	45.90	–	45.90	0.00	45.90	0.00	45.90	0.00	45.50	0.87
$\omega 2$	181.6	–	181.4	0.11	181.2	0.22	180.8	0.44	180.0	0.88
$\omega 3$	265.0	–	264.6	0.15	264.4	0.23	264.2	0.30	262.4	0.98

We further investigated the impact of damage by comparing the frequency response function (FRF) of the structure between the measured responses obtained from the healthy case and four damage cases as shown in Fig. 20.4. It was observed that the damage effects are more evident at high frequency, as the change between the healthy and the damaged structure became more significant. Table 20.1 compares the natural frequencies for the first three modes in the healthy state and three damage cases, as well as the change in frequency of each damage case relative to the healthy state. From Table 20.1, it can be clearly seen that once the severity of damage increases, a higher discrepancy in the first three modal frequencies with respect to the healthy state is obtained.

20.5.1.2   Results

We have applied our proposed damage detection and severity assessment framework (described in Fig. 20.2) onto our specimen dataset. A total of 950 samples were collected in this experiment, where each sample is a measured vibration response of

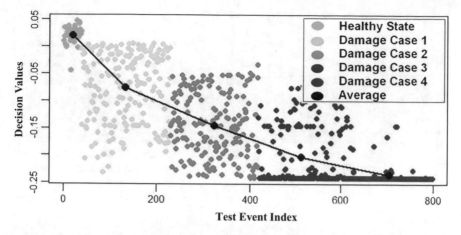

Fig. 20.5 Damage identification results using FDD for feature fusion and extraction

the structure with eight thousand attributes in the frequency domain ($8\,\text{kHz} \times 2\,\text{s} \times$ 0.5 (considering Nyquist frequency)). We separated the data samples into two main groups, healthy samples (190 samples) and damaged samples (760). 80% of the healthy cases data were randomly selected for a training stage, while the remaining 20% of healthy samples and all the damaged cases were used as a test data for validating the proposed approach. Feature extraction and fusion from ten sensors using FDD were initially applied on the training data, and random projection was used for dimensionality reduction. This was followed by calculating the optimal value of σ using the ADES method defined in Eq. 20.11 and constructing a one-class SVM as a damage detection model.

The constructed model was then validated using the test data. Similar to the training steps, the FDD method was initially applied to the test data followed by dimensionality reduction algorithm. The final step was to present the test data onto the constructed one-class SVM model to evaluate its performance in terms of damage detection and severity assessment. As expected, the constructed model was able to successfully detect the damaged cases and produced an F1-score of 0.95. A detailed summary of the results is presented in Fig. 20.5. The figure shows the decision values of all test data, where the black dots represent average decision values for healthy and each damaged cases.

Only three events from the healthy samples were misclassified as damaged. On the other hand, all the damaged samples were correctly classified except for four events in Damage Case 1 that had positive decision values (false negative). This suggests that the model is well generalised on unseen samples and has the ability to detect damaged and healthy samples. It should be emphasised that the level of damage in this case study is considerably small. Moreover, the method also shows a capability to assess a progression of damage (as shown by decreasing decision values for Damage Cases 1 to 4) despite variations in operational conditions. Moreover, the obtained machine learning results match very well with the findings from domain

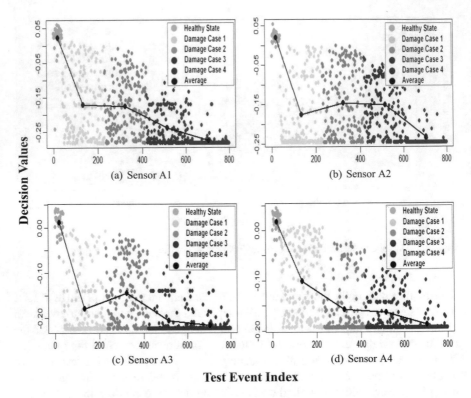

Fig. 20.6 Damage identification results using a separate one-class SVM model for each sensor location

knowledge presented in Table 20.1. A decreasing trend in the ML scores indicates progressive damage in the structure.

To further investigate the effectiveness of feature fusion using FDD, an alternative approach was adopted without using FDD for sensor fusion. Only the frequency features (using FFT) of the acceleration response obtained from each sensor were used to construct a separate damage detection model for each sensor using data from the healthy case.

Damage identification results using this approach are presented in Fig. 20.6 for sensors A1, A2, A3 and A4 (results for other sensors were similar). It can be realised that this approach does not have the capability to monitor the progress of damage. The decision values did not consistently follow the trend of the damage as shown in Fig. 20.6b, c. Based on this, it can be concluded that FDD is robust against excitation variations and can provide reliable information about the severity of damage in the structure.

20.5.2 Substructure Clustering and Anomaly Detection

20.5.2.1 Case Study: The Sydney Harbour Bridge

The goal of this study was to group substructures (i.e. jack arches) with a similar behaviour and then identify substructures with potential anomalies. We used a set of 85 nodes over five structural sections of the SHB, i.e. five different spans of the bridge. These spans were located on the Northern Main Span and the Northern Approach, as illustrated on Fig. 20.1. For each node, we collected 10 min of continuous acceleration data at 1500 Hz over 22 days in July 2015 (as described in Sect. 20.2). We pre-processed this data to identify a continuous 1 min of *ambient* response, i.e. a period where no vehicle was driving over the node. For each of these periods, we computed the spectral moment feature as described in Sect. 20.4.3.1 for accelerations in x, y and z direction (denoted SMx, SMy and SMz), and we averaged them for each node over the 22 days.

We applied our extended k-means – method and its outcome selection criteria (Sect. 20.4.3.2) to this set of spectral moment features. We varied the parameter k (i.e. number of clusters) from 2 to 6, as the studied nodes were spread across five structural sections, and the parameter o (i.e. number of anomalies) from 0 to 4. Finally, we replicated this experiment 10 times. The following subsection reports on the results related to the second order spectral moment. The first and third order moments produced similar results and were not included here.

20.5.2.2 Results

Figure 20.7 shows the Silhouette, Davies-Bouldin, and Dunn indices for each (k, o) pair. Using our selection criteria, we retained the pairs ($k = 2$, $o = 3$), ($k = 2$, $o = 4$), and ($k = 3$, $o = 0$) as they corresponded to the required extremum values. For these pairs, Fig. 20.8 shows the 3D scatterplots for the second order spectral moment in x, y and z, and Fig. 20.8d shows the related index values. The nodes 184, 427, and 433 formed the set of anomalies resulting from the intersection of these pairs as described in Sect. 20.4.3.2.

For ($k = 3$, $o = 0$), the nodes 184 and 427 were in a well-separated group in the 3D feature space, and node 433 was included into one of the other two clusters. This outcome is due to the setting $o = 0$, i.e. the clustering algorithm had to reject any outright outliers (i.e. by-pass step 3 of Algorithm 3). Limiting the range of o to strictly positive integers (e.g. $o \in [1, 4]$) would result in node 433 being identified as an anomaly. However, having $o > 1$ may provide more false positives, as it will force the clustering process to mark the most distant point in a dataset as an anomaly, even if that point is *well* matched to a group. This may be a better decision for a bridge manager, as it could be safer to discard a false positive after a visual engineering inspection than letting a false negative remain undetected.

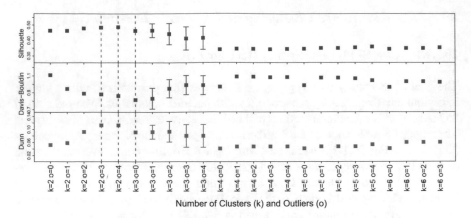

Fig. 20.7 Silhouette, Davies-Bouldin, and Dunn indices for different (k, o) parameters

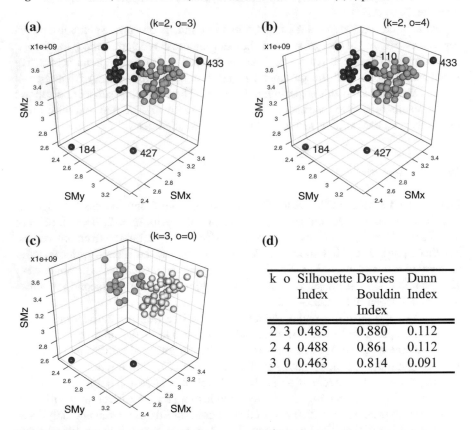

Fig. 20.8 a, b, c Selected 3D scatter plots of spectral moments (SM) for each node, which are coloured based on their cluster membership for specific parameters, and **d** their corresponding performance index values. Cluster groups are coloured in blue, green, and grey, anomalies are coloured in red

Fig. 20.9 Difference between the time interval jitter for the data of a healthy working node 170 and node 433

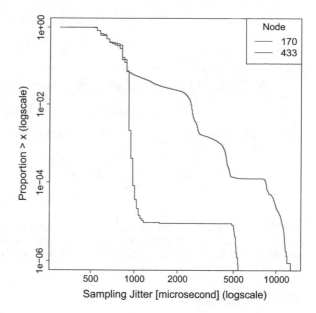

Further engineering investigations of the nodes in the resulting set of anomalies (i.e. 184, 427, and 433) showed that they were all having instrumentation issues during the 22-day period of this study (i.e. sensor defect for 184 and 433, power unit defect for 427) [3]. As an example for node 433, Fig. 20.9 presents the log-scale ECDF of the time interval jitter between two collected data points, as compared to the healthy working node 170. This jitter should be as close to 0 as possible, i.e. for node 170 only 0.01% of the data points had a jitter greater than 1 ms. Node 433 produced in contrast a higher jitter distribution, i.e. more than 1% of the data points had a jitter greater than 2 ms. From a hardware perspective, the cause of such a high jitter could be a failure of the oscillator-based clock of the sensor producing the data. This sensor was marked for replacement.

Figure 20.10 shows the boxplots of second order spectral moment values for each direction and each node in the case of ($k = 2, o = 3$). The nodes are ordered on the x-axis according to their physical location on the SHB from north (left) to south (right). The boxplot for a node is coloured based on its group membership, with the anomalies marked in red. This figure confirms that the nodes that are located on a given structural section are mostly grouped into the same cluster. Indeed most of the North Approach nodes are in the green group, whereas all the Northern Main Span nodes are in the blue group.

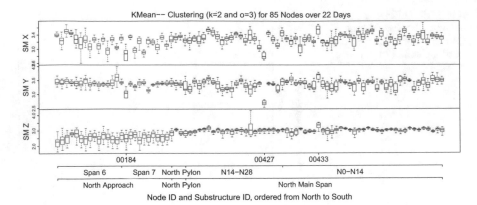

Fig. 20.10 Boxplots of second order X,Y, and Z spectral moment values for ($k = 2$, $o = 3$) for each node. On the x-axis, the nodes are ordered based on their location from north to south. The colours indicate the assigned cluster groups (blue or green) and the anomalies (red)

20.6 Conclusion

This work presents damage identification and substructure grouping approaches for SHM applications using machine learning techniques and features extracted using domain knowledge. The two approaches performed successfully in two case studies using data from a laboratory structure and real data collected from the SHB. Domain knowledge is used in this chapter to show how an SHM problem is formed as a machine learning problem using domain knowledge. It also shows the importance of domain knowledge in extracting damage sensitive features as well as interpreting the results found by machine learning approaches.

In the first approach, a structural benchmark model was built using a self-tuning one-class SVM on a feature space fused and extracted from multiple sensors by FDD, followed by random projection for dimensionality reduction. Then new events were tested against the benchmark model to detect damage. The approach detected damage well with high accuracy and low false positives, even for a small damage case. Moreover, this proposed approach also achieved damage severity assessment using data fusion and decision values from the SVM. In the second approach, a robust clustering technique was utilised on spectral moment features for substructure grouping and anomaly detection. The technique was able to group substructures of similar behaviour on the SHB and to detect anomalies spatially, which were associated with sensor issues from the instrumented substructures.

This work is part of our ongoing effort to build Smart Infrastructures, which bring together data acquisition, data management, and data analytics techniques to optimise their maintenance and services. Our future works include an implementation of the proposed approaches on our production system on the SHB, and applying them using data collected from other structures.

Acknowledgements The authors wish to thank the Roads and Maritime Services (RMS) in New South Wales, Australia for provision of the support and testing facilities for this research work. NICTA is funded by the Australian Government through the Department of Communications and the Australian Research Council through the ICT Centre of Excellence Program. CSIRO's Digital Productivity business unit and NICTA have joined forces to create digital powerhouse Data61.

References

1. Achlioptas, D.: Database-friendly random projections: Johnson-lindenstrauss with binary coins. J. Comput. Syst. Sci. **66**(4), 671–687 (2003)
2. Alamdari, M.M., Li, J., Samali, B.: Frf-based damage localization method with noise suppression approach. J. Sound Vib. **333**(14), 3305–3320 (2014)
3. Alamdarı, M.M., Rakotoarivelo, T., Khoa, N.L.D.: A spectral-based clustering for structural health monitoring of the Sydney Harbour Bridge. Mech. Syst. Signal Process. **87**, 384–400 (2017)
4. Anaissi, A., Khoa, N.L.D., Mustapha, S., Alamdari, M.M., Braytee, A., Wang, Y., Chen, F.: Adaptive one-class support vector machine for damage detection in structural health monitoring. In: Pacific-Asia Conference on Knowledge Discovery and Data Mining, pp. 42–57. Springer (2017)
5. Antoni, J., Randall, R.: The spectral kurtosis: application to the vibratory surveillance and diagnostics of rotating machines. Mech. Syst. Signal Process. **20**(2), 308–331 (2006)
6. Arthur, D., Vassilvitskii, S.: K-means++: The advantages of careful seeding. In: Proceedings of the Eighteenth Annual ACM-SIAM Symposium on Discrete Algorithms, SODA '07. Society for Industrial and Applied Mathematics, pp. 1027–1035. Philadelphia, PA, USA (2007)
7. Banks, H., Inman, D., Leo, D., Wang, Y.: An experimentally validated damage detection theory in smart structures. J. Sound Vib. **191**(5), 859–880 (1996)
8. Benasciutti, D., Cristofori, A., Tovo, R.: Analogies between spectral methods and multiaxial criteria in fatigue damage evaluation. Probab. Eng. Mech. **31**, 39–45 (2013)
9. Bingham, E., Mannila, H.: Random projection in dimensionality reduction: applications to image and text data. In: Proceedings of the seventh ACM SIGKDD International Conference on Knowledge Discovery and Data Mining, KDD '01, pp. 245–250. ACM, New York, NY, USA (2001). DOI https://doi.org/10.1145/502512.502546
10. Brincker, R., Zhang, L., Andersen, P.: Output-only modal analysis by frequency domain decomposition. In: The International Conference on Noise and Vibration Engineering, pp. 717–723 (2001)
11. Cattarius, J., Inman, D.: Time domain analysis for damage detection in smart structures. Mech. Syst. Signal Process. **11**(3), 409–423 (1997)
12. Chawla, S., Gionis, A.: k-means-: A unified approach to clustering and outlier detection. In: Proceedings of the 13th SIAM International Conference on Data Mining, 2–4 May 2013. Austin, Texas, USA, pp. 189–197 (2013)
13. Chen, Y., Zhou, X.S., Huang, T.S.: One-class svm for learning in image retrieval. In: 2001 International Conference on Image Processing, vol. 1, pp. 34–37. IEEE (2001)
14. Curadelli, R., Riera, J., Ambrosini, D., Amani, M.: Damage detection by means of structural damping identification. Eng. Struct. **30**(12), 3497–3504 (2008)
15. CusidÓCusido, J., Romeral, L., Ortega, J.A., Rosero, J.A., Espinosa, A.G.: Fault detection in induction machines using power spectral density in wavelet decomposition. IEEE Trans. Ind. Electron. **55**(2), 633–643 (2008)
16. Davies, D., Bouldin, D.: A cluster separation measure. IEEE Trans. Pattern Anal. Mach. Intell. **1**, 224–227 (1979)
17. Di-Paola, M., Muscolino, G.: On the convergent parts of high order spectral moments of stationary structural responses. J. Sound Vib. **110**, 233–245 (1986)

18. Doebling, S.W., Farrar, C.R., Prime, M.B., Shevitz, D.W.: Damage identification and health monitoring of structural and mechanical systems from changes in their vibration characteristics: a literature review. Technical report. Los Alamos National Laboratory, NM, USA (1996)
19. Dunn, J.: A fuzzy relative of the isodata process and its use in detecting compact well-separated clusters. J. Cybern. **3**, 32–57 (1973)
20. Farrar, C.R., Doebling, S.W., Nix, D.A.: Vibration-based structural damage identification. Philos. Trans. R. Soc. Lond. A: Math. Phys. Eng. Sci. **359**(1778), 131–149 (2001)
21. Farrar, C.R., Worden, K.: An introduction to structural health monitoring. In: Philosophical Transactions of the Royal Society of London A: Mathematical, Physical and Engineering Sciences, vol. 365, pp. 303–315. The Royal Society (2007)
22. Fugate, M.L., Sohn, H., Farrar, C.R.: Vibration-based damage detection using statistical process control. Mech. Syst. Signal Process. **15**(4), 707–721 (2001)
23. Hou, Z., Noori, M., Amand, R.S.: Wavelet-based approach for structural damage detection. J. Eng. Mech. **126**(7), 677–683 (2000)
24. H.Sohn, Farrar, C., Hemez, F., Shunk, D., Stinemates, D., Nadler, B., Czarnecki, J.: A review of structural health monitoring literature: 1996–2001. Los Alamos National Laboratory, USA (2003)
25. Jain, A.K., Murty, M.N., Flynn, P.J.: Data clustering: a review. ACM Comput. Surv. **31**, 264–323 (1999)
26. Jiang, S.F., Zhang, C.M., Koh, C.: Structural damage detection by integrating data fusion and probabilistic neural network. Adv. Struct. Eng. **9**(4), 445–458 (2006)
27. Joachims, T.: Text categorization with support vector machines: Learning with many relevant features. In: European Conference on Machine Learning, pp. 137–142. Springer (1998)
28. Johnson, W.B., Lindenstrauss, J.: Extensions of lipschitz mappings into a hilbert space. Contem. Math. **26**(189–206), 1 (1984)
29. Jolliffe, I.: Principal component analysis. Wiley Online Library (2002)
30. Kemmler, M., Rodner, E., Denzler, J.: One-class classification with gaussian processes. In: Asian Conference on Computer Vision, pp. 489–500. Springer (2010)
31. Khoa, N.L.D., Zhang, B., Wang, Y., Chen, F., Mustapha, S.: Robust dimensionality reduction and damage detection approaches in structural health monitoring. Struct. Health Monit. **13**(4), 406–417 (2014)
32. Law, S., Li, X., Zhu, X., Chan, S.: Structural damage detection from wavelet packet sensitivity. Eng. Struct. **27**(9), 1339–1348 (2005)
33. Lee, U., Shin, J.: A frequency response function-based structural damage identification method. Comput. & Struct. **80**(2), 117–132 (2002)
34. Liberatore, S., Carman, G.: Power spectral density analysis for damage identification and location. J. Sound Vib. **274**(3), 761–776 (2004)
35. Liu, Q.C., Wang, H.P.B.: A case study on multisensor data fusion for imbalance diagnosis of rotating machinery. AI EDAM **15**(3), 203–210 (2001)
36. Long, J., Buyukozturk, O.: Automated structural damage detection using one-class machine learning. In: Dynamics of Civil Structures, Vol. 4, pp. 117–128. Springer (2014)
37. Lu, Y., Michaels, J.E.: Feature extraction and sensor fusion for ultrasonic structural health monitoring under changing environmental conditions. IEEE Sens. J. **9**(11), 1462–1471 (2009)
38. Maia, N., Silva, J., Almas, E., Sampaio, R.: Damage detection in structures: from mode shape to frequency response function methods. Mech. Syst. Signal Process. **17**(3), 489–498 (2003)
39. Makki Alamdari, M.: Vibration-based structural health monitoring. Ph.D. thesis, University of Technology Sydney (2015)
40. Makki-Alamdari, M., Li, J., Samali, B.: A comparative study on the performance of the damage detection methods in the frequency domain. In: Australasian Conference on the Mechanics of Structures and Materials. CRC press/Balkema (2013)
41. Makki Alamdari, M., Samali, B., Li, J., Kalhori, H., Mustapha, S.: Spectral-based damage identification in structures under ambient vibration. J. Comput. Civil Eng. p. 04015062 (2015)
42. Mustapha, S., Hu, Y., Nguyen, K., Alamdari, M.M., Runcie, P., Dackermann, U., Nguyen, V., Li, J., Ye, L.: Pattern recognition based on time series analysis using vibration data for structural health monitoring in civil structures. Special Issue: Electron. J. Struct. Eng. **14**(1) (2015)

43. Nagarajaiah, S., Basu, B.: Output only modal identification and structural damage detection using time frequency & wavelet techniques. Earthquake Eng. Eng. Vib. **8**(4), 583–605 (2009)
44. Pandey, A., Biswas, M.: Damage detection in structures using changes in flexibility. J. Sound Vib. **169**(1), 3–17 (1994)
45. Peeters, B., Maeck, J., De Roeck, G.: Vibration-based damage detection in civil engineering: excitation sources and temperature effects. Smart Mater. Struct. **10**(3), 518 (2001)
46. Petrucci, G., Zuccarello, B.: Fatigue life prediction under wide band random loading. Fatigue & Fract. Eng. Mater. Struct. **27**(12), 1183–1195 (2004)
47. Rousseeuw, P.: Silhouettes: a graphical aid to the interpretation and validation of cluster analysis. J. Comput. Appl. Math. **20**, 53–65 (1987)
48. Runcie, P., Mustapha, S., Rakotoarivelo, T.: Advances in structural health monitoring system architecture. In: International Symposium on Life-Cycle Civil Engineering, pp. 1064 –1071 (2014)
49. Rytter, A.: Vibration-based inspection of civil engineering structures. Ph.D. thesis, University of Aalborg (1993)
50. Salawu, O.: Detection of structural damage through changes in frequency: a review. Eng. Struct. **19**(9), 718–723 (1997)
51. Santos, A., Figueiredo, E., Silva, M., Sales, C., Costa, J.: Machine learning algorithms for damage detection: Kernel-based approaches. J. Sound Vib. **363**, 584–599 (2016)
52. Schölkopf, B., Williamson, R.C., Smola, A.J., Shawe-Taylor, J., Platt, J.C., et al.: Support vector method for novelty detection. In: NIPS, vol. 12, pp. 582–588. Citeseer (1999)
53. Shi, Z., Law, S., Zhang, L.: Structural damage detection from modal strain energy change. J. Eng. Mech. **126**(12), 1216–1223 (2000)
54. Sohn, H., Farrar, C.R.: Damage diagnosis using time series analysis of vibration signals. Smart Mater. Struct. **10**(3), 446 (2001)
55. Sohn, H., Farrar, C.R., Hemez, F.M., Czarnecki, J.J.: A review of structural health review of structural health monitoring literature 1996–2001. Technical Report, Los Alamos National Laboratory (2002)
56. Sophian, A., Tian, G.Y., Taylor, D., Rudlin, J.: A feature extraction technique based on principal component analysis for pulsed eddy current ndt. NDT & e Int. **36**(1), 37–41 (2003)
57. Su, Z., Wang, X., Cheng, L., Yu, L., Chen, Z.: On selection of data fusion schemes for structural damage evaluation. Struct. Health Monit. **8**(3), 223–241 (2009)
58. Sun, Z., Chang, C.: Structural damage assessment based on wavelet packet transform. J. Struct. Eng. **128**(10), 1354–1361 (2002)
59. Sunder, S.S., Grewatz, S.E., Ting, S.K.: Modal identification using spectral moments. Struct. Saf. **3**(1), 1–11 (1985)
60. Vanmarcke, E.H.: Properties of spectral moments with applications to random vibration. J. Eng. Mech. Div. **98**(2), 425–446 (1972)
61. Venkatasubramanian, S., Wang, Q.: The johnson-lindenstrauss transform: An empirical study. In: M. Mller-Hannemann, R.F.F. Werneck (eds.) ALENEX, pp. 164–173. SIAM (2011)
62. Worden, K., Manson, G.: The application of machine learning to structural health monitoring. Philos. Trans. R. Soc. A: Math. Phys. Eng. Sci. **365**(1851), 515–537 (2007)
63. Yao, R., Pakzad, S.N.: Autoregressive statistical pattern recognition algorithms for damage detection in civil structures. Mech. Syst. Signal Process. **31**, 355–368 (2012)

Chapter 21
Domain Knowledge in Predictive Maintenance for Water Pipe Failures

Zhidong Li and Yang Wang

Abstract In this chapter, the water pipe failure prediction is used as an example to show the integration of machine learning and domain knowledge. It is crucial for the risk management strategy of water distribution systems to minimise the water pipe failure impacts. Prediction of water pipe conditions through statistical modelling is an important element for the task. When applying the models to practical problems, domain experts can provide invaluable suggestions that can be used as constraints or informative prior knowledge. Alternatively, the models can also help domain experts to explore more insights. The chapter uses major steps in the water pipe failure prediction, including data review, factor analysis, prediction evaluation and practical use, as examples to illustrate how the domain knowledge is integrated. Then the hierarchical non-parametric model is used as an example model.

21.1 Introduction

21.1.1 Domain Knowledge in Machine Learning

Modern technology makes deploying machine learning algorithms more convenient. For example, the complex but powerful models, such as deep neural network [7] and random Forest [2] can be directly implemented using Python packages. Without the obstacles of implementation, data scientists and analysts are eager to try modern algorithms on different data problems. Data competitions, which provide various data to their competing entrants, is a good example. In these competitions, usually the data

Z. Li (✉) · Y. Wang
DATA61, CSIRO, 13 Garden Street, Eveleigh, NSW 2015, Australia
e-mail: zhidong.li@data61.csiro.au

Y. Wang
e-mail: yang.wang@data61.csiro.au

J. Zhou and F. Chen (eds.), *Human and Machine Learning*, Human–Computer Interaction Series, https://doi.org/10.1007/978-3-319-90403-0_21

are well formatted (the data had been pre-processed by domain knowledge before they were provided), even without meaningful names for features. It has some advantages. First, they do not require the competing entrants to have the domain knowledge so they can proceed them directly and, as domain knowledge is not advocated in testing competitors ability on data analysis, it also provides fairness. However, knowing what is the impact of each feature is vital in real applications. That is why feature engineering is still an essential step to obtain prediction accuracy in the competitions even without using domain knowledge. While some models such as the deep neural network can find optimum feature sets and their combinations, however the actual feature-target relationship is hard to be explained from domain knowledge thus yet to be fully trusted. This also hinders the machine learning algorithms to be used in practice.

In real projects, domain knowledge can shorten the path of determining useful features or producing new features based on the known data, which can be endless trials for computers to exploit. As a result, domain knowledge can either help improve the model performance or explain the results well. In fact, almost all the processes in a real project involve domain knowledge. This could include project value determination, data interpretation for pre-processing, cleaning, quality assessment, and many more. Even in a data competition, preparing the big matrix also requires domain knowledge. In the following section, many examples in different parts of a standard project process are discussed. This chapter focuses on why and how the domain knowledge is needed in different tasks of machine learning and data mining, especially on the infrastructure data, such as the water main maintenance problem.

21.1.2   Water Pipe Failure Prediction Background

The water utilities are responsible for providing an adequate and satisfactory supply of water (mainly for drinking or flushing) to meet the demands of the territory and for maintaining a sound water supply system. To deliver water to consumers, water utilities rely on the due performance of the extensive and complicated water main network (generally buried underground). With the decades of urbanisation, most of the territory network comprises water mains for thousands of kilometres. Some large territories may be maintaining network over ten thousand kilometres.

As most water main systems are build more than 100 years ago. In the recent decades, the condition of more and more mains is deteriorating and maintenance is required. The maintenance of a considerable length of water mains approaching the end of their service life became increasingly difficult and costly. Given the poor condition of the water distribution network, further operations like replacement and rehabilitation (R&R) of the aged water mains was the most effective solution to rejuvenate the water distribution network and arrest the rapidly rising trend of main failures (including bursting and leakage). The R&R program of water mains has been considered by many water utilities in recent years. Because of the high cost and time limitation, predictive maintenance becomes urgent necessity as the water mains will continue to age and deteriorate.

Riding on the growing power of computers, the machine learning technique has been growing rapidly in recent years. Many water utilities are looking into the use of the machine learning technique in prediction of pipe failure probabilities and are planning to engage consultants to carry out a trial of water main failure prediction models. Should the application of the water main failure prediction models to the water distribution network be effective, they may assist in early identification and handling of water mains in poor condition.

For water utilities, the prioritisation step requires a good understanding of the failure risk, and in particular a good estimate of the likelihood of failures, from which potential failure costs can usually be derived easily, based on the area serviced. The mechanisms of water pipe failure have been studied for decades, and various physical and mechanical models, involving pipe wall thickness [4], material deterioration according to environmental conditions and quality of manufacturing [11], and hydraulic characteristics [10], have been developed to estimate the remaining pipe life. However, non-intrusive technologies for pipe condition assessment are still very limited and not cost effective because input parameters such as pipe wall thickness may rely on an inspection step. That latter step, called condition assessment, often requires excavation, the use of specialised analysis equipment, and public disruption. To avoid that, the water utilities are engaging with machine learning scientists for consulting water main failure analysis and prediction by carrying out projects. The main objective of these projects is to test the machine learning based trial of advanced water main failure prediction techniques in real water main data.

Machine learning techniques have their value in the aforementioned problem. Generally, there are two types of models for prediction of water pipe failure: physical models and statistical models. Physical models [6] are significantly influenced by domain knowledge and usually designed to capture the mechanisms of failures due to certain causes, e.g., soil corrosion. But they have significant limitations, e.g. budget restriction for experiments, when applying to a large water mains network with complex factors. In contrast, statistical models usually require fewer resources and can capture hidden statistical failure patterns caused by different physical reasons. Hence, they can be applied to large-scale water main networks for guiding proactive maintenance. The statistical machine learning models are trained by considering historical failure records, physical characteristics of pipes and environmental factors. The value of statistical machine learning techniques is greater if it can be interpreted using domain knowledge. In the following sections, we will discuss why each task needs to be influenced by domain knowledge from the example of water main failure prediction.

This chapter is comprises of five sections, the data is discussed in Sect. 21.2, which also includes how the knowledge is used in data understanding and why domain knowledge is needed to transfer data into the model inputs. Why domain knowledge is essential for data analysis is discussed in Sect. 21.3. In Sect. 21.4, we examine why domain knowledge is important in prediction models, a quite common machine learning task. We consider the Bayesian non-parametric model that includes both the prior knowledge and the flexibility to accommodate the data and evaluation and constraints of the model are spotlighted. Our conclusion are given in Sect. 21.5.

21.2 Data Description

21.2.1 Data Understanding

In most projects, generally there are two main data sets to consider. For example, one example of data set showing in Table 21.1 corresponds to attributes of assets (i.e. elements in water main network, usually each of them is one pipe). The other data set in Table 21.2 contains all the failure records for the assets in recent years (usually left censored). The domain knowledge is important when dealing with such data set.

For the attributes of water mains, it is important that the data scientists understand the meaning of the attribute values. For example, there are numeric values that do not carry any meaningful relations between consecutive numbers (i.e. material = 2 does not mean it has double the materials of material = 1, they only represent different types of materials). The meaning of attributes for the failure records are also important and must be well understood. For example, failure can be caused by a third party (Failure reason = 'R3') rather than corrosion of pipes, so they cannot be combined when predicting.

Table 21.1 The attributes of water mains

Pipe ID	Material	Laid year	Length
1	1	1962	30
2	1	1960	30
3	2	1976	60
4	1	1980	100
5	3	2003	10
6	3	2001	30
7	1	1916	150

Table 21.2 The failure records of water mains

Pipe ID	Failure data	Failure type	Failure reason
1	3/2/2010	Burst	R1
1	11/8/2014	Leak	R2
2	4/2/1998	Burst	R2
2	15/5/2004	Leak	R1
2	30/3/2008	Leak	R3
5	4/4/2011	Burst	R1

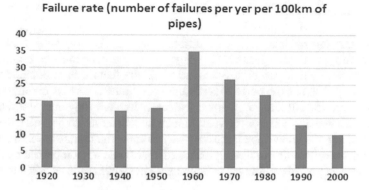

Fig. 21.1 Failure rate versus laid year. Generally, older pipes are more likely to fail, here the observation that pipes laid in 1960 have higher failure rate than pipes laid in 1920 is suspicious so this needs to be confirmed with domain experts

Furthermore, there are censored data in that the observation only contains data from recent years (around 5–20 years). This short period deliver uncertain information when dealing with some water mains whose age is over 100 years. What happened before can only be partly known and put into the model according to domain experts. However, the information could be in fragmented form resulting in much being forgotten or missed. In addition, the data mining and machine learning scientists also have a responsibility to carefully observe the data and raise questions about them, using these questions to obtain as much information as possible from domain experts. For example, we can observe that in Fig. 21.1 more failures occurred for water mains laid between 1950 and 1980, although these pipes are newer than pipes laid between 1920 and 1930. The cause could be missing records, different quality of materials, or different usage habits in the history. However, a reason needs to be discovered and raised to domain experts to obtain more information, otherwise the prediction can be wrong.

21.2.2   Domain Knowledge in Data Pre-processing

After data is understood, the analysts need to convert the raw data to feasible data for further steps. The conversion is referred to as pre-processing and usually domain knowledge is required. For example, to represent the text based unstructured data into word vectors, the special meaning of professional terms must be considered as single element rather than decomposing them. Some common issues in pre-processing are reviewed in this section.

21.2.2.1 Feature Type

Machine learning models can accept different type of features so it is important to know the type of each feature. For example, in the decision tree regression, a feature can be divided into different branches. If the feature is in numeric values, it is meaningful to use the range to represent each branch, such as dividing [1, 10] into [1, 5] and (5, 10]. However, some features, although they are represented by numbers, are actually categorical values, such as 'Material' in Table 21.1. In preprocessing, domain knowledge is the only way to know the feature type. In addition, some numeric values are not linearly arranged. If this can be pointed out by domain experts, we can provide additional column using the sorted rank of this feature.

21.2.2.2 Data Completeness

In a given data set, it is common that not all features values are filled in for each water main. Many of the records are described as missing records because some features are missing. Completeness requires that a particular column, element or class of data is populated and does not have unavailable values or missing values in place of nulls (e.g. N/As). In our case, completeness refers to the percentage of non-empty attributes, such as *facility ID, laid year, material, size, length, failure rate.*

It is important to consider the completeness of data. An option is to use a statistic based imputation. A simple imputation is to fill in the missing features with average or median values. However, this is unsafe as the data could be categorical but labelled with numbers. It is thus important to communicate with domain experts and combine domain knowledge to fill in the missing values. Here is an example of considering data completion with the help of domain knowledge.

Before looking into the data, the analyst does not know which feature is important and will therefore need help from domain experts. In the example, domain experts suggested the features to consider from a big set and point out the reason or confidence for each feature. An example in practice is that we observed that there are many missing values for water main *material*, such as shown in Fig. 21.2. The actual values of *material* can be verified using failure-records-matching filling from the domain knowledge that is learned from their professional activities: for example, the failure records for certain pipes can be determined from on site investigation, then *material* of those water mains can be completed.

21.2.2.3 Data Consistent

Consistent is the data across the different records that hold copies of it. In our case, we check how consistent the data is across water main asset data and failure records data.

Data consistency is necessary before using machine learning algorithms. There are many possibilities that can cause inconsistency but many of them would not be

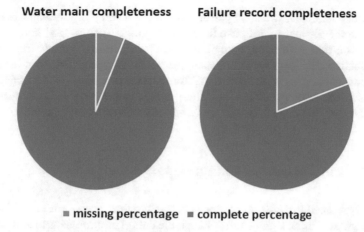

Fig. 21.2 An example for visualising completeness in a data set, both water main attributes and failure records are incomplete

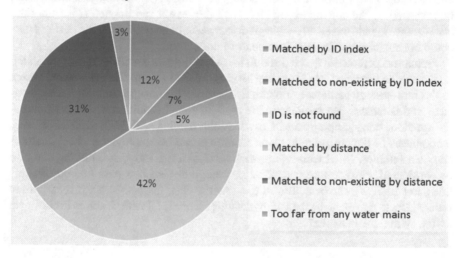

Fig. 21.3 The data matching for a data set, the matching is inconsistent if we only use ID. The matching can be improved using more information such as geological distance

discovered until the trouble they caused made them obvious. In our case, first we need to match the main failures to existing mains. Usually not all failures can be matched to water mains. As an example, Fig. 21.3 gives an example to show the matching quality. From the figure, we can see that many attempts are made to match them. Some of them is based *facility ID*. When *facility ID* cannot be located, it is suggested by the domain expert that some mains could be have been replaced and are not in service. These need to be matched to another data set called Abandoned Mains. In addition, when *facility ID* is unavailable, we discussed with domain experts and obtained the coordinators from geologists to match.

In another example, when we perform our analysis on pipes in major materials, however, some distinct values have the same meaning, such as 'SS' and 'Stainless Steel'. This is due to different regulations when the data are input into the database, since sometimes the data gathering span more than 20 years. They can also be an ambiguous meaning as well, such as Nil for external coating of water mains could mean unknown value or no coating. These factor values need to be confirmed or provided by domain experts before applying the machine learning models.

21.2.3 Data Review by Domain Expert

Data analysts need to make sure the data can still reflect reality after the aforementioned steps which can significantly change the data. This process is usually considered from the commencement of data understanding throughout the pre-processing and cleaning. For example, when checking data consistency, any inconsistency must be reviewed by the domain experts to check the reason and impact. It is important also for the domain expert to review data that seem to be outliers as the outliers data could contain wrong labelling or manner of collection.

Domain experts could find it difficult to review the data due to data volume. Statistical machine learning techniques can be employed to summarise the review, except in the rare case of outliers. For example, statistical moments, such as mean, variance, and skewness, can summarize the cleaned data. In addition, to show structural information, bootstrapping can be used. When dealing with high-dimension data, randomness or dimension reduction techniques can be employed on both features and data samples. Other techniques, such as clustering, and sparse coding can also be considered. Furthermore, visualisation techniques, such as parallel coordinators line and t-SNE [9], can be deployed to show the data. In conclusion, it is important for analysts to represent the data with meaningful or explainable features for efficient review with domain experts.

21.3 Domain Knowledge in Factor Analysis

The purpose of factor analysis is to understand and discover the data insights to support the decision of the domain experts. In addition, the analysis results could be used to build models for prediction or risk analysis. As many analyses are based on statistics, and it is easy to access statistical tools, such as SPSS, domain experts can acquire the basic information from the data. Factor analysis therefore guides the domain experts by providing deep insights, generally through multiple rounds of discussions and reinforced analysis. Sometimes it is found that some discovered insights were actually data issues and we must go back to the previous step. Some examples of the involvement of domain experts in factor analysis are listed.

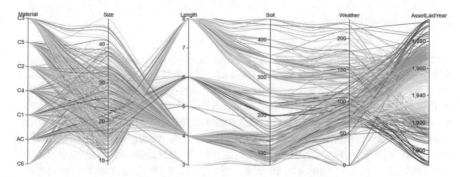

Fig. 21.4 Parallel coordinator to show the different levels of failure rate, the feature subsets with red lines can be the highly interested subsets

1. The factor analyses are usually carried out on all water mains, however, there could be a huge number of categories considering the combination of features. With only a limited budget, the domain experts aim to improving the network performance by seeking a subset among all categories. To provide information for selection, both feature selection and visualisation manners could be used. Figure 21.4 provides an example of parallel coordinator lines to visualise the highly interested subsets.
2. The domain experts know more about which features should be more focused and whether additional data is needed for analysis. For example, weather data could impact the water main failures, however, this data must be additionally extracted from the meteorology department. Since it is not provided in the original data, data scientists do not know this if they have not been mentioned by domain experts.

In this section, we discuss how the domain knowledge is used when analysing some factors, including pressure, geographic, spatial and temporal factors.

21.3.1   Pressure Data Analysis

Many factors cannot be directly applied into analysis, such as pressure. Pressure is the main reason for pipe breaks. However, pressure varies all the time and it can be affected by factors from multiple resources, including ground level of mains, the ground level of reservoirs, how water is transported, such as pumped or gravity. All these data must be pointed out and collected by domain experts so that we can analyze based on the aggregated data. Even so, some data, like the pressure transit which only happened in seconds, although we know it is an important reason, we cannot use the data as they are not easily collected.

21.3.2   Geographic Analysis

As the water mains are buried underground, it is important to analyse the geographic information. The geographic information is collected by geologists, and must be explained by them, combined with the interpretation from domain experts in water utility. For example, soil corrosiveness describes the pitting of pipe (corrosion of metal), which is essentially an electrical phenomenon. We know soil corrosiveness can cause corrosion for uncoated water mains, so combining the data on coating is essential to analyse the soil corrosiveness feature. In another example, soil expansiveness describes the shrinking and swelling of expansive clays in response to moisture content change. From this knowledge, it is essential to combine weather data, such as rainfall level and solar exposure, to analyse soil expansiveness.

Sometimes the soil data is quite sparse, which could lead to problems in analysis. For example, we conducted factor analysis on soil aggressiveness. Soil aggressiveness describes the propensity of soil or water to dissolve concrete structures, which is measured by a range of chemical and physical tests (including pH and resistivity). Domain experts then labelled the *'Aggressive'* or *'Non Aggressive'* values according to their domain knowledge. For a sub-region, the failure rate (number of failures per 100 km per year) for *'Non Aggressive'* is much higher than others. The reason is that the total water main length in the *'Non Aggressive'* area is very small (less than 1 km) and there was only one failure in the *'Non Aggressive'* area. A small denominator leads to a very large failure rate but misleading information.

21.3.3   Spatial and Temporal Analysis

Except for the attributes, failures on certain water mains will have an influence on other pipes. This has also been emphasised by domain experts. This is difficult to notice without domain knowledge since the period of influence is short. It could cause problems if we just assume that they follow an independent Poisson distribution. This is contradicted by the general machine learning settings, which assumes I.I.D. relationship from the observations. The analysis is then performed for this purpose followed by analysis of the temporal dependent and spatial dependent between failures.

To analyse the temporal relationship on the same asset, the intervals between failures are calculated. However, domain experts need to verify the repeated failures carefully as they may include different types of failures as burst versus leak. In the analysis, it is found that the ratio for repeated failures is quite high after certain repeated failures, such as shown in Fig. 21.5. After having them checked by domain experts, it is noticed that the same consecutive events are due to recent maintenance work. This must be differentiated.

For spatial analysis, domain knowledge is essential for determining the spatial relationship. As we know, the water mains are connected so there is existing influence

Fig. 21.5 Failed at least *n* times versus the corresponding probability. For example, about 17% of pipes failed at least once will fail at least twice

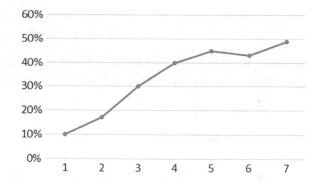

from the connected pipes nearby. The information of the connected network has to be modelled by domain experts. However, the network topography is not static and the status of valves and pumps change over time, which makes the topography dynamic and complex. A lack of knowledge about the hydraulic system for data scientists is a major obstacle to analysis.

21.4   Prediction Models

There are two types of models for water pipe failure predictions: physical models and statistical models. Physical models [6] are usually designed to capture the mechanisms of failures due to certain reasons. But they have significant limitations when applied to a large number of water mains. In contrast, statistical models usually require fewer resources and can capture hidden statistical failure patterns caused by different physical reasons. Hence, they can be applied to large-scale water main networks for guiding proactive maintenance. The statistical models are trained by considering historical failure records, physical characteristics of pipes and environmental factors.

Based on the previous analyses, the data on water pipe failure records show a dramatic difference between failure rates for different categories of pipes. In some categories, e.g., the small-size pipes, a pipe can fail multiple times during the observation period. The model should consider more on the repeated failures. While the pipes in the category of large-size pipes, failed only once or twice during the observation period. For this reason, in the prediction model, we consider different categories of pipes in different groups. The details are discussed in Sect. 21.4.1.

The divide-and-conquer strategy is usually adopted by the proposed methods. It firstly divides water mains into different groups based on their physical attributes. This can involve prior knowledge from domain experts. Then a machine learning model is trained for each group by using physical attributes of a pipe and historical failure records to predict future failures. The model can predict the score of pipe failures by discovering various failure patterns from historical data. It is of significant assistance to water utilities in selecting high-risk pipes for preventative maintenance.

This section discusses some steps in prediction that involve domain knowledge in the model, then an example is given. Based on the model, we show how domain knowledge can be involved in model evaluation and practical use.

21.4.1 Grouping

Since observations are generally limited to a certain short time range compared with the whole life span of water mains, it is difficult to record or predict failures for individual pipes within such a short duration. Therefore, meaningful statistics must consider a set of mains which is grouped across similar pipes. According to the domain knowledge, that the failure patterns are dramatically different for different categories of water mains. In some categories, e.g., the small-size pipes, a pipe can fail multiple times during the observation period, while in some other categories, e.g. large-size pipes, they fail only once or twice during the observation period.

There are two alternatives to determining the grouping based on data. One is based on the attributes. The other is the grouping is based on historical failures.

For the first one, if each distinct feature combination is used as a group, groups with a very small number of water mains may be created that goes against the purpose of grouping. Furthermore, it is difficult to define metrics between attribute values if the attribute is categorical, which can be defined with help from domain experts. The domain knowledge can also be applied to select the most important factors that can split the data set. When the number of attributes is high, the experts can fetch the information quickly based on the visualisation from factor analysis, and determine which water mains can be grouped by considering the actual operations. For example, water mains in close regions can be grouped together so that it is convenient for replacement work.

For the second alternative, the group diversity is undetermined. If the diversity is low, most water mains in a group are almost the same. As the goal of grouping is to learn parameters such as failure rate for the group, in this case, the uncertainty of learned parameters can be lower than the actual uncertainty. However, when the diversity is high, the uncertainty of learned parameters can be higher than the actual uncertainty. Therefore, the most traditional grouping methods must be based on domain knowledge, such as the number of groups. However, a Bayesian non-parametric grouping may alleviate this pain as it controls the group size, number of groups and variance based on data.

21.4.2 Estimate Failure Rate with Bayesian Non-parametric Models

A classic prediction model is to fit the data to a log likelihood estimation, i.e. $logL(X|\theta)$, then determine parameter θ that maximise the log likelihood. Here the domain knowledge can be reflected from the formulation of $L(\cdot)$, such as model is as a Gaussian distribution or Poisson distribution. However, it is important to know that sometimes there is bias in the observation X, which could lead to a wrong estimation. To correct this, another layer of Bayesian prior distribution is used, so that θ can be determined by the posterior:

$$\theta \sim P(\theta|X, \gamma) \propto L(X|\theta)P(\theta|\gamma) = \mathcal{L} \tag{21.1}$$

where γ is the hyper parameter for the Bayesian model. Bayesian prior is a typical example of involving prior knowledge with likelihood function, so that the latent parameters are not only determined by data, but also by the prior knowledge. To solve (21.1) for discrete θ, all values can be tested and the one gives largest $P(\theta|X, \gamma)$ can be selected. However, for continued θ, $P(X)$ must be considered for normalisation, which makes most of the Bayesian models intractable. Therefore, for most prior selections, the conjugated prior is used to obtain a closed form for $P(X)$.

For the Bayesian models, there are still many challenges when working with domain experts. First, in a practical problem setting, we hope to design the model as a tractable model using conjugated prior. However, we hope to represent the domain knowledge in the prior as well. Furthermore, the model must be familiar to domain experts so that they know how to tune the model to reflect their knowledge. The challenge is thus how to help the domain experts understand the model.

On the other hand, both prior and $L(\cdot)$ are designed to reflect domain knowledge. Then the model emphasis the knowledge. However, given the water main failure prediction problem, physical knowledge is not always available to predict failures due to a complexity of factors. Furthermore, there is always a missing piece of domain knowledge if we observe the data carefully. For example, domain knowledge in survival analysis can assert that failures follow the Weibull process [5]. However, it is not the usual case in reality, since we are not aware of all factors nor know about how the factors affect the observation. The data cannot always fit the model setting.

To address these limitations, we propose the use of Bayesian non-parametric learning to predict water pipe condition. Historical water pipe data can be incorporated and the model can grow to accommodate future data as necessary. This novel modelling approach for pipe condition prediction has the potential to work effectively across many different pipe types and local conditions worldwide. Compared to traditional statistical modelling, Bayesian non-paramedic modelling aims to avoid assumptions on the structure of the model at the onset. Non-parametric learning has been applied successfully in various industries, for instance, to predict remission times for leukemia patients, time between explosions in coal mines and weather forecasts [5]. While the general framework of non-parametric learning can be found in the literature of survival analysis and topic modelling [3], to our knowledge the flexibility of using Bayesian non-parametric methods for pipe condition prediction has not been investigated. Our work particularly investigated the hierarchical beta Process (HBP) [12] for the prioritisation step above. The method can be used to predict the failure rate of each individual pipe more accurately by capturing specific failure patterns of different water-pipe groups. Experimental results show that non-parametric modelling outperforms previous parametric modelling for pipe condition assessment. The main aims of this work are: (1) For sparse incident data, develop an efficient approximate inference algorithm based on a hierarchical beta process. (2) Apply the hierarchical beta process based method to the water pipe condition.

21.4.2.1 Hierarchical Beta Process Model for Pipe Condition Assessment

As an example, a model developed in [8] uses the hierarchical beta process to model the water pipe failure problem. A beta process, $B \sim BP(c, B_0)$, is a positive random measure on a space Ω, where c, the concentration function, is a positive function over Ω, and B_0, the base measure, is a fixed measure on Ω. If B_0 is discrete, $B_0 = \sum_k q_k \delta_{\omega_k}$, then B has atoms at the same locations $B = \sum_k p_k \delta_{\omega_k}$, where $p_k \sim Beta(c(\omega_k)q_k, c(\omega_k)(1 - q_k))$, and each $q_k \in [0, 1]$. An observation data X could be modelled by a Bernoulli process with the measure B, $X \sim BeP(B)$, where $X = \sum_k z_k \delta_{\omega_k}$, and each z_k is a Bernoulli variable, $z_k \sim Ber(p_k)$. Furthermore, when there exists a set of categories, and all data belongs to one of them, the hierarchical beta process could be used to model the data. Within each category, the atoms and the associated atom usage are modelled by a beta process. Meanwhile a beta process prior is shared by all the categories. More details could be found in [12]. For a water distribution system, denote π_{ki}, as the probability of failure for a pipe in the kth group. Consider hierarchical construction for pipe condition assessment,

$$q_k \sim Beta(c_0 q_0, c_0(1 - q_0)), \ where \ k = 1, 2, \ldots, K,$$
$$\pi_{k,i} \sim Beta(c_k q_k, c_k(1 - q_k)), \ where \ i = 1, \ldots, n_k, \qquad (21.2)$$
$$z_{k,i,j} \sim Ber(\pi_{k,i})$$

Here q_k and c_k are the mean and concentration parameters for the kth group, q_0 and c_0 are hyper parameters for the hierarchical beta process, $z_{k,i} = \{z_{k,i,j} | j = 1, \ldots, m_{k,i}\}$ is the history of pipe failure, $z_{k,i,j} = 1$ means the pipe failed in jth year, otherwise $z_{k,i,j} = 0$.

For the hierarchical beta process, a set of $\{q_k\}$ are used to describe failure rates of different groups of pipes. For each pipe group, with fixed concentration parameter c_k, our goal is to find $\pi_{k,i}$ for pipe i in group k. This can be estimated from the observation, so we have:

$$p(\pi_{k,i}|z_{k,1:n_k}) = \int p(q_k, \pi_{k,i}|z_{k,1:n_k})dq_k = \int p(\pi_{k,i}|q_k, z_{k,i})p(q_k|z_{k,1:n_k})dq_k$$

$$(21.3)$$

Each term in Eq. 21.3 can be represented by:

$$p(\pi_{k,i}|q_k, z_{k,i}) \sim Beta\left(c_k q_k + \sum_j z_{k,i,j}, \; c_k(1-q_k) + m_{k,i} - \sum_j z_{k,i,j}\right),$$

$$(21.4)$$

and

$$p(q_k|z_{k,1:n_k})(q_k, z_{k,1:n_k}) = p(q_k)\prod_i\left[\int p(\pi_{k,i}|q_k)p(z_{k,i}|\pi_{k,i})d\pi_{k,i}\right]$$

$$\propto q_k^{c_0 q_0 - 1}(1-q_k)^{c_0(1-q_0)-1}\prod_i \frac{\Gamma(c_k q_k + \sum_j z_{k,i,j})\Gamma(c_k(1-q_k) + m_{k,i} - \sum_j z_{k,i,j})}{\Gamma(c_k q_k)\Gamma(c_k(1-q_k))}$$

$$(21.5)$$

In the model, we can see that the group failure rate is controlled by hierarchical level parameters c_0 and q_0. These two parameters can be used for domain experts to determine the group performance without looking into individual pipes. Some details of inference will be discussed in the next section.

21.4.3 Domain Knowledge for Inference

In the inference, if the likelihood is biased, the domain knowledge based prior is very important, since the learned parameters are balanced by both the likelihood and the prior. There are some models using the conjugated prior which can easily infer the posterior of parameters, however, using conjugated prior sometimes cannot reflect the prior knowledge. For example, beta distribution is the conjugate prior for Bernoulli distribution but beta distribution cannot only be interpreted as n succeeds and m failures. It represent the succeeds VS failures given $n + m$ times trials, which is still limited as $n + m$ (observation duration) is small in the water main failure observations. In this manner, the concentration parameter c in HBP model can be roughly calculated using the length of observation duration, whether the short observation duration can reflect the whole life of water mains has to be consulted by domain experts. This is a simplified setting for unknown parameter given domain knowledge, however, in many real cases, the inference can be hard given domain knowledge based prior.

Domain knowledge can also be helpful for direct inference. For example, when the inference is to maximise the likelihood, grid search can be an option when the parameter is not in high dimension. However, the range of parameters cannot be infinity otherwise a grid search is not feasible. Domain knowledge can be deployed to determine the possible and reasonable range. In addition, the density of grids is another important setting that can be induced by domain knowledge.

In this section, for the HBP model, some inference methods are listed and discussed.

21.4.3.1 Learning with Sparse Assumption

In the hierarchical framework, all the observations are generated by Bernoulli distribution which is the likelihood function with parameter π. Then each π is generated by a beta distribution with parameter q and c. Let us consider q here. If q is known, the posterior is also beta distribution as they are conjugated prior. However, q also follows a distribution therefore the posterior must integrate over a Bernoulli distribution and two beta distributions.

The main solution to inference is to use variational inference or sampling based methods but they are complex. The complexity can be reduced by domain knowledge. In the water network, large water mains are mainly made with strong material and well protected. They are very unlikely to break (although leakage is more frequent, the costs are much less than breakage) so the expected number of failures, q, is always very small. That is to say, the variance of q is also limited to a small range. Based on that, limited values $\{q_1, q_2, \ldots, q_t\}$ could be tested for a grid search and then each q_t could be a determined value to be put into the posterior to test the likelihood.

21.4.3.2 Learning with Noise

Although substantial domain knowledge can be incorporated into machine learning models, there is still a large opportunity for something unexpected to happen which can be modelled as uncertainty into the designed model. The uncertainty could be represented by stochastic model as the variance, however, learning the stochastic model is non-trivial. To solve it, the compound probability distribution is generally considered. Therefore the distribution must be carefully chosen to make sure that the loss function is tractable, such as conjugated priors. The computational convenience can violate the requirements from domain knowledge. Also in the Bernoulli distribution, the variance is $\pi(1 - \pi)$, so variance also relates to mean parameter π. This raises the issue that variance is wrongly estimated if the estimation of mean is biased. The strong assumption can be further improved using domain knowledge by setting the variance to be different from $\pi(1 - \pi)$.

21.4.4 Evaluation

In this evaluation, the HBP method was tested and compared with popular survival analysis methods, namely the Cox and Weibull models. The Cox model is usually

Fig. 21.6 Results of water main failure prediction for an example dataset by different models

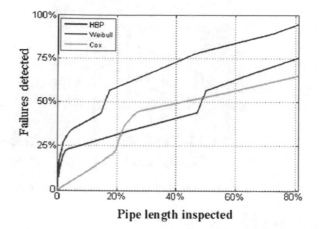

used to model only the first time failure for each pipe, while the Weibull model can deal with multiple failures as same as HBP. The water mains are categorised into different groups according to their coating, region, and laid year. For fair comparison, the other explanatory factors act multiplicatively [1] on the hazard rate in the Cox model or the priors in the Weibull model and the proposed method. Figure 21.6 shows the results of predicting pipe failures in two regions by different models. The test curves exhibit the average performance for the most recent three years. To evaluate the prediction of pipe failures for a given year, all failure records available before that year are used as training data. The x-axis represents the cumulative percentage of inspected water pipes, and the y-axis represents the percentage of detected pipe failures.

21.4.5 Constraints

In certain circumstances, although the prediction algorithm can provide an accurate prediction for each water main, there are still many works to do before interpreting the results and putting them into practical use. Here, domain knowledge must be involved to help the machine learning scientists to find the way to use the results by providing the practical constraints.

21.4.5.1 Budget Constraints

Even when a badly ranked list can be used if the whole network could be replaced without the restrictions of budget, so that any model can achieve the goal of preventing almost 100% failures. However, in reality, the maintenance budget must be limited as the cost of inspecting or replacing pipes is high. The focus therefore is on predicting

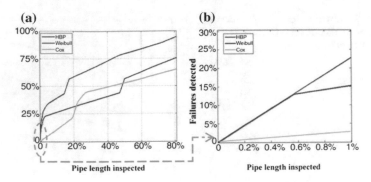

Fig. 21.7 Detection results for first 1% of all water mains in the exampled dataset

the riskiest pipes. As a result, the evaluation of the prediction becomes the ratio of detected failures and corresponding length or number of water mains. The change of evaluation provides the opportunity for algorithms to illustrate its superiority.

Let's now examine the practical implications of the improved prediction provided by the HBP method over the existing models currently used in the risk management process. The budget and resources allocated for pipe condition assessment are usually limited, so that each year only a small fraction of the critical water mains can be physically inspected, typically around 1% of the whole network length. It is hence crucial that the top ranking pipes in the priority list should actually present a need for renewal, otherwise the inspection costs, will be spent to no avail. Figure 21.7 compares the various methods assuming only 1% of mains can be inspected. The HBP outperforms the other methods by predicting almost 25% of the failures, which when extrapolated to the whole urban network (with capital expenditure of about one million dollars on condition assessment per year), represents a saving evaluated to several hundred thousand dollars per year, over its Weibull counterpart. Incidentally, this improvement in prediction accuracy also decreases the number of false negatives for critical mains about to fail, hence avoiding a number of disastrous critical main failures. As the financial and community cost of one critical main break ranges from hundreds of thousands to a few million dollars, this generates estimated savings in excess of a million dollars per year, again calculated over its Weibull counterpart.

21.4.5.2 Spatial Constraints

The most basic use of the prediction results is to make decisions on the most risky water mains for further operations. However, the experienced domain experts have their own interpretation on the meaning of risks and on how best to use the prediction to evaluate the risk of pipes. However, this could be limited as the total number of assets is too high (usually more than 100 k) for manual selection. In this case, they will prefer to make decisions on more coarse granularity, such as zones which contain a set of pipes. Some zones are defined heuristically for experts' operational convenience, while some zones are latent, which means they can be automatically exploited by clustering algorithms. Even in the latter case, domain knowledge must be involved to interpret the learned zones.

Alternatively, for operational efficiency, domain experts may select different levels of assets for different physical maintenances. For example, pipes at higher levels (main distributors in a block of pipes) will be selected or a condition assessment made instead of replacement. However, a higher level unit comprises a 'bag of pipes', where only a limited number of pipes are identified as high risk while the rest are in a good condition. Therefore, there is a trade-off between prediction accuracy and operational constraints: if we focus more on prediction accuracy, selection at the element level performs better while operational efficiency may be lost; if we focus more on operational efficiency, selection at the higher level is better while prediction accuracy may be sacrificed.

To aid the domain experts to make the decision, data scientists can investigate this trade-off, by performing a multi-level constraint based prediction at main, block area, and element levels. At the element level we have only considered those pipes with length equal to above the constraint, and at the higher level we have only considered distributor mains.

21.4.5.3 Length Constraints

Even with the prediction results, how to plan the real maintenance is still based on the domain expert's decision. Usually the actual maintenance can involve many jobs so that the minimum cost is fixed even if it is to maintain a one meter pipe. Therefore, the length constraint is required so that the minimum length of pipes needs to be maintained in the same work. The simple constraint is to consider long pipes only (e.g. pipes that are longer than 200 m). A more robust constraint needs to consider the total length of pipes in a neighbouring area. However, the neighbouring area should cover not only for spatial neighbours but also needs to consider the above-ground situation, such as traffic, terrain, and soil, which may involve various types of domain knowledge.

21.5 Conclusion

This chapter presented how machine learning models can be used with domain knowledge, using the data-driven water main failure prediction as an example. The domain knowledge-based data review, factor analysis and predictions are provided and discussed.

The evaluation criteria for domain experts on specific applications can be very different from the standard performance measurements used in the machine learning domain. For instance, machine learning experts usually use a cut-off point or AUC area of the ROC curve to measure an approach's performance. However, in this work,

Fig. 21.8 Estimated failure probabilities by the proposed method for water mains laid from 1950s to 1970s in the example dataset

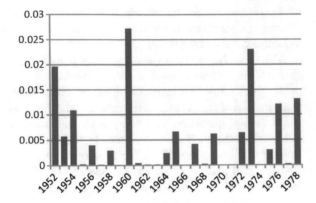

only a small portion of the performance curve (see Fig. 21.7) is of interest, because the number of pipes that can be inspected in practice is only a small percentage of the whole network. Thus, the failure prediction accuracy with 1% of the pipes inspected is the main criteria to measure performance of different approaches. Intermediate experimental statistics are suggestive of the model design. In some sense, it helps to avoid a biased assumption and suggest appropriate modelling. For instance, from the statistics of the pipe failures in different year/age (see Fig. 21.8), we can see the assumption that failure probability increases monotonically with the age of pipe is not always true. The visualisation and presentation of the results need to adapt to the domain experts' habits and technical background. To domain experts, instead of the whole performance curve, only a small portion of the curve (see Fig. 21.7) is of interest. Categorising the data helps to identify subsets of the whole dataset which possess very different failure patterns. It makes the modelling process simpler and more accurate for a system affected by a large variety of factors, especially when some of them are not ascertainable or measurable. Usually water main systems also exhibit those characteristics because they are deployed across large scale areas with very different environmental factors, such as traffic load, soil corrosivity, etc.

References

1. Andreou, S.A., Marks, D.H., Clark, R.M.: A new methodology for modelling break failure patterns in deteriorating water distribution systems: theory. Adv. Water Resour. **10**(1), 2–10 (1987)
2. Breiman, L.: Random forests. Mach. Learn. **45**(1), 5–32 (2001)
3. Chen, X., Zhou, M., Carin, L.: The contextual focused topic model. In: Proceedings of the 18th ACM SIGKDD International Conference on Knowledge Discovery and Data Mining, pp. 96–104. ACM (2012)
4. Ferguson, P., Heathcote, M., Moore, G., Russell, D.: Condition assessment of water mains using remote field technology. WATER-MELBOURNE THEN ARTARMON- **23**, 6–8 (1996)
5. Ibrahim, J.G., Chen, M.H., Sinha, D.: Bayesian Survival Analysis. Wiley, New Jersey (2005)

6. Kleiner, Y., Rajani, B.: Comprehensive review of structural deterioration of water mains: statistical models. Urban Water **3**(3), 131–150 (2001)
7. Krizhevsky, A., Sutskever, I., Hinton, G.E.: Imagenet classification with deep convolutional neural networks. In: Advances in Neural Information Processing Systems, pp. 1097–1105 (2012)
8. Li, Z., Zhang, B., Wang, Y., Chen, F., Taib, R., Whiffin, V., Wang, Y.: Water pipe condition assessment: a hierarchical beta process approach for sparse incident data. Mach. Learn. **95**(1), 11–26 (2014)
9. Maaten, L.v.d., Hinton, G.: Visualizing data using t-SNE. J. Mach. Learn. Res. **9**(Nov), 2579–2605 (2008)
10. Misiūnas, D.: Failure monitoring and asset condition assessment in water supply systems. Vilniaus Gedimino technikos universitetas (2008)
11. Rajani, B., Kleiner, Y.: Comprehensive review of structural deterioration of water mains: physically based models. Urban Water **3**(3), 151–164 (2001)
12. Thibaux, R., Jordan, M.I.: Hierarchical beta processes and the Indian buffet process. In: International Conference on Artificial Intelligence and Statistics, pp. 564–571 (2007)

Chapter 22
Interactive Machine Learning for Applications in Food Science

Alberto Tonda, Nadia Boukhelifa, Thomas Chabin, Marc Barnabé,
Benoît Génot, Evelyne Lutton and Nathalie Perrot

Abstract The apparent simplicity of food processes often hides complex systems, where physical, chemical and living organisms' processes co-exist and interact to create the final product. Data can be plagued by *uncertainty*; *heterogeneity* of available information is likely; *qualitative* and *quantitative* data may also coexist in the same process, from expert perception of food quality to nano-properties of ingredients. In order to obtain reliable models, it then becomes necessary to acquire additional information from external sources. Experts of a domain can provide invaluable insight in products and processes, but this precious knowledge is often available only in the form of intuition and implicit expertise. Including expert insight in a model can be tackled by having humans interacting with a machine learning process, through visualization or via specialists in encoding implicit domain knowledge. In this chapter, three selected case studies in food science portray different success stories of combining machine learning and expert interaction. We show that expert knowledge can

A. Tonda (✉) · N. Boukhelifa · T. Chabin · M. Barnabé · B. Génot · E. Lutton · N. Perrot
INRA, Université Paris-Saclay, 1 av. Brétignières, 78850 Thiverval-Grignon, France
e-mail: alberto.tonda@inra.fr

N. Boukhelifa
e-mail: nadia.boukhelifa@inra.fr

T. Chabin
e-mail: thomas.chabin@inra.fr

M. Barnabé
e-mail: marc.barnabe@inra.fr

B. Génot
e-mail: benoit.genot@inra.fr

E. Lutton
e-mail: evelyne.lutton@inra.fr

N. Perrot
e-mail: nathalie.perrot@inra.fr

© Springer International Publishing AG, part of Springer Nature 2018
J. Zhou and F. Chen (eds.), *Human and Machine Learning*, Human–Computer
Interaction Series, https://doi.org/10.1007/978-3-319-90403-0_22

be integrated at different stages of the modelling process, either online or offline, to initialize, enrich or guide this process.

22.1   Introduction

When dealing with meaningful representations of food systems, several important issues have to be considered: data can be plagued by *uncertainty*, particularly when chemical, physical, and biological phenomena concur to define the process; *heterogeneity* of available information is also likely, as a vegetable involved in a process can be characterised by more than 40,000 genes, whereas the quality of the final product can be assessed using just a few sensory features; *qualitative* and *quantitative* information, from expert perception of food quality, to nano-properties of ingredients, may also coexist in the same process. Consequently, when applying machine learning to agri-food data, the user has to carefully account for variance, manage heterogeneous data, and be able to include both qualitative and quantitative values in the final model.

As gathering data in food science is an expensive and time-consuming process, available datasets are often sparse and incomplete, which poses a challenge to both human modelling practitioners and machine learning algorithms. This issue has been long acknowledged by the community, and ongoing projects have been approved to tackle it, by defining roadmaps to achieve an e-infrastructure for open science,[1] and by fostering cooperation between food scientists and modelling experts.[2] In order to obtain reliable models, it thus becomes necessary to acquire additional information from external sources. Experts in a specific domain can provide invaluable insight into products and processes, but this precious knowledge is often available only in the form of intuition and non-coded expertise. Including expert insight in a model is not a straightforward process, but it can effectively be tackled by having humans interacting with a machine learning process, through visualisation, or via specialists in encoding implicit domain knowledge [17].

In the following, three selected case studies portray different ways of combining machine learning with expert interaction, in the domain of food processing:

- first, a model for Camembert cheese ripening is built, encompassing variables from the micro-scale (presence of bacteria and chemical components) to the macro-scale (sensory evaluations), relying upon experts to help design the structure of a dynamic Bayesian network;
- a second dynamic Bayesian network model is constructed to help winemakers assess the appropriate time for harvesting grapes, depending on weather conditions
- a graphical model based on symbolic regression is used to help experts create a model of bacterial production and stabilisation.

---

[1] eRosa European project, http://www.erosa.aginfra.eu/.
[2] COST Action CA15118 FoodMC, http://www.inra.fr/foodmc.

Day 1

Day ~15

Day >30

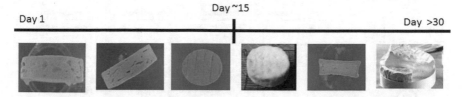

Fig. 22.1 Pictures of Camembert cheese during the ripening process. There are visible changes in the cheese's rind, colour, and aroma during the ripening

Interaction with the experts of each specific process is always mediated by visualisation, complemented by the use of targeted questionnaires (first case study), fuzzy-logic models (second case study), or human-readable equations (third case study). In all considered cases, oriented graphs are used to provide experts with an intuitive and transparent representation of the model under construction. While the models' inner working, ranging from conditional probability inference to computation of free-form equations, is mostly hidden, users can easily interact with oriented graphs, where arcs represent correlation between variables, and modify connections created by learning algorithms, if they are deemed incorrect. For most users, graphs are familiar representations, and manipulating them is intuitive. When users are dealing with graphs that can be considered small, with fewer than 50 variables, node-link diagrams are a well suited portrayal, while matrices become more appropriate for larger or denser graphs [14].

22.2   Dynamic Bayesian Network Model for Camembert Ripening

Cheese ripening is a good example of a process that human practitioners can achieve with success but for which several scientific details remain poorly understood. Nevertheless, even for these processes it is possible to create effective models by harnessing knowledge from experts in the domain and coupling it with experimental data. This can be achieved by using an appropriate machine learning framework, that is able to take into account such heterogeneous information. The work presented in [25] shows how the described methodology can be applied to the case of Camembert, a popular French cheese. The desired model goes from micro-scale properties such as concentration of lactose and bacteria, to macro-scale properties such as color and consistency of the crust, with the goal being to describe the development of the ripening process, up to the prediction of the current phase of ripening. In Fig. 22.1, a few pictures of the cheese ripening process are reported: experts find it useful to divide the ripening into 4 distinct phases.

The approach used in this experiment is a Dynamic Bayesian Network (DBN) [18], a variation on a classical Bayesian network [20]. Bayesian networks are

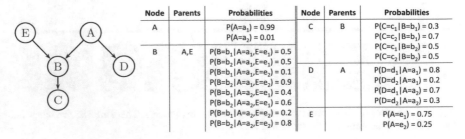

Node	Parents	Probabilities	Node	Parents	Probabilities
A		P(A=a$_1$) = 0.99 P(A=a$_2$) = 0.01	C	B	P(C=c$_1$|B=b$_1$) = 0.3 P(C=c$_2$|B=b$_1$) = 0.7 P(C=c$_1$|B=b$_2$) = 0.5 P(C=c$_2$|B=b$_2$) = 0.5
B	A,E	P(B=b$_1$|A=a$_1$,E=e$_1$) = 0.5 P(B=b$_2$|A=a$_1$,E=e$_1$) = 0.5 P(B=b$_1$|A=a$_1$,E=e$_2$) = 0.1 P(B=b$_2$|A=a$_1$,E=e$_2$) = 0.9 P(B=b$_1$|A=a$_2$,E=e$_1$) = 0.4 P(B=b$_2$|A=a$_2$,E=e$_1$) = 0.6 P(B=b$_1$|A=a$_2$,E=e$_2$) = 0.2 P(B=b$_2$|A=a$_2$,E=e$_2$) = 0.8	D	A	P(D=d$_1$|A=a$_1$) = 0.8 P(D=d$_2$|A=a$_1$) = 0.2 P(D=d$_1$|A=a$_2$) = 0.7 P(D=d$_2$|A=a$_2$) = 0.3
			E		P(A=e$_1$) = 0.75 P(A=e$_2$) = 0.25

Fig. 22.2 On the left, a directed acyclic graph. On the right, the parameters it is associated with. Together they form a Bayesian network BN whose joint probability distribution is $P(BN) = P(A)P(B|A, E)P(C|B)P(D|A)P(E)$

probabilistic models widely used to encode knowledge in several different fields: computational biology and bioinformatics (gene regulatory networks, protein structure, gene expression analysis), medicine, document classification, information retrieval, image processing, data fusion, decision support systems, engineering, gaming and law. BNs are directed acyclic graphs, where each node represents a variable in the problem, and links encode correlations between variables. An example of BN is reported in Fig. 22.2.

Like a BN, a DBN is a graph-based model of a joint multivariate probability distribution that captures properties of conditional independence between variables; in the graph, nodes $X_i(t)$, $i = 1, \ldots, N$, represent random variables, indexed by time t. Differently from a regular BN, a DBN is in fact able to encode dependencies between the same variable over multiple instants of time, providing a compact representation of the joint probability distribution P for a finite time interval $[1, \tau]$ defined as follows:

$$P(X(1), \ldots, X(\tau)) = \prod_{i=1}^{N} \prod_{t=1}^{\tau} P(X_i(t)|Pa(X_i)(t)) \qquad (22.1)$$

where $X(t) = X_1(t), \ldots, X_N(t)$, is called a *slice*, and represents the set of all variables indexed by the same time t. $Pa(X_i)(t)$ denotes the parents of $Xi(t)$. $P(X_i(t)|Pa(X_i)(t))$ denotes the conditional probability function associated with the random variable $X_i(t)$ given $Pa(X_i)(t)$. The joint probability $P(X(1), \ldots, X(\tau))$ represents the beliefs about possible trajectories of the dynamic process $X(t)$. DBNs are useful tools for combining expert knowledge with data at different levels and length scales. The structure of a model (e.g. the directed graph) can be explicitly built on the basis of expert knowledge, or automatically learned from data by an algorithm [6]. In practice, a combination of the two approaches is commonly used, with a first, automatically-learned structure subsequently corrected by humans, resorting to graphical user interfaces such as BayesiaLab[3] or GeNie [12].[4] Once the structure

---

[3]http://www.bayesia.com.

[4]https://www.bayesfusion.com/.

of a DBN is defined, parameters (i.e. conditional probability functions) can be automatically obtained without a priori knowledge on the basis of a dataset, all through a deterministic machine learning procedure known as *parameter learning*.

In this case study, data is gathered from 6 experiments on the cheese ripening process, each experiment lasting 41 days, with a sampling every day. The information obtained concerns the temperature of the ripening chamber (T, °C), relative humidity (RH, %), and the concentration of lactose (lo, g/kg), lactate (la, g/kg), and the bacteria *Kluyveromyces marxianus* (Km, cfu/kg), *Geotrichum candidum* (Gc, cfu/kg), *Penicillium camemberti* (Pc, cfu/kg), and *Brevibacterium aurantiacum* (Ba, cfu/kg). During each experiment, several Camemberts are destroyed to be analysed, with a considerable economic investment for the producer. At the same time, experts are interviewed to provide additional information. The study involves two groups of experts: 4 cheesemakers with over 15 years of expertise in the industry, and 8 scientists with a track record of over 10 years of research on cheese processes. The questions posed to the experts are carefully constructed in order to elicit expert knowledge, with methods ranging from open-ended questions to focus groups. Values of the variables are discretised in 2 to 12 classes each, depending on expert judgment [1].

Following cheesemakers' considerations on the ripening process, the global model is divided into two parts, that are built independently and then linked: **M1** reproduces the temporal links between measured experimental data, simulating how such quantities vary during the ripening process; while **M2** is derived almost entirely from the expert knowledge gathered using questionnaires, and provides a more qualitative assessment between sensory information such as flavour, texture, colour, and the ripening phase. Camembert cheesemakers traditionally identify four different phases in the ripening process. Figure 22.3 shows the final structure of the DBN obtained after the learning process. Variables between **M1** and **M2** are used to link variations in measurable quantities to sensory properties of the cheese.

Figure 22.4 presents an example of predictions of the dynamics in the process. It is noticeable how the model is able to satisfyingly reproduce the dynamics of variables tied to microbial growth, substrate consumption, and sensory properties, for different temperature conditions. Experts ultimately assessed model simulations resorting to classical two-dimensional plots against test data, and were satisfied with the results.

22.3 Decision-Support System for Grape Maturity Prediction

Predicting the right moment to harvest grapes intended for wine production is a task that traditionally is left to specialists in the field. Still, as repercussions of climate change make local weather more unpredictable, experts can use machine learning techniques as a decision support tool, helping them to deal with modified conditions.

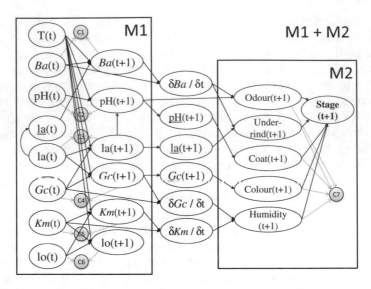

Fig. 22.3 Final DBN model for the Camembert cheese ripening process. The part denominated M1 represents the variables taken mainly from experimental data, whereas part M2 represents variables derived from expert knowledge and assessment. Grey nodes represent constraints defined by experts. Figure redrawn from [25], with permission from Elsevier

Such decision support systems are commonly defined as interactive computer-based systems that help organisations in decision-making activities.

In viticulture, some decision support systems are already in use, for example to prevent mildew [23]. Grape berry maturity is analysed in [10] where the authors built mechanistic models to predict the concentration of sugar in grapes. Other modelling techniques based on spectroscopy predict maturity indicators [13]. These decision support systems are based solely on experimental data, and do not integrate experts' knowledge in order to predict grape maturity. As the human knowledge gained over years of wine production is invaluable and often includes conditions that have not been measured in recent times, it is only sensible to include it as much as possible in the target framework. Expert knowledge handling was already successfully used in the field of viticulture in [7]. Similar to our approach, their model relies on fuzzy logic but to predict vine development with two indicators, vigour and precocity. In order to predict grape maturity, the innovative work presented in [22] offers a good example of how human expertise can be employed to fill the gaps in experimental data, with the final objective of training a machine learning approach. This study represents the basis of our current work.

For this case study, data related to 66 parcels of land in the Loire Valley is collected over the course of 27 years (1988–2015), for a total of 1,086 data points describing weekly average temperature (T, °C), relative humidity (RH, %), insolation (Ins, hours of sunlight received per day, h/day) and rainfall (Pl, mm). Further data on sugar concentration (S, g/l) and acidity (Ac, g/l Eq H_2SO_4) of the grapes are collected every

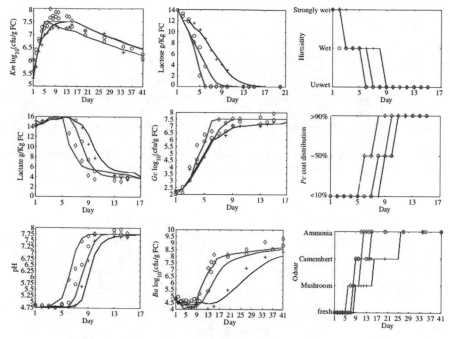

Fig. 22.4 Predictions of the Camembert cheese ripening model for the evolutions of **(top row)** microbial growth (Km, Gc, Ba in decimal logarithm scale); **(middle row)** substrate consumption (lo, la) and **(bottom row)** sensory properties (RH, Pc coat and odor). The DBN model's prediction are represented as lines, versus raw data, represented as points, for three different ripening processes, carried out at $8\,°C$ (marked with $+$), $12\,°C$ (marked with o) and $16\,°C$ (marked with $\diamond$). Figure reproduced from [25], with permission of Elsevier

week, when 200 berries of Cabernet-Franc randomly sampled from the parcels are crushed with a blender and subsequently analysed. It is important to notice again how obtaining data is an expensive and time-consuming process, and it has to be integrated by expert knowledge, in order to improve the knowledge base eventually used for modelling. For this case study, human expertise is collected through a synthesis of the available literature and industrial reports, performed by 4 scientists and 5 winegrowers working in the areas considered in the study.

As for the previous case study, a Dynamic Bayesian Network proves particularly suited for this application, as such a technique makes it possible to employ qualitative and quantitative variables, at different scales, in the same model. The network is designed with the help of the experts, through a trial-and-error process that includes several steps of structure visualisation, correction, and analysis of the predictions, initially presented in [2]: the resulting structure is shown in Fig. 22.7 (top). In this particular case study, even with an established structure, computing the parameters of each node is not trivial. Following experts' assessment, in fact, input is discretised into 8 to 15 classes for sugar, acidity, sugar variation, acidity variation, insolation, pluviometry, humidity and temperature. This discretisation, featuring a relatively

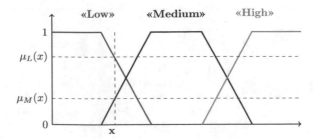

Fig. 22.5 Example of three fuzzy sets *Low*, *Medium*, *High*, with $\mu_L(x)$: the membership degree in the *Low* fuzzy set and $\mu_M(x)$: the membership degree in the *Medium* fuzzy set

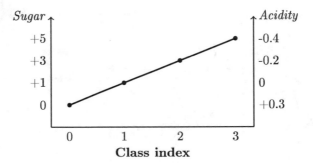

Fig. 22.6 Definition of classes related to meteorological conditions defined into four classes for sugar and acidity concentration evolution expressed in g/L. Class index 0: Bad climatic conditions; Class index 1: Not favourable climatic conditions; Class index 2: Standard climatic conditions; Class index 3: exceptional climatic conditions

high number of classes when compared to more traditional applications of BNs, leads to conditional probability tables with a considerable number of combinations: so many, that some of these combinations are not present in experimental data, and thus probabilities for these cases cannot be straightforwardly learned; resorting to experimental data for parameter learning, only, would leave too many gaps. A possible solution to the issue is to resort to experts again, formalising their knowledge of the process through fuzzy logic mathematical functions.

Fuzzy logic [30] is an extension of the binary logic, where a set is defined by its membership function. A value, x, belongs to a fuzzy set with a membership degree μ_L, with $0 \leq \mu_L(x) \leq 1$, see Fig. 22.5. If we take L a set of *Low* insolation, the membership degree $\mu_L(x)$ of a given insolation value x can be defined as the level up to which insolation x should be considered as *Low*.

Fuzzy sets for the four meteorological variables are then used to build 46 linguistic rules, e.g. *if insolation and pluviometry are Low, then the sugar increase is high*. Each rule is associated by the experts to one of the four classes of meteorological condition, see Fig. 22.6, and is activated according to the activation degree of each rule which define the class. Each class of meteorological condition corresponds to a certain variation of sugar and acidity for one day. The sum of variations on 7 days

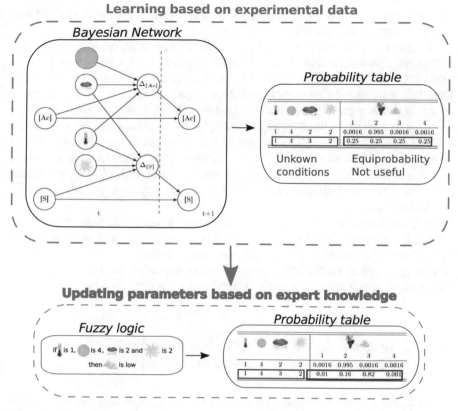

Fig. 22.7 Proposed framework for the prediction of acidity and sugar content in grapes. (top) Structure of the DBN designed for the prediction of acidity (Ac) and sugar content (S) of grapes. (bottom) Parameters of DBN are updated with data produced by expert knowledge, making it possible to learn robust conditional probability tables for the nodes

is performed to produce global variation over the week. This variation of sugar or acidity is added as an input to the DBN.

The fuzzy logic model is created to produce data for combinations of input variables associated to equiprobability in the probability tables of the DBN; equiprobability, in turn, is associated to combination of input variables never observed in experimental data.

The complete structure of the framework, including the coupling fuzzy logic-DBN is shown in Fig. 22.7. The first step (top) corresponds to the DBN learning based on experimental data. This step allows the production of a probability table necessary to perform global predictions. However, some combinations of variable are absent from experimental data. For these specific cases, a probability table is updated using a fuzzy model (bottom). A simulated database is created in variable ranges of interest and variations of sugar and acidity can be produced. These data are included in parallel to experimental data and make it possible to define probabilities in any meteorological conditions necessary.

In order to evaluate the benefit of adding human expertise, the predictions were successively performed with the DBN model, the fuzzy model, and then with combined DBN-fuzzy models, see Fig. 22.8. The best results are obtained by learning from both experimental data and expert knowledge. The resulting model is able to obtain satisfactory predictions, showing good R^2 values (a statistical measure of how close the data are to the fitted regression line) [26] for both sugar content and acidity, with $R_S^2 = 0.85$ and $R_{Ac}^2 = 0.83$, respectively. In comparison, the DBN model alone obtains $R_S^2 = 0.80$ and $R_{Ac}^2 = 0.74$ and the expert model alone obtains $R_S^2 = 0.81$ and $R_{Ac}^2 = 0.83$. Errors of predictions are shown in Fig. 22.8. We can see that at extremes values, the influence of the coupling DBN-Fuzzy approach is visible with significant improvement.

In the current context of climate change, exceptional meteorological conditions are expected to become more frequent. Learning processes performed on experimental data of past years, only, are at risk of being unsatisfactory. The building of fuzzy models to integrate DBNs offers the possibility to enlarge the range of possible meteorological conditions and make the model more flexible and more robust.

22.4 Interactive Symbolic Regression Modelling for Bacterial Production and Stabilisation

Concentrates of lactic acid bacteria are widely used in the food industry for products such as yogurt, cheese, fermented meat, vegetables and fruit beverages. The quality of bacterial starters, defined by the viability and acidification activity of the cells, depends on numerous control parameters across the different steps of the production and stabilisation process, summarised in Fig. 22.9 and described in more detail by Champagne et al. [5]. The bacteria's levels of resistance to the processes is also dependent on the biochemical and biophysical properties and organisation of their membrane [28, 29] which in turn is determined by the genomic expression of the bacteria itself. For these reasons, modelling the bacteria resistance to the process is a complex problem due to many possible non-linear dependencies between the different length scales and steps of the process. In addition, no models are available for several sub-parts of the process, and even those that can be found in literature [19] are often too simple to be included in a wider framework.

One successful approach in modelling complex processes is to stack smaller models such that predictions are propagated between multiple layers formed by these sub-components [8, 9]. In such cases, typically, rich datasets and vast amounts of knowledge are available to describe the stacked components and their interactions. When little data is available, and prior knowledge is limited, mathematical regression techniques can be used to model these complex systems [21]. However, a multitude of candidate models can be obtained through these techniques. Deciding which of

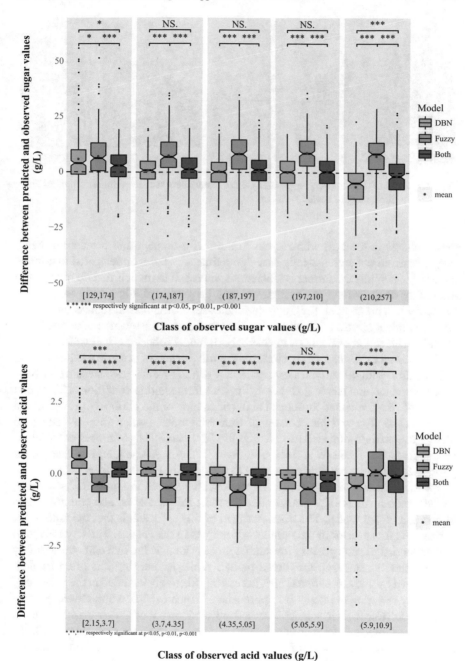

Fig. 22.8 Prediction error according to class of values, for sugar (top) and acidity (bottom). For each class, the error is reported for the DBN model (green), the fuzzy model (orange) and combined model with DBN and fuzzy method (blue). The combined model clearly obtains the best results

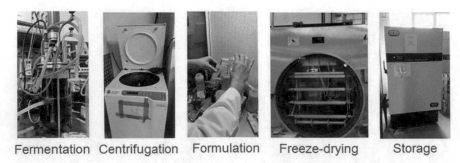

Fermentation Centrifugation   Formulation   Freeze-drying   Storage

Fig. 22.9 Steps of the freeze-drying process. Control parameters at every point in the process chain can influence the quality of bacterial starters

these models is the best with respect to the study domain and problem at hand, may be carried out automatically based on a fitness criteria, or delegated to domain experts [16]. While the former is efficient, it can result in models that do not capture the reality of the underlying system, so may be grounded albeit time-consuming. Similarly to Turkay et al. [27], our approach uses mathematical regression to generate candidate solutions. However, we combine automatic evaluation of candidate models, with expert evaluations to ensure both model robustness and validity.

The dataset in this case study concerns the full process of bacteria production and stabilisation, with 49 variables measured at 4 different steps (two steps of fermentation, freezing, and storage) and at 4 different fermentation conditions (22 °C and 30 °C, with the fermentation stopped at the beginning of the stationary growth phase and 6 h later). The variables consist of transcriptomics, composition of fatty acid membrane, acidification activity and viability [29]. Such a large number of variables requires peculiar methods to deal with them. Using machine learning capacity to provide automatic modelling enables us to find possible dependencies.

From a vast number of possible dependencies between the measured variables, an automatic methodology can identify the most relevant ones, and combine them to obtain a global model. The main problem of this approach is that the number of variables is far superior to the number of samples in the dataset. The key idea is to remember that experts possess invaluable process knowledge that can considerably improve the robustness of the global model. While formalising this often-implicit knowledge is not trivial, experts' insights can be effectively included in the modelling process by resorting to interactive approaches. To achieve these objectives, we proposed *LIDeOGraM* (Life science Interactive Development of Graph-based Models), a semi-supervised model learning framework, based on regression analysis [3, 4]. LIDeOGraM is able to obtain free-form equations for each variable in the process, as a function of all other variables. Each equation, describing a sub-part of the global process, can be considered a local model. Such models should fit the experimental data, and at the same time be deemed plausible by the experts. However, when using an automatic technique without expert guidelines, these two goals are often incompatible: it is always possible to find a polynomial equation that perfectly fits the data points, for example with a complex equation featuring as many parameters as data points available but such an equation could overfit the dataset, failing to represent the underlying relationship between the variables, and ultimately poorly predict the unseen data.

To avoid this issue, every variable in LIDeoGraM is associated with a set of candidate equations, obtained through symbolic regression [15]. Eureqa[5] [24], a commercial software specialised in symbolic regression, is able to obtain a set of possible equations for every variable in a given dataset. A local model can thus be associated to each variable by selecting one of the equations in the set. Symbolic regression makes it possible to effectively search the vast space of all possible mathematical expressions, taking into account both the fitting of the equation and its complexity – indeed, more complex equations tend to be overfitted, while simpler ones are often unable to characterise the data. A collection of local models will then constitute the base for a global model, built using an evolutionary optimisation algorithm [11] that stochastically searches the space of all sets of local models for the one that best fits the global dataset. To evaluate a candidate global model, the input nodes are set to known experimentally-measured values, and the errors in the prediction are averaged over all nodes, thus obtaining a global error, that the evolutionary algorithm aims to minimise.

Human experts are then involved in the modelling process, via a graphical user interface, showing a node-link graph visualisation of the global model, where each node represents a variable, and each link marks a possible dependency between two variables. This interface allows experts to visualise the results from Eureqa, contribute with their knowledge, and finally lead the search for an efficient global model.

For this objective, two views are available. The **Local model view** shows an overall qualitative view of the equation sets given by Eureqa for each variable. This view enables nodes with no satisfactory equation in terms of fitting and/or complexity to be easily spotted. The **Global model view** shows the predictive capability of the current global model, for each variable. This view enables users to rapidly assess which variables in the global model are poorly predicted, but also which ones may be responsible for the poor predictions of their dependent nodes.

LIDeoGraM has several ways to add expert knowledge. First, it is possible to attribute a category to each variable, and specify the available dependencies between categories for the symbolic regression. A category of nodes can represent a step in the process, or a scale of information. This interface is presented in Fig. 22.10.

After obtaining a set of equations for every node, experts can then filter this by specifying that certain kinds of node-to-node dependencies are not allowed. Experts can then manually add new equations in the set of candidate local models for a node, and eventually restart the search for a global model after putting all their constraints in place. With LIDeOGraM, it is possible to learn global models for the production

---

[5]http://nutonian.com/products/eureqa/.

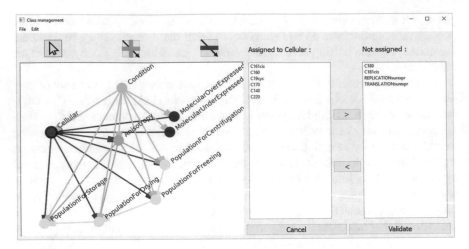

Fig. 22.10 Screenshot of the interface allowing to choose the authorised links between the defined classes. A link between two classes means that all variables associated to the parent class can be used in the equations for all variables associated to the child class. The displayed graph represents the selected constraints chosen for the presented results

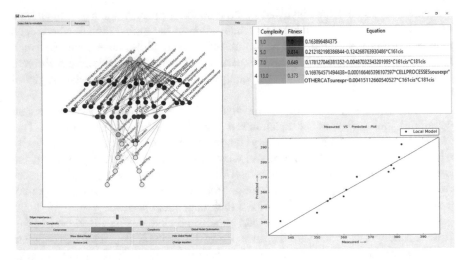

Fig. 22.11 Screenshot of LIDeOGraM. The left side shows a graphical model representing the mean fitness of the local models obtained by symbolic regression. The top-right part is the list of equations proposed by Eureqa for the selected node, and the bottom-right part shows a plot of the measured versus predicted data associated to the selected equation

and stabilisation of bacteria. Such models can then be used to better understand how to preserve the quality of the culture during the process, foster the emergence of new hypotheses, and design new experiments, whose data could in turn be used to further improve the global model. These functionalities are demonstrated in Fig. 22.11.

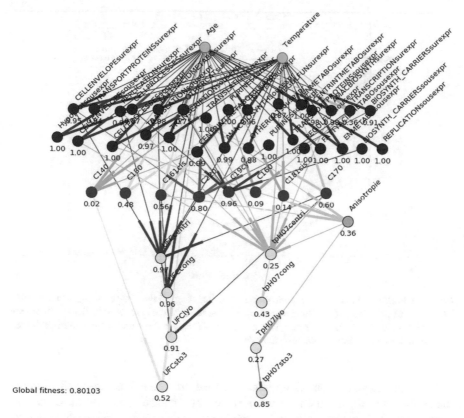

Fig. 22.12 Graphical model generated in LIDeOGraM representing a (optimised) global model. Nodes are organised in 4 categories: experimental conditions, genomic scale, cellular scale, and population scale. A Pearson correlation coefficient, calculated using the predictions from the global model compared to the experimental measurements, is printed below each node. An edge between two nodes means that the parent variable is used in the equation chosen to calculate the child variable. The colour of an edge depends on the Pearson correlation coefficient, which represents the quality of the prediction. The colour varies from red for a poor-quality prediction to green for a satisfying one

Results obtained for the previously described dataset [29] are presented in Fig. 22.12.

In a preliminary experiment on the presented framework, a user with 20 years of experience on freeze-drying process is able to inject their knowledge into the optimisation process. Out of a total of 232 equations generated for the local models, the expert deletes 5 equations, and 2 nodes, removing in turn 14 more equations in which the 2 deleted variables are involved. The expert then restarted symbolic regression on 3 nodes, obtaining 12 new equations. At the end of this process, the global optimisation results are better than those obtained without the expertise, with the average error computed on all nodes being 0.801, using only the automatic approach, and

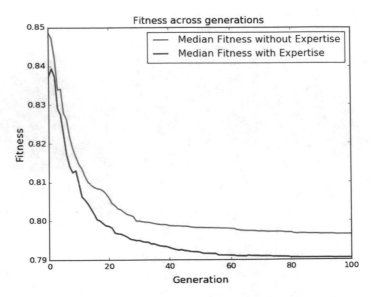

Fig. 22.13 Comparison of an experiment on the learning of the freeze-drying model, using LIDeOGraM with and without human interaction. The term *fitness* here refers to the average error, computed on all variables in the problem. The *generations* are the iterations of the evolutionary algorithm used for optimising the global model

0.787 combining the automatic approach with expert interaction. Figure 22.13 shows the evolution of the mean error per node, for both the automatic and the combined approaches. The results are still not completely satisfactory, as the prediction error for some of the nodes remains large, but the positive influence of the expert on the machine learning process is already substantial. In future works, more data points will be collected, and experiments with several other experts on the freeze-drying process are scheduled.

22.5 Discussion and Guidelines

Computational Modelling is an iterative process that comprises three main activities: *designing* a model where the aim is to define a suitable representation for objects and their relationships; *exploring* the model to understand its behaviour, and *tuning* it to find the best or optimal parameter values to obtain good predictions. Our approach in building interactive machine learning systems for food science and technology focuses on involving experts of the process in one or more stages of this modelling pipeline, facilitating their interactions with the machine learning process through visual representations.

For the first two case studies, on modelling Camembert cheese ripening and grape maturity prediction, expert knowledge is integrated primarily at the design stage of model building. Using established methodologies from the knowledge elicitation domain (e.g. interviews, case studies, and observations), expert knowledge can be collected, coded and formalised into a probabilistic model. The goal, in these cases, is to create a knowledge representation of the process that matches the domain experts mental model.

For the last case study, on modelling bacterial production and stabilisation, experts' knowledge is integrated at each stage of the modelling process. At the design stage, to structure the relationship of variables and system constraints prior to launching the automatic machine learning and optimisation algorithms; and post-model learning through various user interactions via the LIDeOGraM interface. For instance, domain experts can add or remove variables, classes and constraints. They could filter local models, or add new equations to explore how well they fit their data.

While interaction with experts is invaluable even with classical approaches, in the food science domain we argue for a more user-centred design approach to machine learning, whereby users can participate at each stage of the modelling process, from design to exploration and tuning. This involvement not only helps domain experts understand computational models better, but it allows them to confront their domain knowledge and know-how with the results of machine learning, ultimately making machine learning more transparent. Our informal evaluations and discussions with domain experts allowed us to observe the following:

- providing visual representations of machine learning models improves user engage-ment and encourages feedback, especially if domain experts are involved at the design stage and exploration stages.
- graph-based model representations are easy to understand, but multiple linked representations are more helpful when trying to understand the model.
- experts tend to take a multi-step approach to model validation, first to verify exist-ing knowledge (most likely to build trust in the ML algorithm), then to assess new predictions. When doing so, they first look at the general high-level dependen-cies between variables, before looking at detailed information such as values of weights, or data in the conditional probability tables when DBNs are involved.

It remains to prove whether making machine learning more transparent helps domain experts better explore and validate computational models in food science. More research is needed to study whether user-centred design for modelling improves decision making and indeed helps building trust in constructed models. From our experience, we believe this to be the case, but a more formal assessment is required to properly evaluate our intuition.

22.6   Conclusion

In this chapter we illustrated through three case studies from the agri-food domain, how integrating experts knowledge into computational modelling can yield promis-ing results. These real-world case studies portrayed different ways of combining machine learning with experts interaction to design, explore and tune machine learning models. In the first case study, domain experts helped design the structure of a dynamic Baysesian network to predict the Camembert cheese ripening process. In the second case study, winemakers interacted with a dynamic Bayesian Model, to help choose the appropriate time for harvesting grapes. In the third case study, domain experts interacted with a symbolic regression model, to help create a grounded model of bacterial production and stabilisation. Based on our experience in working closely with domain experts, we concluded this chapter with general observations and recommendations. We argue that more research in user-centred design methodologies for machine learning is needed, to enable domain experts to truly become model co-builders.

References

1. Baudrit, C., Sicard, M., Wuillemin, P.H., Perrot, N.: Towards a global modelling of the Camembert-type cheese ripening process by coupling heterogeneous knowledge with dynamic Bayesian networks. J. Food Eng. **98**(3), 283–293 (2010)
2. Baudrit, C., Perrot, N., Brousset, J.M., Abbal, P., Guillemin, H., Perret, B., Goulet, E., Guerin, L., Barbeau, G., Picque, D.: A probabilistic graphical model for describing the grape berry maturity. Comput. Electron. Agric. **118**, 124–135 (2015)
3. Chabin, T., Barnabé, M., Boukhelifa, N., Fonseca, F., Tonda, A., Velly, H., Perrot, N., Lutton, E.: Interactive evolutionary modelling of living complex food systems: freeze-drying of lactic acid bacteria. In: Proceedings of the Genetic and Evolutionary Computation Conference Companion, pp. 267–268. ACM (2017)
4. Chabin, T., Barnabé, M., Boukhelifa, N., Tonda, A., Velly, H., Lemaitre, B., Perrot, N., Lutton, E.: LIDeOGraM: an interactive evolutionary modelling tool. In: Proceedings of the International Conference on Artificial Evolution (Evolution Artificielle) (2017)
5. Champagne, C., Gardner, N., Brochu, E., Beaulieu, Y.: Freeze-drying of lactic acid bacteria. a review. Can. Inst. Food Sci. Technol. J. (Journal de l'Institut canadien de science et technologie alimentaire) (1991)
6. Cheng, J., Bell, D.A., Liu, W.: An algorithm for Bayesian belief network construction from data. In: proceedings of AI & STAT97, pp. 83–90 (1997)
7. Coulon-Leroy, C., Charnomordic, B., Rioux, D., Thiollet-Scholtus, M., Guillaume, S.: Prediction of vine vigor and precocity using data and knowledge-based fuzzy inference systems. Journal International des Sciences de la Vigne et du Vin **46**(3), 185–205 (2012)
8. Cros, M.J., Duru, M., Garcia, F., Martin-Clouaire, R.: A biophysical dairy farm model to evaluate rotational grazing management strategies. Agronomie **23**(2), 105–122 (2003)
9. Dai, Z.W., Vivin, P., Génard, M.: Modelling the effects of leaf-to-fruit ratio on dry and fresh mass accumulation in ripening grape berries. In: VIII International Symposium on Modelling in Fruit Research and Orchard Management, vol. 803, pp. 283–292 (2007)
10. Dai, Z.W., Vivin, P., Robert, T., Milin, S., Li, S.H., Génard, M.: Model-based analysis of sugar accumulation in response to source-sink ratio and water supply in grape (vitis vinifera) berries. Funct. Plant Biol. **36**(6), 527–540 (2009)
11. De Jong, K.A.: Evolutionary Computation: A Unified Approach. MIT Press, Cambridge (2006)
12. Druzdzel, M.J.: Smile: Structural modeling, inference, and learning engine and genie: a development environment for graphical decision-theoretic models. In: AAAI/IAAI, pp. 902–903 (1999)
13. Fadock, M., Brown, R.B., Reynolds, A.G.: Visible-near infrared reflectance spectroscopy for nondestructive analysis of red winegrapes. Am. J. Enology Vitic. (2015)

14. Ghoniem, M., Fekete, J.D., Castagliola, P.: A comparison of the readability of graphs using node-link and matrix-based representations. In: IEEE Symposium on Information Visualization. IEEE
15. Koza, J.R.: Genetic Programming: On the Programming of Computers by Means of Natural Selection, vol. 1. MIT Press, Cambridge (1992)
16. Krause, J., Perer, A., Bertini, E.: INFUSE: interactive feature selection for predictive modeling of high dimensional data. IEEE Trans. Vis. Comput. Graph. **20**(12), 1614–1623 (2014)
17. Lutton, E., Tonda, A., Boukhelifa, N., Perrot, N.: Complex systems in food science: human factor issues. In: Van Impe, J. (ed.) FoodSIM. EUROSIS-ETI (2016)
18. Murphy, K.P.: Dynamic Bayesian networks: representation, inference and learning. Ph.D. thesis, University of California, Berkeley (2002)
19. Passot, S., Fonseca, F., Cenard, S., Douania, I., Trelea, I.C.: Quality degradation of lactic acid bacteria during the freeze drying process: experimental study and mathematical modelling (2011)
20. Pearl, J.: Probabilistic Reasoning in Intelligent Systems: Networks of Plausible Inference. Morgan Kaufmann, Burlington (2014)
21. Pedregosa, F., Varoquaux, G., Gramfort, A., Thirion, B., Grisel, O., Blondel, M., Prettenhofer, P., Weiss, R., Dubourg, V., Michel, V., et al.: Scikit-learn: machine learning in python. J. Mach. Learn. Res. **12**(Oct), 2825–2830 (2011)
22. Perrot, N., Baudrit, C., Brousset, J.M., Abbal, P., Guillemin, H., Perret, B., Goulet, E., Guerin, L., Barbeau, G., Picque, D.: A decision support system coupling fuzzy logic and probabilistic graphical approaches for the agri-food industry: prediction of grape berry maturity. PLOS ONE **10**(7), e0134373 (2015)
23. Raynal, M., Debord, C., Guittard, S., Vergnes, M.: Epicure, a geographic information decision support system risk assessment of downy and powdery mildew epidemics in Bordeaux vineyards (2010). https://doi.org/10.1007/978-1-4302-3031-1
24. Schmidt, M., Lipson, H.: Distilling free-form natural laws from experimental data. Science **324**(5923), 81–85 (2009)
25. Sicard, M., Baudrit, C., Leclerc-Perlat, M., Wuillemin, P., Perrot, N.: Expert knowledge integration to model complex food processes. Application on the camembert cheese ripening process. Expert Syst. Appl. **38**(9), 11804–11812 (2011)
26. Steel, R.G.D., James, H.: Principles and Procedures of Statistics: With Special Reference to the Biological Sciences. McGraw-Hill, New York (1960)
27. Turkay, C., Slingsby, A., Lahtinen, K., Butt, S., Dykes, J.: Supporting theoretically-grounded model building in the social sciences through interactive visualisation. Neurocomputing (2017)
28. Velly, H., Fonseca, F., Passot, S., Delacroix-Buchet, A., Bouix, M.: Cell growth and resistance of Lactococcus lactis subsp. lactis TOMSC161 following freezing, drying and freeze-dried storage are differentially affected by fermentation conditions. J. Appl. Microbiol. **117**(3), 729–740 (2014)
29. Velly, H., Bouix, M., Passot, S., Penicaud, C., Beinsteiner, H., Ghorbal, S., Lieben, P., Fonseca, F.: Cyclopropanation of unsaturated fatty acids and membrane rigidification improve the freeze-drying resistance of Lactococcus lactis subsp. lactis TOMSC161. Appl. Microbiol. Biotechnol. **99**(2), 907–918 (2015)
30. Zadeh, L.: Fuzzy sets. Inf. Control **8**(3), 338–353 (1965)

Index

Printed in the United States
By Bookmasters